North Carolina

William Link examines the fascinating history of North Carolina through the lens of strong, yet seemingly contradictory, historical patterns: powerful forces of traditionalism punctuated by hierarchies of class, race relations, and gender that have seemingly clashed, especially during the last century, with potent forces of modernization and a "progressive" element that welcomed and even embraced change. *North Carolina: Change and Tradition in a Southern State* answers meaningful questions about the history and future of this rapidly growing state.

This second edition includes new coverage while retaining the strengths of the first edition, including its accessible and inclusive coverage of North Carolina's regional diversity. Extending the historical narrative into the twenty-first century, each of the six parts of this new edition conclude with set of primary-source documents selected to encourage students to develop a first-person appreciation for accounts of the past. Considering the North Carolina story from first contact all the way to 2015, this book provides a great resource for all college-level instructors and students of North Carolina history.

William A. Link is Richard J. Milbauer Professor of History at the University of Florida. He is the author of seven books on the history of the South, including *Roots of Secession: Slavery and Politics in Antebellum Virginia* (2003), *Righteous Warrior: Jesse Helms and the Rise of Modern Conservatism* (2008), *North Carolina: Change and Tradition in a Southern State* (2009), and *Links: My Family in American History* (2012). His most recent book is *Atlanta, Cradle of the New South: Race and Remembering in the Civil War's Aftermath* (2013).

North Carolina

Change and Tradition in a Southern State

Second Edition

William A. Link
Richard J. Milbauer Professor of History
University of Florida
Gainsville, FL, USA

This edition first published 2018

Edition History
Harlan Davidson, Inc. (1e 2009)

Registered Office(s)
John Wiley & Sons, Inc., 111 River Street, Hoboken, NJ 07030, USA

Editorial Office
111 River Street, Hoboken, NJ 07030, USA

For details of our global editorial offices, customer services, and more information about Wiley products visit us at www.wiley.com.

Wiley also publishes its books in a variety of electronic formats and by print-on-demand. Some content that appears in standard print versions of this book may not be available in other formats.

Library of Congress Cataloging-in-Publication Data

Names: Link, William A., author.
Title: North Carolina : change and tradition in a Southern state / by William A. Link (Richard J. Milbauer professor of history, University of Florida).
Description: Second edition. | Hoboken, NJ : Wiley, 2018. | Includes bibliographical references and index. |
Identifiers: LCCN 2017030682 (print) | LCCN 2017031230 (ebook) | ISBN 9781118833599 (pdf) | ISBN 9781118833537 (epub) | ISBN 9781118833605 (paperback)
Subjects: LCSH: North Carolina–History. | North Carolina–Social conditions. | Social change–North Carolina–History. | BISAC: HISTORY / United States / General.
Classification: LCC F254 (ebook) | LCC F254 .L56 2018 (print) | DDC 975.6–dc23
LC record available at https://lccn.loc.gov/2017030682

Cover image: © jonbilous / Fotolia
Cover design by Wiley

Set in 10/12pt WarnockPro by Aptara Inc., New Delhi, India

Printed in Singapore by C.O.S. Printers Pte Ltd

1 2018

Contents

Preface and Acknowledgments

This second edition of *North Carolina: Change and Tradition in a Southern State* incorporates a number of significant changes. In this revision, I have attempted to preserve, and even enhance, what I think are the main strengths of this book—its accessibility for students and general readers; its inclusiveness in coverage in terms of social, cultural, economic, and political history; its regional diversity; and its attempt to consider fully North Carolina in the twenty-first century. The historical literature about North Carolina history always was and continues to be extremely rich and productive, and I included the very latest work in my synthesis. Finally, this new edition sees the inclusion of primary-source documents at the end of each of its six sections, added in order to encourage students to explore and understand first-person accounts of the past.

As always, I have relied on the help of others in order to complete this book. The person responsible for its welfare continues to be Andrew Davidson, a good friend and a superb editor. He insured that the edition would have a new home with Wiley-Blackwell. Others at Wiley-Blackwell have been very helpful, including Lindsay Bourgeois, Peter Coveney, Georgina Hickey, Julia Kirk, and Linda Gaio. At the University of Florida, Allison Fredette provided essential help in assembling the documents sections. Ronnie Faulkner volunteered suggestions that I have attempted to incorporate in this version, while John Godwin sent a thorough and very useful critique. I must thank the Center for the Study of the American South for an affiliate that enabled access to the rich resources of the University of North Carolina libraries. I appreciate the assistance of Steven Lawson in helping to understand the nature of voting in early twentieth-century North Carolina. I am also, once again, indebted to my wife, Susannah Link, for her help in clarifying language, thoughts, and organization.

William A. Link

Gainesville, FL

1

European Invasion

One might say that North Carolina history began with a bang, in a clash of cultures spurred by the powerful process of European expansion into the wider world after about 1500. Although scholars used to refer to this process as the "discovery" of the Americas, diverse peoples had inhabited North America's Eastern Seaboard for many thousands of years, with thriving and far-flung cultures. Some Indians were nomadic; others lived in permanent villages. Some engaged in sophisticated forms of agriculture; others fished and trapped shellfish along the coast, and still others subsisted as hunter-gatherers. No matter their economic base, most indigenous peoples engaged in trade with other groups, some over exchange networks extending across thousands of miles.

The Indian groups in North Carolina at the time of first European contact lived in separate, sometimes antagonistic, societies, though all of them would come to share a common historical trauma. What scholars have called an "encounter" of European and Indian cultures is rife with stereotypes and misconceptions. For many years historians commonly portrayed Europeans as civilizing colonists, Indians as savages. More recent scholars have corrected this view and demonstrated the integrity of Indian societies. Older scholars also had a tendency to collapse the "encounter" into a few decades. Rather than a single contact, the cultural, political, and economic exchange between Europeans and indigenous peoples occurred in waves, over many decades, even centuries.

From the outset, European social organization and culture remained hostile to Indian society. At the time of first contact, Europeans were aggressively moving into and seeking to dominate the farthest reaches of the world, where they tried to subdue, or simply remove, the diverse cultures they met. With an expansionist drive, Western Europeans wanted to enrich themselves at the expense of native peoples around the globe, all of whom they tended to view as inferior and barbaric. Most critically, contact between Europeans and indigenous peoples in the Western Hemisphere invariably brought devastating diseases to the latter. The first arrival of English in North Carolina was no exception. Following English visits to Indian villages, wrote English writer Thomas

North Carolina: Change and Tradition in a Southern State, Second Edition. William A. Link.

Hariot, Indians began to "die very fast, and many in short space."[1] Although this demographic crisis weakened their ability to resist European invasion, Indians combatted these onslaughts, both physical and cultural, through different means; they were not simply victims. Indeed, they traded and interacted with the English explorers and settlers, often on terms dictated by the Indians, and their presence defined the character of European colonization.

Physical Geography and Environment

A long series of changes over the millennia combined to create North Carolina's remarkably distinctive geography. Some thirty million years ago, during the Mesozoic Era, much of the eastern third of North Carolina remained under water, but with the onset of the last ice age, some 10,000 years ago, the coastline extended 50 miles east of its present location. With the end of this ice age, the Atlantic Ocean pushed back to the west, filling the river valleys and forming the sounds of eastern North Carolina. Millions of years ago, the present Piedmont region featured immense mountains, the Ocoee Range, which were as high as today's western Rockies. Eon upon eon of erosion wore down these Piedmont ranges to the present elevation of between 350 and 1,800 feet. Composed of mostly rolling countryside, the region still contains small ranges such as the South Mountains in Burke and Rutherford Counties, the Uwharries of Montgomery and Randolph Counties, the Kings Mountain Range of Cleveland and Gaston Counties, and the Sauratown Mountains of Stokes and Surry Counties. West of the Ocoee Range lay a sea whose waters lapped the base of high mountains. About 270 million years ago, during the conclusion of the Paleozoic Era, tectonic pressures caused new mountains to emerge from the sea, the Appalachians, that, in our own time, dominate western North Carolina.

Prior to the Europeans' arrival, North Carolina's coastal areas contained abundant sea life, and its rivers were filled with fish and wildlife. Herds of white-tailed deer foraged river bottoms for food. Across the Carolinas roamed larger grazing animals such as bison and elk; omnivores such as black bears; small mammals such as squirrels and opossum; fowl such as pigeons, doves, and wild turkeys; and various species of reptiles and amphibians. Predators included wolves, panthers, and bobcats, and they helped to keep the population of the grazing animals in check. Creeks, rivers, sounds, and estuaries spawned rich and diverse aquatic life.

North Carolina was also a land of dense forests, which stretched the entire length of the state. In the Coastal Plain, forests of long-leaf pine dominated the landscape, while in northeastern North Carolina, cypress forests prevailed. To the west, pine forests gave way to large stands of uninterrupted hardwood—oak, hickory, and chestnut—deciduous forests that extended from the Coastal Plain to the high ranges of the Appalachians. So thick were the forests of North

Figure 1.1 Bynums Bluff, Mt. Mitchell Reservation. *Source: Library of Congress, National Photo Company Collection, LC-USZ62-100927.*

Carolina that it was said that a squirrel could travel from one end of the state to the other without ever setting foot on the ground.

Possessing these varied characteristics, North Carolina's physical geography had much to do with shaping its distinctive history. Spanning 500 miles in length from the coast to the mountains, and at its widest point nearly 200 miles from north to south, the state is defined by dramatic changes in elevation. In the far West, the Appalachian Mountains cradle a plateau that extends from the Blue Ridge westward to the Great Smokies, which straddle the border with Tennessee. The highest peak of the western mountains, Mt. Mitchell, is the tallest point on the Eastern Seaboard, with an elevation of 6,683 feet above sea level. From the mountains the terrain descends into the Piedmont, at several hundred feet of elevation, and then to the Coastal Plain, lying approximately at sea level.

Water resources also figured prominently in how the history of the state unfolded. In general, North Carolinians suffered from a lack of deep harbors and navigable river systems, hindering transportation of goods and people. The North Carolina coastline is composed of barrier islands to the east and sounds to the west, and most of its intracoastal waterways are not easily navigable. The lack of a good Atlantic harbor—as good, at least, as Boston, New York, Philadelphia, Norfolk, and Charleston—was significant. North Carolina also lacks any large rivers that might have provided a backbone for water-borne transport. In the West, the Little Tennessee, French Broad, and Hiawassee Rivers flow into the Tennessee River system, which drains toward the Gulf of Mexico. Piedmont rivers, such as the Catawba, Yadkin, and Broad, flow from north to south, and eventually into South Carolina. Coastal Plain Rivers such as the Roanoke, Chowan, Tar-Pamlico, Trent, Cape Fear, and Neuse, drain into sounds, but frequently clog with sediment, making them too shallow and tricky for large boats or barge traffic.

North Carolina's geography thus appeared uninviting to prospective colonists, particularly those Europeans who depended on water-borne travel for communication and commerce. At the same time, its propensity for fast-approaching and violent Atlantic storms and its numerous sandbars made—and still make—the North Carolina coast dangerous for shipping. The Outer Banks, a series of barrier islands, vary in width from two miles to only a few hundred feet, and often shift according to the whims of the tides, winds, and waves. Numerous inlets mark places where Atlantic storms have broken through barrier islands and created channels between the ocean and the sounds. At Cape Hatteras, the Gulf Stream, an Atlantic current flowing from the south, mixes with the colder waters of the North Atlantic, forming the notorious Diamond Shoals, where shallow sandbars for centuries awaited ships and their crews. South from Cape Hatteras, the Outer Banks coast extends its treacherous waters to Cape Lookout. Having caused as many as 5,000 reported shipwrecks between the sixteenth century and the present, sailors justly dubbed these waters "the Graveyard of the Atlantic."

Present-day North Carolina is understood to contain three principal geographical regions: the Coastal Plain, the Piedmont, and the Mountains. The Coastal Plain, extending some 150 miles from the coast westward, is defined by the occasions in which the Atlantic Ocean, over many years, spread its waters across the land, leaving terraces of sediment and sand each time it receded. Each of the major rivers of the Coastal Plain includes a "Fall Line," the point at which the Piedmont and Coastal Plain meet and the onset of rapids makes navigation difficult. With the Fall Line constituting its western border, the Coastal Plain, the largest of North Carolina's three major regions, contains sandy soil well suited for agriculture. Immediately adjacent to the coast and extending 30–80 miles inland lies a subregion known as the Tidewater, a low-lying and marshy area in between the sand dunes and the sounds, the place where many of the state's rivers form estuaries. The Tidewater supports a variety of habitats, and includes, in northeastern North Carolina, the Great Dismal Swamp extending between the James River in Virginia and the Albemarle Sound. The Great Dismal Swamp is home to an astounding diversity of plant life such as white cedar, bald cypress, and other wetland trees. The western edge of the Coastal Plain, with a slightly higher elevation and a layer of humus topsoil, became a center for the colony's and later the state's plantation crops.

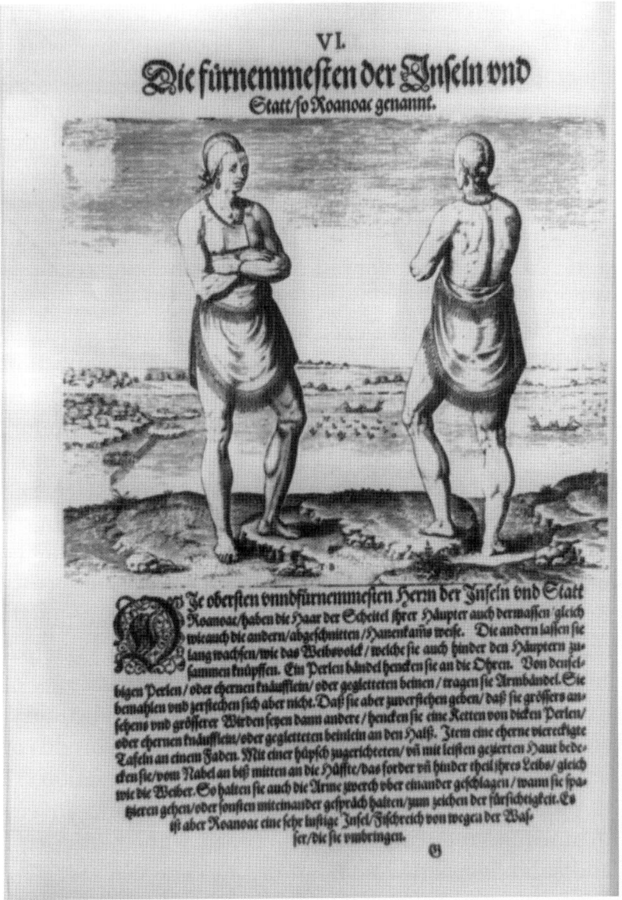

Figure 1.3 A Roanoke chief. Theodor de Bry. *Source: Library of Congress Rare Book and Special Collections Division, LC-USZ62-89909.*

The diversity of language notwithstanding, Indians shared far more cultural characteristics with each other than they did with the invading Europeans, and these differences shaped first contact. Western Europeans were aggressive and expansionist: in their eyes, they had "discovered" the "New World" as part of a historical process in which they would come to dominate most of the planet. During the early 1500s, the Spanish *conquistadors*' victory over the Aztecs in Mexico and the Incas in Peru brought untold millions in gold and silver to Spain, transforming a small nation on the southwestern tip of Western Europe into a leading world power. Spanish expansion into the Americas followed on the heels of the spread of the Portuguese into West Africa and Brazil, but in both cases the solidification of a strong, centralized monarchy presaged efforts at overseas colonization. The growth of the modern nation-state also was instrumental in the colonial successes of the Netherlands and France, both of which had managed to create empires by the end of the sixteenth century. English expansion began later, in the last decades of the 1500s, but it, too, depended on a consolidation of national power—under Queen Elizabeth, especially after the English victory over the Spanish Armada in 1588. As a result, the British colonial empire did not coalesce until the 1600s.

Each of these European powers arrived in the New World possessing militant societies and cultures. In addition, they believed that their Christian religious systems justified, even demanded, cultural domination over subject peoples. Europeans' religious zeal was fueled by the Protestant Reformation, which, in the course of disagreements about the structure, theology, and organization of the western Christian church, brought a continuing breach in the Roman Catholic Church. The Spanish became the leading opponents of the Reformation: their Counter-Reformation proposed a revitalized but expansionist Roman Catholic Church, and the Spanish sought to expand aggressively the reach of the Catholic Church into the Americas. In contrast, the Reformation shaped national development and ideology differently in England. Under Henry VIII, the Church of England split from Rome, and over the next century the Anglican Church became a battleground between reformers and traditionalists. Still, English Christianity, like Spanish Christianity, provided a principal ideological justification for colonization and the conversion to Christianity of native peoples. For the Spanish and the English, their legal systems and cultural values did not easily tolerate cultural differences, and their respective brands of Christianity condemned anything outside the pale of European civilization.

A growing European population, meanwhile, encouraged a class of adventurers to seek their fortunes in colonial endeavors abroad with the hope of exploiting resources and subduing native populations into coerced laborers. During the fifteenth and sixteenth centuries, the population of England grew rapidly, placing terrific pressure on limited land resources. Now those who relied on farming, both rich and poor, were forced to look for a livelihood outside of agriculture. For the poorer English, the line between subsistence and disaster had grown thin indeed. These lower-class English composed the bulk of the servant classes. But even among the aristocracy and landed gentry, social pressures forced change. In order to protect large family estates from division into increasingly smaller portions, upper-class families adopted the practice of bequeathing their entire estates to the eldest son, leaving younger sons without an inheritance. Therefore, many young but landless men began to look to other opportunities, including colonial adventure, as avenues for advancement and fortune.

Thus the two types of societies that were about to meet in North Carolina were quite different. The English were aggressively monotheistic, that is, they believed in only one God; many Indians were pantheistic, meaning, they believed in many gods and spirits that corresponded to animal and plant life, as well as to the forces of nature. The English exalted the individual and one's personal achievement; Indians emphasized a communal identity that put the group first. The English constructed a legal system designed to define and protect private property because they encouraged the acquisition of possessions and wealth. Indians held land in common; rather than individual ownership, all lands belonged to the tribe. The English provided for the inheritance of land through male heirs; according to some scholarly estimates, about half of Indian peoples were matrilineal, and in these instances individual identity and tribal membership followed the mother's family. "It often happens," wrote English colonist John Lawson, that "two Indians that have liv'd together, as Man and Wife, in which Time they have had several Children; if they part, and another Man possesses her, all the Children go along with the Mother, and none with the Father." Lawson noted that in relationships between white traders and Indians, their children always remained with their mother.[2]

Among those Indians with a matrilineal society, their social system ensured that women, especially by comparison with Englishwomen, enjoyed an elevated social status—family identity was linked to the mother. In some Indian societies, women even possessed special economic rights as the managers of agriculture: women were the mainstays of the agricultural system. Tuscarora oral traditions included a creation story in which the Great Chief expelled a pregnant woman who gave birth to twins, the Good Spirit and the Evil Spirit. Good and evil thus arose from women. Algonquians believed that humankind was the fruit of a sexual relationship between a woman and a god, while Sioux speakers believed that all humans originated from four women, Pash, Sepoy, Maraskin, and Askarin, who created four tribes. Many indigenous legends depicted women as originators of life, as connected to nature and its processes, as possessing special powers that made them as important as men, and as communicators between the natural and spirit worlds.

Some Indian women possessed power in their control of the gathering of food and, by the time the Europeans arrived, with their management of agriculture. Women probably led the way in the domestication of key food crops such as corn, squash, and beans, and they remained responsible for the gathering of nuts, berries, and wild vegetables, as well as of clams and oysters. Women supported the hunting activities of men by maintaining camps far away from their villages. The development of ceramic pottery, another area of female activity, was critical to the storage and preparation of food. Ceramics became a critical component of trade—and a way in which women participated in the intertribal economy. Native American women were thus part of a culture that valued communal sharing, that had little concept of the accumulation of private property, and in which women exerted, because of their roles in the economy and their status in a matrilineal society, significant power and agency. One indicator of their autonomy was Indian women's sexual freedom: premarital sex was acceptable, and they were free to take as many partners as they wanted prior to marriage; after marriage, women could freely leave their spouses. Although Europeans like Lawson might "reckon them [Indian women] the greatest Libertines and most extravagant in their Embraces," he admitted that, "they retain[ed] and possess[ed] a Modesty that requires those Passions never to be divulged."[3]

In contrast, the English maintained a patrilineal society, with social identity following the identity of the father. Not only were children named according to their fathers, their wealth and status followed that of their father. Among English upper classes, the prevalence of primogeniture—the legal requirement that an entire estate would go to the eldest male heir—is one such example of the strongly patrilineal and patriarchal qualities of English society. To the English, Indians were simultaneously fascinating and confounding. English visitors often noted Indian women's power and independence in sexuality, courtship, and marriage, practices that they considered far outside the prescribed gender norm, even barbaric. Visitors cited nudity, scant clothing, and what they considered sexual promiscuity as examples of the Indians' savagery. This simultaneous attraction and repulsion toward Native American culture reflected the English belief that they had "discovered" and should rightfully possess—in order to "improve"—Indian lands. In time, these beliefs would also serve to justify, in Europeans' minds, the destruction of Native American civilization.

Diversity and Change among Native Americans

Evidence about pre-contact Indian life is scattered, limited to only a few descriptions penned by European visitors, archaeological fragments, and remnants of the Indians' oral tradition. The picture now emerging is one of conflict and competition among Indians and a variety of responses to the invading Europeans. Indians showed resiliency in adapting to the traumatic changes wrought by first contact and its aftermath. That those changes were traumatic is indisputable, the most important of which was the impact of disease: Native Americans possessed little or no immunity to common European diseases such as the common cold or measles, or more severe viruses such as typhus, influenza, and smallpox. These European diseases swept through Indian villages with epidemic force. Soon after first contact with Europeans, everywhere in the Americas, Indian groups typically experienced an extraordinarily high mortality rate. Indeed, so severe was the loss of life that scholars, without exaggeration, have described this as a holocaust for Indians. Smallpox was probably the deadliest killer: among populations with no previous exposure, the rate of mortality falls somewhere between 50 and 90 percent.

As elsewhere in the New World, North Carolina Indians suffered terrible losses as a result of epidemic disease. In the Carolinas, these diseases probably had their earliest effect after the arrival of the Spanish explorer Hernando de Soto. After the arrival of the Spanish in Florida in 1513, de Soto was leading an expedition throughout the Southeast in search of gold and treasure. During the spring of 1540, he crossed into southwestern North Carolina, visiting the Indian town of Xuala, or Joara (near present-day Hickory); several decades later, in 1566–67 and 1567–68, another Spanish explorer, Juan Pardo, covered much of the same ground. Pardo explored the Catawba Valley and constructed Fort San Juan, near present-day Morganton, along with other forts in western North Carolina. Within a few years, these forts fell victim to Spanish negligence and Indian hostility. During the late 1500s and early 1600s, Spanish traders established contacts with Native Americans in North Carolina and elsewhere in the Southeast, selling horses, weapons, and other goods. They also influenced Indian agriculture, introducing peaches, sweet potatoes, and Irish potatoes, which became important parts of the Native American diet. Without question, Spanish explorers and traders also brought disease to the Native Americans. A chronicler of de Soto's expedition noted that Indians in the Carolina mountains were "very weak," and further contact with the Spanish led to outbreaks of epidemic disease. One missionary commented in the late 1600s that "the Indians die so easily that the bare look and smell of a Spaniard causes them to give up their ghost."[4]

Figure 1.4 Virginia, the Carolinas, and Florida, 1610. *Source: North Carolina Collection, University of North Carolina Library at Chapel Hill.*

The arrival of the English in North Carolina after the mid-1580s occurred *after* the widespread decimation of Indian society was well underway. Data are very scattered and unreliable, but according to one estimate, in 1600, North Carolina contained perhaps 50,000 Native American inhabitants. The Algonquian and Tuscarora numbered perhaps 30,000 in 1660, but within fifteen years these populations had declined by about a third. The advent of settlers into the Albemarle region occurred after about 1660. With Europeans came periodic epidemic outbreaks that further reduced Indian populations. By the turn of the eighteenth century, the total number of Indians living between the Virginia border and the Neuse River was only about 5,000. Although Sioux-speaking Indians and Cherokees remained geographically isolated from Europeans until the mid-1700s, both groups experienced sharp population losses because of disease. During the late 1600s, smallpox reduced the Cherokee population from roughly 30,000 to 15,000 people. Entire villages disappeared because of population losses. During the seventeenth and eighteenth centuries, Catawbas, a Sioux-speaking group, survived by amalgamating other Indian groups on the verge of extinction. According to John Lawson, there was "not the sixth Savage living within two hundred Miles of all our Settlement, as there were fifty Years ago. … These poor Creatures have so many Enemies to destroy them, that it's a wonder one of them is left alive near us."[5]

The main form of contact between Indians and whites was trading. Indians exchanged furs, some food, and war captives sold as slaves; whites offered manufactured items, including tools, metal implements, clothes, and especially guns and ammunition. Over time, Indians came to depend on English goods, but by the 1680s, their exports were chiefly deerskins and beaver pelts, and slaves. Trade undermined the traditional economic bases of Indian society. Increased pressure to provide more and more skins and pelts to trade resulted in the decimation of North Carolina's populations of white-tail deer and beavers, animals upon which the Indians had long relied for food and clothing. The advent of muskets, much desired among Indians, greatly transformed the nature of warfare among Indians. Native Americans had long practiced warfare, with any captives won in battle considered a prize of war and often adopted in the captors' tribe. Continued trade with settlers, however, greatly encouraged warfare for the primary purpose of acquiring captives. European traders urged Indians to "make War amongst themselves," wrote one contemporary, "to get Slaves which they give for our European goods."[6] It is estimated that tens of thousands of captives were sold as slaves to whites, who either kept them in the colony or sold them to Caribbean planters. Native Americans competed furiously to dominate North Carolina's lucrative trade with the English, and the Indian slave trade encouraged wars among Indians who needed greater and greater numbers of captives in order to trade them for the European goods they wanted. Without war, wrote a Cherokee in the early 1700s, they would have "no way in get[t]ing of Slaves to buy am[m]unition and Clothing."[7]

The introduction of alcohol into Indian societies also wreaked havoc. Later, in the eighteenth and nineteenth centuries, the abuse of alcohol among some Indian peoples became epidemic, with profound consequences. But even in the colonial period, the prevalence of rum accounted for widespread social disintegration among Indians, though scholars are uncertain precisely why this was so. To a certain extent, alcohol was incorporated into Native American ceremonies and became an expected part of cultural life. Still, the extent of alcohol consumption clearly went well beyond ritualistic use, as inebriated Indians hurt themselves and others. According to one observer, Indians engaged in "drunken Frolicks" in which they "murder one another, fall into the Fire, fall down Precipices, and break their Necks, with several other Misfortunes which this drinking of Rum brings upon them."[8]

The struggle between Euro-Americans and Indians continued for centuries. As colonists established the Carolina colony, Indians fought to preserve their cultural and political integrity, and they remained an important presence. Indian culture did not disappear with the arrival and settlement of Europeans, and native peoples adapted to the cataclysmic changes wrought by the newcomers. Over the ensuing centuries—and to this day—Indians continued to express a persistent presence in North Carolina life.

Early Attempts at English Colonization

As early as the 1570s, the Elizabethan English became fascinated with the prospect of building an overseas empire that would provide the basis of a new, "mercantilist" economic system that, ideally, would concentrate national wealth through the establishment of colonies. Promoters of this idea, such as two cousins, both named Richard Hakluyt (the "Elder" and the "Younger"), described the link between national greatness and colonial empire. The new empire would seek to convert heathen Indians to Protestant Christianity. At the same time, new colonies could become a safety valve for England's poor and for social distress at home. In developing an economic empire, England would achieve the national independence and military prowess necessary for world greatness. There would be other economic benefits of empire, mercantilists believed. In his *Discourse of Western Planting,* Richard Hakluyt the Younger claimed that North American colonies would send agricultural products such as lemons, rice, silk, sugar, and olive oil to England, products then only available from the Mediterranean. Although incorrect in their understanding of the North American climate—which could not sustain all of these crops—the Hakluyts articulated a mercantilist vision. They believed that by establishing colonies, a mercantilist empire would create a market for exported finished goods abroad and a source of cheap imported raw materials at home. Mercantilism seemed a formula for national greatness.

All of these factors figured into England's first foray into a permanent colonial settlement in North Carolina during the 1580s. Queen Elizabeth awarded Sir Humphrey Gilbert a patent in 1578 to colonize North America, but his efforts failed, and in an attempt to cross the North Atlantic in 1583, he was lost at sea. His half-brother, Sir Walter Raleigh (who was knighted in 1584), an adventurer and a court favorite, organized another attempt at an English settlement. Raleigh was keenly interested in privateering—a form of "legal" pirating in which the Crown empowered entrepreneur sea captains to attack enemy shipping—chiefly against Spain. The English wanted a forward base in the New World that could strike the shipping lanes from Central and South America and the Caribbean on which Spanish treasure ships, laden with silver and gold extracted from their American colonies, routinely traveled. Raleigh looked to Chesapeake Bay, part of a largely uncharted Eastern Seaboard, to establish his colony. Earlier, in 1526, the Spanish had settled at the mouth of the Cape Fear River; in the 1560s, the French established colonies in Florida and South Carolina; and, in 1570–71, Spanish Jesuits landed in the Chesapeake. But by the late 1570s, all of these attempts at settlement had failed: the Spanish drove away the French, while the Indians did the same to the Spanish.

Leaving England on April 21, 1584, Raleigh's first expedition followed the trade winds to the Caribbean and arrived at the Outer Banks on July 13, 1584. Philip Amadas and Arthur Barlowe commanded the expedition. Only 19 years old, Amadas was from Plymouth and was a member of Raleigh's household, as was Barlowe. They did not seek to create a permanent colony. Rather, their chief mission was to examine the area and to determine the best location for a new settlement. Remaining only a few weeks in the area, the Amadas-Barlowe mission brought back enthusiastic but exaggerated descriptions of conditions that became, not surprisingly, part of Raleigh's efforts in England at salesmanship. The area that they had "discovered" was "the most plentiful, sweet, fruitful, and wholesome of all the world," wrote Barlowe, where the "earth bringeth forth all things in abundance, as in the first creation, without toil or labor."[9]

The Amadas-Barlowe mission became especially optimistic about the Native Americans whom they encountered when they visited coastal Carolina. The indigenous people never made "any shewe of feare or doubt," and they were "as mannerly and civil as any of Europe." The people were, Barlowe reported, "most gentle, loving, and faithfull, voide of all guile and treason."[10] Mostly likely, the coastal Algonquians considered the English invited guests who might become allies against Indian enemies and potential trading partners who might supply them with their impressive technology, advanced weaponry, and metal tools. In order to induce further support for their plans in England, Amadas and Barlowe returned with two Indians, Manteo and Wanchese, who were paraded across England. Manteo, belonging to the ruling family of the Croatoans, likely taught expedition chronicler Thomas Hariot to speak Algonquian on the return voyage; Hariot likely taught him English, and Manteo spoke to audiences in

Figure 1.5 Sir Walter Raleigh, c. 1585. *Source: Portrait of Sir Walter Raleigh by Nicholas Hilliard, National Portrait Gallery, London.*

England about his homeland. Wanchese had a different experience. During his visit to England, he became convinced that the English threatened to undermine Indian society, and when he returned he abandoned contact with the colony.

The Amadas-Barlowe expedition recommended a site at Roanoke Island, apparently at the invitation of the Roanoke Indian leader Granganimeo, the brother of a local chief. The expedition, and the publicity it generated, paid off, as Raleigh's efforts to establish a permanent colony attracted support. Queen Elizabeth herself expanded Raleigh's patent by providing him the right to appropriate ships and men, by supplying him a ship of the royal fleet, the *Tiger*, and by releasing one of her military men, Ralph Lane, to serve as military commander of the expedition. Perhaps fearing for his safety, however, Elizabeth prohibited Raleigh from traveling with the colonizing expedition.

On the heels of the Amadas-Barlowe reconnaissance, a full-fledged expedition departed from Plymouth on April 9, 1585, with five ships and two pinnaces (or small ships). Composed of some six hundred men, the expedition contained adventurers, military men, and some male relatives thereof, as well as political cronies of Raleigh. The expedition also included Manteo, who returned with this and a subsequent expedition as guide and interpreter. Raleigh's cousin, Sir Richard Grenville, an aristocratic landowner, officeholder from Cornwall, and former Member of Parliament, commanded the expedition. From the outset, however, the colony was ill-fated. A fundamental division became apparent from the beginning between Grenville and Ralph Lane. Part of the expedition's mission included privateering, which its backers saw as a likely source of profit. At Grenville's insistence the expedition sailed first to the West Indies, partly to rebuild a pinnace destroyed en route and partly to privateer. Delayed by Grenville's privateering, the expedition did not arrive at the Outer Banks until June 26, 1585, at Roanoke Island. They soon realized that this was an unfortunate location for a colony. Lacking access to a deep-water port, with shallow sounds immediately surrounding Roanoke with depths of only 5–9 feet, the larger vessels of Grenville's fleet, such as the fleet's flagship *Tiger*, could only anchor offshore in the dangerous Atlantic. Soon, rough waters forced the *Tiger* toward the dangerous coastline. In order to save the ship, the crew jettisoned food stores meant to sustain the colony. Concluding that the Roanoke site was unsuitable, Grenville then returned to England to attempt a relief expedition that would return sometime during the spring of 1586. Meanwhile, Ralph Lane and about one hundred men remained to construct a fort and an adjoining settlement on the northern end of Roanoke Island.

The remaining men at Roanoke became known as the Lane colony, and it was left to its own resources between the summer of 1585 and the spring of 1586. In order to explore the region, the Lane colony included scientific and artistic participation. John White, an artist who had traveled with the Amadas-Barlowe expedition, and Thomas Hariot, a scientist, were dispatched as part of the Lane colony with instructions to document the New World's natural life. Little is known about White, though his paintings of Indians at Roanoke Island have survived as one of the best records of early Native Americans. Hariot was a well-known mathematician who was a prominent member of Raleigh's household. On his return to England, Hariot published his *Brief and True Report of the New Found Land of Virginia* (1588), one of the earliest accounts of North America.

The combined efforts of Hariot and White produced a wealth of information about the peoples, plants, and animals of sixteenth-century North Carolina.

The Lane colony remained entirely male, composed of 107 military men, gentlemen adventurers, and some commoners. As was true of early English colonial efforts, many of the colonists were veterans of the Elizabethan wars in Ireland. For several decades, the English had been colonizing Ireland and, much as they would in North America, battling a resistant indigenous culture. The Lane colony sought to gather information about the locale and environment, but almost immediately first contact with Native Americans led to conflict. The English had most frequent contact with the Algonquian Indians of the coast and Outer Banks, who were organized around villages, headed by *werowances* (chiefs) that allied themselves with other communities. These alliances were constantly shifting, and when the English arrived in the mid-1580s, the Roanoke werowance Wingina had established local control at Roanoke Island and two mainland villages, Dasemunkepeuc and Pomeiooc, but he was opposed by other warring Indian groups such as the Secotan, Pomeiooc, and Neusioks. Indeed, Wingina had, according to a contemporary English account, recently waged a "mortall warre" with these groups (during the early 1580s).[11]

Warfare among Indian groups in the area was already in progress by the time the English arrived, along with a furious competition for control of prime lands and hunting and fishing grounds. While absorbing the shock of early contact with Europeans, the Algonquians sought to gain advantage over their Indian competitors by virtue of the English presence. In early 1586, colonists traveled north and explored the Chesapeake—visiting with friendly Indians and avoiding the powerful Powhatan Confederacy—and they became convinced of the superiority of this site for future settlement. Meanwhile, Wingina and the Roanokes began to suffer from diseases they had contracted from the English, and became convinced that the encounter with the English meant disaster. Wingina, according to Ralph Lane's account, changed his name to Pemisapan and moved his people from Pomeiooc to Dasemunkepeuc, on the western shore of Roanoke Sound, near present-day Mann's Harbor.

Lane interpreted Pemisapan's departure as evidence of a conspiracy to exterminate the Roanoke Island settlement—a conclusion that Indian enemies likely encouraged. Operating on these faulty assumptions, Lane launched a preemptive attack in June 1586, wounding Pemisapan and then executing him. Lane's unprovoked attack was a turning point; the killing of a werowance resulted in a significant breakdown of Indian-white relations. Facing a likely future of continued resistance from local Indians, Lane and other colonists learned of the arrival of the famous privateer Sir Francis Drake in June 1586. Drake offered to supply Lane with a ship and provisions, but after he accepted the offer, a powerful hurricane struck and inflicted so much damage to the colony that Lane decided to return to England with Drake. Several weeks later a long-awaited relief expedition, led by Sir Richard Grenville, arrived, but Grenville and company quickly returned to England after leaving behind a small force of fifteen men.

The Lane colony failed for obvious reasons. The lack of good harbor facilities created immediate and crucial difficulties of supply and communication. The colonists proved unable to provide themselves with food; for the Lane colony, an important event occurred when the expedition's flagship ran aground, destroying their food supplies. Most important of all in explaining the failure of the Lane colony was the cultural, military, and economic conflict with Native Americans. Lane's massacre of Dasemunkepeuc brought to surface brewing conflicts. Despite an initial friendly posture of the Roanoke Indians, the English, dependent on them for food, alienated their Indian allies by 1586. Indians produced ample quantities of corn and fish, but English colonists, mostly gentlemen or the urban poor, were ill-equipped agriculturalists and fishermen. They were unwilling to farm and produce their own food, preferring to demand it from Indians. The English presence placed a terrific strain on the Indians' ability to feed themselves, which helped to account for the deteriorating relations. The English had little interest in food cultivation: their main interest was in seeking wealth through privateering. Problems with food thus compounded a fundamental problem, the colonists' inability to coexist peacefully with Native Americans. By the time that Drake arrived, the colonists were facing the strong likelihood of a massive Indian attack.

Roanoke Island and the Lost Colony

Despite the failure of the Lane colony, Raleigh sponsored a second colonizing expedition, scheduled to set sail the following spring of 1587 and headed by John White. An artist for the Lane colony, White apparently believed that this attempt to establish a viable colony would represent a significant departure from earlier efforts. More than a hundred colonists agreed to travel; each was promised five hundred acres of land. Unlike the Lane colony, the White colony was composed of men, women, and children, some fourteen families in all. Nonetheless, the colonists were overwhelmingly male, and the men were overwhelmingly single. The colony's objective was to create a permanent "plantation" of English law, culture, and society abroad. Leaving England in early May, a fleet of three ships made the transatlantic crossing by the usual route to the West Indies, arriving at the Outer Banks on July 16, 1587. Despite their intentions to locate the colony on the Chesapeake, the crews transporting the White colony were eager to privateer; quickly leaving, they insisted that the colonists be deposited on Roanoke.

With this inauspicious beginning, White's colony encountered the same difficulties that Lane had experienced. When the White colony arrived, they discovered that the modest military force that Lane had left behind had been wiped out. Unable to feed themselves, the English depended on Native Americans for food, and conflict soon arose. Relations with Indians remained uneasy. Soon after the colonists arrived, Indians killed one of their leaders, George Howe, while he was crab fishing in shallow water. Wanchese, who traveled to England, led hostile Indians. The English responded by attacking an Indian village, but they soon learned that the village they had retaliated against was inhabited by friendly Croatoans. Despite the continuing deterioration in relations with Indians, White's granddaughter, Virginia Dare, was born in Roanoke on August 18, 1587, the daughter of Eleanor and Ananias Dare. Virginia was the first English baby born in North America. In this atmosphere of crisis, the colonists sent a delegation, led by White himself, to lobby for a relief expedition to return to the worried colonists. On August 27, 1587, White reluctantly departed the colony for England in order to seek help.

White's relief expedition experienced a combination of bad fortune and delay. Just before a flotilla of eight ships under Grenville's command prepared to sail for Roanoke in the spring of 1588, authorities seized the ships in order to help defend against the Spanish Armada, a massive (but thwarted) Spanish naval invasion of the British Isles. French privateers captured a subsequent expedition later that year. Not until 1590, three years after he left the Outer Banks, did White return to Roanoke, aboard a privateering expedition bound for the West Indies. Encounters with the Spanish and bad weather off the Carolina coast further delayed the rescue expedition, and when he finally arrived at his colony, White found only dismantled houses, buried chests, scattered metal bars, torn and scattered books, and a few mysterious carvings. White and the colony's ruling council had earlier agreed that, if the colonists were forced to move, they would carve the colony's new location as a guide for White. Since the carvings read "CRO" and "CROATOAN," White and the searchers sailed south to Croatoan Island, but the arrival of bad weather, probably a hurricane, scattered the ships out to sea. White never returned, and so ended the fate of the so-called "Lost Colony" of Roanoke.

The fate of the residents of the "Lost Colony" has remained one of the great mysteries of American history. There were efforts to determine the colonists' fate shortly after the founding of Jamestown and the Virginia colony in 1607, and rumors persisted about how the colonists had amalgamated with local Indians. One tradition has it that the settlers moved north to the Chesapeake but were wiped out by Indians shortly before the arrival of the Jamestown colonists. Nonetheless, the wood carvings that John White saw suggested that the colonists had migrated south. Whatever the fate of the Lost Colonists, the early experiences of the English in eastern North Carolina were hardly auspicious.

* * *

The cultural, political, and economic encounter between Native Americans and invading Europeans had particular consequences for early North Carolina.

Coastal Indians, dispersed politically and lacking military might and technology to blunt the Europeans, were overmatched. Still, the Indian peoples of North Carolina remained diverse and adaptive. Some groups profited from Europeans, using a position as intermediaries in an emerging trade between colonists and interior tribes. The enduring power of Indian groups in the Coastal Plain such as the Tuscarora blunted Europeans' ability to push into the interior, while Indians farther west remained isolated. The prospect of colonizing North Carolina faced other obstacles, the most significant of which were geographical obstacles, such as those posed by the treacherous Carolina coast and the rivers' shallow depth. Because water transport remained the most important form of moving goods and people, colonists would find that making a fortune in North Carolina was far more challenging than in colonies to the north or south.

North Carolina's limited opportunities for the exploitation of land and labor—what elsewhere in the South would become the plantation system—defined the pattern of future colonization. In the aftermath of the failure of the Roanoke colony, the next attempt at English colonization in North America looked north, to the James River and Chesapeake Bay. With broad rivers extending into the interior and one of the best natural harbors in North America, the Virginia colony attracted the primary attention of colonizers in the Southeast for the next few generations. North Carolina developed by fits and start, defined by its isolation and the distinctive social system and political culture that began to emerge.

Notes

1 Quoted in Michael L. Oberg, "Indians and Englishmen at the First Roanoke Colony: A Note on Pemisapan's Conspiracy," *American Indian Culture and Research Journal* 18, 2 (1994): 79.

2 Hugh T. Lefler, ed., *A New Voyage to Carolina, by John Lawson* (Chapel Hill: University of North Carolina Press, 1967), p. 192.

3 Ibid., p. 194.

4 Quoted in Donald Edward Davis, *Where There Are Mountains: An Environmental History of the Southern Mountains* (Athens: University of Georgia Press, 2000), p. 42.

5 Lefler, *A New Voyage to Carolina*, p. 232.

6 Quoted in James H. Merrell, *The Indians' New World: Catawbas and Their Neighbors from European Contact through the Era of Removal* (Chapel Hill: University of North Carolina Press, 1989), p. 37.

7 Quoted in Kirsten Fischer, *Suspect Relations: Sex, Race, and Resistance in Colonial North Carolina* (Ithaca, NY: Cornell University Press, 2002), p. 80.

8 Ibid.

9 Quoted in Karen Ordahl Kupperman, *Roanoke: The Abandoned Colony* (Totowa, NJ: Rowman & Allanheld, 1984), pp. 16–17.

10 Quoted in Kupperman, *Roanoke*, pp. 16–17.

11 Michael Leroy Oberg, "Gods and Men: The Meeting of Indian and White Worlds on the Carolina Outer Banks, 1584–1586," *North Carolina Historical Review* LXXVI no. 4 (October 1999): 371.

2

Origins of North Carolina

In 1607, the Virginia Company founded a new colony at Jamestown at Chesapeake Bay, and within two decades it was attracting a steady flow of migrants. But Jamestown experienced many of the same problems that had plagued the Roanoke colony: early colonists were unable to feed themselves; disease and starvation gripped the colony; relations with Native Americans deteriorated; and an all-out Indian attack (in 1622) nearly wiped out the settlement. The turning point for the Virginia colony occurred with the discovery and development of tobacco as a staple crop. During the first half of the 1600s, Virginians spread the tobacco culture and the plantation system as they colonized the area surrounding Chesapeake Bay. For the most part, England and its American colonists paid little attention to North Carolina in these years, and it was only largely as a result of Virginia's population expansion that settlers began to trickle southward during and after the 1650s.

From the outset, then, North Carolina developed outside the mainstream of emerging South Atlantic plantation economies. Growth of the white population proceeded slowly and haltingly until the early eighteenth century. All of it prior to 1715 was concentrated in northeastern counties east of the Chowan River and north of the Albemarle Sound. Bordered to the north by the Great Dismal Swamp, the Albemarle developed on its own, in isolation from other colonies and with more limited access to the Atlantic economy.

Settlement of the Albemarle and the Carolina Colony

Early attempts by the English to colonize the large, undefined region between Virginia's southern borders and Spanish Florida were disorganized and ineffective. On October 30, 1629, King Charles I of England awarded a charter to the royal attorney-general, Sir Robert Heath, to establish a new colony, Carolana, to be located between 31° and 30° north latitude, from southern Virginia to Florida. Because of the English Civil War and ensuing political

North Carolina: Change and Tradition in a Southern State, Second Edition. William A. Link.

turmoil, however, the Carolana colony never came into existence. Meanwhile, Virginians had explored northeastern North Carolina in 1608, 1622, and 1643, and thereafter trappers and Indian traders ventured into the region.

The first whites who permanently settled North Carolina came from the Virginia frontier after the mid-1650s. Virginia tobacco plantations depended on the importation of white servants traveling to the colony under an "indenture," by which the cost of their transportation to the New World was covered by a master to whom they were bound to service for a term of between five and seven years. During the early years of the Virginia colony, the rate of mortality was so high that many servants did not survive the duration of their indentures. By the middle of the seventeenth century, however, mortality rates declined among all whites; most servants survived their indentures, and the population of the colony increased. Land-hungry settlers now sought land to the north, west, and south, and Virginia migrants began to move down river valleys, across the Great Dismal Swamp, and into the region north of the Albemarle Sound—named after 1663 for the Duke of Albemarle and later known simply as the Albemarle. The new arrivals tended to settle near the head of the Currituck Sound and west of the Chowan and Pasquotank Rivers. By October 1662, their numbers had grown large enough for the Virginia colonial council to appoint Samuel Stephens as the "commander of the southern plantation."

Figure 2.1 The Great Dismal Swamp, 2014. *Source: Public domain image at* http://www.public-domain-image.com/full-image/nature-landscapes-public-domain-images-pictures/wetlands-and-swamps-public-domain-images-pictures/great-dismal-swamp-national-wildlife-refuge.jpg.html

In 1672, George Fox, a founder of the English Society of Friends (or Quakers), visited North America, helping to organize new congregations. In November, he traveled up the Perquimans River to tour the settlements of Quakers, most of whom had migrated from southern Virginia. Fox found the trip hard going, with the region "full of great bogs and swamps; so that we were commonly wet to the knees." Fox also encountered Nathaniel Batts, who was, according to historians, the first permanent settler in the region. A fur trader, Batts constructed a house at the junction of the Chowan and Roanoke Rivers sometime around 1655. He married an Indian woman, serving as the frontier settlement's unofficial governor and intermediary between whites and Indians. Fox described Batts as a "rude, desperate man" who headed what Fox called "Roan-oak."[1]

Batts belonged to a group of white pioneers of the Albemarle whose numbers reached several thousand by the late 1600s. The area, said another contemporary, was populated by "English, intermixt with the native Indians to a great extent."[2] Often portrayed as outcasts and misfits, the early Albemarle settlers are better understood as frontierspeople. They had migrated to a profoundly isolated region. As in the case of the failed colony at Roanoke, the treacherous Carolina Atlantic coast shaped the nature of the Albemarle settlement. The Albemarle settlers had come from a society in which economic opportunity was associated with tobacco culture, but lacking good transportation facilities, they turned primarily to subsistence farming. Between 1655 and 1710, white settlement spread across northeastern North Carolina; nearly all of the settlers were second- or third-generation Virginians. Many of them were of modest means; popular lore that describes the Albemarle as composed of runaway servants, misfits, and rogues is only partly an exaggeration. Many settlers were Quakers who left southeastern Virginia during the late seventeenth century because of mounting religious persecution. The Quaker presence would figure prominently, as we shall see, in the early history of the colony. In sum, unlike other British mainland colonies, no significant migration occurred directly from England to North Carolina, a fact that made the Albemarle what one historian has described as the first "truly American" settlement of the Eastern Seaboard.[3]

The English social system followed a rigid patriarchy in which the political, legal, and economic dominance of men was built into the system. Not surprisingly, the Albemarle frontier possessed a social structure that, in the late 1600s, remained in flux. Landownership, political representation, and legal identity all followed the heads of households, and, in married couples, men were always heads of household. On the Carolina frontier these gender roles often became blurred. Men and women were entitled to headright land grants; as in Virginia and England, in Carolina if women were single, and especially if they were widows, they could own land independently of men as heads of households. In this way, two migrants from Virginia in the 1660s, Mary Fortsen and Katherine Woodward, received land grants. Fortsen gained her grants by virtue of the fact that she was a widowed head of household. For most white women, the opportunities for some degree of independence were enhanced by high mortality rates, especially among males. Frequent remarriages among women enhanced the possibility of acquiring property and increasing status, and widowhood provided an unexpected path for social upward mobility. Women thus sometimes exercised political and economic independence: Ann Marwood Durant, wife of tobacco exporter George Durant, operated an inn in Perquimans precinct, and at court proceedings that sometimes met there she represented her husband's legal and business interests. Ann Durant even acted as an attorney in the court, and she successfully argued cases during the 1670s and 1680s. In the fluctuating social environment of the Albemarle, other women served as executrices for estates in local courts, while others even prosecuted civil cases involving property disputes. Once court proceedings met in formal courthouses, and as the legal system became more institutionalized and settled in the early 1700s, women's political and economic power receded.

Black women on the Carolina frontier, as it evolved in the late seventeenth century, encountered harsher challenges. Most black women arrived in small groups as enslaved chattel, brought south from Virginia by masters. A lopsided male to female gender ratio that prevailed at the time meant that black family units were often disparate and dispersed across plantations. Enslaved women functioned in a fluid social system; the institution of slavery remained undefined, and enslaved people functioned in a world where racial hierarchies were not rigidly defined. Yet chattel slavery imposed serious obstacles to the integrity of family, as the sales of slaves often separated husbands from wives, parents from children. The case of "Manuell & Frank his wife," the first recorded slave in North Carolina, is instructive. Listed among the possessions of Gov. Seth Sothel on his death in 1695, Manuell and his wife were inherited by Thomas Pollock, a large landowner in Chowan County. Manuell and Frank had five children, and they hired themselves out to other planters; they also had some possessions, including a gun, clothing, and a bed. But when Pollock divided his estate among his sons in 1709, some time after Manuell had died, Frank and her children were separated.[4]

Not long after Virginia frontiersmen first reached the Albemarle, a new Carolina colony was established. While the Albemarle settlement occurred as an extension of Virginia's southern frontier by people of modest means, some of the wealthiest citizens of England created a new colony in Carolina. Beginning in 1651, Parliament enacted a series of Navigation Acts creating a new mercantilist empire in which England and its colonies existed in a self-sufficient isolation from the rest of the world. On the assumption that there was a limited amount of wealth in the world, this mercantilist system sought to establish a protected and insulated economic system in which colonies shipped raw, unfinished products to England, which controlled manufacturing and shipping—and thereby gained a favorable balance of trade.

In 1660, the end of the English Civil War brought the restoration of the Stuart monarchy and of Charles II to the throne—it also brought a new approach to empire. Charles's Restoration supporters acquired special privileges of colonies, trade, and wealth. The creation of the Royal African Company and the Barbados Company, two enterprises that produced great profits for their stockholders, went to Charles's allies. So, too, did the newly organized proprietary colonies in North America. Earlier, both James I and Charles I had established that the southern boundaries of Virginia existed near the Albemarle Sound. The Carolana colony had encompassed a vast territory existing only in theory; in its aftermath, Charles II, in 1663, announced the creation of the Carolina colony. Like many other early English colonies, this was a proprietary colony. And, as in other proprietary colonies, the British Crown bestowed the power of colonial administration, land management, and government upon those favored by the monarch. What was most unusual—and ultimately unwieldy—about the Carolina proprietary was its shape and organization. First, rather than a single proprietor, Charles awarded control of the new colony to eight Lords Proprietors, all of whom were important Restoration figures. The colony's royal charter empowered the proprietors to organize government, dispose of land, provide for military protection, and levy taxes. Subsequently, the Lords Proprietors issued several documents—one of which was written by the famous English political philosopher John Locke—laying out their vision for the colony. These documents, known as the Fundamental Constitutions, established the colony's constitutional boundaries. In some respects, the Fundamental Constitutions reasserted English constitutional traditions; the document reaffirmed the recognized right to representative government. But the Fundamental Constitutions broke new ground in other respects. Notably, they recognized slavery, for most of the Lords Proprietors were deeply involved in the Atlantic slave trade and Caribbean slavery. The most remarkable provisions of the Fundamental Constitutions were its attempts to provide for religious toleration, but also to establish the Church of England—that is, make it a state-supported institution. The proprietors further envisioned a system of manors headed by landed aristocrats who would preside over manorial courts that would serve as the basis of civil government. Clearly, however, these portions of the Fundamental Constitutions bore little relationship to the realities of settlement and daily life in the Carolina colony.

The Carolina proprietors focused their efforts on the establishment of a colony at Charles Town (now Charleston, South Carolina) in 1670. It attracted the attention of slaveholding sugar planters from the English Caribbean colony of Barbados. With a deep-water harbor and thus excellent trade facilities—in contrast to the Albemarle—Charles Town quickly became a thriving commercial hub for the Carolina colony. In its early years, from the 1670s to 1690s, Charles Town was a center for the fur trade and Indian slave trade, as well as for the production of foodstuffs, especially livestock, for the food-hungry Caribbean colonies. Near the beginning of the eighteenth century, however, the introduction of rice cultivation ushered in an economic boom. Slavery spread rapidly, and the prevalence of large rice plantations, with a growing slave population, enriched white rice planters and their English merchant benefactors. By

1700, the Carolina colony contained widely divergent interests: two Carolinas were emerging. Charles Town was a society of extreme differences, with a large slave majority encircling a wealthy planter society that was connected to Atlantic trade and capitalism. In contrast, Albemarle remained isolated, poor, and disconnected, and its political culture was profoundly antiauthoritarian.

The proprietors themselves recognized the reality of these two worlds during the late 1680s, when they authorized separate governments, with the

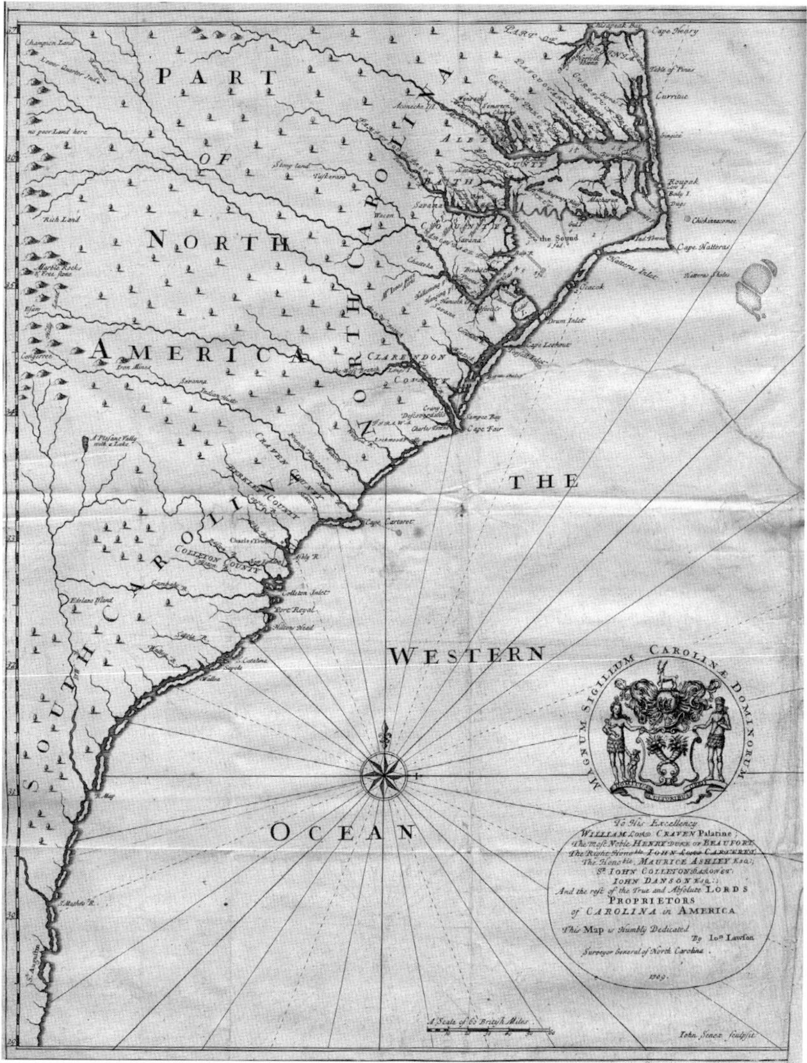

Figure 2.2 John Lawson's map of Carolina, 1709. *Source: North Carolina Collection, University of North Carolina Library at Chapel Hill.*

appointment of a deputy governor and local assembly to rule a "North Carolina" associated with the Albemarle and a governor and assembly to rule a "South Carolina" connected to Charles Town. The Albemarle, between the arrival of the first white settlers in the 1650s and the beginning of the Tuscarora War in 1711, experienced a profound period of isolation, political instability, and economic stagnation. Nonetheless, during this period the characteristics of North Carolina's distinctive social and political culture began to emerge.

Political Instability

Soon after their arrival, Albemarle pioneers experienced problems. While the Lords Proprietors saw the Charles Town colony as a source of wealth, they regarded the Albemarle as troublesome and unprofitable. North Carolina remained economically underdeveloped and politically neglected for good reasons. Hemmed in by a treacherous coastline that denied them and their agricultural products easy access to the outside world, settlers found tobacco cultivation unrewarding. Inhabiting a region with an ill-defined boundary, many settlers owned land under unclear circumstances, with deeds coming from both Virginia and Carolina authorities. These economic insecurities helped to foster a culture of frontier-minded independence and an ingrained instability that infused social life, politics, and everyday life. North Carolina's development diverged significantly from that of the Charles Town colony, and proprietary officials ruled the former only with difficulty.

The tenuousness of proprietor rule in the Albemarle was particularly apparent during the last third of the 1600s. Between 1677 and 1711, no fewer than three rebellions against the legally established government occurred in North Carolina: Culpeper's Rebellion (1677), Gibbs's Rebellion (1689), and Cary's Rebellion (1708–11). All three uprisings reflected weak political authority, an antiauthoritarian political culture, and an almost endemic strand of instability. In December 1677, a complicated series of events led to Culpeper's Rebellion, but the basic issue involved the proprietors' attempt to enforce the Navigation Acts and the British colonial system. Under these laws, English merchants and ships would control all trade within the empire. North Carolina's geography of shallow coves and inlets provided an ideal harbor for the smaller ships that carried the "coastwise" (or intercoastal) trade among colonists in North America as well as trade from English North America to the West Indies. The Navigation Act of 1660, for example, banned direct trade with non-English ports in the Caribbean and elsewhere, and prohibited any trade but that carried in English vessels. During the next decades, smuggling of tobacco and livestock grew into a cottage industry in North Carolina. When local smuggler and political figure George Durant was arrested in 1677, his fellow residents,

Figure 2.3 The Newbold White House, the oldest brick house in North Carolina. It was built in 1730 by Abraham Sanders, a Quaker farmer, on the banks of the Perquimans River. *Source: Keith D Beecham/Shutterstock.*

led by John Culpeper, rose up and overthrew the proprietary governor, Thomas Miller.

Culpeper's Rebellion challenged the Lords Proprietors, who remained in England and cared little for the situation in Albemarle. In North Carolina, the pro-smuggling faction sometimes opposed proprietary authority, sometimes not: the ousted Governor Miller himself changed sides several times. When the highest English colonial authority, the Privy Council, finally considered Culpeper's Rebellion in 1679, they refused to reinstate Miller. And so it went in the Albemarle of the late 1600s: weak and indifferent proprietary authority, inept and often corrupt governors, and a rebellious and alienated population all resulted in a series of rebellions. England's Glorious Revolution in 1688–89 sparked uprisings across colonial North America, North Carolina included. In 1689, a local ship's captain, John Gibbs, overthrew the appointed proprietary authorities and briefly declared himself governor. Although Gibbs's Rebellion lasted only a few days, it suggested broad, underlying trends of social and political instability.

Just as smuggling was an indicator of social conditions and a rebellious political culture, so was religion a lightning rod for larger issues. The English Parliament enacted legislation in the late 1600s requiring all subjects to pledge loyalty, by means of an oath, to the Church of England. Those who refused to do so became "dissenters," and thereby lost the ability to vote or hold political office. In North Carolina, efforts to establish Anglicanism encountered powerful opposition from the colony's Quakers, who had suffered persecution in England and Virginia and migrated to Albemarle precisely because of Carolina's policy of religious toleration announced in the Fundamental Constitutions. By the early 1700s, several thousand Quakers inhabited the Albemarle, and there they organized three monthly meetings and occupied important political leadership positions. John Archdale, who had converted to Quakerism in 1674 and purchased a share of the Carolina proprietary in 1678, lived in the Albemarle between 1683 and 1686. Archdale became governor of the Carolina colony in Charles Town, and he appointed another Quaker, Thomas Harvey, as deputy governor in charge of the Albemarle. In general, Quakers dominated the Albemarle's council and assembly for much of the 1680s.

After Archdale's return to England in 1698, the Anglican forces went on the offensive. The deputy governor Henderson Walker and his successors, Robert Daniel, Thomas Cary, and William Glover, sought to uproot Quaker influence by sponsoring Anglican missionaries to come to Carolina and encouraging the assembly to pass new legislation establishing the Church of England as the official church. The Vestry Acts of 1701 and 1703 expanded Anglican influence by laying out parishes and vestries, creating churches, and requiring financial support, or "establishment," through public taxation, and placing political disabilities on religious dissenters.

The Quakers resisted these efforts by lobbying hard with the proprietors, who voided the Vestry Act of 1701 and, in 1705, removed Daniel and Cary from power. In 1706, matters became more complicated when Cary, a Charles Town merchant and son-in-law of John Archdale, led a revolt against Glover, unseating him and installing a new government. After elections in 1708, an assembly endorsed Cary. He then held power, under dubious legal authority, for the next three years. The appointment in 1711 of Cary's successor, Edward Hyde, changed little: Hyde also enforced anti-Quaker policies. Now both the pro- and anti-Quaker factions took up arms. What became known as Cary's Rebellion only ended after Alexander Spotswood, the governor of Virginia, dispatched a man-of-war and troops to the Albemarle. The troops dispersed the rebels, described by Spotswood as "a mob up in arms obstructing the cause of justice."[5] Cary was shipped to London under charges of rebellion and sedition. The political ascendancy of the North Carolina Quakers ended and disfranchisement of dissenters became standard policy in the colony.

The Tuscarora War

Since the arrival of immigrants from Virginia during the 1650s, the white population had been confined to four precincts (later counties) whose boundaries were defined by the Albemarle Sound to the south and the Chowan River to the west. Rivers separated the four precincts—Currituck, Pasquotank, Perquimans, and Chowan—and planters remained isolated from each other. The Albemarle's confinement reflected the continued military power of the largest Indian group in eastern North Carolina, Tuscaroras. Calling themselves, Unkwa-hunwa, which meant "the Royal People," Tuscaroras were Iroquois-speaking Indians, related linguistically to the powerful Five Iroquois Nations to the north. They had migrated to central North Carolina by AD 600, establishing villages on the river valleys of that region. Engaged in agriculture and hunting, the Tuscarora inhabited fifteen towns from the Tar-Pamlico River south to the Neuse River. They were known as fearsome fighters, quick to seek revenge. Christoph von Graffenried described their "strong anger, which generally becomes wrath," while another white observer recounted how they made "personal murders oftentimes [into] national quarrels."[6]

For a time, these Indians profited from the presence of Euro-Americans. Their enemies among Algonquian tribes had suffered precipitous losses soon after whites arrived; in particular, Chowanoke Indians, who competed with Tuscaroras for territory, saw their ranks severely depleted. Tuscaroras also profited as intermediaries between colonists seeking trade in furs, salt, and copper, and their trade connections extended as far as the Gulf Coast and the Great Lakes. Trade ties between Carolinians and Indians also encouraged the spread of Indian slavery. Warfare and raiding among Native Americans of the region became common practice in order to generate captives and slaves for slave markets to the south, in Charles Town. The slave trade became an all-consuming activity among Indians, and the Southeast developed the largest traffic in enslaved Indians during this period. Slavery served further to destabilize and fragment Indian society and, ultimately, to exacerbate Indian-white tensions and resentment about the growing economic, cultural, and political presence of the Carolinians.

By signing a treaty with settlers in 1672 as well as through informal understandings, Tuscaroras succeeded for the next generation in restricting the white population to the northern banks of the Albemarle Sound. This limitation resulted in a land shortage among colonists that figured into internal conflicts and political strife in early North Carolina. Various forces altered this balance of power. First, Tuscaroras, through contact with Euro-Americans, experienced changes. They, too, suffered a population decline because of disease; a smallpox epidemic in 1707 devastated the tribe. Tuscaroras also experienced differences among themselves. Each town was an autonomous political entity which a *teethha*, or king, governed. Over time, the northern and southern Tuscarora experienced contact with Euro-Americans. It is important to keep in mind that there was no single Tuscarora tribe: like most American Indian groups, they were an assemblage of allied or confederated villages who shared a common culture and language. Northern Tuscaroras, led by Tom Blunt, lived on the shores of the Pamlico River, in the town of Ucouhnerunt. This group existed in closest proximity to settlers and was linked to Virginia traders to the north. With intermarried, mixed-race families, the northern Tuscaroras possessed ties of kin and trade to the Albemarle settlement. Many of them had adopted English ways.

At the same time, southern Tuscarora villages, led by a chief known as King Hancock, were relatively more isolated from the influence of settlers, and they felt more threatened by white expansion. Meanwhile, increased pressures arose among white settlers to "open up" Native American lands for encroachment. Within the colony, there had long been pro- and anti-expansionist factions; some favored an active policy designed ultimately to drive Indians from their land. The North Carolina colony expanded southward with the establishment of white settlement along the Pamlico and the founding of the town of Bath in 1705. By 1711, forty or fifty families lived in this region, which was divided into three precincts.

With the support of this land-hungry faction, several new immigrant groups arrived in the North Carolina colony. There were plans to establish a settlement of French Protestants, or Huguenots, along the lower Trent River in 1708. Though nothing came of these plans, another group of Protestant refugees like the Huguenots were Swiss immigrants from the section of the Rhine Valley called the Palatinate. They obtained a grant of 17,500 acres from the Lords Proprietors to establish a settlement, known as New Bern, on a tract between the Neuse and Trent Rivers. Under the direction of Baron Christoph von Graffenried, the New Bern settlement began with 100 settlers in September 1710. Although the lands were supposedly unoccupied, New Bern was located at the site of a former Neusioc town, Chattooka, or Cartouca. John Lawson, who arrived in 1700 and subsequently traveled across North Carolina, became surveyor general of the colony in 1708. He became responsible for supervising the move of von Graffenried's Palatines to New Bern, and it has been said that Lawson drove off the resident Native Americans and sought to profit by land development in the region.

Trouble was brewing between whites and Indians. Traders, often from Virginia and South Carolina, created a web of dependency among Native Americans, who came to rely on supplies of English goods such as metal knives and axes for use in hunting and warfare. Traders also supplied Indian groups with firearms and gunpowder, as well as rum. In exchange, Indians supplied the traders' caravans with deerskins and slaves. Over time, the trading relationship became mutually dependent, and the Tuscarora were deeply immersed in the economic network. The demand for manufactured goods drove Indians to deplete deer herds, because they had become dependent on metal tools, utensils, and weapons. The expanding Indian slave trade encouraged constant slave raiding and warfare by competing groups of Indians. The prevalence of rum fostered the spread of alcoholism with multiple adverse social consequences for Indian society. Trade and contact brought exposure to European diseases to Indian groups and, periodically, devastating epidemics. Traders were the main contact between white and Indian societies, yet these individuals were known for having rough-hewn, abusive personalities. Often they cheated or price-gouged. Finally, Englishmen, traders and others, often mistaking Indian sexual practices as promiscuousness, had little compunction about sexually assaulting Indian women.

The New Bern settlement posed an immediate threat to southern Tuscaroras. There is some evidence that the factionalization of the North Carolinians evident in Cary's Rebellion affected attitudes toward Indians. Von Graffenried would later claim that those "few rioters" who were Cary supporters had "kindled" Indian resentment. Virginia governor Alexander Spotswood chimed in that Cary and his allies had "greatly encouraged" the "unnatural Divisions and Animosities" among Indians.[7] Whether the Cary insurgents actually encouraged resentment is uncertain, but some Indians no doubt recognized, and sought to exploit, differences among the Carolinians.

The event that precipitated conflict occurred in September 1711, when Lawson and von Graffenried traveled up the Neuse River, probably in search of locations for further white expansion. Tuscaroras regarded this as an insulting intrusion and a threat, especially coming from Lawson, who had become known as an advocate of expansionism. The Indians captured Lawson and von Graffenried and took them to a war council convened by King Hancock, the leader of southern Tuscaroras. Hancock, a moderate in his posture toward whites, was under considerable pressure from his younger warriors to launch an attack to limit white expansion, or at least to teach the settlers a lesson. Other Indian allies closer to white settlers, those living in the region between the Neuse and Pamlico Rivers, such as the Cores, Bear River Indians, Pamlicos, Weetocks, Neusiocs, and Machapungas, were fed up with intrusions on their lands. The Indians took Lawson and von Graffenried captive, keeping them in Catechna, Hancock's town on Contentea Creek, where the intruders were questioned before a meeting of forty elders, including Tuscarora and other tribes. Although the Tuscaroras originally intended to set both men free, the Core King of Chattooka, known as Core Tom, became involved in a violent argument with Lawson, who, according to von Graffenried, denounced the Indian king, saying "we would avenge ourselves on the Indians."

The Indians now condemned both men to death. Lawson and a black slave with him were executed. Some accounts reported that Lawson was tortured to death, using pine splinters stuck into his skin and then slowly set on fire. Other accounts stated that the Indians slit his throat. According to Virginian William Byrd, the Tuscarora "resented their wrongs a little too severely upon Mr. Lawson, who under colour of being Surveyor Gen'l had encroached too much upon their territories."[8] After killing Lawson—whose account of his travels throughout the Carolinas remains one of the fullest about Native American life at the time—the Indians eventually set von Graffenried free. But Lawson's murder marked the beginning of hostilities, with the southern Tuscaroras convinced that the New Bern settlement represented a violation of the traditional understanding that whites would not invade Indian lands south of the Albemarle. Perhaps hoping to end white settlement and to negotiate a more secure treaty, Hancock expected to take advantage of the division in white ranks evident in Cary's Rebellion. At dawn on September 22, 1711, Tuscaroras and their Core, Matchapunga, Pamlico, Bear River, and Neusioc allies—some 500 warriors in all—gathered at Catechna and, sweeping down the south banks of the Neuse and the Pamlico Rivers, launched three days of attacks on white settlements on the Neuse and the Pamlico. Within two hours of the attacks, 130 colonists lay dead, an equal number were wounded, and scores had been taken captive.

Stunned, the whites responded with a counterattack intended to exterminate all southern Tuscaroras. The whites retreated to eleven garrisons in the Albemarle, but with depleted resources and a divided colony, they were unable to mount an effective offensive. King Hancock may have hoped that negotiations would follow his surprise attack. He also might have hoped that northern Tuscaroras would join his confederacy, but they remained neutral spectators throughout the war. Meanwhile, out of desperation, white North Carolinians appealed for aid from Virginia and South Carolina. While the Virginians reacted equivocally and slowly, South Carolina responded by appropriating £4,000 and raising a relief expedition under the command of Colonel John Barnwell, which was composed of some 500 Indians and 30 whites.

Barnwell and his expedition wanted booty: Indian allies were promised cash and captives whom they could sell as slaves. Arriving in North Carolina in January 1712, the Barnwell expedition included nearly a thousand warriors from Waterees, Corsaboys, Congarees, Waxhaws, Pee Dees, Sagarees, Catawbas, Suterees, Apalachees, and Yamasees. Half of the Indian allies deserted after a difficult crossing of the Cape Fear River, but the remaining forces helped Barnwell attack Tuscarora towns, wreaking havoc, while the Tuscaroras retreated to nine forts located in close proximity to one another. Barnwell took the Tuscarora fort at Nahunta, on the Neuse River, on January 20, 1712. He proceeded east in search of Hancock's town, but with the passage of time, many of his remaining Indian allies abandoned him, taking captives and booty (much of which had been taken from Carolinians by the Tuscaroras in their initial attack) with them.

Pushing forward to Catechna, Barnwell ran low on provisions and now oversaw a depleted force of 94 whites (including 67 North Carolinians) and 148 Indians. The North Carolinians refused to provision Barnwell and did little to support his expedition. Reaching Hancock's town on March 5, 1712, Barnwell found a well-entrenched and fortified enemy, on the creek bank opposite

Catechna, manned by 130 Indians. The fortifications included high palisades and earthen ramparts, perhaps the work of a runaway slave from Virginia named Harry, who had learned about constructing these types of fortifications and may have been working with the Tuscaroras. Despite several assaults, Barnwell could make little progress against Hancock's forces. After negotiations in March and April 1712, Barnwell agreed to lift his siege and make a truce with Tuscaroras, who were holding white and black hostages whom they threatened to kill. With a dwindling force and only scant support from North Carolina, Barnwell concluded this unauthorized treaty. The Tuscaroras freed twenty-four children who had been held captive, along with two slaves, while nearly all of the Indians' plunder had already been sold to Virginia traders. Meanwhile, Hancock fled to Virginia, and North Carolina governor Edward Hyde denounced the peace and bitterly criticized Barnwell. Soon thereafter, the Indian allies, who remained in the vicinity, launched attacks against the Tuscarora, plundered the countryside, and searched the area for captives. The remaining Tuscaroras retaliated by attacking white settlements.

North Carolinians again appealed for help from South Carolina, and in December 1712, Col. James Moore arrived with a force of 33 whites and 850 Indians, mostly Catawbas and Yamasees. Moore's forces marched to Hancock's fort at Neoheroka, and, after a three-day battle in which Moore's forces used artillery to reduce the Tuscaroras, the Carolinians prevailed. On March 20, 1713, Tuscaroras suffered a major defeat, with a loss of 950, about half of whom were killed, the rest enslaved. Many of the surviving southern Tuscaroras fled the area and moved to join the Iroquois' Five Nations Confederacy in New York. In the meantime, Tom Blunt caught Hancock and handed him over to the Carolinians, who immediately murdered him, and Blunt's northern Tuscaroras signed a new treaty recognizing Blunt as Tuscarora leader and seeking to oblige all members of the tribe to live under his supremacy. Those who refused to do so were declared outlaws; about fifty Tuscaroras held out. These guerrilla fighters killed some twenty whites living on the Alligator River in the spring of 1713; they killed another twenty-five on Roanoke Island. Retreating to the swamps of North Carolina, the outlaw band of Tuscaroras resisted capture until Blunt led an all-out effort to kill or capture them. The last phase of the Tuscarora War occurred on February 11, 1715, when Tuscaroras signed a treaty that established a reservation in Bertie County.

The Pirate Colony

The same conditions that fostered political instability also made North Carolina a center of North American piracy. The Albemarle's geographical isolation made it an ideal place of operation for smugglers and a physical haven for pirates. But piracy would not have thrived in North Carolina were there not already a political culture that welcomed it: the proprietors' weak political grip, the endemic antiauthoritarianism, and prevalent corruption all created conditions that fostered piracy. This was, in addition, at a time when the line between legally sanctioned and unlawful theft on the high seas remained murky. Between the late sixteenth and the early eighteenth centuries, privateering thrived as an officially sanctioned instrument of national policy, and European monarchs continued to use it as a way to harass and disrupt enemy shipping when they lacked adequate naval forces. In England, monarchs issued Letters of Marque and Reprisal that empowered merchant seamen to capture enemy ships and their cargoes during wartime. These "prizes" were sold, with the profits divided between the government and the seamen, and privateering provided a great source of income for shipowners and crews. During the early 1700s, privateering no longer occupied a place in the new English mercantilist empire, and, with no royal sponsorship, many of the *privateers* suddenly became *pirates*.

Undaunted, many persons chose piracy as the path of social mobility. Pirate crews attracted outcasts—runaway servants, lower-class seamen, and African Americans—and piracy held out the promise of instant wealth, though at a high risk. Not all pirates were male. Anne Bonny (or Bonney) was born in Ireland but migrated with her father, a lawyer, somewhere in Carolina. Known to possess a "fierce and courageous" disposition, Bonny fell in love with a poor sailor. When her father opposed the match, she ran away with the sailor to the West Indies and there began a life as a pirate, serving with Capt. John Rackham, "Calico Jack." Leaving her husband, she joined several pirate crews, fell in love with another pirate—who turned out to be a woman, Mary Read—and enjoyed a notorious reputation. Most of Bonny's career was spent in the West Indies, though some of it may have occurred off the Carolina coast. She probably died after her apprehension as a pirate.

Pirate ships were relatively democratic, especially compared to the highly regimented and brutally oppressive national navies. Captains were often elected, and they could lose their ships if they became too unpopular. Other officers were also elected, and the pirate crew enjoyed extraordinary powers of governance. At the same time, the pirate crews were only rarely whipped, in stark contrast to seamen of this era, who were brutally flogged for even the most minor offenses. As a sociological phenomenon, piracy was not new; pirates—and theft on the high seas—have existed as long as recorded human civilization. During the 1600s, much of the pirate trade was concentrated in the Caribbean, where pirates temporarily controlled islands which they used as bases to prey on the Spanish galleons en route from the American colonies to Spain. Hispaniola, Jamaica, Tortuga, and New Providence (now Nassau, Bahamas) all became piracy centers that were tolerated by the English as weapons in their world power struggle against Spain.

Caribbean pirates eventually became a nuisance even to the English, whose shipping was the subject of attacks, and they made a concerted effort to eradicate piracy. To lead this effort English authorities in 1717 appointed Capt. Woodes Rogers, a former privateer, as governor of the Bahama Islands. Many pirates had already relocated to North America, where between about 1690 and 1720 they participated in the so-called "Golden Age of Piracy." Pirates enjoyed the unofficial protection of the merchants and colonial governments. Pillaging and stealing on the high seas, they found a market for their goods in major North American ports such as Boston, Providence, New York City, Philadelphia, and Charleston. Pirates found particular advantages in basing their activities out of North Carolina. Pirate ships were smaller and faster than most ocean-going craft, and they were ideally suited to navigate the shallow sounds and coves of the North Carolina coast, which made excellent hiding places.

The best-known Carolina pirates were Stede Bonnet and Edward Teach. Bonnet had an atypical background for a pirate. Born to a sugar-planter family in Barbados, he had achieved the rank of major in the island militia and was at least of moderate means. Then Bonnet experienced what today might be described as a "midlife" crisis. Perhaps because of marital problems—what one contemporary called "some Discomforts he found in the married state"—sometime in early 1717 Bonnet fled his home and family and became a pirate. Purchasing his own ship—something of a rarity among pirates—Bonnet outfitted it himself, naming it the *Revenge*, while he hired his own crew and paid their wages himself. Late one evening in the summer of 1717, Bonnet departed the Barbados port of Bridgetown for the open Atlantic and began work off the capes of Virginia. Bonnet's career was a prolific one. Plundering vessels in the Atlantic, he took his stolen booty to New York City, where merchants routinely trafficked with pirates. After a costly encounter with a Spanish man-of-war, the *Revenge* was badly damaged and Bonnet, severely injured, was faced with the loss of half of his men. Meeting the notorious pirate Blackbeard in the Bahamas in September 1717, Bonnet allied himself with Blackbeard's expanding flotilla, which preyed on scores of ships in the South Atlantic. Off the coast of the present-day Central American country of Belize, Bonnet's crew was on the verge of mutiny when Blackbeard took over the *Revenge*. Later, when this ship ran aground off Topsail Island in North Carolina, Bonnet fled to the town of Bath and temporarily took an oath of allegiance to the Crown. After Bonnet, using another ship, made further depredations based at the mouth of the Cape Fear River, Col. William Rhett, receiver-general of South Carolina, led an expedition that captured Bonnet in late September 1718, and he was taken to Charleston, tried, and hanged on November 8, 1718.

Without question the best-known pirate of the Golden Age of Piracy was Blackbeard. His origins remain obscure (he was born either in Bristol, England, or in Jamaica), and there remains real uncertainty about his name (alternatively, Edward "Teach" or, less commonly, "Thatch"). A large man, Teach earned his

Figure 2.4 Hanging of Stede Bonnet, 1718, Charleston, SC.

nickname because of his dark black beard, which he braided and often tied with ribbons. An account written not long after his death described him in this way:

> This Beard was black, which he suffered to grow of an extravagant Length; as to Breadth, it came up to his eyes; he was accustomed to twist it with Ribbons, in small Tails; … his Eyes naturally looking fierce and wild, made him altogether such a Figure, that Imagination cannot form an Idea of a Fury, from Hell, to look more frightful.[9]

Figure 2.5 Bell recovered from a wreck reputed to be Blackbeard's ship, *Queen Anne's Revenge*. *Source: North Carolina Department of Natural and Cultural Resources.*

Blackbeard emerged as a pirate after working for the famous English privateer, Benjamin Hornigold. Blackbeard's greatest successes as a pirate came in actions in the Caribbean and off the Carolina coast during 1717–18. Probably as a stopgap measure, Blackbeard took refuge in the town of Bath, where he applied for a pardon under the Act of Grace, which Parliament had enacted in 1717. Under terms of the act, all pirates were eligible for a royal pardon by renouncing piracy and taking an oath of allegiance to the Crown. Blackbeard took the oath and became a citizen of Bath, and ingratiated himself with the leading figures of the town, including Gov. Charles Eden and Secretary and Collector of Customs Tobias Knight. Soon local officials found that Blackbeard, who had no intention of renouncing piracy, sought what one contemporary called "a more favorable Opportunity to play the same Game over again"[10] by providing a lucrative trade in stolen goods. Blackbeard quickly achieved respectability: spreading money around the colony, he married the 16-year-old daughter of a local planter—with the marriage ceremony performed by Governor Eden. Working out of Bath and another base at Ocracoke Island, Blackbeard enjoyed the unofficial protection of the North Carolina government, and during the next several months preyed on shipping in the South Atlantic.

Eventually, Blackbeard's depredations became so extensive and included so many colonial and English ships that even North Carolina merchants and planters became determined to eradicate him. Realizing that they would get nowhere with their own government, they dispatched a secret delegation to the Virginia governor and longtime pirate-fighter, Alexander Spotswood. Two Royal Navy ships, the *Pearl* and the *Lyme*, were in Chesapeake Bay, but the governor instead hired two sloops, the *Jane* and the *Ranger*, because they were smaller and better suited for North Carolina's shallow waters. Led by Lt. Robert Maynard, the expedition departed in November 1718; that the expedition occurred without the knowledge of North Carolina's authorities and involved the transgression of Virginia authority into North Carolina reflected the reality of Blackbeard's collusion with local officials. Maynard fought a pitched battle with the pirate chieftain, and, after terrific losses on both sides in hand-to-hand fighting, Blackbeard was killed and the pirates vanquished.

The surviving pirates—four of whom were African American—were tried and executed in Williamsburg in March 1719. Documents discovered aboard Blackbeard's ship, the *Adventure*, implicated leading North Carolinians, especially the Secretary of the colony, Tobias Knight. Searches by Maynard's forces discovered stores of stolen sugar in Knight's possession, while a number of captured pirates testified about their involvement with North Carolina officials. Nonetheless, though Virginia officials recommended that Knight be indicted for piracy and though Governor Eden appeared implicated, neither man was ever convicted for any crime. This may reflect the circumstantial nature of the evidence, or it might reflect the murky area of collusion in which both men were engaged.

* * *

The demise of Bonnet and Blackbeard marked the passing of an era. Piracy was made possible by the existence of conditions endemic to early North Carolina: a particular geography defined by a hazardous coast that provided easy escape routes for pirates; the longtime existence of smuggling as a local industry; and, above all, a fragile and weakly established social and political order. These particular conditions defined the distinctive qualities of social life and political culture in the Albemarle region of the late seventeenth and early eighteenth centuries. The end of piracy marked a move away from these conditions. A key to economic development in the South Atlantic colonies of Virginia and South

Carolina—both of which had well-established economic, social, and political systems by the early eighteenth century—lay in the introduction of African slavery. Slavery, well established as part of the North Carolina legal, political, and social system since the establishment of the proprietary colonies, expanded significantly after 1715, growing with a rising white population and the size of the colony. The social system that accompanied slavery depended on plantations and the exploitation of land and labor which accompanied it. Beyond this, it defined the social system.

Notes

1 Bland Simpson, *The Inner Islands: A Carolinian's Sound Country* (Chapel Hill: University of North Carolina Press, 2006), p. 25; Journal of George Fox, http://docsouth.unc.edu/csr/index.html/document/csr01-0085.

2 Noeleen McIlvenna, *A Very Mutinous People: The Struggle for North Carolina, 1660–1713* (Chapel Hill: University of North Carolina Press, 2009), p. 21.

3 Wesley Frank Craven, *The Colonies in Transition, 1660–1713* (New York: Harper & Row, 1967).

4 Margaret Supplee Smith and Emily Herring Wilson, *North Carolina Women Making History* (Chapel Hill: University of North Carolina Press, 1999), p. 24.

5 Stephen Jay White, "From the Vestry Act to Cary's Rebellion: North Carolina's Quakers and Colonial Politics," *Southern Friend* 8 (Autumn 1986): p. 18.

6 David La Vere, *The Tuscarora War: Indians, Settlers, and the Fight for the Carolina Colonies* (Chapel Hill: University of North Carolina Press, 2013), p. 46.

7 Allan Gallay, *The Indian Slave Trade: The Rise of the English Empire in the American South, 1670–1717* (New Haven, CT: Yale University Press, 2002), p. 262.

8 La Vere, *Tuscarora War*, p. 67.

9 Lindley S. Butler, *Pirates, Privateers, & Rebel Raiders of the Carolina Coast* (Chapel Hill: University of North Carolina Press, 2000), p. 31.

10 Quoted in Butler, *Pirates*, p. 40.

3

A Slave Society

After 1720, a new era in North Carolina history dawned. With the crushing defeat of the southern Tuscaroras, white settlers, no longer facing any Indian threat in eastern North Carolina, poured across the boundaries of the colony. During the next generation, eager migrants raced from the coast to the Appalachian foothills. From the geographically restricted region of the Albemarle Sound, settlers moved south and west, toward the interior of the Coastal Plain. Meanwhile, a number of South Carolinians moved north and established a society of rice and indigo plantations in the Lower Cape Fear valley. The rush of settlers would push farther westward from the 1740s to the 1770s, as white, largely non-English migrants moved down the Great Valley extending from Pennsylvania into Maryland and Virginia. These migrants, part of a distinctive pre-Revolutionary backcountry society, traveled on the Great Wagon Road across the Blue Ridge into the Carolinas.

Despite this era of intense change, many ingredients of Albemarle social and political culture endured during the 1700s: residents of the colony remained staunchly antiauthoritarian, and successive colonial governors exercised tenuous power and exerted weak authority. This antiauthoritarianism reflected the persisting reality of North Carolina's geography and the obstacles that it created for the profitable exploitation of land and labor embodied in the plantation. Antiauthoritarianism also became imbedded in the insular culture of rural areas, where the vast majority of whites lived.

The most important change of the post-1715 era was the importation of a large African enslaved population. Despite the presence of slaves since the 1670s, prior to the eighteenth century, the enslaved population was scattered and small. That changed radically after 1715. A rush of new, coerced Africans that peaked during the 1770s remade life and redefined society. North Carolina moved from a society with slaves to a slave society, in which politics, culture, the economy, and the social system depended on the presence of an enslaved population.

North Carolina: Change and Tradition in a Southern State, Second Edition. William A. Link.

Origins of African Slavery

Across the southern British colonies on the Eastern Seaboard, a crucial transition occurred during the seventeenth century: the main form of labor in the plantation economy became enslaved African Americans. An intense demand for labor in the Chesapeake colonies of Virginia and Maryland followed the robust and expanding tobacco-plantation system. Although during the early years, white indentured servants fulfilled the labor demand, planters began to import slave laborers from Africa and the Caribbean in ever-increasing numbers. By the early 1700s, the Chesapeake had fully and enthusiastically converted to slavery and the social, political, and economic system that accompanied it.

Without question, the adoption and extensive use of chattel slavery were based on race: all enslaved people were Africans or of African origin. As the system of slavery became accepted by custom and law in British North America, moreover, it relied on a cultural, social, and political system of race prejudice. The prevalence of slavery provided a foundation for racism and white supremacy. In North Carolina, the origins of race slavery differed significantly from the instance of the Chesapeake: the system of enslavement was already well established, and the early white colonizers from Virginia and South Carolina were either slaveholders or eager to become slaveholders. Chattel slavery was a given from the beginning in North Carolina, although it provided a linchpin for the emerging racial hierarchy.

In contrast to that of Virginia, the charter of the Carolina colony (in 1663) had expressly condoned African American slavery. The original eight Lords Proprietors were deeply involved in expanding both the Atlantic slave trade and the sugar and slaveholder bastion of Barbados, in the Caribbean. Early on, the Carolina proprietors employed the headright system, which also existed in Virginia. Under the headright system, first announced by the proprietors in 1665, anyone immigrating to the colony could receive 50 acres of land. In addition, those who paid the passage of immigrants—either white servants or African American slaves—received 50 acres per person. The headright system thus subsidized slavery. In 1669, the Fundamental Constitutions affirmed the existence of slavery and embedded it into the constitutional structure of the new colony. All Carolina whites would have "absolute power and authority" over their slaves, it stated. A key component of this political structure was the creation of chattel slavery: that is, not only would slaves remain in servitude for their lifetime, but so would their descendants. The Fundamental Constitutions affirmed chattel slavery by stating that even those slaves converting to Christianity would remain in bondage.

These early provisions for chattel slavery in the Carolina colony reflected the influence of Barbadian colonists/proprietors, who sought to transplant Caribbean slave culture. Their efforts proved fantastically successful in Charles

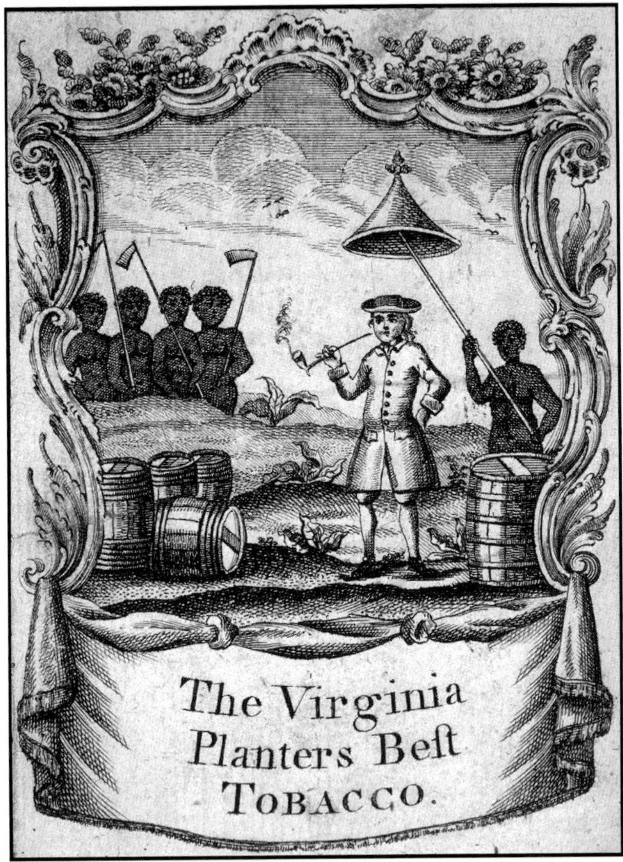

Figure 3.1 Planter, slaves, and tobacco barrels. *Source: Accession #1980-165, image #C1980-884, no.16. The Colonial Williamsburg Foundation.*

Town. Within the space of a generation—from Charles Town's founding in the 1670s to the early 1700s—South Carolina became a thoroughly slave society. Early on, Charles Town was a leading center of the trade for enslaved Indians. Then, the introduction of rice cultivation in the 1690s encouraged a rush of African slaves, as plantations spread in the marshy but agriculturally rich lands of the low country. In South Carolina's plantation districts, slavery soon assumed Caribbean proportions, as enslaved Africans outnumbered whites by a margin of nine to one.

Slavery existed from the early days of the Albemarle settlement, as immigrants from Virginia brought their chattel slaves with them. Yet the settlement's underdeveloped economy retarded the growth of slavery, and in the Albemarle virtually all slaves lived in small groupings, working not only with tobacco but grains such as corn and wheat and livestock such as hogs and cattle. The slave population of the Albemarle remained small relative to that of the burgeoning Charles Town colony: in 1710, for example, an early population count in two northeastern North Carolina counties, Pasquotank and Currituck, found an overall slave population of perhaps 800, along with 1,871 whites.[1] While South Carolina was rapidly moving toward majority-slave status, North Carolina's approximately 1,000 slaves in 1705 composed about a fifth of the total population.

Between the 1720s and 1750s, the population of the North Carolina colony grew, as its economy began to diversify. By 1754, there were 15,000 African Americans, as compared with 62,000 whites. In the next decades both the white and black population doubled, and slaves composed about a quarter of the total population. By mid-century, whites occupied most of the lands between the Atlantic shore and the Fall Line, with several zones of occupation. The Albemarle population spread westward and southward, up river valleys with rich alluvial soils. These settlers took with them tobacco culture, which expanded during the period, and used slaves as their primary source of labor. Plantation agriculture also spread into southeastern North Carolina, near the mouth of the Cape Fear River (and present-day Wilmington). In the marshy areas immediately bordering South Carolina in the Lower Cape Fear valley, a small area of rice culture—perhaps no more than 500 acres—comprised larger holdings of slaves.

Towns, which had not existed during the early years of the colony's history, began to develop. Bath was the colony's first town, chartered in 1705. New Bern was founded four years later, while Beaufort was chartered in 1715. Edenton, the most important town of the Albemarle Sound area, was founded in 1722. In northeastern North Carolina, these towns played important roles as ports for export of the burgeoning forest products industry, as well as for the export of tobacco, livestock, grains, and fish. North Carolina's economic growth was tied, as well, to imperial policies that encouraged the growth of naval stores such as turpentine, tar, and pitch. In the late 1600s, these naval stores were mostly imported from Scandinavia and the Baltic States. But imperial authorities were determined that naval stores, strategic materials vital for the Royal Navy, should originate from within the British Empire. After 1705, Parliament paid a substantial subsidy (or "bounty") for naval stores, producers of which received subsidies of £1 per ton for bowsprits, yards, and masts, £4 per ton on tar and pitch, £3 per ton on turpentine and rosin, and £6 per ton on hemp; these imperial bounties, though reduced in 1729, survived for most of the pre-Revolutionary period. The abundant pine forests of the Lower Cape Fear, from Wilmington to Cross Creek (present-day Fayetteville) supplied raw materials for the emerging naval stores industry, and African American slaves provided the labor. In the generation before the Revolution, North Carolina became the top producer of naval stores in the British Empire, accounting for half of turpentine, 70 percent of tar, and a fifth of pitch. By the mid-1700s, as a result, the Lower Cape Fear had developed the largest concentration of slave population, with most slaves working in the lumber or naval stores industries. By the outbreak of the American Revolution, slaves comprised about three-fifths of the total population in this region.

The enslaved population played an instrumental role in the agricultural system of colonial North Carolina. Rice planters could not have cultivated their crop without African Americans' skill and hard work; the enslaved workers had transported their knowledge of rice culture from West Africa. Rice cultivation could only occur in bogs and marshes, unhealthy places in which to work. During spring, slaves planted rice seeds in trenches, using the African practice of covering them with their feet. Following the flooding of the fields, slaves maintained the seedlings through the spring and summer, while during the autumn they drained the rice fields, harvested the rice, and then threshed and packed the crop. The work was very arduous, but that on tobacco plantations was no easier. Slaves nurtured tobacco seedlings in rich mold, transplanted seedlings to fields in late spring, once they had grown to 4–5 inches in height, maintained them as they grew during the summer, then cut and stacked the mature leaves in August and September. Finally, slaves packed the tobacco products into hogsheads (barrels) for shipment to market.

The most significant difference between rice and tobacco culture, however, was that, while rice could only be cultivated on large plantations, tobacco could, and often was, produced on small holdings. Thus, on tobacco plantations, many slaveholders owned relatively few slaves but were able to use them profitably. The differences in the cultivation of tobacco and rice also had important implications for the sort of slave community that emerged in the respective areas. Whereas tobacco planters supervised their slaves on a regular basis, rice planters relied on a task system of labor that provided considerably greater freedom for slaves.

Much of the slaves' labor was expended toward nonagricultural activities. Slaves, for example, were intricately involved in maritime activities as fishermen, boatmen, and ferry operators. They were also especially involved in the processing of lumber products and naval stores. North Carolina's abundant pine forests, especially longleaf pines, provided raw materials for the burgeoning industry; wood products and naval stores supplied full-time, year-round employment. The cycle of labor adhered to the following pattern: during springtime, slaves cut slashes into the bark of long leaf trees, a process known as "boxing" the trees because the collection points were called "boxes." Slaves awaited the flow of sap, or turpentine, which they ladled into barrels; the turpentine was then distilled. The life span of tapped pine trees was approximately three years; after that, they were felled and used to make tar. According to contemporary John Brickell, pine logs "split about the thickness of the small of a Man's leg, and two or three Feet in length" were tossed into kilns built "on some

Figure 3.2 Although this photograph was taken in North Carolina circa 1903, it shows men and women gathering crude turpentine by the same "boxing" method used by slaves in the colonial period. *Source: Library of Congress Prints and Photographs Division, LC-USZ62-71812.*

rising Ground or Earth." In order to contain the heat, the kilns were covered with "Clay, Earth, or Sods," and while the fire burned, over the course of several days, slaves collected the accumulating tar into barrels. Typically a portion of tar was placed into kettles and boiled into pitch.[2] In these unpleasant and arduous processes, slaves performed all of the labor. Other enslaved workers labored in the hardwood and cypress forests of northeastern North Carolina to produce lumber, shingles, and barrel staves.

The post-1720 expansion of the North Carolina colony brought a rapid expansion of its slave population. The growth of slavery paralleled the physical expansion of the colony between 1720 and 1775. Indeed, as we shall explore in Chapter 4, North Carolina experienced a veritable population explosion. In 1675, approximately 4,000 whites lived in North Carolina; by 1730, this number had increased to perhaps 40,000. By 1770, the total white and black population had grown exponentially, to as many as 185,000 inhabitants. Put another way, the overall population in North Carolina doubled between 1730 and 1750 and tripled between 1750 and 1770.

The African American population, most of which was enslaved, grew at a similarly rapid rate. In 1730, the black population was approximately 6,000. Twenty-five years later, in 1755, there were nearly 19,000 African Americans in the colony. The expansion of the slave population was particularly rapid during the 1750s and 1760s, and by 1767 the number of slaves had increased to more than 40,000. Representing an annual population increase of 6 percent—compared with a 4 percent rate of increase for the white population—the growth in North Carolina's slave population constitutes a genuine population explosion. By the time of the first federal census, in 1790, there were more than 100,000 slaves in North Carolina, along with more than 288,000 whites. By the late 1700s, slaves in the colony constituted more than a third of the total population.

The slave population was widely, though unevenly, dispersed across the colony. West of the Fall Line, slavery existed in relatively small patches: only about 10 percent of backcountry Orange County households were slaveholding in 1755, for example. In contrast, both northeastern and southeastern North Carolina possessed significant slave populations. About 52 percent of Chowan County households owned slaves in 1766, while in New Hanover County (which surrounded Wilmington) the same proportion was nearly 55 percent. The largest portion of slaves lived in northeastern North Carolina: in 1767, almost two-fifths of North Carolina's black population resided there, while the Lower Cape Fear's slaves constituted only 12 percent of the total. Slavery rapidly expanded west of the Albemarle, and the northern Coastal Plain became a tobacco plantation region. At the same time, southeastern North Carolina slaveholders tended to have larger numbers of slaves, and there the proportion of slaves to overall population was high. The number of slaves living in families with more than ten slaves increased from 51 percent in 1748–55 to 62 percent in 1763–71, while slaves toiling under "great" planters—those slaveholders owning more than twenty slaves—rose during the same period from 19 to 29 percent.

Several factors underlay the rapid growth of slavery in North Carolina. For the most part, the number of slaves directly imported from Africa or the Caribbean remained small, especially compared with South Carolina, where thousands of imported slaves arrived. In contrast, North Carolina, complained a governor of the colony, had fewer numbers of slaves who were imported "directly from Affrica," and whites were forced to "buy the refuse, refractory, and distemper'd Negroes" brought in from other colonies. According to one estimate, perhaps 3,000 slaves reached North Carolina via its ports.[3] Most of the rise in North Carolina's slave population thus came from natural increase and importation from Britain's other North American colonies. By the middle of the eighteenth century, sex ratios among slaves—the proportion of men to women—had stabilized, and family units were becoming more common. Meanwhile, migrants from Virginia and South Carolina brought slaves with them, and slaveholders obtained slaves from both of these colonies. In addition, an active intercolonial slave trade developed in the years leading up to the Revolution. The most intense period of slave immigration occurred between 1750 and 1770, when more slaves (about 25,000) immigrated to North Carolina than anywhere in the British American colonies, with the exception of Jamaica.[4]

Solidifying the Slave Society

By the time of the American Revolution, North Carolina had become a slave society. Slavery was a vital part of the economic expansion of the colony: status and wealth depended on slaveholding. Slavery spread to the reaches of the colony, as well. Although still weak in the backcountry, slavery had tightened its hold on the socioeconomic system of the coast and Coastal Plain. With this solidification of slavery, North Carolina became a society whose social and political bases were rooted in the slave system.

While slavery was expanding, the legal system changed so as to provide increased protections for North Carolina slaveholders. In 1715, the colony's assembly (which had been in existence since 1665) enacted its first slave code, which prohibited blacks or those of mixed race (along with Native Americans) from voting. Additional legislation attempted, for the first time, to define the status of slaves in a variety of areas—and to distinguish the status and rights of slaves and freed people. The assembly limited slaves' physical mobility, prohibited blacks from traveling without the consent of their masters, and instituted a pass system regulating slaves' physical mobility. The new slave code also sought to draw sharp lines between slaves and white indentured servants. The law imposed a £50 fine on whites marrying "any Negro, Mulatto or Indyan Man or Woman" as well as on anyone caught performing an interracial marriage ceremony. White women bearing the children of nonwhite fathers were subjected to a £6 fine, and, if they were unable to pay the fine, would be required to serve four years as indentured servants, with their children bound until the age of 31. Fearful of possible insurrection, the 1715 slave code banned the unauthorized meetings of slaves. Wilmington expanded these limitations in a 1765 ordinance. There, groups of more than three slaves found "playing, Riotting, or Caballing" could be arrested and whipped. Harsher penalties, including mutilation and hanging, were imposed on slaves who violently rebelled against masters, and between 1738 and 1779, according to one estimate, about 100 slaves were hanged, castrated, or beheaded for assault, murder, and attempted murder.[5] The ordinance also included a curfew. Seven years later, in 1772, town authorities strengthened this ordinance by prohibiting slaves from trading on street corners.

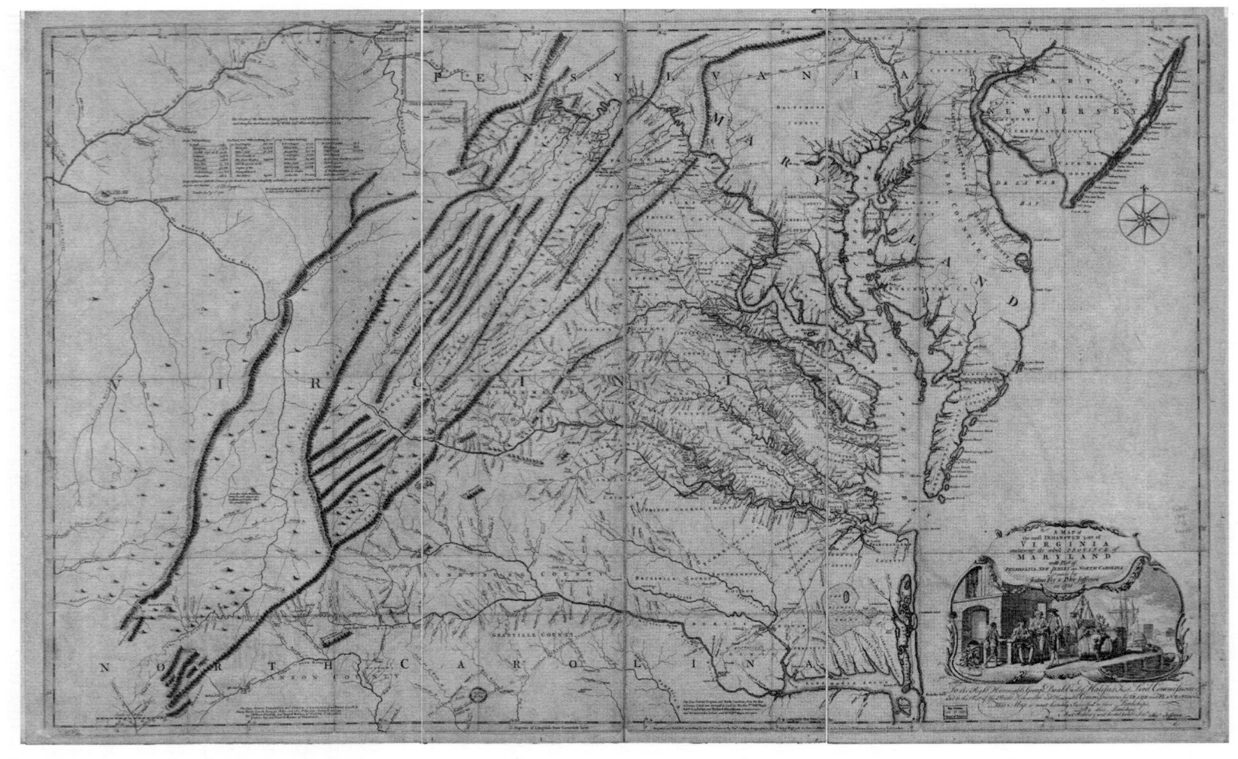

Figure 3.3 Detail of the cartouche from the Fry-Jefferson map of 1751, showing a wharf scene in which a planter negotiates with a ship's captain while slaves load the tobacco on to the ships. *Source: Library of Congress, Geography and Map Division, Access #2189, Special Collections, University of Virginia Library (Map Call # G3880 1755.F72 Vault).*

African Americans were stripped of their legal rights: slaves accused of crimes, previously tried in regular courts, now came under the jurisdiction of special courts composed of three magistrates and three landowners, and whites were granted wide discretion in pursuing runaways, defending against possible uprisings, and punishing slaves. Slaves enjoyed few of the privileges of Anglo-American legal tradition: no jury trials, little regard for due process, and restricted ability to defend themselves in the courts. Charging and trying a slave usually meant conviction: one historian has estimated that as many as 97 percent of slaves charged with crimes were found guilty.[6] Moreover, the special "negro courts"—which existed until 1807, when cases involving African American crime were returned to the regular court system—were awarded sweeping powers of punishment, including mutilation, castration, and even burning alive.

It is always difficult to determine whether a divergence existed between the law and actual practice, for in many instances the slave code might well have been ignored. Nonetheless, the passage of this new system of laws suggests a general tightening of legal controls over the status of black people. This became particularly true with the increase in the slave population. Masters were determined to maintain control, and they sought a legal and political system to preserve their dominance, which included sanctioning their brutality. John Brickell, a visitor to North Carolina in the late 1730s, commented that he frequently witnessed slaves whipped so severely that large pieces of skin fell off of their backs.[7] Executions of slaves were not uncommon. When a slave known as Peter escaped from his master and traveled to Wilmington in 1788, he was tried and executed for running away and for raiding and stealing a chicken. Even as late as 1812, a slave in Wake County was sentenced to burn publicly for murdering his master.[8]

Two forms of slave resistance most concerned slaveholders: running away, which might cost them valuable property, and insurrections, which might cost them their lives. Accordingly, the law provided protections against both, requiring the apprehension of fugitive slaves and providing harsh penalties against violent slave resistance. In the most extreme instances, according to the 1715 law, the colony provided compensation for the masters of executed slaves. Brickell noted that there was considerable justification for slaveholders' concerns. Despite "many severe Laws," he wrote, slaves would sometimes "rise and Rebel against their Masters and Planters, and do a great deal of mischief." As a result, "mild laws" were of "no use against them." This meant that masters very often carried out their own form of justice: in instances in which a slave assaulted whites and bloodshed resulted, according to Brickell, masters would "immediately meet and order him to be hanged, which is always performed by another *Negroe*, and generally the Planters bring most of their *Negroes* with them to behold their fellow *Negroes* suffer, to deter them from the like vile Practice." Without severe punishment, masters feared that slaves would "overcome the *Christians* in theirs and most of the other Provinces in the Hands of the *English*."[9]

The slave system thus became more fully developed and solidified, and the slave code was expanded in 1741. Though amended in 1753, 1758, and 1764, the slave code remained the basic body of law regarding slaves until the Revolution. With the mid-century explosion in slave population, masters grew even more determined to impose security through a clear, though harsh definition of the slave system. After the Stono Rebellion, a famous slave uprising in South Carolina that resulted in the death of more than twenty whites, in 1739, North Carolina slaveholders were highly concerned about their security. Now they extended the slave code greatly. Interracial marriages were denounced as "an abominable Mixture," mulatto children as "spurious issue." The expanding numbers of free blacks in North Carolina also attracted the legislators' attention. The 1715 Act had limited manumission, or the freeing of slaves, to those performing "honest and Faithful service." In 1741, the law restricted manumission to slaves performing "meritorious Services," as determined by county court, requiring that manumitted slaves leave the colony within six months or face re-enslavement. Like the 1715 law, the 1741 Act severely restricted the physical mobility of slaves: legislators hoped to prevent nighttime assemblies of slaves. Earlier, in 1729, a law declared that blacks found at large at night or in white residences should receive as many as forty lashes. Whites—described as "loose, disorderly, or suspected person"—in the company of slaves could be arrested and whipped.[10]

With restrictions on physical freedom came limitations on economic freedom. During the first decades of North Carolina slavery, masters often permitted their slaves to own and maintain small plots of land and to manage livestock herds. As the slave population increased, however, and slaveholders became determined to impose more controls over the system, they sought legal restrictions over slaves' economic freedoms. New legislation also reflected the increasing frequency of masters' complaints about how slaves had stolen their livestock and incorporated the animals into their own herds. In 1715, the assembly restricted the ability of slaves to trade goods without the consent of their masters. The 1741 law went much further: it prohibited the ownership of any private property by any slave and imposed harsh penalties for theft: any blacks or Indians who stole or killed livestock and attempted to sell it illegally could be publicly whipped and have their ears cut off. A second offense could lead to capital punishment.

Slaveholders also restricted hunting by slaves. Hunting provided an opportunity for a degree of physical freedom, and masters feared that slaves hunting in the field might steal their livestock. Hunting also enabled slaves to carry arms, often in groups, which could conceivably form the seeds of insurrection. In 1729, the North Carolina Assembly prohibited slaves from hunting, except under white supervision, with dogs, guns, or any weapon outside of their masters' property. The slave code of 1741 strengthened this prohibition by requiring that slaves caught hunting illegally be given twenty lashes. Despite these restrictions, slaves, with their masters' connivance, continued to hunt and to bear arms; the 1741 law, complained one contemporary, had been "ineffectual" in restraining "many slaves in divers parts of this province from going armed, which may prove of dangerous consequences."[11] In 1753, the assembly modified the law by requiring masters to be responsible in overseeing the disarming of slaves. No slave could hunt in the woods until masters had provided a bond for good behavior; anyone injured by the slave could sue masters for damages. Finally, the law provided that slaves could be armed only under limited circumstances.

Into the Revolutionary era, the rapid growth of the slave population resulted in even harsher and more restrictive legal controls over slaves. Masters relied on such controls: like slaveholders in other colonies, they depended particularly on compensation for executed slaves. In North Carolina, however, rising prices for slaves, combined with larger numbers of executions, led to considerable financial pressure; during the French and Indian War (1756–63), the state had begun to castrate slaves rather than execute them, except for the most heinous crimes. Castration of slaves for crimes ended in 1764, when the assembly began to impose legal limits on the amount of compensation that could be paid to the owners of executed slaves.

Slave Community, Slave Resistance

Matched against the increasing harshness of the institution of American slavery was the emergence of an independent and, to a degree, autonomous slave community. As the slave system expanded and became more explicitly defined, African Americans became an important presence in North Carolina life. From the outset African Americans contested enslavement. Most slaves challenged the brutality and cruelty of the system, though most did not do so violently. There were numerous instances of slaves fighting back against violent masters or overseers, but the most common forms of resistance were nonviolent ones. The persistence of slave resistance coincided with another important development: the transition of North Carolina from a "slaveholding" state to a "slave" society.

Slaves resisted the system in ways both blatant and subtle. Many masters complained about the "insolence" of their slaves, who clearly performed their duties with displeasure. In some instances, insolence led to assaults, poisoning, and arson—all very serious crimes under the slave regime. Other slaves were found guilty of "malingering," a deliberate effort to sabotage or slow down the work process. Masters also complained about the inefficiency of enslaved workers, as slowing down on the job or purposely breaking tools became a common form of resisting an oppressive system. In many instances, slaves stole from their masters in order to subvert the system. Despite efforts to legislate controls over slaves' ability to sell stolen goods, a black market operated in North Carolina, especially in towns. When slaveholders bemoaned the loss of their crops, tools, or personal items, they frequently blamed their own slaves. Livestock, including horses, cattle, and hogs, also might disappear into the underground slave economy. It was in response to such theft that colonial assemblies enacted legislation restricting slaves' ability to own and maintain private property. Slaveholders recognized all of these as crimes that sought to undermine the security of the slave system. In 1741, the assembly enacted legislation making it a crime for three or more slaves to "conspire to make insurrection," punishable by execution.

A serious form of slave resistance remained the act of running away. From the advent of slavery in the late 1600s, slaves had fled their masters. In the early years of the Carolina colony, the swamps and isolated communities of the Albemarle provided sanctuary for fugitive slaves from Virginia, and North Carolina slaves found a welcoming hideaway in the Great Dismal Swamp, which contained a maroon colony of escaped slaves. It has been estimated that slaveholders lost several hundred thousand dollars per year through slaves absconding to the Great Dismal Swamp, and whites feared venturing too far into maroon territory. "Traveling here without pistols" was thought to be "very dangerous owing to the great number of runaway Negroes," wrote one visitor of the swamp in February 1817, which, he said, was "inhabited almost exclusively by run away Negroes, bears, wild cats & wild cattle."[12] Another observer noted that, in the swamps, fugitives became "perfectly safe" from apprehension and could "elude the most diligent search of their pursuers." Many of the runaway communities existed for years outside of white control.[13]

Generally North Carolina's isolated geography provided an ideal habitat for runaways, and slaves could "lay out" for extended periods of time to escape oppressive masters. Woods often provided one such refuge: slaves would, according to Brickell, "make use of … Advantages in the Woods, where they will stay for Months together before they can be found out by their Masters."[14] Swamps dotted eastern North Carolina, the bogs and marshy areas around Wilmington becoming refuges for runaways. In 1795, complaints about runaways raiding plantations near Wilmington grew so common that the town government created a night guard. In 1821, the Onslow County militia, near Wilmington, was dispatched to suppress a band of runaways who were stealing from local whites and even burning their houses. Despite these efforts, the guerrilla bands were never completely uprooted.

Runaways, and disaffected slaves generally, found more hospitable circumstances in towns, where the degree of control by the slave regime was less strict. Urban areas were home to the colony's (and later the state's) growing free black population—potential allies for those on the lam. There were significant free black populations in the larger coastal towns—Edenton, New Bern, and Wilmington—and these increasingly autonomous communities supplied a sanctuary for runaways, who could meld into the local setting. As ports, these towns also hosted vessels which harbored runaways and, in some instances, employed them as seamen. The problem of slaves absconding by water was considered so serious that in 1791 the legislature criminalized seamen who harbored or employed fugitives. The law also prohibited slaves from boarding vessels without a pass. The laws notwithstanding, North Carolina towns, with a large artisan and seaport population of watermen, simply absorbed many runaways into their ranks.

Slaves fled from their masters for various reasons. In general, those with fewer family connections on the plantations or farms on which they lived—wives, children, and siblings—were more likely to run. Naturally, then, more recently arrived Africans were the most likely to flee, and males in general escaped more often than did women. Artisans and some literate slaves possessed sufficient independence to make this move. For whatever reasons, the decision to run away always entailed considerable risk. Those slaves apprehended were brutally whipped; thirty-nine lashes at the whipping post was the standard punishment. Chronic runaways faced leg-irons, amputation of limbs, and even execution. In some instances, whites employed Indians to track down runaways, and Indians were notoriously brutal in their treatment of captives. Native Americans, according to Brickell, possessed a "natural aversion to the *Blacks*, that they commonly shoot them when ever they find them in the Woods or solitary parts of the Country." At the same time, however, there is little evidence that Indians regarded African Americans with any greater antipathy than they perceived any other outsider group. Some Indian tribes were known to harbor runaways or to adopt free blacks.[15]

In response to the problem of absconding slaves, the legal system increasingly focused on runaways. As early as 1699, the North Carolina Assembly enacted legislation penalizing whites who harbored runaways. In 1715, as part of the initial creation of a slave code, the law provided incentives for whites to apprehend and return slaves by rewarding them and reimbursing them for their expenses. It established a pass system by which slaves needed the written permission of their masters—including the slave's name and destination—in order to travel unsupervised. In 1729, the assembly strengthened the travel regulation by stipulating that slaves found traveling at night without a pass could receive forty lashes. Masters faced a fine of five shillings for violating the law. In general, all whites were required to make every effort to arrest slaves without passes and to arrest any undocumented slaves.

The creation in 1753 of a system of local slave patrols—which at first were called "searchers"—became part of efforts to defend the slave regime. Under the law enacted in that year, county magistrates could divide their counties into districts and appoint three white freeholders in each as "searchers." Patrollers exerted wide powers. Four times annually they could search slave quarters for arms; if they deemed it necessary, they could conduct even more frequent *in the Power of every Body to ſettle their Accompts.*

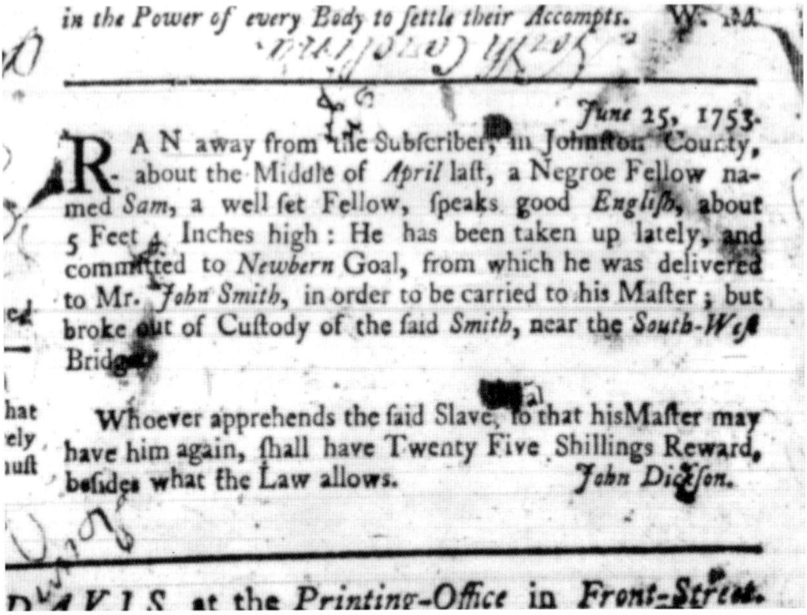

June 25, 1753.

RAN away from the Subſcriber, in *Johnſton* County, about the Middle of *April* laſt, a Negroe Fellow named *Sam*, a well ſet Fellow, ſpeaks good *Engliſh*, about 5 Feet 4 Inches high: He has been taken up lately, and committed to *Newbern* Goal, from which he was delivered to Mr. *John Smith*, in order to be carried to his Maſter; but broke out of Cuſtody of the ſaid *Smith*, near the *South-Weſt* Bridge.

Whoever apprehends the ſaid Slave, ſo that his Maſter may have him again, ſhall have Twenty Five Shillings Reward, beſides what the Law allows. *John Dickſon.*

... at the *Printing-Office* in *Front-Street.*

Figure 3.4 Runaway slave ad, *North Carolina Gazette*, July 7, 1753. *Source: http://libcdm1.uncg.edu/cdm/singleitem/collection/RAS/id/1149/rec/3*

searches for "guns, swords, and other weapons." Fears of slave insurrection, combined with a desire to apprehend runaways, motivated the creation of the patrol system, but patrollers became a regular part of slaveholding in North Carolina. The system was reformed and expanded in 1779, when the assembly required that slave quarters be searched once a month and that patrollers be empowered to treat slaves lacking passes as runaways—with the same reward for their apprehension. Still another act in 1794 provided for even more frequent searches and gave patrollers the power to whip slaves traveling without passes. As fears of insurrection grew, patrollers exercised greater powers, and they were widely feared and hated in the slave community, who rightly saw themselves as the victims of unrestrained vigilante justice. As one historian put it, the patrol was an "institution which the slave eventually learned to dread perhaps next to the bloodhounds."[16]

As North Carolina's slave system acquired definition, the social system moved away from what one historian has called a "society with slaves" to a "slave society":[17] while slaves had been present in North Carolina since the end of the 1600s, by the outbreak of the Revolution slavery had become a fundamental part of the colony's legal and political system. The colony's political leadership considered the control of its slaves and the protection of slaveholders as top priorities. From the slaves' point of view, the creation of a slave society meant changes. Along with harsher punishments for threats real and imagined, the arrival of a slave society also brought changes within the slave community. Over time, the heavy rush of slave immigrants subsided, and African American communities became more "creolized"—that is, they developed societies and cultures that had adapted to the North Carolina environment. From the masters' point of view, creolization meant, to a degree, that slaves learned to cope with the system. Slaveholders described this as "seasoning"—a term suggesting a degree of acceptance of the institution by slaves. Slaves born in North Carolina, as Brickell put it, were "more industrious, honest, and better slaves than any brought from *Guinea*."[18]

The "creolization" of North Carolina slaves was perhaps best exemplified in the development of slave religion. During the period of heavy immigration, slaves brought African religions with them, including traditional animism—which emphasized pantheistic religion with many gods, tied to nature—and Islam. African slaves maintained their faith in old charms, the presence of spirits, and various rituals that were common in Africa. Medicine men became "obeah" men, headmen with religious authority. Protestant denominations in North Carolina began efforts to convert slaves to Christianity, with mixed results; the Church of England, for example, made little progress, while Baptists and Methodists were far more successful during the last half of the eighteenth century. The attraction of the latter denominations for African Americans paralleled their popularity among whites: both offered a democratic, accessible faith that could adapt itself to the local geographical as well as racial differences. Until the 1800s, Methodists were antislavery, and their message was one of human equality. Baptists, meanwhile, preached a message of fellowship and equality before God that slaves found appealing.

Christianity eventually became the most powerful cultural expression of the enslaved African American community. Independent Methodist and Baptist churches came into existence in towns, but on plantations slaves developed their own distinctive variety of Christianity. Although the law prohibited slaves from holding separate worship services and though slaveholders attempted to sponsor slaves in segregated facilities in white churches, they nonetheless worshipped apart from white control. Slave music was largely religious, and the themes of spirituals emphasized liberation, deliverance, and redemption from slavery. The cultural leaders of the black community, by 1800, were also their religious leaders.

* * *

The evolution of North Carolina into a slave society helped to define the colony and state's social, cultural, and political maturation. By the time of the American Revolution, slaves were numerically important, and in the plantation districts of coastal North Carolina the population of enslaved persons approached a majority. Wealth and power became associated with slaveholding, which became an essential ingredient in the pre-Revolutionary economy. As time passed, moreover, the legal, political, and constitutional system was shaped to recognize slavery's primacy and to institutionalize the imperative of protecting the special rights of slaveholders. The transformation of North Carolina into a slave society was part of a growing consciousness and self-confidence, as the colony became a place where fortunes could be made. While slavery grew to dominate the social life and political institutions of coastal North Carolina, another world was emerging in the rapidly developing frontier. There, in the backcountry, a very different society came into existence.

Notes

1 These figures are from Jeffrey J. Crow, *The Black Experience in Revolutionary North Carolina* (Raleigh, NC: Division of Archives and History, 1977).

2 John Brickell, *The Natural History of North Carolina* (orig. published 1737; Murfreesboro, NC: Johnson Publishing, 1968), pp. 265–66.

3 Marvin L. Michael Kay and Lorin Lee Cary, *Slavery in North Carolina, 1748–1775* (Chapel Hill: University of North Carolina Press, 1995), p. 21.

4 David Galenson, *White Servitude in Colonial America: An Economic Analysis* (Cambridge: Cambridge University Press, 1981), pp. 217–18.

5 Cindy Hahamovitch, "Crime, Law, and Authority in Colonial North Carolina, 1700–1750," M.A. thesis, University of North Carolina, 1987, p. 55.

6 Kay and Cary, *Slavery in North Carolina, 1748–1775*, p. 72.

7 Brickell, *Natural History*, p. 272.

8 R. H. Taylor, "Humanizing the Slave Code of North Carolina," *North Carolina Historical Review* 2, no. 3 (July 1925): 324–25.

9 Brickell, *Natural History*, pp. 272–73.

10 John Spencer Bassett, *Slavery and Servitude in the Colony of North Carolina* (Baltimore, MD: Johns Hopkins University Press, 1896), p. 39.

11 Quoted in Bassett, *Slavery and Servitude in the Colony of North Carolina*, p. 37.

12 Freddie L. Parker, *Running for Freedom: Slave Runaways in North Carolina, 1775–1840* (New York: Garland Publishing, 1993), pp. 33–35.

13 Quoted by Kay and Cary, *Slavery in North Carolina, 1748–1775*, p. 101.

14 Brickell, *Natural History*, p. 263.

15 Quoted in Crow, *The Black Experience in Revolutionary North Carolina*, p. 45; James H. Merrell, "The Racial Education of the Catawba Indians," *Journal of Southern History*, 50 (August 1984):363–84.

16 Bassett, *Slavery and Servitude in the Colony of North Carolina*, p. 38.

17 Ira Berlin, *Many Thousands Gone: The First Two Centuries of Slavery in North America* (Cambridge, MA: Harvard University Press, 2000).

18 Brickell, *Natural History*, p. 272.

Suggested Readings, Part 1

Chapter 1

Donald Edward Davis, *Where There Are Mountains: An Environmental History of the Southern Mountains* (Athens: University of Georgia Press, 2000).

Kirsten Fischer, *Suspect Relations: Sex, Race, and Resistance in Colonial North Carolina* (Ithaca, NY: Cornell University Press, 2002).

James Horn, *A Kingdom Strange: The Brief and Tragic History of the Lost Colony of Roanoke* (New York: Basic Books, 2011).

Jack Temple Kirby, *Poquosin: A Study of Rural Landscape and Society* (Chapel Hill: University of North Carolina Press, 1995).

Karen Ordahl Kupperman, *Roanoke: The Abandoned Colony*, 2nd ed. (Lanham, MD: Rowman & Littlefield Publishers, 2007).

Enoch Lawrence Lee, *Indian Wars in North Carolina, 1663–1763* (Raleigh, NC: Carolina Charter Tercentenary Commission, 1963).

Hugh T. Lefler, ed., *A New Voyage to Carolina, by John Lawson* (Chapel Hill: University of North Carolina Press, 1967).

James H. Merrell, *The Indians' New World: Catawbas and Their Neighbors from European Contact through the Era of Removal* (Chapel Hill: University of North Carolina Press, 1989).

Michael L. Oberg, "Indians and Englishmen at the First Roanoke Colony: A Note on Pemisapan's Conspiracy," *American Indian Culture and Research Journal* 18, 2 (1994): 79.

Michael L. Oberg, "Gods and Men: The Meeting of Indian and White Worlds on the Carolina Outer Banks, 1584–1586," *North Carolina Historical Review* LXXVI no. 4 (October 1999): 371.

Theda Perdue, *Slavery and the Evolution of Cherokee Society, 1540–1866* (Knoxville: University of Tennessee Press, 1979).

Theda Perdue, *Native Carolinians: The Indians of North Carolina* (Raleigh, NC: Division of Archives and History, 1985).

Theda Perdue, *Cherokee Women: Gender and Culture Change, 1700–1835* (Lincoln: University of Nebraska Press, 1998).
David B. Quinn, *Raleigh and the British Empire* (New York: Macmillan, 1949).
David B. Quinn, *Set Fair for Roanoke: Voyages and Colonies, 1584–1606* (Chapel Hill: University of North Carolina Press, 1985).
Douglas L. Rights, *The American Indian in North Carolina* (Winston-Salem: J. F. Blair, 1957).
Timothy Silver, *A New Face on the Countryside: Indians, Colonists, and Slaves in South Atlantic Forests, 1500–1800* (Cambridge: Cambridge University Press, 1990).
David Stick, *Graveyard of the Atlantic: Shipwrecks of the North Carolina Coast* (Chapel Hill: University of North Carolina Press, 1952).
David Stick, *Roanoke Island: The Beginnings of English America* (Chapel Hill: University of North Carolina Press, 1983).

Chapter 2

John Spencer Bassett, *The Constitutional Beginnings of North Carolina, 1663–1729* (Baltimore, MD: The Johns Hopkins University Press, 1894).
Warren M. Billings, "Sir William Berkeley and the Carolina Proprietary," *North Carolina Historical Review* 72 (July 1995): 329–42.
Alan Vance Briceland, *Westward from Virginia: The Exploration of the Virginia-Carolina Frontier, 1650–1710* (Charlottesville: University Press of Virginia, 1987).
Lindley S. Butler, "The Early Settlement of Carolina: Virginia's Southern Frontier," *Virginia Magazine of History and Biography* 79 (January 1971): 20–28.
Lindley S. Butler, *Pirates, Privateers, & Rebel Raiders of the Carolina Coast* (Chapel Hill: University of North Carolina Press, 2000).
E. Lawrence Lee, Jr., *The Lower Cape Fear in Colonial Days* (Chapel Hill: University of North Carolina Press, 1965).
Paul M. McCain, *The County Court in North Carolina before 1750* (Durham, NC: Duke University Press, 1954).
Noeleen McIlvenna, *A Very Mutinous People: The Struggle for North Carolina, 1660–1713* (Chapel Hill: University of North Carolina Press, 2009).
Thomas C. Parramore, "With Tuscarora Jack on the Back Path to Bath," *North Carolina Historical Review* 63 (April 1987): 115–38.
William S. Powell, *The Proprietors of Carolina* (Raleigh, NC: Division of Archives and History, 1968).
Hugh F. Rankin, *The Pirates of Colonial North Carolina* (Raleigh, NC: Division of Archives and History, 1960).
Hugh F. Rankin, *Upheaval in Albemarle: The Story of Culpeper's Rebellion, 1675–1689* (Raleigh, NC: Carolina Charter Tercentenary Commission, 1962).

Margaret Supplee Smith and Emily Herring Wilson, *North Carolina Women Making History* (Chapel Hill: University of North Carolina Press, 1999).

Stephen Jay White, "From the Vestry Act to Cary's Rebellion: North Carolina's Quakers and Colonial Politics," *Southern Friend* 8 (Autumn 1986): 3.

Chapter 3

John Spencer Bassett, *Slavery and Servitude in the Colony of North Carolina* (Baltimore, MD: The Johns Hopkins University Press, 1896).

John Brickell, *The Natural History of North Carolina* (orig. published 1737; Murfreesboro, NC: Johnson Publishing, 1968).

Jeffrey J. Crow, *The Black Experience in Revolutionary North Carolina* (Raleigh, NC: Division of Archives and History, 1977).

David Galenson, *White Servitude in Colonial America: An Economic Analysis* (Cambridge: Cambridge University Press, 1981).

Cindy Hahamovitch, *"Crime, Law, and Authority in Colonial North Carolina, 1700–1750,"* M.A. thesis, University of North Carolina, 1987.

Cecily Jones, *Engendering Whiteness: White Women and Colonialism in Barbados and North Carolina, 1627–1865* (Manchester: Manchester University Press, 2007).

Marvin L. Michael Kay and Lorin Lee Cary, *Slavery in North Carolina, 1748–1775* (Chapel Hill: University of North Carolina Press, 1995).

David La Vere, *The Tuscarora War: Indians, Settlers, and the Fight for the Carolina Colonies* (Chapel Hill: University of North Carolina Press, 2013).

James H. Merrell, "The Racial Education of the Catawba Indians," *Journal of Southern History*, 50 (August 1984): 363–84.

Philip D. Morgan, *Slave Counterpoint: Black Culture in the Eighteenth-Century Chesapeake and Lowcountry* (Chapel Hill: University of North Carolina Press, 1998).

Thomas D. Morris, *Southern Slavery and the Law, 1619–1860* (Chapel Hill: University of North Carolina Press, 1996).

Freddie L. Parker, *Running for Freedom: Slave Runaways in North Carolina, 1775–1840* (New York: Garland Publishing, 1993).

R. H. Taylor, "Humanizing the Slave Code of North Carolina," *North Carolina Historical Review* 2, no. 3 (July 1925): 323–31.

Document Section, Part 1
Native Americans in Eighteenth-Century North Carolina: European Views

The following documents explore the interactions between Native Americans and Europeans in colonial North Carolina. Beginning with the Roanoke Island colony in the 1580s, what historians traditionally call the "first encounter" or "first contact" shaped the course of the evolution of the colony. As in other places in the New World where Indians interacted with Europeans, contact meant a steady process of erosion of Indian societies because of disease, economic dislocation, and warfare. In North Carolina the process took centuries, and for much of the early history of colony, Indians held the upper hand. During North Carolina's first fifty years, white settlement was confined to a few counties in the northeastern portion of the colony. Not until the Tuscarora War of 1711–15 did whites establish military dominance sufficient to permit colonization of the interior.

The documents below offer a representation of eighteenth-century white views of Indian society. Historians rely on white descriptions of Indian society because of the paucity of evidence, but students of the subject must be careful in using these materials. While reading these materials, pay careful attention to Euro-Americans' attitudes toward race and culture, and ponder how these attitudes shaped their accounts.

North Carolina: Change and Tradition in a Southern State, Second Edition. William A. Link.

Baron Christoph von Graffenried's drawing, "The Death of John Lawson," depicts von Graffenried, his servant, and John Lawson being held captive by Tuscarora Indians shortly before Lawson's death. *Source: Illustration by Christopher von Graffenried. NC Archives,* http://www.learnnc.org/lp/multimedia/8938.

INDIAN VILLAGE OF SECOTON (no. 38 A, cf. pl. 135)

Watercolor drawing "Indian Village of Secoton" by John White (created 1585–1586). Licensed by the Trustees of the British Museum. ©Copyright the British Museum.http://www.virtualjamestown.org/images/white_debry_html/white35.html

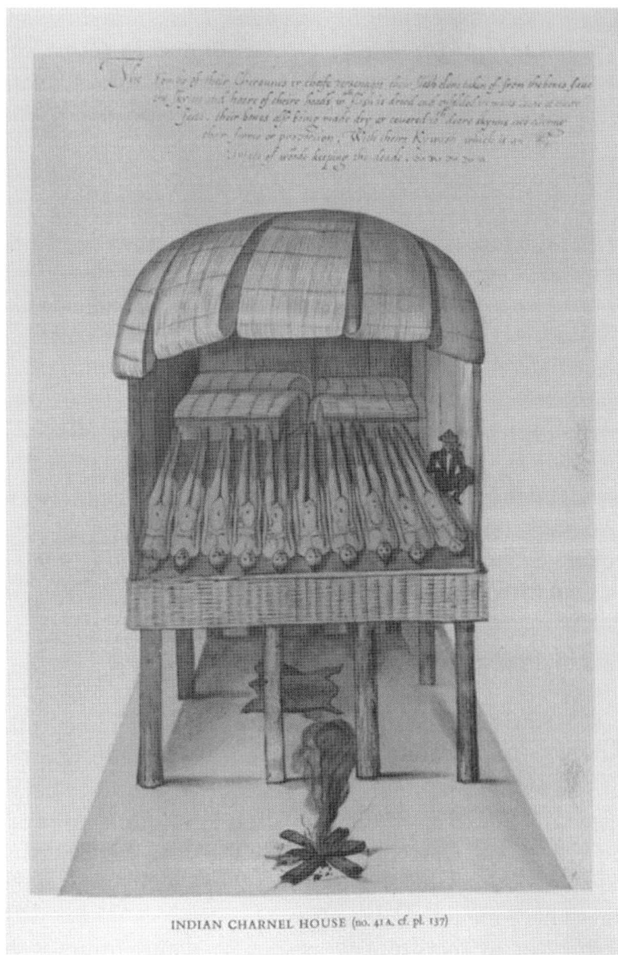

INDIAN CHARNEL HOUSE (no. 41A, cf. pl. 137)

Watercolor drawing "Indian Charnal House" by John White (created 1585–1586). Licensed by the Trustees of the British Museum. ©Copyright the British Museum.

John Lawson, *A New Voyage to Carolina* (1709)[1]

One of the better first-person accounts that we have is John Lawson's A New Voyage to Carolina. *Lawson first arrived in North Carolina in the early 1700s. He had an active career as an explorer, naturalist, surveyor, and organizer of new colonies. The Lords Proprietors commissioned him to survey the colony's interior;*

1 http://docsouth.unc.edu/nc/lawson/lawson.html.

Lawson began his first expedition in December 1700. Traveling for fifty-seven days and 550 miles from Charleston through the North Carolina Piedmont, Lawson moved by canoe with a party of five whites and four Indians through the Catawba and Yadkin River valleys and then moved eastward to the coast. Lawson meticulously recorded plant and animal life he observed, collecting specimens along the way. Lawson was also an acute and often perceptive observer of Indian life.

The rivers that Lawson traversed were named according to neighboring Indian tribes, including the Santee, the Congaree, the Wateree, the Waxhaw, the Catawba, the Eno, the Meherrin, the Neuse, the Sapona, and the Pamlico. Lawson in many ways expressed the cultural prejudices that English commonly possessed about native peoples. Yet the mass of detailed observations it comprises make A New Voyage *essential reading for early-American historians.*

Lawson was captured and killed by the Tuscarora Indians with the outbreak of the Tuscarora War. He died an especially gruesome and painful death, according to one account, having pitch pine splinters stuck into his body that were subsequently set on fire.

In this section, Lawson describes social organization and customs among the Waxhaws, a Sioux-language tribe that lived in the Catawba River valley.

Sexual Practices among the Waxhaws[2]

He that is a good Hunter never misses of being a Favourite amongst the Women; the prettiest Girls being always bestow'd upon the chiefest Sports-Men, and those of a grosser Mould, upon the useless Lubbers. Thus they have a Graduation amongst them, as well as other Nations. As for the Solemnity of Marriages amongst them, kept with so much Ceremony as divers Authors affirm, it never appear'd amongst those many Nations I have been withal, any otherwise than in the Manner I have mention'd hereafter.

The Girls at 12 or 13 Years of Age, as soon as Nature prompts them, freely bestow their Maidenheads on some Youth about the same Age, continuing her Favours on whom she most affects, changing her Mate very often, few or none of them being constant to one, till a greater Number of Years has made her capable of managing Domestick Affairs, and she hath try'd the Vigour of most of the Nation she belongs to; Multiplicity of Gallants never being a Stain to a Female's Reputation, or the least Hindrance of her Advancement, but the more Whorish, the more Honourable, and they of all most coveted, by those of the first Rank, to make a Wife of. The Flos Virginis, so much coveted by the Europeans, is never valued by these Savages. When a Man and Woman have gone through their Degrees, (there being a certain Graduation amongst

---

2 Ibid., pp. 33–36.

them) and are allow'd to be House-Keepers, which is not till they arrive at such an Age, and have past the Ceremonies practis'd by their Nation, almost all Kingdoms differing in the Progress thereof, then it is that the Man makes his Addresses to some one of these thorough-paced Girls, or other, whom he likes best. When she is won, the Parents of both Parties, (with Advice of the King) agree about the Matter, making a Promise of their Daughter, to the Man, that requires her, it often happening that they converse and travel together, for several Moons before the Marriage is publish'd openly; After this, at the least Dislike the Man may turn her away, and take another; or if she disapproves of his Company, a Price is set upon her, and if the Man that seeks to get her, will pay the Fine to her Husband, she becomes free from Him: Likewise some of their War Captains, and great Men, very often will retain 3 or 4 Girls at a time for their own Use, when at the same time, he is so impotent and old, as to be incapable of making Use of one of them; so that he seldom misses of wearing greater Horns than the Game he kills. The Husband is never so enrag'd as to put his Adulteress to Death; if she is caught in the Fact, the Rival becomes Debtor to the cornuted Husband, in a certain Quantity of Trifles valuable amongst them, which he pays as soon as discharg'd, and then all Animosity is laid aside bewixt the Husband, and his Wife's Gallant. The Man proves often so good humour'd as to please his Neighbour and gratify his Wife's Inclinations, by letting her out for a Night or two, to the Embraces of some other, which perhaps she has a greater Liking to, tho' this is not commonly practis'd.

Warfare[3]

Therefore, they inflict on them Torments, wherein they prolong Life in that miserable state as long as they can, and never miss Skulping of them, as they call it, which is, to cut off the Skin from the Temples, and taking the whole Head of Hair along with it, as is it was a Night-cap. Sometimes, they take the Top of the Skull along with it; all which they preserve, and carefully keep by them, for a Trophy of their Conquest over their Enemies. Others keep their Enemies Teeth, which are taken in War, whilst others split the Pitch-Pine into Splinters, and stick them into the Prisoners Body yet alive. Thus they light them, which burn like so many Torches; and in this manner, they make him dance round a great Fire, every one buffeting and deriding him, till he expires, when every one strives to get a Bone or some Relick of this unfortunate Captive. One of the young Fellows, that has been at the Wars, and has had the Fortune to take a Captive, returns the proudest Creature on Earth, and sets such a Value on himself, that he knows not how to contain himself in his Senses. The Iroquois, or Sinnagars, are the most Warlike Indians that we know of, being always at

3 Ibid., pp. 198–99.

War, and not to be persuaded from that Way of Living, by any Argument that can be used. If you go to persuade them to live peaceably with the Tuskeruros, and let them be one People, and in case those Indians desire it, and will submit to them, they will answer you, that they cannot live without War, which they have ever been used to; and that if Peace be made with the Indians they now war withal, they must find out some others to wage War against; for, for them to live in Peace, is to live out of their Element, War, Conquest, and Murder, being what they delight in, and value themselves for. When they take a Slave, and intend to keep him to Work in their Fields, they flea the Skin from the Setting on of his Toes to the middle of his Foot, so cut off one half of his Feet, wrapping the Skin over the Wounds, and healing them. By this cruel Method, the Indian Captive is hinder'd from making his Escape, for he can neither run fast or go any where, but his Feet are more easily traced and discover'd. Yet I know one Man who made his Escape from them, tho' they had thus disabled him, as you may see in my Journal.

The Indians ground their Wars on Enmity, not on Interest, as the Europeans generally do; for the Loss of the meanest Person in the Nation, they will go to War and lay all at Stake, and prosecute their Design to the utmost; till the Nation they were injur'd by, be wholly destroy'd, or make them that Satisfaction which they demand. They are very politick, in waging, and carrying on their, War, first by advising with all the ancient Men of Conduct and Reason, that belong to their Nation; such as superannuated War-Captains, and those that have been Counsellors for many Years, and whose Advice has commonly succeeded very well. They have likewise their Field Counsellors, who are accustomed to Ambuscades, and Surprizes, which Methods are commonly used by the Savages; for I scarce ever heard of a Field-Battle fought amongst them. . . .

Community[4]

The Victuals is common, throughout the whole Kindred Relations, and often to the whole Town; especially, when they are in Hunting-Quarters, then they all fare alike, whichsoever of them kills the Game. They are very kind, and charitable to one another, but more especially to those of their own Nation; for if any one of them has suffer'd any Loss, by Fire or otherwise, they order the griev'd Person to make a Feast. . . . The same Assistance they give to any Man that wants to build a Cabin, or make a Canoe. They say, it is our Duty thus to do; for there are several Works that one Man cannot effect, therefore we must give him our Help, otherwise our Society will fall, and we shall be depriv'd of those urgent Necessities which Life requires. They have no Fence to part one anothers Lots in their Corn-Fields; but every Man knows his own, and it scarce ever happens,

4 Ibid., pp. 178–79, 225.

that they rob one another of so much as an Ear of Corn, which if any is found to do, he is sentenced by the Elders to work and plant for him that was robb'd, till he is recompensed for all the Damage he has suffer'd in his Corn-Field; and this is punctually perform'd, and the Thiese held in Disgrace, that steals from any of his Country-Folks. It often happens, that a Woman is destitute of her Husband, and has a great many Children to maintain; such a Person they always help, and make their young men plant, reap, and do every thing that she is not capable of doing herself; yet they do not allow any one to be idle, but to employ themselves in some Work or other.

Leadership[5]

The King is the Ruler of the Nation, and has others under him, to assist him, as his War-Captains, and Counsellors, who are pick'd out and chosen from among the ancientest Men of the Nation he is King of. These meet him in all general Councils and Debates, concerning War, Peace, Trade, Hunting, and all the Adventures and Accidents of Humane Affairs, which appear within their Verge; where all Affairs are discoursed of and argued pro and con, very deliberately (without making any manner of Parties or Divisions) for the Good of the Publick; for, as they meet there to treat, they discharge their Duty with all the Integrity imaginable, never looking towards their Own Interest, before the Publick Good. After every Man has given his Opinion, that which has most Voices, or, in Summing up, is found the most reasonable, that they make use of without any Jars and Wrangling, and put it in Execution, the first Opportunity that offers.

Disease and Alcoholism[6]

The Indians are very careless and negligent of their Health; as, by Drunkenness, Wading in the Water, irregular Diet and Lodging, and a thousand other Disorders, (that would kill an European) which they daily use. . . . The Small-Pox has been fatal to them; they do not often escape, when they are seiz'd with that Distemper, which is a contrary Fever to what they ever knew.

Most certain, it had never visited America, before the Discovery thereof by the Christians. Their running into the Water, in the Extremity of this Disease, strikes it in, and kills all that use it. Now they are become a little wiser; but formerly it destroy'd whole Towns, without leaving one Indian alive in the Village. The Plague was never known amongst them, that I could learn by what Enquiry I have made: These Savages use Scarrification almost in all Distempers. Their

5 Ibid., p. 195.
6 Ibid., pp. 223–25.

chief Instruments for that Operation is the Teeth of Rattle-Snakes, which they poison withal. They take them out of the Snake's Head, and suck out the Poison with their Mouths, (and so keep them for use) and spit out the Venom, which is green, and are never damag'd thereby. The Small-Pox and Rum have made such a Destruction amongst them, that, on good grounds, I do believe, there is not the sixth Savage living within two hundred Miles of all our Settlements, as there were fifty Years ago. These poor Creatures have so many Enemies to destroy them, that it's a wonder one of them is left alive near us.

William Bartram, *Travels* (1791[7])

While John Lawson provided an early eighteenth-century account of Indian life, nearly a century later, naturalist and traveler William Bartram provided a detailed description of Indian life. Born near Philadelphia, Bartram was the son of John Bartram, himself a distinguished naturalist. Traveling to Florida in 1760 with his father, William conducted his own travels throughout the Southeast after 1770. His Travels through North and South Carolina (1791) *thoroughly examined natural life, but it also involved frequent observations about Indian life.*

pp. 350–354

I passed through and continued three miles farther to Nucasse, and three miles more brought me to Whatoga: riding through this large town, the road carried me winding about through their little plantations of Corn, Beans, &c. up to the council-house, which was a very large dome or rotunda, situated on the top of an ancient artificial mount, and here my road terminated; all before me and on every side appeared little plantations of young Corn, Beans, &c. divided from each other by narrow strips or borders of grass, which marked the bounds of each one's property, their habitation standing in the midst: finding no common high road to lead me through the town, I was now at a stand how to proceed farther, when observing an Indian man at the door of his habitation, three or four hundred yards distance from me, beckoning to come to him, I ventured to ride through their lots, being careful to do no injury to the young plants, the rising hopes of their labour and industry, crossed a little grassy vale watered by a silver stream, which gently undulated through, then ascended a green hill to the house, (where I was cheerfully welcomed at the door and led in by the chief, giving the care of my horse to two handsome youths, his sons). During my continuance here, about half an hour, I experienced the most perfect and agreeable

7 http://docsouth.unc.edu/nc/bartram/menu.html.

hospitality conferred on me by these happy people; I mean happy in their dispositions, in their apprehensions of rectitude with regard to our social or moral conduct: O divine simplicity and truth, friendship without fallacy or guile, hospitality disinterested, native, undefiled, unmodifyed by artificial refinements.

My venerable host gracefully and with an air of respect, led me into an airy, cool apartment, where being seated on cabins, his women brought in a refreshing repast, consisting of sodden venison, hot corn cakes, &c. with a pleasant cooling liquor made of hommony well boiled, mixed afterwards with milk; this is served up either before or after eating in a large bowl, with a very large spoon or ladle to sup it with.

After partaking of this simple but healthy and liberal collation and the dishes cleared off, Tobacco and pipes were brought, and the chief filling one of them, whose stem, about four feet long, was sheathed in a beautiful speckled snake skin, and adorned with feathers and strings of wampum, lights it and smoaks a few whiffs, puffing the smoak first towards the sun, then to the four cardinal points and lastly over my breast, hands it towards me, which I cheerfully received from him and smoaked, when we fell into conversation; he first enquired if I came from Charleston? if I Knew John Stewart, Esq,? how long since I left Charleston? &c. Having satisfied him in my answers in the best manner I could, he was greatly pleased, which I was convinced of by his attention to me, his cheerful manners and his ordering my horse a plentiful bait of corn, which last instance of respect is conferred on those only to whom they manifest the highest esteem, saying that corn was given by the Great Spirit only for food to man. . . .

This prince is the chief of Whatoga, a man universally beloved, and particularly esteemed by the whites for his pacific and equitable disposition, and revered by all for his exemplary virtues, just, moderate, magnanimous and intrepid.

He was tall and perfectly formed; his countenance cheerful and lofty and at the same time truly characteristic of the red men, that is, the brow ferocious and the eye active, piercing or fiery, as an eagle. He appeared to be about sixty years of age, yet upright and muscular, and his limbs active as youth.

After leaving my princely friend, I travelled about five miles through old plantations, now under grass, but appeared to have been planted the last season; the soil exceeding fertile, loose, black, deep and fat. I arrived at Cowe about noon; this settlement is esteemed the capital town; it is situated on the bases of the hills on both sides of the river, near to its bank, and here terminates the great vale of Cowe, exhibiting one of the most charming natural mountainous landscapes perhaps any where to be seen; ridges of hills rising grand and sublimely one above and beyond another, some boldly and majestically advancing into the verdant plain, their feet bathed with the silver flood of the Tanase, whilst others far distant, veiled in blue mists, sublimely mount aloft, with yet greater majesty lift up their pompous crests and overlook vast regions. . . .

On my arrival at this town [Cowe] I waited on the gentlemen to whom I was recommended by letter, and was received with respect and every demonstration of hospitality and friendship.

I took my residence with Mr. Galahan the chief trader here, an ancient respectable man who had been many years a trader in this country, and is esteemed and beloved by the Indians for his humanity, probity and equitable dealings with them, which to be just and candid I am obliged to observe (and blush for my countrymen at the recital) is somewhat of a prodigy, as it is a fact, I am afraid too true, that the white traders in their commerce with the Indians, give great and frequent occasions of complaint of their dishonesty and violence; but yet there are a few exceptions, as in the conduct of this gentleman, who furnishes a living instance of the truth of the old proverb, that "Honesty is the best policy," for this old honest Hibernian has often been protected by the Indians, when all others round about him have been ruined, their property seized and themselves driven out of the country or slain by the injured, provoked natives. . . .

pp. 356–358

We returned to our trusty servants that were regaling themselves in the exuberant sweet pastures and strawberry fields in sight, and mounted again; proceeding on our return to town, continued through part of this high forest skirting on the meadows; began to ascend the hills of a ridge which we were under the necessity of crossing, and having gained its summit, enjoyed a most enchanting view, a vast expanse of green meadows and strawberry fields; a meandering river gliding through, saluting in its various turnings the swelling, green, turfy knolls, embellished with parterres of flowers and fruitful strawberry beds; flocks of turkies strolling about them; herds of deer prancing in the meads or bounding over the hills; companies of young, innocent Cherokee virgins, some busily gathering the rich fragrant fruit, others having already filled their baskets, lay reclined under the shade of floriferous and fragrant native bowers of Magnolia, Azalea, Philadelphus, perfumed Calycanthus, sweet Yellow Jessamine and cerulian Glycine frutescens, disclosing their beauties to the fluttering breeze, and bathing their limbs in the cool fleeting streams; whilst other parties, more gay and libertine, were yet Collecting strawberries or wantonly chasing their companions, tantalising them, staining their lips and cheeks with the rich fruit.

This sylvan scene of primitive innocence was enchanting, and perhaps too enticing for hearty young men long to continue idle spectators.

In fine, nature prevailing over reason, we wished at least to have a more active part in their delicious sports. Thus precipitately resolving, we cautiously made our approaches, yet undiscovered, almost to the joyous scene of action. Now, although we meant no other than an innocent frolic with this gay assembly of hamadryades, we shall leave it to the person of feeling and sensibility to form an idea to what lengths our passions might have hurried us, thus warmed and excited, had it not been for the vigilance and care of some envious matrons who lay in ambush, and espying us gave the alarm, time enough for the nymphs to rally and assemble together; we however pursued and gained ground on a group of them, who had incautiously strolled to a greater distance from their guardians, and finding their retreat now like to be cut off, took shelter under cover of a little grove, but on perceiving themselves to be discovered by us, kept their station, peeping through the bushes; when observing our approaches, they confidently discovered themselves and decently advanced to meet us, half unveiling their blooming faces, incarnated with the modest maiden blush, and with native innocence and cheerfulness presented their little baskets, merrily telling us their fruit was ripe and sound.

We accepted a basket, sat down and regaled ourselves on the delicious fruit, encircled by the whole assembly of the innocently jocose sylvan nymphs; by this time the several parties under the conduct of the elder matrons, had disposed themselves in companies on the green, turfy banks.

My young companion, the trader, by concessions and suitable apologies for the bold intrusion, having compromised the matter with them, engaged them to bring their collections to his house at a stipulated price, we parted friendly.

And now taking leave of these Elysian fields, we again mounted the hills, which we crossed, and traversing obliquely their flowery beds, arrived in town in the cool of the evening.

pp. 366–371

The town of Cowe consists of about one hundred dwellings, near the banks of the Tanase, on both sides of the river.

The Cherokees construct their habitations on a different plan from the Creeks, that is but one oblong four square building, of one story high; the materials consisting of logs or trunks of trees, stripped of their bark, notched at their ends, fixed one upon another, and afterwards plaistered well, both inside and out, with clay well tempered with dry grass, and the whole covered or roofed with the bark of the Chesnut tree or long broad shingles. This building is however partitioned transversely, forming three apartments, which communicate with each other by inside doors; each house or habitation has besides a little conical house, covered with dirt, which is called the winter or hot-house; this stands a few yards distance from the mansion-house, opposite the front door.

The council or town-house is a large rotunda, capable of accommodating several hundred people; it stands on the top of an ancient artificial mount of earth, of about twenty feet perpendicular, and the rotunda on the top of it being above thirty feet more, gives the whole fabric an elevation of about sixty feet from the common surface of the ground. But it may be proper to observe, that this mount on which the rotunda stands, is of a much ancienter date than the building, and perhaps was raised for another purpose. The Cherokees themselves are as ignorant as we are, by what people or for what purpose these artificial hills were raised; they have various stories concerning them, the best of which amounts to no more than mere conjecture, and leave us entirely in the dark; but they have a tradition common with the other nations of Indians, that they found them in much the same condition as they now appear, when their forefathers arrived from the West and possessed themselves of the country, after vanquishing the nations of red men who then inhabited it, who themselves found these mounts when they took possession of the country, the former possessors delivering the same story concerning them: perhaps they were designed and appropriated by the people who constructed them, to some religious purpose, as great altars and temples similar to the high places and sacred groves anciently amongst the Canaanites and other nations of Palestine and Judea.

The rotunda is constructed after the following manner, they first fix in the ground a circular range of posts or trunks of trees, about six feet high, at equal distances, which are notched at top, to receive into them, from one to another, a range of beams or wall plates; within this is another circular order of very large and strong pillars, above twelve feet high, notched in like manner at top, to receive another range of wall plates, and within this is yet another or third range of stronger and higher pillars, but fewer in number, and standing at a greater distance from each other; and lastly, in the centre stands a very strong pillar, which forms the pinnacle of the building, and to which the rafters centre at top; these rafters are strengthened and bound together by cross beams and laths, which sustain the roof or covering, which is a layer of bark neatly placed, and tight enough to exclude the rain, and sometimes they cast a thin superficies of earth over all. There is but one large door, which serves at the same time to admit light from without and the smoak to escape when a fire is kindled; but as there is but a small fire kept, sufficient to give light at night, and that fed with dry small sound wood divested of its bark, there is but little smoak; all around the inside of the building, betwixt the second range of pillars and the wall, is a range of cabins or sophas, consisting of two or three steps, one above or behind the other, in theatrical order, where the assembly sit or lean down; these sophas are covered with matts or carpets, very curiously made of thin splints of Ash or Oak, woven or platted together; near the great pillar in the centre the fire is kindled for light, near which the musicians seat themselves, and round about this the performers exhibit their dances and other shews at public festivals, which happen almost every night throughout the year.

About the close of the evening I accompanied Mr. Galahan and other white traders to the rotunda, where was a grand festival, music and dancing. This assembly was held principally to rehearse the ball-play dance, this town being challenged to play against another the next day.

The people being assembled and seated in order, and the musicians having taken their station, the ball opens, first with a long harangue or oration, spoken by an aged chief, in commendation of the manly exercise of the ball-play, recounting the many and brilliant victories which the town of Cowe had gained over the other towns in the nation, not forgetting or neglecting to recite his own exploits, together with those of other aged men now present, coadjutors in the performance of these athletic games in their youthful days.

This oration was delivered with great spirit and eloquence, and was meant to influence the passions of the young men present, excite them to emulation and inspire them with ambition.

This prologue being at an end, the musicians began, both vocal and instrumental, when presently a company of girls, hand in hand, dressed in clean white robes and ornamented with beads, bracelets and a profusion of gay ribbands, entering the door, immediately began to sing their responses in a gentle, low and sweet voice, and formed themselves in a semicircular file or line, in two ranks, back to back, facing the spectators and musicians, moving slowly round and round; this continued about a quarter of an hour, when we were surprised by a sudden very loud and shrill whoop, uttered at once by a company of young fellows, who came in briskly after one another, with rackets or hurls in one hand. These champions likewise were well dressed, painted and ornamented with silver bracelets, gorgets and wampum, neatly ornamented with moccasins and high waving plumes in their diadems, who immediately formed themselves in a semicircular rank also, in front of the girls, when these changed their order, and formed a single rank parallel to the men, raising their voices in responses to the tunes of the young champions, the semicircles continually moving round. There was something singular and diverting in their step and motions, and I imagine not to be learned to exactness but with great attention and perseverance; the step, if it can be so termed, was performed after the following manner, i. e. first, the motion began at one end of the semicircle, gently rising up and down upon their toes and heels alternately, when the first was up on tip-toe, the next began to raise the heel, and by the time the first rested again on the heel, the second was on tip toe, thus from one end of the rank to the other, so that some were always up and some down, alternately and regularly, without the least baulk or confusion; and they at the same time, and in the same motion, moved on obliquely or sideways, so that the circle performed a double or complex motion in its progression, and at stated times exhibited a grand or universal movement, instantly and unexpectedly to the spectators, by each rank turning to right and left, taking each others places; the movements were managed with inconceivable alertness and address, and accompanied with an instantaneous and universal elevation of the voice and shrill short whoop.

The Cherokees besides the ball play dance, have a variety of others equally entertaining; the men especially exercise themselves with a variety of gesticulations and capers, some of which are ludicrous and diverting enough; and they have others which are of the martial order, and others of the chace; these seem to be somewhat of a tragical nature, wherein they exhibit astonishing feats of military prowess, masculine strength and activity. Indeed all their dances and musical entertainments seem to be theatrical exhibitions or plays, varied with comic and sometimes lascivious interludes; the women however conduct themselves with a very becoming grace and decency, insomuch that in amorous interludes, when their responses and gestures seem consenting to natural liberties, they veil themselves, just discovering a glance of their sparkling eyes and blushing faces, expressive of sensibility.

Part 2

The Revolutionary Republic

4

Immigrants and the Backcountry World

While the slave system expanded to such an extent that the colony was well on its way to becoming a slave society, a steady stream of immigrants entered North Carolina, accounting for the dramatic increase in the white population. During the generation before the Revolution, among the most important changes affecting North Carolina was the rapid increase of the white population. Many of these immigrants were ethnically non-English; they included Scotch-Irish, Scots, and Germans. Most of them settled in the Carolina interior, the "backcountry," where a land rush was underway by the 1740s. The rise of backcountry society was spurred by liberal land practices that dispensed land to immigrants on easy and inexpensive terms. Still the land boom did not benefit everyone equally, and with the rise of the Regulators, the backcountry became a hotbed of political crisis.

Carolina Society in the Eighteenth Century

In 1728–29, when the Virginian William Byrd II served on a boundary commission to resolve the "dividing line" between North Carolina and Virginia, he found a folk culture that was stubbornly isolated and antiauthoritarian. The Carolina colony had two charters, in 1663 and 1665, neither of which established clear borders. As a result, along the Virginia-North Carolina border, land titles were uncertain and taxes difficult to collect. Both colonies sought to end this chaotic situation.

In his *History of the Dividing Line*, Byrd provided a half-satirical, half-truthful depiction of North Carolina life. "The only business here is raising of hogs," he wrote, which was "managed with the least trouble, and affords the diet they are most fond of." North Carolinians ate so much fresh pork, he claimed with considerable exaggeration, that country folk were victims of "gross humours," and the "highest taint of scurvy" that could lead to the yaws, or "country distemper," that sometimes undermined the "foundation" of the nose. "This calamity

North Carolina: Change and Tradition in a Southern State, Second Edition. William A. Link.

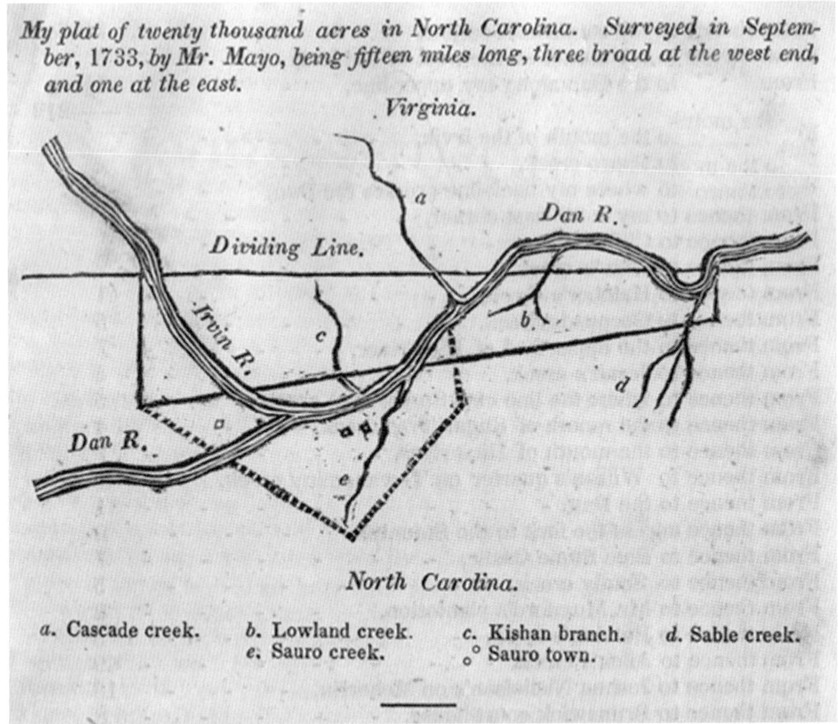

Figure 4.1 William Byrd's *History of the Dividing Line*. Source: North Carolina Collection, University of North Carolina Library at Chapel Hill. *Source:* http://www.docsouth.unc.edu/nc/byrd/ill1.html

is so common and familiar here, that it ceases to be a scandal, and in the disputes that happen about beauty, the noses have in some companies much ado to carry it." After three good pork years, according to Byrd, it was said that a member of the North Carolina Assembly made a motion that anyone with a nose should be "incapable of holding any place of profit in the province; which extraordinary motion could never have been intended without some hopes of a majority."[1]

Byrd's account was, of course, over the top, and it suggests the haughty pretensions of a Virginia grandee over what he considered an inferior, frontier society. But by the time Byrd visited North Carolina, in the late 1720s, a new white society was emerging, one that would possess distinctive cultural characteristics. As Byrd suggested, pork was an essential part of the diet of North Carolinians. The word *barbecue*, according to some accounts, came from the Spanish, who first observed natives in the West Indies preparing meat on wooden sticks suspended over a fire, a method for which the Indian word was *barbacoa*. Indians in eastern North Carolina used a similar method of cooking meat, and the Anglo-American colonists began to call this "barbecue." By the eighteenth century, hogs had become the most common form of livestock in North Carolina, some of them raised for export to markets in Virginia and the West Indies but most of them consumed locally. At the time, the most marketable form of pork was salted pork, which Gov. Josiah Martin described as "made in vast quantities."[2]

Throughout the eighteenth century, the great majority of North Carolinians lived in rural areas, remotely located from the few existing towns. Naturalist and physician Johann David Schoepf described North Carolina in the 1770s as "a continuous, measureless, forest, an ocean of trees." The colonists had founded settlements interspersed within dense forests, what one observer called "cultivated spots, ... plantations ... scattered about in these woods at various distances, 3–6 miles, and often as much as 10–15–20 miles apart." In between farms were crossroads, courthouse towns, and taverns. Rural roads ran "constantly thro' woods," wrote another observer, "which tho' they are generally pretty open, yet objects at any considerable distance are intercepted from the eye, by the trees crowding into the line of direction as the distance increases."

Much of the colony remained remote and, to many travelers, wild and uncivilized. This was a world in which the social system was "still in a state of infancy," according to a Spanish visitor.[3] William Byrd provided a much harsher description. "Surely there is no place in the world where the inhabitants live with less labor than in North Carolina," he wrote of a culture he claimed was fueled by "the great felicity of the climate, the easiness of raising provisions, and the slothfulness of the people." The average family lived on a diet of cornmeal, sweet potatoes, greens, and pork, and "a little pains will subsist a very large family with bread, and then they may have meat without any pains at all, by the help of the low grounds, and the great variety of mast that grows on the high land." With a "thorough aversion to labor," rural Carolinians, Byrd charged, "loiter away their lives, like Solomon's sluggard, with their arms across, and at the winding up of the year scarcely have bread to eat."[4]

The social structure of this rural society—where 98 percent of North Carolina's population lived—divided according to a class structure. A large portion of the population, about half, were either landless or enslaved. Another large portion was composed of small, generally self-sufficient landholders. "Every proprietor of ever so small a piece of land," said an English visitor, raised "some Indian corn and sweet potatoes and breeds some hogs and a calf or two, and a man must be very poor who walks on foot."[5] Households were scattered, some simple log cabins with dirt floors, a few, mostly in the plantation regions of eastern North Carolina, having more architectural pretensions. Values of honor, resistance to outside authority, and hospitality—values that sometimes lay at odds with one another—prevailed among North Carolinians.

Rural folk organized themselves locally, although militia gatherings, days on which county courts met, and elections provided occasions for social interaction. Men worked together in corn husking and barn raisings, women in quilting bees. In these settings recreation focused on hunting, fishing, horse racing, and cockfighting, usually accompanied by gambling. Horse racing, a popular sport in England, was practiced across colonial North Carolina. As the traveler John Brickell wrote in the 1730s, North Carolinians were "fond" of horse racing "for which they have Race-Paths near each town and in many parts of the Country." Races were often conducted at taverns or village crossroads, and informal "jockey clubs" organized competitions that typically comprised a race of a quarter mile on a country road. In North Carolina, according to a British visitor:

> They are much addicted to quarter-racing … and they have a breed which performs it with astonishing velocity, beating each other for that distance with great ease. … I am confident that there is no horse in England nor perhaps in the whole world than can excel them in rapid speed.[6]

Another popular sport in North Carolina during the colonial period and into the nineteenth century was cockfighting. This blood sport pitted against one another two specially bred gamecocks (often imported from England or Ireland) that fought until one had killed the other. Cockfighting attracted widespread interest and support among the Carolina gentry, but it also drew the intense interest of gambling spectators. Another blood sport, gouging, was especially popular in eighteenth-century North Carolina. One traveler described a gouging contest in which two men were

> fast clenched by the hair, and their thumbs endeavoring to force passage into each other's eyes, while several of the bystanders were betting upon the first eye to be turned out of its socket. At length the combatants fell to the ground and in an instant the uppermost sprang up with this antagonist's eye in his hand! The savage crowd applauded while, sick with horror, we galloped away from the infernal scene.

This violent sport combined wrestling, boxing, and all-out combat. Gouging grew so popular among poorer Carolinians that Gov. Gabriel Johnson condemned the "barbarous and inhuman manner of Boxing, which so much prevails among the lower Sort of People." Three years later, the General Assembly prohibited sports that "cut out the Tongue, or pull out the Eyes."[7]

Immigration and the Land Rush

At the beginning of the eighteenth century, approximately several thousand whites lived in North Carolina; by 1730, this number had increased to as many as 35,000; by 1750, to 75,000. Although the population explosion is attributable in part to the fact that, at the time, North Carolinians, like most Americans, tended to have large families, this was not the principal factor. Rather, most of the population increase in the pre-Revolutionary era resulted from a rush of migrants into the Carolinas from other colonies.

Many of the newcomers arrived from Virginia, where population expansion had placed new pressures on land resources. Many Virginians—most of whom had an English heritage—migrated south, peopling North Carolina's Coastal Plain. Of the 175,000 North Carolinians in 1770, about 45,000 lived in the backcountry, all of them migrants and the majority non-English—ethnic Scotch-Irish and Germans—who came in large numbers after 1750 by way of Pennsylvania. They arrived via the Great Wagon Road, which extended 735 miles from Philadelphia to Georgia. Its route ranged from Pennsylvania south to western Maryland, then down the Shenandoah Valley of Virginia. Near the present-day city of Roanoke, the route turned southeast, following the Staunton River gap, turning south across the Dan River into North Carolina and, eventually, South Carolina. The earliest immigrants traveled the Great Wagon Road to North Carolina as early as the 1740s, and by the 1750s and 1760s a rush of immigrants flowed south into the Yadkin River country then spread in all directions across the backcountry. Between 1754 and 1770, the total population of Rowan County, a sprawling county in the western backcountry, quadrupled.

The surge of white immigrants into the backcountry coincided with the decimation of the indigenous societies. In the backcountry, a dispersed group of tribes, linked linguistically by the Sioux language, had organized themselves into compact villages founded several hundred years before the arrival of Euro-Americans to North Carolina. As already discussed in Chapter 1, the advent of European diseases wreaked a holocaust on these societies, and by the mid-1700s the backcountry was virtually depopulated of its Indian inhabitants. A prominent exception was the Catawbas, who organized themselves from the remnants of a number of other tribes and continued to persist into the nineteenth and twentieth centuries. The population explosion of migrants into the backcountry thus met very little resistance from Indian groups.

Numerous commentators of the day took note of the rush of immigrants. Benjamin Franklin asserted in 1763 that nearly 40,000 immigrants had recently departed Pennsylvania for North Carolina. Another observer remarked, "There is scarce any history, either ancient or modern, which affords an account of such a rapid and sudden increase of inhabitants in a back frontier country as that of North Carolina." He found the growth in population and the "flourishing" condition of the North Carolina backcountry through immigration to be "surprising and astonishing."[8] In the early years of settlement, the migrants hunted the remaining big game animals for meat and pelts, which found buyers in Charleston, but the wild herds soon became virtually extinct. The economic base of this "flourishing" society, by the 1750s, was agriculture, but migrants to the backcountry had taken the mixed farming

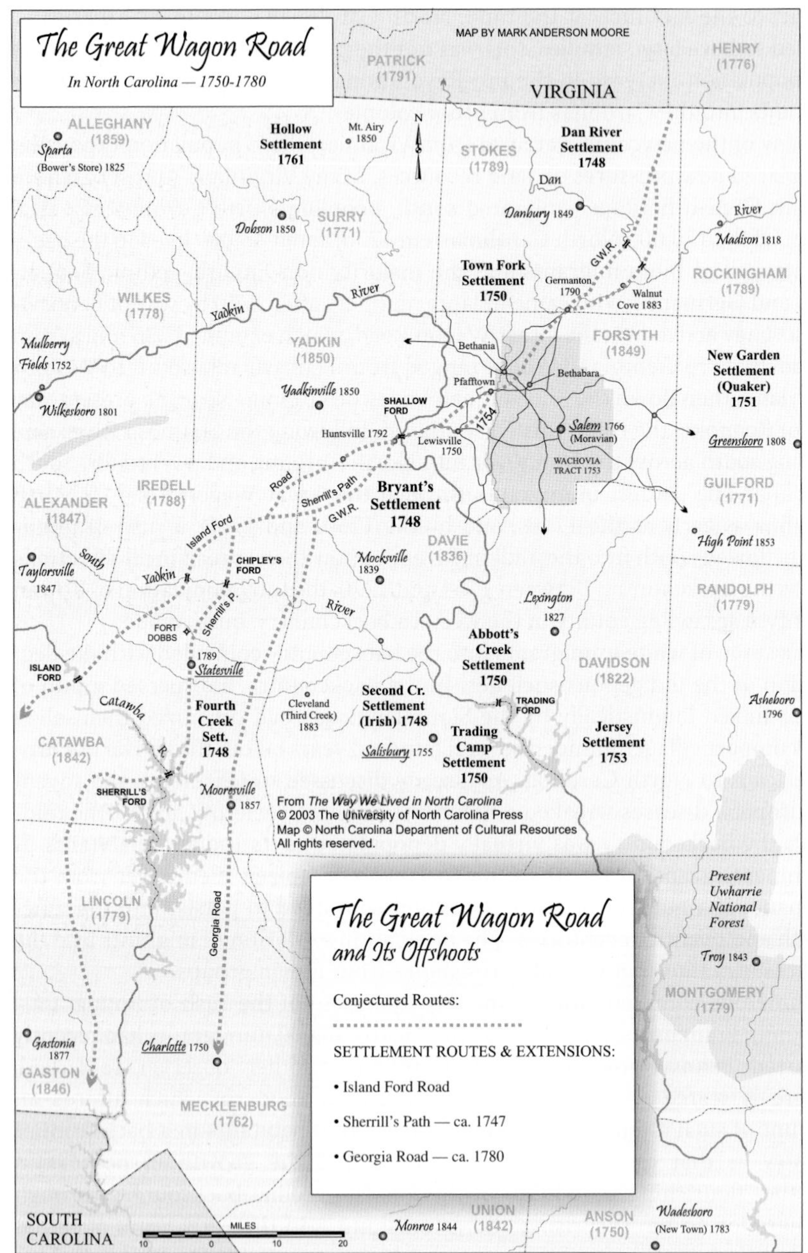

Figure 4.2 Great Wagon Road, and its offshoots.

practices of Pennsylvania and the Great Valley with them. Although some of the newcomers grew tobacco, the majority grew grains such as corn and wheat, as well as barley, oats, and rye. Most backcountry farmers also kept livestock, and they raised cattle and hogs. By this time both beef and pork could be sold in markets in eastern North Carolina.

The Carolina population explosion resulted in the organization of new counties and the establishment of new towns. Responding to the influx, in 1750 the assembly created a large western county, Anson, and, two years later, it established Orange County. Over the next two decades, both Anson and Orange Counties were divided into Guilford, Mecklenburg, Rowan, Tryon, and Surry Counties. Meanwhile, new towns—Hillsborough, Salem, Salisbury, and Charlotte—sprang up. Though not particularly large—none of these towns comprised more than a few hundred residents—they served as centers in the backcountry. Hillsborough and Salisbury, both founded in 1754, were located on major trading routes—the Indian Trading Path, which went north to Virginia, and the Salem-Cross Creek Road, which went east. Both towns also benefited from the rush of migrants and the land boom. Hillsborough and Salisbury also served as governmental centers. They originated as county seats, Hillsborough of Orange County and Salisbury of Rowan County, and also served as meeting places for superior courts. The Moravian settlement of Salem, founded in 1766, became the most important trade center in the northern backcountry. Making routine runs to Charleston, South Carolina, Moravian wagons also carried the products of the northern backcountry for transshipment to Fall Line towns, especially after the road connecting Salem to Cross Creek was completed in 1770. Charlotte, first settled in 1750 and incorporated in 1768, became the leading town of the southern Piedmont, though in terms of size and economic importance it was the least significant backcountry town.

Backcountry towns also expanded because they were home to an aggressive core of merchants linked to eastern towns and economic centers that included towns on the Fall Line, such as Cross Creek (later Fayetteville) or, to the north, Halifax. Backcountry merchants were the western outliers of a larger network that extended farther east: the most dominant mercantile community was the merchant town of Wilmington, which by the Revolution had become the largest town in North Carolina.

The New Immigrants

The development of the backcountry was of great significance for the history of North Carolina. Rapid population growth occurred in the coastal counties of the colony, to be sure, where a rise in the white population and especially the surge of the African American population brought on expansion. But the backcountry developed quite differently: the land rush came first, followed by the

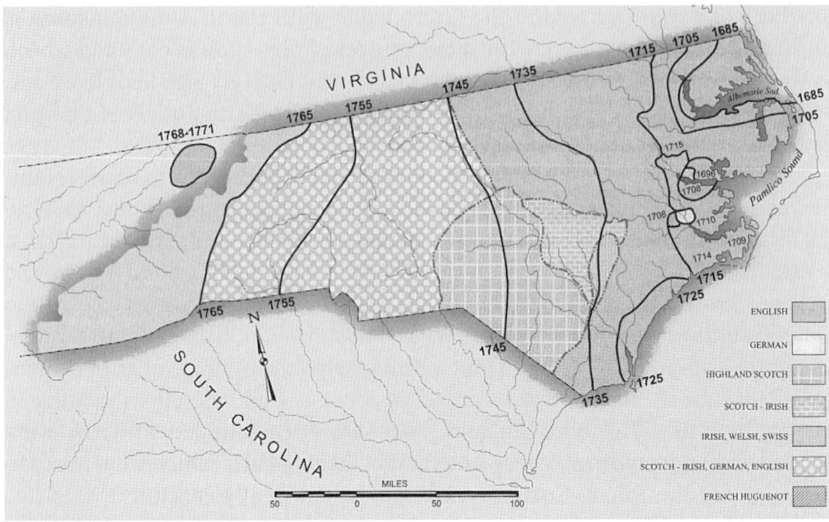

Figure 4.3 Progress of European settlement, 1685–1771. Map by Mark Anderson Moore. *Source: North Carolina Office of Archives and History.*

sudden influx of white migrants over a relatively short span of time; in addition, by no means were all of the whites who poured into the backcountry English. Between the 1750s and 1770s, backcountry population grew quickly, with white populations increasing in many instances by fourfold or more. Nearly all of this population increase occurred as a result of the immigration of four key ethnic groups: English, Germans, Scottish Highlanders, and Scotch-Irish.

What gave the backcountry region its particular flavor was the presence of these non-English immigrants, part of a significant migration stream arriving in British North America from the early 1700s to the American Revolution. Among these were Gaelic-speaking Highland Scots, who began to arrive in North Carolina after 1732. Nearly all of them traveled to North Carolina by way of Wilmington and Brunswick and settled in the Upper Cape Fear valley. By the time of the Revolution, with 10,000 Highland Scots, North Carolina possessed the largest concentration of these migrants in the thirteen colonies. Germans and Scotch-Irish migrated to North Carolina in a migration stream that extended from Pennsylvania through Maryland and Virginia, along the Great Wagon Road. The Germans were mostly Protestant Lutherans who left because of the warfare and economic distress that characterized their homeland in the Rhine region of Germany.

The Scotch-Irish came originally from the province of Ulster, an area occupied by English and Scottish Protestants beginning in the Elizabethan Era: Northern Ireland, England's first colonial experiment, involved an attempt to transform the hostile Roman Catholic population of Ulster through a process of "plantation" and colonization. By the early 1700s, the English colonial experiment in Ireland had reached a dead end. Most of the Protestants, now third-generation Irish, were "dissenting" Protestants, for the most part Reformed Presbyterians, and they existed apart from the Church of England. In the late seventeenth century, the English-imposed restrictions on the political power of dissenters meant that the Presbyterian Irish were barred from voting, office-holding, and the professions. Economic pressures figured importantly, as well. Rising population placed pressures on land, and the largely dispossessed Ulster Scots faced a rapid increase in the rents that they had to pay as tenants. Even more serious was the impact of the English mercantile empire as established by the Navigation Acts of the late 1600s. These Acts, seeking to divert mercantile activity and control of trade from the colonies to England, had the effect of wiping out the Ulster woolens industry. These developments, in combination with a high rate of population growth in Northern Ireland, led to a new migration stream in which approximately 250,000 Scotch-Irish arrived in the American colonies by the time of the Revolution.

The Granville District

The rapid development of the North Carolina backcountry was tied to the creation of a unique administrative arrangement: the Granville District. The English Crown, chiefly for reasons of efficiency and better colonial administration, sought to absorb the proprietary colonies of British North America: between the 1680s and 1720s, most of its proprietary colonies became royal colonies. In the case of North Carolina, royal officials negotiated with the heirs of the Lords Proprietors to sell their shares; most of the heirs had little interest in maintaining their control. In July 1729, all but one of the eight proprietors, John Carteret—the great-grandson of the original proprietor—agreed to do so, and Parliament provided £2,500 along with £5,000 for unpaid quitrents (an ancient form of tax revenue) to each heir. But Carteret asserted a claim to retain control over one-eighth of the original Carolina colonies and, fifteen years after the establishment of the royal colony of North Carolina, on September 17, 1744, the British Crown recognized his claim and established a new proprietary grant. Under the terms of the agreement, Carteret (who in 1744 became the Earl of Granville) received approximately 26,000 square miles, extending from the southern boundary of Virginia 60 miles south to 35° 34′ north latitude. The precise boundaries of this grant were determined by a boundary commission that surveyed the area and reported to the Privy Council in December 1743, and in both 1746 and 1753, the boundary was extended westward. The administrative and governmental structure of what became known as the Granville District was highly unusual; nothing like it existed anywhere else in British North

Figure 4.4 John Carteret, Earl of Granville. *Source: North Carolina Collection, University of North Carolina Library at Chapel Hill.*

America. For his part, Carteret had no desire to exert governmental control over his micro colony: the grant mandated that the Granville District possessed no power to levy taxes, administer justice, or perform any other governmental functions. Its sole functions were to sell land and to collect quitrents.

After 1751, when Carteret's land agents opened their offices, the Granville District, which comprised approximately the northern half of North Carolina, became a magnet for new immigrants to the colony. A land boom ensued, which the attractive policies of Granville's agents encouraged. Between 1748 and 1763—during which time Granville's land office was open—three million acres were sold in about 4,400 land grants. The lands became available in fee-simple form—rather than through any sort of leasing arrangement—and the quitrents were no higher than for Crown lands. Granville's agents also offered land at cheap rates. They charged a modest fee of £4 19s (Virginia currency) for each tract, no matter the size. Although technically the holders of Granville's land patents were his tenants, in effect they became freeholders under relatively generous terms. In the land-hungry society of British North Carolina, migrants flocked to the Granville District because good lands could be had there at a cheap cost.

Granville himself never set foot in North Carolina, and his chief interest was in securing a source of revenue. As early as 1730, he had anticipated that the proprietary was "capable of Such improvements ... as were likely to make it as valuable an Estate to my Family, as any Subject had in America."[9] Although Granville sought an annual revenue of several thousand pounds sterling, his hopes were never realized. Partly, this reflected malfeasance on the part of his land agents, Edward Moseley and Robert Halton, who after 1749 were followed by Francis Corbin and Thomas Child. These land agents administered the Granville District's land offices in a notoriously corrupt fashion. Between 1751 and 1756, Corbin's office sent only £4,000; after 1756, no further revenues came Granville's way. Corbin's system of corrupt administration also affected the migrants, as his network of local deputies, or "agents," were generally careless about maintaining land records and imposed excessive fees in order to line their pockets. Granville land agents routinely charged high fees for surveys and deeds and patents. In numerous instances they sold multiple patents for the same tracts of land, and in some cases they collected fees for deeds but never issued patents for the land. Among the most notorious of Corbin's local land agents was James Carter, who served as a surveyor in Orange and Rowan Counties. Carter was well known for collecting excessive fees for surveys and deeds but also for defrauding settlers of their land. According to one account, he had "exacted and extorted considerable sums of Money from several Persons," but the settlers possessed no legal deed.[10] Despite numerous complaints about Corbin and his deputies, Granville, himself aware of the extent of the corruption, did nothing to reform the administration of the Granville District.

At the same time, Granville's agents were embroiled in an ongoing dispute with Scottish merchant Henry McCulloh, who, through influence-peddling and maneuvering, had purchased large tracts of land in the Upper Cape Fear valley and the central and southern Piedmont in the 1730s, amounting to 1.2 million acres. The massive McCulloh grants came with highly favorable terms: promising to absorb the costs of surveying these lands, he was excused from quitrents during the initial decade of settlement (this provision was subsequently extended to 1760). Of these lands, however, 475,000 acres lay in the proprietary grant of the Granville District. Although Granville was willing to resolve matters with McCulloh in England, Corbin defied Granville and deliberately undermined any settlement, as Granville agents busily sold deeds to lands under McCulloh's control and demanded quitrents from McCulloh's

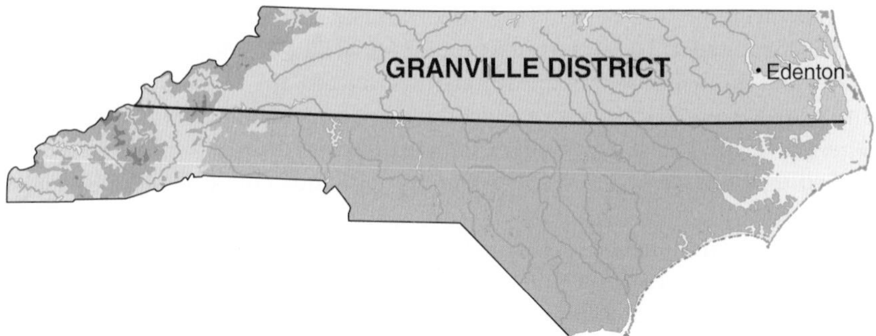

Figure 4.5 The Granville District.

settlers. In June 1755, surveyors sent by McCulloh were attacked by Granville supporters. While the conflict extended to provincial-level politics—Assembly Speaker John Campbell was allied with McCulloh—the Granville-McCulloh dispute cast a shadow over the legitimacy of landholdings in the area.

The legacy of the Granville District thus remained mixed. Without question, it played an important role in the rapid development of North Carolina and the influx of white settlers, mostly new, non-English immigrants or first-generation Pennsylvanians who came to the backcountry in search of opportunity through cheap land. Clearly, however, the boom had adverse consequences. Seemingly overnight, the backcountry was filled with men on the make, hucksters who took advantage of the boom and sought to make fast money. Other men accumulated large holdings in the land rush. But most of the new settlers had come for purely legitimate reasons and possessed no special access to power, were modest in their landholdings, and suffered under the obnoxious public malfeasance that seemed to dominate backcountry life. Granville District corruption was connected to corruption at the provincial level: Corbin dispensed extensive patronage that enhanced his standing in the assembly, and a number of assemblymen even served as Granville deputies. There was also a growing disjuncture during the 1750s between the new migrants and Granville agents and local officials, who were closely attached to the slave-based political culture of coastal North Carolina.

Backcountry immigrants' frustration with the misadministration of the Granville District began to manifest itself politically. In November 1758, nearly 500 Granville residents petitioned the assembly to investigate malfeasance and mismanagement, and the assembly organized a committee to investigate. But its report did little to address the petitioners' grievances and specifically acquitted Corbin of any wrongdoing. Naturally, the report did little to quiet the immigrants' outrage. When the former assemblyman and Corbin deputy John Haywood died in early 1759, locals dug up his body to make sure his death was not a hoax. Anti-Granville resentment also led to the famous Enfield Riot. On January 25, 1759, a group from the Granville District visited Corbin at his Edenton home, abducted him along with one of his agents, Joshua Bodley, and transported them to Enfield, in Halifax County, 75 miles west. The mob was composed mostly of farmers of moderate means who could no longer tolerate Corbin's corrupt behavior. Another prominent rioter was Edgecombe County's Alexander McCulloh, nephew of Henry McCulloh, who probably participated out of frustration with the inability of Corbin and Granville agents to settle their dispute with his uncle. The rioters confined the two men for four days until they agreed to open up their records for public inspection and to return the exorbitant fees that Corbin's operation had collected.

Although the demands of the mob had been met, the Enfield Riot solved few of the Granville District's problems. Even after Granville suspended Corbin and Bodley, the problems of malfeasance and ambiguous land titles continued. Even worse, when Granville died in 1763, the Granville District's land offices closed, meaning that no more of its land was distributed and many of its deeds remained unissued. As a result, many backcountry residents would never enjoy any security regarding the legality of their landholdings. Although Gov. William Tryon subsequently would propose purchasing the Granville District for £68,000 from Granville's family, its status remained in limbo until the Revolution, and the backcountry continued as a breeding ground for discontent.

Religious Discontent

The booming Carolina backcountry also became the scene of intense religious change during the three decades before the American Revolution. From the arrival of the first white settlers in the 1650s through the mid-1700s, religion played only a small part of life among white North Carolinians. The only religious presence was the Church of England, which existed sporadically in eastern North Carolina. The first parish church was established in the town of Bath in the early 1700s, and, from England, the Anglican Society for the Propagation of the Gospel (SPG) dispatched missionaries. Yet the Anglican Church enjoyed, at best, a tenuous foothold in the colony, and the backcountry boom created opportunities for non-Anglican religious groups to flourish.

In part, the religious diversity reflected the ethnic diversity of the immigrants, who brought new faiths to the frontier. The Scotch-Irish and Scottish Highlanders practiced an active Presbyterian faith, and Presbyterianism, with a Calvinist theology that emphasized the sovereignty of God, predestination, and the certainty of justification (or salvation) by faith alone, became firmly rooted in the backcountry. Some German immigrants, like the Presbyterians, adhered to a Calvinist Reformed faith, though most Germans were Lutherans. The Pietist Dunkers, also Germans, who believed in the innate goodness and godliness of people and who were active pacifists and preferred a simple religion that rejected affluence and power, created several active communities in the western backcountry. A distinctive German-speaking group was the Moravians, who originated in eastern Bohemia, in central Europe, in the mid-1400s, and by 1517 the Unity of the Brethren, or Moravians, included 200,000 members and more than 400 parishes. Having organized even before the advent of the Reformation, the Moravians favored reforms in the church. But during the next three centuries, suffering persecution, they developed a highly unique form of Christianity that led to the creation of separate communities in which they sought to exist largely apart from the evil of the world. Stressing individual faith and an emotional connection to God, the Moravians refused to participate in offensive wars. Without private real property (though individuals owned personal property), a typical Moravian colony lived under a hierarchical social order in which the brethren's elders determined work, allocation of resources, housing, and marriages. Establishing colonies around the world, the German-speaking Moravians purchased 100,000 acres from the Granville District in 1752—which they called "Wachovia"—and created thriving towns in Bethania, Bethabara, and, eventually, Salem.

North Carolina had long possessed large and active Quaker communities: the Society of Friends became established in northeastern North Carolina in the late 1600s. The backcountry attracted a new rush of Quakers moving south from Maryland and Pennsylvania after the 1740s. Quakers lived in communities that rejected the trappings of material life, and they were devout pacifists. Unlike other Protestants, they did not have ministers and believed that all Christians could receive God's "inner light." Church services followed the "inner lights" rather than a rigid liturgy: church governance was highly decentralized and democratic. During the 1750s and 1760s, backcountry Quakers organized themselves into eight meetings, their basic unit of church government.

Adding to the backcountry's mixture of religious denominations was the explosive presence of evangelicalism, a new movement in Protestantism that emphasized individual conversion and revivalism. As early as 1739, the English Methodist revivalist George Whitefield visited North Carolina, and his methods and approach, which emphasized working outside the bounds of the church to achieve a rebirth of Christians' faith, encouraged new evangelicals across British North America. By the 1760s and 1770s, these evangelicals were having a marked impact. Their message extended the Protestant themes of individual salvation, congregational independence, and the centrality of faith, but evangelicals took these in new directions. Rejecting the older convention of mainline Protestantism, evangelicals embraced a new, more enthusiastic practice of faith that stressed the presence of the Holy Spirit and made faith and the experiential dimensions of Christianity paramount. Evangelicalism tended to move across denominations, splitting churches and denominations, and its leaders actively sought ecumenical alliances. Particularly important in organizing evangelical organizations were the Presbyterians, many of whom had become active converts in the 1740s in the mid-Atlantic colonies and took their faith with them to the Carolinas in the 1760s and 1770s.

Still another important cross-denominational group was the Separate Baptists. First arriving in North Carolina in 1755, Shubal Stearns and Daniel Marshall led a small group of Connecticut evangelicals who had been converted during one of Whitefield's tours to New England and had left the Congregational Church to organize the evangelical Separate Baptists. After his conversion and baptism, Stearns had migrated to Virginia in the early 1750s. Joining up with Marshall, the group established a new community at Sandy Creek, on the Deep River, in present-day Randolph County near the town of Liberty. The North Carolina Separate Baptists were the most enthusiastic evangelicals of the backcountry, and they aggressively sought out new converts and founded new churches, planting forty-two new churches by 1772. Enthusiastic in their church practices, the Separate Baptists were also highly democratic and advocated an egalitarian approach to church membership and government. In the backcountry, they soon attracted scores of new members and churches across the Piedmont and, within only a few years, into Virginia, South Carolina, and Georgia in what one contemporary described as a "mighty rushing wind."[11]

By the late 1760s, the backcountry thus contained a highly diverse mix of religious groups that partly matched the region's ethnic diversity. But the new religions soon transcended ethnicity or backgrounds. Increasingly the various Protestant groups embraced an evangelical culture that shared beliefs in spiritual rebirth, the scriptural basis of faith, and the need to spread the word of God to a wider audience. Separate Baptists were the most spectacularly successful of the new evangelicals, but other denominations such as Presbyterians and Quakers at least partially adopted evangelical methods.

This new, collective backcountry evangelical culture, moreover, created a new dichotomy, one that provided the basis for challenges to the established social order of colonial North Carolina. Coastal North Carolina remained hierarchical and slaveholding; the backcountry was more egalitarian and largely nonslaveholding. Coastal North Carolinians were ethnically English, while the majority of backcountry residents were non-English. Not the least important, coastal folk were Anglican and largely indifferent to religious faith, while backcountry people embraced a form of religious fervor that spilled over into political radicalism. Increasingly, backcountry residents challenged the ways of coastal Carolinians, and their challenges culminated in the sudden emergence of the Regulators.

The Rise of the Regulators

In the spring of 1765, William Tryon arrived in North Carolina to become the colony's fourth royal governor, succeeding Arthur Dobbs. Tryon's administration was a tumultuous one. Not long after he became governor, the English Parliament enacted the Stamp Act, and a storm of resistance erupted all over British North America to what was perceived as a usurpation of the traditional rights of taxpayers (for more extended discussion of the Stamp Act crisis, see Chapter 5). In the Stamp Act crisis, which ended with Parliament's repeal of the law in the spring of 1766, a struggle erupted between an emerging American political leadership eager for autonomy and British royal authorities determined to exert control over royal administration. In North Carolina, as in most other colonies, the Revolutionary struggle involved an internal contest for power. Many years ago, the progressive historian Carl Becker wrote that the American Revolution was not one conflict but two conflicts: a struggle not only over home rule but over who shall rule at home. The dual nature of the American Revolution—an imperial crisis and an internal battle among Americans—became especially apparent in North Carolina with the rise of Regulators, which became the most important internal uprising in British North America during the years prior to the Revolution.

The Regulators arose out of the particular conditions of the Carolina backcountry. The corrupt administration of the Granville District affected the thousands of immigrants who arrived during the 1750s and 1760s; as mentioned, they suffered from misadministration, excessive fees, and the malfeasance of both the Granville agents and North Carolina governmental officials. In addition, the explosion of evangelicalism onto the scene helped to foster a sense of alienation between backcountry and coastal North Carolina. It is no coincidence that religious radicalism soon converged with political radicalism. Not long after the resolution of the Stamp Act, in August 1766, a group of Orange County citizens formed the Sandy Creek Association. Prominent among the associators was Herman Husband, who subsequently became the most important Regulator leader. Like many people who became Regulators, Husband had not come from desperate poverty. Born in Maryland, he migrated to Orange County, North Carolina, in 1755, where he eventually accumulated more than 10,000 acres of land. Unconventional in his religious habits, Husband had become a converted evangelical during one of Whitefield's visits to Maryland, and on his arrival in North Carolina he became active in the local Quaker meeting. In 1764, Husband was disowned, or expelled, from the meeting because of his radicalism. Two years later, he was instrumental in organizing the Sandy Creek Association. In August 1766, Husband and other locals took the extraordinary step of appearing before the Orange County court and reading a list of grievances about the nature of local government, making a declaration in open court and summoning their fellow citizens forward to inquire "whether the free men of this county labor under any abuses of power or not."[12] Appealing to the example of North Carolinians' resistance to the Stamp Act and their quest for liberty, Husband and company denounced the corruption that dominated and oppressed backcountry life.

By 1768, this growing movement became known as the Regulation. It was so named because backcountry residents sought to "regulate" the honesty of local officials. The movement spread across the backcountry, with major uprisings in Orange, Rowan, and Anson Counties and with a lesser uprising in Granville, Mecklenburg, and Johnston Counties. From the outset, the Regulator movement was dispersed and decentralized, as Regulators sought to protest the payment of taxes, petition officials, and disrupt the administration of justice at their own local levels. Nonetheless, the movement attracted widespread attention and support, with a large portion of backcountry Carolinians attracted to the cause. According to one estimate, as much as three-quarters of the backcountry's adult white male population was sympathetic to or actively involved in the Regulation.[13]

Its leadership was horizontal rather than hierarchical: Regulators consciously avoided ostentatious pretensions. Husband became the best-known Regulator; not long after the collapse of the movement, he would publish his account of the uprising. Next in importance to Husband was James Hunter, a Presbyterian who, like Husband, had been a member of the Sandy Creek Association. A large number of Separate Baptists, most of them more modest in social origins, became active Regulators: Baptist preachers James Billingsley, Nathaniel Powell, Francis Dorsett, James Younger, and James Stewart all thus became involved.

Much of the backcountry frustration expressed class resentments against a new elite emerging in North Carolina. These frustrations culminated in open conflict during the spring of 1768. First came news that the colonial assembly had appropriated funds to build a residence for Governor Tryon which would also serve as a provincial capital. This was regarded as an example of legislative excess, and there was considerable unhappiness over high taxes and the unresponsiveness of the political system. Then, on May 3, 1768, Orange County official Edmund Fanning attempted to arrest Husband and William Butler, a fellow Regulator. Earlier, after local officials had confiscated some of a Regulator's possessions and sold them to pay his taxes, a group went to Hillsborough and discharged their weapons outside of Edmund Fanning's house. To Regulators, Edmund Fanning represented all that was wrong with Carolina society. With the rapid development of the backcountry, a class of people on the make had arrived on the scene, of whom Fanning seemed to be the ultimate example. Born in 1737 as the fifth son of a British army officer, Fanning attended Yale, where he graduated in 1757, and Harvard, where he received the M.A. degree. Arriving in Carolina at the age of 23, he settled near Hillsborough and soon established a law practice and promoted himself politically, becoming town commissioner and Orange County representative to the assembly. Thereafter, he held a succession of other public offices: prosecutor for the Crown, county public register, judge of the superior court, and officer of the county militia. Fanning was also very close to Governor Tryon, serving as his private secretary. In part because of his political influence, Fanning was conspicuously wealthy: by 1770, he owned more than 10,000 acres in Orange, Anson, and Rowan Counties, along with twenty-nine lots in Hillsborough, New Bern, Charlotte, Cross Creek, and Salisbury. Fanning was notorious for charging high fees for land registration—more than double the usual rate—and Regulators seized on Fanning as an archvillain of public corruption, and he soon became widely detested in the backcountry.

When Fanning attempted to arrest Husband and Butler, widespread public discontent ensued. Word quickly spread about the arrests, and 700 Regulators appeared in Hillsborough and forced Husband's release; officials, meanwhile, promised that they would consider the Regulators' grievances. Tryon, repudiating any direct negotiations with the Regulators, remained determined to thwart this uprising. On the other hand, he issued a proclamation pledging a crackdown on public corruption, banning the taking of excessive fees, and promising future prosecutions against transgressors. The governor then sponsored proceedings against Fanning, who was charged with extortion. He also personally visited Hillsborough in July and organized a force of militia to protect court proceedings against Husband and Butler in September 1768. After a tense standoff between 1,419 militia and 3,700 Regulators, Husband was acquitted, while Butler and Fanning were convicted but given light sentences. Although violence had been avoided, the Regulator movement—and open defiance of authority—thereafter only grew stronger. For example, in Johnston County, eighty Regulators assaulted members of a court in session, while in Anson County protesters disrupted the meeting of the county court. In both instances, Regulators were objecting to excessive fees and high taxes. Elsewhere, Regulators continued to mock court proceedings and to defy the very legitimacy of government.

In September 1770, Regulator defiance reached a peak at Hillsborough, in what became known as the Hillsborough Riot, when 150 Regulators burst into the courtroom of Superior Court judge Richard Henderson. Brandishing sticks and switches, the mob, led by Husband, Butler, and James Hunter, drove Henderson from the bench, whipped a local attorney, and dragged the future signer of the Declaration of Independence William Hooper through the streets of Hillsborough and ridiculed him. But the worst of the mob's fury was unleashed on Edmund Fanning. Taken from the courtroom and whipped, Fanning watched as the mob stormed his Hillsborough house, burned his papers, wrecked his furnishings and furniture, and then destroyed his house. The Hillsborough Riot was the worst event in a series of Regulator assaults on the legitimacy of provincial government, and it constituted a very serious challenge to the social and political order.

Meeting in December 1770, the North Carolina legislature, worried that a Regulator army would soon march on the capital in New Bern, enacted the Johnston Riot Act. Sponsored by future Revolutionary leader Samuel Johnston, the Act empowered the governor to suppress the Regulator insurgency. Regulators, responding to the Johnston Act, grew even more defiant, and in the spring of 1771 a military confrontation seemed likely. Tryon personally organized and led a militia army, which he marched to the backcountry in May 1771. The militia force, numbering about 1,000 men, confronted a Regulator group about twice that size at Great Alamance Creek. The Regulators lacked ammunition, organization and discipline, and, above all, military leadership; highly democratic, many Regulators refused to accept command of troops. Despite mediation attempts by Guilford County Presbyterian minister David Caldwell—who had opposed the Regulators—Tryon's militia attacked on May 16 and, after a two-hour battle, the disorganized and ill-trained Regulators were decisively routed. During the next few weeks, Tryon invited Regulators to come forward, surrender their arms, and take an oath of allegiance. Regulator leaders, such as Herman Husband and James Hunter, fled the colony. After summarily executing one of the Regulators on the day of the battle, twelve more were taken to Hillsborough, convicted, and sentenced to death. Six of them were hanged, six others pardoned.

* * *

On the eve of the Revolution, the rise and fall of the North Carolina Regulators raised serious questions about the stability of the colony's political leadership and the hold of its social elite. In 1772, when Josiah Martin became governor of North Carolina, he visited the backcountry and discovered a lingering hostility among many of its residents. In 1775, with the Revolution underway, many former Regulators became either neutral or supported the Crown, and patriots were worried enough about the stability of the backcountry that the Continental Congress hired two Presbyterian ministers to "use their pastoral Influence to work a change in the disposition of the people."[14] In truth, the rapid expansion of the colony during the mid-1700s had placed severe strains on its social and political structure. The flood of immigrants into the backcountry had created a separate and very distinct world, one decidedly different from the plantation society of eastern North Carolina. The provincial elite had not solidified its grip on the power structure, and during the 1760s and 1770s, as North Carolina moved into a continent-wide imperial crisis, serious divisions remained.

Notes

1 William Byrd II, *The History of the Dividing Line Betwixt Virginia and North Carolina: A Journey to the Land of Eden, A.D. 1733; and a Progress to the Mines, Written from 1728 to 1736, and Now First Published* (Petersburg, VA: Edmund and Julian C. Ruffin, 1841), pp. 16–17.

2 Alice Elaine Mathews, *Society in Revolutionary North Carolina* (Raleigh, NC: Division of Archives and History, 1976), p. 12.

3 Ibid., pp. 48–49; Alexander Schaw, in Evangeline Walker Andrews and Charles Mclean Andrews, eds., *Journal of a Lady of Quality; Being the Narrative of a Journey from Scotland to the West Indies, North Carolina, and Portugal, in the Years 1774 to 1776* (New Haven, CT: Yale University Press, 1921), p. 280.

4 Byrd, *History of the Dividing Line*, pp. 27–28.

5 Andrews and Andrews, eds., *Journal of a Lady of Quality*, p. 281.

6 "Smyth's Travels in Virginia, in 1773," in *Virginia Historical Register and Literary Companion*, IV (Richmond, VA: MacFarlane & Fergusson, 1853), p. 17.

7 Jim L. Sumner, *A History of Sports in North Carolina* (Raleigh, NC: Division of Archives and History, 1990), pp. 3–5; entry on gouging, William S. Powell, ed., *Encyclopedia of North Carolina* (Chapel Hill: University of North Carolina Press, 2007), p. 515.

8 Quoted in Harry Roy Merrens, *Colonial North Carolina in the Eighteenth Century: A Study in Historical Geography* (Chapel Hill: University of North Carolina Press, 1964), p. 54.

9 Quoted in A. Roger Ekirch, *"Poor Carolina": Politics and Society in Colonial North Carolina* (Chapel Hill: University of North Carolina Press, 1981), p. 128.

10 Quoted in Marjoleine Kars, *Breaking Loose Together: The Regulator Rebellion in Pre-Revolutionary North Carolina* (Chapel Hill: University of North Carolina Press, 2002), p. 33.

11 Quoted in ibid., p. 87.

12 Quoted in John Spencer Bassett, "The Regulators of North Carolina (1765–1771)," in *Annual Report of the American Historical Association for the Year 1894* (Washington, DC: Government Printing Office, 1895), p. 162.

13 Ekirch, *"Poor Carolina,"* p. 165.

14 Kars, *Breaking Loose Together*, p. 214.

5

The Age of Revolution

In 1763, the conclusion of the French and Indian War brought on a crisis in British North America. England triumphed over its wartime adversaries, France and Spain, in Europe and America, yet the war also raised serious questions about imperial roles and responsibilities. The Treaty of Paris (1763) secured British control of French Canada and the vast region between the Appalachians and the Mississippi River. But the war was very expensive; the peace highlighted the money drain that the North American colonies had become to the imperial treasury. After 1763, the British thus sought to redefine relations with the colonists in such a way as to increase their contribution to the costs of maintaining the empire. But no longer satisfied with their status as imperial dependents, the colonists were aggrieved at unilateral British attempts to alter their relationship.

Aftermath of the French and Indian War: The Stamp Act Crisis

The Americans, for their part, came of age during the French and Indian War (1757–63). Beginning in the 1740s, the North Carolina Assembly became more assertive. North Carolina had been a reluctant participant in the French and Indian War, and the assembly and Arthur Dobbs, the royal governor, had squabbled over a variety of money issues associated with the war. North Carolina sent about 750 troops to fight the French and their Indian allies in the Ohio country in 1754, but there was virtually no military conflict in North Carolina until midway into the war, in the winter of 1760, when Cherokee forces began a series of attacks in South Carolina. Though more isolated than Coastal Plain or Piedmont Indians, Cherokees had suffered from European diseases and had begun to adopt white ways. In 1738, a smallpox epidemic resulted in the death of half of the Cherokee population and undermined traditional social and political institutions. Conflicts with encroaching Anglo-American

North Carolina: Change and Tradition in a Southern State, Second Edition. William A. Link.

settlers, especially those arriving northwest from the South Carolina Piedmont, prompted Cherokees to ally themselves with the French when war began in 1756. In 1760, British forces attacked and captured and then murdered Cherokee leaders in North Carolina, setting off a general war. Indians retaliated with an attack on whites in Tennessee and South Carolina, and in North Carolina along the Yadkin, Catawba, and Broad Rivers. On February 27, 1760, Cherokee raiders struck at Fort Dobbs (near present-day Statesville), which had been erected four years earlier, in 1756, as a frontier outpost. About seventy Cherokee warriors attacked fifty defenders, who managed to hold the fort and repulse the attack.

An all-out war with Cherokees continued through much of the western backcountry, with Indian attacks occurring as far east as the confluence of the Mayo and Dan Rivers, near the Virginia border. During the summer of 1761, 2,000 volunteers from South Carolina under the command of Col. James Grant attacked the heartland of Cherokees, the Middle Towns, laying waste to villages, cornfields, and orchards. Forced to sue for peace in 1761, the Cherokees ended their participation in the French and Indian War in complete defeat. The Treaty of Paris, which concluded the war, secured the expulsion of the French from most of North America. But, as part of the agreement, the British also issued the Proclamation Line of 1763 (a north-south line running roughly down the spire of the Appalachians), which promised Indians west of the line protection from any further white encroachment on their lands.

Although some whites in North Carolina saw the Proclamation Line as an unwanted, even meddling, measure of post-1763 imperial policy, in general, it provoked little reaction. Soon thereafter, in the Sugar Act of 1764, the British attempted to increase revenue by reducing by half the duty on imported sugar and molasses imposed in 1733, while at the same time providing for better enforcement—meaning strict collection of the remaining duties on items the colonists were forced to import. Some North Carolinians objected to the trade regulation provisions of the Sugar Act, which required that all lumber shipments to Europe be transshipped via Britain. But because North Carolinians did not import sugar or molasses in significant amounts, no one there organized any resistance to the Act. The Currency Act of 1764, which forbade the issuance of bills of credit in the colonies, also remained of little concern to North Carolinians, who evaded the law through the issuance of treasury notes and notes of credit that served as a kind of currency. Similarly, with no British regulars stationed in the colony prior to 1776, the Quartering Act of 1765, which decreed that colonists were required to board British soldiers in their homes, evoked no popular opposition.

Of far greater significance was the Stamp Act, which Parliament enacted on March 22, 1765, and which was scheduled to take effect on November 1, 1765. The Stamp Act marked a turning point in North Carolina and in British North America. The first direct tax ever levied on the American colonists, its creators in Parliament envisioned it as a means of financing the empire. They hoped that it would also maintain a permanent redcoat garrison on the western frontier of British North America. The law required that a stamp duty, paid in currency only, be levied on playing cards, legal documents, ship clearances, and newspapers. By providing that courts of the vice-admiralty rather than juries would try violators, the law also established a separate enforcement machinery, accountable only to royal authorities, that bypassed colonial courts. British officials anticipated little resistance, but potent opposition emerged by the summer of 1765.

Like other American colonists, many North Carolinians regarded the Stamp Act as a matter involving both constitutional privilege and raw political power. Although colonists believed that Parliament had the right to tax trade, they saw "internal" taxes, such as a stamp duty, as the exclusive prerogative of the lower houses of the assembly, which represented the colonies' landholders and taxpayers. Protest arose not long after news of the new law arrived in North Carolina. During the summer of 1765, Maurice Moore, a Lower Cape Fear judge and well-to-do member of the assembly, published a pamphlet decrying the practice of taxation without representation. Born in New Hanover County about 1735, Moore belonged to one of Cape Fear's wealthiest families. He had served in the lower house of the assembly for numerous sessions during the 1760s and 1770s, and in the assembly Moore had led opposition to the Regulators. He also served as a judge of the superior court. In his pamphlet, Moore challenged the notion of virtual representation, in which English constitutionalists had claimed that Parliament represented the entire nation—including the colonies—even without doing so directly. Such a notion was absurd, he said, as English authorities had long provided that colonists could elect assemblies to levy taxes. Moore asserted, moreover, that colonies should be "taxed only with their own consent." He described the Stamp Act as "impolitic" and "inconsistent with the rights of the Colonists." Thoroughly infused with a knowledge of British constitutional law, Moore provided an intellectual basis for the resistance that subsequently developed in the Lower Cape Fear area.

Because the North Carolina Assembly remained out of session, the colony sent no representatives to the continent-wide Stamp Act Congress in New York in 1765. Only recently, early in that year, William Tryon had arrived as the colony's new governor, and resisting the Stamp Act challenged his leadership. He responded forcefully, dissolving the assembly soon after it enacted an anti-Stamp Act resolution in May 1765 and prevented it from convening during the remainder of the crisis. Although Tryon deprived anti-Stamp Act protesters of a provincial forum, fierce opposition emerged. As assembly Speaker Samuel Ashe put it, the colony intended to resist the law and "fight it to the death." Between July and November of 1765, sporadic public protests occurred at Cross Creek (later Fayetteville), Edenton, New Bern, and Wilmington. By late

1765, a full-fledged movement had developed with new leaders, the vanguard of a group promoting revolution.

With the stamps due to arrive on November 1, 1765, the core of the new anti-Stamp Act leadership, which was determined to thwart the execution of the law, emerged in southeastern North Carolina, near Tryon's home at "Bellefont" in Brunswick. As early as October 19, 1765, an anti-Stamp Act protest of 500 people assembled in the colony's largest town and leading port, Wilmington, in which the crowd hung British prime minister John Stuart, the Earl of Bute, in effigy, lit a bonfire, and toasted liberty. About two weeks later, on Halloween, in another protest of the stamp duty, a similar group staged a mock funeral for "Liberty." After November 1765, opposition in the Lower Cape Fear focused on subverting the implementation of the Stamp Act. The law required that stamps be affixed to all legal documents and publications. But since the official stamps had yet to arrive from Britain, Governor Tryon suspended the courts, halted trade from incoming vessels, and ceased publication of newspapers. When Duplin County surgeon William Houston, who had been appointed stamp duty collector, visited Wilmington on November 16, he encountered a hostile mob of perhaps 400 members of the new anti-Stamp Act group, the Sons of Liberty. Intimidated by this mob, in which many of Wilmington's leading citizens participated, Houston resigned his office.

Tryon responded by attempting to rally public opinion behind the law. Inviting leading citizens to his home in Brunswick on November 18, 1765, he urged his guests to refrain from violence. Should North Carolinians support him, the governor added, he would seek to exempt the colony from the Stamp Act. But Tryon's appeal garnered little support: at his inaugural speech as governor about a month later, on December 20, he was booed and hissed when he urged use of the stamps. During the fall and winter of 1765–66, as business and legal transactions came to a standstill and as British naval vessels arrived in Wilmington to deliver the stamps but met no local stamp master to receive them, the situation slipped further into crisis. In January 1766, at Brunswick, Capt. Jacob Lobb, master of the British ship *Viper*, seized two colonial ships, the *Dobbs* and the *Patience*, because their clearance papers were unstamped. Wilmington residents responded by refusing to send supplies to royal naval vessels and closing the port. Thereafter, mob activity by the Sons of Liberty increased, as anti-Stamp Act protesters sought to block the removal of the *Dobbs* and the *Patience*. On February 18, leaders from across the Lower Cape Fear gathered. They included influential locals such as Hugh Waddell, John Ashe, Cornelius Harnett, along with eight justices of the peace—William Campbell, John DuBois, Alexander Duncan, Frederick Gregg, Alexander Lillington, John Lyon, William Purviance, and Moses John DeRosset. In a meeting held in Wilmington, the group announced its intention to prevent "entirely the operation of the Stamp Act." A day later, on February 19, a mob of 100 marched to Brunswick, surrounding Tryon's home in search of Captain

Lobb of the *Viper*. Unable to locate him, the crowd imprisoned Governor Tryon in his own home for most of the night, but he managed to escape in the early morning after the "guard" dispersed. Subsequently, on February 21, Cornelius Harnett led a group of several hundred citizens seeking to intimidate several local officials and thus prevent them from enforcing the Stamp Act. The crisis subsided only after Captain Lobb agreed to release the two ships.

By the late winter of 1766, the deadlock over the stamp duty continued to paralyze trade and commerce, as ordinary business remained suspended. Success emboldened anti-Stamp Act leaders; they realized that mob violence and intimidation effectively prevented the implementation of the law. Under siege in Brunswick and surrounded by anti-Stamp mobs, Tryon eventually persuaded the assembly to move the capital to New Bern, to the great consternation of southeastern North Carolina leaders. In early 1766, Tryon was contemplating requesting troops when, on March 18, 1766, Parliament repealed the Stamp Act. Retreating from the brink, Parliament also enacted the Declaratory Act, which reiterated its right—and, presumably, its intent—to enact further revenue measures.

In fact, Parliament had not relinquished its quest to seek revenue from the colonies, but, equally important, the colonial leadership that emerged during the Stamp Act crisis was still determined to assert itself. In 1767, when Parliament enacted the Townshend Act, which imposed import duties on various goods imported into British North America, North Carolina Speaker John Harvey approved an address to King George III on November 11, 1768, opposing the Act because it violated the British constitutional concept of no taxation without representation. Tryon responded by dissolving the assembly, which met anyway, independent of the governor's authority. In October 1769, the assembly endorsed the organization of nonimportation associations under which North Carolinians agreed not to import or purchase any goods bearing Townshend duties. Subsequently, in December 1773, the Revolutionary leadership in North Carolina established a committee of correspondence composed of John Harvey, Robert Howe, Richard Caswell, Edward Vail, John Ashe, Joseph Hewes, and Samuel Johnston. This group linked the North Carolina patriot leadership with Revolutionaries elsewhere in British North America.

The emerging Revolutionary leadership also mobilized North Carolina women. The "Edenton Tea Party" marked increased assertiveness by women in the public sphere. On October 25, 1774, fifty-one women from at least five counties, led by Penelope Barker (wife of Thomas Barker, North Carolina's colonial agent), circulated resolutions declaring their determination "to do everything, as far as in us lies, to testify to our sincere adherence to [whatever] … appears to affect the peace and happiness of our country." The Edenton Tea Party became an early example of women's political activity in British North America.

Figure 5.1 Penelope Barker. *Source: 1758 Cupola House Association, courtesy of NC Museum of History.*

Josiah Martin and the Revolutionary Crisis

When William Tryon left North Carolina to become governor of the New York colony in 1771, he left behind a colony seemingly at peace after the recent turmoil of the Regulator insurgency. Yet appearances, in this case, were deceiving: within three years of the arrival of Tryon's successor as governor, Josiah Martin, North Carolina erupted in revolution. What occurred in North Carolina in some sense mirrored developments in the other colonies: across British North America, patriots mobilized enough public opinion to move toward independence. But what galvanized North Carolina public opinion was the growing conflict between Martin and the legislature.

Martin inherited a festering situation that the afterglow of good relations between Tryon and the legislature could only thinly mask. Martin, as a new governor, faced serious problems: the bitter legacy of the Regulators, continuing boundary problems with South Carolina, and a persisting degree of factionalism and political instability in the North Carolina Assembly. Further complicating matters for Martin was the foreign attachment controversy. When Martin arrived in 1771, he had received instructions from royal officials, which were explicit and binding. Martin was instructed to seek revisions in the North Carolina court system; royal officials were particularly interested in an obscure provision of law dealing with the attachment of foreign debts. Under earlier statutes establishing the court system, the North Carolina Assembly had required that in all disputes between North Carolina creditors and British debtors—an unusual situation, since in most instances North Carolinians borrowed from British creditors—jurisdiction would lie with North Carolina courts. That is, should a dispute over a debt arise in which a North Carolina creditor sought to "attach" (seize) the property of a British debtor, the dispute would be settled in North Carolina rather than British courts. English colonial officials regarded this as an anomaly; they believed that all jurisdiction in disputes between British and colonials properly resided in British courts. Although this was a largely hypothetical situation, what became known as the foreign attachment controversy would seriously undermine the Martin administration.

Martin proposed a new court bill that would remove the foreign attachments provisions of the expiring court act. The assembly resisted Martin's proposals, claiming that the Crown would replace a locally controlled with a royally imposed judicial system. In the contest between Martin and the legislature, no court bill was enacted. The result was that North Carolina's judicial system—and the legal basis for commerce—came to a halt. When Martin blundered further by attempting to establish royal courts by edict, many North Carolinians feared that the governor's actions were part of a larger effort to subvert colonists' traditional liberties. By 1774, just as the Revolutionary crisis was spreading throughout British North America, North Carolina was experiencing its own peculiar paralysis of government that boosted the patriots' move toward independence.

In resisting royal authorities, patriot leaders during the 1770s were beginning to create their own forms of government. In a number of communities, Sons of Liberty organizations created local associations that tried to enforce the American boycott of British goods that paid Townshend duties. These associations steadily expanded their powers; by 1774, they were drafting documents that formed the basis of Revolutionary government. Although Martin had dissolved the assembly in order to keep it out of session, North Carolina patriots organized the First Provincial Congress in 1774, and this meeting fully committed the colonial leadership to the patriot cause. Electing John Harvey as Speaker, the congress declared its loyalty to King George III, asserting that provincial assemblies "solely and exclusively" possessed the right to tax. The congress also criticized Parliament's high-handedness in dealing with rebellious Massachusetts by imposing the punitive Coercive Acts that followed the Boston Tea Party. Perhaps most important, the group elected three delegates, William Hooper, Richard Caswell, and Joseph Hewes, to represent the colony at the Continental Congress meeting in Philadelphia.

Figure 5.2 William Hooper's home in Hillsborough. *Source: Historic American Buildings Survey. Library of Congress.*

In the spring of 1775, when British redcoats and Americans began a shooting war in Massachusetts at Lexington and Concord, North Carolinians had already organized a rudimentary Revolutionary government. In response to Lexington and Concord, on April 3, 1775, John Harvey summoned a Second Provincial Congress to elect delegates to the Second Continental Congress and "to act in union with our neighboring colonies." A day later, on April 4, Governor Martin, in a vain attempt to forestall the emergence of Revolutionary leadership, summoned the assembly into session, but its composition was virtually identical to that of the Provincial Congress. Reporting to his superiors in England that royal authority was effectively nonexistent, Martin dissolved the assembly after it met for only four days. Meanwhile, among the most important actions of the Second Provincial Congress was its authorization of local committees of safety. Already in existence in a number of North Carolina towns in 1774–75, committees of safety had drafted their own "associations," or documents defining the Revolutionary cause and serving as a constitutional basis for their authority. The Provincial Congress authorized the creation of new committees in each of the colony's counties, along with one for each town, one for each of the six military districts, and a council of safety for the entire province. By 1775, eighteen counties and four towns had established committees of safety, and in many of these areas, they became the effective government.

Martin, for his part, faced a depressing situation. North Carolina had no occupying British troops; local militias were increasingly hostile; and the committee of safety of New Bern—the provincial capital—had become a menacing presence. On May 23, 1775, Martin's wife and children left the colony for New York; on June 2, 1775, the governor himself fled New Bern for Fort Johnston, at present-day Southport, and then took refuge on the British ship *Cruizer*. Martin moved to New York with his family, returning to North Carolina late in the war to organize loyalist forces. But with his departure from New Bern in June 1775, royal authority in North Carolina had come to an end.

The Emergence of Revolutionary Government

With royal authority in tatters, a new Revolutionary regime took charge. On June 19, 1775, North Carolina's delegates to the Continental Congress urged the committees of safety to support the cause. On August 8, Martin issued his "Fiery Proclamation," which denounced the committees of safety and the Revolutionaries generally. It was in this context that 184 delegates assembled at the Third Provincial Congress at Hillsborough on August 20, 1775. Because John Harvey had died the previous May, the congress elected Samuel Johnston of Edenton as Speaker. The meeting, dominated by patriots, almost immediately pushed for revolution. Stopping short, all of the delegates signed an oath declaring their allegiance to the Crown but dismissing outright parliamentary taxation of the colonies.

More important, the Third Provincial Congress began to create a provisional independent state government. The congress established a committee to obtain arms and ammunition and to determine the cost thereof. Additional committees sought to oppose Martin's effort to recruit supporters. Thus, members of this committee sought out two groups particularly susceptible to Martin's overtures, the Scottish Highlanders and the surviving Piedmont Regulators. Responding to Martin's "Fiery Proclamation" on August 25, the Third Provincial Congress asserted that the governor had "deserted" the colony and that the congress could properly exercise functions of government in order to preserve law and order. The Provincial Congress then organized itself by creating a provincial council, which would serve as the colony's chief executive and administrative authority and be composed of thirteen members representing the entire province. The congress also expanded its military reach by creating committees of safety for each of the colony's six military districts.

Meanwhile, the Third Provincial Congress began a general military mobilization. It permitted Col. James Moore of New Hanover County and Col. Robert Howe of Brunswick County to organize two regiments, each containing

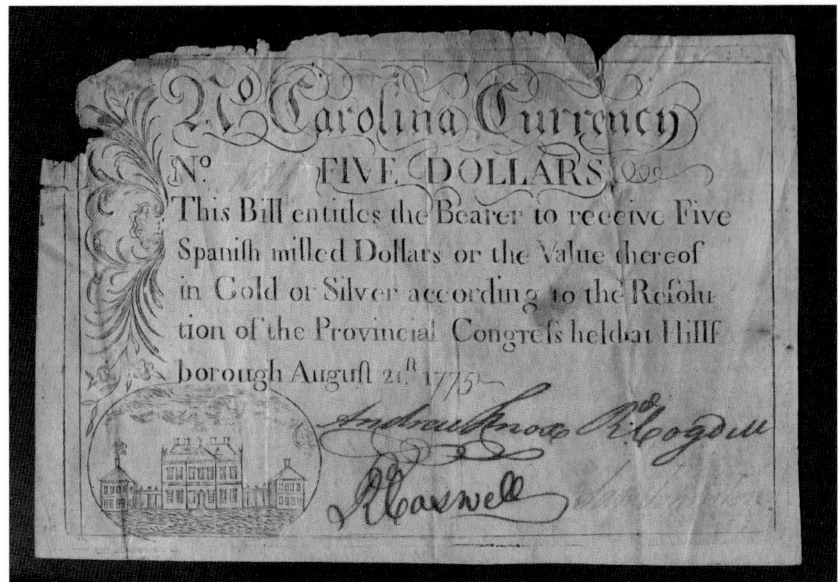

Figure 5.3 Counterfeit money printed by loyalists during the Revolution. *Source: Accession #1973.67.1 Photo by the North Carolina Museum of History.*

500 men, to become part of the regular army in the Continental Line. Each of North Carolina's six military districts created a battalion of 500 militia; the congress appointed field commanders of each of these units. Perhaps the most active was the unit in Wilmington, which constructed defenses, seized loyalists, and evacuated noncombatants. In New Bern, Richard Caswell assumed command of local forces. The New Bern committee of safety had instructed him to obtain all necessities of warfare, and units from Dobbs, Johnston, Pitt, and Craven Counties joined Caswell's force. By 1775, North Carolina's leadership was committed to participating in a war of independence. These rapid movements enjoyed substantial popular support, as small farmers, artisans, and large landholders joined the cause.

But there were also significant numbers of people remaining loyal to the Crown, and these "loyalists," or "Tories," opposed armed resistance or a war of independence. North Carolina loyalists included a number of wealthy merchants, those who had served in provincial government, some large planters, as well as some professional men. In addition, in the Upper Cape Fear, most of the Scottish Highlanders in this region remained loyal, as did many settlers in the Piedmont, some of them former Regulators, who remained angry at the eastern leaders who had defeated them in 1771. While patriots and Tories began to announce their loyalties in the spring and summer of 1775, many others—perhaps a majority of North Carolinians—remained neutral. This was particularly true among some religious and ethnic groups: many Quakers, for example, were pacifists, while German settlers, especially Moravians, also resisted taking sides.

Although the patriot, or "Whig," leadership initially attempted conciliation with loyalists, soon the conflict in North Carolina became an armed civil war, with each side giving little quarter. Now military necessity governed the situation. In November 1775, Whig units participated in efforts to the north, in the Norfolk area, to drive royal authorities' forces from the Virginia Tidewater. Subsequently, in December 1775, other North Carolina units combined with South Carolina forces in what became known as the "Snow Campaign." Josiah Martin had not been idle during this period. On June 30, 1775, in a letter to Lord Dartmouth, secretary of state for the colonies, he outlined an ambitious plan that included organizing a large loyalist military force; in support of these efforts, Martin requested weapons and supplies. After Martin sent a delegation to lobby Dartmouth, he and the Privy Council approved it.

Martin, from the security of his position aboard a royal sloop, organized loyalist military efforts during 1775–76. He maintained a steady correspondence with Regulators, Highlanders and British military authorities in Boston under the command of Gen. Thomas Gage. In July 1775, Gage dispatched Maj. Donald MacDonald and Capt. Alexander McLeod to the Upper Cape Fear in order to organize a Royal Highland Emigrant Regiment composed of loyal Scots by promising each volunteer 200 acres of land, remission in arrears of quitrents, and twenty years' tax exemptions. The response was heartening to the British, as many recent immigrants from Scotland, men without much property, joined the cause. Ultimately, Martin envisioned the organization of a military force composed of 3,000 Highlanders, 3,000 Regulators, and 3,000 other Tories. In addition, Martin requested the assemblage of substantial British forces, including several thousand redcoats and a Royal Navy flotilla. These forces were to be assembled by early 1776, and on January 10, 1776, Martin issued a proclamation calling on all loyal subjects to converge on Brunswick on February 15, 1776.

In part, Martin succeeded in exploiting significant internal differences—ethnic, cultural, and political—among North Carolinians. In addition, the patriots' efforts at controlling the loyalists were lax at best; local committees of safety did little in late 1775 to prevent Tories from openly organizing in the Upper Cape Fear and even in the Whig stronghold of Wilmington, where loyalist leaders such as Alex McLean, Samuel Campbell, and Robert Hogg maintained contacts with Governor Martin during the winter of 1775–76. McLean, who helped to organize loyalist forces in the Upper Cape Fear, was a British officer on half-pay, and he operated with only minimal opposition from the Wilmington committee of safety. Meanwhile, Wilmington loyalist merchants, under the noses of these committees, provided sizeable amounts of supplies and money for the organization of the Highlander army. In large part, the paralysis of the Wilmington committees reflected a general weakness and lack of enthusiasm among Revolutionaries, as some Whigs moved back to the loyalist cause. For example, James Hepburn of Cumberland County, though a delegate to the Third Provincial Congress, became a leading loyalist in February 1776.

By mid-February 1776, the loyalist army, composed of approximately 1,600 Highlanders and led by Donald MacDonald, marched from Cross Creek down the Cape Fear River toward Wilmington. Patriot forces under the command of James Moore sought to prevent the Highland regiment from reaching Wilmington and to capture the loyalist stronghold of Cross Creek. With Moore and his unit assuming a position at Elizabeth Town, Moore dispatched units under Richard Caswell's command to secure Corbett's Ferry on the Black River, while Cols. James Martin and James Thackston moved toward Cross Creek, where Col. Alexander Lillington awaited them. Meanwhile, James Ashe reinforced Caswell's position. This combined Whig force marched toward Moore's Creek Bridge, 18 miles north of Wilmington. On February 26, 1776, Caswell reached the bridge with about 1,100 men; after an all-night march through the swamps and woods, the Highlanders reached the bridge at dawn; the fighting began immediately. Caswell's men had obstructed the bridge, making it nearly impossible to cross, and there Revolutionary units caught the Highlanders in a brief but devastating cross-fire. In the Battle of Moore's Creek Bridge, the patriots lost only one man with one other wounded, while the Highlanders lost around fifty men, killed or wounded; McLeod was the first to fall dead. Stunned, the Tories fled back into the swamps, with Moore's men in pursuit.

In the summer of 1776, the Whigs struck at another group with questionable loyalties, the Cherokees, who had allied themselves with the British. Gen. Griffith Rutherford, in August, led a force of North Carolinians against thirty-six Cherokee towns in the river valleys of the Oconaluftee and Tuckasegee in North Carolina, along with the Hiwasee and Little Tennessee in Tennessee. The force of North Carolinians systematically burned crops and destroyed villages, with the objective of driving the Cherokees from the region. Suffering similar genocidal attacks at the hands of South Carolinians, the Cherokees suffered a terrific blow and were effectively removed as a military force during the Revolution. Forced to sue for peace, the Indians relinquished claim to what remained of their ancestral lands in western North Carolina.

The Fourth Provincial Congress and Independence

With the onset of armed conflict in North Carolina and the rest of British North America, there was a concerted move toward independence. At the Fourth Provincial Congress, which met at Halifax between April 4 and May 15, 1776, the chief issue was whether to support a declaration of independence severing formal ties with England. Since the Revolutionary crisis began, there had remained a strong feeling of support for the Crown, even as many patriots opposed the actions of the English Parliament. Now, with the deepening military conflict and the emergence of a provisional Revolutionary government, North Carolina Whigs were more willing to take the drastic step of independence. On April 12, the Provincial Congress adopted the Halifax Resolves, which declared that the Continental Congress in Philadelphia should be authorized to seek "Independency" and the "right of forming a Constitution and laws for this Colony." The Halifax Resolves marked a turning point for the Revolutionary cause, and, with the adoption of the Declaration of Independence—which North Carolina delegates Joseph Hewes, William Hooper, and John Penn signed on July 4, 1776—a path had been cleared toward statehood and the formation of a new independent republic. After the North Carolina provincial council of safety endorsed the declaration on July 22, Whig leader Cornelius Harnett gave its first public reading on August 1, 1776.

Having made the decision for independence, Revolutionary leaders were faced with the necessity of governing. The Fourth Provincial Congress had not created a state constitution; indeed, in the Anglo-American world at the time, the very idea of a written constitution was a novel idea. Instead, a provisional regime was established, with Cornelius Harnett serving as president and with a provincial-wide council of safety exercising political control of the new state, in conjunction with local committees. Sensing the need for a written constitution, on August 9, the provincial council ordered elections, to be held on October 15, 1776, that would select delegates for a Fifth Provincial Congress, which would also meet in Halifax. With its main work the writing of a permanent state constitution, the congress split into conservative and radical factions. Conservatives, led by Samuel Johnston, James Iredell, William Hooper, and Archibald Maclaine, were mainly eastern planters and slaveholders. They favored a government that would protect property—especially slave property—and guard against the excesses of popular control. They sought a strong executive, an independent judiciary with life tenure, the protection of property rights, and property qualifications for voting and officeholding. In contrast, radicals such as Willie Jones, Thomas Person, and Griffith Rutherford favored a strong legislature, along with a weak executive subordinate to the legislature. Representing divergent religious groups, radicals also advocated religious freedom with no state-supported or established church.

Meeting between November 12 and December 23, 1776, the Fifth Provincial Congress was dominated by this conservative-radical power struggle. After Richard Caswell was unanimously chosen as president, a Committee of Eighteen drafted a constitution and bill of rights. The new state constitution was presented on December 6, 1776, a bill of rights nine days later, and they were adopted on December 17–18. The Constitution of 1776—which remained the governing document of the state for the next sixty-nine years—represented

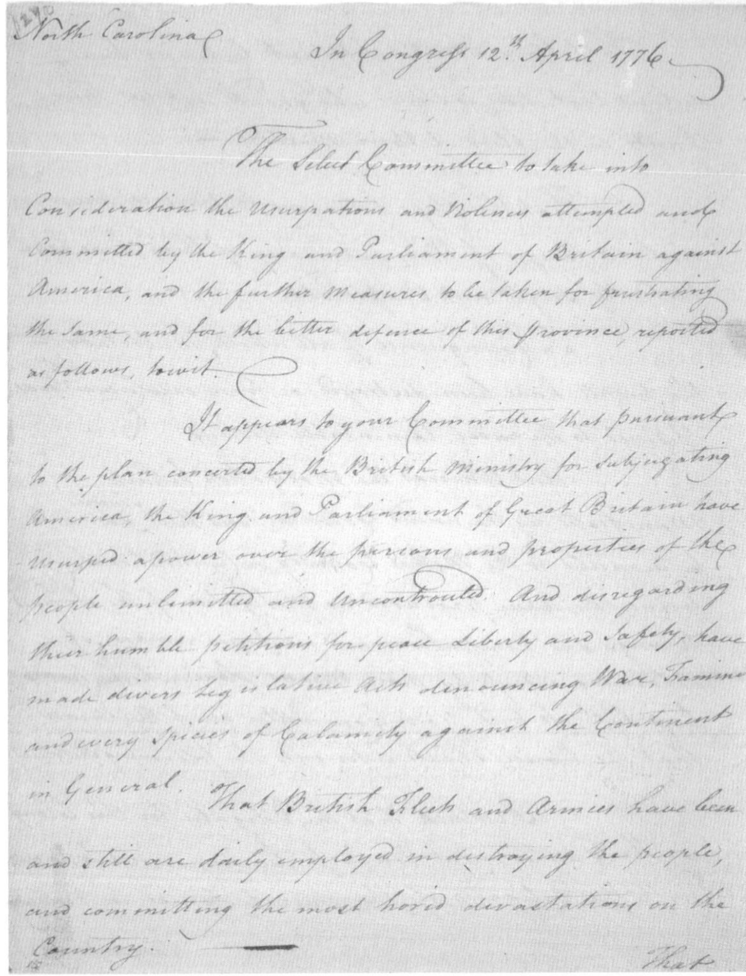

North Carolina In Congress 12th April 1776

The Select Committee to take into Consideration the Usurpations and Violences attempted and Committed by the King and Parliament of Britain against America, and the further Measures to be taken for frustrating the same, and for the better defence of this Province reported as follows, towit.

It appears to your Committee that pursuant to the plan concerted by the British Ministry for subjugating America, the King and Parliament of Great Britain have usurped a power over the persons and properties of the people unlimitted and uncontrouled. And disregarding their humble petitions for peace Liberty and Safety, have made divers Legislative Acts denouncing War, Famine and every Species of Calamity against the Continent in General. That British Fleets and Armies have been and still are daily employed in destroying the people, and committing the most horrid devastations on the Country. —

That

Figure 5.4 Halifax Resolves. *Source: National Archives and Records Administration.*

a new departure in North Carolina's constitutional history. It authorized the election of delegates to the Continental Congress: delegates were chosen by joint ballot of the legislature, could serve three successive terms, and were subject to legislative recall.

The new constitution also established a permanent rubric for state government. It created a general assembly, composed of a senate and a house of commons that were annually elected. The constitution imposed property qualifications for officeholders: each senator, one per county (regardless of that county's population), was required to own at least 300 acres of land. At the same time, voters for state senators were required to own at least 50 acres. Two members of the house represented each county, while each borough town received one seat. Each house member was required to own at least 100 acres. Voters for house members were not required to own property but they had to be taxpayers. Both houses in joint session annually elected the governor, council of state, attorney general, judges, and high-ranking military officers. With the governor and council of state annually elected (though eligible for reelection for three years in any six successive years), the executive remained weak. Governors could initiate policies, offer recommendations, offer pardons and reprieves, and serve as commander of state military forces, but beyond these responsibilities they possessed little power. Governors were required nonetheless to own at least £1,000 in property. The constitution also created a system of state courts, but these were subservient to the legislature, which annually elected the state's judges of Supreme Courts of Law and Equity as well as local justices of the peace. The justices of the peace, as they had during the colonial period, served as the basic unit of local government.

With the Fifth Provincial Congress's adoption of the new constitution—which was not submitted to the voters for ratification—the first General Assembly was elected and met in New Bern on April 7, 1777. Choosing Abner Nash of Craven County as house Speaker and Samuel Ashe as Speaker of the senate, the legislature elected Richard Caswell as North Carolina's first governor, James Glasgow as its first secretary of state, and Cornelius Harnett, Thomas Eaton, William Dry, William Haywood, Edward Starkey, and Joseph Leach as members of its first council of state. The constitution was a mixed document: it provided for a weak executive and legislative dominance. At the same time, it did little to change the political structure of power in place since the colonial era. The county-based system of representation ensured eastern domination of the legislature; new counties were created, but for every one in the West, several were divided in the East. Thus, by 1799, there were forty-six eastern counties and thirty-four western counties. Very soon westerners nursed a festering—and genuine—grievance about the inequitable distribution of political power. Although most whites lived in the Piedmont and Mountain West, easterners enjoyed a 33–19 majority in the senate and a 70–40 majority in the house.

At the same time, the executive's limited powers restricted the Whigs' ability to wage war. The first governor, Richard Caswell, complained about the weakness of the governor's office, although he had been the chairman of the committee that created the office. After 1780, when the legislature created a board of war, some criticized this as a further erosion of the governor's powers. In 1781, the state government nearly collapsed with the capture of Gov. Thomas Burke by Tory forces under the command of David Fanning, and bitter political rivalry punctuated this entire early phase of state government.

Not only did the new state government reflect sectional differences, it also faced, along with a restive and resistant slave population, a large Tory population. Wartime provided opportunities for enslaved North Carolinians to fight against the system, and throughout the Revolution slaveholders lived in constant fear of insurrection. Those fears appeared to have a basis in the declaration of Virginia royal governor John Murray, Earl of Dunmore, on November 7, 1775. Dunmore's Proclamation—issued from the British sloop the *William* in Norfolk harbor—promised freedom to any slaves "able and wiling to bear arms." Slaves in North Carolina responded enthusiastically, and scores of African Americans joined the British forces; by late 1775, an "Ethiopian Regiment," composed of about one thousand black troops, had been organized, wearing uniforms with "Liberty to Slaves" written across their chests. Later, when British troops invaded and occupied North Carolina, moreover, they freed slaves as a way to undermine the Revolutionary regime.

The fledgling state government faced a continuing threat from loyalists, who were especially emboldened by the arrival of British forces in the Carolinas and felt aggrieved at the Whigs' conscription and impressment policies, which forced men into the Revolutionary army and confiscated North Carolinians' property. In many localities, Tory militia and volunteers conducted assaults on their neighbors, destroying their belongings and homes, and killing Whig sympathizers. Against this violent backdrop, the original patriot policy of conciliation gave way to unrestricted warfare against Tories. In 1776, the North Carolina Provincial Congress ordered that those fighting at the Moore's Creek campaign should be imprisoned. In November 1777, the new state government demanded that all males over the age of 16 swear an oath of allegiance to the Whig cause or face exile, imprisonment, and the confiscation of their property. Those loyalists who had fled North Carolina were also subject to property seizures. In 1779, the state government declared the property of sixty-eight Tories and "all others who come within the meaning of the confiscation acts" subject to confiscation; the list included former royal governor William Tryon, Governor Josiah Martin, and other leading figures including Edward Dobbs, Henry McCulloh, and Judge Martin Howard. Although John Carteret, the Earl of Granville—who owned the much-disputed Granville District—was not named on this list, his land was also seized. The legislature appointed commissioners who identified the landholdings and then sold them. By the late 1770s, a general exodus of loyalists from North Carolina had begun.[1]

The other major challenge facing the new state government was the financing of the war. The government paid for the war by means of paper currency, beginning with £125,000 in 1775; by 1781, the state government was issuing £26,250,000. The paper currency schemes were mostly a failure. While North Carolinians increasingly refused to accept the currency, counterfeiting became common and inflation skyrocketed. Because soldiers were paid in what soon became worthless money, morale plummeted and desertion became commonplace. The civilian population also chafed under the severe inflation: by 1780, the price of corn had reach £100 a bushel and beef £48 per pound.

The Whig regime had no choice but to rely on paper currency because of its failure to create an adequate source of revenue. In April 1777, the General Assembly implemented a property tax—the first ever in North Carolina. Although taxes rose steadily during the war years, the state succeeded in collecting only a small amount of money. By 1780, with invasion by British forces imminent, the state adopted additional revenue schemes by imposing a "special provisions tax" on all state inhabitants. A better source of revenue became the confiscation of Tory property, which was sold in parcels of 640 acres in public auction: by November 1783, the state collected £583,643 from the sale of the confiscated property of Tories.

North Carolina's economy suffered terrific losses during the war years. Merchants, especially in the backcountry, experienced a collapse in trade; those agricultural products depending on the export trade saw an acute decline in their markets. During the war, shipment of naval stores ground nearly to a halt, while food exports were also sharply curtailed. On the other hand, tobacco exports increased, aided in part by Virginia planters' determination to evade the British naval blockade of the Chesapeake. Ocracoke and other North Carolina ports maintained a lively wartime trade, and shipbuilding remained a major industry in Edenton, Beaufort, New Bern, and Wilmington. At the same time, privateers of the state included the vessels *Sturdy Beggar*, *Chatham*, *Bellona*, *Rainbeau*, *Fanny*, *Betsy*, *General Nash*, *Lydia*, and *Nancy*, and other ships brought in a regular supply of British prizes captured on the high seas.

The British Invasion

North Carolina Revolutionaries struggled for the duration of the Revolution to achieve a credible military force. At first, North Carolina Whigs depended on volunteers, but they soon relied on other methods: by 1778, enlistments had declined, and the state began to employ a system of bounties, which steadily increased during the war years. In 1780, North Carolina provided £500 upon initial enlistment and £500 at the conclusion of each year's service, two hundred acres of land, plus the gift of a slave after the war ended. A year later, in 1781, the bounty increased to £3,000 and land allotment to 640 acres, along with an additional bounty of three barrels of corn. With the declining value of currency, the land bounty figured more significantly as a recruitment incentive. In 1782, the legislature created a scale based upon rank in which privates received 640 acres and commissioned and noncommissioned officers from 1,000–1,200 acres.

These inducements helped to stimulate enlistments. Although the Continental Congress called for the state to supply nine regiments, the North Carolina Provincial Congress had already raised two of them, one commanded by James Moore, the other by Robert Howe. The remaining regiments were created in 1776, with Jethro Sumner, Thomas Polk, Edward Buncombe, and Alexander

Lillington serving as their commanders. By November, three additional regiments were raised under the command of James Hogun, James Armstrong, and John Williams. Subsequently, the Continental Congress authorized a tenth regiment under the command of Col. Abraham Shepperd. By the end of the Revolutionary War, somewhere between 5,000 and 8,000 North Carolinians served in the Continental army, and these forces were supplemented by militia, which the legislature authorized in 1777. In general, militias were erratically and poorly trained, and regarded as unreliable by Continental commanders. It was "impossible to carry on the war any length of time with the militia," Gen. Nathanael Greene, who commanded military forces in the Carolinas in the early 1780s, wrote to Gen. George Washington in early 1781. American arms, he said, should not be placed into the hands of these "doubtful characters; for you may depend upon it, such will never be useful in this hour of difficulty."[2]

The Revolutionary War was fought actively in North Carolina territory. As mentioned, after 1776, North Carolina patriots, along with military forces from South Carolina and Virginia, attacked the Cherokees, who were allied with the British, destroying some thirty-six of their towns. In a treaty signed on July 20, 1777, the Cherokees relinquished claim to all lands east of the Blue Ridge as well as the lands bordering the Watauga, Nolichucky, Holston, and New Rivers. A particularly active phase of the war in the South began in late 1778, as British forces under the command of Sir Henry Clinton mounted an attack on Georgia, capturing Savannah on December 29, 1778, and Charleston—after a siege that lasted nearly three months—on May 12, 1780. Satisfied with his victory, Clinton, on June 5, 1780, left more than 8,300 soldiers under the command of the newly appointed commander for the South, Charles, Lord Cornwallis. His mission was to subdue the rest of South Carolina by seizing such strategic centers as Ninety Six and Camden, and then to invade North Carolina.

The British campaign in the Carolinas comprised three elements. First, British forces under the command of Maj. James Craig captured Wilmington in January 1781, guaranteeing the British a supply port to provision the extensive inland campaign and protecting the right flank of Cornwallis's main force. Second, Cornwallis took his main force and marched from Camden through Charlotte, thence on to Hillsborough, where the Tory forces were to create a supply depot for the army in advance of his arrival. Third, to protect his left flank, raise additional loyalist support, and stave off the partisans, Cornwallis sent Lt. Col. Patrick Ferguson, who departed from the town of Ninety Six with approximately nine hundred men, almost entirely Tory.

Responding to the British invasion, patriots dispersed guerrilla forces that fought loyalists and conducted hit-and-run attacks on British forces. Former governor Richard Caswell, who was appointed by the legislature as major-general in command of militia forces, led forces in eastern North Carolina, while Gen. Richard Butler led North Carolinians at Hillsborough. In the West, partisan leaders conducted a highly effective guerrilla war in which irregulars

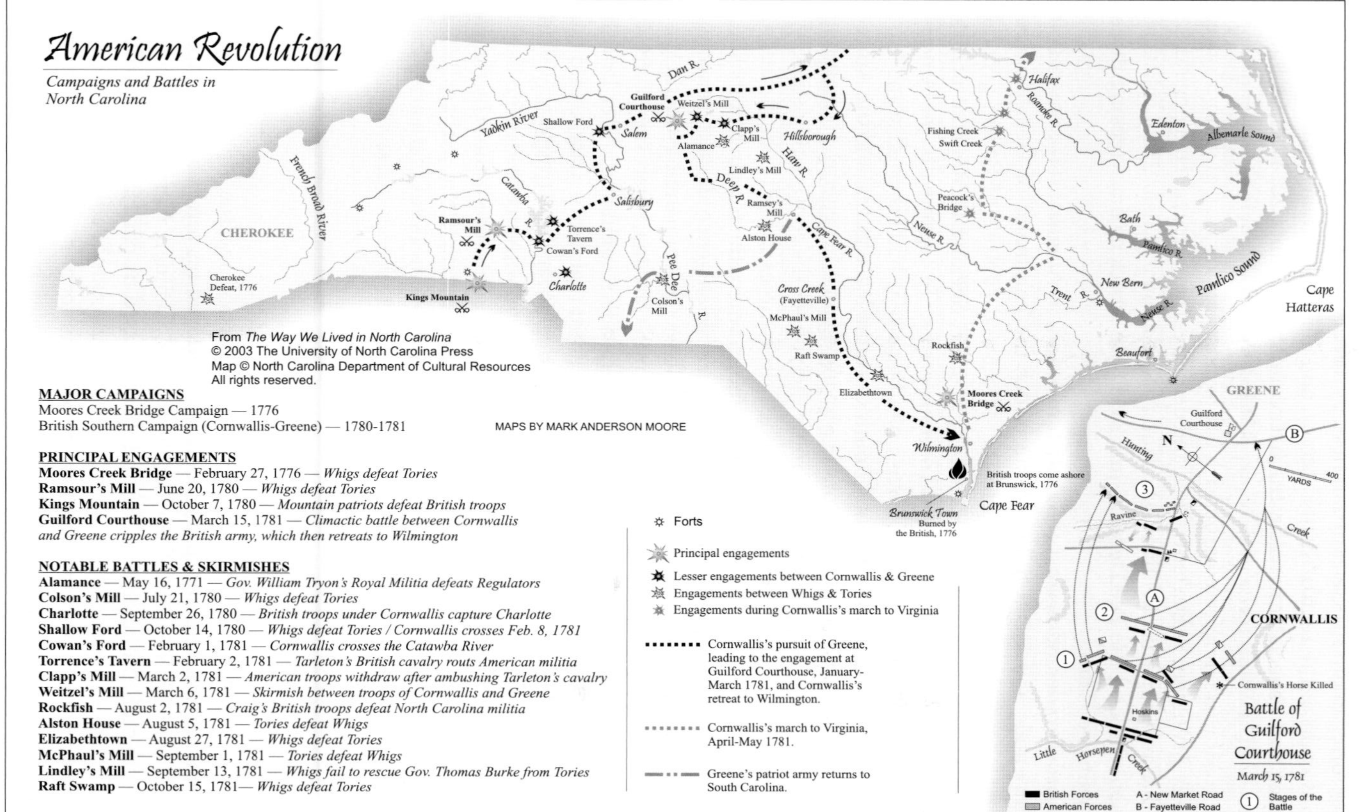

American Revolution
Campaigns and Battles in North Carolina
CHEROKEE
French Broad River
Cherokee Defeat, 1776
Kings Mountain
Ramsour's Mill
Catawba R.
Torrence's Tavern
Cowan's Ford
Charlotte
Yadkin River
Shallow Ford
Salem
Salisbury
Guilford Courthouse
Weitzel's Mill
Dan R.
Clapp's Mill
Alamance
Hillsborough
Lindley's Mill
Haw R.
Deep R.
Ramsey's Mill
Alston House
Pee Dee
Colson's Mill
Cape Fear R.
Cross Creek (Fayetteville)
McPhaul's Mill
Raft Swamp
Elizabethtown
Rockfish
Moores Creek Bridge
Wilmington
British troops come ashore at Brunswick, 1776
Brunswick Town Burned by the British, 1776
Cape Fear
Halifax
Roanoke R.
Fishing Creek
Swift Creek
Peacock's Bridge
Neuse R.
Edenton
Albemarle Sound
Bath
Pamlico R.
New Bern
Trent R.
Neuse R.
Pamlico Sound
Beaufort
Cape Hatteras
From The Way We Lived in North Carolina
© 2003 The University of North Carolina Press
Map © North Carolina Department of Cultural Resources
All rights reserved.
MAPS BY MARK ANDERSON MOORE
MAJOR CAMPAIGNS
Moores Creek Bridge Campaign — 1776
British Southern Campaign (Cornwallis-Greene) — 1780-1781
PRINCIPAL ENGAGEMENTS
Moores Creek Bridge — February 27, 1776 — Whigs defeat Tories
Ramsour's Mill — June 20, 1780 — Whigs defeat Tories
Kings Mountain — October 7, 1780 — Mountain patriots defeat British troops
Guilford Courthouse — March 15, 1781 — Climactic battle between Cornwallis and Greene cripples the British army, which then retreats to Wilmington
NOTABLE BATTLES & SKIRMISHES
Alamance — May 16, 1771 — Gov. William Tryon's Royal Militia defeats Regulators
Colson's Mill — July 21, 1780 — Whigs defeat Tories
Charlotte — September 26, 1780 — British troops under Cornwallis capture Charlotte
Shallow Ford — October 14, 1780 — Whigs defeat Tories / Cornwallis crosses Feb. 8, 1781
Cowan's Ford — February 1, 1781 — Cornwallis crosses the Catawba River
Torrence's Tavern — February 2, 1781 — Tarleton's British cavalry routs American militia
Clapp's Mill — March 2, 1781 — American troops withdraw after ambushing Tarleton's cavalry
Weitzel's Mill — March 6, 1781 — Skirmish between troops of Cornwallis and Greene
Rockfish — August 2, 1781 — Craig's British troops defeat North Carolina militia
Alston House — August 5, 1781 — Tories defeat Whigs
Elizabethtown — August 27, 1781 — Whigs defeat Tories
McPhaul's Mill — September 1, 1781 — Tories defeat Whigs
Lindley's Mill — September 13, 1781 — Whigs fail to rescue Gov. Thomas Burke from Tories
Raft Swamp — October 15, 1781— Whigs defeat Tories
Forts
Principal engagements
Lesser engagements between Cornwallis & Greene
Engagements between Whigs & Tories
Engagements during Cornwallis's march to Virginia
Cornwallis's pursuit of Greene, leading to the engagement at Guilford Courthouse, January-March 1781, and Cornwallis's retreat to Wilmington.
Cornwallis's march to Virginia, April-May 1781.
Greene's patriot army returns to South Carolina.
GREENE
Guilford Courthouse
Hunting
Creek
Ravine
Hoskins
Little Horsepen Creek
CORNWALLIS
Cornwallis's Horse Killed
0 YARDS 400
Battle of Guilford Courthouse
March 15, 1781
British Forces
American Forces
A - New Market Road
B - Fayetteville Road
Stages of the Battle

Figure 5.5 The American Revolution in North Carolina.

struck, often under the cover of darkness, by threatening Tory support, delaying the invasion of the regular British forces, and generally buying time. Partisan fighting was especially fierce in the backcountry. On June 20, 1780, at Ramsour's Mill, a Whig force of perhaps 300 led by Col. Francis Locke and Maj. Joseph McDowell defeated around 1,100 loyalists led by Lt. Col. John Moore. On July 2, William R. Davie attacked and defeated Tory forces at Hanging Rock, South Carolina, while William Davidson routed a force of near 250 loyalists at Colson's Mill on the Pee Dee. On July 31, Davie struck again, wrecking three companies of Tories.

In order to defend against the British invasion, in August 1780, some 3,000 Continentals and 1,200 militia came under the command of Gen. Horatio Gates, who had led Americans in the defeat and capture of British general John Burgoyne at Saratoga, New York, in 1777. Seeking to stop the British invasion, Gates committed several serious errors. To begin with, the American army was seriously underprovisioned because it had received scant support from the North Carolina and South Carolina legislatures, and the American forces suffered from low morale. Moving against his enemy prematurely without adequate supplies and on a route then under the control of hostile loyalists, Gates misjudged the strength of the British forces and left behind most of his cavalry—a critical mistake in the Piedmont, where the terrain lent itself to mobile horsemen, who could provide important intelligence about the enemy's whereabouts and whose effectiveness in battle was instrumental. Nonetheless, Gates led his pared-down force to Camden, South Carolina, where they suffered a rout at the hands of 2,000 men under Cornwallis's command. After British redcoats from the Twenty-Third and Thirty-Third regiments charged into the militia forces, Americans fled the scene. Although Maryland troops waited in reserve, they were undermanned; lacking cavalry and with an exposed left flank, a cavalry attack led by British Lt. Col. Banastre Tarleton sent the Americans in flight. With some 800 Americans dead on the battlefield and perhaps 1,000 taken prisoner, Whig forces fled the scene. Horatio Gates's southern army had been cut to pieces.

Toward Yorktown

The disastrous defeat at Camden provoked a crisis, and the North Carolina government was near collapse as Cornwallis moved his forces and attempted to meet up with loyalists. Traveling north from Camden, Cornwallis reached Charlotte on September 26, 1780, but was harassed by partisans. On October 7, the Whigs experienced a major victory with the annihilation of Patrick Ferguson and his men at Kings Mountain. In the summer of 1780, Ferguson's forces had sought to attack western Whigs and rally Tories, but he met a determined force of some 900 patriots. Advancing on the Tory force under cover of the trees, the Americans used their skill as hunting sharpshooters to deadly effect on Ferguson's men. The battle turned when Ferguson was mortally wounded and his force dissolved into rout. The battle was a decisive Whig victory, with 120 loyalists killed, another 123 wounded, and 664 captured. The attackers lost only 28 men killed and suffered 62 wounded.

The Battle of Kings Mountain was a turning point in the southern campaign. The ability of North Carolina Tories to continue to participate militarily in the British invasion had been dealt a severe blow. Devastated by the death of Ferguson, one of his trusted subordinates, Cornwallis had lost an important component of his invasion plan. As a result, he was forced to retreat to Winnsboro near Camden, where he gathered his forces for a later attempt. Meanwhile, in December 1780, Gen. Nathanael Greene assumed command of American forces in the Carolinas. Perhaps the most effective commander in the Continental army besides George Washington, Greene was dispatched south to revive the southern war effort. Arriving in Charlotte on December 2, 1780, he discovered a dispirited remnant composed of 2,307 men, more than half of whom were militia, approximately 300 of whom possessed no weapons, and only about 800 of whom remained fit for service. Serving under Greene was a mix of veteran Continental soldiers and experienced partisan fighters: Daniel Morgan, William Washington, "Light Horse Harry" Lee, Polish nobleman Thaddeus Kosciusko, and William Smallwood. William R. Davie served as commissary general.

Figure 5.6 Nathanael Greene. *Source: Portrait of Nathanael Greene by Charles William Peale c 1783 oil on canvas/Alamy Images.*

Greene's strategy sought to force Cornwallis into a battle emphasizing American strengths. He relied especially on intelligence and a thorough mapping of the region, particularly its river system. Lacking the forces for a direct engagement, Greene relied on hit-and-run tactics; in the backcountry this meant knowing precisely where to cross the rivers and having pre-positioned canoes and rafts. Unable to mount a direct assault, Greene was willing to take the potentially risky move of dividing his forces in two; one portion, under his command, operated on the Pee Dee River in South Carolina, the second unit of about 1,300 men, under the command of Daniel Morgan, was sent to the town of Ninety Six. Cornwallis's response was to remain at Winnsboro, South Carolina, while he sent Tarleton to pursue Morgan. These British and American forces met at Cowpens, South Carolina, on January 17, 1781, with Tarleton suffering an overwhelming defeat.

Profoundly outraged at the defeat of Tarleton, Cornwallis resolved to lure Greene into a battle so that he might destroy the patriot force. Cornwallis pursued Morgan and his men, but they retreated back to Charlotte. Greene, realizing that he had provoked his enemy, ordered Isaac Huger to move from Cheraw, South Carolina, to Guilford County Courthouse in North Carolina. Meanwhile, Greene, moving from the west and covering 125 miles in three days, united with Morgan at Sherrill's Ford on the Catawba River on January 28, 1781. Cornwallis then pursued Greene deep into the Carolina interior, away from both his base at Winnsboro and supply lines from Wilmington, and the Americans avoided engagement while building up their forces. Northward the chase began, with Greene successfully outdistancing his pursuers. This was no simple feat: because of winter precipitation, the Catawba and Yadkin Rivers were difficult to cross. After a chase of twenty-two days, Greene, Morgan and their army rendezvoused with Huger at Guilford Courthouse, with Cornwallis 25 miles behind at the Moravian settlement at Salem. Leaving Guilford Courthouse and traveling north across the Dan River into southern Virginia on February 13, Greene drew Cornwallis more than 200 miles north of his supply bases.

Worse still for Cornwallis, Greene's successes at evading the British general had drawn attention across North America and Great Britain. With a larger army than he had begun with in the autumn of 1780, Greene now willingly engaged Cornwallis at Guilford Courthouse on March 15, 1781, where 4,500 Americans—2,200 of them Continentals, the remainder militia—fought 2,253 British soldiers. Greene placed the militia in front of the regulars. Told to fire three volleys at the British, the militia began to disperse almost as soon as the British forces came into sight. At this point the battle was joined by the Continentals. After ferocious fighting, Greene tallied his losses at 1,255, including 576 missing militia who fled the battlefield and 290 killed. Though he retained possession of the battlefield, Cornwallis had lost 93 killed, 413 wounded, and 26 missing. The British had paid a high price in this engagement, for their losses were difficult to replace. Cornwallis subsequently ended operations in the North Carolina interior and moved his forces to Wilmington.

* * *

The outcome of the Battle of Guilford Courthouse might have been a British victory, but it effectively stalled the British advance into the Carolinas. The fighting in the backcountry continued throughout 1781, and guerrilla fighting—what one historian calls "civil warfare"—persisted unabated into 1782 as large parts of the backcountry remained locked in the lingering bitterness surrounding the conflict.[3] Indeed, 1782 was probably the most violent year of Tory-Whig conflict, and it set the stage for bitter feelings. In late 1781, Cornwallis advanced his force back toward the Virginia Tidewater and, finding himself surrounded by a combination of American infantry and French naval forces at Yorktown in October 1781, he was forced to surrender. The defeat and capture of Cornwallis's army ended formal hostilities, and nearly two years later, in September 1783, the Treaty of Paris granted American independence.

North Carolina, by participating in the Revolution, became part of a larger American republic. Independence was of profound importance for the new state. It reinforced the powerful traditions of localism and antiauthoritarianism dominating colonial life; indeed, the Revolution built these traditions into the constitutional and legal system. North Carolinians proved reluctant partner in the establishment of a new nation, at least one endowed with much power over states and localities. Most voting North Carolinians opposed in particular the new federal constitution of 1787, and antistatism and localism became parts of state residents' political rhetoric and ideology. The next few generations following the Revolution thus brought the dawn of a new era, but one in which North Carolinians began to explore conflicting meanings of independence and republicanism.

Notes

1 Isaac S. Harrell, "North Carolina Loyalists," *North Carolina Historical Review* 3 no. 4 (October 1926): 582.

2 Nathanael Greene to George Washington, January 31, 1781; Greene to Abner Nash, February 9, 1781.

3 Ronald Hoffman, "The 'Disaffected' in the Revolutionary South," in Alfred F. Young, ed., *The American Revolution: Explorations in the History of American Radicalism* (DeKalb: Northern Illinois University Press, 1976), p. 295.

6

The New Republic

After the 1780s, North Carolinians discovered that the long-fought, costly, and ultimately successful struggle against Great Britain raised troubling questions. How would North Carolinians construct their new republic? What did republicanism—the belief system behind independence—mean? How should republican citizens fashion their political system? How would it differ from the familiar but, in their minds, flawed English political system? How would independent North Carolinians most effectively protect their hard-fought liberties? Should the new state join up with a new Union of American states and, if so, to what extent did North Carolinians belong to it? Finally, what would North Carolina's relationship be toward the new federal system established at Philadelphia in 1787?

When fighting stopped and a peace was signed in 1783, independence took on new implications. Revolutionary libertarianism in North Carolina involved an intense obsession with liberty, and the defense of liberty was the central ideological premise of the war with Britain. But this obsession meant white liberty, developed against the context of a slave society. Patriots realized contradictions between black slavery and a revolutionary/libertarian ideology, and the clash between ideology and reality provided a creative tension in the new republic. There was yet another dimension to the paradox of slavery and freedom, and that was the oligarchic political structure that had long prevailed in North Carolina. Local elites, allied with provincial authorities, dominated the colony, and they exercised power by controlling county courts that were appointed by the colonial assemblies and that served as the basic unit of local government. Oligarchy was clothed in a language of local control and freedom. The Revolutionary constitution of 1776 included a Declaration of Rights whose twenty-five sections affirmed traditional constitutional liberties and asserted protections from tyranny.

Restructuring provincial-level government, the constitution of 1776 severely limited executive power and established legislative supremacy. The General

North Carolina: Change and Tradition in a Southern State, Second Edition. William A. Link.

Assembly included a lower house (the house of commons), which was composed of two members from each county and one from each town, and an upper house (the senate), which contained one member from each county. But because the east contained many more counties than the rest of the state, political power in the legislature was skewed, and this inequitable system of apportionment overvalued the political power of eastern slaveholders. The constitution specified property qualifications for voting, and under this political system not everyone could vote—all women were excluded from the political system, though most white males were enfranchised. The county courts remained unchanged; though establishing the offices of justice of the peace, sheriff, coroner, and constable, the constitution said nothing about local government.

Constitutional Beginnings

North Carolina emerged from the end of the Revolutionary War, like many other new states, having endured considerable stress and strain. The Whig hold on the state during the Revolution remained tenuous; North Carolina possessed a sizeable population of neutralists and loyalists, and the British invasion of the Carolinas during the early 1780s exposed internal class and regional conflicts. The state government pursued draconian measures against loyalists; thousands were driven into exile. Never enjoying solid popular support and suffering from bitter internal divisions, the Revolutionary regime was blamed for the problems of economic recession and inflation that plagued the 1780s. The new state government faced immediate decisions about the treatment of veterans, imprisoned prisoners of war, confiscations of loyalist property, and determining a location of a new state capital. But the 1776 constitution had created a structure in which any decision-making would be difficult.

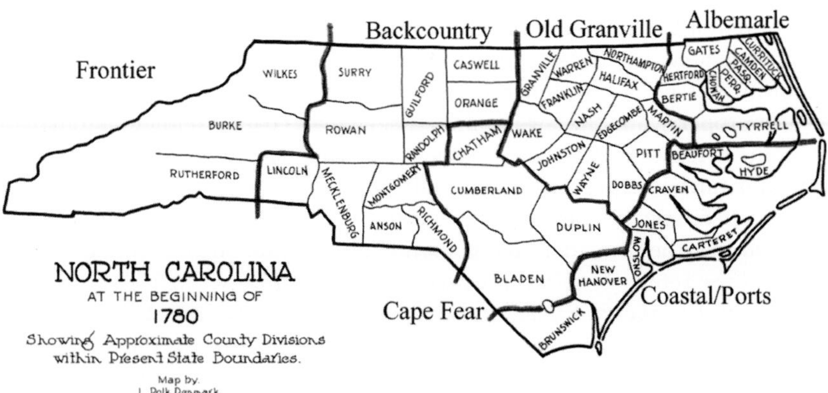

Figure 6.1 Map of North Carolina, c. 1780.

The 1780s political scene was thus highly confused. Whig leadership split into two general groups, known as "conservatives" and "radicals," though these were not in any sense organized political parties. Leading conservatives included prominent Revolutionary leaders such as Samuel Johnston, James Iredell, Hugh Williamson, William R. Davie, and William Hooper; the best-known radicals were Willie Jones, Thomas Person, Samuel Spencer, and Timothy Bloodworth. Unified by an attachment to the commercial economy, conservatives drew from North Carolina's elites, and they were composed of town residents, lawyers, shippers, large planters, and speculators. Radicals, in contrast, generally existed on the margins of the market economy. Radicals included subsistence farmers and artisans, and they especially predominated in backcountry areas isolated from the commercial economy. Not surprisingly, conservatives and radicals held different notions of the role of government. Conservatives feared unrestricted democracy, and they wanted protections for property holders in the form of a stronger state executive, an enhanced court system, and an empowered national government that would, in place of the decentralized Articles of Confederation, successfully check what they called "mob" excesses. Conservatives feared the consequences of radical policies. For example, radicals favored an easy money policy in which the state government printed paper money. The result of this policy was price inflation, which decreased the value of debts but, conservatives believed, violated the property rights of lenders and debased the currency. Conservatives feared other radical policies, including the confiscation of loyalist property and their refusal to pay pre-Revolutionary debts to British lenders. Conservatives saw these radical measures as mob excess and as examples of democracy run amok.

The treatment of loyalists and neutralists remained among the most important issue of the 1780s. During the war, many North Carolinians, including significant numbers of Quakers, Mennonites, and Dunkards, refused participation for religious reasons. In 1779, the legislature targeted pacifists by taxing those exempt from military service. During the war years, pacifists were only barely tolerated. Loyalists experienced even harsher treatment. In the Confiscation Act of 1777, the General Assembly provided for the expropriation of loyalist property, and the law required that all males over 16 either take an oath of loyalty or leave the state. A subsequent Confiscation Act, passed in 1779, provided for further expropriation and sale of loyalist lands, and thereafter radicals sought to seize property as retribution against loyalists. The Treaty of Paris required that the Confederation government recommend an end to confiscation and the return of seized property. While another Act in 1781 protected most loyalist property, a year later the General Assembly reinstituted confiscations and created a special commission to enforce the law. The radicals in the assembly favored wholesale expropriations and a vindictive policy toward loyalists, and they were bitterly opposed by conservatives, who believed that the confiscations were illegal. The radicals were nothing more than a "parcel of profligate scoundrels," said conservative Archibald Maclaine, and they could not "possibly do anything for the benefit of the public."[1] In 1784, the legislature provided for the sale of the remaining loyalist property in the state, and North Carolina officials continued selling loyalist lands until 1787. During the 1780s, thousands of North Carolina loyalists fled to England, Scotland, Florida, and Lower Canada.

Out of the controversy over loyalists emerged an important constitutional principle when the state supreme court, in *Bayard* v. *Singleton* (1787), declared that the Confiscation Acts were unconstitutional. The case involved Elizabeth Bayard, the daughter of wealthy New Bern merchant and loyalist Samuel Cornell, who sued to obtain the return of his confiscated property that was now deeded to her. Under the terms of the state Confiscation Act as redrawn in 1785, Spyers Singleton had purchased Cornell's confiscated holdings in New Bern. With the case argued by prominent jurists and conservatives Johnston, Davie, and Iredell, the state supreme court, while striking down the 1785 law, refused to return the property to Bayard. But the court had made an important point, which the General Assembly accepted—that the courts had the right to review the constitutionality of legislation.

Other important issues of the 1780s included veteran benefits, a new state university, and the location of a new state capital. In the Bonus Act of 1780, the legislature created a large reserve of western lands for veterans, and new legislation in 1782 provided for 640 acres for each common soldier and 12,000 acres for each brigadier general. Beginning in 1782, a state commission oversaw the surveying of these lands, while a subsequent commission addressed monetary losses suffered by North Carolina officers and continentals. Conservatives (and later federalists) were the strongest supporters of establishing a state university, whose legitimacy was based on Section 41 of the constitution of 1776. Radicals, in contrast, viewed a new state university as an unnecessary and frivolous expenditure of taxpayers' money. After opponents defeated one proposal in the General Assembly in 1784, William R. Davie renewed the fight, and in December 1789, the legislature authorized the establishment of a University of North Carolina. Stalled by the lack of financial support, a university trustees' committee nonetheless obtained a 1,380-acre site for a campus on a central location in Orange County, in New Hope Chapel (later, Chapel Hill). Admitting its first student, Hinton James, in February 1795, the new university became the first state university in the United States to open its doors.

About a decade before the Revolutionary War began, New Bern had become the capital of the province of North Carolina. While this served well the interests of the eastern planters who ran the assembly, after the war there was widespread discontent with this location, and many westerners favored establishing a new, more centrally located capital. Nearly every town in the state—even several farther east than New Bern—campaigned for the honor; among the leading contenders were Fayetteville, Tarboro, and Hillsborough. After New

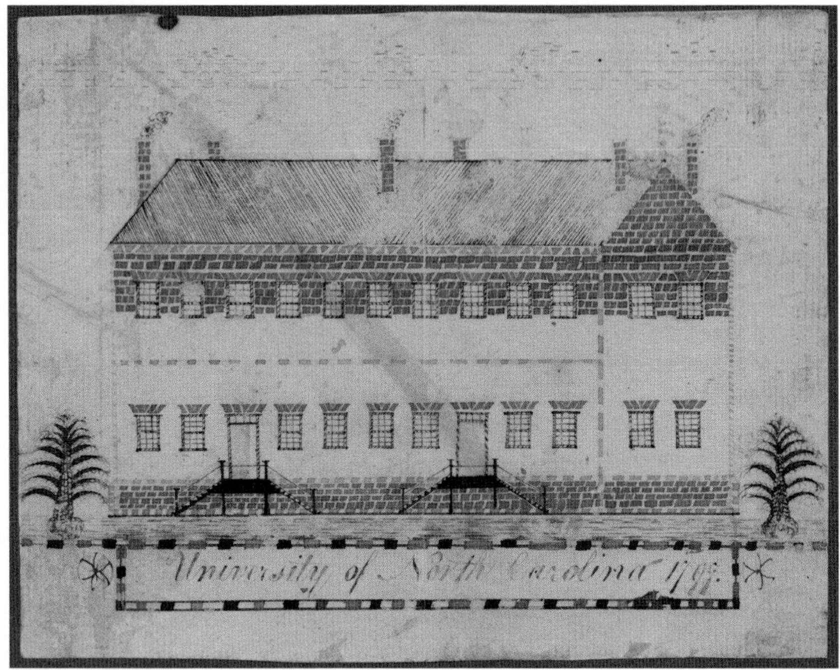

Figure 6.2 Old East, the first building at UNC. By John Pettigrew, c. 1797. *Source: North Carolina Collection, University of North Carolina at Chapel Hill.*

Bern ceased serving as the state capital after 1778, the legislature debated the issue off and on for the next thirteen years. In 1781, the legislature named Hillsborough, but it soon rescinded that decision, and the legislators subsequently met at Halifax, Smithfield, Fayetteville, New Bern, Tarboro, and the Wake County courthouse. At the Hillsborough Convention, which met in 1788 to consider ratification of the federal constitution, delegates voted to locate a new capital in Wake County, but the convention left the precise location to the legislature. The Hillsborough Convention had not, however, arrived at the decision easily; some 119 of the 268 delegates protested the choice, with most of the dissenters favoring Fayetteville because of its location at the upper end of the navigable portion of the Cape Fear River. Facing dissension over the location of the capital, the legislature did not act until 1791, when it appointed a commission to purchase land for a new capital city, and in March 1792 it bought Joel Lane's 1,000-acre plantation for £1,378. With William Christmas of Franklin County as the surveyor, the new capital included five public squares (Union, Caswell, Burke, Nash, and Moore) and eight streets—Edenton, New Bern, Hillsborough, Halifax, Salisbury, Fayetteville, Wilmington and Morgan—named for the state's judicial districts. While other streets were named North, East, South and West, still others were named for house speakers William Lenoir, Stephen Cabarrus, Joel Lane, and William R. Davie. Choosing the name "Raleigh" for the new city, the legislature first met in the new capital on December 30, 1794, and the statehouse structure was completed two years later.

North Carolina during the Articles of Confederation

After independence, the most important decision confronting North Carolinians concerned their relationship to the American Union. Whigs remained fervent opponents of a strong executive, and during the 1770s and 1780s in state politics they opposed the concentration of power in an executive branch of the government. The radical/conservative debate spilled over into the arena of national politics. While conservatives tended to favor a strong national government, radicals stood opposed to any further loss of state privileges and power. Continuing through much of the 1780s, this debate reached a peak with the struggle over ratification of the new federal constitution adopted at Philadelphia in July 1787.

The Articles of Confederation, which were drawn up in the aftermath of the Declaration of Independence on July 4, 1776, created a weak national government. Establishing the Continental Congress as the sole repository of most of the powers of the government, the Articles did not provide for an independent executive or judiciary. The states retained ultimate sovereignty, and all laws enacted by Congress required the states' cooperation in enforcement. Nor was the national government granted taxing powers. Deprived a source of revenue, the federal government struggled to assert much authority. The Articles deliberately made it difficult for the Continental Congress to pass laws—the assent of nine states was required, while amending the Articles required the approval of all thirteen states. Not surprisingly, reform efforts during the 1780s failed. For the most part, North Carolina's political leaders favored a weakened national government; some North Carolinians, such as Thomas Burke, believed that even the Articles went too far in providing for national power at the expense of the states. When the Articles were debated in 1776–77, some North Carolinians favored limiting the Confederation government's power over western lands, taxes, interstate and foreign commerce, and tariffs.

The North Carolina government also issued paper currency not backed by gold or silver specie, and abundant paper currency spurred inflation. This policy of "fiat finance" advantaged debtors—whose debts decreased with inflation—while disadvantaging the monied class. The declining currency, and fiat financing, became another major disagreement between conservatives and radicals: while conservatives were appalled at what they considered the expropriation of private property, radicals sought easy money as a way to ease the burden of servicing the debt the state had incurred during the Revolution. But fiat financing was also a major source of conflict between North Carolina and the national government during the 1780s.

Throughout the 1780s, the status of western lands remained a contentious issue for North Carolinians. In a land boom, North Carolina attracted thousands of migrants. This influx did not end with the Revolution, but many of the new arrivals pushed farther westward. Hugh Williamson described how the "Spirit of Migration" that was "making new States" had reached "epidemic" proportions. Williamson warned that troublemakers were encouraging the settlers to revolt and establish independent states. Convinced that the source of the turmoil was land speculators and not the settlers themselves, he urged North Carolina officials to head off any such movement in the far western "Tennessee Country" so that North Carolina's western "Subjects" would be "among the last to run riot." In response to the flood of migrants, the North Carolina legislature established the new counties of Washington (1777), Sullivan (1779), Greene (1783), and Davidson (1783). In 1783, Davidson County was divided, with part of it becoming Sumner County, while part of Sullivan County became Hawkins County. A year later, in 1784, Davidson was again divided, with a portion of it going into the new Tennessee County. These seven counties remained part of North Carolina until the cession of the western (Tennessee) lands to the federal government on December 22, 1789. The "Tennessee Country" became available to any North Carolinian or American who paid land agents £10 (about fifty dollars) in gold or silver per 100 acres.

The disposition of these western lands—including the present state of Tennessee, then under the control of North Carolina—became a major issue of the political economy of the 1780s. Some saw the western lands, and the willingness of the new states to cede them to the national government, as a source of revenue for the entire nation. After Virginia led the way by ceding most of its western lands in 1784, there was considerable pressure for North Carolina to follow suit. During the Revolution, North Carolina delegates to the Continental Congress opposed cession. Many of them believed that control of western lands would provide the state a source of revenue to pay off the Revolutionary debt. In 1782, North Carolina proposed cession but under strict conditions that provided that Congress should make an "actual valuation" of the western lands, that state debt should remain separate from Confederation debt, and that any new state formed out of the western lands would be required to assume a portion of the state debt.

The issue of western lands continued to figure prominently in state politics during the 1780s. Hoping to reduce the state tax burden and its Revolutionary debt, easterners remained unsympathetic to cession. In contrast, North Carolinians in the Piedmont and Appalachian West favored a lenient, cheap land policy that they believed would accompany cession. Westerners, resenting eastern domination, also sought better military protection as they attempted to move Indians off of their lands. Without the protection of a stronger national government, some westerners worried that the region might gravitate toward the Mississippi Valley and Spanish domination. The issue remained bitter: though the legislature enacted a Cession Act in April 1784 providing for cession, several months later, in October 1784, conservatives in the General Assembly repealed the law.

On August 23, 1784, settlers in seven western counties organized a convention led by John Sevier supporting cession to take place at Jonesborough. The North Carolina government, the settlers charged, had neglected the interests of westerners, and they urged Congress to accept the Cession Act. After the Act was subsequently repealed, the state legislature attempted to placate the western counties by creating a judicial district of Washington and establishing a separate western military district with John Sevier as a brigadier general. But these efforts failed to head off the separatists, who were outraged by the refusal of eastern North Carolinians to endorse cession. The West was now split between supporters of John Tipton, who wanted to remain part of North Carolina, and John Sevier and his supporters, who favored immediate secession and the formation of a new state. On December 14, 1784, a third meeting was held and two constitutions were created, one for each of the factions. While one constitution established a state of "Frankland," the other, championed by Sevier and modeled on the North Carolina constitution of 1776, created the state of "Franklin." In November 1785, yet another convention adopted the Sevier constitution, named him governor, and sent a delegate to the Continental Congress. In this self-proclaimed fashion, thus came into existence the new state of Franklin.

Franklin's independent existence was short-lived, however. The new state posed a threat not only to the North Carolina leadership, but to Virginia, whose own frontierspeople in the southwestern county of Washington shared grievances about a distant eastern government. Leaders of the Continental Congress, even those favoring cession, no doubt cast a wary eye toward the troublesome frontier. Because the North Carolina General Assembly had already repealed the Cession Act, the Continental Congress refused to recognize the new state. North Carolina governor Alexander Martin issued a stinging manifesto denouncing the new state of Franklin as a "mock government" and warning that its existence might lead to civil war. Although the state of Franklin quickly folded and Sevier was elected to the legislature to represent the dissident seven counties, the region remained divided, as the intense factional conflict between supporters of Sevier and those who backed Tipton continued through the remainder of the 1780s. The far western frontier region only stabilized after North Carolina ceded this region to the United States after ratifying the federal constitution in 1789, the Tennessee territory was formed in 1790, and the state of Tennessee was admitted to the Union as the sixteenth state in 1796.

The Federal Constitution and the Ratification Debate

During the 1780s and 1790s, Americans remained deeply divided about the meaning of the American Revolution. Conservatives believed that the Revolution had liberated Americans from the yoke of oppression, but they feared excessive democracy and mob rule. Fiat finance and the state of Franklin suggested mob rule and the consequences of majority rule; conservatives believed that a stronger national government could check democratic excesses at the state level. Radicals, in contrast, favored the autonomy and sovereignty of the states, opposed executive power, and resisted any further delegation of power to the national government. Radicals constructed a political appeal that resonated with plain folk and fed into ordinary whites' suspicions about outsiders. Radicals, for the most part, held sway over public opinion during the 1780s, while conservatives were dispersed and ineffective.

For most of the sessions of the Continental Congress, only one person, or no one at all, represented North Carolina. When a group of nationalists met at the Annapolis Convention in 1786 in order to revise the Articles of Confederation, North Carolina failed to send a delegate; Governor Richard Caswell had appointed five delegates, but only Hugh Williamson even made an attempt to attend, and by the time he reached Annapolis the meeting had adjourned. When nationalists organized a new constitutional convention that met in Philadelphia in May 1787, for most of the meeting North Carolina representatives essentially did not participate, mostly out of inactivity. On January 6, 1787, the North Carolina legislature selected as delegates William R. Davie, Richard Dobbs Spaight, Governor Richard Caswell, Alexander Martin, and Willie Jones. These men were affluent and conservative, and they disproportionately represented the slaveholding plantation and commercial interests of coastal North Carolina. None of them represented majority public opinion—that is, the great mass of yeoman, noncommercial farmers of the state's interior regions.

Most North Carolinians had little interest in creating a stronger national government, and the Philadelphia Convention that drew up a new federal constitution in 1787 had only scant North Carolina representation. The leading radical of the day, Willie Jones, refused to serve. Richard Caswell resigned because of ill health. Neither his replacement, John Gray Blount, nor Alexander Martin did much at the Philadelphia Convention. William R. Davie delivered five short speeches and represented North Carolina on the committee that fashioned the so-called "Great Compromise"—which created a Congress that balanced equal small-state representation in the Senate with a House of Representatives based entirely on population. Richard Dobbs Spaight opposed the Great Compromise and delivered four speeches and proposed provisions for the election of senators and the power of presidents to make recess appointments. The leading North Carolina delegate at the Philadelphia Convention was Hugh Williamson.

He made numerous speeches, served on five committees, and proposed provisions of the new constitution that included the details of senators' terms (six years), procedures for impeachment, the census, and apportionment.

North Carolina delegates favored constitutional provisions protecting slavery. Like other representatives from the slave South, they favored the "three-fifths" clause, which counted three-fifths of the slave population for purposes of representation and apportionment in congressional districts and the distribution of taxes. The three-fifths clause, a major compromise with the nonslaveholding states, institutionalized slaveholders' political power. So did constitutional requirements for the return of fugitive slaves, and a mandate to end further importation of slaves. North Carolina delegates opposed the creation of an independent and potentially powerful presidency. In the end, Blount, Williamson, and Spaight signed the constitution for North Carolina; Davie and Martin were absent. The distinct lack of enthusiasm for the new federal constitution set the stage for the coming political battle in which conservatives, generally more affluent, from commercial classes, and now known as "federalists," generally supported ratification. In contrast, radicals or "antifederalists," who opposed ratification, tended to live in more remote areas of the state that were detached from the commercial economy. North Carolina antifederalists maintained the upper hand from the outset. Hoping that ratification in other states would fail, opponents of the federal constitution pursued a policy of delay. Though distinctly in the minority, federalists nonetheless pressed for ratification.

The ratification debate exposed a major fissure in post-Revolutionary North Carolina. Although the commercial economy was thriving in North Carolina—largely in plantations, coastal ports, and inland towns—the vast majority of North Carolinians still lacked good transportation facilities and remained more or less isolated from the commercial economy. Those associated with the commercial sector, most of whom lived close to coastal ports or interior towns, favored an empowered national government and identified with a new sense of national identity and citizenship. These federalists vigorously favored ratification. In contrast, the antifederalist appeal was rooted in a political culture of majoritarianism, independent freeholding, and the primacy of state rights. The federal constitution, antifederalists maintained, stripped ordinary white people of control over their government, and they pointed to the constitution's creation of a powerful executive (the presidency) and the Senate as examples of the authoritarianism. The federal government, they feared, would simply become too strong and threaten to swallow up state governments. Timothy Bloodworth predicted that a strong national government meant the coming of an "autocratic tyranny." Antifederalists further warned of federal intervention in monetary policy, which they saw as excessive favoritism toward the commercial sector at the expense of those Carolinians—the majority of the state's population—who by and large existed outside of the market economy. Antifederalists were also strong libertarians, and they demanded that the new constitution should include explicit protections of personal liberty in a bill of rights.

After the Philadelphia Convention submitted the constitution to the states for ratification, the North Carolina legislature met at Tarboro to consider the matter on November 19, 1787. Opponents of ratification employed every means at their disposal to delay consideration, but the legislature called for an election on the last Friday and Saturday in March 1788 to elect delegates—five representatives from each of the counties and one delegate from each of six towns—to a ratification convention. Ordering the publication of 1,500 copies of the new constitution, the legislature ruled that the convention should meet on July 21, 1788. This long, four-month interlude provided the occasion for a lengthy debate about ratification, and it provided ample opportunity for the more numerous antifederalists to rally their forces.

Antifederalists conducted a vigorous campaign. Revolutionary general and antifederalist Thomas Person described federalist George Washington as "a damned rascal, and traitor to his country for putting his hand to such an infamous paper as the new Constitution." Most of the federalist support came from the eastern part of the state and from North Carolinians of money, social standing, and education, such as planters, merchants, and professionals. Antifederalists, appealing to backcountry farmers and those on the periphery of the commercial economy, won the majority of seats in the convention, 184 to 83, virtually guaranteeing defeat for the document. Federalists elected to the ratification convention included Iredell, Davie, Richard Dobbs Spaight, and John Gray Blount. But more shocking were those leading federalists who went down in defeat. William Blount and Alexander Martin (both delegates to the Philadelphia Convention), Declaration of Independence signer William Hooper, and former governor Richard Caswell all lost to antifederalist opponents. The Hillsborough Convention would be dominated by leaders who included Willie Jones, Timothy Bloodworth, David Caldwell, William Lenoir, and James Galloway.

From Nonadoption to Ratification

The antifederalists entered the ratification convention at Hillsborough, which met on July 21, 1788, firmly in control. Although the convention's first action was to elect prominent Revolutionary leader Samuel Johnston president, its real business was weightier. By July 1788, eleven states had already ratified the federal constitution and, since only nine ratifying states were needed, advocates of the new constitution had already triumphed. Only North Carolina and Rhode Island remained nonratifiers, so the actions of the Hillsborough Convention had no bearing on the formation of the new federal Union. The main question facing the Hillsborough Convention was whether North Carolina could exist

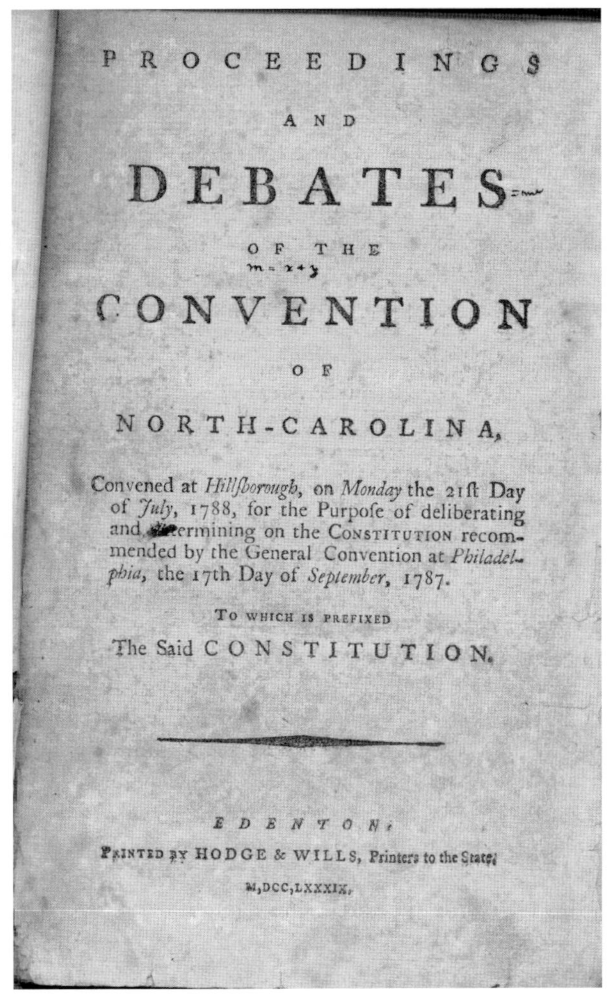

PROCEEDINGS

AND

DEBATES

OF THE

CONVENTION

OF

NORTH-CAROLINA,

Convened at *Hillſborough*, on *Monday* the 21ſt Day of *July*, 1788, for the Purpoſe of deliberating and determining on the CONSTITUTION recommended by the General Convention at *Philadelphia*, the 17th Day of *September*, 1787.

TO WHICH IS PREFIXED

The Said CONSTITUTION.

EDENTON:

PRINTED BY HODGE & WILLS, Printers to the State.

M,DCC,LXXXIX.

Figure 6.3 Hillsborough Convention, 1788. *Source: North Carolina Collection, University of North Carolina Library at Chapel Hill.*

on its own, outside the United States, without the protection of any national government. Antifederalist leaders realized that North Carolina could not do so, and their strategy from the outset was to delay ratification until they could obtain maximum concessions. Above all they feared that the new federal structure provided few protections for states' rights and individual liberties.

Although antifederalists such as Willie Jones considered adjourning the convention on its first day, they permitted federalists such as James Iredell and others to conduct a full discussion of the federal constitution. In a debate lasting a full two weeks, supporters of the new constitution ranged freely in making a case for ratification, though they realized the futility of their cause.

Antifederalists objected to what they perceived as federal control of taxation, debt, western lands, and the court system. "I can see no power that can keep up the little remains of the power of the states," warned Samuel Spencer. "Our rights are not guarded." He favored a "declaration of rights, to secure to every member of the society those unalienable rights which ought not to be given up to any government."[2] Indeed, the most important proposal emerging from the Hillsborough Convention concerned the need to protect liberties through the addition of a bill of rights. Antifederalists argued that a bill of rights would provide a written, concrete guarantee for future generations. At the conclusion of this debate, by a vote of 184 to 83, the convention refused to ratify. Support for the federal constitution was limited to the Albemarle-Pamlico Sound region and most of North Carolina's towns, while the rest of the state remained solidly antifederalist.

Reflecting its indecision regarding North Carolina's future identity in the new nation, the convention neither rejected nor ratified the federal constitution. Rather it chose a course of "non-adoption," in which the convention issued a declaration of rights closely resembling similar documents passed earlier by the Virginia ratification convention. Leading antifederalist Willie Jones spearheaded this nonadoption. On July 31, he told the convention that Thomas Jefferson, in a letter to the Virginia ratification convention, declared that nine states should adopt the constitution to preserve the Union, but that four states should reject it "that there might be a certainty of obtaining amendments." In spite of the certainty of ratification, Jones declared, "I would rather be eighteen years out of the Union than adopt it in its present defective form." The convention thus demanded the holding of a new national convention that would revise the federal constitution to contain a bill of rights including some twenty-six amendments protecting civil liberties, including freedom of speech, the press, religion, and states' rights. Careful to avoid antagonizing the other states, both federalists and antifederalists cooperated with the new Union. For example, the convention specified that if the national government imposed a tariff on imported goods, North Carolina agreed to collect the duty and supply the revenue to Congress. Meanwhile, Hugh Williamson, a former delegate to the Philadelphia Convention, served as a liaison to the new national government while living in New York City in 1788–89. Federalists such as Iredell, Davie, and Archibald Maclaine remained determined, meanwhile, to press their case, and they campaigned for a second state convention to correct what they saw as the "mistake" of Hillsborough. Federalists' support for a list of the rights of the individual was reinforced by the announcement of James Madison of Virginia, in early May 1789, that he would submit a series of constitutional amendments to Congress. He presented the same to Congress on June 8, 1789, and in August and September ten constitutional amendments were distilled from the total of seventy-eight proposed by the various state ratifying conventions. In September, these amendments—which became known as the Bill of Rights—were sent to the states in what was described as an "accommodation" for antifederalists nationwide.

In November 1788, a newly elected legislature ordered elections, by a narrow margin, for a second convention to be held in Fayetteville, but antifederalists succeeded in delaying the convention for another year. By this time a new political atmosphere in North Carolina made ratification quite probable; inveterate antifederalist Willie Jones, realizing the inevitable, refused to run as a convention delegate. Meeting from November 21 to 23, 1789, the Fayetteville convention included a large number of sitting legislators (about half of the convention), while more than 40 percent of those seated also had been delegates to the Hillsborough Convention. The leading federalists in attendance included prominent figures such as Johnston, Davie, Blount, but also Williamson and John Sevier. Antifederalists included old stalwarts such as Timothy Bloodworth, Samuel Spencer, William Lenoir, and David Caldwell. On November 21, 1789, moving quickly, the convention ratified the "Constitution and form of government" embodied in the federal constitution by a vote of 195 to 77, and on December 22, 1789, the North Carolina legislature—with the state now again part of the Union—approved the Bill of Rights. Support for the federal constitution in 1789 spread across the state, as forty-five counties favored and fifteen opposed ratification. In general, there was a decisive shift toward federalism across western North Carolina, with only a few exceptions, and antifederalist holdouts persisted in the Wilmington area, scattered Upper Cape Fear counties, some counties in the northern Piedmont, and in the far West's Sullivan County (now in Tennessee).

In the end, North Carolina's transformation in the fifteen months between nonadoption of the U.S. Constitution at Hillsborough in July 1788 to ratification at Fayetteville in November 1789 resulted from several factors. It had become obvious that the new Union would survive quite well without North Carolina—the only other state that had refused ratification was Rhode Island—and that the state needed the new nation more than the new nation needed North Carolina. The new national government imposed tariff duties on imports, and although duties on North Carolina were suspended while the state remained out of the Union, they were scheduled to take effect on January 15, 1790. North Carolina federalists worked assiduously to change public opinion through newspaper editorials. Residents of the state were, moreover, Americans, with a shared national identity forged during the common Revolutionary experience. That American national identity seemed already to have concrete benefits. The new national government received some credit for the return of good times from the severe economic downturn of 1785–86, while the radical state government in North Carolina was blamed for continuing problems of fiat currency. Westerners saw this national identity in concrete terms, as the national government could protect settlers from Indians and British and Spanish agents. The visit of President George Washington, who visited North Carolina as part of his national tour in 1791, reminded North Carolinians of this national identity embodied in the hero of the Revolution. Federalists such as James Iredell and William R. Davie were insistent advocates of ratification in letters and essays; many opponents of ratification, meanwhile, realized that the advantages of a strong national government—an improved currency and a stronger military defense of the western frontier—could serve their interests. By early 1790, North Carolina had joined the Union as the twelfth state, having elected senators and congressmen, ratified the Bill of Rights, and ceded western lands to the national government.

Social Change and the Transportation Revolution

During the generation after North Carolina joined the Union, the state began to establish a new transportation infrastructure. In December 1815, state senator Archibald D. Murphey submitted a report to the North Carolina legislature's Committee on Inland Navigation. The report, which, along with subsequent recommendations, became known as the Murphey Program, proposed major changes. Two years later, in 1817, Murphey urged the General Assembly to create a system of public schools, which he foresaw as essential to the modernization of the state.

Figure 6.4 Archibald de Bow Murphey. *Source: North Carolina Collection, University of North Carolina Library at Chapel Hill.*

No such thing as a public school system existed in colonial North Carolina. Formal schooling took place only if planters with the means to do so arranged for tutors for their children. Charity, or "free," schools (mostly held in churches) existed only in those localities willing to support them. A large portion of the state's population, probably a majority of whites and nearly all African Americans, remained illiterate. In 1800, an observer writing in the *Raleigh Register* complained that 90 percent of the population lived in "brutish ignorance."[3]

The establishment of a public school system was tied to Archibald Murphey's ideas about transforming North Carolina. Between 1802 and 1838, the legislature frequently considered, but did little about, establishing a public school system. Murphey's report on public schools in 1817 called for the establishment of an outline of a state school system that included a common school fund and a state education board, and he envisioned a combination of primary schools and academies that would feed into the state university. Although Murphey's proposals went nowhere, more than twenty years later, in 1839, the General Assembly adopted legislation that divided the state into districts that contained a primary school supported by the state's Literary Fund (which had been established in 1825 and had grown to several million dollars by the late 1830s) and local authorities to run them. Needless to say, these "common" schools were for whites only.

The new common school system grew slowly in the 1840s. The new system had, as mentioned, some state funding, but its success depended on the ability of local communities to build schools and provide much of the subscription and tax support to sustain them. In 1853, the appointment of Calvin H. Wiley as the first state school superintendent provided some momentum toward school expansion. Wiley, a native of Guilford County, was a lawyer, Presbyterian minister, and political figure who became an enthusiastic evangelist for public schools, traveling the state exhorting North Carolinians to support education. By the beginning of the Civil War, North Carolina had 3,082 schools, 2,752 licensed teachers, and 118,852 children attending schools regularly, and the state was spending $278,000 on common school education.

Murphey believed that his ambitious program of reform depended on economic change, which in turn hinged on altering the state's system of transportation. Over the past quarter century, Murphey declared, more than 200,000 North Carolinians had left the state, many of them "driven away by the prospect of poverty." Agriculture had reached a standstill and farmers realized that they had little future living off the land. A "perversion of things" was undermining public morality, and it was "converting the character which we bore of being industrious, enterprising farmers and thriving mechanics, into that of shopkeepers and speculators." Previously, North Carolinians had "not availed ourselves of the means which Providence has thrown in our way," and, as a result, had "suffered year after year to pass by without seizing opportunities to improve our condition."

Murphey's solution lay in public support for improving transportation facilities—what were then known as "internal improvements." These were "essential to our prosperity." It was

> surely worse than folly to expect the rewards of industry without its toils, or national prosperity without exertion; and we ought always to bear in mind, that it is the duty of the government to aid the enterprise of its citizens, and to afford to them facilities of disposing, to advantage, of the products of their industry.

Through improved transportation, he asserted,

> one or more large commercial cities would grow up; markets would be found at home for the productions of the State; foreign merchandize would be imported into the State for the demands of the market; our debts would be contracted at home; and our Banks would be enabled to change their course of business.

He proposed that the state government plan and fund transportation that would improve the state's access to markets through its rivers, sounds, and harbors.[4]

Although Murphey's proposals to the North Carolina legislature did not go anywhere, he had identified a critical problem in the state's economic development. With often unnavigable rivers and shallow harbors, water transportation—the staple of preindustrial economies—remained inferior in North Carolina. Only one of the state's river systems—the Cape Fear—flowed directly into the Atlantic, while three others emptied west into Tennessee (the French Broad), or south toward South Carolina (the Catawba and the Yadkin). Three other rivers, the Neuse, Tar, and Roanoke, flowed into sounds. Interior North Carolinians, who were removed from river systems, remained isolated from access to good markets for their products and goods. Anyone living "west of a hundred miles from the sea," declared an internal improvements convention in January 1829, was "habitually suffering the most injurious consequences from the want of a monied market, to which he may carry his productions with profit."[5]

The advent of overland transportation, especially railroads, promised to overcome the difficulties of water-borne commerce. During the next generation, North Carolinians embraced internal improvements with the same fervor as did other Americans. As early as 1790, efforts to improve water transportation began with the establishment of the Dismal Swamp Canal Company, which sought to improve connections to Norfolk by connecting the Pasquotank River in North Carolina with the Elizabeth River in Virginia. The canal opened for business on December 31, 1828. In 1855, the Virginia legislature provided for the creation of the Albemarle and Chesapeake Canal, seeking to improve water traffic between the sounds of northeastern North Carolina and the Chesapeake Bay, and the North Carolina legislature later authorized the canal. The canal, 75 miles long with 14 miles through land, opened on the eve of the Civil War, in January 1859. After 1815, other efforts were made to better the navigation of the Roanoke, Tar, Neuse, and Cape Fear Rivers, and to increase access to ports through the inlets of the Outer Banks through dredging and other methods. Many of these projects, funded through public subscription and joint-stock companies, received a modest amount of state support through an internal improvements fund that drew money from the sale of the former lands of the Cherokees.

Despite these considerable efforts in improving water routes, more significant changes in transportation occurred in overland transport. The state invested some money in the construction of turnpikes; some twenty-three roadways received public support in the antebellum era. But turnpikes in North Carolina remained what the state geologist called "at best, good dirt roads."[6] County roads were even worse: usually little more than bumpy pathways swamped with mud and water during thaws and hard-packed and deeply rutted during much of the rest of the year. Farmers depended on these roads to transport their goods to market, but, as a result, still had no reliable and inexpensive way of reaching markets beyond their immediate neighborhoods. Stagecoach travel was lengthy and laborious. When the noted traveler and landscape architect Frederick Law Olmsted toured the American South in the 1850s, he found that his stagecoach had left the eastern North Carolina town of Weldon without him. Running after the stage, he soon caught up to the slow-moving contrivance! The road, he wrote, was "as bad as anything under the name of a road can be conceived to be."[7]

During the 1840s and 1850s, North Carolina took part in a national construction boom in plank-road turnpikes. The legislature awarded charters to private companies to build the turnpikes, the maintenance of which was supported by tolls and subscriptions by farmers along their routes. Plank roads were intended to overcome notoriously bad dirt roads by providing a type of highway one could traverse even in bad weather. They were constructed on graded roadways, typically 8–10 feet in width. Large timbers were placed lengthwise, while planks of heart pine were laid across parallel stringers and covered with sand and wood shavings. Plank roads served to connect the Fall Line river towns with the interior portions of North Carolina; six of the plank roads converged in Fayetteville from various points, the longest of which was the Fayetteville and Western Plank Road, which extended to Salem and ran for 129 miles. It was incorporated in 1849, with the state contributing $120,000 of the $200,000 in stock. "All classes profited," according to a contemporary account describing the plank roads, and "their peculiar merit was the diminution of friction, by which a horse was able to draw two or three times as great a load as he could

Figure 6.5 Country road near New Bern, NC, log road, bridge, c.1900. *Source: Courtesy of the State Archives of North Carolina.*

on an ordinary road."[8] Between 1849 and 1861, some eighty-four plank-road companies were chartered with 500 miles of road constructed and maintained.

The plank-road movement, peaking in the 1850s, was connected to the expansion of the railroad system in the last decades of the antebellum era. In the 1830s, the North Carolina legislature chartered two railroads, the Raleigh & Gaston and Wilmington & Weldon, both of which were completed in 1840. While the former linked the town of Raleigh with the Roanoke River at Gaston to the north, the latter connected Wilmington, in a line that extended 161 miles, with the same river at Weldon. During the 1850s, by means of the Wilmington & Weldon, Wilmington established rail connections to markets in Petersburg and Norfolk and points north, resulting in a surge of exports. Wilmington further consolidated its position with the construction of the Wilmington, Charlotte, and Rutherfordton Railroad, which extended to the southern Piedmont, and the Wilmington and Manchester Railroad, which established a connection south to Charleston, South Carolina. By 1860, the exportation of cotton and wheat from Wilmington exceeded that of naval stores, and the city became the dominant port in eastern North Carolina.

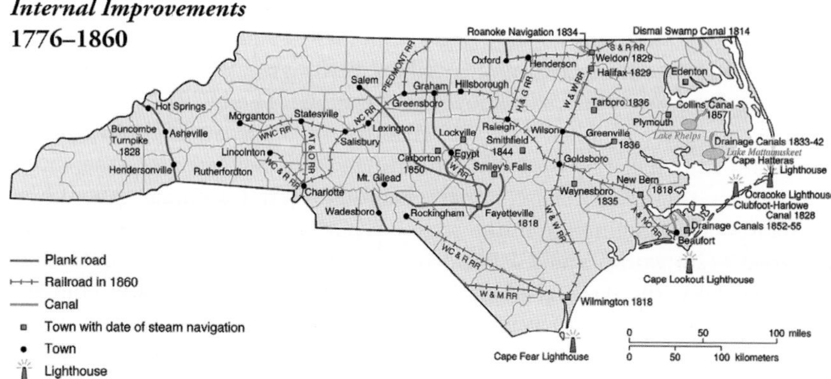

Figure 6.6 Map, internal improvements. *Source: A. Coates, ed.,* Talks to Students and Teachers *(Chapel Hill: Creative Printers, 1971) as shown in North Carolina Atlas, ed. by Douglas M. Orr, Jr., and Alfred W. Stuart (Chapel Hill: UNC Press, 2000).*

The most important railroad of the antebellum era—and the state's most significant antebellum internal improvements project—was the North Carolina Railroad. Chartered in 1849, the NCRR was provided with $2 million in public aid, which became available only after another $1 million had been raised by public subscription. The railroad was supposed to link eastern and western North Carolina, from Goldsboro to Charlotte, extending in a crescent-shape across the Piedmont region. Exalted as a backbone of transportation, supporters claimed the NCRR would enhance trade but divert much of it to the ports of coastal North Carolina.

After a massive construction effort that began with groundbreaking in July 1851, with most of the labor coming from hired slaves, the NCRR was completed in January 1856. Crews working on lines from the east and west met between Greensboro and Jamestown, with David F. Caldwell driving in the last spike. Reputedly the longest railroad in the world, the North Carolina Railroad extended over 223 miles through the state. Meanwhile, additional lines were opened. The Atlantic and North Carolina Railroad, finished in 1858, connected the NCRR from Goldsboro east to Beaufort; the rail terminus became Morehead City, named in honor of John Motley Morehead, governor and a leading figure in the railroad movement. The Western North Carolina Railroad was formed to link the NCRR at Salisbury west to the Tennessee line, but by 1861 it had extended only as far as Morganton.

The completion of the NCRR had an immediate impact in reducing travel time for passengers and lowering costs of sending goods to market by about one-half. Trains departing from Goldsboro at 6:30 a.m. arrived in Greensboro by 3:30 p.m. and Charlotte by about 9:15 in the evening, with the train averaging

15 miles per hour en route. Overall, the 1850s saw a railroad boom, and during that decade, rail lines in the state grew from 283 to 922 miles of track. There were limitations to railroad growth, perhaps most significant the inconsistency of the width between the rails, known as the gauge. The NCRR track was, for example, an inch and a half narrower than the rail lines coming into Greensboro from Danville, Virginia, to the north, and to Charlotte from the south. Nonetheless, there was a sense of marvel among North Carolinians about how railroads were changing life in the state. "What North Carolinian can survey this great State work," said a Hillsborough newspaper, "without emotions of pride that Old 'Rip' has waked up and in her strength presumes to compete with sister States in the great improvements of the age." "Whose heart would not beat with quickened vibration," declared a resident of Asheville, "at the idea of meeting his brethren from all parts of the State at Raleigh in 12, in 14 hours! What poor man could not then visit his friends and relatives, and make life more social and endurable?"[9]

* * *

Despite social and political change in the new republic, there remained a strong residue of suspicion in North Carolina toward the national government, which remained a fixed part of the state's political culture. An entrenched localism and antiauthoritarianism had long characterized the state's political culture. Nonetheless, changes were in the offing. The generations of North Carolinians who came of age in the years after the Revolution oversaw great improvements in transportation, laying the foundation of a modernized infrastructure. At the same time, slavery and racial prejudice remained a mainstay of social life and the economy. Indeed, during the years between the Revolution and the Civil War, North Carolina saw slavery, and its social and political trappings, spread to every corner of the state.

Notes

1 Isaac S. Harrell, "North Carolina Loyalists," *North Carolina Historical Review* 3 no. 4 (October 1926): 585.

2 See the ratification debates of the Hillsborough Convention, at http://www.constitution.org/rc/rat_nc.htm (accessed December 16, 2007).

3 Guion Griffis Johnson, *Ante-Bellum North Carolina: A History* (Chapel Hill: University of North Carolina Press, 1937), p. 259.

4 Archibald D. Murphey, "Report of the Committee on Inland Navigation," December 6, 1815, *North Carolina Senate Journal, 1815*, in William Henry Hoyt, ed., *The Papers of Archibald D. Murphey*, 2 vols. (Raleigh, NC, 1914), II, 20.

5 Quoted in Alan D. Watson, "Battling 'Old Rip': Internal Improvements and the Role of State Government in North Carolina," *North Carolina Historical Review* 77 (April 2000): 181.

6 Ibid., p. 197.

7 Quoted in Allen W. Trelease, *The North Carolina Railroad, 1849–1871, and the Modernization of North Carolina* (Chapel Hill: University of North Carolina Press, 1991), p. 9.

8 Quoted in Thomas H. Clayton, *Close to the Land: The Way We Lived in North Carolina, 1820–1870* (Chapel Hill: University of North Carolina Press, 1983), p. 81.

9 Quoted by Trelease, *The North Carolina Railroad*, p. 41.

Suggested Readings, Part 2

Chapter 4

John Spencer Bassett, *The Regulators of North Carolina, 1765–1771* (Washington, DC: Government Printing Office, 1895).

John Buchanan, *The Road to Guilford Courthouse: The American Revolution in the Carolinas* (New York: Wiley, 1997).

Michael Crawford, *The Having of Negroes Is Become a Burden: The Quaker Struggle to Free Slaves in Revolutionary North Carolina* (Gainesville: University Press of Florida, 2010).

Elisha P. Douglass, *Rebels and Democrats: The Struggle for Equal Political Rights and Majority Rule during the American Revolution* (Chapel Hill: University of North Carolina Press, 1955).

A. Roger Ekirch, *"Poor Carolina": Politics and Society in Colonial North Carolina* (Chapel Hill: University of North Carolina Press, 1981).

Elizabeth A. Fenn, *Natives & Newcomers: The Way We Lived in North Carolina before 1770* (Chapel Hill: University of North Carolina Press, 1983).

Ian C. C. Graham, *Colonists from Scotland: Emigration to America, 1707–1783* (Ithaca, NY: Cornell University Press, 1956).

Carl Hammer, Jr., *Rhinelanders on the Yadkin: The Story of the Pennsylvania Germans in Rowan and Cabarrus Counties, North Carolina* (Salisbury, NC: n.p., 1943).

Marjoleine Kars, *Breaking Loose Together: The Regulator Rebellion in Pre-Revolutionary North Carolina* (Chapel Hill: University of North Carolina Press, 2002).

Enoch Lawrence Lee, *The Lower Cape Fear in Colonial Days* (Chapel Hill: University of North Carolina Press, 1965).

Wayne E. Lee, *Crowds and Soldiers in Revolutionary North Carolina: The Culture of Violence in Riot and War* (Gainesville: University Press of Florida, 2001).

Harry Roy Merrens, *Colonial North Carolina in the Eighteenth Century: A Study in Historical Geography* (Chapel Hill: University of North Carolina Press, 1964).

Duane Meyer, *The Highland Scots of North Carolina, 1732–1776* (Chapel Hill: University of North Carolina Press, 1961).

Paul David Nelson, *William Tryon and the Course of Empire: A Life in British Imperial Service* (Chapel Hill: University of North Carolina Press, 1990).

Robert Ramsey, *Carolina Cradle: Settlement of the Northwest Carolina Frontier, 1747–1762* (Chapel Hill: University of North Carolina Press, 1964).

Blackwell P. Robinson, *The Five Royal Governors of North Carolina* (Raleigh, NC: Division of Archives and History, 1963).

Jon F. Sensbach, *A Separate Canaan: The Making of an Afro-Moravian World in North Carolina, 1763–1840* (Chapel Hill: University of North Carolina Press, 1998).

Donna Spindel, *Crime and Society in North Carolina, 1663–1776* (Baton Rouge: Louisiana State University Press, 1989).

Daniel B. Thorp, *The Moravian Community in Colonial North Carolina: Pluralism on the Southern Frontier* (Knoxville: University of Tennessee Press, 1989).

Alan D. Watson, *Money and Monetary Problems in Early North Carolina* (Raleigh, NC: Division of Archives and History, 1980).

Chapter 5

Lindley S. Butler, *North Carolina and the Coming of the Revolution, 1763–1776* (Raleigh, NC: Division of Archives and History).

Robert M. Calhoon, *The Loyalists in Revolutionary America, 1760–1781* (New York: Harcourt Brace Jovanovich, 1973).

Robert M. Calhoon, *Religion and the American Revolution in North Carolina* (Raleigh, NC: Division of Archives and History, 1976).

Jeffrey J. Crow, *A Chronicle of North Carolina during the American Revolution, 1763–1789* (Raleigh, NC: Division of Archives and History, 1975).

Jeffrey J. Crow, *The Black Experience in Revolutionary North Carolina* (Raleigh, NC: Division of Archives and History, 1983).

Chalmers Davidson, *Piedmont Partisan: The Life and Times of Brigadier-General William Lee Davidson* (Davidson, NC: Davidson College, 1951).

Robert O. De Mond, *The Loyalists in North Carolina during the Revolution* (Durham, NC: Duke University Press, 1940).

Robert L. Ganyard, *The Emergence of North Carolina's Revolutionary State Government* (Raleigh, NC: North Carolina Dept. of Cultural Resources, Division of Archives and History, 1978).

Jack P. Greene, *The Quest for Power: The Lower Houses of Assembly in the Southern Colonies, 1689–1776* (Chapel Hill: University of North Carolina Press, 1963).

Isaac S. Harrell, "North Carolina Loyalists," *North Carolina Historical Review* 3 (October 1926): 582.

Don Higginbotham, *Daniel Morgan: Revolutionary Rifleman* (Chapel Hill: University of North Carolina Press, 1961).

Enoch Lawrence Lee, Jr., "Days of Defiance: Resistance to the Stamp Act in the Lower Cape Fear," *North Carolina Historical Review* 43 (April 1966): 186–202.

Enoch Lawrence Lee, Jr., *Indian Wars in North Carolina, 1663–1763* (Raleigh, NC: State Division of Archives and History, 1968).

John R. Maass, "All This Poor Province Could Do: North Carolina and the Seven Years' War, 1757–1762," *North Carolina Historical Review* 79 (January 2002): 50–89.

Alice E. Mathews, *Society in Revolutionary North Carolina* (Raleigh, NC: Division of Archives and History, 1976).

John Oliphant, *Peace and War on the Anglo-Cherokee Frontier, 1756–63* (Baton Rouge: Louisiana State University Press/Basingstoke: Palgrave, 2001).

John S. Pancake, *This Destructive War: The British Campaign in the Carolinas, 1780–1782* (Tuscaloosa: University of Alabama Press, 1985).

William S. Price, Jr., *Not a Conquered People: Two Carolinians View Parliamentary Taxation* (Raleigh, NC: Division of Archives and History, 1975).

Hugh F. Rankin, "The Moore's Creek Bridge Campaign, 1776," *North Carolina Historical Review* 30 (January 1953): 23–60.

Hugh F. Rankin, *The North Carolina Continentals* (Chapel Hill: University of North Carolina Press, 1971).

Hugh F. Rankin, *Greene and Cornwallis: The Campaign in the Carolinas* (Raleigh, NC: Division of Archives and History, 1976).

Charles G. Sellers, Jr., "Making a Revolution: The North Carolina Whigs, 1765–1775," in *Studies in Southern History*, ed., J. C. Sitterson (Chapel Hill: University of North Carolina Press, 1957): 23–46.

J. Russell Snapp, *John Stuart and the Struggle for Empire on the Southern Frontier* (Baton Rouge: Louisiana State University Press, 1996).

Chapter 6

Kevin Barksdale, *The Lost State of Franklin: America's First Secession* (Lexington: University Press of Kentucky, 2009).

Sarah McCulloh Lemmon, *Frustrated Patriots: North Carolina and the War of 1812* (Chapel Hill: University of North Carolina Press, 1973).

John R. Maass, *"'A Complicated Scene of Difficulties': North Carolina and the Revolutionary Settlement, 1776–1789,"* Ph.D. diss., Ohio State University, 2007.

Blackwell P. Robinson, *William R. Davie* (Chapel Hill: University of North Carolina Press, 1954).

Louise Irby Trenholme, *The Ratification of the Federal Constitution and North Carolina* (New York: Columbia University Press, 1932).

Henry M. Wagstaff, *State Rights and Political Parties in North Carolina, 1776–1861* (Baltimore, MD: Johns Hopkins Press, 1906).

Harry Watson, *An Independent People: The Way We Lived in North Carolina, 1770–1820* (Chapel Hill: University of North Carolina Press, 1983).

Document Section, Part 2
The Debate about the Federal Constitution

In North Carolina, the American Revolution spawned an intense opposition to centralized political authority. In some respects, this antiauthoritarianism reflected longstanding political culture in the colony. With a dispersed settlement and weakly established colonial political authority, North Carolinians had long resisted the exertion of external control. The Whig government in North Carolina adopted a constitution in 1776 that established absolute legislative supremacy in the running of state government, with a weak governor possessing no veto power, few powers of appointment, and annual elections by the legislature. State courts were similarly under legislative domination, while local government officials were appointed by the legislature.

In this context, it should come as little surprise that people of North Carolina were reluctant participants in the organization of a new national government. No North Carolina delegates attended the Philadelphia convention that adopted a new federal constitution in the summer of 1787. And this Constitution, which provided for a much stronger national government than had existed under the Articles of Confederation, met strong opposition from North Carolina's leaders when it was submitted to the states for ratification. Unsurprisingly, antifederalists, opponents of the federal Constitution, constituted a large portion of the North Carolina leadership.

These documents explore the debate over ratification of the Constitution. When reading the documents, consider what antifederalists most objected to, and how they framed their case.

North Carolina: Change and Tradition in a Southern State, Second Edition. William A. Link.

Federalists Present the New Constitution for Adoption, September 18, 1787[1]

North Carolina's delegation to the Philadelphia convention presented the new federal Constitution in September 1787. The convention created a mechanism for ratification in which three-quarters of the states needed to meet in convention, composed of elected delegates. In these documents, the nascent North Carolina federalists made their case.

In the course of four Months severe and painful application and anxiety, the Convention have prepared a plan of Government for the United States of America which we hope will obviate the defects of the present Federal Union and procure the enlarged purposes which it was intended to effect. Enclosed we have the honor to send you a Copy, and when you are pleased to lay this plan before the General Assembly we entreat that you will do us the justice to assure that honorable Body that no exertions have been wanting on our part to guard and promote the particular interest of North Carolina. You will observe that the representation in the second Branch of the National Legislature is to be according to numbers, that is to say, According to the whole number of white Inhabitants added to threefifths of the blacks; you will also observe that during the first three years North Carolina is to have five Members in the House of Representatives, which is just one-thirteenth part of the whole number in that house and our Annual Quota of the National debt has not hitherto been fixed quite so high. Doubtless we have reasons to believe that the Citizens of North Carolina are more than a thirteenth part of the whole number in the Union, but the State has never enabled its Delegates in Congress to prove this Opinion and hitherto they had not been Zealous to magnify the number of their Constituents because their Quota of the National Debt must have been Augmented accordingly. We had many things to hope from a National Government and the chief thing we had to fear from such a Government was the Risque of unequal or heavy Taxation, but we hope you will believe as we do that the Southern States in general and North Carolina in particular are well secured on that head by the proposed system. It is provided in the 9th Section of Article the first that no Capitation or other direct Tax shall be laid except in proportion to the number of Inhabitants, in which number five blacks are only Counted as three. If a land tax is laid we are to pay the same rate, for Example: fifty Citizens of North Carolina can be taxed no more for all their Lands than fifty Citizens in one of the Eastern States. This must be greatly in our favour for as most of their Farms

---

1 William Blount, Richard Dobbs Spaight, and Hugh Williamson to Richard Caswell, September 18, 1787, in William Clark, ed. *The Colonial Records of North Carolina*, vol. 20 (Raleigh, NC: P. M. Hale, Printer to the State, 1902), pp. 777–79, http://docsouth.unc.edu/csr/index.html/document/csr20-0197.

are small & many of them live in Towns we certainly have, one with another, land of twice the value that they Possess. When it is also considered that five Negroes are only to be charged the Same Poll Tax as three whites the advantage must be considerably increased under the proposed Form of Government. The Southern States have also a much better Security for the Return of Slaves who might endeavour to Escape than they had under the original Confederation. It is expected a considerable Share of the National Taxes will be collected by Impost, Duties and Excises, but you will find it provided in the 8th Section of Article the first that all duties, Impost and excises shall be uniform throughout the United States. While we were taking so much care to guard ourselves against being over reached and to form rules of Taxation that might operate in our favour, it is not to be supposed that our Northern Brethren were Inattentive to their particular Interest. A navigation Act or the power to regulate Commerce in the Hands of the National Government by which American Ships and Seamen may be fully employed is the desirable weight that is thrown into the Northern Scale. This is what the Southern States have given in Exchange for the advantages we Mentioned above; but we beg leave to observe in the course of this Interchange North Carolina does not appear to us to have given up anything for we are doubtless the most independent of the Southern States; we are able to carry our own produce and if the Spirit of Navigation and Ship building is cherished in our State we shall soon be able to carry for our Neighbors. We have taken the liberty to mention the General pecuniary Considerations which are involved in this plan of Government, there are other Considerations of great Magnitude involved in the system, but we cannot exercise your patience with a further detail, but submit it with the utmost deference, and have the Honor to be,

Your Excellency's Most Obedient Humble Servts,
WM. BLOUNT,
RICH'D D. SPAIGHT,
HUGH WILLIAMSON.

Debating the Constitution, Hillsborough Convention, July 24, 1788[2]

In response to the presentation of the Constitution for adoption, the North Carolina legislature provided that elections would be held for a convention. That

---

2 *Proceedings and Debates of the Convention of North-Carolina, Convened at Hillsborough, on Monday the 21st Day of July, 1788, for the Purpose of Deliberating and Determining on the Constitution Recommended by the General Convention at Philadelphia, the 17th Day of September, 1787: To Which is Prefixed the Said Constitution* (Edenton, NC: Hodge & Wills, Printers to the State, 1789), pp. 36–44, http://docsouth.unc.edu/nc/conv1788/conv1788.html.

convention met in Hillsborough in July 1788. Federalists enjoyed ample opportunity to make their case, here presented by William Richardson Davie. Born in 1756, Davie emigrated with his family from England to background South Carolina in 1763. Educated at the College of New Jersey (later Princeton University), Davie served in the Revolution on the patriot side, rising to the rank of colonel. Elected to the North Carolina house of commons, he led legislative efforts to charter the University of North Carolina and laid its cornerstone in 1793. Davie attended the Philadelphia constitutional convention in 1787, but left before he could sign the document. Nonetheless, he was an outspoken federalist.

Mr. Davie—Mr. Chairman. After repeated and decisive proofs of the total inefficiency of our general government, the states deputed the Members of the Convention to revise and Strengthen it: And permit me to call to your consideration, that whatever form of confederate government they might devise, or whatever powers they might propose to give this new government, no part of it was binding until the whole Constitution had received the solemn assent of the people. What was the object of our mission? "To decide upon the most effectual means of removing the defects of our federal union." … Perhaps it may be necessary to form a true judgment of this important question, to state some events, and develope some of those defects which gave birth to the late Convention, and which have produced this revolution in our federal government. With the indulgence of the committee I will attempt this detail with as much precision as I am capable of. The general objects of the union, are, 1st. To protect us against foreign invasion. 2d. To defend us against internal commotions and insurrections. 3d. To promote the commerce, agriculture and manufactures of America. These objects are requisite to make us a safe and happy people, and they cannot be attained without a firm and efficient system of union.

As to the first, we cannot obtain any effectual protection from the present Confederation. It is indeed universally acknowledged that its inadequacy in this case, is one of its greatest defects. Examine its ability to repel invasion. In the late glorious war its weakness was unequivocally experienced: It is well known that Congress had a discretionary right to raise men and money, but they had no power to do either. In order to preclude the necessity of examining the whole progress of its imbecility, permit me to call to your recollection one single instance. When the last great stroke was made which humbled the pride of Britain, and put us in possession of peace and independence, so low were the finances and credit of the United States, that our army could not move from Philadelphia, until the Minister of his most Christian Majesty was prevailed upon to draw bills to defray the expence of the expedition: These were not obtained on the credit or interest of Congress, but by the personal influence of the Commander in Chief … The next important consideration which is involved in the external powers of the union, are treaties. Without a power in the federal government to compel the performance of our engagements with foreign nations, we shall be perpetually involved in destructive wars. The

Confederation is extremely defective in this point also. I shall only mention the British treaty, as a satisfactory proof of this melancholy fact. It is well known, that although this treaty was ratified in 1784, it required the sanction of a law of North-Carolina in 1787: And that our enemies, presuming on the weakness of our federal government, have refused to deliver up several important posts within the territories of the United States, and still hold them, to our shame and disgrace. It is unnecessary to reason on facts, the perilous consequences of which must in a moment strike every mind capable of reflection.

The next head under which the general government may be considered, is the regulation of commerce. The United States should be empowered to compel foreign nations into commercial regulations, that were either founded on the principles of justice or reciprocal advantages. Has the present Confederation effected any of these things? Is not our commerce equally unprotected abroad by arms and negociation? Nations have refused to enter into treaties with us. What was the language of the British Court on a proposition of this kind? Such as would insult the pride of any man of feeling and independence—"You can make engagements, but you cannot compel your citizens to company with them; we derive greater profits from the present situation of your commerce, than we could expect under a treaty; and you have no kind of power that can compel us to surrender any advantage to you." This was the language of our enemies; and while our government remains as feeble as it has been, no nation will form any connexion with us, that will involve the relinquishment of the least advantage. What has been the consequence? a general decay of trade, the rise of imported merchandise, the fall of produce, and an uncommon decrease of the value of lands. Foreigners have been reaping the benefits and emoluments which our citizens ought to enjoy. An unjustifiable perversion of justice has pervaded almost all the states, and every thing presenting to our view a spectacle of public poverty and private wretchedness.

While this is a true representation of our situation, can our general government recur to the ordinary expedient of loans? During the late war, large sums were advanced to us by foreign states and individuals. Congress have not been enabled to pay even the interest of these debts with honour and punctuality. The requisitions made on the states have been every where unproductive, and some of them have not paid a stiver. These debts are a part of the price of our liberty and independence; debts which ought to be regarded with gratitude and discharged with honour. Yet many of the individuals who lent us money in the hour of our distress, are now reduced to indigence in consequence of our delinquency. So low and hopeless are the finances of the United States, that the year before last Congress were obliged to borrow money even to pay the interest of the principal which we had borrowed before. …

There are several other instances of imbecility in that system. It cannot secure to us the enjoyment of our own territories, nor even the navigation of our own rivers. The want of power to establish an uniform rule of naturalization through the United States is also no small defect, as it must unavoidably be productive of disagreeable controversies with foreign nations. The general government ought in this, as in every other instance, to possess the means of preserving the peace and tranquility of the union. …

The encroachments of some states on the rights of others, and of all on those of the confederacy, are incontestible proofs of the weakness and imperfection of that system. Maryland lately passed a law granting exclusive privileges to her own vessels, contrary to the articles of the Confederation: Congress had neither power nor influence to alter it, all they could do, was to send a contrary recommendation. It is provided by the 6th article of the Confederation, that no compact shall be made between two or more states without the consent of Congress; yet this has been recently violated by Virginia and Maryland, and also by Pennsylvania and New-Jersey. North-Carolina and Massachusetts have had a considerable body of forces on foot, and those in this state raised for two years, notwithstanding the express provision in the Confederation that no forces should be kept up by any state in time of peace.

As to internal tranquility, without dwelling on the unhappy commotions in our own back counties, I will only add, that if the rebellion in Massachusetts had been planned and executed with any kind of ability, that state must have been ruined, for Congress were not in a situation to render them any assistance. …

These are some of the leading causes which brought forward this new Constitution. It was evidently necessary to infuse a greater portion of strength into the national government: But Congress were but a single body, with whom it was dangerous to lodge additional powers. Hence arose the necessity of a different organization. In order to form some balance, the departments of government were separated, and as a necessary check the legislative body was composed of two branches. Steadiness and wisdom are better ensured when there is a second branch to balance and check the first. The stability of the laws will be greater, when the popular branch, which might be influenced by local views, or the violence of party, is checked by another, whose longer continuance in office will render them more experienced, more temperate and more competent to decide rightly.

The Confederation derived its sole support from the state Legislatures; this rendered it weak and ineffectual: It was therefore necessary that the foundations of this government should be laid on the broad basis of the people. Yet the state governments are the pillars upon which this government is extended over such an immense territory, and are essential to its existence. The House of Representatives are immediately elected by the people. The Senators represent the sovereignty of the states; they are directly chosen by the state Legislatures, and no legislative act can be done without their concurrence. The election of the Executive is in some measure under the controul of the Legislatures of the states, the Electors being appointed under their direction.

The difference in point of magnitude and importance in the members of the confederacy, was an additional reason for the division of the Legislature into two branches, and for establishing an equality of suffrage in the Senate. The protection of the small states against the ambition and influence of the larger members, could only be effected by arming them with an equal power in one branch of the Legislature. On a contemplation of this matter, we shall find, that the jealousies of the states could not be reconciled any other way. The lesser states would never have concurred unless this check had been given them, as a security for their political existence against the power and encroachments of the great states. It may be also proper to observe, that the Executive is separated in its functions from the Legislature as well as the nature of the case would admit, and the Judiciary from both.

Another radical vice in the old system, which was necessary to be corrected, and which will be understood without a long deduction of reasoning, was, that it legislated on states instead of individuals; and that its powers could not be executed but by fire or by the sword; by military force, and not by the intervention of the civil magistrate. Every one who is acquainted with the relative situation of the states, and the genius of our citizens, must acknowledge, that if the government was to be carried into effect by military force, the most dreadful consequences would ensue. It would render the citizens of America the most implacable enemies to one another. If it could be carried into effect against the small states, yet it could not be put in force against the larger and more powerful states. It was therefore absolutely necessary that the influence of the magistrate should be introduced, and that the laws should be carried home to individuals themselves.

In the formation of this system, many difficulties presented themselves to the Convention. Every member saw that the existing system would ever be ineffectual, unless its laws operated on individuals, as military coercion was neither eligible nor practicable. Their own experience was fortified by their knowledge of the inherent weakness of all confederate governments: They knew that all governments merely federal, had been short-lived; or had existed from principles extraneous from their constitutions; or from external causes which had no dependence on the nature of their governments. These considerations determined the Convention to depart from that solecism in politicks, the principle of legislation for states in their political capacities.

The great extent of country appeared to some a formidable difficulty; but a confederate government appears at least in theory, capable of embracing the various interests of the most extensive territory: Founded on the state governments solely, as I have said before, it would be tottering and inefficient. It became therefore necessary to bottom it on the people themselves, by giving them an immediate interest and agency in the government. There was however, some real difficulty in conciliating a number of jarring interests, arising from the incidental, but unalterable, difference in the states in point of territory, situation, climate, and rivalship in commerce. Some of the states are very extensive, others very limited: Some are manufacturing states, others merely agricultural: Some of these are exporting states, while the carrying and navigation business are in the possession of others. It was not easy to reconcile such a multiplicity of discordant and clashing interests. Mutual concessions were necessary to come to any concurrence. A plan that would promote the exclusive interests of a few states, would be injurious to others. Had each state obstinately insisted on the security of its particular local advantages, we should never have come to a conclusion; each therefore amicably and wisely relinquished its particular views. The federal Convention have told you, that the Constitution which they formed, "was the result of a spirit of amity, and of that mutual deference and concession, which the peculiarity of their political situation rendered indispensable." I hope the same laudable spirit will govern this Convention in their decision on this important question.

The business of the Convention was to amend the Confederation by giving it additional powers. The present form of Congress being a single body, it was thought unsafe to augment its powers, without altering its organization. The act of the Convention is but a mere proposal, similar to the production of a private pen. I think it a government which, if adopted, will cherish and protect the happiness and liberty of America; but I hold my mind open to conviction; I am ready to recede from my opinion if it be proved to be ill-founded. I trust that every man here is equally ready to change an opinion he may have improperly formed. The weakness and inefficiency of the old Confederation produced the necessity of calling the federal Convention: Their plan is now before you, and I hope on a deliberate consideration every man will see the necessity of such a system. It has been the subject of much jealousy and censure out of doors. I hope gentlemen will now come forward with their objections, and that they will be thrown out and answered with candour and moderation.

Debating the Constitution, Hillsborough Convention, July 26, 1788[3]

Although federalists made their case to the convention, opponents of the Constitution held the upper hand. Samuel Spencer, born in Virginia, was educated at Princeton and moved to Anson County in 1760 to practice law. Elected to the North Carolina Assembly in 1769, he became a prominent Revolutionary leader. In 1777, Spencer became a North Carolina Superior Court judge, holding that

3 *Proceedings and Debates of the Convention of North-Carolina, Convened at Hillsborough,* pp. 102–3, http://docsouth.unc.edu/nc/conv1788/conv1788.html.

seat until his death in 1794. In 1788, Spencer emerged as one of the leaders of the North Carolina antifederalists at the Hillsborough Convention. Here, he outlines his case against adoption.

Mr. Spencer—Mr. Chairman, I cannot, notwithstanding what the gentleman has advanced, agree to this clause unconditionally. The most certain criterion of happiness that any people can have, is, to be taxed by their own immediate Representatives—By those Representatives who intermix with them, and know their circumstances—not by those who cannot know their situation. Our federal Representatives cannot sufficiently know our situation and circumstances. The worthy gentleman said, that it would be necessary for the general government to have the power of laying taxes, in order to have credit to borrow money. But I cannot think, however plausible it may appear, that his argument is conclusive. If such emergency happens as will render it necessary for them to borrow money, it will be necessary for them to borrow before they proceed to lay the tax. I conceive the government will have credit sufficient to borrow money in the one case as well as the other. If requisitions be punctuality complied with, no doubt they can borrow, and if not punctually complied with, Congress can ultimately lay the tax.

I wish to have the most easy way for the people to pay their taxes. The state Legislature will know every method and expedient by which the people can pay, and they will recur to the most convenient. This will be agreeable to the people, and will not create insurrections or dissentions in the country. The taxes might be laid on the most productive articles: I wish not, for my part, to lay them on perishable articles. There are a number of other articles besides those which the worthy gentleman enumerated. There are besides tobacco, hemp, indigo, and cotton. In the northern states, where they have manufactures, a contrary system from ours would be necessary. There the principal attention is paid to the giving their children trades. They have few articles for exportation. By raising the tax in this manner, it will introduce such a spirit of industry as cannot fail of producing happy consequences to posterity. He objects to the mode of paying taxes in specific articles: May it not be supposed that we shall gain something by experience, and avoid those schemes and methods which shall be found inconvenient and disadvantageous? If expences should be incurred in keeping and disposing of such articles, could not those expences be reimbursed by a judicious sale? Cannot the Legislature be circumspect as to the choice and qualities of the objects to be selected for raising the taxes due to the continental treasury? The worthy gentleman has mentioned, that if the people should not comply to raise the taxes in this way, that then if they were subject to the law of Congress, it would throw them into confusion. I would ask every one here, if there be not more reason to induce us to believe that they would be thrown into confusion in case the power of Congress was exercised by Congress in the first instance, than in the other case. After having so long a time to raise the taxes, it appears to me that there could be no kind of doubt of a punctual compliance. The right of Congress to lay taxes ultimately, in case of non-compliance with requisitions, would operate as a penalty, and would stimulate the states to discharge their quotes faithfully. Between these two modes there is an immense difference. The one will produce the happiness, ease, and prosperity of the people; the other will destroy them, and produce insurrection.

Debating the Constitution, Hillsborough Convention, July 31, 1788[4]

Among the most prominent antifederalists was Willie Jones. Born in southern Virginia in 1741, Jones grew up in Northampton County. Eventually moving to Halifax, he became one of the largest landholders and slaveholders in eighteenth-century North Carolina. Jones was also a fierce defender of liberty for whites. Elected to the assembly in 1766, he became an ardent Revolutionary, and later became an outspoken antifederalist. His comments at the convention appear below.

Mr. Willie Jones—Mr. Chairman, The gentleman last up has mentioned the resolution of Congress now lying before us, and the act of Assembly under which we met here, which says that we should deliberate and determine on the Constitution. What is to be inferred from that? Are we to ratify it at all events? Have we not an equal right to reject? We do determine by neither rejecting nor adopting. It is objected we shall be out of the union. So I wish to be. We are left at liberty to come in at any time. It is said we shall suffer a great loss, for want of a share of the impost. I have no doubt we shall have it when we come in, as much as if we adopted now. I have a resolution in my pocket, which I intend to introduce if this resolution is carried, recommending it to the Legislature to lay an impost for the use of Congress on goods imported into this state, similar to that which may be laid by Congress on goods imported into the adopting states. This shews the committee what is my intention, and on what footing we are to be. This being the case, I will forfeit my life that we shall come in for a share. It is said that all the offices of Congress will be filled, and we shall have no share in appointing the officers. This is an objection of very little importance. Gentlemen need not be in such haste. If left eighteen months or two years without offices it is no great cause of alarm. The gentleman further said, that we could send no Representatives, but must send Ambassadors to Congress as a foreign power. I assent the contrary, and that whenever a Convention of the states is

---

4 *Proceedings and Debates of the Convention of North-Carolina,* pp. 252–54, http://docsouth.unc.edu/nc/conv1788/conv1788.html.

called, North-Carolina will be called upon like the rest. I do not know what these gentlemen would desire. I am very sensible that there is a great majority against the Constitution. If we take the question as they propose, they know it would be rejected, and bring on us all the dreadful consequences which they feelingly foretell, but which can never in the least alarm me. I have endeavoured to fall in with their opinions, but could not. We have a right in plain terms to refuse it, if we think proper. I have in my proposition adopted word for word the Virginia amendments, with one or two additional ones. We run no risk of being excluded from the union when we think proper to come in. Virginia our next neighbour will not oppose our admission. We have a common cause with her. She wishes the same alterations. We are of the greatest importance to her. She will have great weight in Congress, and there is no doubt but she will do every thing she can to bring us into the union. South Carolina and Georgia are deeply interested in our being admitted. The creek nation would overturn these two states without our aid. They cannot exist without North-Carolina. There is no doubt we shall obtain our amendments and come into the union when we please. Massachusetts, New-Hampshire and other states have proposed amendments. New-York will do so also if she ratifies. There will be a majority of the states, and the most respectable, important and extensive states also, desirous of amendments, and favourable to our admission. As great names have been mentioned, I beg leave to mention the authority of Mr. Jefferson, whose great abilities and respectability are well known. When the Convention sat in Richmond, in Virginia, Mr. Madison received a letter from him. In that letter he said he wished nine states would adopt it; not because it deserved ratification, but to preserve the union. But he wished that the other four states would reject it, that there might be a certainty of obtaining amendments. Congress may go on and take no notice of our amendments. But I am confident they will do nothing of importance till a Convention be called. If I recollect rightly, the Constitution may be ratified either by Conventions or the Legislatures of the states. In either case it may take up about eighteen months. For my own part, I would rather be eighteen years out of the union than adopt it in its present defective form.

Part 3

The Civil War Crisis

7

Social Change in Antebellum North Carolina

In 1860, wrote Guion Griffis Johnson in her classic study, *Ante-Bellum North Carolina* (1937), North Carolinians had witnessed extensive social, cultural, and economic changes. They had, she wrote, "lived to see the results of the inventions of the steam engine and of the spinning-jenny," while they had also seen telegraph cables linking them inside and outside the state. Stagecoaches gave way to "miles of railroads stretching north and south, east and west." The extension of political democracy was significant, as was the growth of educational facilities. After a "convulsion of religious emotion at the opening of the century," Protestantism gained new vigor and cultural authority. In short, according to Johnson, North Carolina was transformed from "a body politic emerging from the simplicities of the frontier to the complexities of civilized life," and "prophetic fingers" indicated a new future. The antebellum period "shaped the future; it was a time of origins which still control many ways of life in North Carolina."[1]

Between the Revolution and the Civil War, North Carolina underwent a significant social transformation. In the 1800s, North Carolina became known as the "Rip Van Winkle" State, so named because, like Washington Irving's fictional character, this was a state that had fallen asleep for many years and now awakened to a new, changed world. Long isolated geographically, the advent of the transportation revolution affected the state and its inhabitants with important consequences. Railroads, which were first constructed in North Carolina during the 1830s and spread across the state during the next three decades, meant greater ease and speed of movement for the people of every region. From the Appalachians to the Piedmont to the Atlantic coast, improved transportation brought increased contact with the national and international markets, ushering in heightened commercialization of agriculture and the stirrings of industrialization. At the same time, white and black migrants moved across the state, and North Carolina's population continued to grow substantially. But there were also real limits to the changes of the antebellum era. Despite economic expansion, much of the state remained outside of the market economy.

North Carolina: Change and Tradition in a Southern State, Second Edition. William A. Link.

During these years, a large portion of the state's white and black population left North Carolina to take up residence in the booming cotton regions of the Deep South. Although slavery spread into the interior and across much of the state, large portions remained fiercely nonslaveholder. North Carolina was a state of distinct contrasts, and the antebellum era ended as the tensions these constraints spawned boiled over into crisis.

Economic Change in the Antebellum Era

Although transportation improvements helped bring increasingly more North Carolinians into the market economy, traditional economic activities remained important. North Carolinians continued to produce large amounts of corn; even in the late stages of the Civil War, the state's corn crop fed half of Robert E. Lee's Army of Northern Virginia. Naval stores, historically the dominant extractive industry of the Cape Fear valley, remained important, and on the eve of the Civil War, some 1,500 distilleries produced more than 65 percent of the turpentine produced in the United States.

Antebellum North Carolina also became a major producer of gold during the 1820s and 1830s. One newspaper in 1831 described it as the "golden state, from the great lumps of precious metal found there."[2] Before 1829, North Carolina produced all of the gold coined at the Philadelphia Mint, and in the 1830s gold mining was next to agriculture in terms of its economic importance. Gold was first discovered in 1799 in North Carolina by John Reed, a Hessian soldier who had taken up residence in Cabarrus County. His son found a shiny object while fishing, and the family used it as a doorstop for a few years. In 1802, Reed took the large nugget to a jeweler in Fayetteville, who melted it down and made it into a bar six inches long. The jeweler gave Reed $3.50 for the gold, though it was reportedly worth $8,000. Reed then searched neighboring creeks, and in the next few years found more nuggets, the largest of which weighed 28 pounds. Reed organized a mining company, which by 1848 had extracted as much as $10 million in gold.

A gold rush swept the southern Piedmont during the 1820s, with prospecting and mining in Cabarrus, Burke, Anson, Mecklenburg, and Montgomery Counties. "I have heard scarce anything since my arrival, except gold," wrote a visitor in 1829.

> Nothing before has ever so completely engrossed the attention of all classes of the community in this section ... Those who have been esteemed prudent and cautious, embark in speculation with the greatest enthusiasm—bankrupts have been restored to affluence, and paupers turned nabobs.

PERSONAL.

Hon. Samuel J. Pemberton was here Tuesday.

Mr. John Correll went to Albemarle Tuesday to live.

Mr. Jno. A. Barnhardt, of Pioneer Mills, was here yesterday.

Mrs. Jas. C. Gibson spent Tuesday afternoon in Charlotte.

Judge Montgomery is attending court at Shelby this week.

Mr. Parks King, of Davidson College, was home several days this week.

Dr. and Mrs. A L. Petrea, of Charlotte, were visiting here this week.

Mrs. Dr. Garrison returned to her home at Bessemer City last Saturday.

Mrs. C. F. Ritchie, of Salisbury, was visiting at her father's, Mr. G. W. Patterson.

Miss Ivy Cross, of China Grove, was visiting last Sunday at her father's in No. 1.

Mr. T. L. Ross, superintendent of the cotton factory at China Grove, was here Monday.

Miss Jessie Deaton left yesterday for Lynchburg, Va., where she will visit Mrs. N. T. Smith.

Mrs. W. R. Kindley, of Mt. Pleasant, is visiting her daughter, Mrs. L. E. Heilig, at Salisbury.

Miss Laura Parish, who has been teaching school at Weaverville, returned home here Saturday night.

—Miss Blanche McAllister, of Mt. Pleasant, and Miss Lula Cook, of St. John's, were visiting in Concord Tuesday.

Mrs. Graham, who has been visiting her sister Mrs. Dr. J. P. Gibson, returned to her home in Lexington, Va., yesterday morning.

Mr. T. E. Smith, of Stockholm, Sussex county, N. J., who has been here for several weeks with Mr. W. S. Bingham hunting snipe, left last night for home.

Democratic Ward Meetings.

The Democratic primaries of the town of Concord met in the various wards Monday night to select candidates for aldermen and school commissioners. They were all well attended, and the Democrats are enthusiastic.

The following men were chosen from the various wards:

Ward No. 1—Aldermen, L. D. Duval and W. C. Houston. School commissioner, W. R. Odell.

Ward No. 2—Aldermen, Jas. C. Fink and R. F. Coble. School commissioner, D. B. Coltrane.

Ward No. 3—Aldermen, Jno. K. Patterson and R. A. Brown. School commissioner, Jno. A. Cline.

Ward No. 4—Aldermen, C. W. Swink and M. L. Brown. D. B. Morrison, school commissioner.

The following were appointed delegates to the town convention next Saturday night in the court house:

No. 1—S. L. Montgomery, T. C. Wilson, Robert Duval, Harry Deaton, J. P. Hornbukle, W W. Deaton, Jas. F. Hurley, Andrew Grier, W. A. Wilkinson, J. F. Harris, John Creech and F. B. Haydock.

No. 2—All Democrats were appointed delegates.

No. 3—John R. Patterson, A. G. Bost and C. M. Sappenfield.

No. 4—D. P. Dayvault, Col. Paul B. Means, Charles Dry, Elam King, W. W. Stuart, A. B. Young and Dr. J. E. Smoot.

Let every Democrat attend the convention next Saturday night. Mayor

A 22-POUND GOLD NUGGET.

FOUND AT THE REED MINE IN NO. 9 LAST THURSDAY.

Mr. J. L. Shinn the Lucky Finder—Description of the Find, and Other History of This Famous Mine.

On last Thursday morning about 11 o'clock a nugget of gold weighing 22½ pounds Troy was found at the already famous Reed mine in No. 9 township, this county. Messrs. Jacob L. Shinn, D. M. Cox, Jesse Cox and Adam Canup were working the mine at the time. They were digging about three and a half feet under the surface. Mr. Shinn unearthed the precious nugget, and came near casting it aside. He took a second look at it, however, and its appearance made him examine it more closely. He alone (the others not knowing about his find) took it to the branch and washed it. He at once saw what he had found, and cried out: "Boys, I've got it!" The other men went to where he was, and when they saw the treasure they could hardly contain themselves.

Dr. Lisle, one of the owners of the mine, who lives near, was at once informed, and they say the doctor was almost as much excited as uncle Jesse Cox, whose excitement and joy found expression in continued shouts. One of the other men told him if he didn't hush he would alarm the neighborhood, but Dr. Lisle told him to shout on, as he had something to shout for.

The men worked on until 4 o'clock in the afternoon, when Dr. Lisle had his conveyance hitched up and carried them and their find over to Georgeville. As they entered the village Mr. Cox heralded the fact as he went, and soon the whole neighborhood was all excitement. Hundreds of people went to Widenhouse & Shinn's store to examine the nugget.

The nugget weighs 17 pounds avoirdupois, or 22½ pounds Troy. As there are 240 pennyweights in a Troy pound, there would therefore be 5400 pennyweights in the chunk. At 90 cents a pennyweight the nugget would, if it were all gold, be worth $4,866. It is estimated that there are at least five pounds of quartz in the nugget.

Dr. Lisle came up to Concord on Saturday bringing the nugget with him. It was deposited in the Concord National Bank for safe keeping for the present. It is about 4 inches in diameter and 10 inches long. If it were not for a few shining spots over it, it would look like a common flint rock. Its weight, however, tells the tale, as a rock of the same would not weigh over five pounds. Dr. Lisle took the nugget to Charlotte yesterday.

The Reed mine is now owned by Messrs. O. S. and O. W. Kelley, and Dr. J. D. Lisle, of Springfield O. Dr. Lisle lives near the mine. The mine was being operated by Messrs. J. L. Shinn, D. M. and Jesse Cox and Dr. J. R. Jerome, who got half the output. Each man will, therefore, get one eighth the amount the nugget brings, the owners getting one-half. The day before the nugget was found Mr. Jesse Cox offered to sell out to Dr. Jerome for five dollars.

The first gold ever discovered in the United States was found at the Reed mine, and also the largest nugget. The last discovered nugget is the second largest ever found in the country.

The present nugget will no doubt be sold for much more than its intrinsic value, as it will be valuable as a curiosity for all time to come, and will be much sought after.

We find in Wheeler's History of North Carolina the following history of the Reed mine, furnished that book by

mine. After referring to the facts above, he says:

"So much for the facts in the written history of this mine. But there is an unwritten history. Tradition says that there was found more than fifty years ago a piece much larger than any above mentioned. It is said that Mr. Martin Phifer, once associated with Mr. Reed, for many years bought the products of the mine—that he bought three pieces from three different parties—that these pieces fitted together exactly, showing that they had been cut apart with a chisel or some sharp instrument, but the fourth piece, which had been cut from them and was evidently of the same size and weight, never came to hand- was never heard of. These three pieces weighed 60 pounds, and of course the other being of the same size and weight of the other three, the entire nugget weighed eighty pounds!

"This statement will not be accepted as true, but many people in this vicinity believe it. Three of the Messrs. Widenhouse, in and around Georgeville, say they have heard their late venerable father say many times that he knew Reed and Phifer well, and that he had heard both of them, especially Mr. Phifer, tell the story of the large nugget, and vouched for the truth of the statement."

The following telegram from Springfield, O., the home of the owners, appeared in the daily papers of Tuesday:

A syndicate of Ohians who began prospecting in North Carolina about three years ago for gold have struck it rich. Ex-Mayor O. S. Kelley, the millionaire manufacturer, who was recently appointed a commissioner to the Mexican exposition by Gov. Bucknell, who is a member of the syndidate, received a telegram from Dr. J. D. Lisle, late of this city, who has been superintending the mining for the last eight months, stating that a chunk of ore, almost a nugget, weighing 21 pounds and 2 ounces had been found, which an assay showed to be worth over $4,000. Other finds of lesser richness, but at the same time very profitable, have been found and as a consequence excitement is running high.

Just before the war broke out capitalists began working the locality for gold, but with the internecine strife raging work was abandoned and not until a few months ago were any further efforts made to find the hidden treasure. It was in the vicinity of the Concord mines that the largest nugget known was found back in the fifties.

A big rush to the new eldorado is expected. It is probable that people from here will go to Concord at an early date. Besides the ex-Mayor and Dr. Lisle, Warren Kelly, a well known manufacturer, also of this city, is in the syndicate.

The Salisbury Herald has this:

It must be remembered that the Reed mine is not the only North Carolina property that produces big nuggets. In late years an 8lb., 4lb. 3oz. and a 2lb. piece has been found at the Sam Christian mine in Montgomery county. A 9lb., 3½ lb., 1½ and 1¼ pound piece at the Parker and 2¼ lb., 3½ lb. and a 10 lb. piece at the Crawford, a 1¾ lb. piece at the Fesperman, in Stanly county, and a 2½ lb. piece at the Nugget mine in Cabarrus county, about a mile and a half from the Reed mine.

A writer in yesterday's Charlotte Observer gives us the following:

As to gold nuggets, the largest found in the United States was that discovered in Sierra county, California, August 21, 1857, by one J. J. Finney. Its weight was about 343 pounds and value nearly $90,000. Several other nuggets and masses of gold with quartz attached

Chairman Holton Here.

Mr. A. E. Holton, of Winston, Chairman of the Republican State committee, was here Monday in conference with the faithful. He was on a mission to feather his own and Dockery's nest. He had a conference in the afternoon at Patterson's Hall with a dozen or more prominent Republicans, most of whom were colored.

Holton thinks he has gotten where he can defy Butler now. In talking recently regarding Butler's statement that there were no conditions as to his election to the Senate, Holton said:

"I don't want to discuss this matter with Senator Butler in advance of a meeting of the committees of the two parties but when he lays down his terms and declares that Republicans must come up and take his test oath, which virtually puts them out of their party and one that no self respecting Republican will think of accepting, and no Populist who desires co-operation would think of demanding, he is going too far.

"The only hope for Populists and Republicans to have co-operation this year is for Senator Butler to either get out of the way himself or abandon his position. I don't believe he has any idea of fusing with us. He wants to build up his own party on silver lines, drawing from Republicans and Democrats, for he is no sucker; any man, to make such demands as he has recently, expecting to get them from the Republican organization, is wanting in ordinary intelligence, and this we do not accuse him of."

No. 6 News.

Farmers are busy planting corn, and getting ready to plant cotton seed.

There will be a good deal of fertilizer used in our community, and a large crop of cotton will be planted this spring.

Mr. William A. Foil, has returned to school at N. C. College, Mt. Pleasant.

The exhibition at the Cruse school house, was a grand success to teacher and scholars and was enjoyed.

Dr. Woods, and Col. Propper, of Colorado were in our community a few days ago hunting up mining property.

Mr. Goodman and family, of Forest Hill, were in our community Sunday, their old home.

The J. C. Watts gold mine was bonded to Dr. Woods, and will be worked by Col. Propper of the Culp mine. Work will begin in a few days.

A rich mine of gold was discovered on the land of Mr. Wellington Moose a few days ago.

THE TIMES is a welcome visitor and we hope it will always succeed.

The politicians must be dead in our part of the country or keeping very quiet. No. 6 is pretty well represented, we have Reps, Pops and Dems.

DEMOCRAT.

The Times Till After the Election for 50 Cents.

We will send THE TIMES from now until after the November election for only 50 cents. This is going to be an exceedingly lively campaign—probably the most interesting we have ever known, and everybody ought to have a paper. We propose to keep up with the procession and keep our readers thoroughly posted about what is going on. The above price is very low—over seven months for only half a dollar. Make us up a club of six and we will send an extra copy free.

When Traveling.

Whether on pleasure bent, or business, take on every trip a bottle of Syrup of Figs, as it acts most pleasantly and effectually on the kidneys, liver, and

Figure 7.1 Newspaper article announcing the discovery of a 22-pound gold nugget at the Reed Mine. *Source: Courtesy of the State Archives of North Carolina.*

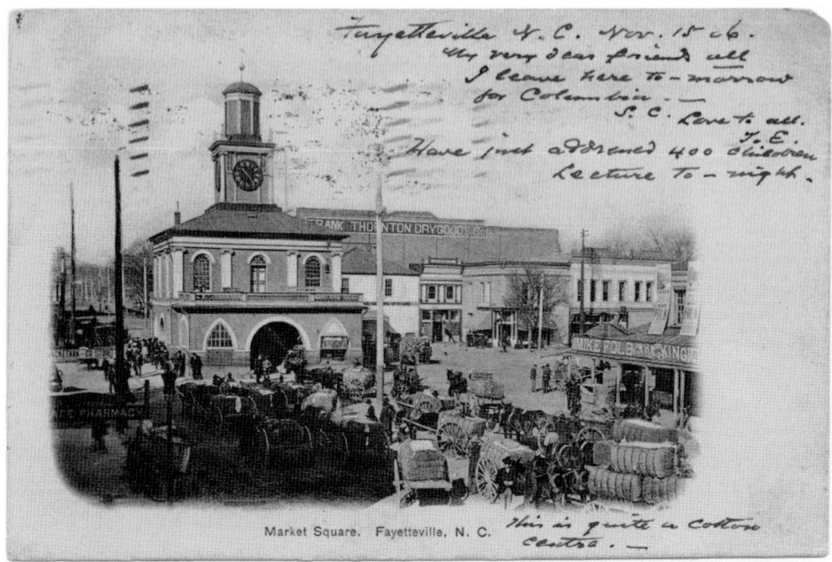

Figure 7.2 Commercial activity in Market Square, Fayetteville, 1832. *Source: North Carolina Collection, University of North Carolina Library at Chapel Hill.*

By the 1830s, 30,000 people were working in gold mining in North Carolina, with some of the largest mines employing as many as 1,000 workers. Boom towns housed workers and supplied the mining camps. A number of these towns sprang up and went out of existence in short order, though two that survived, Charlotte and Morganton, continued as significant urban centers. Men and women alike worked in the mines; women were described as having "great acumen in selecting the best gold-bearing lands and … very expert in panning it." Thousands of African American slaves worked in the mines, side by side with whites. The mines also attracted temporary immigrants, including Welsh, Scottish, Cornish, Irish, Swedish, Polish, Italian, and Portuguese miners, among other ethnic groups.[3]

At the same time, the expanding marketplace opened up opportunities for commercialized agriculture. In the antebellum era, the spread of commercial crops followed railroads, and in interior North Carolina, the most important of these crops were bright leaf tobacco and cotton. By the 1820s, older areas of traditional tobacco cultivation were in decline, as demand abroad stagnated for pipe and chewing tobacco. In short, tobacco planters never recovered from the American Revolution, which ended the protected status for their crop within the British Empire. Especially in eastern North Carolina, soil exhaustion also contributed to the decline of tobacco culture. At the turn of the nineteenth century, tobacco planters faced declining yields and low prices. But by the end of the antebellum period, tobacco revived with a rise in the demand for bright leaf and flue-cured tobacco. In northern Piedmont North Carolina counties extending from Halifax and Granville to Caswell to the west, a small boom in tobacco cultivation occurred in the 1840s.

Meanwhile, the rise of cotton spread to portions of North Carolina. The invention of the cotton gin in 1793 by Eli Whitney provided a way to remove mechanically cotton seeds from short-staple cotton, a strain more frost-resistant and better suited to the upland South. While one laborer could hand-pick a pound or two of cotton per day, after the invention of the cotton gin, one worker could clean 350 pounds a day. As in much of the South, cotton was "king," but it spread only to those portions of North Carolina with access to railroads and proper soil and weather conditions. The centers of cotton production were confined to portions of the eastern Coastal Plain and the Piedmont counties bordering South Carolina. The expansion of cotton culture was especially marked during the 1850s, when production in North Carolina doubled.

Indians in the Age of Jackson

The growth of the market economy, and the spread of white population across the state, brought additional pressures on North Carolina Indians. Since first contact in the late 1500s, despite widespread social dislocation, Indians had found ways to adapt and survive. Indian peoples regrouped into new confederations. The Catawba Nation, for example, was originally a Sioux-speaking group in an area spread across the Catawba River valley, in the Piedmont region of North Carolina and South Carolina. After the Yamasee War of 1713, which pitted Indians against lowcountry South Carolinians, Catawbas absorbed the remnants of some thirty different refugee Indian tribes. After several devastating epidemics, their population had been reduced to around 500 people by 1759. Siding with patriots during the Revolution, a choice that helped them to survive, the Catawbas retreated in the face of a growing white presence into an enclave after 1840 on the western banks of the Catawba River. Though reduced in numbers, Catawbas have maintained their identity to the present day.

Similarly, in Robeson County, Indians had lived since the 1600s in semi-independent bands outside of white control. As they were known in the twentieth century, Lumbees shared a group identity and a sense of their past. Some would later claim that Lumbees were descended from the Lost Colonists of Roanoke, while others would suggest that they were related to Cherokees and Tuscaroras. The most likely explanation, however, is that, like the Catawba Nation, the Lumbees were an amalgamated group of refugee Indians, many of them originally Sioux-speaking, who acquired a new, collective identity in the region in which the Lumbee River empties into the upper Pee Dee. Local whites, for their part, had trouble putting Lumbees into a racial category, and, beginning in 1835, the constitution of that year classified them as "free persons of color," taking away their right to vote and denying them the right to bear arms; in essence, white North Carolina lumped all nonwhites into a single category. Not until 1885 did a special Act of the North Carolina General Assembly recognize these Indians as the Croatan Indians of Robeson County, and in that year school officials established separate and segregated schools for Indians. Moreover, the state established the Croatan Normal School to train Indian teachers; this institution eventually became UNC-Pembroke. While from 1911 to 1913, the designation was changed to "Indians of Robeson County," after 1913 they became the Cherokee Indians of Robeson County. In 1953, the legislature recognized the group as the Lumbee Indians. Though the federal government recognized Lumbees as a tribe in 1956, they specifically excluded them from the rights and privileges extended to other Indians. Since then, Lumbees, though they are the largest group of Indians on the Eastern Seaboard, have attempted unsuccessfully to obtain full federal recognition and the benefits that come with it.

During the 1820s and 1830s, land-hungry whites sought Indian lands. North Carolina Cherokees, after their disastrous alliance with the British during the Revolution, were a conquered people, and their lands remained under the control of the new federal government. During the 1790s, federal officials began efforts to "civilize" Cherokee culture and society. The Cherokees seemed open to the idea, with many of them adopting white ways, including sedentary agriculture, trade with whites, and even slaveholding. During the 1820s, an educator named Sequoyah created a Cherokee syllabary in which the syllables of their language were reduced to eighty-five symbols to produce a written language. The *Cherokee Phoenix*, published in English and Cherokee, first appeared in 1828.

But the adoption of white culture did not stem the further erosion of Cherokee landholding, primarily in Georgia, South Carolina, and western North Carolina, and between 1783 and 1819 they lost some 69 percent of their lands. Also by this time, a significant number of Cherokees, about a quarter of

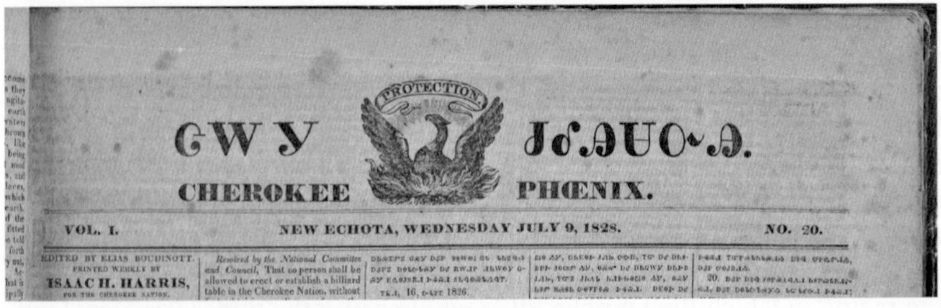

PROTECTION

ᏣᎳᎩ ᏧᏬᏪᎳᏅᎯ.

CHEROKEE PHŒNIX.

VOL. I. NEW ECHOTA, WEDNESDAY JULY 9, 1828. NO. 20.

EDITED BY ELIAS BOUDINOTT.
PRINTED WEEKLY BY
ISAAC H. HARRIS,
FOR THE CHEROKEE NATION.

Figure 7.3 Masthead for the *Cherokee Phoenix*. *Source: American Antiquarian Society.*

the population, were of mixed-race ancestry. Protestant missionaries sought to convert Indians to Christianity and to establish schools, and about 12 percent of the Cherokee Nation by 1860 had become Christian. Some Cherokees also became slaveholders and took up plantation agriculture. A series of treaties with the United States government after 1791 offered federal protection in exchange for further cessions of land and the guarantee of new lands west of the Mississippi. In 1819, still another treaty was negotiated, which resulted in the cession of another 4 million acres of Cherokee lands to whites, but at this point the Cherokee National Council announced its determination to resist any further loss of land.

Andrew Jackson, elected president of the United States in 1828 with a promise to expand lands available to whites at the expense of southeastern Indians, pursued a policy of removal. Reflecting a frenzy for land and development, and a new, frankly racist posture toward Indians, removal marked an important change in Indian-white relations. Between 1796 and 1833, about 4,000 Cherokees—sensing the hostile mood of the United States government and people—had voluntarily moved to lands in present-day northeastern Oklahoma. Under Jackson, federal authorities intended to force the rest of the Cherokees to move. In 1830, Congress enacted the Indian Removal Act, which provided for the forcible relocation of thousands of Cherokees across the Southeast to lands west of the Mississippi. In May 1838, the Cherokees came under military rule, as Gen. Winfield Scott led a force of soldiers that interned Cherokees from North Carolina and surrounding states in three relocation camps. Many remained under poor and insanitary conditions for much of the summer of 1838, with many of them dying in the wake of epidemic diseases that swept through the squalid camps. About 15,000 Indians were then led on a forced march west, despite bad planning and a lack of supplies, in an event that became known as the infamous Trail of Tears, in which approximately 4,000–5,000 Indians died before, during, or immediately after undertaking their arduous journey. One soldier remarked: "I fought through the Civil War and have seen men shot to pieces and slaughtered by the thousands, but Cherokee removal was the cruelest work I ever knew."[4]

While most North Carolina Cherokees were deported in the Trail of Tears in 1838, some resisted the move. About 300–400 Indians sought refuge in the mountains. This small band was headed by the Indian leader Tsali. Although he was eventually caught and executed by federal forces, a contingent of Cherokees remained in the area. They eventually purchased a tract from local whites of about 83 square miles, most of it in present-day eastern Swain County and northern Jackson County, known as the Qualla Boundary. These Cherokee were permitted to remain and became known as the Eastern Band of the Cherokee Indians, though they were unaffiliated with the Cherokee Nation in Oklahoma. In 1924, the Qualla Boundary came under federal protection and was held in trust.

Table 7.1 The Expansion of Slavery, 1790–1860

	Whites	Free Blacks	Slaves	Total
1790	288,204	4,975	100,572	393,751
1800	337,764	7,043	133,296	478,103
1810	376,410	10,266	168,824	555,500
1820	419,200	14,612	205,017	638,829
1830	472,823	19,534	245,601	737,987
1840	484,870	22,732	245,817	753,419
1850	553,028	27,463	288,548	869,039
1860	629,942	30,463	331,059	992,622

The Growth of Slavery

During the 1700s, North Carolina had experienced rapid population expansion, with a stream of non-English immigrants flooding its interior regions. Meanwhile, large numbers of African and African American immigrants arrived with the spreading institution of slavery.

Overall, the slave population grew from more than 100,000 in 1790 to more than 331,000 in 1860, and, as a percentage of the total population, from about a quarter to about a third during the same period. The spread of commercial agriculture, mercantile activity, town growth, and industry—in short, any form of capitalist enterprise—brought more slaves into the state. As the river valleys of Piedmont and western North Carolina saw heightened commercial activity, they also experienced increased numbers of slaves. As cotton culture spread to the southern Piedmont counties of Mecklenburg, Anson, and Union, slavery came along with it.

Slavery's expansion was uneven across North Carolina. In the western third of the state, slightly more than 10 percent of the population was enslaved in 1860. But slavery's extent increased as one moved east. In 1860, slightly more than a quarter of the population in the Piedmont was enslaved, while during the same year slaves composed more than two-fifths of the population of eastern North Carolina. Although slavery became firmly established in North Carolina, its uneven presence reflected the mixed impact of the commercial economy. A small portion of households, between a quarter and a third, owned slaves in 1860—on the lower end of such proportions in the slaveholding South. Put another way, 72 percent of white families in the state owned no slaves in 1860. The slave population, although spreading westward, remained highly concentrated in the older plantation counties of eastern North Carolina. The largest numbers of slaves were located in regions with rapidly expanding populations: in the cotton-producing counties of the southern Piedmont and the bright-leaf tobacco-producing counties of the northern Piedmont that bordered Virginia.

Figure 7.4 Harriet Jacobs, 1894. *Source: Cabinet photograph by Gilbert Studios, Washington, D.C. Gold-toned albumin print. By permission. Public Domain.*

The growth of slavery coincided with the development of an African American community in North Carolina, and cultural institutions such as the family and religion became bastions of independence in an otherwise hard and humiliating situation. To be sure, as they always had, slaves actively resisted the institution in the antebellum era. Enslaved North Carolinians often committed petty crime against slaveholders' property, and slaves would sometimes pilfer livestock, food, or supplies as a way of compensating for the system's oppressive and exploitative nature. Slaveholders frequently complained about slaves' propensity for theft, and occasionally they brought them to court for punishment. Slaves were "sure to steal" their masters' food, said one contemporary, "believing that he has a right to do so; and pray who is there to dispute his right?"[5]

One of the most telling indictments against slaveholder society came from Harriet Jacobs, who in 1861 published *Incidents in the Life of a Slave Girl, Written by Herself.* Written under the pseudonym "Linda Brent," Jacobs's work has become perhaps the best-known account of slavery by an enslaved woman. Born and raised in Edenton, Jacobs described her path from slavery to freedom. She taught herself to read, and her literacy became a way of resisting the system. Managing to turn back the unwelcome sexual advances of her master, Dr.

James Norcom, Jacobs had an affair with an Edenton lawyer, Samuel Tredwell Sawyer, with whom she bore two children: far from a dalliance, the affair was, in her words, a "deliberate calculation" in which she had used her sexual power as a woman to liberate herself from bondage. "So much attention from a superior person was, of course, flattering," Jacobs recalled, and she "felt grateful for his sympathy, and encouraged by his kind words." There was "something akin to freedom," she wrote, "in having a lover who has no control over you, except that he gains by kindness and attachment." But Jacobs also recognized that this "educated and eloquent gentleman" was "too eloquent, alas, for the poor slave girl who trusted in him," and an "impassable gulf between us." Such was the condition of an enslaved woman, who "confuses all principles of morality, and, in fact, renders the practice of them impossible."[6]

Still threatened by Norcom, Jacobs took a further step toward freedom by escaping and eluding his control. In *Incidents*, she detailed how she spent about seven years hidden in her grandmother's attic in Edenton, stowed away with only enough space to lie down. Sawyer purchased her children, and eventually let Jacobs's daughter travel north. In June 1842, Jacobs left Edenton, departing by boat to Philadelphia, and thence on to New York City. Harriet Jacobs eventually settled in Rochester, New York, and along with her reunited family, worked in the abolitionist cause, speaking and promoting her life story.

While some enslaved people, like Jacobs, found freedom by running away, others resisted through other methods. When John Myrick, a white resident of Hertford County, tried to return home from Norfolk with some runaway slaves he had captured in December 1850, he was astonished to be insulted by a group of blacks, who not only jostled with him verbally but struck him with a brick. Myrick would have shot his black attackers "on the spot," according to one account, if he were not concerned for the well-being of innocent bystanders. Other forms of violent resistance went even further. As in other portions of the South, slave conspiracies were periodically exposed—though often alleged plots were more the product of slaveholder paranoia than reality. Slaveholders naturally feared insurrections, and they had vivid images of the consequences (for themselves and family members) of such upheaval in the 1791 uprising on the French Caribbean sugar island of Saint Domingue in which slaves burned some 300 plantations and brutally murdered whites, including women and children. After foiled slave revolts in Virginia—Gabriel's Rebellion in August 1800 and Nat Turner's uprising in August 1831—North Carolina slaveholders swiftly and brutally acted to repress any supposed insurrection. Like masters in any slave society, slaveholders in North Carolina lived in fear of insurrection, and in many localities periodic scares did occur. In December 1825, for example, Edgecombe County whites feared a slave insurrection that had been encouraged, a petition claimed, by "those preachers who under the semblance of religious worship instill into the minds of the blacks, the most diabolical opinions & prepare them for the perpetration of the most horrible crimes."[7]

Slavery and the Antebellum Social System

Slaveholder paranoia, though often exaggerated, was also reinforced by much evidence of slave restiveness. In 1816, authority for trying capital slave crimes was transferred from county courts to superior courts, while lesser crimes—for which the punishment was whipping—remained with county authorities. Various laws regulated slaves' behavior with whites: insolence toward whites, trespassing, sexual relations between black men and white women, teaching slaves to read and write, gambling, and holding religious services outside of white control. Whites in coastal North Carolina were especially susceptible to resistant slaves exerting freedom of movement aboard ships, and incoming ships often provided an avenue of escape—or of subversive behavior. Northern shipmasters were, by law, forbidden to have slaves or freed people aboard their vessels after sunset. Slaves' economic and spatial freedoms were restricted in other ways, as slaves were prohibited from owning property and keeping farm plots or raising livestock. The slave patrol, which had been established in 1753, gained wider powers and freedom to punish slaves who traveled at large, without their masters' permission, in legislation of 1779 and 1794. In response to the insurrection scare of 1802, the patrol system was authorized to conduct regular searches, and patrols could operate over several counties. In 1830, the slave patrols gained enlarged powers of arrest, and patrollers were instructed to disperse slave assemblies, apprehend runaways, combat slave theft, and arrest whites who bought or sold goods from slaves.

In 1829, the appearance of David Walker's *Appeal in Four Articles* created a furor in North Carolina. Walker (1785–1830) was an African American born in Wilmington who lived in Boston, where he sold secondhand clothing. Walker's *Appeal* provided a rousing call for slaves to resist their oppressors. "Are we MEN!!—I ask you, O my brethren! Are we MEN?" Walker declared. "Did our Creator make us to be slaves to dust and ashes like ourselves? Are they not dying worms as well as we? Have they not to make their appearance before the tribunal of Heaven, to answer for the deeds done in the body, as well as we?" African Americans should not "be so submissive to a gang of men" who had "always been an unjust, jealous, unmerciful, avaricious and blood-thirsty set of beings, always seeking after power and authority." Slaveholders might "want slaves, and want us for their slaves, but some of them will curse the day they ever saw us." Walker foresaw a coming cataclysm in which slaves rose up against their masters. "As true as the sun ever shone in its meridian splendor," he wrote, "my colour will root some of them out of the very face of the earth."[8]

Although Walker died mysteriously three months after his pamphlet was published, the adverse reaction among North Carolina slaveholders to the prospect of slave rebellion and insurrection suggested in Walker's *Appeal* was widespread and pervasive. The *Appeal* reached Wilmington in the summer of 1830, supposedly smuggled in on visiting ships and distributed by slaves.

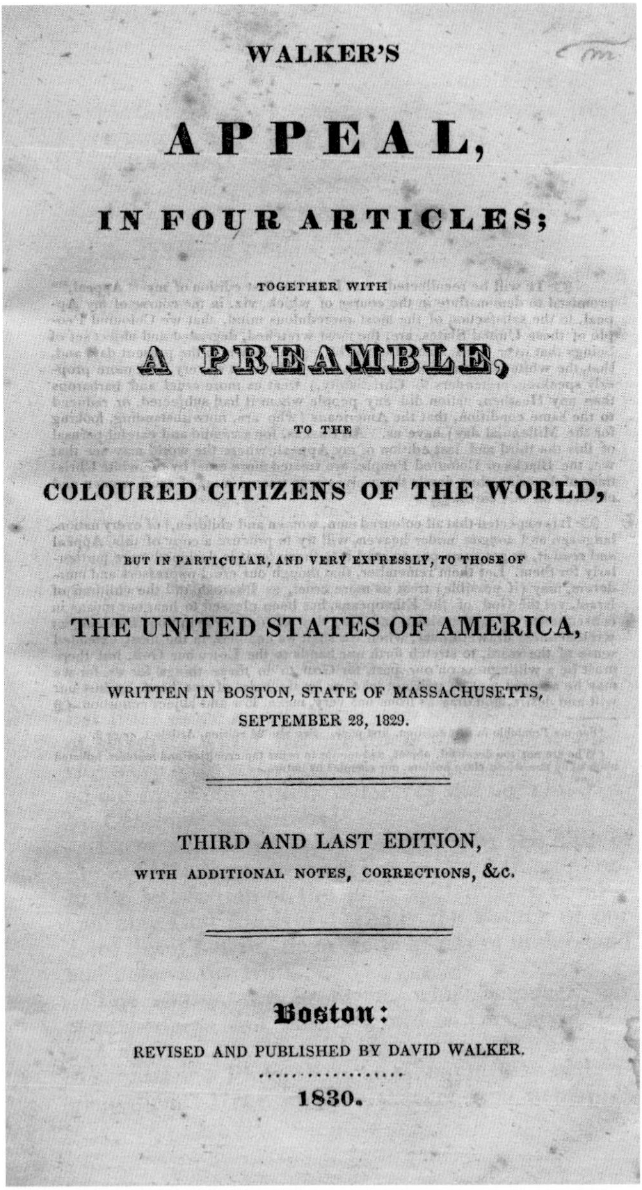

WALKER'S

APPEAL,

IN FOUR ARTICLES;

TOGETHER WITH

A PREAMBLE,

TO THE

COLOURED CITIZENS OF THE WORLD,

BUT IN PARTICULAR, AND VERY EXPRESSLY, TO THOSE OF

THE UNITED STATES OF AMERICA,

WRITTEN IN BOSTON, STATE OF MASSACHUSETTS,
SEPTEMBER 28, 1829.

THIRD AND LAST EDITION,
WITH ADDITIONAL NOTES, CORRECTIONS, &c.

Boston:
REVISED AND PUBLISHED BY DAVID WALKER.
....
1830.

Figure 7.5 David Walker's *Appeal*, title page. *Source: North Carolina Collection, University of North Carolina Library at Chapel Hill.*

Outraged and fearful, whites around the state demanded action, and Governor John Owen asked the General Assembly to address the matter in November 1830, when it convened in Raleigh. The legislature, meeting in secret session, enacted harsh measures designed to control the slave population, including prohibitions against teaching slaves to read and write, along with strict measures against the distribution of seditious literature. Manumissions of slaves were further limited, and freedom of movement by slaves and free blacks was now greatly restricted. In addition, all blacks entering North Carolina were quarantined, and contacts between blacks and those on visiting ships (presumably because they might possess the infectious spirit of the *Appeal*) were banned.

The pervasive fear that something might threaten slavery shaped the attitudes of North Carolina leaders. The views of Thomas Ruffin, the North Carolina supreme court judge who is generally regarded as one of the greatest jurists in the history of the state, are suggestive. Ruffin is often remembered for his decision in *State* v. *Mann* (1829), in which a white man was charged with assaulting a hired slave, Lydia. When she resisted a beating, he responded by shooting the woman in the back. The white man charged with murder, John Mann, possessed the same power as the master over the slave, according to Ruffin, and because the killing took place in an assertion of slaveholder authority, he had committed no crime. The institution of slavery required that the law "recognize the full dominion of the owner over the slave." The master's authority should not be undermined by courts. "The slave," said Ruffin, "to remain a slave, must be made sensible, that there is no appeal from his master; that his power is in no instance, usurped; but is conferred by the laws of man at least, if not by the law of God." Despite the right of slaves to life and the desire to protect them from abuse, "the power of the master must be absolute, to render the submission of the slave perfect."[9]

Subsequent cases did not completely sustain Ruffin's legal reasoning. In one of the best-known cases in North Carolina legal history, *State* v. *Will* (1834), a slave in Edgecombe County, Will, was convicted of murder when he killed a white overseer attempting to whip him. Will's defense attorney, B. F. Moore, argued that there were limits to which the master's authority could be exerted "without recurring responsibility." When the case went to the North Carolina Supreme Court, Judge William Gaston reversed the lower court decision. Although slaves owed unconditional submission to slaveholder authority, it was "certain that the master has not the right to slay his slave," Gaston wrote, "and I hold equally certain that the slave has a right to defend himself against the unlawful attempt of the master to deprive him of his life."[10]

Slaveholders in antebellum North Carolina were also uneasy about the growing free-black population. Although as early as 1715, the colonial assembly had made it illegal to manumit slaves except for meritorious conduct, numerous slaves were freed by masters, with the consent of county courts, over the course of the next 150 years. Manumitted slaves were required to leave the state within six months of obtaining their freedom. Some groups, such as Quakers, actually bought slaves and manumitted them and organized a North Carolina Manumission Society, which expanded during the 1820s and by 1826 had some twenty-three branches in the state. Moreover, the legislature continued to manumit slaves for meritorious service by special act, and petitions to the General Assembly for freeing slaves continued through the eighteenth and nineteenth centuries. In many other instances, slaves obtained freedom because they were the children of white fathers. Although the offspring of liaisons between white men and slave women were by law enslaved, in some instances white fathers made provisions for their children by freeing them.

Manumission thus continued to exist as a route to freedom. In 1833, Ned Hyman, a slave of Martin County, sought his freedom. He had gathered property, he said, and an estate worth five to six thousand dollars; the property was in his wife's name, a free black.[11] One of the best-known free blacks of antebellum North Carolina, John C. Stanly of New Bern, obtained his freedom in 1798 by a special act of the legislature. He then accumulated considerable property, bought and owned a number of slaves, and freed other slaves on his own. Like Hyman and Stanly, other free blacks succeeded in acquiring property and status, and some even owned slaves. Thomas Blacknall of Granville County was a slave and a skilled blacksmith and bell-maker. He bought his freedom for 1,000 acres of land and five slaves that he had accumulated. Perhaps the best-known free black in antebellum North Carolina was John Chavis. Born in Halifax County, Chavis served in the Revolution in the Fifth Virginia Regiment; after the war he was manumitted. He attended the Presbyterian Washington Academy (now Washington and Lee University) in Lexington, Virginia; it is possible that Chavis studied with John Witherspoon, president of Princeton, as a private student at the College of New Jersey. Chavis later served as a missionary for the Presbyterian Church and moved to North Carolina. In an extraordinary accomplishment for an African American during the slave regime, Chavis had become perhaps the best-educated black person of his day. Though a preacher, he was best known for the school he established in Raleigh in 1808. Teaching white students by day and black students by night, Chavis taught his students in Wake, Granville, and Chatham Counties.

Despite the accomplishments of individual free blacks, the late antebellum period saw white paranoia reach a new level. Even more new measures sought to restrict African American privileges. The constitutional convention of 1835 ended the possibility of free blacks voting; the constitution of 1776 had not specifically excluded African Americans from the franchise, and some blacks voted in early nineteenth-century North Carolina, to which many whites in North Carolina objected. Permitting free blacks to vote, said a group of New Bern petitioners in 1832, would "excite and cherish a spirit of discontent and disorder among the slaves." If a slave could regard a free black as "his associate

Figure 7.6 Plaster of bust of John Chavis. *Source: Commissioned artwork for Washington & Lee University, Lexington, Virginia.*

and equal … thus respectfully treated by men of high character," was the "barrier of opinion which alone keeps him in subjection … not effectively undermined?"[12] After the 1820s, various groups of North Carolina whites worked to colonize free blacks in West Africa; the American Colonization Society sponsored the emigration of 1,363 North Carolina African Americans between 1825 and 1860. Throughout the 1850s, there were proposals in the legislature to remove by force the free-black population from North Carolina. In 1859, the General Assembly enacted a new free-black code that restricted physical mobility, economic status, and legal rights of freed people of color. The new code limited the ability of free blacks to serve as preachers; it was a common fear among whites that black preachers would lead insurrection.

Women and Families

For most families, the basic units of social interaction and work were the household and the agricultural economy. Farmers, whether rich or poor, extended values of hospitality. Even the poorest of families would invite visitors to share in their meal of hominy and salt pork. Social life centered on the farm. Men amused themselves with communal activities such as corn shucking, whereas prosperous farmers might invite neighbors over to a large meal of meat, sweet potatoes, and pies, along with plenty of whiskey and brandy to drink. Men frequently gathered to hunt and fish, both of which were considered traditional rights of white males in the state. Taverns or inns, scattered in rural areas throughout the state, offered males another gathering space, as did courthouse towns during days on which the militia assembled for musters—at least twice a year—or on election days. Sports were part of male recreation at these gathering places, where horse racing, wrestling, bandy (a game related to golf), and "fives" (a game of hand tennis) were popular activities.

Women organized quilting bees that brought neighbors together. It was not uncommon at these events for women to dip snuff: commonly, the practice among rural North Carolina women was to dip a stick into a snuffbox, and then rub the stick along their teeth. By some accounts, dipping snuff was common among women of all classes across antebellum North Carolina. Women maintained responsibility for household management, and they worked arduously in cleaning, keeping fires (which meant hauling in wood), cooking (which usually entailed hauling in water), and caring for children—all very labor-intensive activities in an era in which all cleaning and laundry had to be done by hand, the only indoor heating came from fireplaces or stoves, and the only light from lamps or candles. Household management, complained one male planter after managing his home in his wife's absence for a few days, was "dirty, demoralizing & debasing in a high degree."[13]

In the antebellum era, most women lived in a highly patriarchal society, with well-defined, gender hierarchies that awarded control of economic resources and political power exclusively to men. At the same time, as improved transportation broke down the stifling effects of living in isolated regions and brought more goods, a market economy, and outside cultural influences to North Carolina, traditional gender roles underwent some pressure to change.

North Carolina women, like American women generally, lived in families that provided men nearly absolute legal, political, and economic power. The head of the family household was always male; legally, married women possessed no independent legal identity, though widows and single adult women could be heads of household. Nonetheless, courtship and marriage were crucial ingredients in the establishment of women's status, especially for property-holding families—even though marriage legally ended a woman's independent legal identity. Planter families followed elaborate courtship rituals, the most important being that prospective suitors meet the parents' standards of social and economic status. Typically, marriages occurred only after fathers provided their blessing, and parents were reluctant to approve of marriages across class lines. One suitor was thus described by a father as objectionable because he was "of the lower class & not such as can be agreeable to [our] character and disposition." Among planters, there was a frequent conflict among parents determined to maintain the family status through marriage, and their children, who were often guided by motives of love and affection. In the localized rural society that most white North Carolinians inhabited, there was also a limited pool of suitors, and there was a high incidence of intermarriage. Although the state legislature in 1841 declared that marriages of first cousins or closer first cousin were illegal, marriages of distant cousins or closer were not unusual.

By law, married women, with no independent legal identity, could not sue or be sued and could not own property separate from their husbands (this remained the case in North Carolina until 1911). Husbands were held responsible for their wives' actions; according to common law, if wives slandered or assaulted anyone, husbands had to pay damages. Husbands also owed their wives' debts, and if wives committed a misdemeanor, husbands remained accountable. By law, moreover, husbands possessed near-absolute physical power over their wives, and local authorities intervened in cases of domestic abuse only in the most extreme cases. In 1827, Thomas Ruffin noted that "altho' in civilized society it was universally considered as dishonorable and disgraceful for persons in elevated situations to lift their hands against their wives, yet the law was made for the great bulk of mankind." The only question, Ruffin said, was whether domestic abuse was "excessive, barbarous, and unreasonable."[14]

North Carolinians, white and black, defined themselves by kin and kinship connections, with family serving as the basis of education, socialization, and work, both farm work and the running of small businesses. In North Carolina, families were typically large. The average family size during the antebellum period remained between five and six children per family, but families exceeding ten children were not unusual. Families remained large, owing to the labor required in the household economy. Family members, especially for yeoman farmers without slaves, served as economic assets—and meant a larger work force. According to common law, children owed their fathers their labor, and their wages belonged to their fathers until majority, or the age of 21. Fathers had the right to require work from their children, either on their own farms or those of others. The trend of large families also reflected the reality of the high rate of childhood mortality, owing to poor sanitation and the prevalence of disease in North Carolina. According to one estimate, as many as one in four children did not live to the age of 5.

Yet family was also shaped by factors of race and class. Among slaves, the very existence of families was constantly undermined, as masters sold off their slaves and divided husbands from wives, children from parents. The concept of family varied according to social station. Planter families, especially the "great" planters owning significant numbers of slaves, began to see families as units of affection and nurturing—something akin to modern conceptions. Planter families adopted a different approach to childrearing, and among this class a kind of youth rebellion even began to manifest during the last part of the antebellum period. Children, complained one observer, "now treat parents, their relatives, their masters, with contempt." Children were permitted to "indulge a violent temper without punishment," complained a professor at the University of North Carolina, and "to domineer over slaves, and even fight their mothers, when they attempted to control them."[15] Yeoman families tended to see families as economic units in which the work force lay in the household unit of labor that included women and children. North Carolina white families were bound together by a concept of honor, and for planters and yeomen alike defending family honor and kinship connections was a cornerstone value that involved males. Honor thus formed a part of a patriarchal value system that pervaded society.

Evangelicalism and Cultural Change

Between the Revolution and the Civil War, the most important cultural influence in antebellum North Carolina was the spread of evangelical Christianity. During the colonial period, North Carolinians had remained a mostly unchurched people. Visitors often commented on the absence of churches and the hostility of locals to missionary activities. Beginning in the 1780s and 1790s, the arrival of evangelicals changed things. James McGready, a Presbyterian evangelist from Guilford County, helped to establish an interdenominational evangelical alliance in Piedmont North Carolina, and, along with evangelical leaders such as William McGhee and Barton Stone, helped to proselytize Orange County. In August 1801, McGready, McGhee, and Stone all participated in a massive revival at Cane Ridge, Kentucky. Carefully planned, even orchestrated, the famous meeting at Cane Ridge was the result of an interdenominational alliance of Baptists, Methodists, and Presbyterians. The event occurred over several days and attracted, according to some accounts, as many as 30,000 people who traveled some distance and stayed in tents. The revival was characterized by feverish emotionalism, as participants fell to the ground and exhorted others to embrace the feeling of the Holy Spirit.

Cane Ridge set off a wave of revivals across the South, the phenomenon sweeping through North Carolina soon thereafter (1801–02). This wave of revivals was followed by subsequent ones in 1829–35, the 1840s, and 1857–61. In North Carolina, the revivals became almost ritualized occurrences. Often set in the Cane Ridge "camp meeting" setting—complete with tents and itinerant ministers—the revivals enjoyed the support of Protestant denominations, who embraced evangelicalism as a way to expand their influence by reaching rural North Carolinians. Revivals emphasized individual conversion and spectacular, sometimes supernatural evidence of God's presence. Commonly, the events featured evangelical "exercises" that included dancing, jerking, wheeling, laughing, falling, and even barking. The Rev. Joseph Travis, an evangelical revivalist in North Carolina, described how participants in a meeting were "stricken

Figure 7.7 Camp meeting revival about 1801. *Source:* http://www.learnnc.org/lp/editions/nchist-newnation/4505

to the floor, as if shot by a deadly arrow" and for "an hour or so remained speechless, breathless, pulseless, and, to all appearances, perfectly dead."[16]

The popularity of the revival meetings transformed Protestantism in North Carolina. Evangelicalism succeeded in expanding church membership, but it also cemented evangelicalism as an organizing force in the state—and across the South. Evangelical churches gladly embraced their expanded social role, and they became enforcers of a new social code of behavior. Among evangelicals in North Carolina, evangelical churches impressed a code of individual piety and personal morality—rather than a social sense or an emphasis on community redemption. The records of one Methodist church in Person County, in northeastern North Carolina, bear this out. Like other Methodist churches, it operated a church court that tried infractions by its members. Between 1791 and 1860, the church court tried 501 cases. Twenty-one percent of the cases were for drunkenness, but a significant number included attempts to regulate personal morality, and included infractions such as promiscuity, illegitimate births, and marital conflict. In contrast, a relatively small number, about 13 percent, involved direct offenses against the church. In short, evangelical churches, which long had been on the fringes of the social order, were moving into an establishment position by the antebellum period.

The impact of evangelicalism was not confined to whites, as African Americans also participated in revivals. White evangelicals actively proselytized slaves, who saw an appealing message in revivalism. Early evangelicals promised equality of all people before God, a radical concept, a message that transcended traditional racial barriers. But because slaves were often barred from attending services with whites, black evangelicalism evolved on its own, becoming yet another bulwark of an independent and resistant slave culture.

At the same time, white evangelicals' position on slaves and slavery became another benchmark of the changing character of Protestantism in North Carolina. Evangelicalism had gone from a countercultural movement to a central part, even a pillar, of the mainstream society. Early evangelicals were, in fact, strongly antislavery. Methodists, for example, refused to permit their ministers to own slaves and applied strong pressures against those church members who did so. In 1780, a conference of North Carolina Methodists declared that slavery was "contrary to dictates of conscience and pure religion" and against the "laws of God, man and nature, and hurtful to society." Other evangelicals, to varying extents, expressed similar sentiments. Yet by the 1830s and 1840s, white evangelicals in North Carolina and elsewhere in the South had reversed themselves: rather than decrying slavery as immoral, they now ardently defended the institution. It is fair to say that the evangelical churches *had* to embrace slavery if they wanted to keep their powerful role in North Carolina society.

* * *

North Carolina underwent important social changes during the antebellum period, as the advent of a market economy exposed Tar Heels to a host of new forces. Farmers increasingly grew crops for consumption outside of their immediate community—for cash rather than subsistence—thanks to the ease of shipping their products at a more reasonable cost. The market also spurred the expansion of slavery: if anything, the slave society grew in importance and power wherever the market economy spread. A new ethos of race appeared to grip the state, typified by the Indian removal of the 1830s, and further solidification of the slave system. Women's status in the new economy changed, as old patterns of life eroded. At the same time, cultural life in North Carolina became more unified and interconnected through evangelicalism, which came to dominate not only religious life but social life. Meanwhile, social changes coincided with political changes, as North Carolinians faced, in the coming Civil War, the gravest crisis in their history.

Notes

1 Guion Griffis Johnson, *Ante-Bellum North Carolina: A History* (Chapel Hill: University of North Carolina Press, 1937), pp. vi–ix.

2 Fletcher M. Green, "Gold Mining: A Forgotten Industry of Ante-Bellum North Carolina," *North Carolina Historical Review* 14, no. 1 (January 1937): 3.

3 Ibid., pp. 10, 14.

4 William G. McLoughlin, *The Cherokees and Christianity, 1794–1870: Essays on Acculturation and Cultural Persistence* (Athens: University of Georgia Press, 1994), p. 95.

5 Johnson, *Ante-Bellum North Carolina*, p. 506.

6 Harriet A. Jacobs, *Incidents in the Life of a Slave Girl, Written by Herself* (Boston: Published for the Author, 1861), pp. 83–88.

7 Ibid., pp. 507, 515.

8 David Walker, *Walker's Appeal, in Four Articles* (Boston: n.p., 1830), pp. 19–20, 24.

9 *State* v. *Mann*, 13 N.C. 263 (1829); Sally Hadden, "Judging Slavery: Thomas Ruffin and *State* v. *Mann*," in Christopher Waldrep and Donald G. Nieman, eds., *Local Matters: Race, Crime, and Justice in the Nineteenth-Century South* (Athens: University of Georgia Press, 2001), pp. 1–2.

10 R. H. Taylor, "Humanizing the Slave Code of North Carolina," *North Carolina Historical Review* 2, no. 3 (July 1925): 327–28.

11 James Blackwell Browning, "The Free Negro in Ante-Bellum North Carolina," *North Carolina Historical Review* 15, no. 1 (January 1938): 27.

12 John Hope Franklin, *The Free Negro in North Carolina, 1790–1860* (Chapel Hill: University of North Carolina Press, 1943), pp. 107–8.

13 Johnson, *Ante-Bellum North Carolina*, p. 237.

14 Ibid., p. 242.

15 Ibid., p. 253.

16 Ibid., p. 398.

8

Political Parties and the Coming of the Civil War

The governmental and constitutional system in antebellum North Carolina was dominated by slavery: the constitution and the law protected slaveholders from slave rebellion, while also preserving a special status for the slaveholders (typically the upper class) in the political and legal system. In the early American republic, politics became democratized around the participation of white males, as, over time, restrictions limiting voting and officeholding for this group were loosened. By the 1830s, accompanying this expansion in white-male democracy was an intense and widespread interest in politics, featuring two aggressive political parties, the Whigs and the Democrats, and a deeply divided partisan culture sustaining voter interest. On the eve of the Civil War, however, the political system, especially on the national level, no longer accommodated sectional differences, and white North Carolinians saw the Union as a tightening noose that imperiled the liberty and political stronghold of white men.

From the Early Republic to the Jacksonian Era

In North Carolina, the constitution of 1776 had institutionalized the supremacy of the legislature, which exerted uncontested power over state courts and the executive by annually electing governors and appointing superior court judges. Legislative supremacy reinforced local hierarchies: local magistrates were also appointed by the legislature, and county courts appointed all local officials except for constable and sheriff. Most magistrates were slaveholders, even in counties with relatively few slaves; in antebellum North Carolina, slaveholding was tied to wealth, status, and political power. Since election to the General Assembly depended on the support of local grandees, the system was self-perpetuating (though there were periodic revolts against such control), with local oligarchies and statewide political power dependent on legislative supremacy.

North Carolina: Change and Tradition in a Southern State, Second Edition. William A. Link.

From the 1790s until the 1820s, one-party political control dominated politics in North Carolina. In national politics, the advent of Federalist policies such as the chartering of a national bank and raising the import tariff on foreign-made goods in order to stimulate American industry seemed to favor northern business interests over those of southern agriculturalists. The opponents of the Federalist regime, rallied by Thomas Jefferson and James Madison, became known as Republicans, and their states'-rights message had a strong appeal to Tar Heel voters. Republicans attracted their strongest support in the northern counties bordering Virginia. Federalists persisted in pockets of North Carolina—in towns and commercial centers, in the northeastern part of the state, in Fayetteville and the Upper Cape Fear valley, and in the southern Piedmont. Not surprisingly, these were all areas with a significant loyalist presence during the Revolution. The great majority of North Carolina's voters became Jeffersonian Republicans, though Federalists remained a competitive minority until after the War of 1812. As late as 1816, Federalists held 40 percent of the seats in the legislature's lower house, the house of commons.

The career of Nathaniel Macon, one of the most important figures of the Jeffersonian era, exemplified Republican dominance in North Carolina. Born in Warren County in 1758, Macon attended the College of New Jersey (later Princeton University) and entered state politics in 1781, when he was elected to the state senate. A follower of antifederalist Willie Jones, Macon served from 1791 to 1815 in the US House of Representatives, where he emerged as a powerful Jeffersonian Republican. After holding numerous powerful committee chairmanships in the House, Macon served as Speaker of the House. In 1815, he left the House and gained a seat in the US Senate, where he served for the next thirteen years. Along with other so-called Old Republicans, Macon opposed expanding the power of the federal government.

One-party Republican control began to recede in the 1820s, when the Revolutionary generation receded and the country began moving toward a new, post-Revolutionary era. The Republican congressional caucus backed Georgia congressman William H. Crawford for the presidency in the election of 1824, but an insurgent "Peoples'" ticket backed Tennessee war hero Andrew Jackson. Riding a political wave and carrying forty-two of North Carolina's counties, Jackson captured 57 percent of the popular vote in the state. Although Jackson would eventually lose the presidential election of 1824—which was decided in the House of Representatives—to John Quincy Adams, "Old Hickory's" appeal to ordinary folk and those who had previously found themselves shunted to the political periphery by the rich and powerful was nothing short of spectacular. Indeed, Jackson had spearheaded a political revolution that smashed the one-party Republican control of politics. The dawn of the so-called Jacksonian era ushered in a new age in democracy. The advent of the market revolution and the first stage of US industrialization posed new challenges to public policy and raised important new questions. What role would state governments play in the economic expansion? How much and to what extent should states encourage and foster their own economic growth? To what extent was the construction of a transportation system the responsibility of government, and which portions of the population should receive governmental support and subsidy? What role should government play in banking?

An equally important political issue was the future of the relationship between slavery and the federal government. During the Missouri Compromise crisis of 1819–21, Congress became paralyzed over whether slaveholders could transport their slave property to the newly acquired Louisiana Territory and whether or not the new states organized out of the territorial governments would permit slavery. Although the crisis was solved through a political compromise that established a boundary of 36' 30", north of which slavery could not expand, it also raised fundamental issues about the need to protect slavery and slaveholders. The Missouri Compromise effectively suppressed further discussion of slavery at a national level for another generation, but it also added a new urgency and importance to politics and the political system of the 1820s and 1830s. Fears of expanded powers of the national government—for example, in the form of a protective (import) tariff or a series of federal internal-improvements policies, many of which were undertaken in the Northeast—were usually wrapped up into fears about the imposition of limitations on slaveholders.

Four years after his defeat in the presidential election of 1824, Jackson was swept into the White House in 1828, taking practically everything outside of New England. In North Carolina, Jackson won in a landslide, attracting 75 percent of the state's popular vote and carrying fifty-five of the state's sixty-three counties. Accompanying Jackson's 1828 landslide was a surge in interest and participation in politics. Between 1824 and 1828, voter turnout increased by 44 percent; voters took a deep interest in the issues of the day and Jackson's combative political style. Reelected in 1832, Jackson left a permanent imprint on politics in North Carolina and the nation. Yet Old Hickory's controversial personality and his all-or-nothing political style further divided voters. Jackson, for example, vehemently opposed the rechartering of the Bank of the United States, mounting a populist, anti-elitist campaign to destroy its power. In so doing he alienated commercial interests, including residents of North Carolina's towns, who saw the Bank as a stabilizing financial institution. On the other hand, Jackson stridently opposed South Carolina's attempt to nullify, or declare void, the federal tariffs of 1828 and 1832, and he asserted the right of the US government to suppress the South Carolinians' nullification of federal legislation. The South Carolinians provoked the nullification crisis because of their fears about stronger federal authority—and the ability of a strong national government to restrict slavery. The conflict over nullification also became subsumed into a personality conflict between Jackson and South Carolina senator John C.

Calhoun. While Jackson's strong position on nullification rallied Unionists, it alienated advocates of states' rights in North Carolina and the rest of the South.

The Constitution of 1835

The Jacksonian era exposed the antiquated nature of North Carolina's constitution. Not only did the constitution of 1776 institutionalize oligarchic control by county elites, it also skewed political power toward the slaveholding counties of eastern North Carolina. The constitution established a county basis for representation in which each county, regardless of population, sent the same number of representatives and senators to the legislature. This system naturally led to inequitable political representation. By 1815, although a majority of the state's whites lived west of Raleigh, most political power remained with easterners. In 1816, North Carolina had a total white population of nearly 387,000: that year, thirty-seven counties comprising almost 153,000 whites were represented by 111 legislators, while the other 234,000 whites living in the other twenty-five counties had only 75 legislators. In other words, roughly one-third of the state managed to elect a majority in the General Assembly.

As early as 1801, North Carolinians began to call for constitutional revisions, and these calls picked up after the War of 1812. Thereafter, North Carolina legislatures, in East-West votes, defeated proposals to call a constitutional convention to revise the document. In the face of solid eastern opposition, proreform groups organized a movement to pressure the legislature to act on the matter. A convention of forty-seven reformers met in Raleigh in November 1823 and demanded the convening of a convention, but the legislature rejected their plea. In the early 1830s, President Andrew Jackson's appeals to political egalitarianism gave the reformers additional momentum. Westerners insisted on change; some even threatened revolutionary measures. Sectional solidarity eroded when easterner townspeople supported constitutional reform because it might stimulate state support for internal improvements, or publicly subsidized transportation facilities such as roads, canals, and, eventually, railroads.

In January 1835, the legislature finally gave way and approved a bill authorizing the meeting of a state constitutional convention. The bill required that delegates to the convention own at least 100 acres of land, and it forbade the convention from altering the property-holding qualifications governing the election of state senators. In contests for the house of commons, it should be noted, voters could be propertyless, as long as they were at least 21 years old, male, a resident of the state for a year, and had paid some taxes. The constitution of 1776 did not explicitly require that voters be white, and free blacks could in some instances qualify to vote. On the other hand, the North Carolina senate remained a bastion of property and slaveholding, even after the constitutional convention of 1835, when only half of white males could vote in state senate

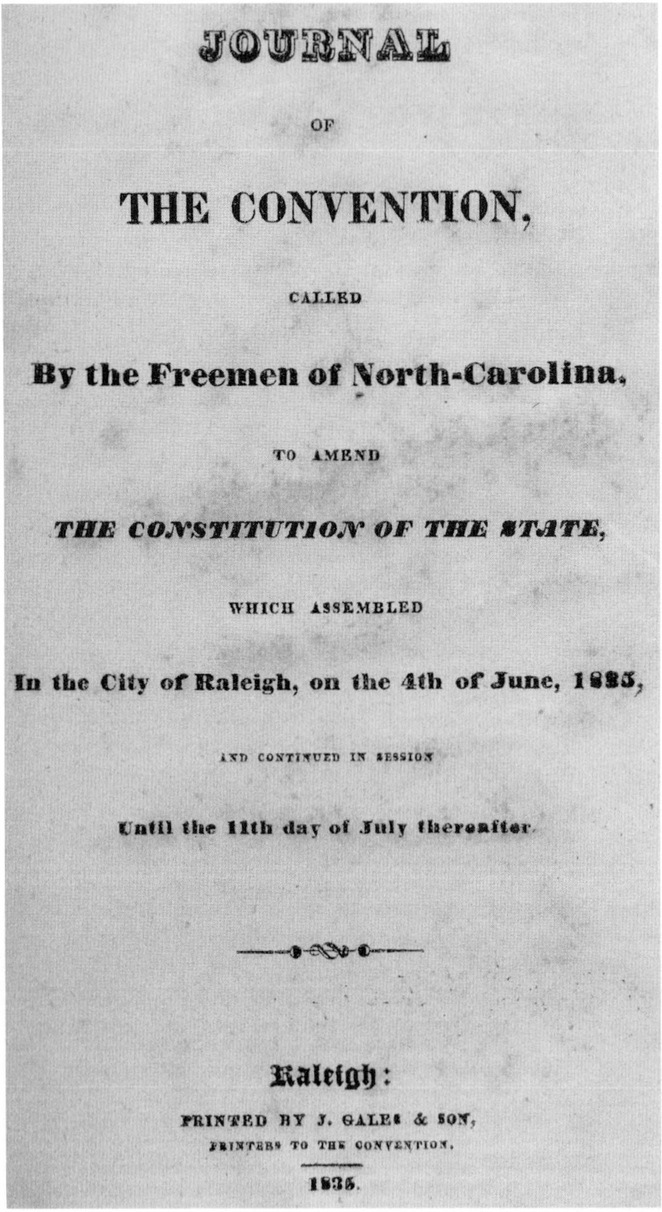

JOURNAL

OF

THE CONVENTION,

CALLED

By the Freemen of North-Carolina,

TO AMEND

THE CONSTITUTION OF THE STATE,

WHICH ASSEMBLED

In the City of Raleigh, on the 4th of June, 1835,

AND CONTINUED IN SESSION

Until the 11th day of July thereafter.

Raleigh:

PRINTED BY J. GALES & SON,

PRINTERS TO THE CONVENTION.

1835.

Figure 8.1 Constitutional Convention of 1835. *Source: North Carolina Collection, University of North Carolina Library at Chapel Hill.*

elections. The Convention Act of 1835 stipulated that the General Assembly's lower house, the house of commons, would be composed of members apportioned according to the federal census, which enhanced slaveholder representation through the clause in the US Constitution that counted a slave as three-fifths of a person—the notorious three-fifths clause—while the state senate was apportioned according to wealth. The latter provision ensured continued dominance, through control of the state senate, of the General Assembly by wealthier eastern slaveholding counties.

Endorsed in a popular referendum by a margin of 27,550 to 21,694, the convention met in Raleigh between June 4 and July 11, 1835. Although the issue of legislative apportionment was already decided before the meeting convened, other key changes in the constitutional structure emerged from the proceedings. The convention abolished the special seats in the house of commons that existed for seven towns. Although the constitution stipulated that all free white men could vote, it simultaneously disfranchised free blacks. The constitution of 1835 further stipulated that the governor would henceforth be elected by a statewide, popular vote for a two-year term, rather than by vote of the legislature and a one-year term, as specified by the old constitution.

There were, however, limits to constitutional change: with continued control of the state senate and a weighted representation through the federal model of apportionment, eastern slaveholders maintained political power for the foreseeable future. The new constitutional structure also preserved property qualifications for officeholders: members of the house of commons were required to own 100 acres of land, state senators 300 acres. The new constitution reinforced the oligarchic system of local government, thus ensuring slaveholders' lock on power. Indeed, for the remainder of the antebellum period, slaveholders dominated membership in the legislature. In 1850, for example, although only about a quarter of white families in North Carolina owned slaves, about 81 percent of the members of the General Assembly were slaveholders. This was the highest rate of slaveholding by any legislature in the South; in 1850, no other southern legislature was more than 70 percent slaveholder. In 1860, the proportion of slaveholders in the North Carolina legislature remained essentially the same: 81 percent of legislators owned slaves, but only about 35 percent of them owned more than twenty slaves.

The predominance of slaveholder power in the North Carolina legislature was no accident; it represented longstanding trends by which the state's slaveholding elite held political power. The constitution of 1835 retained limitations over the amount of taxation future legislatures could levy on slaves, a measure that preserved a telling inequity in public finance. The new constitution also limited the amendment process, as state conventions could be convened only with the agreement of two-thirds of the legislature, or by act of legislature only after a three-fifths vote by both houses, followed by a two-thirds vote two years later and a popular referendum following that.

Still, the constitution of 1835 unquestionably inaugurated a new period of political life in North Carolina. Although African Americans were effectively disfranchised, the convention had raised the subject of property qualifications for voting for the state senate and set an agenda for the future liberalization of the franchise, meaning that nearly all white males could vote in statewide and legislative elections. The constitutional restructuring of the office of the governor also was significant. The governor gained little additional ability to govern—the legislature retained all important forms of power—but the requirement that gubernatorial elections occur every two years helped to stimulate popular interest in a statewide electoral system based on active party competition. In conjunction with the emergence of a new national partisan system of Whigs and Democrats, gubernatorial elections provided new momentum toward the formation of political parties in North Carolina.

The Second Party System

Two strong political parties competed for voters' allegiances in antebellum North Carolina—the Democrats and the Whigs. Utterly devoted to Andrew Jackson, the Democratic Party favored individualism, minimal government, and states' rights. Advertising themselves as the party of ordinary white men, Jacksonian Democrats advocated limited government. They had welcomed President Jackson's Bank War as a struggle against monopolistic corruption—the collusion of government and big business—while they favored low tariffs and free-trade policies that would benefit southern agricultural interests that exported crops to European markets. Democrats also wanted the opening up of western lands: Jacksonians wanted cheap land on which white migrants could settle. They enthusiastically supported Jackson's policy of Indian removal from all of the southeastern United States, including North Carolina, in order to provide the dispossessed Indians' lands at a discount to land-hungry whites.

The Whigs, in contrast, opposed Andrew Jackson on all of these issues. Where Democrats exalted individualism and states' rights, Whigs preferred constitutionalism and a strong central government to foster social cohesion. Endorsing a national banking policy, they opposed Jackson's Bank War. Whigs preferred a protective import tariff that would shelter American manufacturers. They were uneasy about the legality of Jackson's Indian removal policies, and they worried about some of the president's other extraconstitutional activities as well. Whigs favored land distribution policies that charged higher prices for public lands, with the revenue the sales generated distributed to the various states to use for internal improvements and education. The differences between Democrats and Whigs were profound, and the two parties offered voters distinctively different visions of the American Republic.

Figure 8.2 Whig Party banner, c. 1840. *Source: North Carolina Museum of History.*

The emergence of a competitive political system during the Jacksonian era resulted in a surge of interest in the political system among white males. In 1828, some 54 percent of eligible North Carolina voters voted in the presidential election, the largest rate of participation ever recorded in the state. Voter turnout subsequently grew even larger. Opposition to Jackson's banking policies among urban North Carolinians, along with resentment over his strong stance against South Carolina during the 1832–33 nullification crisis, created a strong anti-Jackson backlash in North Carolina. In addition, Whigs' support for political reform identified them as the party of constitutionalism. North Carolina Whigs became strong supporters of expanded state support for internal improvements, a position that was popular among isolated residents of the state eager to connect to the expanding marketplace. Whigs assembled a political coalition based in North Carolina's towns, the Upper Cape Fear counties, the central Piedmont (especially counties with a large Quaker population), the region surrounding the Albemarle Sound, and the mountainous West.

The Second Party System—which followed the First Party System of Federalists versus Republicans—thus took shape in North Carolina by the late 1830s. Creating a highly effective grassroots structure that mobilized their supporters and turned them out at the polls, the Whigs were the first political party to exploit mass politics. Democrats responded in kind, working equally hard to marshal their constituencies. In the gubernatorial and presidential elections of

1840, voter mobilization efforts yielded unprecedented levels of political participation. In that year, 84 percent of adult white males voted in the presidential election, while 83 percent voted in the contest for governor. In statewide elections during the 1840s and 1850s, voter turnout fell below 70 percent only twice. Slightly more successful in getting their voters to the polls, North Carolina Whigs won every gubernatorial election between 1836 and 1848, and their presidential candidates carried the state between 1840 and 1848. Although the 1840s was a decade of Whig dominance, their majorities remained slender, and the party system was characterized by intense competitiveness. Whigs controlled the General Assembly by slim margins in 1840, 1844, and 1846, lost control in 1842 and split power in 1848.

Whigs maintained narrow control over politics because of superior organization, vigorous leadership, and close attention to issues. Whigs such as Edward Dudley, John Motley Morehead, and William Alexander Graham articulated a political vision that attracted popular support. Advocating federal support for internal improvements through the distribution of public revenues from the sales of western lands—the so-called "distribution" issue—became a successful rallying point. Although Democrats opposed distribution because they instead preferred cheap western lands and resisted providing federal authorities with the power to provide revenue, North Carolina Whigs advertised the program as an inexpensive way to provide much-needed public subsidies for transportation infrastructure. The Whigs' emphasis on economic issues and their advocacy of programs that would drive economic development proved to be powerful issues among North Carolina voters.

Although the overall pattern of intense competitiveness remained—in which core Democratic and Whig counties retained their partisan loyalties—by the late 1840s Democrats began to win elections more frequently. Between 1848 and 1852, Democratic candidates for governor attracted an increasing percentage of the statewide vote. In those years, their share of the gubernatorial vote thus increased from 49.5 percent to 53 percent. Democratic resurgence resulted partly from their success in promoting further political reform. Beginning in 1848, Democrats wholeheartedly embraced a platform of "Equal Suffrage," and over the next decade they campaigned on a platform of universal white manhood suffrage and criticized the Whigs for their support of the existing system. Equal suffrage provided Democrats with considerable political traction, and, in close contests, contributed to narrow majorities.

Democrats also benefited by issues and political developments at the national level. The War with Mexico (1846–48) and the peace that followed brought a large cession of territory—what amounted to the entire American Southwest—but it also raised troubling questions about the sectional balance and the rights of slaveholders. Congress remained deadlocked for two years about whether the new territorial governments of the West should permit slavery. Although the deadlock had been broken by the Compromise of 1850, the issue persisted through the 1850s. James B. Shepard, a Democratic state senator, offered resolutions in late 1850, asserting secession "as an extreme remedy" in the case of sectional tyranny. Although Shepard's resolutions were defeated and Whigs prevailed by favoring compromise and constitutionalism, the party leadership was sorely weakened by what appeared to be weakness on the issue of slavery extension, while Democrats aggressively asserted "southern rights" throughout the decade.[1]

The Crisis of the 1850s

Throughout the 1850s, Democrats pressed hard on state issues of equal suffrage and the national issue of slavery extension. During the 1848 gubernatorial campaign, Democratic candidate David S. Reid, a former congressman from Rockingham County, raised the suffrage issue during a debate with Whig candidate Charles Manly. Calling for a constitutional amendment that would eliminate the 50-acre property qualification for voting for the state senate, Reid announced a campaign motto of "equal suffrage." "We hold that all men are free and equal," said the Democratic newspaper, the *New Bern Republican*, and that "each man possesses an equal share of political liberty, and that any distinction between one citizen and another ... is a variation from this spirit of political liberty and equality." While Democrats advocated a political system in which all white men would have access to voting, Whigs attacked the notion as radical and undermining political stability. Equal suffrage was a "lawless desire for leveling all the bulwarks which are raised for the protection of individual rights," said the Whig *Wilmington Commercial*.[2]

Although Reid was narrowly defeated in the gubernatorial election of 1848—he lost by only 845 votes—the Democrats had discovered, in equal suffrage, a winning political issue. Whigs, opposing equal suffrage because they believed that property restrictions added more balance to the political system, were easily portrayed as elitist and aristocratic. When Reid ran again two years later, in 1850, the equal-suffrage issue helped to sweep Democrats to their first victory in a gubernatorial election in more than a decade. Democrats pursued the lengthy legislative process of amending the constitution, and equal suffrage was adopted by popular referendum in 1857. Ironically, equal suffrage did nothing to change the wealth and status of state senators, whose average income actually rose after 1856.

Meanwhile, Whigs fought back, using the issue of apportionment. Claiming that the 1835 constitutional revision had weighted apportionment toward wealthy, slaveholding counties, Whigs proposed a "white basis" of apportionment—that representation should be apportioned entirely on the basis of white population. Democrats, enjoying support in eastern North Carolina, favored retaining the status quo that privileged slaveholders, and in this debate it was the Whigs who appeared more egalitarian. The debates over equal suffrage during the 1850s suggested something about the politics of slavery in North Carolina. Both parties represented slaveholders, but both were also sensitive to the political leanings of the state's large population of nonslaveholders. Mass democratic politics cast a spotlight on North Carolina's constitutional system and the ways in which it placed power in the hands of slaveholders.

There were some antislavery activists, especially among Quakers and Wesleyan Methodists in the northern Piedmont; a few of them were even abolitionists. The North Carolina Manumission Society, founded by Quakers in 1816, claimed 1,000 members by 1825. Nevertheless, the vast majority of white North Carolinians remained committed to the preservation of slavery, and by the 1850s the state's majority was increasingly unwilling to tolerate dissenting opinions. In 1830, the General Assembly enacted the Incendiary Publications Act, which prohibited the publication and distribution of abolitionist literature. During the late antebellum period, the Wesleyan Methodists, an antislavery denomination, sent missionaries across North Carolina, and they found fertile ground in northern Piedmont counties such as Guilford and Randolph. Enjoying the support of Quakers, the Wesleyans used their meetinghouses to espouse abolitionist teachings. Two Wesleyan missionaries, Adam Crooks and Jesse McBride, attracted a hostile reception in September 1850, when the *Greensboro Patriot,* a Whig newspaper, attacked them as subversive incendiaries. McBride was arrested and convicted in October of illegally distributing abolitionist literature and sentenced to twenty lashes and a year in prison. Subsequently, in May 1851, McBride fled the state for his native Ohio. Shortly thereafter Crooks also left North Carolina.

Although North Carolina refused to tolerate any antislavery dialogue, there were a significant number of dissenters in the state. In 1856, University of North Carolina professor Benjamin Sherwood Hedrick, a Davidson County native, was forced to leave the state after it became known in August 1856 that he supported John C. Frémont, the Republican presidential nominee in 1856. By that year, Whigs were no longer a unified national political party, and the new Republican Party, founded in the mid-1850s, was dedicated to opposing the westward expansion of slavery. The *North Carolina Standard,* the state's leading Democratic newspaper in Raleigh, conducted a campaign demanding Hedrick's dismissal. "No man who is avowedly for John C. Frémont," it editorialized, "ought to be allowed to breathe the air or tread the soil of North Carolina."[3] After Hedrick defended himself in print on October 8, 1856, UNC students burned him in effigy, and the university trustees dismissed him. When he returned home to Salisbury, Hedrick narrowly avoided being tarred and feathered by a mob. Other antislavery dissenters, such as Daniel R. Goodloe and Hinton Rowan Helper, realized that they could only criticize slavery by leaving the state. Goodloe, a native of Louisburg, moved north to become editor of the antislavery *National Era* and an abolitionist pamphleteer. Born near

Figure 8.3 Benjamin S. Hedrick. *Source: North Carolina Collection, University of North Carolina Library at Chapel Hill.*

Mocksville, Helper had migrated to California during the Gold Rush of the 1850s. In 1857, Helper published *The Impending Crisis of the South,* which argued that it was in the interests of nonslaveholders to oppose slavery. *The Impending Crisis,* a sensation in the North, sold more than 150,000 copies and was even distributed as Republican Party campaign literature. Helper's book became a scandal in North Carolina because it seemed to suggest a possible nonslaveholder rebellion and, even worse, an alliance with the antislavery Republican Party. *The Impending Crisis* was banned in the state, and anyone possessing a copy was threatened with arrest. Helper, said Sen. Asa Biggs, was an "apostate son" of North Carolina who was "catering to a diseased appetite at the north, to obtain a miserable living by slanders upon the land of his birth."[4]

Repression and paranoia about abolitionist subversion continued to dominate public life in North Carolina, especially after October 1859, when abolitionist John Brown raided the federal armory at Harpers Ferry, Virginia, in a failed attempt to ignite a slave insurrection. In North Carolina, postmasters were forbidden from delivering incendiary publications such as *The Impending Crisis* or the *New York Tribune*. In December 1859, Daniel Worth, a Wesleyan minister and representative of the antislavery American Missionary Association who had been born in Guilford County but had moved to Indiana, was arrested in Greensboro and charged with distributing copies of the *Tribune* and *The Impending Crisis*. Worth was also accused of encouraging slaves and free blacks to reject the slave regime. Worth was a bold opponent of slavery, which, he wrote, he "denounced … at every point … with whatever … language and emphasis I could command." Often, Worth told his audiences that

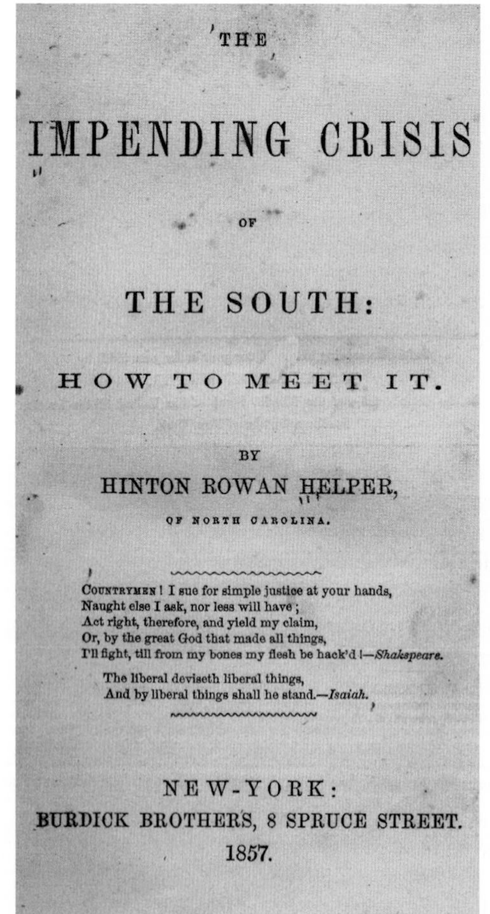
THE

IMPENDING CRISIS

OF

THE SOUTH:

HOW TO MEET IT.

BY

HINTON ROWAN HELPER,

OF NORTH CAROLINA.

COUNTRYMEN! I sue for simple justice at your hands,
Naught else I ask, nor less will have;
Act right, therefore, and yield my claim,
Or, by the great God that made all things,
I'll fight, till from my bones my flesh be hack'd!—*Shakspeare.*

The liberal deviseth liberal things,
And by liberal things shall he stand.—*Isaiah.*

NEW-YORK:
BURDICK BROTHERS, 8 SPRUCE STREET.
1857.

Figure 8.4 Hinton Helper's *The Impending Crisis. Source: North Carolina Collection, University of North Carolina Library at Chapel Hill.*

the leaders of North Carolina were nothing more than "drunkards, gamblers, and whoremongers."[5]

For nearly a year, Worth had been under attack in the *North Carolina Presbyterian*, which asserted that the state should be protected "against cut-throats and assassins, and the sword of the civil magistrate is the instrument which God had appointed for their punishment." Other secular newspapers took up the campaign. "Why is this man not arrested?" declared the *Weekly Standard*. "If the law will not take hold of him," it warned, "let the strong arm of an outraged people be stretched forth to arrest him in his incendiary work."[6] In the subsequent weeks, five of his Wesleyan followers were also arrested, and mob action was threatened against them. Worth was tried and convicted under the state Incendiary Publications Act in Asheboro in March 1860 and under the same act in Greensboro a month later. Sentenced to a year in prison, Worth chose instead to leave the state for the North, where he became a star on the lecture circuit.

Although a consensus about preserving slavery prevailed among most white North Carolinians, there was less enthusiasm about secession. By the mid-1850s, the Whig Party had ceased to exist as a national party. Whigs nonetheless remained a presence in states of the Upper South, including North Carolina, where voters expressed a contrarian view. Although Democrats dominated statewide gubernatorial and presidential elections, North Carolina Whigs continued to pursue two issues of particular saliency. First, they argued for compromise regarding the sectional crisis. During the late 1850s, as a guerrilla war was raging in Kansas and as the nation was sliding toward disaster, Whigs defended the rights of slaveholders but urged the preservation of the Union. Over time, Whigs were growing stronger in elections in North Carolina. In 1859, in congressional elections Whig candidates, running on a platform of Unionism and compromise, gained four seats. A year later, in the crucial presidential election of 1860, Southern Democratic candidate John C. Breckinridge carried North Carolina by only 848 votes, narrowly defeating Whig candidate John Bell.

Whigs continued to make a case for equity in slaveholder-nonslaveholder relations. In the 1850s, the expansion of state-subsidized internal improvements put a strain on revenue and increased state debt. According to the constitution, slaves were subject to a flat capitation tax. The capitation levy did not tax slaves' value as property—which was rising rapidly in the 1850s—and young and old slaves were excluded; by making the tax the same for whites and slaves, slaveholders protected themselves against a tax increase on their human property.

In the 1858–59 legislature, Whigs, led by state senator Moses A. Bledsoe of Wake County, proposed a new system of ad valorem taxation in which slaves would be taxed according to their value as property, a reform that would significantly change the tax burden toward slaveholders. Although tax reform failed in the legislature, during the gubernatorial election of 1860, North Carolina

Whigs—running under the Opposition Party ticket—argued for a restructuring of the tax system. Rallying behind candidate John Pool, Whigs made ad valorem taxation into a major campaign issue. In Pool's campaign, Whigs adopted the slogan "equal taxation"—a twist on the Democrats' earlier campaign for "equal suffrage." Democrats, supporting the incumbent John W. Ellis, argued against ad valorem taxation, claiming that taxes would be levied on the value of all property, including even the poor man's "tin cups." But the issue raised the question of class relations in the slaveholder republic. How fair was a system that taxed land but excluded slaves' real value as property? Whigs narrowly lost the gubernatorial election of 1860, but they won on the ad valorem taxation issue, which helped provide momentum for a Whig resurgence on the eve of the Civil War. In May 1861, the secession convention amended the state constitution to enable ad valorem taxation, and the legislature enacted tax reform in 1863.

The Secession Crisis

The resurgence of North Carolina Whiggery provided the context for the unfolding of the secession crisis. The election of a Republican, Abraham Lincoln, to the presidency in November 1860, resulted in calls for secession. Southern Rights Democrats decried Lincoln's election as proof of a new era of Republican tyranny, the limitation of slavery in the western territories, and the erosion of southern rights (especially the rights of slaveholders) within the Union. On December 20, 1860, South Carolina became the first state to secede, and conventions in Deep South states resulted in the formation of the Confederate States of America in February 1861. In contrast, Upper South and Border states that possessed strong Whig opposition resisted the drive to secession. North Carolina Whigs argued that Lincoln's election, though calamitous, was an insufficient cause to abandon the Union. Better, they argued, that North Carolinians adopt a wait-and-see approach, in the hope that slaveholders' rights could be defended inside the Union. As long as Lincoln operated within the Constitution, respected their understanding of states' rights, and did not attempt to invade the South, they supported continued participation in the Union. Who could support secession, said William Alexander Graham, "upon the ground that we have been out-voted in an election in which we took the chances of success?"[7]

During the winter of 1861, the revitalized Whigs successfully stalled secession in North Carolina. When Democratic governor John W. Ellis proposed a bill convening a convention and organizing and equipping a state military force of ten thousand men, Whigs, aided by the constitutional provision requiring two-thirds assent for a constitutional convention, delayed deliberation in the legislature for six weeks. Not until January 29, 1861, was the bill enacted. By then, the public mood had turned decidedly Unionist, despite the secession of the Deep South. In general, Unionists were divided between those opposing secession under any conditions—unconditional Unionists—and those who saw secession as a last resort against northern military invasion. The centers of unconditional Unionism lay in the areas of Whig political support—the central Piedmont and in some western mountainous counties. The Convention Bill provided for a vote on February 28, and during the ensuing campaign Unionists argued that secession would provoke an unnecessary war when compromise was still possible. If secession occurred, said the *Fayetteville Observer*, "war must follow" and the "eventual destruction of that great interest"—slavery—"whose safety is made the pretext for destroying the Government which protects it."[8] In the Convention Bill, Whigs insisted on a popular referendum on holding a convention, and the results yielded a narrow Unionist majority. North Carolina thus had no sitting convention as the dramatic events of March and April 1861 unfolded.

Even so, secessionists continued to press their case by holding rallies, forming vigilance committees, and organizing militia units. South Carolina's bombardment of federal forces at Fort Sumter, on April 12, 1861, changed matters completely. On April 15, responding to South Carolina's attack, Lincoln issued a proclamation calling for seventy-five thousand volunteers to suppress the threat to the Union. Most conditional Unionists saw Lincoln's proclamation as the beginning of a Northern invasion of the South. North Carolina's fourteen Unionist newspapers all changed their stance, now endorsing disunion. One Yadkin County Whig, Josiah Cowles, explained his changed position in the following manner. "I was as strong a union man as any in the state," he wrote to his son, "up to the time of Lincoln's proclamation calling for 75,000 volunteers. I then saw that the south had either to submit to abject vassalage or assert her rights at the point of the Sword." Lincoln's resort to coercion against secession, Cowles believed, amounted to the destruction of white liberty.[9] With this swing in public opinion, Governor Ellis summoned the legislature into special session, and it enacted a law calling a convention that would on May 13 elect delegates to meet in Raleigh on May 20, 1861. The elections returned an overwhelmingly pro-secession convention, partly because the state's remaining Unionist minority boycotted the election. During the convention's opening day, it unanimously voted an ordinance of secession, and the state later joined the Confederacy. Even while conditional Unionists swung in line behind the Confederacy, a number of unconditional Unionists continued to object. As the secessionist government moved toward war, anti-Confederate groups such as the Heroes of America came into existence in Union areas across the state.

But even as North Carolina joined the Confederacy and its war with the United States, it did so with prominent internal divisions and differences between it and the other Confederate states that would persist throughout the conflict. During the late antebellum era, these points of contention had already been laid bare. North Carolina was a state in which slaveholders held unquestioned political power, but it was also a place where nonslaveholders were numerous and growing more vocal. Economic development spawned by the transportation revolution and the spread of the market economy had reshaped life, but it had done so with uneven effects, with sprawling gaps between rich and poor and between developed and undeveloped counties. Slavery had spread throughout North Carolina, but, as in other Southern states, slaveholders lived with the daily challenges and fears of maintaining control over an increasingly resistant enslaved population.

Notes

1 William C. Harris, *North Carolina and the Coming of the Civil War* (Raleigh, NC: Division of Archives and History, 1988), p. 17.
2 Marc Kruman, *Parties and Politics in North Carolina, 1836–1865* (Baton Rouge: Louisiana State University Press, 1983), pp. 87–88.
3 Guion Griffis Johnson, *Ante-Bellum North Carolina: A History* (Chapel Hill: University of North Carolina Press, 1937), p. 567.
4 Ibid., p. 568.
5 Clement Eaton, "The Freedom of the Press in the Upper South," *Mississippi Valley Historical Review* 18 (March 1932): 483; Claude R. Rickman, "Wesleyan Methodists in North Carolina, 1847–1902," MA thesis, University of North Carolina at Chapel Hill, 1952, p. 26.
6 Noble J. Tolbert, "Daniel Worth: Tar Heel Abolitionist," *North Carolina Historical Review* 39, no. 3 (July 1962): 291–92.
7 Kruman, *Parties and Politics in North Carolina*, p. 201.
8 Ibid., pp. 208–9.
9 Ibid., p. 219.

9

The Civil War

Zebulon Vance, a Whig congressman who later became North Carolina governor and senator, recalled that news of the onset of war came in April 1861, when he was speaking to a crowd and "canvassing for the Union with all my strength." He had his arms extended when news of the Fort Sumter firing and Lincoln's call for volunteers came by telegraph. When Vance's hand came down, he recalled, "it fell slowly and sadly by the side of a Secessionist."[1] Although most North Carolinians were reluctant to join the Confederacy prior to the outbreak of fighting after the attack on Fort Sumter, the beginning of a shooting war changed things. But the war also exposed and aggravated tensions in the social structure of the state, and in many respects, the Civil War spawned turmoil and internal warfare among North Carolinians. By joining the Confederacy, the state government now became committed to a full-scale struggle for survival. It faced Union invasion, the need to provide thousands of its young men to the Confederate army, and increasing hardship and privation for people at home. The war also focused attention on the institution of slavery, and the eventual Union victory brought freedom for all of North Carolina's enslaved people.

It is perhaps ironic that North Carolina, a state that entered the Civil War only reluctantly, became a major contributor to the war effort. The state possessed one-ninth of the Confederacy's population, but it sent roughly one-sixth of the men serving in the Confederate armies. Nearly every adult white male served: some 110,000 volunteers and conscripts, in a state in which only 115,000 people could vote in 1860. The Civil War exacted a high price from North Carolinians: 40,275 men died of their wounds or of disease, a number that exceeded any other Southern state.

North Carolina: Change and Tradition in a Southern State, Second Edition. William A. Link.

Invasion, War, and Coastal North Carolina, 1861–63

Soon after the attack on Fort Sumter, President Abraham Lincoln imposed a Union blockade of all the seaports of the Deep South; eight days later, he extended it to Virginia and North Carolina. The Union's eventual goal was to choke off the Confederacy's access to both markets and resupply from the outside world. In the spring of 1861, during the secession crisis, local militia seized federal forts in coastal North Carolina, and Confederate authorities erected fortifications to protect the state's harbors in Wilmington and elsewhere. About 600 Confederates, including 350 men from the 7th North Carolina Regiment, guarded Hatteras Island. Also defending against invasion was the "Mosquito Fleet," a ragtag collection of five shallow-draft vessels that had served as tugboats and small trading vessels before they were commandeered and converted into a makeshift navy. The Mosquito Fleet disrupted Union commerce by privateering along the Atlantic coast, and during the summer of 1861 the Outer Banks became a staging ground for attacks on shipping to Northern ports. As a result, Union forces under the command of General Benjamin Butler organized an invasion force to capture forts at ocean and sound sides of Hatteras Inlet. Intending to end privateering and establish an invasion route to the interior of North Carolina, Butler led an opening assault on the coastal region.

In late August 1861, a Union naval force under the command of Commodore Silas Stringham and an invading force of 900 men under Butler's command sailed for Hatteras. With the Confederate forces undermanned and ill-equipped—Confederate authorities in Richmond had provided few reinforcements, despite reports of an invasion and pleas for help—they faced naval bombardment and a superior Union force. The invaders quickly took control of Fort Clark and then surrounded Fort Hatteras. On August 27, 1861, the Confederate commander, Samuel Barron, surrendered his force of 600 soldiers to Butler. The brief battle constituted the first Union victory of the Civil War, and it brought good news after the disastrous Northern defeat inflicted in the First Battle of Manassas, in northern Virginia, about a month earlier, in late July 1861. Soon after Butler captured Hatteras, Confederate forces withdrew from forts at Oregon Inlet and Ocracoke Island, in fact, abandoning control of access from sound to ocean on the northern North Carolina coast.

Union forces, now in the form of a larger Coast Division under the command of Brig. Gen. Ambrose Burnside, expanded this foothold. In January 1862, a force of 13,000 men and nearly 100 ships sailed from Annapolis and, braving Atlantic storms and treacherous shoals, assaulted Roanoke Island. The 1,400 men under the command of Colonel Henry W. Shaw of the 8th North Carolina Regiment defending Roanoke, lightly equipped, could do little to stop the invaders. In operations lasting about a week, Burnside's forces routed the Mosquito Fleet and ended the Confederate naval presence in northeastern North Carolina, capturing the coastal towns of Elizabeth City and Edenton.

Figure 9.1 Bombardment of New Bern during the Burnside Expedition. *Source: North Carolina Collection, University of North Carolina Library at Chapel Hill.*

Raleigh officials were terrified about the prospect of a Union march through eastern North Carolina, and enlistees began to pour in to defend against further losses. Only now did authorities in Richmond, the capital of the Confederacy, finally send reinforcements. Burnside's coastal invasion continued when the brightly uniformed New York Zouaves under the command of Rush C. Hawkins sailed up the Chowan River and looted and burned the town of Winton. The culmination of Burnside's campaign came on March 11, 1862, when 11,000 Northern troops left Roanoke, crossed the sound, and invaded New Bern. By March 14, Burnside's troops occupied the town, pillaging it and liberating slaves. About a month later, on April 25, Burnside captured Fort Macon and secured control of the North Carolina coast north of Wilmington.

Although there were complaints about the Richmond government's neglect of the defense of North Carolina, manpower shortages made it impossible for the Confederacy to protect all of its borders, and the attempt to do so early in the war resulted in the piecemeal destruction of scattered Southern forces. Burnside's campaign thus yielded significant results. In the summer of 1862, the coast, sounds, and outlets of the state were under Union control and would remain so until the end of the war. Supply lines to Robert E. Lee's army to the north were threatened, and access to the world was partially limited. Thirteen counties, 119,000 whites, and 50,000 slaves were now behind Union lines, while the eastern towns of New Bern, Edenton, Beaufort, Elizabeth City, and Washington were all under occupation. Following the summer of 1862, the Union offensive stalled. In part, this reflected stiffened Confederate resistance and a renewed determination to prevent further inroads into the North Carolina interior. Also significant, Burnside and a large portion of his invading force were withdrawn in order to reinforce Federal forces in Virginia. What remained in eastern North Carolina was an occupying force with little offensive power.

The Inner Civil War

Even while it rallied many of the state's white residents around a new Confederate identity, the Civil War exposed deep fissures in North Carolina society. In December 1861, the secession convention reassembled into a kind of constitutional convention; the purpose of the meeting was to provide for a legal government during wartime. Avid supporters of the war—adherents of a "Confederate" party—introduced resolutions endorsing the all-out prosecution of the war. Introduced by Asa Biggs, the resolutions empowered the state government to suppress any opposition to the war by requiring a test oath and imprisoning any disloyal North Carolinians for sedition. The Biggs resolutions encountered strong opposition, however, and those opposing them became known as part of the "Conservative" party. The Biggs resolutions were stalled, but they suggested how these philosophical and practical differences fractured the home front and divided North Carolinians about whether there should be any restraints in how the war was conducted.

The opposition to an all-out war reflected the extent to which North Carolina's political culture of dissent survived into the conflict. Although the Confederate government abandoned partisan identities, political divisions remained, and, in general, Democrats regrouped under the name "Confederate" and Whigs under the designation "Conservative." Confederates favored an unrelenting prosecution of the war; Conservatives were more cautious, and, on occasion, critical of the powers exercised by the Richmond government. The Conservatives rallied around former conditional Unionists—those North Carolinians who had opposed secession as long as Lincoln refrained from coercion—the most important of whom was Zebulon Vance. Like many other antebellum Whigs, Vance, from western North Carolina's Buncombe County, had originally opposed secession but then supported it after Lincoln threatened military invasion. Soon after the war began, Vance was elected colonel of the 26th North Carolina Regiment, and he saw action in the Union attack on New Bern in March 1862 and at Malvern Hill, in Virginia, in the Seven Days battles of June 25–July 1, 1862. Vance emerged from both encounters with a reputation for decisive leadership and popularity among his troops.

In the gubernatorial election of 1862, Vance was opposed by William Johnston, a former Whig, railroad president, and ardent secessionist who ran on a plank endorsing an unqualified war effort. Johnston favored, according to the platform nominating him, "an unremitting prosecution of the war to the last extremity; complete independence; eternal separation from the North; no abridgement of Southern territory; no alteration of Southern boundaries; no compromise with enemies, traitors, or tories." For his part, Vance appealed to North Carolinians' unwillingness to award sweeping powers to a central government. In addition, Vance enjoyed popular, even enthusiastic, support among North Carolina troops. Running as a Conservative candidate for governor, Vance was decisively elected in August 1862, by a margin of 55,282 to 20,813.

Once in office, Vance tried to unify the Confederates and Conservatives without sacrificing North Carolina's military contribution to the war. Assuming office in September 1862, he reaffirmed his allegiance to the Confederacy. Secession, he declared in his inaugural address, was "not a whim or sudden freak, but the deliberate judgment of our people." Any alternative to joining the Confederacy meant the "deepest degradation" and the "vilest dishonor." North Carolinians accepted the "inevitable consequences" of secession, a "long and bloody war." Vance's governorship was marked by a series of conflicts with the Confederate government in Richmond. After the Union invasion of eastern North Carolina, many had criticized the Confederate government's slow and ineffective response in providing troops and supplies; it seemed to some that the government's mismanagement of the war contributed to Northern victories. Others complained that North Carolinians had been passed over in appointments to important Confederate offices. Soon after his inauguration in September 1862, Vance objected to the suspension of habeas corpus, which the Confederate Congress empowered Confederate president Jefferson Davis to invoke (although he never did in North Carolina). Vance enforced the Confederate Conscription Act of April 16, 1862—and North Carolina eventually supplied about one-quarter of Southern conscripts, or 21,000 men—but the draft law remained unpopular. Conscription, said newspaper editor William W. Holden, was tyrannical. The Civil War was a "war of people against arbitrary power—let it be fought by volunteers." Conscripted armies, he concluded, were "the adjuncts and supporters of despotism."[2] Even more unpopular were the provisions in the conscription act that permitted the hiring of substitutes and exempted slaveholders owning more than twenty slaves—both of which excused the wealthy (should they wish) but left poor men little choice but to serve.

Indeed, the war inflicted great hardship on North Carolina's nonslaveholding yeomen, who, as the war dragged on, disproportionately contributed manpower and suffered casualties. Nearly the entire adult male population served in the Confederate armies, and in a society that depended on the labor of young men, the war created a terrific labor shortage. War profiteering became a problem, as greedy merchants took advantage of shortages and began to charge greatly inflated prices for basic necessities by early 1863. Confederate policies, which reflected the scarcity of resources throughout the South, only intensified hardships at home. Authorities freely exercised the power to impress crops and goods, which they paid for in devalued Confederate scrip. In addition, Richmond authorities imposed a tax-in-kind levy that required farmers to provide one-tenth of their crops to the government. These measures hurt poor families with soldiers in the field, but the government needed to supply its troops, and the Richmond regime saw little alternative but to impose these policies.

As much as any other Confederate state, a groundswell of resentment existed in North Carolina about the war. In the interior regions of the state, sporadic protests erupted. As early as the summer of 1862, during elections to the legislature, one candidate in the Piedmont declared his support for peace and reunion with the Union. Desertion and draft evasion were constant problems, and in the Piedmont and Mountain counties, war resisters tried to avoid pursuit by the local Home Guards; antiwar sentiment was concentrated in the northern Piedmont "Quaker Belt" counties of Randolph, Guilford, Davie, and Forsyth. Deserters worried about the welfare of their families returned to their farms, and did their best to avoid local authorities. Periodically, Vance sent troops to put down draft resisters and deserters. Shortly after the elections of 1862, deserters were pursued by troops in Wilkes and Yadkin Counties, while later troops were sent to mountainous Madison County, where large portions of territory were under the control of guerrilla bands of deserters. In April 1863, Vance appealed to Confederate general D. H. Hill for regular troops to suppress deserters in Randolph because, he declared, the outliers could "lick my militia in a fair fight."[3]

As the Confederate military cause absorbed major defeats at Gettysburg and Vicksburg, the rate of desertion by North Carolinians rose significantly, and during the summer of 1863 there were reports of 500 deserters in mountainous Wilkes County and as many as 1,100 organized and armed outliers in the region between Randolph, Moore, and Chatham Counties. Among the best-known and most extreme guerrilla leaders was William Owens of Randolph County, who, though eventually captured in April 1864, kidnapped militiamen and forced them to swear oaths of loyalty to the Union. Some of these groups, especially in the Quaker Belt, were associated with the Heroes of America (HOA), a secret organization founded in early 1861 to resist the Confederacy. Claiming as many as 10,000 members in North Carolina, the HOA supported war resisters and sometimes even surreptitiously aided Union forces. In late 1863, Gen. Robert Hoke was dispatched to suppress these guerrilla bands. In some instances, efforts to suppress war resisters often led to extremes, with local militias and Home Guards committing atrocities against civilian populations. Antiwar sentiment in the mountains of North Carolina, South Carolina,

Georgia, and Alabama, reported the Confederate assistant secretary of war, "menaces the existence of the Confederacy as fatally as either of the armies of the United States."[4]

The Struggle for the Confederacy

In July 1863, not long after the defeat of Robert E. Lee's invading Army of Northern Virginia at Gettysburg, Pennsylvania, William Wagner, a Catawba County nonslaveholding yeoman farmer, wrote to his wife. "I Believe we are whipt, but I hope and trust to God it will End before long yet I cant see how it will be don[e]." Later he added, "I got hope and trust in my God to save and pertect me through this cruil war."[5] Wagner's sense of despair extended to popular resentment about the war, which boiled over in North Carolina after 1863 with the eruption of widespread protests and the emergence of an organized political movement that sought to take the state out of the war. Although these movements failed to dislodge North Carolina from the Confederacy, they provided hard evidence of the extent to which the war's sacrifices had exacerbated internal tensions in the state.

In March 1863, anger boiled over in Salisbury, when a group of forty to fifty wives of soldiers converged on merchants demanding that they sell food at reasonable prices. Protesting price inflation and devaluation of the Confederate currency, the women moved from merchant to merchant, informing them of a fair price for flour and threatening to seize food and provisions. When a merchant protested that he himself had paid a higher price, they responded, according to one account, that "they were determined to have the flour, and would take it, unless he would sell." Becoming known as the Salisbury food riot, the episode indicated the extent of privation among the civilian population and the widespread resentment about the inequality of the war's impact.

Other spontaneous protests occurred in other parts of North Carolina, including Greensboro and in present-day Durham, and these were also led by groups of aggrieved women. In Johnston County, women broke into a corncrib and seized food in order to provide for their families. In late 1864, a group of women appeared at a government warehouse in Yancey County, taking sixty bushels of wheat. Months later, in western Piedmont North Carolina's Yadkin County, yet another group of women appeared at Jonesville, the county seat, and seized supplies of corn. Elsewhere in North Carolina, hungry women raided public stores and warehouses to obtain food.[6] In Robeson County, meanwhile, Indians—who later became known as Lumbee Indians—resisted Confederates who had impressed them into work on forts defending Wilmington. Along with some escaped Union prisoners of war, guerrilla bands of Indians resisted Confederate Home Guards in the swamps near the Lumber River. Under the command of Lumbee leader Henry Berry Lowery, this

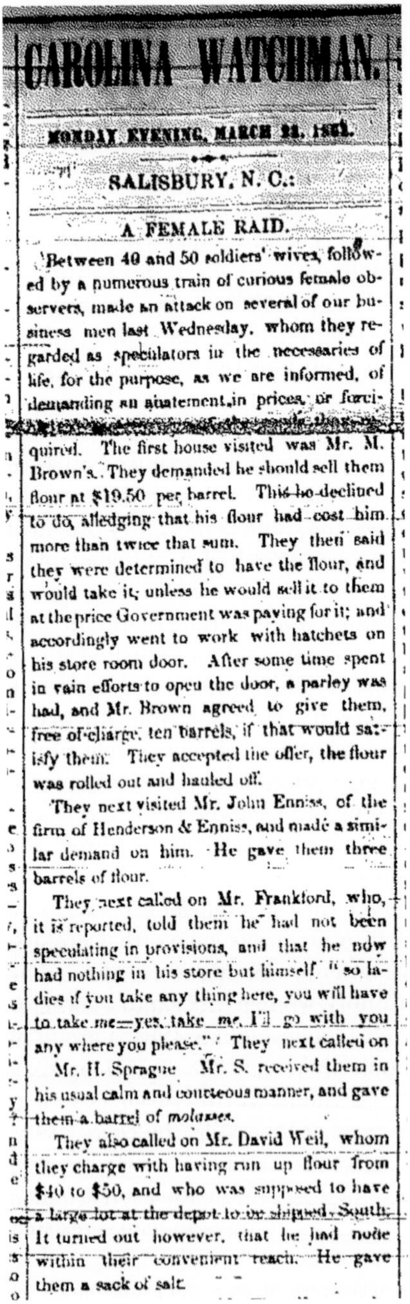

CAROLINA WATCHMAN.

MONDAY EVENING, MARCH 23, 1863.

SALISBURY, N. C.:

A FEMALE RAID.

Between 40 and 50 soldiers' wives, followed by a numerous train of curious female observers, made an attack on several of our business men last Wednesday, whom they regarded as speculators in the necessaries of life, for the purpose, as we are informed, of demanding an abatement in prices, or forci- [illegible] quired. The first house visited was Mr. M. Brown's. They demanded he should sell them flour at $19.50 per barrel. This he declined to do, alledging that his flour had cost him more than twice that sum. They then said they were determined to have the flour, and would take it, unless he would sell it to them at the price Government was paying for it; and accordingly went to work with hatchets on his store room door. After some time spent in vain efforts to open the door, a parley was had, and Mr. Brown agreed to give them, free of charge, ten barrels, if that would satisfy them. They accepted the offer, the flour was rolled out and hauled off.

They next visited Mr. John Enniss, of the firm of Henderson & Enniss, and made a similar demand on him. He gave them three barrels of flour.

They next called on Mr. Frankford, who, it is reported, told them he had not been speculating in provisions, and that he now had nothing in his store but himself. "so ladies if you take any thing here, you will have to take *me*—yes, take *me*, I'll go with you any where you please." They next called on Mr. H. Sprague Mr. S. received them in his usual calm and courteous manner, and gave them a barrel of *molasses*.

They also called on Mr. David Weil, whom they charge with having run up flour from $40 to $50, and who was supposed to have a large lot at the depot to be shipped South. It turned out however, that he had none within their convenient reach. He gave them a sack of salt.

Figure 9.2 Report of Salisbury Bread Riot, *Carolina Watchman*, March 1863. *Source: North Carolina Collection, University of North Carolina Library at Chapel Hill.*

"Lowery Band" persisted even after the war was over to contest white control of the area; not until 1874 did the Lowery Band disperse, after Lowery was caught and executed. Whatever the form, these outbreaks of discontent were severe enough to provoke a response from Vance, who issued a proclamation describing the conditions of "scarcity of provisions and threatened famine" affecting most North Carolinians but also urging North Carolinians to refrain from mob violence. "Broken laws will give you no bread, but much sorrow," he wrote. "When forcible seizures have to be made to avert starvation, let it be done by your County or State agents."[7]

The worst example of opposition to the war and efforts to repress them occurred in the mountains of Madison County, northeast of Asheville, during the winter of 1863. In January, a group of about fifty deserters with Unionist sympathies seized salt supplies in a raid on the town of Marshall, a pro-Confederate stronghold; salt, an essential preservative, was in short supply in wartime North Carolina. In the raid, the attackers shot a Confederate soldier who was in town, stole supplies from local residents, and abandoned two children, who later died of exposure to the elements, out in the cold. The Unionist raid opened up wounds in Madison County, and the 64th North Carolina Regiment, then in Saltville, Virginia, was dispatched to hunt down the raiders. The 64th entered the Shelton Laurel neighborhood of the county, a center of anti-Confederate discontent, and rounded up fifteen men and boys. After two of their alleged traitors escaped, they massacred the remaining thirteen. Although Vance was outraged by the incident, none of the soldiers or their commanders was ever brought to justice by Confederate authorities.

Popular discontent with the war culminated in an organized peace movement of 1863–64. During the spring of 1863, some newspaper editors called for peace, though most refused to accept the end of slavery or reunion—the two conditions upon which President Lincoln insisted. Others, however, were willing to take things further. In May 1863, former state senator and large slaveholder James Thomas Leach called for a cessation of hostilities and peace according to the principle of "the Constitution as it is, the Union as it was." The loudest advocate of peace was William W. Holden, former Southern Rights Democrat and editor of the *North Carolina Standard* in Raleigh. Born in Hillsborough in 1818, Holden had a long and interesting career during which he was often accused of political opportunism. In the 1840s, he had begun as a Whig and then became a Southern Rights firebrand in the 1850s. After the Civil War, in still another political incarnation, Holden would be elected governor as a Republican. In asserting leadership over the peace forces, Holden may have had motives of political advantage uppermost in his mind.

In the summer of 1863, following a series of Confederate defeats, Holden issued a call for peace. The "great mass" of the state, he wrote, wanted negotiations. "We favor peace," he said, "because we believe that peace now would save slavery, while we very much fear that a prolongation of the war will obliterate

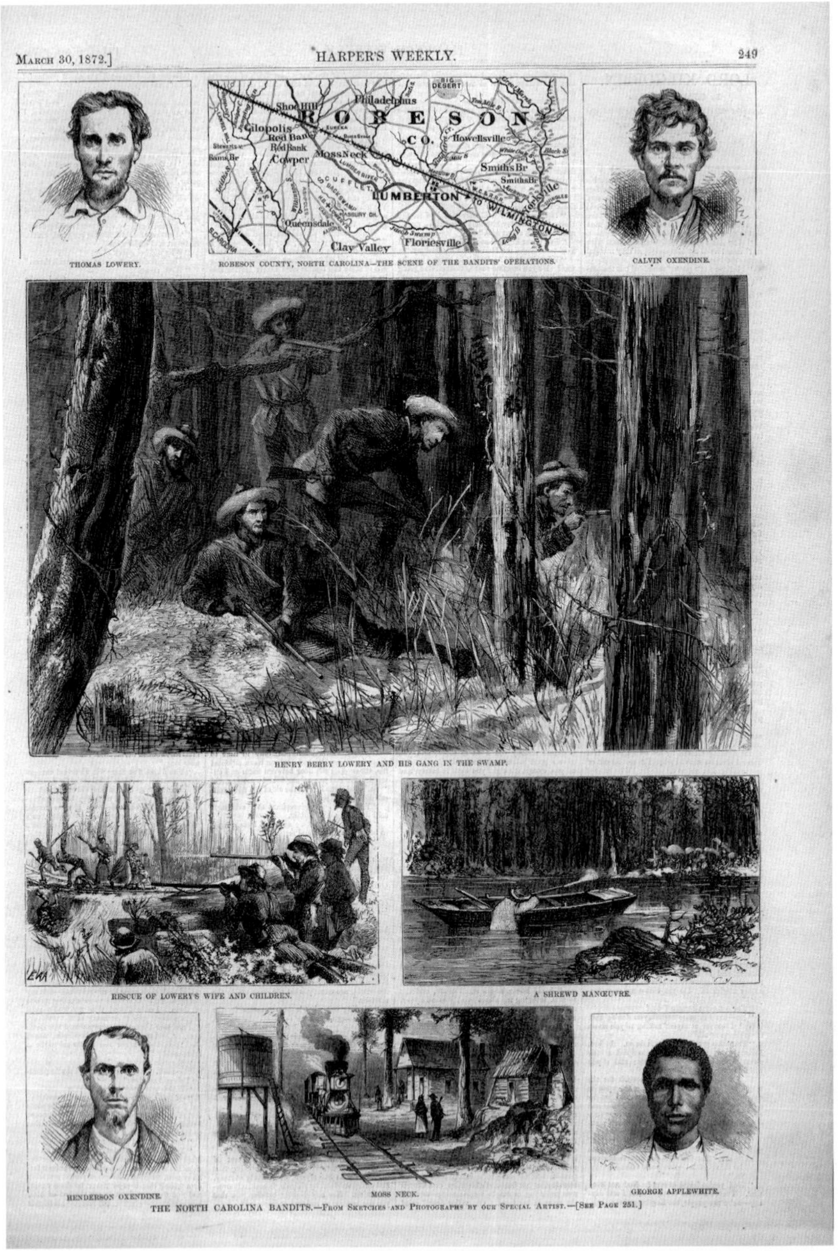

MARCH 30, 1872.] HARPER'S WEEKLY. 249

THOMAS LOWERY.

ROBESON COUNTY, NORTH CAROLINA—THE SCENE OF THE BANDITS' OPERATIONS.

CALVIN OXENDINE.

HENRY BERRY LOWERY AND HIS GANG IN THE SWAMP.

RESCUE OF LOWERY'S WIFE AND CHILDREN.

A SHREWD MANŒUVRE.

HENDERSON OXENDINE.

MOSS NECK.

GEORGE APPLEWHITE.

THE NORTH CAROLINA BANDITS.—FROM SKETCHES AND PHOTOGRAPHS BY OUR SPECIAL ARTIST.—[SEE PAGE 251.]

Figure 9.3 *Harper's Weekly*, Henry Lowery drawings, March 30, 1872. *Source: North Carolina Collection, University of North Carolina Library at Chapel Hill,* https://cwnc.omeka.chass.ncsu.edu/items/show/170

Figure 9.4 Shelton Laurel Massacre, January 18, 1863. *Source: Skedaddle/Public Domain.*

the last vestige of it." It was "time to consult reason and common sense." Voters should elect representatives to the Confederate Congress who would seek "to make an honest effort to stay the effusion of blood by an honorable adjustment." Holden advocated, if necessary, a separate peace, what he called "negotiations with a view to separation." Holden's peace declarations were vague, and no one was sure, not even his supporters, what would constitute the terms of peace.

On the heels of Holden's call for negotiations, peace conventions were held across the state. At one such convention in Wake County, attendees demanded any peace that would provide the South with equality within the Union, and they urged the cessation of hostilities and a national convention. Not all reaction to Holden's peace movement was positive: on September 9, 1863, a Georgia brigade spent the night in Raleigh, and, while there, sought out Holden at his home. When they failed to find him there, the soldiers sacked the offices of the *North Carolina Standard*. A few days later, an Alabama regiment rode through Raleigh threatening Holden. The next day, Holden's supporters retaliated by sacking the offices of the pro-Confederate *State Journal*. During elections held for the Confederate Congress in the fall of 1863, five of the ten openly elected candidates favored a negotiated peace. Even Vance was convinced that discontent had reached a critical point.[8]

The organized peace campaign continued into 1864. In the winter of that year, resolutions were introduced in the legislature calling for a convention to reconsider secession. One such resolution, denouncing the "alarming and fearful tendency of the Confederate Government towards military despotism by the enactment of unjust and oppressive laws," urged negotiations. In May 1864, Holden decided to mount a gubernatorial challenge come August, when Vance ran for reelection. But Vance, sensing that North Carolinians' discontent was not necessarily Unionist, outmaneuvered Holden by portraying himself as an avid defender of North Carolina's interests in the Confederacy. Vance published his letter to Confederate president Jefferson Davis, in which he called for negotiations, and he emphasized his differences with the Confederate government. In general, while Holden ran an inept campaign, Vance had already become one of the more effective politicians of his generation. A captivating speaker, Vance conducted his campaign by speaking six days a week for two months in the summer of 1864, and in his speeches he was careful to maintain that he, too, opposed the excesses of the Richmond government. The Union offensive in Virginia remained stalemated during the summer of 1864, and this military situation benefited Vance politically. Holden's peace movement also stirred a backlash among North Carolinians in the Confederate army, and they would vote in large numbers for Vance. The result was a landslide Vance victory, as the incumbent won the race by a margin of 44,664 to 12,608, and he carried all but three counties.

The Destruction of Slavery

Slaveholders were acutely aware of the threat the Civil War posed to the institution of slavery. Northern abolitionists, warned one North Carolina newspaper, were "agents for propagating insurrection."[9] Much of this sort of language was paranoid hyperbole, but the war did bear out whites' fears. Although Abraham Lincoln in the early phases of the war took a qualified approach to slavery—preferring, for the most part, to support gradual emancipation and African colonization—by 1863, the war had become one for emancipation. Wherever Union armies invaded and occupied, they disrupted master-slave relations, prompting enslaved people to flee bondage and spurring masters to "refugee" their slaves by moving them safely beyond the front lines of battle. Ironically, action taken by the North Carolina government, especially its impressment policies, also helped to undo the stability of slavery. In need of labor to erect fortifications in battle areas, state authorities made free use of slaves by impressing their labor. In late 1862, the legislature empowered the governor to impress slaves to work on defensive fortifications, and although the law stipulated that masters should be compensated and slaves returned to them after the completion of work, frequently neither occurred. Separated from their families and fearful of their treatment near the battle zone, slaves had little to lose and considerable incentive to flee to Union forces. In addition, slave

Figure 9.5 Freedmen's Colony, Roanoke Island. *Source:* Report of the Services Rendered by the Freed People to the United States Army, in North Carolina, in the Spring of 1862, After the Battle of Newbern, *by Vincent Colyer (1864).*

impressments usually occurred against the will of the slaveholders. On a personal, day-to-day level, both masters and slaves realized that the war already had indelibly changed things.

The Northern occupiers discovered that enslaved North Carolinians saw the war as providing an opportunity for freedom. General Burnside of the US Army, after invading and occupying coastal North Carolina, promised masters that he would respect slave property. But the arrival into his camp of a growing number of escaped slaves undermined Burnside's position. "Stealing in from every direction by land & sea," wrote one observer, escaping slaves "come and dump themselves by the side of the fence and 'wait orders from Mr. Burnside.'" Runaway slaves were "continually coming in," reported a northern soldier, "in squads of men from one to a dozen threading their way through the swamps at night, avoiding pickets, they at last reach our lines." New Bern, according to still another observer, offered freedom and sanctuary, becoming a "Mecca of a thousand aspirations."[10]

African Americans' "self-emancipation" coincided with congressional intervention. In March 1862 Congress forbade their return to their masters, while in July it passed the Second Confiscation Act, granting freedom for all slave fugitives. Burnside believed that eastern North Carolina could serve as an outpost for Unionist North Carolinians, and soon after New Bern was occupied, Lincoln appointed Edward Stanly the military governor of North Carolina, on the premise that it would be possible to organize loyal forces and rally them around the Union. But Stanly's government in New Bern was a complete failure, partly because it lacked much appeal to North Carolina whites, and also because of its opposition to emancipation. In part, this reflected the ineptness of Stanly, a former five-term Whig congressman from North Carolina who had moved to California in 1857 and campaigned unsuccessfully as a Republican candidate for governor of that state. Returning to North Carolina in May 1862, Stanly wrote to Vance in October, offering to meet with him to help negotiate a peace. Vance wrote back, denouncing Stanly, whose name, he said, was "execrated and pronounced with curses in North Carolina."[11] Stanly later departed as military governor because he protested Lincoln's Emancipation Proclamation.

The most immediate impact of the erosion and ultimate destruction of slavery came in those areas threatened by Union invasion, in eastern North Carolina, after the summer of 1861. In the East, freedpeople worked to subvert slavery, in some instances by aiding the Northern war effort by serving as scouts, guides, and spies for raiding parties. In plantation districts masters found that their slaves began to challenge their authority, and thousands of bondspeople fled slavery for freedom behind Union lines. Slaves streamed into occupied North Carolina after the summer of 1861. By summer 1862, there were 10,000 former slaves behind Northern lines, and two years later this number had increased to more than 17,000, including nearly 8,600 at New Bern, 2,500 at Beaufort, 2,700 at Roanoke Island, and 2,700 at Tarboro. With these fleeing African Americans possessing a nebulous status, the Northern military was forced to define their position. Early on, Benjamin Butler, in command of occupying forces in southeast Virginia and eastern North Carolina, applied the ambiguous term "contrabands of war" to describe the slave runaways, but eventually they came to gain greater status under Northern military protection. In the late spring of 1862, there were 1,000 runaways at Roanoke Island, and by the end of the year, contrabands became a decided presence. Slaves flooded into New Bern, after Union forces captured the town in March 1862. "When the Yankees took New Bern," remembered an ex-slave, "all who could swim … and get to the Yankees were free." There was "perhaps not a slave in North Carolina who does not know he can find freedom in New Bern," wrote a Union army officer, "and thus New Bern may be Mecca of a thousand noble aspirations."[12] The military began to supervise various programs involving the labor of the contrabands, as well as to house them in camps, eventually located in Beaufort, New Bern, Plymouth, Roanoke Island, and Tarboro. The military paid contrabands $10 a month for men and $4 a month for women. In these areas, Northern missionaries entered the state and created new schools to educate freedpeople.

New Bern, which by the war's conclusion housed nearly 11,000 fugitive slaves, became a headquarters of the freedpeople's community. South of town, Union officials established a freedmen's village near the junction of the Neuse

Figure 9.6 Impact of the Emancipation Proclamation, New Bern. *Source:* Harper's Weekly, *February 21, 1863, North Carolina Collection, University of North Carolina Library at Chapel Hill.*

and Trent Rivers. Containing some 800 cabins, there were about 2,800 freedpeople in the community. Horace James, a Northerner who headed up missionary activities for freedpeople in North Carolina, described the "settlement, located healthfully on the banks of the Trent" as a "model for imitation." The New Bern African American community survived the end of war, despite local whites' efforts to reassert ownership. In 1893, when a local court threw the freedpeople off the land, the community possessed a strong enough identity that it relocated to an all-African American community, James City.[13]

An important part of the destruction of slavery was the recruitment of ex-slaves into the Union military. Some 6,000 black North Carolinians, participating in four regiments, would join the Union army, out of the 179,000 black troops who served. Following the Emancipation Proclamation, recruiting black troops became a formal part of Northern policy, and in December 1863, Butler instructed the command in southeastern Virginia and North Carolina actively to seek enlistment of freedpeople. "Every negro able to work who leaves the rebel lines," Butler wrote, "diminishes by so much the producing power of the rebellion to supply itself with food and labor necessary," and the Union gained "either a soldier or a producer." Now Butler ordered all forces to seek "by every means in his power, the coming of all colored people within the Union lines"; all military should "bring in with them all the negroes possible, affording them transportation, aid, protection, and encouragement." Butler further pledged to provide for women and children of black recruits; he even promised to house and feed women and children of any slaves, on the theory that their presence would encourage husbands and fathers to flee to Union lines. "However far south his master may drive him," Butler observed, "he will sooner or later return to his family."[14]

Meanwhile, black North Carolinians were also actively recruited by the abolitionist governor of Massachusetts, John A. Andrew. Working with Andrew was a fellow abolitionist, George L. Stearns, who by 1863 had created a network of recruiting agents seeking out ex-slaves to join the ranks. Opposition in the Union army slowed Andrew's and Stearns's efforts, but blacks in coastal North Carolina continued to serve as spies and scouts. Some African Americans were even sent behind enemy lines to encourage slaves to leave their masters. In the summer of 1862, two black men were apprehended and hanged by Confederate forces when they were found to be "emissaries to induce others … to run away and enlist."[15]

As a result of Andrew's and Stearns's activities, the Union army authorized Col. Edward A. Wild to organize an "African brigade" of three regiments of North Carolina African Americans, combined with the Massachusetts 55th Regiment, an all-black unit that followed the creation of the legendary Massachusetts 54th Regiment. The North Carolina troops became the 1st, 2nd, and 3rd Regiments of the North Carolina Colored Volunteers. Wild operated a recruitment office out of New Bern, and the town became a center of black military participation. Commanded by white officers, these black troops saw their first significant action in December 1863. Two regiments of the African Brigade, raiding Confederate guerrillas operating in northeastern North Carolina, tried to reopen traffic on the Dismal Swamp Canal. In this campaign, black troops freed 2,500 slaves, captured weapons and supplies, and took prisoners, but they also struck terror among whites. Locals complained that "bands of armed Negroes domineer in the homes of their masters and spread terror over the land," and one resident called General Wild a "monster of humanity" for commanding black troops.[16] Nonetheless, Confederates treated African American soldiers as illegal war participants. In April 1864, after the battle for Plymouth, Confederates massacred captured black prisoners of war.

The Collapse of the Confederacy

By late 1864 and early 1865, the Confederacy's ability to sustain resistance against Union forces was eroding, and in Virginia the (Federal) Army of the Potomac made a relentless advance against the (Confederate) Army of Northern Virginia. From the beginning of 1865 until Gen. Robert E. Lee's surrender at Appomattox, Virginia, in April, North Carolina experienced steady, unrelenting military pressure. Union forces surrounded Wilmington, which by war's end remained the last open Confederate port and a hub of blockade-running. Nearly 100 blockade runners operated out of Wilmington, and between December 1861 and December 1864 blockade runners arrived more than 300 times in the city's port. In late December 1864, a large Union naval armada, backed by 6,000 men, attacked 650 Confederate soldiers manning Fort Fisher, which protected Wilmington at the mouth of the Cape Fear River and was known as the "Gibraltar of the Confederacy." But reinforcement from a Southern brigade under the command of North Carolinian Robert F. Hoke and fierce resistance from the defenders of the fort stalled the assault, and the armada pulled back. The Union forces returned in mid-January and renewed the assault on the entrenched Southern forces at Fort Fisher. Between January 13 and 15, 1865, a naval bombardment combined with the landing of Northern troops finally demoralized and weakened the defenders. Late in the evening of January 15, those inside the fort surrendered. With the fall of Fort Fisher and the infusion of more Union troops, the surrender of Wilmington became a certainty, and the town lay in Northern hands by February 22, 1865.

To the horror of its white inhabitants and the delight of local blacks, among the Union forces that marched into Wilmington was a contingent of African American troops. The United States Colored Troops 37th Regiment, which was organized from North Carolina recruits, played a prominent part in the assault on Fort Fisher. After the fall of Wilmington, black troops were among the first to enter the city. Wilmington's African Americans celebrated wildly. Some were in tears, while others were "shouting and singing, dancing and hugging each other, and showing the gladness of their hearts." Local whites were dismayed and shocked at the appearance of black troops. One resident described himself as "completely heartbroke, can't eat, or sleep."[17]

The collapse of the Confederacy was completed in the spring of 1865. In his March to the Sea, Union general William T. Sherman, leading a 60,000-strong army, devastated Georgia and South Carolina in late 1864. After occupying Savannah, Georgia, on December 21, Sherman moved north through upcountry South Carolina, scouring the countryside for provisions. Burning Columbia, South Carolina, on February 17, 1865, Sherman moved northeast. He intended to capture Goldsboro in order to shut off a vital rail supply to Lee's army in Virginia and, eventually, to link up with Grant's army in Virginia and obliterate the vestiges of the Confederate military. Sherman expected, but did not receive, a hero's welcome from North Carolina Unionists, and he was opposed by a ragtag army of about 21,000 men assembled by Gen. Joseph E. Johnston, who took command of all remaining Confederate forces in the Carolinas on February 25, 1865. Sherman's army, accompanied by 20,000–30,000 slave refugees that followed him from Georgia and South Carolina, moved into the state on March 8, 1865, and a few days later occupied Fayetteville, destroying the Confederate arsenal and the town's two textile mills. Sherman

Figure 9.7 Battle of Bentonville, March 19–21, 1865. *Source:* http://cfnelson.everythingesteban.com/march-1865.

then crossed the Cape Fear River and headed toward Goldsboro, hoping to unite with Union forces coming east from Wilmington. On March 19, the Confederate and Union armies engaged at the Battle of Bentonville, in the largest battle ever fought in North Carolina. The battle battered both sides, but it confirmed that nothing would stop Sherman's further advance and the continued collapse of Southern resistance.

During the early spring of 1865, North Carolina also experienced military pressure from the west, as Union forces from the Army of the Ohio dispatched 6,000 cavalry forces—most of them Unionists from eastern Tennessee and western North Carolina under the command of George Stoneman—to sweep through western and Piedmont North Carolina. On March 28, Stoneman's forces entered North Carolina and captured Boone. Living on forage, the Yankee troops proceeded through the Yadkin valley, crisscrossing northward into Virginia. On April 10, Stoneman struck south again, reaching Germantown and Salem, where his army burned 7,000 bales of cotton. At this point Stoneman dispatched part of his force east toward Greensboro and another through Forsyth County. His forces succeeded in cutting rail connections, including the vital link between Greensboro and Danville, by destroying a bridge at Reedy Fork, 10 miles north of Greensboro. The bridge was destroyed only an hour after President Jefferson Davis and the Confederate cabinet had made their escape by rail from Richmond, south through Greensboro.

A major objective of Stoneman's raid originally had been to liberate the 10,000 Northern prisoners being held under horrific conditions at Salisbury. The facility there had been established as a small prison to hold Confederate soldiers under detention, but in November 1864 Rebel authorities transferred 8,000 prisoners of war whom they detained without shelter, many of them living in holes in the ground and without any supplies of fresh water. Stoneman attacked Salisbury on April 12, but found that the vast majority of the Northern prisoners had already been transferred from the camp. Nonetheless, Stoneman destroyed ammunition supplies, food, and other provisions that might have sustained the Confederate war effort. In his final blow, on April 13, 1865, Stoneman entered Statesville, burning the rail depot, destroying supplies, and burning the offices of a local pro-Confederate newspaper.

Though successful, Stoneman's raid occurred after the war essentially had ended. On April 9, 1865, Gen. Robert E. Lee surrendered the Army of Northern Virginia to the forces of Gen. Ulysses S. Grant. In early April, Vance sent out feelers to Sherman indicating that the North Carolina government might negotiate—an effort which earned him widespread scorn. Davis and the Confederate government fled to Greensboro on April 11, and two days later Joseph Johnston recommended that he surrender his forces to Sherman. The surrender then proceeded quickly after a meeting between Johnston and Sherman at Bennett Place, and Sherman extended generous terms that included the continued power by existing governments across the South, including North Carolina, and a general amnesty for most Confederates—terms that were immediately repudiated by Washington authorities. But, by mid-April 1865, with Davis in flight, the state government in tatters, and the last of the military disintegrating, the Confederacy had collapsed.

The end of the Civil War left North Carolina devastated. The state had suffered considerable privation, and the losses of its youth were horrific. The war had exposed major divisions in the state, and it had destroyed the institution of slavery. After peace came in the spring of 1865, many questions loomed large. Not the least of these was the position that African Americans would occupy in the postwar South and how white North Carolinians would accommodate themselves to the new circumstances that accompanied freedom for all.

Nonetheless, the Civil War helped to solidify North Carolina's identity as a southern state, and from this point on it is said the term "Tar Heel" came into currency to describe the state's residents. According to other accounts, the term was used to mock North Carolinians in the Civil War by Virginians who urged them to "clap your foot down and stick" in battle. The earliest written use of the term occurred in February 1863, when 2nd Lt. William B. A. Lowrance, serving in the 46th Regiment North Carolina Troops, recorded the term in his diary. "I know now," he wrote, "what is meant by the piney woods region of North Carolina and the idea occurs to me that it is no wonder we are called 'tar heels.'" Although originally an insult, the name survived—and became a badge

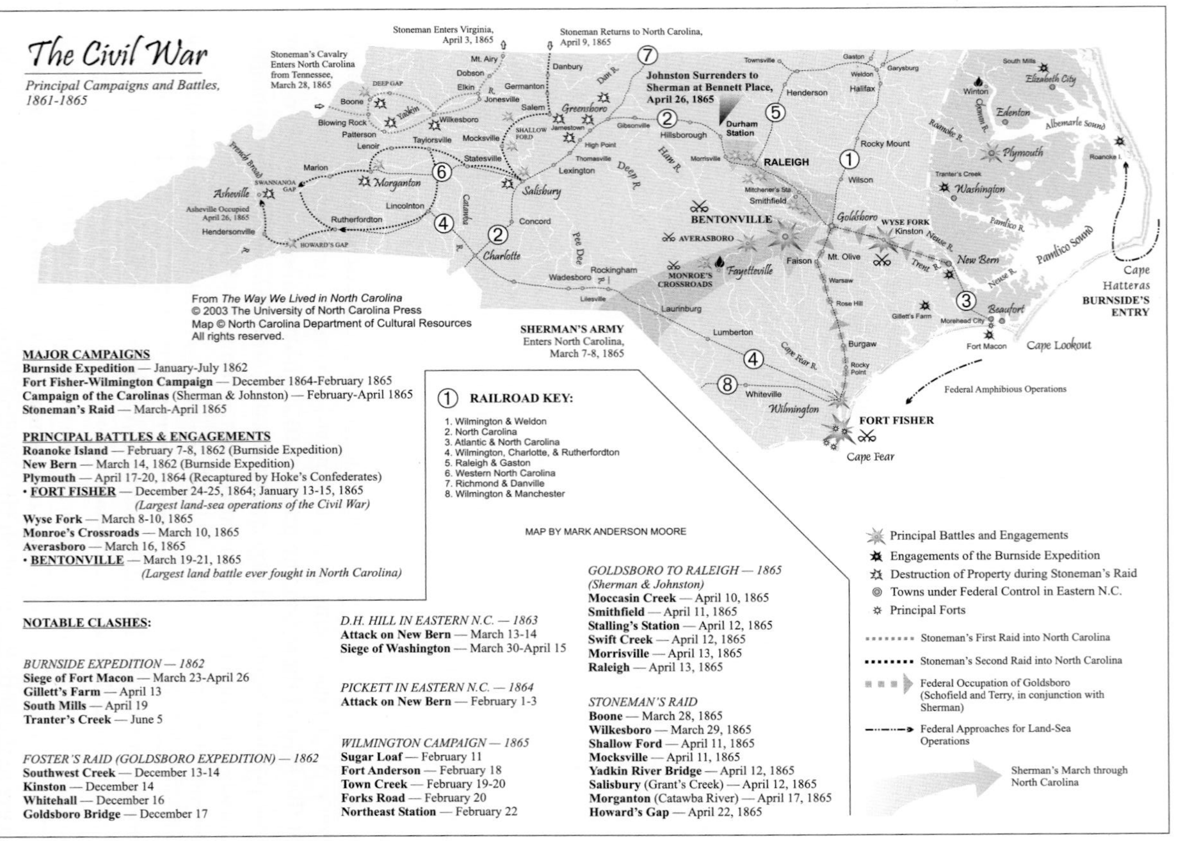

Figure 9.8 The Civil War in North Carolina.

of honor during the Civil War. In March 1864, when Governor Vance visited North Carolina troops, he addressed them as "Fellow Tar Heels." The war thus helped forge a particular Tar Heel identity that became an important legacy.

Notes

1 Gordon D. McKinney, *Zeb Vance: North Carolina's Civil War Governor and Gilded Age Political Leader* (Chapel Hill: University of North Carolina Press, 2004), p. 76.

2 Jennifer Van Zant, "Confederate Conscription and the North Carolina Supreme Court," *North Carolina Historical Review* LXXII, no. 1 (January 1995): 54.

3 William R. Trotter, *Silk Flags and Cold Steel: The Civil War in North Carolina: The Piedmont* (Winston-Salem: John Blair, 1988), p. 154.

4 Paul Escott, *Many Excellent People: Power and Privilege in North Carolina, 1850–1900* (Chapel Hill: University of North Carolina Press, 1985), p. 65.

5 William F. Wagner to N. M. Wagner, July 16, 1863, in Joe M. Hatley and Linda B. Huffman, eds., *Letters of William F. Wagner, Confederate Soldier* (Wendell, NC: Broadfoot's Bookmark, 1983), pp. 56–57.

6 Escott, *Many Excellent People*, pp. 65–67.

7 McKinney, *Zeb Vance*, p. 163.

8 Escott, *Many Excellent People*, pp. 45–46.

9 B. H. Nelson, "Some Aspects of Negro Life in North Carolina in the Civil War," *North Carolina Historical Review* 25, no. 2 (April 1948): 150.

10 Quoted in Judkin Browning, *The Union Occupation of North Carolina* (Chapel Hill: University of North Carolina Press, 2011), p. 85.

11 McKinney, *Zeb Vance*, p. 126.

12 John S. Carbone, *The Civil War in Coastal North Carolina* (Raleigh, NC: Division of Archives and History, 2001), p. 93.

13 Patricia C. Click, *Time Full of Trial: The Roanoke Island Freedmen's Colony, 1862–1867* (Chapel Hill: University of North Carolina Press, 2001), p. 12.

14 Benjamin Butler, "Order by the Commander of the Department of Virginia and North Carolina," December 5, 1863, in Ira Berlin et al., eds., *Freedom: A Documentary History of Emancipation, 1861–1867, Series II: The Black Military Experience* (New York: Cambridge University Press, 1982), pp. 135–38.

15 Richard Reid, "Raising the African Brigade: Early Black Recruitment in Civil War North Carolina," *North Carolina Historical Review* 70 (July 1993): 272.

16 Donna Johanna Benson, "'Before I Be a Slave': A Social Analysis of the Black Struggle for Freedom in North Carolina, 1860–1865." Ph.D. diss., Duke University, 1984, p. 127.

17 Richard M. Reid, *Freedom for Themselves: North Carolina's Black Soldiers in the Civil War Era* (Chapel Hill: University of North Carolina Press, 2008), pp. 183–84.

Suggested Readings, Part 3

Chapter 7

Bess Beatty, *Alamance: The Holt Family and Industrialization in a North Carolina County, 1837–1900* (Baton Rouge: Louisiana State University Press, 1999).

Charles C. Bolton, *Poor Whites of the Antebellum South: Tenants and Laborers in Central North Carolina and Northeast Mississippi* (Durham, NC: Duke University Press, 1994).

James Blackwell Browning, "The Free Negro in Ante-Bellum North Carolina," *North Carolina Historical Review* 15, no. 1 (January 1938): 27.

Cornelius O. Cathey, *Agricultural Development in North Carolina, 1783–1860* (Chapel Hill: University of North Carolina Press, 1956).

David Cecelski, *The Waterman's Song: Slavery and Freedom in Maritime North Carolina* (Chapel Hill: University of North Carolina Press, 2001).

Bill Cecil-Fronsman, *Common Whites: Class and Culture in Antebellum North Carolina* (Lexington: University Press of Kentucky, 1992).

Jane Turner Censer, *North Carolina Planters and Their Children* (Baton Rouge: Louisiana State University Press, 1984).

Thomas H. Clayton, *Close to the Land: The Way We Lived in North Carolina, 1820–1870* (Chapel Hill: University of North Carolina Press, 1983).

Paul D. Escott, *Slavery Remembered: A Record of Twentieth-Century Slave Narratives* (Chapel Hill: University of North Carolina Press, 1979).

Jeff Forret, *Race Relations at the Margins: Slaves and Poor Whites in the Antebellum Southern Countryside* (Baton Rouge: Louisiana State University Press, 2006).

John Hope Franklin, *The Free Negro in North Carolina, 1790–1860* (Chapel Hill: University of North Carolina Press, 1943).

Fletcher M. Green, "Gold Mining: A Forgotten Industry of Ante-Bellum North Carolina," *North Carolina Historical Review* 14, nos. 1 and x (January and April 1937): 1–19 and 135–55.

Guion Griffis Johnson, *Ante-Bellum North Carolina: A Social History* (Chapel Hill: University of North Carolina Press, 1937).

Sally Hadden, "Judging Slavery: Thomas Ruffin and *State v. Mann*," in Christopher Waldrep and Donald G. Nieman, eds., *Local Matters: Race, Crime, and Justice in the Nineteenth-Century South* (Athens: University of Georgia Press, 2001).

Edward W. Phifer, "Slavery in Microcosm: Burke County, North Carolina," *Journal of Southern History* 28 (1962): 137–60.

Joseph C. Robert, *The Tobacco Kingdom: Plantation, Market, and Factory in Virginia and North Carolina* (Durham, NC: Duke University Press, 1938).

Rosser H. Taylor, "Humanizing the Slave Code of North Carolina," *North Carolina Historical Review* 2, no. 3 (July 1925): 327–28.

Rosser H. Taylor, *Slaveholding in North Carolina: An Economic View* (Chapel Hill: University of North Carolina Press, 1926).

Nannie May Tilley, *The Bright-Tobacco Industry* (Chapel Hill: University of North Carolina Press, 1948).

Allen W. Trelease, *The North Carolina Railroad, 1849–1871, and the Modernization of North Carolina* (Chapel Hill: University of North Carolina Press, 1991).

Herbert S. Turner, *The Dreamer: Archibald De Bow Murphey, 1777–1832* (Verona, VA: McClure Press, 1971).

Alan D. Watson, "Battling 'Old Rip': Internal Improvements and the Role of State Government in North Carolina," *North Carolina Historical Review* 77 (April 2000): 181.

Charles C. Weaver, *Internal Improvements in North Carolina Previous to 1860* (Baltimore, MD: The Johns Hopkins University Press, 1903).

Timothy J. Williams, *Intellectual Manhood: University, Self, and Society in the Antebellum South* (Chapel Hill: University of North Carolina Press, 2015).

Chapter 8

Clement Eaton, "The Freedom of the Press in the Upper South," *Mississippi Valley Historical Review* 18 (March 1932): 479–99.

Fletcher Green, *Constitutional Developments of the South Atlantic States, 1776–1860* (Chapel Hill: University of North Carolina Press, 1930).

Joseph Gregoire de Roulhac Hamilton, *Party Politics in North Carolina, 1835–1860* (Durham, NC: Seeman Printery, 1916).

William C. Harris, *North Carolina and the Coming of the Civil War* (Raleigh, NC: Division of Archives and History, 1988).

William S. Hoffmann, *Andrew Jackson and North Carolina Politics* (Chapel Hill: University of North Carolina Press, 1958).

Thomas E. Jeffrey, *State Parties and National Politics: North Carolina, 1815–1861* (Athens: University of Georgia Press, 1989).

Burton Alva Konkle, *John Motley Morehead and the Development of North Carolina, 1796–1866* (Philadelphia, PA: William J. Campbell, 1922).

Marc Kruman, *Parties and Politics in North Carolina, 1836–1865* (Baton Rouge: Louisiana State University Press, 1983).

Herbert Dale Pegg, *The Whig Party in North Carolina* (Chapel Hill: Colonial Press, 1968).

J. Herman Schauinger, *William Gaston: Carolinian* (Milwaukee, WI: Bruce Publishing, 1949).

J. Carlyle Sitterson, *The Secession Movement in North Carolina* (Chapel Hill: University of North Carolina Press, 1939).

Michael Thomas Smith, *A Traitor and a Scoundrel: Benjamin Hedrick and the Cost of Dissent* (Newark: University of Delaware Press, 2003).

Noble J. Tolbert, "Daniel Worth: Tar Heel Abolitionist," *North Carolina Historical Review* 39, no. 3 (July 1962): 291–92.

Harry L. Watson, *Jacksonian Politics and Community Conflict: The Emergence of the Second American Party System in Cumberland County, North Carolina* (Baton Rouge: Louisiana State University Press, 1981).

Timothy J. Williams, *Intellectual Manhood: University, Self, and Society in the Antebellum South* (Chapel Hill: University of North Carolina Press, 2015).

Gail Williams O'Brien, *The Legal Fraternity and the Making of a New South Community, 1848–1882* (Athens: University of Georgia Press, 1986).

Chapter 9

Daniel W. Barefoot, *General Robert F. Hoke: Lee's Modest Warrior* (Winston-Salem, NC: John F. Blair Publisher, 1996).

William L. Barney, *The Making of a Confederate: Walter Lenoir's Civil War* (New York: Oxford University Press, 2008).

John G. Barrett, *Sherman's March through the Carolinas* (Chapel Hill: University of North Carolina Press, 1956).

John G. Barrett, *The Civil War in North Carolina* (Chapel Hill: University of North Carolina Press, 1963).

Donna Johanna Benson, *"'Before I Be a Slave': A Social Analysis of the Black Struggle for Freedom in North Carolina, 1860–1865,"* Ph.D. diss., Duke University, 1984.

Ira Berlin et al., eds., *Freedom: A Documentary History of Emancipation, 1861–1867, Series II: The Black Military Experience* (New York: Cambridge University Press, 1982).

Mark L. Bradley, *This Astounding Close: The Road to Bennett Place* (Chapel Hill: University of North Carolina Press, 2000).

Mark L. Bradley, *Bluecoats and Tar Heels: Soldiers and Civilians in Reconstruction North Carolina* (Lexington: University Press of Kentucky, 2009).

Louis A. Brown, *The Salisbury Prison: A Case Study of Confederate Military Prisons, 1861–1865* (Wendell, NC: Avera Press and Broadfoot's Bookmark, 1980).

Judkin Browning, *Shifting Loyalties: The Union Occupation of Eastern North Carolina* (Chapel Hill: University of North Carolina Press, 2011).

John S. Carbone, *The Civil War in Coastal North Carolina* (Raleigh, NC: Division of Archives and History, 2001).

David S. Cecelski, *The Fire of Freedom: Abraham Galloway and the Slaves' Civil War* (Chapel Hill: University of North Carolina Press, 2012).

Patricia C. Click, *Time Full of Trial: The Roanoke Island Freedmen's Colony, 1862–1867* (Chapel Hill: University of North Carolina Press, 2001).

Archie K. Davis, *Boy Colonel of the Confederacy: The Life and Times of Henry King Burgwyn* (Chapel Hill: University of North Carolina Press, 1985).

Wayne K. Durrill, *War of Another Kind: A Southern Community in the Great Rebellion* (New York: Oxford University Press, 1990).

Paul Escott, *Many Excellent People: Power and Privilege in North Carolina, 1850–1900* (Chapel Hill: University of North Carolina Press, 1985).

Paul Escott, *North Carolinians in the Era of the Civil War and Reconstruction* (Chapel Hill: University of North Carolina Press, 2008).

Gary W. Gallagher, *Stephen Dodson Ramseur* (Chapel Hill: University of North Carolina Press, 1985).

Joe M. Hatley and Linda B. Huffman, eds., *Letters of William F. Wagner, Confederate Soldier* (Wendell, NC: Broadfoot's Bookmark, 1983).

Richard B. McCaslin, *The Last Stronghold: The Campaign for Fort Fisher* (Abilene, TX: McWhiney Foundation Press, 2003).

Gordon D. McKinney, *Zeb Vance: North Carolina's Civil War Governor and Gilded Age Political Leader* (Chapel Hill: University of North Carolina Press, 2004).

Memory Mitchell, *Legal Aspects of Conscription and Exemption in North Carolina, 1861–1865* (Chapel Hill: University of North Carolina Press, 1965).

Joe A. Mobley, "War Governor of the South": North Carolina's Zeb Vance in the Confederacy (Gainesville: University Press of Florida, 2005).

B. H. Nelson, "Some Aspects of Negro Life in North Carolina in the Civil War," *North Carolina Historical Review* 25, no. 2 (April 1948): 150.

Phillip Shaw Paludan, *Victims: A True Story of the Civil War* (Knoxville: University of Tennessee Press, 2004).

Richard Reid, "Raising the African Brigade: Early Black Recruitment in Civil War North Carolina," *North Carolina Historical Review* 70 (July 1993): 272.

Richard Reid, *Freedom for Themselves: North Carolina's Black Soldiers in the Civil War Era* (Chapel Hill: University of North Carolina Press, 2008).

David Silkenat, *Moments of Despair: Suicide, Divorce, and Debt in Civil War Era North Carolina* (Chapel Hill: University of North Carolina Press, 2011).

William R. Trotter, *Silk Flags and Cold Steel: The Civil War in North Carolina: The Piedmont* (Winston-Salem: John Blair, 1988).

Jennifer Van Zant, "Confederate Conscription and the North Carolina Supreme Court," *North Carolina Historical Review* LXXII, no. 1 (January 1995): 54.

Document Section, Part 3
Voices of the Enslaved

The experience of slavery is often told from the point of view of masters and slaveholders. In large part, this reflects the nature of the sources: in other words, it was whites who wrote most contemporary accounts that still survive. But the differences between how slavery was understood among slaves and masters differed radically. Most descriptions from slaveholders tend to paper over the harsh, demeaning, and humiliating qualities of life for the enslaved. Most say little about the system's brutality, how masters frequently resorted to the lash to preserve their often tenuous authority, to maintain work discipline and insure that slaves worked, and how often slaves gave clear evidence of their intense desire for freedom. The documentary record from the enslaved is fragmentary, though compelling. During the 1920s and 1930s, researchers, many funded by agencies created by the New Deal, interviewed scores of ex-slaves, writing down their accounts and preserving their memories. Legal documents are also useful, especially when they include the testimony of black people.

Numerous narratives of former slaves were published during the antebellum years, written by those able to escape slavery to the North and Canada. These have also become an invaluable source from African Americans' point of view. There were around one hundred such narratives published, many of them involving North Carolina ex-slaves. Often written in collaboration with white and black abolitionists, the published narratives are unabashedly antislavery; their purpose was to expose slavery's evils to a broad, national public. They also vary in quality and in the extent to which voices of those who had been enslaved emerge (they were often ghost-written). But a number of the slave narratives, such as those written by Frederick Douglass, Moses Grandy, Solomon Northup, and Harriet Jacobs are powerful—and obviously personal—descriptions of the horrors of slavery and how individuals were able to escape enslavement.

In this section's documents, we hear from the voices of the enslaved. The first selection describes the worst of slavery's abuses—the separation of families through forced sale, a frequent occurrence in North Carolina. The second

North Carolina: Change and Tradition in a Southern State, Second Edition. William A. Link.

document provided a detailed account of the desire for freedom—and how one slave obtained it.

Thomas H. Jones's Slave Narrative[1]

One of the most common—and wrenching—experiences under slavery was the separation of families. This became especially common in North Carolina, a major slave-exporting state in the antebellum period. Born in 1806 near Wilmington, Thomas H. Jones, was sold at the age of 9 to a Wilmington storekeeper. After his master's death in 1829, Jones was sold to Owen Holmes, who hired him out as a stevedore. Jones's first marriage ended when his wife, Lucilla Smith, and his three children had no choice but to move (away from him) with Lucilla's master to Alabama.

Jones married again in the mid-1830s; he was able to purchase his wife, and they lived in Wilmington's free-black community. With his children by this marriage still slaves, Jones naturally worried about their status and the possibility that they, too, might be sold away from him and out of his life.

Here, Thomas H. Jones explains the impact of the slave trade on his family. In 1849, he sent his family to freedom in the North. Still a slave himself, Jones then stowed away on a brig, absconding to New York City. His narrative describes his recollections of enslavement.

I was born a slave. My recollections of early life are associated with poverty, suffering and shame. I was made to feel, in my boyhood's first experience, that I was inferior and degraded, and that I must pass through life in a dependent and suffering condition. The experience of forty-three years, which were passed by me in slavery, was one of dark fears and darker realities. John Hawes was my first master. He lived in Hanover County, N. C., between the Black and South Rivers, and was the owner of a large plantation called Hawes' Plantation. He had over fifty slaves. I remained with my parents nine years. They were both slaves, owned by John Hawes. They had six children, Richard, Alexander, Charles, Sarah, myself, and John. I remember well that dear old cabin, with its clay floor and mud chimney, in which, for nine years, I enjoyed the presence and love of my wretched parents.

Father and mother tried to make it a happy place for their dear children. They worked late into the night many and many a time to get a little simple furniture for their home and the home of their children; and they spent many hours of

---

1 Thomas H. Jones, *Experience and Personal Narrative of Uncle Tom Jones; Who Was for Forty Years a Slave. Also the Surprising Adventures of Wild Tom, of the Island Retreat, a Fugitive Negro from South Carolina* (Boston: H. B. Skinner, [185-?]), pp. 7–10, http://docsouth.unc.edu/neh/jonestom/jones.html.

willing toil to stop up the chinks between the logs of their poor hut, that they and their children might be protected from the storm and the cold. I can testify from my own painful experience, to the deep and fond affection which the slave cherishes in his heart for his home and its dear ones. We have no other tie to link us to the human family, but our fervent love for those who are with us and of us in relations of sympathy and devotedness, in wrongs and wretchedness. My dear parents were conscious of the desperate and incurable woe of their position and destiny; and the lot of inevitable suffering in store for their beloved children. They talked about our coming misery, and they lifted up their voices and wept aloud, as they spoke of our being torn from them and sold off to the dreaded slave trader, perhaps never to see them or hear from them a word of fond love. I am a father, and have had the same feelings of unspeakable anguish, as I have looked upon my precious babes, and have thought of the ignorance, degradation and woe which they must endure as slaves. The great God who knoweth all the secrets of the earth, and He only, knows the bitter sorrow I now feel, when I think of my four dear children who are slaves, torn from me and consigned to hopeless servitude by the iron hand of ruthless wrong. I love those children with all a father's fondness. . . .

Thus passed nine years of my life; years of suffering, the shuddering memory of which is deeply fixed in my heart.

These nine years of wretchedness passed, and a change came for me. My master sold me to Mr. Jones of Washington, N. C., distant forty-five miles from Hawes' plantation. Mr. Jones sent his slave driver, a colored man, named Abraham, to conduct me to my new home in Washington. I was at home with my mother when he came. He looked in at the door, and called to me, "Tom, you must go with me." His looks were ugly and his voice was savage. I was very much afraid, and began to cry, holding on to my mother's clothes and begging her to protect me, and not let the man take me away. Mother wept bitterly, and, in the midst of her loud sobbings, cried out in broken words, "I can't save you, Tommy; master has sold you, you must go." She threw her arms around me, and while the hot tears fell on my face, she strained me to her heart. There she held me, sobbing and mourning, till the brutal Abraham came in, snatched me away, hurried me out of the house where I was born, my only home, and tore me away from the dear mother who loved me as no other friend could do. She followed him, imploring a moment's delay and weeping aloud, to the road, where he turned around, and striking at her with his heavy cowhide, fiercely ordered her to stop bawling, and go back into the house.

Thus was I snatched from my loving parents, and from the true affection of the dear ones of home. For thirteen weary years did my heart turn in its yearnings to that precious home. And then at the age of twenty-two, I was permitted to revisit my early home. I found it all desolate; the family all broken up; father was sold and gone; Richard, Alexander, Charles, Sarah, and John were sold and gone. Mother prematurely old, heart-broken, utterly desolate, weak and dying, alone remained. I saw her, and wept once more on her bosom. I went back to my chains with a deeper woe in my heart than I had ever felt before. There was but one thought of joy in my wretched consciousness, and that was, that my kind and precious mother would soon be at rest in the grave. And then, too, I remember, I mused with deep earnestness on death, as the only friend the poor slave had. And I wished that I too, might lie down by my mother's side, and die with her in her loving embrace.

James Curry's Slave Narrative[2]

Most slaves possessed few options to resist the oppressive system. Violent resistance prompted beatings; insurrections were usually suicidal. The most effective means of resistance proved to be running away. Although most slaves did not abscond, enough did to worry slaveholders about the loss of profits and investment. James Curry was born in 1815 in Person County. His father was free, his mother enslaved; that meant that he was a slave. At the age of 22, Curry escaped, eventually settling in Canada. In 1840, he published his narrative. In it, he describes his flight. Curry's departure, as was true of many slaves, came after a beating; he responded spontaneously, as a way to strike back against the system.

I was born in Person County, North Carolina. My master's name was Moses Chambers. My mother was the daughter of a white man and a slave woman. She, with her brother, were given, when little children, to my master's mother, soon after her marriage, by her father. Their new master and mistress were both drunkards, and possessed very little property besides these two slaves. My mother was treated very cruelly. Oh! I cannot tell you how dreadful her treatment was while she was a young girl. It is not proper to be written; but the treatment of females in slavery is very dreadful. When she was about fifteen years old, she attempted to run away. She got about fifteen miles, and stopped at the house of a poor white woman, with the intention of staying there four weeks, until her brother, who had a wife near there, came down to see her, which he did once in four weeks. She could not bear to go farther without hearing from her mother, and giving her intelligence of herself. She also wished to procure herself some clothes, as she was very destitute. At the end of three weeks, there came in a white man, who knew and arrested her, and returned her to her master. She soon afterwards married a slave in the neighborhood. Her mistress did not provide her with clothes, and her husband obtained for her a wheel, which she

---

2 James Curry, *Narrative of James Curry, A Fugitive Slave, The Liberator*, January 10, 1840, http://docsouth.unc.edu/neh/curry/curry.html.

kept in her hut, for the purpose of spinning in the night, after her day's work of her cruel mistress was done. This her mistress endeavored to prevent, by keeping her spinning in the house until twelve or one o'clock at night. But she would then go home, and, fixing her wheel in a place made in the floor to prevent its making a noise, she would spin for herself, in order that she might be decently clad in the daytime. Her treatment continued so bad that she, with her sister, who was the slave of her mistress's sister, resolved to run away again. Her sister had a husband, who concluded to go too; and then my mother informed her husband, and they all four started together. Not knowing any better, they went directly south. After traveling two or three nights, Ann's husband thought they could travel safely by day, and so they walked on in the morning. They had got but little way, when they met a white man, who stopped and asked them, 'Are you travelers?' They answered, 'Yes, sir.' 'Are you free?' 'Yes, sir.' 'Have you free papers?' 'Yes, sir.' (They got some person to furnish them before they started.) 'Well,' said he, 'go back to the next village, and we will have them examined.' So he took them before a magistrate, who examined the papers and said, 'these won't do.' He then said to the girls, 'Girls, we don't doubt that you are free, and if you choose, you may go on; but these boys you have stolen from their masters, and they must go to jail.' (Then, before the laws against emancipation were passed, bright mulattoes, such as these girls were, would be allowed to pass along the road unmolested, but now they could not.) The girls, being unwilling to part with their husbands, went to jail with them, and being advertised, their masters came after them in a few days. This ended my mother's running away. Having young children soon, it tied her to slavery....

From my childhood, the desire for freedom reigned predominant in my breast, and I resolved, if I was ever whipped after I became a man, I would no longer be a slave. When I was a lad, my master's uncle came one day to see him, and as I was passing near them, the old man took hold of me and asked my master if this was one of Lucy's boys. Being told that I was, he said, 'Well, his father was a free man and perhaps when he gets to be a man, he'll be wanting to be free too.' Thinks I to myself, indeed I shall. But if he had asked me if I wanted to be free, I should have answered, 'No, Sir.' Of course, no slave would dare to say, in the presence of a white man, that he wished for freedom. But among themselves, it is their constant theme. No slaves think they were made to be slaves. Let them keep them ever so ignorant, it is impossible to beat it into them that they were made to be slaves. I have heard some of the most ignorant I ever saw, say 'it will not always be so, God will bring them to an account.' I used to wonder why it was that our people were kept in slavery. I would look at the birds as they flew over my head or sung their free songs upon the trees, and think it strange, that, of all God's creatures, the poor negro only was held in bondage. I knew there were free states, but I thought the people there did not know how we were treated. I had heard of England, and that there, there were no slaves; and I thought if I could only get there and tell my story, there would immediately be something done which would bring freedom to the slave.

The slaves, altho' kept in the lowest ignorance in which it is possible to keep them, are, nevertheless, far more intelligent than they are usually represented, or than they ever appear to white people. (Of course, in this and every thing else, I speak only so far as my knowledge extends.) The few faculties they are allowed to cultivate are continually exercised, and therefore greatly strengthened; for instance, that of providing comforts for themselves and those they love, by extra work, and little trade. Then they are generally brought together from distant places and communicate to each other all the knowledge they possess. The slaves also from neighboring plantations hold frequent intercourse with each other, and then they cannot help learning white people talk. For instance, just before the last presidential election, there came a report from a neighboring plantation, that, if Van Buren was elected, he was going to give all the slaves their freedom. It spread rapidly among all the slaves in the neighborhood, and great, very great was the rejoicing. One old man, who was a christian, came and told us, that now, all we had got to do, was, as Moses commanded the children of Israel on the shore of the Red Sea, 'to stand still and see the salvation of God.' Mr. Van Buren was elected, but he gave no freedom to the slaves. . . .

In May, 1837, just after I was 22 years old, the overseer sent a boy to me one evening, with a horse, bidding me go with him to feed him. It was then between nine and ten o'clock at night. I had toiled through the day for my master, had just got my dinner, and was on my way to the hatter's shop for my night's work, when the boy came to me. I did not think it necessary for me to go with him, so I told him where to put the horse, and that the feed was all ready and he might throw it in; and then I went to my work at the shop, where I was allowed to make hats, using nothing of my master's, except tools and the dye, which would be thrown away after my uncle had done with it. In a few minutes, the overseer came in and asked me why I did not go with the boy. . . . He then swore that he would flog me because I had not obeyed his orders. He took a hickory rod and struck me some thirty or forty strokes, over my clothes. My first impulse was to take the stick out of his hand, for I was much stronger than he. But I recollected that my master was in the house, and if I did so, he would be called, and probably I should be stripped and tied, and instead of thirty or forty, should receive hundreds of stripes. I therefore concluded it was wisest to take quietly whatever he choose to inflict, but as the strokes fell upon my back, I firmly resolved that I would no longer be a slave. I would now escape or die in the attempt. They might shoot me down if they chose, but I would not live a slave. The next morning, I decided, that, as my master was preparing for one of his slave-driving expeditions to Alabama, I would wait until he was gone; that when he was fairly started on his journey, I would start on mine, he for the south, and I for the north. In the meantime, I instructed my two younger brothers in my plans. It happened that on the afternoon of the 14th of June, about three weeks after the whipping I received, and just after my master had set off for Alabama, as we were going to the field after breakfast, to ploughing, the overseer got very angry with me and my two brothers, and threatened to whip us before night. He said that as he could not do it himself, there were men in the neighborhood he could get to help him, and then he walked away. This was our opportunity. We took our horses round to the road fence and hitched them, and ran for my wife's house. There I changed my clothes, and took my leave of her, with the hope of being soon able to send for her from a land of freedom, and left her in a state of distress which I cannot describe. We started without money and without clothes, except what we wore, (not daring to carry a bundle,) but with our hearts full of hope. We travelled by night, and slept in the woods during the day. After travelling two or three nights, we got alarmed and turned out of the road, and before we turned into it again, it had separated, and we took the wrong road. It was cloudy for two or three days, and after travelling three nights, we found ourselves just where we were three days before, and almost home again. We were sadly disappointed, but not discouraged; and so, turning our faces again northward, we went on. I should have said before, that I knew the way to Petersburgh, Va. having been several times sent there by my master with a team. Near Petersburgh, we passed a neat farm-house, with every thing around it in perfect order, which had once been shown to me by a slave, as I was driving my master's team to the city. 'That,' said he, 'belongs to a Friend; they never hold slaves.' Now I was strongly tempted to stop there, and ask instruction in my northward course, as I knew the way no farther; but I dared not. So, not knowing the north star, we took the two lower stars of the great bear for our guide, and putting our trust in God, we passed Petersburgh. We suffered much from hunger. There was no fruit and no grain to be found at that season, and we sometimes went two days, and sometimes three, without tasting food, as we did not dare to ask, except when we found a slave's, or free colored person's house remote from any other, and then we were never refused, if they had food to give. Thus we came on, until about forty-five miles from Washington, when, having in the night obtained some meal, and having then been three days without food, my poor brothers begged me to go out of the woods in the day time, and get some fire in order to bake us some bread. I went to a house, got some and returned to the woods. We made a fire in the hollow stump of a tree, mixed our meal with water, which we found near, and wrapping it in leaves, threw it in and baked it. After eating heartily, we began to bake some to carry with us, when, hearing a noise in the bushes, we looked up, and beheld dogs coming towards us, and behind them several white men, who called out, 'O! you rascals, what are you doing there? Catch him! catch him!' The dogs sprang towards us. My feelings I cannot describe, as I started, and ran with all my might. My brothers, having taken off their coats and hats, stopped to pick them up, and then ran off in another direction, and the dogs followed them, while I escaped, and never saw them more. I heard the dogs barking after them, when I had got as much as a mile from where we started. Oh! then I was most miserable, left alone, a poor hunted stranger in a strange land—my brothers gone. I know not how to express the feelings of that moment.... That night [I] crossed a branch of the Potomac. Just before I reached the town of Dumfries, I came across an old horse in a field with a bell on his neck. I had been warned by a colored man, a few nights before, to beware of Dumfries. I was worn out with running, and I took the bell off the horse's neck, took the bell collar for a whip, and putting a hickory bark round his head for a bridle, I jumped on his back, and thus mounted, I rode through Dumfries. The bull-dogs lay along the street, ready to seize the poor night traveller, but, being on horse-back, they did not molest me. I have no doubt that I should have been taken up, if I had been on foot. When I got through the town, I dismounted, and said to my horse, 'go back to your master, I did not mean to injure him, and hope we will get you again, but you have done me a great deal of good.' And then I hastened on, and got as far from him as I could before morning. At Alexandria, I crossed the Potomac river, and came to Washington, where I made friends with a colored family, with whom I rested eight days. I then took the Montgomery road, but, wishing to escape Baltimore, I turned off, and it being cloudy, I lost my course, and fell back again upon the Potomac river, and travelled on the tow path of the canal from Friday night until Sunday morning, when I lay down and slept a little, and then, having no place to hide for the day, I determined to go on until I could find a place of safety. I soon saw a man riding towards me on horse-back. As he came near, he put his eyes upon me, and I felt sure that he intended to question me. I fell to praying to God to protect me, and so begging and praying fervently, I went forward. When he met me, he stopped his horse, leaned forward and looked at me, and then, without speaking, rode on again. I still fully believe it was at first his intention to question me. I soon entered a colored person's house on the side of the canal, where they gave me breakfast and treated me very kindly. I travelled on through Williamsport and Hagerstown, in Maryland, and, on the 19th day of July, about two hours before day. I crossed the line into Pennsylvania, with a heart full of gratitude to God, believing that I was indeed a free man, and that now, under the protection of law, there was 'none who could molest me or make me afraid.' In the course of the morning, I was spoken to by a man, sitting at the window of a house in Chambersburg, who asked me if I wanted a job of work. I replied that I did, and he took me into his garden, and set me to work. When the job there was done, he told me I might clean his carriage. At dinner, I ate in the kitchen with a colored woman. She inquired where I came from, I told her the name of the town in Pennsylvania. Said she, 'I didn't know but you came from Virginia, or Maryland, and sometimes, some of our colored friends come from there hither, and think they are free, but the people about here are very ugly, and they take them and carry them back; and if you haven't sufficient free papers, I would advise you not to stay here to-night.' This was enough for me. I had discovered that the man was very curious about me, and seemed disposed to keep me at work upon little jobs until night. I went out, and jumped over the garden wall, and was soon on the turnpike road. I was very fearful, and came on tremblingly; but near Philadelphia, I fell in with members of the Society of Friends, whom I never feared to trust, who 'took in the stranger,' and I worked for them until Christmas.

After finding, to my great disappointment, that I was now a free man, and that I could not send for my wife from here, I determined to go to Canada. But the situation of that country at that time was such, that my friends thought it not best for me to go immediately, and advised me to come into the State of Massachusetts, as the safest place for me until the difficulties in Canada were passed away. I was taken by kind friends to New York, from whence the Abolitionists sent me to Massachusetts, and here I have found a resting place, and have met with friends who have freely administered to my necessities, and whose kindness to the poor fugitive I shall ever remember with emotions of heartfelt gratitude. And here I have fulfilled the promise made in slavery to my Maker, that I would acknowledge him before men, when I came into a land of freedom. And although I have suffered much, very much in my escape, and have not here found that perfect freedom which I anticipated, yet I have never for one moment regretted that I thus sought my liberty.

Part 4

Reconstruction and Its Aftermath

10

Reconstruction

By end of the Civil War, North Carolina had suffered terrific human losses, more than 40,000 dead and thousands of others maimed for life. The state's economy lay in ruins, with the value of property in the state having been reduced by half. Money and credit were hard to come by, and commerce, trade, and manufacturing had ground to a halt. Not only was industry defunct, but the railroad transportation system lay in ruins, and agriculture was in a state of disarray. Not only had crops gone to feed armies, with many a field exhausted, but much of the state's livestock had been wiped out, either by hungry North Carolinians or Sherman's invaders. With the surrender of Confederate armies, state and local governments lacked any authority, and North Carolina, occupied by Union troops, lay under military rule.

On the heels of the Civil War, pressing questions accompanied North Carolina's return to the Union in a process known as "Reconstruction." Under what circumstances would North Carolinians return to the Union? How would the federal government treat former Confederate officeholders, elected representatives, and military leaders—those who, for the most part, represented the state's governing elite? To what extent would this old guard be included in the future leadership of the state? The most important constellation of issues, however, surrounded the fate of the more than 350,000 former slaves, now freed by the Union victory, a status soon to be made permanent by the ratification of the Thirteenth Amendment. What place would the freedpeople occupy in postwar North Carolina society? What civil rights would they possess? And would they participate in the political system?

North Carolina African Americans and Freedom

As slavery disintegrated throughout the course of the war, spurred by Lincoln's Emancipation Proclamation in 1863, then received its death sentence with the passage of the Thirteenth Amendment, black people in North Carolina began

North Carolina: Change and Tradition in a Southern State, Second Edition. William A. Link.

Figure 10.1 St. Stephen AME Church, Wilmington, formed by ex-slaves. *Source: Tim Buchman, courtesy of Preservation North Carolina.*

to construct new institutions. Those portions of North Carolina under Union occupation experienced this process earlier, as emancipated slaves began to explore freedom, but North Carolina's entire black population did not realize slavery's end until the spring of 1865, in some cases, months after the conclusion of the war. At the grass-roots level, most African Americans focused on three basic social institutions: family, church, and school. Under slavery, the state's legal system had not recognized the legitimacy of slave marriage, though slaves had created a viable system of common-law marriage nonetheless. Nor did the slave code recognize the legitimacy of children. Still, despite the frequency of family breakups—with masters often selling husbands away from wives, children away from parents—the African American family remained a source of support and independence. With emancipation came efforts by thousands of freedpeople to seek out displaced loved ones, enter into legalized marriages, choose legal names, and forge stable family units.

After emancipation, former slaves organized their own independent church congregations, which had been prohibited in antebellum North Carolina. Antebellum white churches had accepted slaves but insisted on their segregation during worship services and their subservience within the church structure. Slaves, meanwhile, created an alternative version of Christianity that thrived in underground congregations outside the control of whites. Former slaveholders were shocked when African Americans left white churches in droves, but former slaves wanted control of their congregations. In all of the major Protestant denominations, therefore, black churches separated into distinct entities soon after the Civil War ended.

In another form of institution-building, freedpeople flocked into schools organized by northern white missionary groups and the Freedmen's Bureau. Congress had established the Freedmen's Bureau in March 1865 to coordinate various efforts—in education, as well as in work and health—to facilitate the transition from slavery to freedom, first, among slaves fleeing their masters during the war and then the entire ex-slave population thereafter. In education, the Bureau sponsored schools in North Carolina and across the South. Beginning during the war, groups such as the northern American Missionary Association had made the establishment of schools for freedpeople a chief priority. By 1867, 13,039 black children were attending Freedmen's Bureau and missionary schools in the state, about 10 percent of the African American school-age population.

Institution-building by North Carolina African Americans led, almost inevitably, to political involvement. Leaders emerged from the prewar free black population and returning black Union army veterans. In organizations such as the Union League, which first appeared in 1866 and grew rapidly after 1867, African Americans used grass-roots political organization to press for civil and political rights. During the years immediately after the end of the war, black veterans paraded, sometimes even armed, on occasions such as the Fourth of July. One such parade occurred in Raleigh in July 1865, when 2,000 African Americans, many of them veterans, paraded in front of the state capitol. Later, African Americans organized their first statewide freedmen's convention, with mass meetings throughout the state. One such local meeting was held in New Bern, with a call to "rise up in the dignity of men" and "to strike one blow to secure those rights of Freedmen that have been so long withheld from us." In another meeting, in Tarboro, some 1,500 freedmen attended.[1] Throughout the state, African Americans sought civil rights and the vote, measures they considered essential to protecting their freedom.

This freedmen's convention, which met in Raleigh on September 29, 1865, included representatives from thirty-four counties, mostly from eastern North Carolina. Assembling at the African Methodist Church—and coinciding with the all-white constitutional convention then in session— the freedmen's convention elected as president Rev. James W. Hood, a Pennsylvania native and African Methodist Episcopal (AME) minister who had moved to New Bern and later Fayetteville after that town was occupied by Union forces in March 1865. Hood called for equal rights, including the ability for African Americans to testify in courts of law, serve on juries, and, above all, vote. Abraham Galloway, another convention leader, was born in southeastern North Carolina's Brunswick County to a 17-year-old slave mother and a wealthy white father,

Figure 10.2 Abraham H. Galloway (1837–70), fugitive slave, Union war veteran, and Reconstruction-Era leader. *Source: North Carolina Museum of History.*

John Wesley Galloway. Working as a slave artisan as a brick mason, in June 1857, Abraham escaped on a ship to Philadelphia, moving to Ontario and becoming an outspoken abolitionist. During the war, he enlisted in the Union army and worked as a spy for Union forces, returning to North Carolina in 1862–63, where he also recruited African Americans into the northern army. A noted orator, Galloway was a leader in the National Equal Rights League, and he became one of the prominent North Carolina African Americans pressing for civil and political rights for freedmen. During the spring of 1864, he visited the White House to urge Abraham Lincoln to support black suffrage. When he died suddenly in April 1868, 6,000 people attended his funeral in Wilmington.

Also prominent in the Raleigh meeting was James H. Harris. Born in Granville County, Harris had attended Oberlin College's preparatory school in Ohio, and he later traveled to Canada and Africa (Liberia and Sierra Leone) where some American blacks had become colonists. On his return to the United States in 1863, Harris helped to organize the Twenty-Eighth Regiment of Colored Troops, and became involved in the Union League and Republican Party politics. Resolutions adopted by the freedmen's convention endorsed emancipation as a "bright page in the history of progressive civilization," and they called on Congress to "secure to the colored citizen his rights through the actions of Congress."[2] But in a subsequent address to the all-white constitutional convention (then meeting in Raleigh), the convention struck a moderate stance, saying nothing about political rights, instead calling for harmonious relations between former masters and slaves, expanded educational opportunities for black children, and fairness in new work arrangements.

Even as white leaders sought to impose a new pattern of race relations, African Americans remained determined to preserve their hard-fought freedom by pursuing a program of civil and political rights. The freedmen's convention adjourned with the organization of a new group, the North Carolina State Equal Rights League. Meanwhile, whites' attempts to enforce the Black Code, defining the social, political, and economic roles of slaves, at the local level—especially in areas such as southeastern North Carolina that had a large black population—encountered stiff resistance. For this reason, white authorities' efforts to regulate black employment remained ineffective. North Carolina whites regarded this resistance as evidence of the breakdown of law and order, which many of them attributed to "uppity" freedpeople. Among African Americans, the newly established local authorities simply appeared to be trying to reestablish vestiges of slavery.

Self-Reconstruction

The collapse of state and local government accompanied the surrender of Confederate armies in April and May of 1865. Fleeing the advancing troops of William T. Sherman, who occupied Raleigh on April 13, 1865, Gov. Zebulon Vance was apprehended and arrested in Statesville on May 14, and then briefly imprisoned in Raleigh. Sherman's troops served as a temporary government; when Sherman left the state in April, he left Gen. John Schofield in charge.

Andrew Johnson, who became president after the death of Abraham Lincoln in April at the hands of an assassin, moved to restore civilian rule in North Carolina and elsewhere in the occupied South. Extending Lincoln's policy of leniency toward former Confederates, Johnson provided what historians later called "self-Reconstruction," which meant the northern victors permitted southern whites to manage the process of Reconstruction. On May 29, 1865, Johnson issued a proclamation that applied to North Carolina but quickly became a model for his Reconstruction policy across the South. The president extended an amnesty and pardon to all former rebels who agreed to take an oath of allegiance to the United States and accept the end of slavery; his proclamation excluded those who had held high political and military offices in the Confederacy. Johnson also appointed William W. Holden as provisional governor of North Carolina and empowered him to exercise "all the powers necessary and proper"[3] to organize a provisional government composed of "loyal persons," create a new constitution, and restore the former Confederacy to the Union. Holden had led a delegation that had met with President Johnson in mid-May in Washington, urging, to no avail, immediate restoration of the state to the Union, and Johnson was impressed with Holden as a like-minded leader.

On June 12, after his appointment as provisional governor, Holden issued a proclamation laying out his plans for the restoration of constitutional government. Within a year, he had appointed more than 3,000 "loyal" justices of the peace, who reinstituted local government. On August 8, Holden summoned a state convention to create a new structure for local and state government. Elections were held on September 21, 1865, with only those voters eligible for the franchise prior to the war participating; excluded from the vote were not only fourteen classes of Confederate officials but also all of the state's African American males. All who wished to vote had to take an oath of loyalty to the Union. A flood of North Carolinians sought and obtained pardons from President Johnson; by July 1866, the number of such pardons reached nearly 2,000.

Meeting in Raleigh on October 2, 1865, the so-called Holden Convention included mostly familiar faces: two delegates had served as members of the Confederate Congress, twelve had sat with the 1861 secession convention, and three had participated in the constitutional convention of 1835. The convention's main charge from the Union occupiers was to repudiate secession, ratify the end of slavery, and repudiate the debt incurred by the state Confederate government. In this capacity, the Holden Convention subscribed to the Reconstruction policies of Abraham Lincoln and Andrew Johnson—known generally as "presidential Reconstruction." In North Carolina, as in the other former states of the Confederacy, presidential Reconstruction brought no substantive changes in the social and political system, with the newly freed slaves left in a subordinate position, roughly equivalent to the status of free blacks during the antebellum era.

Nonetheless, the convention moved quickly. First, it repealed the ordinance of secession; then, after some discussion, the delegates voted to repudiate all debts incurred by the Confederate government. Beyond this, the convention, which was dominated by prewar Whig Unionists, left the state's constitutional structure essentially unchanged. On October 9, 1865, the convention announced that slavery was "forever prohibited"[4] in the state, but it ignored calls for the political empowerment of freed slaves. Instead, the delegates endorsed the creation of a commission that would eventually propose a new system of laws—the Black Code—defining the social, political, and economic position of freedpeople. Without having altered the antebellum system of government, the convention adjourned until May 1866. It ultimately revised the constitution of 1835 in only minor respects: representation for the state house was now based on (white) population; the office of lieutenant governor was established; slavery was abolished; and an oath of allegiance to the Union was now required of all voters. While property requirements for officeholding remained, black males were excluded from the electorate. Even so, when the new constitution was submitted to the voters, it aroused considerable opposition from critics asserting that it changed things too much, and voters rejected ratification by a narrow majority of about 2,000 votes out of more than 41,000 cast. With Union forces still exerting some jurisdiction and lacking a clear constitutional basis for government, the political situation remained murky at best.

Even before it had rewritten the constitution, the Holden Convention called for immediate elections, which were held on November 9, 1865. Although

Holden ran for governor, he had made too many enemies statewide and his pardon policy, some charged, penalized his political opponents. Holden was defeated by the state treasurer and former Whig Unionist from Randolph County, Jonathan Worth, who, though enjoying the support of former secessionists, supported Johnson's presidential Reconstruction policies. The legislature, in turn, elected former Whigs William A. Graham (who was also a former Confederate senator) and John Pool as US senators, but Congress refused to seat them. By early 1866, Congress had made clear that it did not consider the North Carolina government—which had sprung out of Andrew Johnson's desire to effect Reconstruction as quickly and painlessly as possible—a legitimate aspirant to the restored Union. In their eyes, the United States had not waged the bloodiest war in its history only to see the immediate return of the status quo in former Confederate states.

Meeting in late 1865 and early 1866, the newly elected North Carolina government occupied a perilous position. Meanwhile, Johnson's presidential Reconstruction policies faced powerful opposition from Congress. Andrew Johnson was eager to restore "loyal" white southerners to head up new governments. But neither Johnson, nor Holden, nor Worth gave any consideration to the status of freedpeople. Although the North Carolina legislature ratified the Thirteenth Amendment to the US Constitution in December 1865, it would go no further in extending rights to freedpeople. Still, the issue of the status of freed slaves would not go away. For one thing, African Americans continued to press their demands for full civil, political, and economic rights. Johnson's congressional opponents were demanding a different approach, and they sought to assert control over the Reconstruction process. These tensions focused on two particular issues: the Black Code and the Fourteenth Amendment.

The Black Code emerged from a shared desire among North Carolina's white leaders to clarify the status of freedpeople in the postslavery era. The 1865–66 state convention appointed a three-person committee to provide a new legal structure for freedpeople, and on January 23, 1866, the commissioners provided a report recommending nine new laws, known as the "Black Code," which the legislature eventually enacted in early March 1866. Although the code nominally provided the same legal rights for whites and blacks—and enabled African Americans to testify in court in limited fashion—these provisions were intended for northern consumption. Compared to legislation enacted by other southern states, North Carolina's Black Code was lenient; most of its provisions were not explicitly aimed at black people, though authorities possessed sufficient leeway to focus these laws on blacks. But in other respects, the new code was offensive and clearly sought to curtail black freedom. The law reaffirmed North Carolina's antebellum free-black code, replacing "slaves and free Negroes" with "persons of color." It defined persons of color to the fourth generation, so that any person one-sixteenth black was defined as black. Freedpeople could testify in courts, but only against other people of color; testimony against whites required special consent. Freedpeople were barred from executing a contract for activities worth more than $10, unless the contract was witnessed by a literate white. No provision was made for black jurors. A series of work laws sought to regulate African American labor. An apprenticeship law enabled county courts to compel freedpeople under the age of 21 to work for someone of the court's choosing. Local courts of wardens were empowered to declare undocumented freedpeople "orphans" and to assign them to the supervision of a white warden, usually former slaveholders. County courts also gained the power to declare unemployed people "vagrants" and to force them to work, to maintain wardens of the poor, and to establish workhouses. The Black Code forbade interracial marriage and provided for a death penalty for any black man convicted of raping a white woman, while it legalized all slave marriages. Other provisions of the code limited the physical freedom of black people and prohibited their ownership of firearms.

The enactment of the Black Code suggested to African Americans and their supporters in the North that the restored North Carolina government at best cared little for freedpeople's rights and at worst was attempting to reimpose slavery. In the spring of 1866, the state's constitutional convention reconvened. It softened the most discriminatory sections of the Black Code, finalized a constitutional structure, and provided for another round of elections, which were held in November 1866. North Carolina voters once again defeated the revised constitution in a statewide referendum, but they did reelect Governor Worth and elect a new legislature, which included thirty-five Confederate veterans. The new legislature believed that sufficient concessions had been made to the North, and they greeted Congress's submission to them of the Fourteenth Amendment with hostility. This amendment, enacted by Congress and submitted to the states in early 1866, sought to revolutionize federal-state relations and to guarantee full political and civil rights for African Americans. The amendment would establish the supremacy of the federal government, and it created a national definition of citizenship: all native-born Americans, regardless of race, were automatically citizens, entitled to the equal protection of the laws. The Fourteenth Amendment ran contrary to efforts by the southern white governments established during presidential Reconstruction to institutionalize white supremacy, and all the states of the former Confederacy, with the exception of Tennessee, rejected the amendment.

In North Carolina, there was little question that the legislature would refuse ratification, even though Holden, out of office but enjoying some political influence, announced his support for the amendment in the summer of 1866. In transmitting the amendment, Worth urged rejection; speakers of both houses were opposed; and a thirteen-member joint committee recommended rejection. Only two members of the legislature spoke in favor, and the North Carolina senate rejected the amendment by a vote of 46 to 1, the house by a vote of 102 to 10. To many in the North and in the state—especially Unionists and African Americans—it seemed as if the Civil War had changed little.

Radical Reconstruction

The clash between white and black expectations came to a head in early 1867 with the imposition of what scholars refer to as Radical Reconstruction. The advent of African American political power forced the issue, but the rejection of the Fourteenth Amendment by North Carolina and most of the rest of the South occasioned a profound backlash in northern public opinion during the congressional elections of 1866. The Congress that convened in March 1867 was determined to reassert control over the Reconstruction process and move matters in an entirely different direction. The Reconstruction Acts of March 2, 1867, which were passed over Andrew Johnson's veto, declared the state governments established during presidential Reconstruction as illegitimate. Now Congress organized the ten southern states that had rejected the Fourteenth Amendment into five military districts, each under the command of a major general in the US Army. North Carolina and South Carolina were combined into a single Second Military District under the command of Gen. Daniel E. Sickles, a former New York politician who had lost a leg at Gettysburg, and Gen. Edwin R. S. Canby, who succeeded Sickles in August 1867. Military rule—which involved only about 1,600 occupying troops in the state—coincided and mostly cooperated with the civilian Worth government, which served a caretaking function, but its most important duty was to register African American voters. During 1867–68, 72,000 new black voters were added to the rolls. Under this new electorate, nineteen North Carolina counties, all in the eastern part of the state, now contained African American majorities, and in the fall of 1867 elections under this regime of universal suffrage were held for an entirely new constitutional convention, which met in January 1868.

These elections returned a convention that was overwhelmingly Republican. Of the convention's 120 delegates, 107 were members of the newly created Republican Party, which was founded in North Carolina in March 1867 and had organized itself across the state during the following summer. Its leadership was varied. Most Republican voters were African Americans, but there was also prominent white participation. William W. Holden, in yet another political transfiguration, became the Republicans' most important state leader, and he was instrumental in organizing the new party. Republicans also drew white leaders among so-called carpetbaggers, a derogatory term used by opponents of Reconstruction to describe northern whites who had migrated to the South. Carpetbaggers did not provide large numbers of voters. Though they were represented in Republican leadership circles in disproportionate numbers, they often allied themselves with African Americans; among whites, they were the

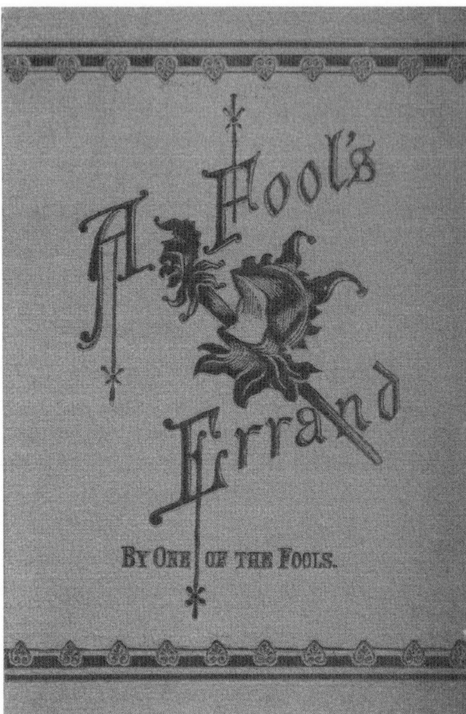

Figure 10.3 Original book cover, Albion W. Tourgée's *A Fool's Errand*. *Source: North Carolina Collection, University of North Carolina Library at Chapel Hill.*

most insistent advocates of equal rights. Carpetbaggers included people of varied backgrounds. Gen. Joseph Carter Abbott, a Union officer from New Hampshire who, after the Civil War, participated in the lumber business in Lower Cape Fear North Carolina, became a leader in the North Carolina Republican Party. Samuel Stanford Ashley, a northern minister who served with the Freedmen's Bureau, became North Carolina's Reconstruction state superintendent of schools. Probably the best example of a carpetbagger was Albion Winegar Tourgée, an Ohioan, who moved to Greensboro, became active in Republican politics, served as a state superior court judge, and then left the state and wrote several novels, including *A Fool's Errand*, which described his Reconstruction experiences.

Republicans could not hope to win elections in North Carolina without wider white support, and a final component of this political coalition was native-born whites, the so-called scalawags. These native-born white Republicans included the few North Carolinians who had actively supported the Union, but they also included others living in more-remote counties, most of which had low African American populations. In many instances, former Whigs in the Piedmont North Carolina counties of Randolph, Davidson, and

Forsyth became Republicans during the Reconstruction era. Scalawags became a major presence in party ranks. Of the 107 Republican delegates sitting in the constitutional convention from January to March 1868, seventy-seven were scalawags—compared with eighteen carpetbagger and fifteen African American delegates.

The 1868 convention wrote a constitution that would provide the basic governmental structure for North Carolina for the next one hundred years. With the opponents of Reconstruction—who by now were calling themselves "Conservatives"—sitting out the election, Republicans completely dominated the meeting, and the new document that they composed constituted a more modern and certainly more democratic instrument of government. The constitution of 1868 revised the court system by providing for a new system of superior court judges, who were popularly elected to eight-year terms. Revolutionary changes affected voting and representation: the constitution formalized universal male suffrage for both whites and blacks, while it instituted the principle of equal representation based on population. The constitution of 1868 also abolished all property requirements for officeholding. In local government, the constitution did away with the antebellum county-court system, replacing it with elected county commissioners. This meant that, for the first time in North Carolina history, democratically elected local government would run local affairs.

Equally revolutionary were the new state services incorporated into the constitution. The constitution revamped the state's prison system; in 1884, a new state penitentiary was completed in Raleigh. Even more important was the constitutional provision for universal public education for all of the state's children (though the constitution scrupulously avoided the question of whether these schools would be integrated). On the heels of the adoption of the new constitution, in April 1868, Holden was elected as North Carolina's first Republican governor, while a new Republican legislature was swept into office. After his inauguration, Holden convened the new legislature; and one of its first actions, on July 2, 1868, was to ratify the Fourteenth Amendment. Several months later, in November 1868, the Republican candidate and Union Civil War hero Ulysses S. Grant carried the state in the presidential election with 53 percent of the vote.

Republicans extended their revolution to other areas as well. The legislature established a new public school system—for the most part, that included only elementary schools—that provided for both white and black children. That system subsequently suffered from disorganization and inadequate funding; 49,000 out of 330,000 school-age students regularly attended school in 1870. Local government was completely reformed, while the state government abolished the antebellum system of the whipping post—which had obviously been applied disproportionately against African Americans—and began a new state prison system. Holden appointed blacks to important offices: for example, African American leader James W. Hood was appointed assistant

Figure 10.4 James W. Hood. *Source: Kellenberger Room, New Bern-Craven County Public Library.*

superintendent of public instruction. Many other North Carolina blacks were elected to local offices, especially in the eastern part of the state, while nineteen African Americans were elected to the legislature in 1868.

Once in power, Republicans suffered from two ugly problems. The first was corruption. Most of the Republican officeholders were new to officeholding and for some of them political power and the lure of railroad money proved irresistible. During 1868–69, the Republican government issued some $28 million in state bonds, apparently as the result of extensive lobbying and the expenditure of some $200,000 by New Yorker Milton S. Littlefield, a former Union army officer, and his North Carolina ally George W. Swepson. But state borrowing far exceeded the ability to pay off the bonds, the value of which soon plunged after the state defaulted on payment. By June 1869, the value of the bonds had declined to 28 percent of par, and North Carolina's credit lay in tatters.

The second political problem was even more serious: the growing insurgency, led by the new Ku Klux Klan, which in the late 1860s was conducting a terror campaign against the Republican Party. "Conservatives" included most of the white political talent of postwar North Carolina, who had regrouped after 1868 and were determined to overthrow Radical Reconstruction. Newspaper editors such as Josiah Turner, editor of the Conservative *Raleigh Sentinel*, launched a

Figure 10.5 Ku Klux Klan costumes, probably late 1860s. *Source: New York Public Library.*

no-holds-barred campaign against Republicans, unleashing a steady stream of political invective focused personally on Governor Holden. The Klan served as a paramilitary, terrorist wing of the Conservative political effort. First created in eastern Tennessee in 1867, the Klan arrived in North Carolina sometime in 1868, attracting mostly Confederate veterans who were grimly determined to end "Negro rule" and destroy the Republican infrastructure. At its peak, the North Carolina Klan included perhaps 40,000 members—as much as one-third of all adult white males. During the next four years, until 1872, the Klan was responsible for systematic terror—whippings, beatings, and murders—across Piedmont North Carolina.

The Klan became most active in counties where Republicans competed for the white vote, not in those counties (such as in southeastern North Carolina) where an African American majority prevailed. Thus, Republican presidential candidate U. S. Grant carried Alamance County, a hotbed of terror activity, by only fifteen votes in the elections of 1868. Klan activities were focused on Piedmont counties where racial polarization would likely benefit the opponents of Reconstruction. In a well-coordinated strategy, the Klan conducted a campaign of terror that began in May 1869, when Klansmen murdered a carpetbagger

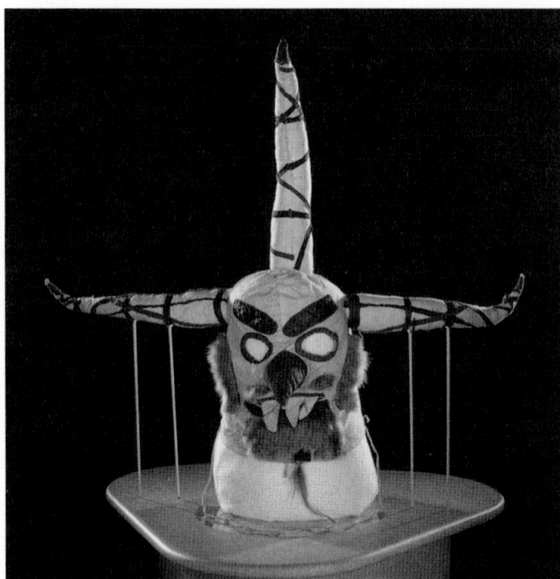

Figure 10.6 Ku Klux Klan mask, Reconstruction Era. *Source: North Carolina Museum of History.*

sheriff and his black associate in Jones County. By the fall, violence had broken out in Lenoir, Chatham, and Orange Counties. Governor Holden responded by issuing a proclamation in October 1869 calling for an end to the violence, but he lacked sufficient police force—or military support from Washington—to quell the violence in those areas where local law enforcement worked in concert with the Klan. He sought to strengthen his hand by organizing a state militia and endorsing the Shoffner Act, enacted in January 1870, which empowered Holden to employ military force against the Klan insurrection.

By early 1869, the epicenters of Klan violence had become Alamance and Caswell Counties, in the Piedmont. Two particularly egregious outrages forced Holden's hand. On May 21, 1868, white Republican state senator John W. "Chicken" Stephens was abducted and murdered in broad daylight in the courthouse at the Caswell County town of Yanceyville. Born in Guilford County in 1834, Stephens had worked in Yanceyville as an agent of the Freedmen's Bureau and became a leader of the Union League and the Republican Party. Elected to the state senate in 1868, Stephens became the object of hatred. During a meeting of the county Democratic Party, Frank Wiley, a former Caswell County sheriff, organized Stephens's killing. Not until sixty-five years after the murder did the details—and the extent of local involvement—become public.

Two years later, the murder of black Republican activist Wyatt Outlaw forced Governor Holden to take action. The son of a white slaveholder and an enslaved mother, Wyatt Outlaw joined the Union army, served in the 2nd Regiment US Colored Cavalry, and was mustered out in February 1866.

Returning to Alamance County, Outlaw became a town commissioner and one of three black constables in the county seat, Graham. He also served as a prominent black leader and an organizer of the Republican Party in the county. On February 26, 1870, Klansmen stormed into Outlaw's house in Graham, hanging him in plain view of the county courthouse. The perpetrators attached a sign to his dangling corpse that read, "Beware, ye guilty, both black and white." Republicans, black and white, were outraged at this brazen show of terror.

In response to the assassination, Holden unsuccessfully attempted to persuade local authorities to take action; although federal authorities sent forty troops to Alamance, his pleas for additional troops fell on deaf ears. Stephens's assassination, which occurred as the August 1870 campaign was gearing up for the legislature, forced Holden to organize a state militia under the command of George W. Kirk, who had commanded a regiment of North Carolina Union troops during the Civil War. Kirk's troops, many of whom had been in the thick of the bitter partisan warfare in western North Carolina, marched east. A ragtag collection of troops, the militia oversaw the suspension of habeas corpus in Piedmont counties, as well as the hasty arrest and imprisonment of Klan suspects and the imposition (sometimes arbitrary) of military justice. There were a number of conspicuous incidents of heavy-handedness by the occupying militia in Alamance and Caswell Counties, and a popular backlash in the Piedmont soon developed. As part of Holden's campaign against Klan terror, *Raleigh Sentinel* editor Josiah Turner was apprehended and jailed.

Although what became known as the "Kirk-Holden War" broke the back of the Klan in Alamance and Caswell, it spelled doom for Holden's political career. The Kirk-Holden War sparked a white backlash against Holden in the Piedmont. While Republican corruption and higher taxes alienated many voters, the racial polarization and fears of Holden's designs on civil liberties created a Conservative landslide. In the contests for the General Assembly, a Conservative tide swept the state, as anti-Reconstruction candidates captured two-thirds of the seats and Conservative candidates won most of North Carolina's congressional seats. Republicans maintained control in the predominantly African American eastern counties, and the party remained viable in statewide elections, but in the Piedmont white voters shifted en masse to the Democratic ranks. In addition, ten of the fifteen North Carolina counties that shifted from Republican to Conservative between 1868 and 1870 experienced significant Klan activity.

In December 1870, when the newly elected legislature convened, Conservatives focused their political hostility on Holden by leading an effort to impeach and remove him from office. On December 19, 1870, the state house adopted a resolution seeking to impeach Holden; on the same day, the house also adopted eight articles of impeachment that detailed the crimes for which they believed Holden should be removed from office. Most of these charges focused on the Kirk-Holden War. Holden's impeachment and trial in the state senate occurred between February 2 and March 22, 1871. African Americans realized that the removal of Holden would mean a blow against their political rights. On January 13, 1871, a group of black legislators published an address declaring a day of "fasting and prayer" and warning that the attack on Holden signified an attack on equal rights. "When Gov. Holden is disposed of," they warned, "those whom he protected will be the next victims." This "murderous host" had taken such drastic measures because "we refuse to bow the knee to them."[5] Despite a spirited defense, on March 22, 1871, Holden was convicted by a vote of the state senate, thus becoming the first and only North Carolina governor ever removed from office in this manner.

The Klan continued to operate in other Piedmont counties—it was particularly strong after 1871 in the southwestern Piedmont, in Rutherford and Cleveland Counties—but it eventually came under the scrutiny of federal authorities. Although President Grant had provided inadequate military support for Holden in 1869–70, after 1871, he and his attorney general mounted a serious campaign to uproot Klan influence. A federal Ku Klux Klan Act, passed in 1871, criminalized Klan terror and authorized full-scale federal military intervention in Klan-infested areas of the South. It further permitted the suspension of habeas corpus and the use of federal marshals. Federal authorities mounted a determined prosecution in Cleveland and Rutherford, and eventually some 1,400 people were indicted, thirty of whom were convicted. The most famous of these was Randolph A. Shotwell, a newspaper editor active in Klan affairs, who was convicted under the Ku Klux Klan Act and sentenced to six years in prison. Federal anti-Klan efforts were highly effective: the North Carolina Klan was eradicated, gone from the state until it was revived during World War I. But the damage had already been done. The Klan had succeeded in stalling Reconstruction, causing the impeachment of a Republican governor, and intimidating scores of whites and African Americans active in Republican politics across the state.

North Carolina Redeemers

Holden's impeachment and removal from office constituted only one part of the Conservative assault on Reconstruction. Between 1871 and 1875, these "Redeemers"—so named because they proclaimed it their mission to "redeem" North Carolina from the evils of Reconstruction—sought to eradicate Republican influence throughout the state. In large part, their concern was racial: Redeemers wanted to restore "white man's government" and eliminate "Negro rule." Thus, southeastern North Carolina, the seat of African American political power, became a target. During the mid-1870s, the Conservative legislature divided Republican New Hanover County—which included Wilmington—by creating a new Pender County, in the hopes of reducing Republican political

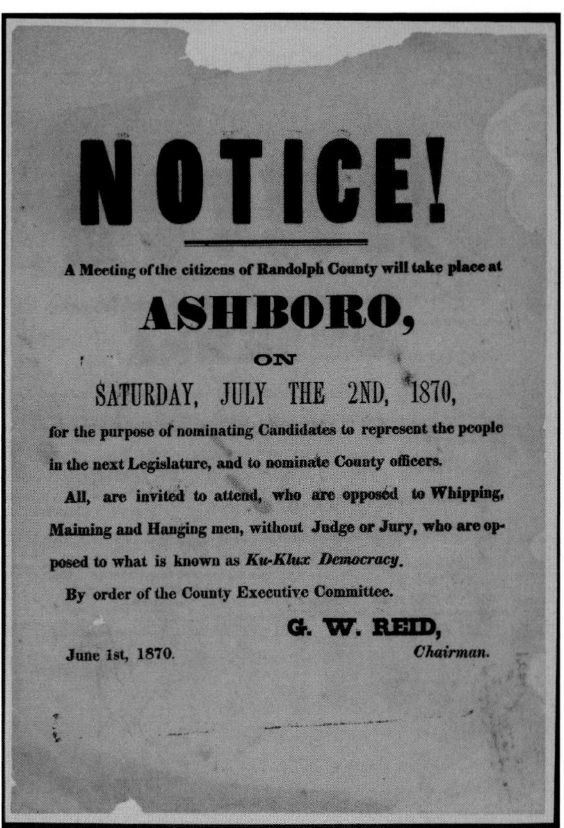

NOTICE!

A Meeting of the citizens of Randolph County will take place at

ASHBORO,

ON

SATURDAY, JULY THE 2ND, 1870,

for the purpose of nominating Candidates to represent the people in the next Legislature, and to nominate County officers.

All, are invited to attend, who are opposed to Whipping, Maiming and Hanging men, without Judge or Jury, who are opposed to what is known as *Ku-Klux Democracy*.

By order of the County Executive Committee.

G. W. REID,
Chairman.

June 1st, 1870.

Figure 10.7 Anti-Klan broadside, Randolph County, 1870. *Source: North Carolina Collection, University of North Carolina Library at Chapel Hill.*

power. But Conservative hopes were frustrated when Pender continued to vote Republican. The General Assembly meanwhile gerrymandered a Conservative majority in Wilmington's local government. The Conservatives' venom toward Reconstruction encompassed the entire Republican Party: they targeted white as well as African American Republicans. In control of the legislature after 1870, the Redeemers sought to control the governorship and the courts. Their principal objective was to repudiate the symbol of Reconstruction, the constitution of 1868.

The Redeemers discovered, however, that realizing their goals was not going to be easy. In August 1871, voters defeated a popular referendum seeking to hold a new constitutional convention by a vote of 95,252 to 86,007. Klan terror had worked effectively to diminish the Republican vote in Piedmont North Carolina, but elsewhere strongholds of Republicanism remained. After the impeachment of Holden, Lt. Gov. Tod R. Caldwell became governor. In 1872, Caldwell ran for reelection in his own right; he was opposed by Conservative western North Carolinian Augustus S. Merrimon. Despite an all-out campaign by the Conservative/Redeemers in which the race issue figured prominently, in elections held in August 1872 Caldwell carried the state by nearly 2,000 votes. Although Merrimon carried fifty-four counties, heavy black voting in eastern North Carolina turned the tide for Caldwell, while the Redeemers' majorities in both houses of the legislature were reduced. In the presidential campaign that followed three months later, in November, incumbent Republican U. S. Grant carried the state by the wide margin of nearly 25,000 votes. Clearly, Republicans were still able to win statewide elections in North Carolina.

Heartened by legislative elections in 1874 that returned a solid two-thirds majority in the legislature, Redeemers again attempted constitutional revision. The General Assembly provided for elections to a new constitutional convention in August 1875, and the weeks prior to the election brought intense confrontation. The race issue again appeared as the dominant consideration. "Let the line be drawn," declared the Redeemer *Albemarle Register*. "Are you in favor of the white man's government? This will be the only question in the future." This was a "white man's government," declared the *Charlotte Democrat*, "framed by the wisdom of the white men, and secured by the blood of the white race."[6]

But the race issue cut both ways, for it served to mobilize African American voters against a rollback of Reconstruction's gains. The elections for the convention produced a razor-thin difference separating the two parties: in the convention vote, Republican candidates outpolled Conservatives by a total of only 154 votes. After the death of prominent Conservative leader William A. Graham, the constitutional convention of 1875, which met between September 2 and October 11, 1875, was divided evenly between fifty-eight Democrats, fifty-eight Republicans, and three independents. From the outset, Republican delegates fought to preserve the constitutional structure established in 1868. In the end, the convention, unable to repudiate the constitution of 1868, adopted thirty amendments, with concessions to both sides. Republicans, looking for protections against terror, obtained amendments condemning secret societies and empowering the legislature to ban the carrying of concealed weapons. Conservatives obtained more significant changes. They managed to ban interracial marriage as well as integrated public schools. The court system, both superior and supreme courts, was changed through the reduction of the number of judges (which ended up eliminating Republican judges), the provision for statewide election of judges, and a new system providing for the rotation of superior court judges. The single most important change affecting local government was a constitutional amendment empowering the General Assembly to end democratically elected local government.

Still, constitutional revision in 1875 represented only a partial victory, and the Democrats—as Conservatives were now calling themselves—believed that Reconstruction would only be ended once the Republicans were denied control

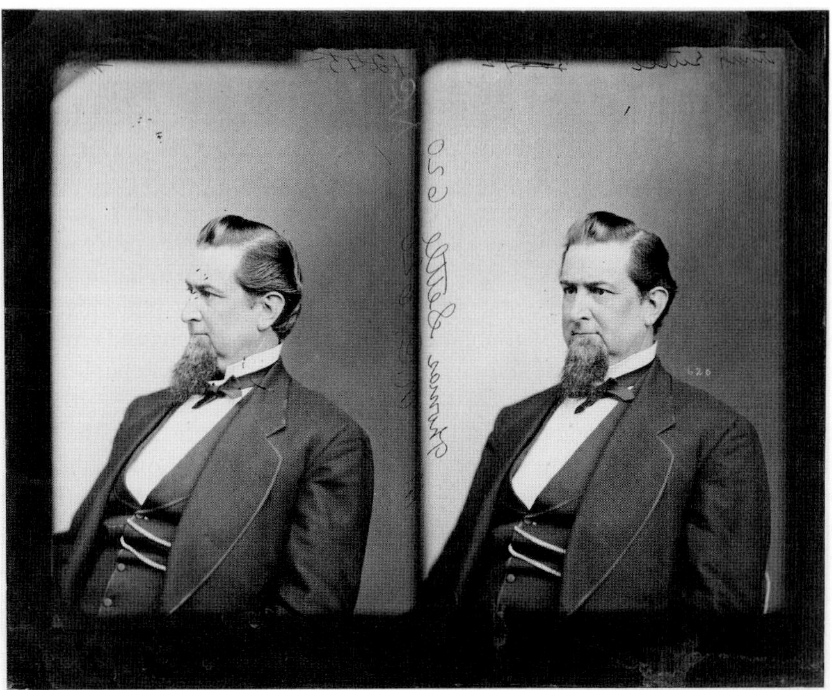

Figure 10.8 Thomas Settle. *Source: Library of Congress.*

of the governorship. The consensus Democratic candidate was Zebulon Vance, the wartime governor whom Congress had already declined to seat as a US senator. Running as the Republican candidate was Thomas Settle. The gubernatorial campaign of 1876 became an intense battle in which the race issue figured prominently. Republicans reminded voters that a Democratic victory would threaten African American civil and political rights; they also emphasized their party as supporters of the Union. Democrats, as they would for the next generation, campaigned against the dangers of "Negro rule" and favored limiting black voting and officeholding. Vance and Settle engaged in a speaking tour across the state, conducting debates in sixty-four counties. With a reputation as a renowned orator, Vance attracted huge crowds. According to one estimate, he reached as many as 125,000 listeners. In elections in August 1876, Vance defeated Settle, gaining a majority of about 13,000 out of almost 234,000 votes cast. Democrats strengthened their control over the legislature and, in November 1876, elected seven out of eight congressmen and provided a majority to the Democratic presidential candidate, Samuel Tilden of New York.

With Vance's victory in 1876, the last holdout of Republican power— the governorship—fell, and Democrats sought to consolidate their power. The

Democratic legislature gerrymandered legislative districts so as to minimize Republican power, while the Democratic majority also exploited its control of the electoral machinery to its fullest advantage. Using the power flowing from the constitutional amendments of 1875—which were ratified in the elections of 1876—the legislature enacted the Local Government Act of 1877, which eliminated elective home rule in local government. In order to ensure that white Democrats would dominate the black majority districts of eastern North Carolina, the law empowered the legislature to appoint justices of the peace who, in turn, would choose county commissioners. Once inaugurated in January 1877, Vance fired nearly all of the state's Republican officeholders, replacing them with loyal Democrats. The new regime instituted strict economy and retrenchment, drastically cutting the state services expanded under the Republicans.

The Redeemer government, during the 1870s, repudiated other vestiges of Republican rule. Working under a Republican executive until 1877, the legislature stripped the governor's office of much of its appointive power and abolished various offices that Republicans had occupied. Redeemers repudiated the scandal-laden debt incurred in railroad bonds during the 1868–70 legislature, while they drastically cut property taxes—so much so, in fact, that by 1890 only one other state in the Union had lower property tax rates than North Carolina. Among their targets were the public schools, symbols of Republican Reconstruction. Redeemers undermined the system of public financing by drastic reductions that eliminated any centralized state supervision over schools and returning complete control to localities. Thus, school boards now came under the direct control of the Democratically appointed boards of county commissioners.

One measure of the oppressive environment of post-emancipation North Carolina was a surge of emigration from the state. In 1880, the African American leader of Raleigh, James H. Harris, convened a meeting to examine "the causes contributing to the emigration of colored people from the state." The convention named five chief causes: (1) high rents that white landlords imposed on black tenants in the countryside, which were "sucking the life's blood from the colored sons of toil"; (2) the prevalence of appointed magistrates with "no sympathy with the colored laborer"; (3) a general prohibition of black jurors in North Carolina courtrooms; (4) the inability of black parents to choose black teachers for their children in public schools; and (5) the absence of "fair and impartial trials" for black people in white-dominated courts.

Some North Carolina blacks were interested in emigration to Africa, but most in the 1870s and early 1880s joined a new wave of migration from southern to northern states. Although migration in this period was much smaller than the numbers of black people who left North Carolina in the mid-twentieth century, a significant number departed. In the heavily black districts of eastern North Carolina, there seemed to have been a general exodus of a small but steady number of African Americans. According to one estimate, nearly

100,000 blacks left North Carolina between 1876 and 1894. The growth rate of black population declined from a 36 percent increase in the 1870s to a 6 percent increase during the 1890s. While African Americans composed 52.6 percent of the population of eastern North Carolina's Lenoir County in 1880, that proportion had declined to 42.8 percent in 1890.[7]

* * *

Reconstruction had proven politically and racially divisive, and it had left many questions unresolved. The most important of these questions concerned the status of African Americans, and the transition from slavery to freedom became the central, dominating thread of the Reconstruction years, as well as the years thereafter. Despite emancipation and federally established civil and political rights, black people in North Carolina faced a terrifically oppressive environment. Despite the fact that some African Americans acquired property and literacy, the black masses of North Carolina remained largely at the mercy of the white majority, and, without federal protection, lived under a system that denied them true equality. Not until many years later would African Americans in North Carolina finally realize the promise of freedom.

Notes

1 Quoted in William C. Harris, *William Woods Holden: Firebrand of North Carolina* (Baton Rouge: Louisiana State University Press, 1987), p. 163; Roberta Sue Alexander, *North Carolina Faces the Freedmen: Race Relations during Presidential Reconstruction, 1865–1867* (Durham, NC: Duke University Press, 1985), p. 33.

2 Quoted in Harris, *Holden*, p. 187.

3 Quoted in Alexander, *North Carolina Faces the Freedmen*, p. 12.

4 Ibid., pp. 26–27.

5 Quoted in Harris, *Holden*, p. 304; Catherine S. Silverman, "'Of Old Wealth, Virtue, and Intelligence': The Redeemers and Their Triumph in Virginia and North Carolina, 1865–1877," Ph.D. diss., City University of New York, 1971, pp. 199–200.

6 Joseph G. De Roulhac Hamilton, *Reconstruction in North Carolina* (New York: Columbia University Press, 1914), pp. 633–34, 636.

7 Frenise A. Logan, "The Movement of Negroes from North Carolina, 1876–1894," *North Carolina Historical Review* 33, no. 1 (January 1956): 46–47, 65.

11

Social Change in the Post-Reconstruction Era

During the late antebellum years, North Carolinians had constructed a new railroad system, which would eventually become the state's dominant system of transportation. After their near destruction during the Civil War, railroads were rebuilt and expanded across the state. Railroad growth brought immediate and wide-ranging consequences, the most important of which was the spread of a new economic system based on the market. In agriculture, the market revolution helped to spread commercially-based farming. Areas that had previously been isolated because of poor transportation now grew crops for external consumers. Drawn into the market system, farmers in all regions of the state found themselves more dependent on credit and more exposed to the ups and downs of national, even international, market cycles. Meanwhile, the market revolution also spread to non-agricultural pursuits, as an increasing number of North Carolinians moved into urban areas, where they found industrial jobs and took up new lifestyles. The combined revolution in transportation and the market economy enabled the emergence of industrialized manufacturing, particularly in cotton textiles, while it also fostered a startling growth in new towns and cities across the state.

The Growth of Railroads

For centuries, North Carolinians had little choice but to depend on erratic and unpredictable water-borne traffic. Unlike any other state on the Atlantic seaboard, North Carolina lacked a good deep-water port, a fact that kept the state's products less competitive until well into the nineteenth century. North Carolina's river transportation was equally inadequate: no great river systems traversed the state, and goods moved across the rocky and often obstructed rivers of the Piedmont only with great difficulty. The state's roads, meanwhile, were at best poorly maintained and at worst nonexistent. The advent of railroads during the late antebellum period was thus of particular significance in

Figure 11.1 The 86-mile line of the Raleigh & Gaston Railroad was begun in 1836 and completed in 1840. In this 1857–58 photograph, the RGRR president (standing on engine) and treasurer (in top hat) show off the new locomotive, Romulus Sanders. *Source: History NC.org.*

North Carolina history; the construction of a dependable statewide transportation system would eventually transform commerce, social life, and residential patterns in the state.

As mentioned, by the Civil War, the rudiments of a railroad network had existed. The Wilmington and Weldon Railroad constructed in the 1840s linked Wilmington to interior plantation regions, while the North Carolina Railroad, built during the 1850s, crisscrossed the Piedmont, connecting it with external markets. Railroads recovered in the aftermath of the devastation of the Civil War. During Reconstruction, Republicans expanded the antebellum program of internal improvements by issuing $28 million in state aid in the form of publicly-supported bonds for railroad expansion. The fiscally conservative Redeemers, however, took a different approach, and between the 1870s and 1890s they made it their policy to withdraw public involvement in railroads by leasing state-owned rail lines to private investors. In 1871, the state leased the North Carolina Railroad, established in the 1850s as the crown jewel of the state's program of internal improvements, to the Richmond and Danville Railroad for thirty years for $260,000 in annual rent. In 1880, the state sold the publicly-owned Western North Carolina Railroad, the designated beneficiary of the failed state bonds of the Republican regime, to New York investors, and in 1883 the Richmond and Danville acquired its assets. In 1894, northern capitalist J. P. Morgan organized the Southern Railway Company, a mammoth new railroad conglomerate. A year later, Southern Railway officials negotiated a new 99-year agreement to lease the North Carolina Railroad's tracks. In 1904, the financially troubled Atlantic and North Carolina Railroad was leased to a private company and, in 1910, was absorbed into the Norfolk and Western Railroad system.

The last twenty years of the nineteenth century witnessed the greatest period of railroad growth in North Carolina history. According to the most basic measure of railroad capacity—miles of track in operation—this period witnessed a major expansion. In 1880, at the start of the period, North Carolina had about 1,500 miles of track, a figure that grew to 3,000 miles in 1890 and to nearly 4,000 miles in 1900. State leasing of public rail lines coincided with the consolidation of control of railroads in North Carolina and elsewhere in the nation. By the time the United States entered World War I, most lines had been consolidated into several highly capitalized railroad systems. These included the Southern Railway system, created in 1894, which operated the east-west connections of the North Carolina Railroad and the north-south connections of the Richmond and Danville; the Atlantic Coast Line system, created in 1900, which included the Wilmington and Weldon Railroad and its Coastal Plain network; and the Seaboard Airline system, established in 1900, which acquired the Raleigh and Gaston and eventually connected Charlotte with Atlanta. All of these systems were integrated into a larger regional railroad transportation network.

Where only a generation earlier railroads were still considered an exotic novelty, by 1900, most communities in North Carolina possessed at least some access to railroad transportation. Railroads offered a cheaper, more efficient, and more reliable form of transportation than had ever before been available. The costs of transporting goods to market declined precipitously, and store-bought goods now penetrated into Carolina hinterlands. The social, economic, and cultural implications of this newfound mobility were stunning to North Carolinians, who, along with new access to outside markets, suddenly felt the relentlessly intense competition of a national market economy.

Railroads helped to pioneer an emerging tourist industry. With their arrival, tourism became a larger, more nationalized industry that especially included sites in the South. In 1869, the Western North Carolina Railroad completed a link between Morganton and Old Fort, NC, cutting through foothills and high mountains to the Blue Ridge. In 1880, the rail line was completed to Asheville, opening that growing tourist town to travelers. Six years later, the Asheville and Spartanburg Railroad was finished, creating a new path for visitors to western North Carolina. South Carolinians had traveled to the region since the antebellum era; towns such as Flat Rock were filled with lowcountry planters. Now railroads opened up the region to even more visitors. Hotels expanded, as did an

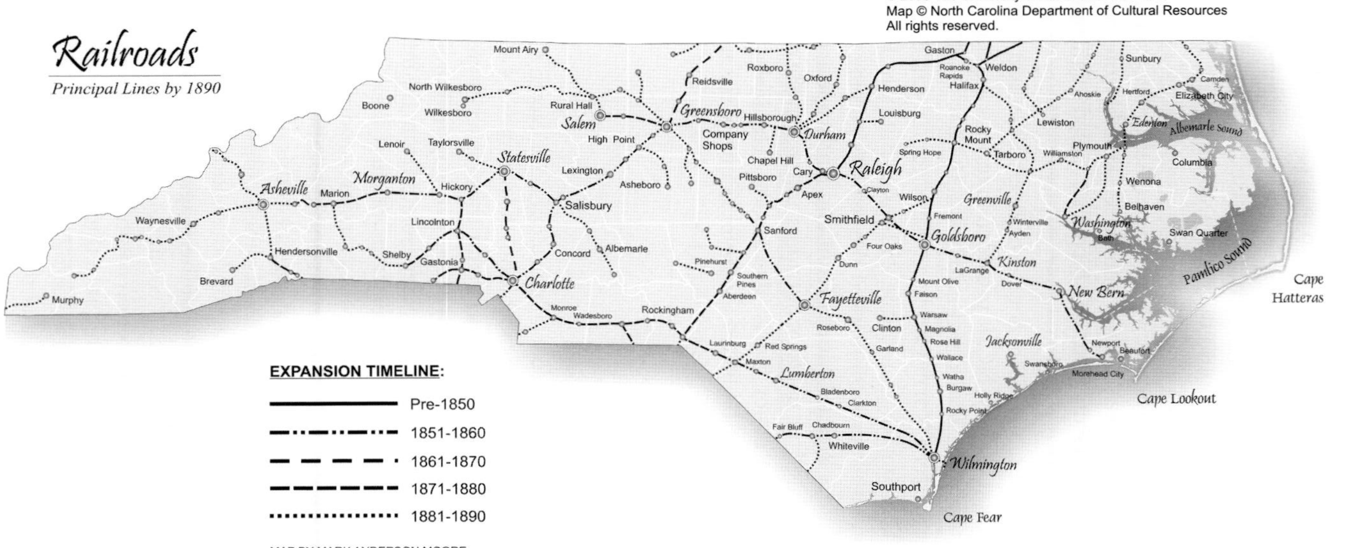

Figure 11.2 Railroads in North Carolina.

entire service industry radiating in and around Asheville, which grew in population from 1,450 in 1870 to 50,193 in 1930. The city's Battery Park Hotel, constructed in 1886 as Asheville's first resort hotel, contained amenities such as running water and steam heat. It advertised itself as "the acknowledged center of fashionable life in the South during the summer."[1] By 1890, the city had twelve hotels and many more boardinghouses.

Hotels and resorts sprang up elsewhere beyond Asheville. Two entrepreneurs from Kansas, Samuel T. Kelsey and Clinton C. Hutchinson, constructed an entire community in Macon County which they called Highlands. The town drew thousands of visitors and summer residents. Thirty-five miles to the north, in Hot Springs, in 1890, northern investors constructed Mountain Park Hotel, Madison County, NC. It provided luxurious accommodations that offered visitors stunning vistas and outdoor activities. During the hot East Coast summers, western North Carolina offered tourists an escape from heat and humidity. The construction of the 250-room Biltmore Estate by George Washington Vanderbilt in 1895 marked the region's coming of age. Biltmore, designed by architect Richard Morris Hunt and landscape architect Frederick Law Olmsted, indicated the depth of outsiders' interest in the mountains. It also immediately became a major tourist destination. The opening of Asheville's Grove Park Inn in 1913 established the hotel as one of the most luxurious in the South.

Market Agriculture

The impact of railroads was especially profound for North Carolina farmers. Because of inadequate water transportation, the commercial economy long had been confined to towns, coastal ports, and those interior plantation regions with access to navigable rivers. Much of the state's agricultural economy, existing in pockets of self-sufficiency, remained isolated from the influences of external markets. For many people, the patterns of rural life had not changed in generations. In this world, North Carolina farmers produced enough for themselves and their families, with any surpluses sold locally. Yet the penetration of the new railroad network began to change all of this. Farmers, whether or not they wanted to do so, faced a harsh reality: their crops had to compete with the same agricultural products grown around the nation and even the world.

The end of slavery had reshaped southern agriculture, but it did not mean the end of the plantation system. In combination with new modes of transportation, by which tobacco and cotton could be moved to market, hinterland acres of farmland were incorporated into the plantation system. The expanding market economy in rural North Carolina helped to expand the reach of crops such as cotton and tobacco, and the plantation system adapted to post-emancipation realities. Country stores and merchants became centers of the market economy; by offering their customers finished goods, supplies, feed, and fertilizers, merchants provided a vital connection to the resources of the outside world. Furnishing merchants also extended credit to previously noncommercial farmers, who used this capital to buy goods without much cash at hand. Planters, sometimes merchant-planters, continued to use poor and marginally poor African American and white farmers as their labor force, but they discovered a new means of tying them to the land through sharecropping, tenancy, and the crop-lien system.

Sharecropping was a system of land tenure by which poor black and white farmers rented their farms from merchants or planters who provided them with seeds, fertilizers, and other supplies. In exchange, sharecroppers promised a portion of their harvest to the merchant as payment for the use of the land and the supplies. Like "croppers," farm "tenants" also rented their land for a fixed cash amount, but tenants were responsible for all their own tools and supplies. Like sharecroppers, they often ended the year still in debt to the landlord, especially when harvests were poor. Both sharecroppers and tenants, in this way, became subject to a system of debt known as the crop lien. Serving as a means of credit, the crop lien enabled sharecroppers and tenants—who were not good credit risks—to borrow from landlords, who were legally allowed to put liens on the farmers' future crops. But because sharecroppers and tenants were frequently unable to settle their debts come the end of the year, the crop-lien system became a form of financial oppression and poverty from which farmers could only hope to escape by producing increasingly larger amounts of cash crops such as cotton. Over time, desperate farmers grew cotton at the expense of needed food crops—even as their families suffered and their overall economic status deteriorated.

The most important plantation crops were cotton and tobacco. While cotton production tripled between 1860 and 1880, tobacco production nearly quadrupled between 1860 and 1900. The growth of cotton culture paralleled the extension of cotton across the post-Reconstruction South. The growth of plantation agriculture was also accompanied by increasing levels of debt and rising rates of farm tenancy and sharecropping. Thousands of farmers thus participated in market agriculture, but could do so only by perpetuating a ceaseless cycle of indebtedness in order to finance the crop and rent farm lands. With their ever-mounting debt, small farmers felt compelled to produce ever-higher quantities of cash crops in order to have any hope of escaping their financial burden. "The dog that chases his tail fails to make both ends meet," observed an Edgecombe County newspaper, and "so does the poor farmer who buys protected products and sells unprotected crops to pay the debt. He works as hard as the dog and gets about the same sort of shadowy reward."[2]

The growth of tobacco in North Carolina was linked to the development of a national market for bright-leaf tobacco, which, to reach its marketable form, required a new flue-curing process for cigarette production. Flue-curing was

Figure 11.3 Farm workers in Pitt County tobacco field. *Source:* Joyner Library, East Carolina University.

an arduous, multistep task that consumed the labor of the entire farm family, fathers and mothers, sons and daughters. The work was divided by gender. The process began during the spring with seedlings, which the men cultivated and transplanted to the fields. The female family members then maintained the plants by weeding, plucking off the energy-sapping stems called suckers, looking for insects, and harvesting the crop into individual "hands," or leaves, which could then be hung over sticks to be dried and cured inside tobacco barns. Males performed the more physically demanding task of topping the plants before they went to seed; men also harvested the crop. The curing typically consumed five entire days, during which fires that produced the smoke and heat that colored and cured the tobacco leaves had to be continuously maintained. Because the tobacco curing involved barns heated by metal pipes, or flues, this became known as "flue-curing." Finally, men and women graded the leaves according to size and quality, and men took the product to market.

Beginning in the 1850s, flue-cured tobacco appeared in northern Piedmont counties—the center of production was in Caswell County—and the growth of the bright leaf spread across eastern and central North Carolina. The expansion of tobacco traced the northern lines of the North Carolina Railroad's corridor, starting at the new town of Durham, which became a major warehousing center for cured tobacco and a prime location for tobacco-product manufacturing. Tobacco farming continued to expand until World War I, when, stimulated by an agricultural boom during the war, it pushed into the "new belt" region of

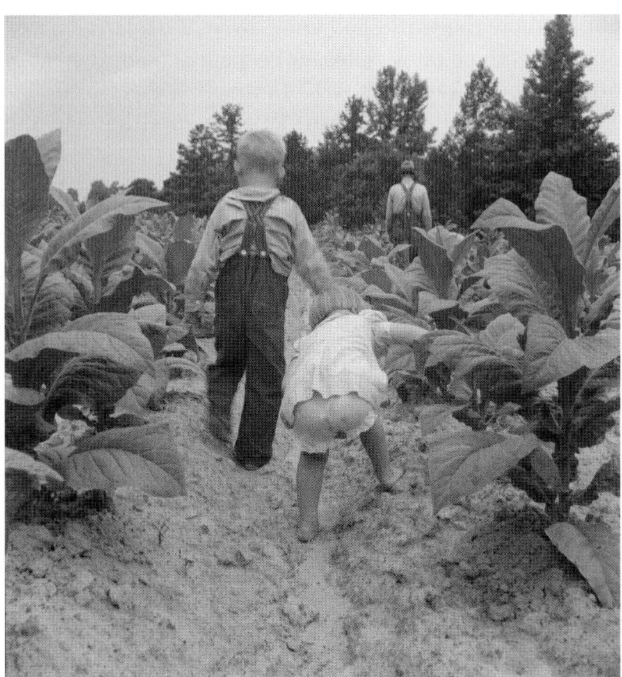

Figure 11.4 Sharecropper family, working tobacco fields, 1930s. *Source: Farm Security Administration image by Dorothea Lange. Library of Congress.*

eastern North Carolina. Between 1916 and 1919, the number of acres devoted to tobacco in North Carolina doubled, and tobacco prices increased from prewar levels of around 10 cents per pound to more than 50 cents per pound. The tobacco boom, at least in eastern North Carolina, resulted in the displacement of cotton by tobacco as the more profitable crop.

Paradoxically, the spread of the market revolution to farming brought greater misery for rural North Carolinians. By 1900, farm life had become visibly harder, especially by comparison with life in the state's towns and cities. For the great bulk of North Carolinians living in the countryside, the advent of commercial agriculture was, in other words, a mixed blessing. On many fronts, North Carolina farmers by the 1890s felt besieged. Now connected to the market system, farmers experienced a generation of sharp price declines in farm products (other than tobacco, which maintained its prices); these price declines undermined the income of farmers, especially cotton farmers, and impoverished many of them. "When a man mortgages his property," wrote one farmer in 1891, "he can't help thinking about it, consequently he can't work like a free man." Another commented that rural Carolinians were "mortgaged to a few merchants and capitalists," with "middle men" capitalists exploiting rural folk.[3] The arrival of railroads was a key development, but by the late 1800s they had simply become a symbol of how the world had gone awry. With farmers frequently complaining about their high rates, railroads became a concrete symbol of how the external forces of the marketplace were dominating their lives.

No better example of the adverse intersection between rural life and the market revolution existed than in the controversy over fencing laws. Following ancient traditions of livestock-keeping, small farmers since colonial times had enjoyed access to common pastures for their herds. The most important of the state's livestock were hogs, and North Carolina farmers—especially yeoman and landless farmers—let their pigs run free during much of the year, and then conducted round-ups and slaughters. Although farmers fenced in crops, rural North Carolinians with little or no pastureland also had access to this open range for hunting and fishing. The open range also included, by tradition, access to forest resources, especially wood. Two new developments forced changes after the Civil War. First, railroads, experiencing frequent collisions between their locomotives and free-ranging livestock, sought legal protection. Second, commercial farmers sought to restrict foraging livestock. Both powers supported fencing laws, which would reverse the old order of things.

The fence, or stock, laws were typically local legislation, and each community, generally townships and counties, considered these measures. Fencing laws pitted the new economic order against the old one. Commercial farmers and railroads saw laws limiting the rights of freely ranging livestock as a symbol of modern civilization. Many other North Carolinians, perhaps a majority of white farmers, saw the fence laws as an example of the erosion of traditional rights and privileges at the hands of government and its partners in big business. Not only was the old system of herding basically undermined—for the free-range hogs could not survive without forage and poor farmers could hardly afford to purchase feed for their hogs year-round—but the new laws also limited access to hunting and fishing and prohibited ordinary folk from using forest resources. Opposition to attempts to enact stock laws was fierce. Nonetheless, in the 1870s and early 1880s, legislation was occasionally enacted over the objections of the representatives of various counties, mainly because of the political power of railroads and larger farmers. In 1885, the General Assembly enacted legislation that empowered county commissioners to impose stock-law districts if a majority of voters petitioned in favor of the measure. But this law, and the ensuing local elections, created even further rancor between commercial interests and many rural North Carolinians, as farmers continued to resent the loss of traditional privileges.

The Advent of Industrialization

"When an old state," such as North Carolina, wrote an observer in 1906, "builds almost two hundred cotton mills within twenty years, and also enters largely into other manufactures, evidently a great economic change is indicated." North Carolina had historically been rural and isolated, but the observer estimated that more than 150,000 people had moved into industrial centers, where they received wages rather than commodities. A formerly rural population, rather than "living remote from neighbors" and working "in the open air with a few simple tools," were now crowded into factories working for bosses. In this new environment, the North Carolina proletariat faced a "radical change in manner of life [that] must affect them physically and mentally."[4]

In the post-Civil War generation, the market revolution spurred on the rapid industrialization of Piedmont North Carolina. Before 1865, cotton-textile mills first appeared in the Piedmont. The shallow, fast-moving rivers and streams of the region—including the Dan, Deep, Haw, Mayo, Smith, Yadkin, and Catawba Rivers—coursed through layers of rock in such a way as to create rapids and falls. The Fall Line, where the Piedmont gave way to the Coastal Plain, typically featured falls on its eastern edge. These conditions, which long had made using these rivers for water-borne transportation difficult, rendered them ideal for powering mills. As early as 1813, Michael Schenck, a Lincoln County merchant and investor, constructed the state's first textile mill. After 1830, entrepreneurs such as Edwin Michael Holt in Alamance County and John Motley Morehead in Leaksville (later Eden) developed water-powered mills in the rural Piedmont. By 1840, North Carolina could claim twenty-five mills with 50,000 spindles and 700 looms. During the next two decades, water-powered cotton mills expanded into rural areas, the great majority of which employed local whites or slaves. Often these mills belonged to a mixture of other enterprises such as sawmills, grist mills, or cotton gins. In some instances, mill owners began to construct mill villages that provided housing for the "public work" that rural whites were now taking up, often as family units. Some of the products of North Carolina cotton-textile manufacturers—such as Salem Jeans, produced in factories owned by Moravians Henry and Francis Fries, or the Alamance Plaid, a woven, dyed-cotton cloth produced by the factories of Edwin M. Holt—acquired a regional, even national, reputation.

North Carolina's antebellum textile industry laid the basis for subsequent expansion. Despite setbacks during the Civil War, cotton textiles grew after 1865, for the most part, along previously established patterns. Edwin Holt expanded his mill capacity during the 1870s, constructing the state's first planned community at Glencoe, which opened in Alamance County along the Haw River in 1879. During that same decade, manufacturers built mills and hired workers along the Haw and Deep Rivers in the central Piedmont, the South Fork of the Catawba in Gaston and Lincoln Counties, and at the Fall-Line towns of Rocky Mount and Fayetteville. The spurt in cotton-mill construction acquired rapid momentum during the 1880s, as a crusade occurred across the towns of the central part of the state to establish mills. With the antebellum textile entrepreneur class leading the way, cotton mills became symbols of progress

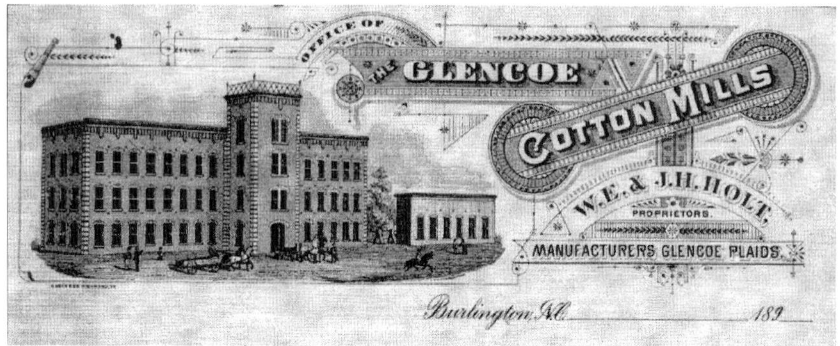

Figure 11.5 Glencoe Mills letterhead. *Source: Textile Heritage Museum, Glencoe, North Carolina.*

and accomplishment, serving in North Carolina as the advance agents of industrialization. During the late nineteenth century, more than 200 mills were constructed, and nearly 200,000 North Carolinians migrated from the countryside to work in them. The number of mills increased from 60 to 318 between 1885 and 1915. During this period, while the workforce grew from 10,000 to 51,000, the industrial capacity rose rapidly, from 200,000 to 3.88 million spindles and from 2,500 to 67,288 looms.

Mid-nineteenth-century mills typically were small operations, primarily involving the spinning of cotton thread. Startup financing typically came from local capital. By World War I, textile operations had become more highly capitalized, larger, and more complex. The increased complexity of post-Civil War textile mills had significant implications. Mills now required a more regular and efficient source of energy; most mills switched from water to steam power, and eventually to electricity, as their chief power source for factory machinery. Relatively cheap textile machinery available on generous terms of credit from northern manufacturers encouraged the growth of mills. By 1900, North Carolina textile mills dominated the production of "low numbered," or lower quality, cotton yarn, and the advent of the Northrup loom in the 1880s, which became widely available, required only unskilled labor, pushing many skilled weavers out of the picture. As mills became less dependent on water power, they moved away from rivers and toward railroad lines and towns—though typically remaining on the periphery of urban areas. Mill architecture changed, as did mill villages. Factories became typically brick, resembling New England factories. Isolated in rural areas a good distance from nearby towns, mill villages were created outside of town limits. Growing urban centers such as Burlington, Greensboro, Gastonia, and Roanoke Rapids developed much larger-scale mill housing on a planned scale. These mill villages were run in paternalistic fashion, under the nearly complete control of such owner-manufacturers as the Cone family in Greensboro, the Carrs in Durham, or Cannons in Concord. The new, post-1890 generation of mills was closely connected to railroads, and towns such as Gastonia, Kannapolis, and Burlington grew into mill centers because of their proximity to major railroad lines. In the northern Piedmont, Greensboro became a dominant textile city, while Charlotte's rise to prominence as North Carolina's leading city (it became the state's largest community in 1930) reflected its strategic position in the southern Piedmont textile belt.

The mill villages possessed a distinctively rural/pastoral character, yet the factories were thoroughly industrial. Mill owners also began to employ more modern business methods, and through the position of an industrial manager began to adopt more bureaucratic methods of business organization, one emphasizing profits and efficiency. But even as mill operations became more complex, owners continued to preach to the workers in the same language of paternalism. Ostensibly, owners offered mill families protection and benevolent leadership in exchange for their unquestioning loyalty—yet the profit motive undoubtedly drove the enterprise. Paternalism survived as a powerful ideology in textiles, even as it was undermined by its evolution into a modern industry.

During this time, a class of so-called New-South "boosters" began to praise the cotton-mill crusade in newspapers, speeches, and even from the pulpit. Hoping to attract northern capital and even the relocation of businesses and factories in the South, newspaper editors such as Henry Watterson of Louisville, Kentucky, and Henry Grady of Atlanta espoused a New-South message to northern audiences, one that promised a rejection of slavery and the Old South in favor of modernized agriculture and a cheap and loyal labor force, both black and white. Perhaps the best-known New-South booster in North Carolina was Daniel Augustus Tompkins, a businessman, newspaper editor, and publicist. An engineer by training and a South Carolinian by birth, Tompkins had moved to Charlotte in 1883 while working for the Westinghouse Machine Company, a main supplier of mill equipment for the expanding southern textile industry. Tompkins became the owner of three mills in North Carolina, and in the 1880s, he worked as southern correspondent for the *Manufacturers' Record*, edited by Richard H. Edmonds. Eventually he bought controlling interest in the *Charlotte Daily Observer* and the *Greenville* (South Carolina) *News*.

Cotton mills were the best, though not the only, example of the first phase of industrial manufacturing in North Carolina. As bright-leaf tobacco became an important commercial cash crop after 1865, small-scale tobacco factories sprang up across the Piedmont between the new railroad towns of Durham to the east and Winston to the west. In Durham, a local merchant entrepreneur, Julian S. Carr, purchased what became the Blackwell Durham Tobacco Company from two peddlers and developed Bull Durham into a dominant brand of pipe and plug, or chewing, tobacco. Carr's operation was highly capitalized and involved nationwide marketing. By 1884, his factory employed more than 1,000 workers and produced nearly 5 million pounds of Bull Durham tobacco. More

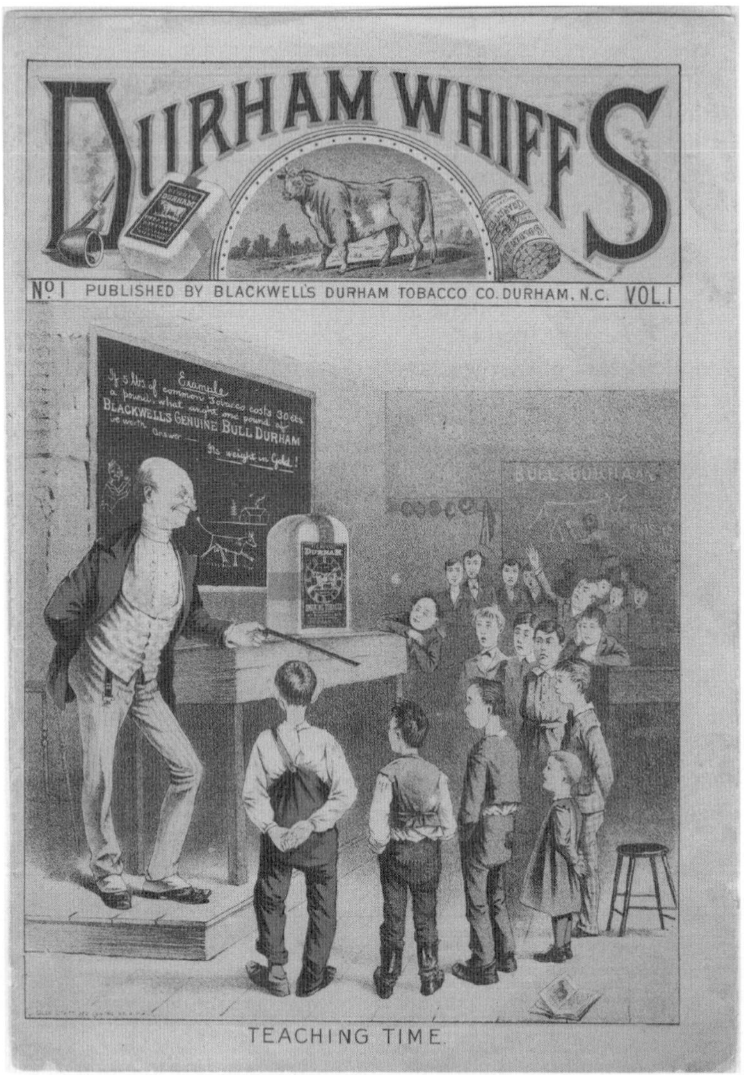

Figure 11.6 Advertisement for Blackwell's Genuine Bull Durham. *Source: David M Rubenstein Rare Books and Manuscript Library, Duke University.*

important was an Orange County entrepreneur, Washington Duke, who, along with his sons Benjamin and James Duke, during the 1880s organized a tobacco manufacturing operation focusing on cigarette production. The Dukes' factories used new Bonsack machines that enabled mass production of cigarettes, and the family established highly capitalized and productive manufacturing

Figure 11.7 Bird's eye view of Durham, NC, manufacturing district. *Source:* http://dc.lib.unc.edu/cdm/singleitem/collection/nc_post/id/7833/rec/13

operations in New York City that, along with facilities in North Carolina, were aided by mass advertising. With the organization of the American Tobacco Company in 1890, the Dukes achieved almost complete domination of the industry.

Although the U.S. Supreme Court, in a major antitrust decision, split the American Tobacco Company in 1911 into the American Tobacco, Liggett & Myers, P. Lorillard, and R. J. Reynolds Tobacco companies, tobacco manufacturing remained an important industrial enterprise in North Carolina. By World War I, in the new railroad town of Winston— which was the industrial counterpart of the Moravian town of Salem—a tobacco industry arose out of the factories organized by entrepreneur R. J. Reynolds. The tobacco factories of the R. J. Reynolds Company, and other tobacco companies, differed in their industrial organization from textile factories in an important respect: unlike the all-white cotton mills, tobacco factories hired significant numbers of African American workers.

The Impact of Industrialization

The advent of factories and industrialized manufacturing resulted in changes in the social life of thousands of North Carolinians. The spread of railroads spurred the growth of towns. After 1870 especially, North Carolina underwent a process of urbanization, the chief manifestation of which was the emergence of small and mid-size towns, along with a few large towns and small cities. Overall, the proportion of North Carolinians living in urban communities—which the federal census defined as communities of more than 2,500 people—grew appreciably. At the same time, larger towns such as Durham, Greensboro, Winston-Salem, and Charlotte became the state's largest cities. The extent of urban growth was most marked where the railroad had made its most decided appearance, in Piedmont North Carolina, and in no instance did urbanization occur without the presence of railroads.

Urbanization was also inextricably connected to the new work habits of the factory. Thousands of North Carolinians took the major step of embracing "public work" and abandoning rural communities in order to migrate to a factory setting where they became wage laborers and, increasingly, residents in the town environment. As part of this migration and social relocation, two forces—the decline of traditional farming and the rise of the industrial workplace—converged to create a new social environment in North Carolina. The new industrial workforce was simultaneously driven out of the countryside by deteriorating conditions and drawn to towns and cities by the cash income provided by the expanding factories. Therefore, the small farmers, white and black, who long had composed the agricultural workforce, were the very people most affected by the market revolution in rural North Carolina.

During the history of most migrations, young males typically arrive first, followed by their families. In post-1880 North Carolina, in contrast, migration to towns involved women and children from the start; the migration was most often composed of entire families, with a workforce including men, women, and children. This in part reflected the preferences of rural folk: the agricultural economy traditionally depended on family labor, with husbands, wives, and children all contributing to the agricultural process. North Carolinians were determined to preserve their rural ways, even as they migrated to mill villages, and recruiters for cotton textiles found it easier to attract mill laborers to mills as family units. Finally, since mills paid notoriously low wages, entire families had to work in order to survive. Workers existed at subsistence or barely above it; housing was barely adequate. Claims of mill paternalism in many instances rang hollow. In the first generation of post-Civil War cotton mills, family labor meant an exceptionally high rate of child labor in mills.

Despite this family system of labor, on the job, mill workers were segregated by gender, and it became generally acknowledged that mills should keep "men's work" separate from "women's work." Women worked in traditionally feminine parts of the work process that dated back to the preindustrial pattern of "piecemeal" work, like spinning and weaving, performed in the home: women thus performed "light" work, men "heavy" work. Managers strictly respected these gender divisions, though the presence of married women in the workforce admittedly violated the Victorian taboo of married women working outside the home. Unlike in tobacco factories, in cotton mills the work process was less hierarchical, with few differences between prefabrication and fabrication; because of this, white women were interspersed as tenders of machines throughout. Nonetheless, this was obviously a patriarchal system of labor.

A somewhat similar pattern of migration and workplace conditions existed in tobacco factories. Like cotton textiles, tobacco manufacturing grew out of antebellum patterns: particularly important was the use of African American slaves and then freedpeople in the work process. Black women did much of the unskilled labor of sorting, picking, and stemming, while black men performed the harder physical labor. With the expansion of cigarette production during the 1880s, white men and women worked in the more skilled phases of production and in the tending of the Bonsack machines. Rural whites moved to tobacco factories, as they did to cotton mills, because of declining traditional agriculture and the devastating impact of market agriculture, and their presence created a two-tiered work hierarchy based on race as well as gender. In tobacco factories, the two races were thus strictly segregated. In the R. J. Reynolds tobacco factories—which produced the highly popular Camel cigarette after 1913—manufacturing was divided into prefabrication and manufacturing. In prefabrication, which employed an all-black workforce, workers, mostly women, took unprocessed leaf and stemmed and removed external parts in order to prepare it for manufacturing; by the 1900s, much of stemming was mechanized. Black men, meanwhile, lifted, hauled, and maintained shredding machines—all tasks that required heavy manual labor. White men and women worked in manufacturing and in the processes by which the processed leaf was transformed into cigarettes, pipe tobacco, and chewing tobacco.

These industrial work processes in tobacco manufacturing were part of the social transformation of industrialization by which the work experience, as well as social life, changed radically. The expanding plantation system had impoverished a large portion of rural white and black North Carolinians, many of whom responded by migrating to the new towns spawned by railroads and industry. Rapidly expanding locales such as Durham contained both tobacco factories and cotton mills, and it was composed almost entirely of rural migrants—men and women, African American and white, who came to town in search of work with their families in tow.

Workers in tobacco factories and cotton mills—despite major differences in the two work environments—shared a common experience of adapting to the industrial workplace. Farm life was different: it was geared to the natural, seasonal rhythms of peak periods of planting and harvesting, with slack time in between. The rural world of small farms—at least as it existed before the advent of market agriculture—was the last vestige of a powerful culture of independence and self-sufficiency. Farmers produced crops for themselves and their families and existed largely in isolation; whatever surplus they produced went to market. Market agriculture changed things dramatically, with its insistence on cash crops and its introduction of debt and store-bought goods. Factory work and life in mill villages and towns presented an even more profound change. Workers labored for cash wages, were responsible for defined working hours, experienced the authority of owners and managers and were expected to obey factory whistles and punch time clocks. Workforces were strictly segregated by race and gender, while factory overseers and managers sought to control the workforce through a mixture of paternalism that sought to "protect" workers and strict, sometimes even harsh, discipline.

In the industrial North Carolina of the post–Civil War era, the advent of this new world of factories and mills only hardened lines of race and class. The new working class possessed a distinctive cultural identity: workers retained their rural traditions but recreated them as a way to assert dignity and independence in the face of the hostile industrial environment. North Carolina industrial workers spoke differently, dressed differently, attended their own public schools, bought supplies from the company store, and lived differently from other residents of the growing urban centers of the Piedmont. For the most part, though workers sometimes became factory overseers, these people had little chance of upward social mobility. The managerial class, all white males, defined themselves as distinctly different, while owners occupied a place at the top of the social ladder. Access to the upper class of the industrial world came only through correct family background, education, and connections. The management/owner class used different language and lived in a completely different cultural world.

Workers expressed these class differences in various ways. Managers increasingly found the mill village a confounding, disturbing, and confusing place that they failed to understand fully. Nonetheless, until the 1920s, unions made little headway in North Carolina industrial workplaces. An exception was the Knights of Labor, which organized in North Carolina during the 1880s, garnering the largest state chapter of any southern state outside of Virginia. Protest instead assumed other forms. Among African American tobacco workers, strong, independent communities emerged in the leading tobacco towns, Winston-Salem and Durham. In Durham, the black community, Hayti, became a center of a vibrant African American culture. In both communities, black family units, churches, and other cultural institutions formed the basis of a kind of racial and class solidarity. Strong family units became cultural refuges that existed outside of the control of the managerial class. Most mill workers remember that a general "family" atmosphere characterized the textile-worker community. In many mill villages, religion and churches provided powerful vehicles of cultural independence, and the early twentieth century witnessed

Figure 11.8 St. Joseph's AME (African Methodist Episcopal) Church. African American church constructed during the 1890s in Durham's Hayti neighborhood.

the rapid spread of new evangelical groups such as Nazarene and Pentecostal churches that had a distinct working-class character and emphasis. Still more common was the increased mobility of workers. By World War I, managers often complained about the propensity of workers to change jobs, and they sought ways to limit their physical mobility.

* * *

On the eve of the twentieth century, few parts of North Carolina had remained unaffected by the market revolution, a process that began to manifest itself before the Civil War but became fully formed during the 1880s and 1890s. Spearheading economic change was the transformation of transportation with the advent and spread of a dependable rail network, which enabled North Carolina to overcome its historically inferior system of often unnavigable rivers, harbors, and waterways. Farmers, exposed to market pressures, were drawn into a new system of commercial farming, and thousands abandoned the subsistence or semi-subsistence agriculture that had dominated life. Rural North Carolinians were also drawn to dynamic economic activity in manufacturing, and the majority of the workers laboring in the new textile and tobacco factories came from the countryside. The market revolution thus presaged a wider transformation of life in North Carolina.

Notes

1 Richard D. Starnes, *Creating the Land of the Sky: Tourism and Society in Western North Carolina* (Tuscaloosa: University of Alabama Press, 2005), p. 29.

2 Quoted in Kent Redding, *Making Race, Making Power: North Carolina's Road to Disfranchisement* (Urbana: University of Illinois Press, 2003), p. 77.

3 Quoted in Dolores E. Janiewski, *Sisterhood Denied: Race, Gender, and Class in a New South Community* (Philadelphia, PA: Temple University Press, 1985), pp. 12–13.

4 Holland Thompson, *From the Cotton Field to the Cotton Mill: A Study of the Industrial Transition in North Carolina* (New York: Macmillan Company, 1906), pp. 1–5.

12

Populism and the Crisis of the 1890s

At the close of the nineteenth century, farmers experienced disruptive changes in the expansion of the railroad network and the extension of market agriculture, and they felt increasingly aggrieved about the new social system that seemed to oppress them. For many farmers, post-Reconstruction politics no longer represented their interests. Political parties appeared less relevant than they had during the Jacksonian Era. The Redeemer leadership that ran state government after the 1870s preached economy, white supremacy, and economic development. But these leaders, many farmers believed, had become too cozy with industrial interests. Farmers thus turned to desperate measures. In the 1880s, they embraced an independent style of politics challenging the orthodoxy of unquestioning support for the Democratic Party. The arrival of a new protest organization, the Farmers' Alliance, provided a mouthpiece for agrarian frustration. By the early 1890s, Alliance leaders helped to found a new third party, the People's Party, and it brought seismic changes when Populists created a coalition that was swept into power after 1894.

Agrarian Discontent and the Farmers' Alliance

The late 1880s and early 1890s were tough times for North Carolina farmers. In the 1880s, railroads reshaped life, drawing much of the state into a market economy. But participation in the market meant an environment of deflated prices for farm goods, cyclical boom and bust, and the extreme volatility of the financial markets and banking resources. While more farmers became a part of market agriculture, a severe price decline occurred in the cotton economy. Until the 1870s, cotton prices ranged between 12 and 18 cents per pound. Then, after 1883, cotton prices collapsed to 8 cents per pound by 1890 and 5 cents per pound by 1894. Meanwhile, the plantation system continued to expand: between 1870 and 1890, the production of cotton doubled. North Carolina farmers experienced dislocation and bewilderment about the changing scene, and these feelings came to fruition during the 1880s. "If Miss Prosperity has made her appearance in this section," wrote one farmer, "she certainly has appeared wrong end forward, for there never has been, since Adam was a boy, such weeping, wailing and gnashing of teeth … among the poor."[1]

In addition to this general dissatisfaction with the market revolution, rural North Carolinians grew unhappy with the Democratic Party. Although that party consolidated power in 1876—in the so-called "redemption" of the state from Republican rule—it adopted a number of policies that placed it at odds with its traditional constituencies. During the late 1870s and 1880s, the legislature often considered fence or stock laws; because this legislation was considered local, the fence issue became a regular matter before the legislature. In general, Democrats sided with commercial and railroad interests, despite the strong opposition of ordinary white farmers, many of whom were loyal Democratic voters. This grassroots disgruntlement began to undermine the Democratic appeal in many parts of the state.

Redeemers in North Carolina thus faced potent problems. Republicans managed to remain a presence in state politics throughout the generation after Reconstruction, as a solid core of African American voters, most of whom continued to participate politically, challenged white control. Statewide turnout of black voters was, for example, more than 80 percent in 1880 and above 60 percent in 1892.[2] Between 1877 and 1890, fifty-four African Americans were elected to the North Carolina legislature; overall, 113 blacks served between 1860 and 1900. During this same period, the Second Congressional District, encompassing much of heavily black eastern North Carolina, regularly elected an African American to the United States Congress. In addition, pockets of white Republicanism persisted in Piedmont and western North Carolina. This meant the Democratic margin of victory remained narrow during the post-Reconstruction era: in elections taking place between 1880 and 1896, Democratic majorities never once exceeded 54 percent. In statewide elections, Democrats maintained control by what was the narrowest margin in the South. As a result, North Carolina Democrats took extraordinary measures to maintain their control, but in doing so they were caught in a difficult position: maintaining power meant passing measures that were unpopular with and alienated some of their traditional constituencies.

An obvious example of the Redeemer Democrats' increasing unpopularity was the changes that they initiated in local government. The constitutional convention of 1875 had authorized an important change in local government by eliminating elections for county government and empowering the legislature to appoint the county commissioners. In 1877, the legislature in a local government act eliminated home rule, a measure that ensured Democratic control of majority black and Republican districts in eastern North Carolina. At the same time, the Local Government Act was highly unpopular in the largely white counties of Piedmont and western North Carolina, and ordinary white voters—again, the backbone of the Democratic constituency—considered this a betrayal of Democratic ideals.

Democrats also were forced to exert strong and sometimes clumsy control over the electoral machinery in order to guarantee political power. The General Assembly of 1877 enacted a new electoral law that established county boards of elections to administer and supervise the electoral process. The members of these boards were named by the legislature, who appointed loyal partisans in order to ensure that their party would remain in power. The Democrats' control of the electoral machinery wore thin during the 1880s. By this time, ordinary North Carolina voters had begun to view the party leadership suspiciously.

In many respects, that leadership had grown old and somewhat out of touch, while the party itself suffered from severe factionalization. The Redeemers had brought together, in the Democratic Party, much of the antebellum political leadership class. Prewar Whigs coexisted with prewar Democrats, but their coexistence in the party was at times uneasy. Antebellum Whigs favored a high tariff, antebellum Democrats a low one. Former Whigs favored government sponsorship of economic development, which in the post-Reconstruction era meant unqualified support for railroad expansion. But traditional Jacksonian Democrats were uneasy with any appearance of a governmental alliance with "monopolies," the "money trust," and "big business," and tensions over these and other issues hardened divisions within the party. So divided was the party that it lost an absolute majority in the elections for the North Carolina legislature in 1886, with slates of independent legislators, who had bolted from the Democratic Party, holding the balance of power in the General Assembly.

Against this background of Democratic weakness, the Farmers' Alliance appeared on the scene in North Carolina. Originating in Texas in the late 1870s, by the mid-1880s the Farmers' Alliance had emerged as a major protest group of farmers discontented with what they perceived as the ill effects of the market revolution. The Alliance drew disaffected cotton farmers from east Texas, and it attracted members through a protest message that promised, through cooperatives that marketed the cotton crop and then bypassed the crop-lien system, to break the stranglehold of rural merchants and agricultural debt. In 1887, the Alliance decided to expand nationwide by sending out lecturers across the South, and it found an especially receptive audience among southern farmers. Organizers in North Carolina worked with existing agrarian groups such as the Grange, or Patrons of Husbandry, which was organized nationally in 1867 and first arrived in North Carolina in 1873 with the founding of a local chapter in Guilford County. "In essentials, unity," went the Grange's motto, "in non-essentials, liberty—in all things, clarity."[3] The Grange formally became a statewide organization in February 1875 by legislative statute of incorporation, at which point North Carolina had about 500 local lodges and 15,000 members. Appealing mostly to larger, more commercial farmers, the Grange's main objectives included the establishment of a state department of agriculture,

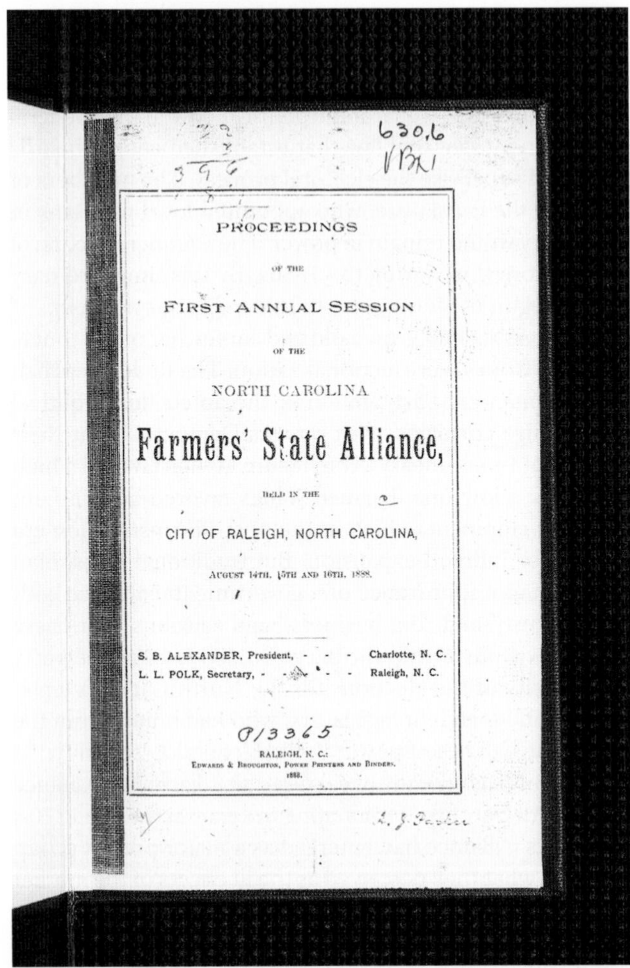
PROCEEDINGS

OF THE

FIRST ANNUAL SESSION

OF THE

NORTH CAROLINA

Farmers' State Alliance,

HELD IN THE

CITY OF RALEIGH, NORTH CAROLINA,

AUGUST 14TH, 15TH AND 16TH, 1888.

S. B. ALEXANDER, President, - - - Charlotte, N. C.
L. L. POLK, Secretary, - - - - Raleigh, N. C.

RALEIGH, N. C.:
EDWARDS & BROUGHTON, POWER PRINTERS AND BINDERS.
1888.

Figure 12.1 Proceedings of Farmers' Alliance meeting, Raleigh, 1888. *Source: North Carolina Collection, University of North Carolina Library at Chapel Hill.*

which the legislature created in 1877. In April of that year, Leonidas LaFayette Polk, Confederate veteran and editor of the agricultural newspaper, *Progressive Farmer* in Raleigh, became North Carolina's first commissioner of agriculture and served until 1880. But thereafter the Grange declined in North Carolina and during the late 1880s the more militant agrarian protest organization, the Farmers' Alliance, offered a wider appeal to farmers. After 1887, the Alliance grew quickly in North Carolina, with more than 1,000 "sub-alliances" (or local Alliance organizations) and more than 42,000 members in over fifty-two counties in the first year. By 1890, the Alliance claimed somewhere between two and three million members nationwide, with 100,000 of them in North Carolina. The Alliance appealed to the mass of farmers—men and women, black and white—discontented with the eroding status of rural life, and it was strongest in the cotton counties of the state.

The appeal of the Alliance was not simply based on class: many of the leading figures in the order were substantial planters and members of the state's rural elite. The state chapter enjoyed strong leadership from Polk, who was later president of the national Alliance. As Alliance leader, he earned widespread popularity for his leadership, but he was clearly not from the bottom rung of the social order. The Alliance's appeal at least partly lay in the creation of a statewide cooperative and in the establishment of several tobacco warehouses. The Alliance enjoyed its strongest support in North Carolina—as in the rest of the South—in cotton-producing areas. Originating in seven cotton counties, after 1887, it extended its dominance to forty-six additional nearby counties.

Describing itself as a nonpolitical organization, the Alliance reassured rural North Carolinians that it was not seeking to disrupt racial unity and white supremacy. It worked in combination with the Democrats, and in congressional elections in 1890, the Alliance helped to elect a number of candidates from across the South who were pledged to enact the Alliance's subtreasury plan, the farm group's primary objective in Congress during the early 1890s. In North Carolina, four of the state's elected congressmen actually belonged to the Alliance, while the speaker of the state house of representatives in 1891 was a member of the order. Responding directly to rural problems of credit, the subtreasury plan proposed to establish government-guaranteed agricultural warehouses that would store farm products (ideally until prices for them were favorable) and, in the interim, extend credit to farmers. The subtreasury plan sought to overcome the perennial problem of rural debt and the lack of an adequate money supply. When the subtreasury plan was proposed in Congress in 1890, however, it encountered immediate opposition. The North Carolina's Senator and Redeemer Zebulon Vance, working with Alliance president Polk, introduced the Subtreasury Bill but then opposed it, effectively sabotaging whatever chance it had of passage. "I never gave any one reason to suppose that I [wanted] the Bill," Vance wrote, "and only introduced it because in courtesy I could not refuse to do it." But the Alliance considered Vance's switch treacherous, and a farm leader condemned his position as in "open opposition to the Alliance."[4]

Populism and Fusion

In 1891, a "farmers' legislature" enacted legislation targeted at the Alliance and its rural constituency; of the General Assembly's 170 members, 110 belonged to the order. North Carolina farmers often expressed hostility toward railroads,

Figure 12.2 North Carolina Agricultural and Mechanical Colored College (later A&T State University), Greensboro, early 1900s. *Source: North Carolina Collection, University of North Carolina Library at Chapel Hill.*

which they regarded as the source of their troubles. Railroads, while fueling the spread of the market economy, also brought heightened competition and lowered agricultural prices. In the 1880s, especially, railroads spread to the farthest reaches of rural North Carolina, but they became a symbol of the oppressive qualities of the new, post-Civil War economy. In the eyes of many farmers, the railroads charged high freight rates with impunity, even as they provided preferential, lower rates to shippers transporting goods for longer hauls. Railroads also exercised considerable political influence in North Carolina and nationally through lobbying, a liberal distribution of money, and the awarding of free passes for travel by legislators. Responding to antirailroad sentiment, the legislature—much like other legislatures in the South—created a state railroad commission with some power to regulate rates and to prevent discriminatory practices. Much of the emphasis of this session of the legislature was on education, as it established in Greensboro a state agricultural college for blacks, the Agricultural and Mechanical College for the Colored Race (later North Carolina A&T State University). In 1890, the legislature created, also located in Greensboro, a new institution of higher learning for white women, the State Normal and Industrial School.

In part, because of the failure of the subtreasury plan in Congress and in part because farm leaders believed that the Democratic Party no longer served their interests, the North Carolina Alliance contemplated radical measures by 1891–92. Some leading and articulate Alliancemen, such as Polk, Pitt County's Harry Skinner, and Sampson County newspaper editor Marion Butler, advocated organizing a new People's Party. This party came into existence at a convention in Cincinnati, Ohio, in 1891; North Carolina Alliance leaders played a principal role, and North Carolina sent the largest delegation of any state to that meeting. In 1892, the Populists came together in a national nominating convention in Omaha, Nebraska. The consensus favorite as the party's presidential nominee was Polk, but he died suddenly in May 1892. As a result, the convention, while articulating a wide-ranging platform of reform, nominated James B. Weaver of Iowa for president. Weaver, a former Union army general, had little appeal in North Carolina or the South, but Populists nevertheless became a presence in state politics. Meeting in a statewide convention in August 1892, North Carolina Populists also fielded a statewide ticket in elections for the legislature and governorship, nominating W. P. Exum of Wayne County.

Although Democrats maintained control of state government in the elections of 1892—in part by nominating and electing former Alliance state president Elias Carr—they faced a serious challenge in Populism. The new party elected fourteen new members of the legislature, and it succeeded in fashioning a strong appeal to white farmers, especially in the Piedmont. As Populist candidate for governor, Exum attracted almost 48,000 votes, or 18 percent of the total; the third party won majorities in Chatham, Nash, and Sampson Counties and a near-majority in Brunswick and Hyde. Resentment against Democrats, combined with a severe depression that followed a global financial panic in 1893, further eroded their support. In 1894, moreover, Populists, led by state chairman Marion Butler, reached a crucial decision: they allied themselves in a "fusion" coalition with the Republican Party. In elections that year for the General Assembly, the Fusionists were swept to power.

That new legislature, now under a Fusionist majority of 74–46, elected Populist Marion Butler and Republican Jeter C. Pritchard to seats in the United States Senate (incumbent senator Zebulon Vance had died in 1894). The legislature enacted measures designed to benefit farmers, such as legislation establishing a maximum credit rate of 6 percent annually and raising taxes on railroads. After the election of Republican Daniel L. Russell as governor in 1896, the Fusion coalition tried to revoke what they called the "unholy" 99-year lease by which Democratic governor Elias Carr had agreed in August 1895 to turn over the assets of the North Carolina Railroad to the Southern Railway conglomerate. In his inaugural address, Russell denounced the lease and promised to make these "foreign corporations" pay a higher rent for the railroad.[5]

The Fusionist victory also meant an entirely new approach to state government. Public schools benefited by receiving an increased state appropriation, a $25,000 lump sum that Congress had refunded to the state, and authorization for local tax districts (a measure that sought to increase public tax support for education). Fusionists also sought to break down the Redeemer power structure by eliminating the repressive measures that Redeemers used to maintain their tenuous hold over state government. The Fusionist legislature repealed the Local Government Act of 1877 and restored a system of democratically elected local government; county commissioners, for the first time since 1876, were chosen by a popular vote rather than by appointment. For good measure, the legislature provided for the popular election of district school-board members. The legislature also enacted a new election law that overturned Democratic measures of 1886 and 1889 that had imposed firm partisan control over the electoral process. Under the Payne law, enacted in 1889, Democratic registrars had gained wide latitude in disfranchising African American voters if they were unable to validate their identities, age, or residence, and to document their birthplace in "satisfactory" fashion. The law was applied with equal effectiveness against African American and poor white voters. The Payne law also empowered election boards—under the control of a partisan majority—to disqualify votes or adjust vote totals at their own discretion.

In March 1895, the Fusionist legislature repealed the Democratic electoral system that had been established between 1877 and 1889. They replaced it with a new law that stipulated that local elections boards should represent all parties, permitted a ballot with party symbols and insignia (which would assist illiterates in voting), and limited the ability of registrars to throw out votes on an arbitrary basis. The results were impressive: counties with a large African American electorate increased their vote total from 18,543 to 33,900 between 1892 and 1896. In sixteen counties with the largest black population, the vote total during the same period increased by more than 15,000.

By 1896, Fusionism was at high tide in North Carolina. Unlike in any other southern state, the Redeemer Democratic regime had been utterly repudiated by popular vote: along with the election of Russell, in 1896 the popular vote returned a legislature that was 78 percent Fusionist. Meanwhile, Populists controlled five out of eight congressional seats in the same election. Thereafter, however, this coalition began to suffer from serious strains. Some of these were internal and intrinsic: in 1896, at the national level, Populists and Republicans opposed each other, while Democrats fused with Populists to nominate William Jennings Bryan (of Nebraska) for president. Although state elections occurred in August and the presidential election in November, in a number of counties "Fusion" tickets included a Populist/Republican coalition in state elections and a Populist/Democratic coalition in the presidential election. In the presidential election, Populists and Democrats favored "free silver," which meant using silver as a form of hard currency in order to expand the money supply for cash-starved farmers in a deflated economy. Since most farmers carried debt, inflation—and cheaper money—actually made their debts easier to pay off. Republicans, in contrast, favored retaining the gold standard as the single form of specie or hard currency. Although in North Carolina the

Populist and Republican executive committees agreed to cooperate in September 1896, tensions existed in the gubernatorial elections, as Daniel L. Russell ran as the Republican candidate and Durham attorney William A. Guthrie ran as a Populist, who denounced Fusionism, and, during the campaign's late stages, opposed Fusion with Republicans and urged a return to Democratic ranks.

At least some of the tensions in the Fusion coalition were racial. Populists were nearly entirely white, Republicans overwhelmingly black. At both the state and federal levels, black officeholding increased. George White, elected twice from eastern North Carolina's Second Congressional District, was an articulate and well-known black leader. Wake County's James Young became the best-known African American leader in the legislature. A newspaper editor, Young figured importantly in Republican politics as an advocate of Fusion in 1894; he would later lead a North Carolina black regiment organized to fight in the Spanish-American War of 1898. Elected to the state house in 1894, he became a supporter of public education and especially black education. Other black Republican leaders included state house members William H. Crews of Granville County and John T. Howe of New Hanover County, along with state senators William L. Person of Edgecombe County and W. B. Henderson of Warren and Vance Counties.

Figure 12.3 George H. White. *Source: North Carolina Collection, University of North Carolina Library at Chapel Hill.*

Fusionist leaders realized that the race issue could destroy the coalition. Daniel L. Russell was elected as a Republican governor despite the misgivings of some African Americans about him. Russell's inaugural address, in a reference to black voters, warned that ordinary citizens needed protections against "the danger of misrule by propertyless and ignorant elements."[6] In early 1897, the Fusionist breach spilled over into the reelection of Jeter C. Pritchard, who in 1895 filled Vance's unexpired term. As part of the Fusion coalition, Republicans and Populists had agreed to elect one Republican and one Populist to the Senate. Pritchard, a gold-standard man, was opposed by a bloc of Populists—including the other US senator, Marion Butler—who favored Alliance leader and doctor Cyrus Thompson of Onslow County. Although Pritchard won reelection through the support of several bolting Populists, including Pitt County Populist Harry Skinner, an open break had occurred from which the Fusion coalition would never recover. Not only were Republicans and Populists at odds, but Populists remained seriously divided between "regular" (who supported Butler) and "bolter" (who supported Skinner) factions.

The White Supremacy Campaign and the Wilmington Massacre

Following the electoral debacle they had suffered in 1896, in which they lost both the legislature and the governorship to Fusionists, the Democratic leaders were determined to regain power. During the mid-1890s, a new generation was rising to the leadership of the Democratic Party. Gone were Redeemers such as Zebulon Vance. In his place stood figures such as former congressman and future senator Furnifold M. Simmons, an eastern North Carolina Democratic leader; Josephus Daniels, owner/editor of the fledging *Raleigh News and Observer*; and Charles B. Aycock, a reform-oriented partisan from Goldsboro. Other "new" Democrats included future governors Robert B. Glenn, Claude Kitchin, Locke Craig, and Cameron Morrison. While Furnifold M. Simmons, Democratic Party chairman after 1892, took charge of reorganizing the party, Daniels and Aycock communicated a new message to voters. These newer and younger Democratic leaders decided on a strategy emphasizing race—holding up the prospect of the social, political, and sexual threat of "black rule" through the Fusion coalition. During 1896–97, the Democratic press, led by Daniels, warned that the rape of white women by black men would be the fruit of African American political power. In a few instances, black males so accused were lynched: in Asheville, for example, an angry mob lynched accused rapist Bob Brackett in August 1897. Alleged sexual assaults by African Americans were presented to voters in such a way as to emphasize black bestiality and brutality and the need for white manhood to protect their women from attack. In this way, during the notorious "White Supremacy" campaign of 1898–1900,

Figure 12.4 Furnifold M. Simmons (1854–1940). *Source: North Carolina Collection, University of North Carolina Library at Chapel Hill.*

the Democratic opponents of Fusionism tried to link fears about gender and sexuality with fears about race in the minds of white men.

Anticipating legislative elections in that year, the Democratic Party in May 1898 adopted a platform accusing the Fusion government of "Negro domination" and pledging a return to "rule by the white men of the State."[7] Without evidence of its existence, Democratic newspaper editors launched a campaign after 1898 suggesting that a black crime wave—featuring widespread sexual assault of white women by black males—had resulted from the Fusionist regime. Black "insolence" and "uppitiness," Democrats suggested, had upset the social order and were creating widespread chaos: simply put, "black rule" was the chief source of North Carolina's problems. Like their portrayal of an alleged crime wave, the Democrats' description of "black rule" was wildly off the mark: between 1895 and 1899 only eleven African Americans served in the North Carolina General Assembly. Although there were black officeholders at the county level, their numbers were also limited. Nonetheless, in the columns of the *Raleigh News and Observer*, Josephus Daniels produced a regular amount of copy, distributed by Simmons and others, in a well-organized effort to unite Democratic partisans across the state.

Daniels persuaded a former cartoonist for the *News and Observer*, Norman E. Jennett, to return to the state, and Jennett composed lurid, openly racist cartoons emphasizing the dangers of "Negro rule." Jennett's cartoons, along with other white-supremacist materials, were sent to 100,000 voters across the state. Between August and November, scores of articles, most of them based on fabricated or grossly exaggerated evidence, were distributed throughout the state. Echoing the successful effort by Redeemers to overthrow Reconstruction, the new Democrats also embraced terror and violence. They organized White Government Unions calling for an end to African American political participation and calling for a reinstatement of white supremacy. The campaign, by spreading news of the ill effects of African American "rule," most of it fabricated, sought to split the coalition of the mostly white Populists with the mostly black Republicans. Just as Redeemers had used Klan violence to

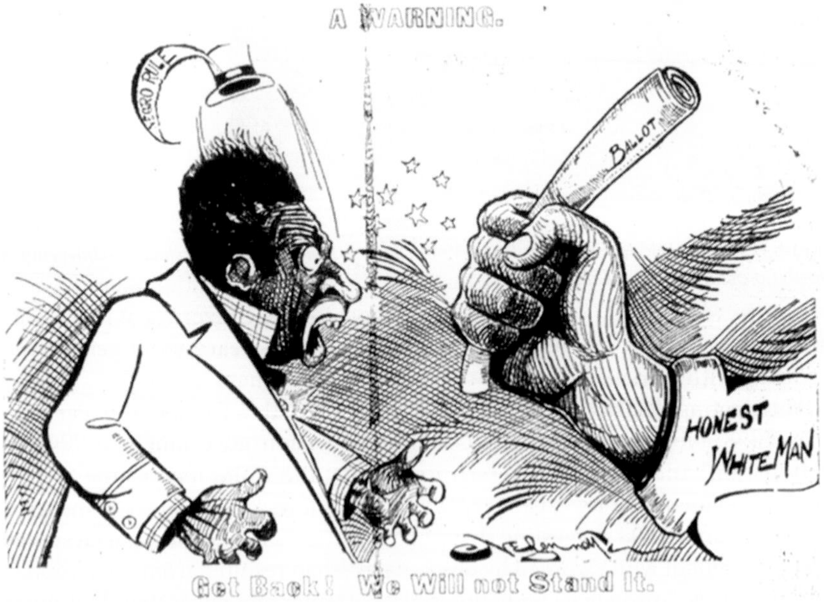

Figure 12.5 Cartoon from *Raleigh News and Observer*, 1898 campaign. *Source: North Carolina Collection, University of North Carolina Library at Chapel Hill.*

split the biracial Reconstruction coalition, the new Democrats exploited largely manufactured fears about race and gender to destroy the Fusion coalition.

Particularly important were newly organized terrorist groups that sought to mobilize white voters on the race issue and to intimidate African American voters. Along with White Government Unions, Democrats formed local groups known as the Red Shirts, and during the late stages of the campaign, in October 1898, they orchestrated local efforts that erupted into violence. The North Carolina Red Shirts were modeled on the Red Shirt organization created by South Carolina governor and white supremacist Benjamin Tillman, and they operated mostly in the heavily black counties of southeastern North Carolina. Red Shirts often rode into Republican areas in dramatic fashion, carrying Winchester rifles. Without question this was a campaign, Simmons announced in an address sent to 100,000 voters statewide, to "restore the state to the white people." Whites, "by the irresistible power of fusion laws and fusion legislation," had been "placed under the control or dominion of that race which ranks lowest ... in the human family." White women were routinely arrested by black constables and tried by black judges, he claimed.

> The battle has been fought, the victory is within our reach. North Carolina is a WHITE MAN'S STATE, and WHITE MEN will rule it, and they will crush the party of Negro domination beneath a majority so overwhelming that no other party will ever dare to establish Negro rule here.[8]

The Democrats' immediate strategy was to recapture control of the legislature in the election of November 1898. Democrats enjoyed the solid support of North Carolina business interests, who had been thoroughly alarmed by the Populists' anticorporate rhetoric. Simmons, who dispatched former governor Thomas L. Jarvis to meet with railroad, financial, and textile concerns in the state, assured business leaders that under Democratic rule business taxes would remain low, and they responded by bankrolling the party's expensive campaign efforts. Simmons also forged a secret alliance with denominational interests, who wanted to restrict state support for the University of North Carolina, the growth of which threatened enrollments at church-related colleges. In exchange for their support, he promised to oppose any proposed increases in funding for the University of North Carolina. Their strategy paid off, as Democrats were swept to power in August 1898. In the aftermath of the election, Democrats occupied 94 of the 120 seats in the state house and 40 of 50 seats in the state senate.

The Democratic victory occurred in the context of a pivotal development in North Carolina history: the illegal overthrow of local government in Wilmington on November 10, 1898, two days after the elections. Since Reconstruction, Wilmington had been a center of African American social and political life; the city was known for its black skilled workers, businessmen, and professionals such as ministers, attorneys, and physicians. During the Fusion years, black political culture fully blossomed. The city and the surrounding counties furnished black legislators to Raleigh, and a number of local officeholders—including offices such as county treasurer, assistant sheriff, jailer, and coroner—were black. After 1877, the Democrats ensured white control of the city by appointing local city government, but the Fusionist victory, and the return to home rule in local government, changed matters. In 1897, the General Assembly adopted a new charter for Wilmington, establishing a governing board of aldermen composed of five elected members and five members appointed by the governor. In elections in March 1897, four of five aldermen elected were African American; Governor Russell appointed one black and four white aldermen. The aldermen then selected a Republican mayor. Local white leaders challenged the constitutionality of the new charter, but the North Carolina supreme court unanimously upheld it.

Local whites regarded this board of aldermen, which was composed of five whites and five blacks, as an example of intolerable "black rule." In addition, African American journalist Alex Manly edited the *Wilmington Record* in a bold style that, in an era of white supremacy, challenged common assumptions about black culture and asserted racial equality. Local whites regarded Manly as inappropriately insolent, another example of the excesses of "black rule." In 1898, the Georgia suffragist and prohibitionist Rebecca Latimer Felton delivered a speech at a farmers' convention that was reprinted in a Wilmington Democratic newspaper. In pointing out the problem of rural poverty among families, Felton asserted that white males inadequately protected their women: black males threatened white womanhood, she believed, and strong action, even lynching, was necessary. In August 1898, Manly responded in a locally published editorial that white supremacists republished and ridiculed widely. Black males were not, he said, the only sexual predators. Just as white males conducted interracial sexual relationships with black women, Manly claimed, why was it not possible that black males might have such relationships with white females? While white males' relationships with black females were often nonconsensual, Manly said, white females' relationships with black males were sometimes consensual. In many instances, white women participated in interracial relationships; once exposed, they claimed rape. He suggested that lynching was driven by this double standard. Whites seeking to "guard their women closely," he said, reflected poor white males' inclination to leave their "goods out of doors and then complain because they are taken away."[9]

Many whites considered Manly's editorial highly inflammatory. In it, he suggested that all white women were not sexually pure, that a genuine attraction might exist between black men and white women, and that any emotional attachment by no means constituted rape—all assertions that most North Carolina whites deemed unacceptable. In the context of the widespread reporting by the press of a supposed increase in sexual crimes across the state, Manly's editorial seemed to encourage the alleged gender and racial disorder of the late 1890s. In the aftermath of Manly's editorial, the atmosphere in Wilmington during the days before the election grew extremely tense.

The statewide White Supremacy campaign certainly inflamed matters in Wilmington. The city's white press reported regularly on alleged black insults to white womanhood, insisting on the need to expel the African American male leadership in the city. Across Wilmington, whites and blacks alike began to arm themselves in anticipation of an outbreak of violence. Wilmington black women, for example, assembled the Organization of Colored Ladies, which called on all African Americans to vote Republican; those who did not would be "branded a white-livered coward who would sell his liberty."[10] Whites in the city, said Alfred Moore Waddell, a local white leader of the White Government League, extended a "Macedonian call" to all whites to rescue the city from black domination. "We will not live under these intolerable conditions," for "no society can stand it." Local whites, he warned, would change things, even "if we have to choke the current of the Cape Fear River with negro carcasses."[11]

White leaders then conspired to ensure the triumph of their cause. Sometime before November, a group known as the "Secret Nine" drew up plans for an uprising. In a "Declaration of White Independence," the group denounced rule by the African American political majority, asserting that white males rightfully deserved "a large part of the employment" and demanding that the *Record* be shut down and that Manly be expelled (though he had already left the city). The "Secret Nine" organized a twenty-five-person committee, chaired by Waddell, which convened a meeting attended by 1,000 Wilmington whites; on November 8, 1898, the committee presented their declaration to African American leaders, whom they gave two days to respond. When their response failed to arrive, Waddell led a band of armed whites composed of many of Wilmington's leading citizens, which proceeded to Manly's office and torched it. Mayhem and random violence against the black community of Brooklyn followed, as many blacks fled to the nearby woods. Meanwhile, a company of the recently mobilized Wilmington Light Infantry joined the fray, and they turned their full force, including a rapid-fire machine gun and two cannon, against the city's African Americans.

Despite appeals from North Carolina Republicans, the administration of President William McKinley refused to intervene. The black leadership of Wilmington became a special target of the white mob, and the board of aldermen elected in 1897 was forced to resign and driven from the city. After the *coup d'état,* Waddell installed himself as mayor and his supporters back into office as a new city government. The death toll of the Wilmington Massacre is unknown. More than a century later, in 2006, a legislative commission estimated it at least twenty-five and perhaps as many as sixty African American deaths. Whatever its precise extent, the mayhem in Wilmington was a carefully calculated attack on the center of North Carolina's black political culture.

Figure 12.6 Destruction of the offices of Alex Manly's *Wilmington Record* on November 10, 1898. *Source: Courtesy of New Hanover County Public Library.*

The Wilmington Massacre proved to be a pivotal event. Defining a new period of white supremacy, it ushered in an era of one-party (Democratic) rule that would dominate the entire state for much of the next century. The four hundred or so Wilmington whites participating in the violence had very specific objectives: to end black influence, restore white supremacy, and expel the leading African American males of that city. "The white people of Wilmington intended to remove all the able leaders of the colored race," remembered a black minister who fled the city,

> stating that to do so would leave them better and obedient servants among the Negroes; and all the better class of the colored citizens were driven from the city, showing to the world that they were not after the criminal and ignorant class of Negroes, but the professional and business men ... These and many others with them were driven and sent away from the city.[12]

Triumphant White Supremacy

The illegal *coup d'état* in Wilmington was only a symptom of a larger disease: the triumph of white supremacy that had occurred in North Carolina was suggestive of trends across the United States, and it was perhaps fitting that one of the nation's best examples of white supremacy triumphant was a North

Carolinian, Thomas Dixon. Born near Shelby, in Cleveland County, in 1864, Dixon was highly intelligent and incredibly prolific. Graduating with two bachelor's degrees from Wake Forest College in 1883 at the age of 19, he reputedly earned the best academic record of any student ever at that institution. Thereafter, he studied for the doctorate (though he never completed it) in political science at Johns Hopkins, where a fellow student and friend was future president Woodrow Wilson. Trained in the law, Dixon was elected to the North Carolina legislature in 1884 and served one term. He subsequently had various careers as a minister (he was ordained in 1886) in North Carolina and New York City. By 1895, he switched careers again, becoming a popular lecturer, novelist, actor, playwright, business entrepreneur, and impresario of the infant motion-picture industry. He achieved national fame for his novels; he published some twenty-two works of fiction between 1902 and 1939. The mercurial Dixon spent money as fast as he made it, and later in life he would end up bankrupt in a North Carolina courtroom.

Dixon is perhaps best known, however, as a popularizer of the new, angry mood of white racism. Between 1902 and 1907, he published a trilogy of novels about Reconstruction and race—*The Leopard's Spots* (1902), *The Clansman* (1905), and *The Traitor* (1907)—that derided what he suggested was the hasty emancipation of African Americans and their supposed corruption of southern public life. Dixon maintained that the policies of Reconstruction had been a tragic mistake and that black political equality had led to "social equality" and sexual race-mixing. Like other scientific racists of the day, Dixon urged racial purity, insisting that white women must be "protected" from black sexual predators. Just as the Wilmington Massacre had been sparked by an alleged assault on white manhood—and ironically portrayed African Americans as a menacing presence in the South—Dixon warned in his novels that black men threatened sexual mastery over white women.

Dixon's imagery was powerful, and his fictitious Klan trilogy attracted a large, national readership. But Dixon sought to expand his reach, and during the early 1900s he promoted a stage version of *The Clansman*. Then, in the most ambitious production of his career, Dixon developed a film version of *The Clansman*. Known as a pioneering work in American film history, *The Birth of a Nation,* released on February 8, 1915, was directed by D. W. Griffith, the Kentucky-born son of a Confederate war hero and one of Hollywood's most successful filmmakers. The film portrayed American history as a struggle between the races, with its culmination occurring during Reconstruction, when, according to the film's account, the Klan saved white womanhood from the threat of unrestrained black sexuality. All the main African American male characters in the film—played by white actors in black face—wanted one thing: a white woman. Encountering widespread protests by civil-rights groups and a boycott by the newly founded National Association for the Advancement of Colored People (NAACP), *The Birth of a Nation* nonetheless enjoyed widespread popularity, in large part because it reflected the prevailing racism prevalent throughout the country.

In North Carolina, the elections of 1898 secured overwhelming Democratic control of the legislature and finally wrecked the Fusion coalition. With large majorities in both houses, the Democratic General Assembly repealed the Fusionist reforms and restored partisan control over the state: the legislature of 1899 revised thirty-three sections of the North Carolina Code, while it rewrote fifty-three laws enacted by the Fusionist legislatures of 1895–97. Local government was revised yet again: the Democratic legislature provided for both appointment and election of county commissioners, but in the end about two-thirds of the state's local governments came under the control of the legislature. Just as important, Democrats returned the election system to their control and restored their party's domination of the election boards and registrars; this system, once again, worked to exclude black and Republican voters.

But the General Assembly went further. Democratic leaders imposed a permanent system of white supremacy by effectively removing African Americans from the political system through disfranchisement, using means both legal and otherwise. Already there were models for accomplishing the task. Beginning with Mississippi in 1890, during the next fifteen years most of the South adopted some form of suffrage restriction through the use of new electoral devices that targeted black voters. In contrast to the Reconstruction Era, southern white disfranchisers now realized that they could operate without much chance of northern interference, for northern white Republicans, no longer interested in protecting black rights, had largely abandoned the goal of enforcing the Fourteenth and Fifteenth Amendments. Southern white supremacists eagerly exploited this opportunity to restore their power. The most common of these electoral devices included the poll tax and the literacy test. The poll tax imposed a tax on voting, granted registrars wide leeway in enforcing it, and then provided that voters could be excluded if they had not paid the taxes. The literacy test required that voters demonstrate reading and writing ability in a test administered by local officials (who invariably were white Democrats); it sought not only to exclude illiterate voters but essentially to prohibit blacks from voting. Such devices—as well as intimidation at polling places that often included violent tactics—appeared across the South during the 1890s and early 1900s.

Along with other southern disfranchisers, North Carolina Democrats envisioned radical measures: in the end, they would seek to exclude about half of the electorate. The vast majority of these voters would be black, but their ranks would include Republicans, and disfranchisement would secure the one-party rule of the Democrats until the last third of the twentieth century. The 1899 General Assembly soon contemplated an amendment to the state constitution institutionalizing black disfranchisement. Francis D. Winston, who had helped to organize the White Supremacy clubs, and George Rountree, one of the Wilmington conspirators, played leading roles in writing North Carolina's disfranchisement amendment and in steering it through the legislature. The most important features of this amendment were the requirements of the payment of a poll tax and the completion of a literacy test, administered by local registrars. In order to make it more acceptable to illiterate whites, the disfranchisers included a "grandfather clause," which exempted anyone who was eligible to vote, or whose ancestors had been eligible to vote, on January 1, 1867. The grandfather clause was extended to all white registrants prior to December 1, 1908. Since all North Carolina whites would be so eligible, they would be nominally exempted from the literacy test, which thereby could, its advocates claimed, be applied exclusively to nearly all black voters (there were a handful of black voters still alive who had voted before 1835). In actual fact, the grandfather clause was only rarely invoked, and the literacy test had a devastating effect on both white and black voters. The net result, as historian John Spencer Bassett wrote in February 1899, was "an enameled lie" that educated "our people that it is right to lie, to steal, and to defy all honesty in order to keep a certain party in power."[13]

The North Carolina disfranchisement amendment was submitted to the voters in August 1900. The Democrats' White Supremacy campaign continued, as the statewide press urged white voters to rid the political system of African American males for good. Once again, as they had two years earlier, Red Shirts appeared in majority African American counties in order to intimidate potential opposition. Meanwhile, Democratic reformer Charles Brantley Aycock, campaigning as a progressive reformer but also a white supremacist, was swept into office, as Republicans lost control of the governor's office. Republicans and blacks appealed for federal intervention. In the end, with a substantially suppressed electorate, the disfranchisement amendment passed overwhelmingly, by a margin of 59 to 41 percent.

The advent of disfranchisement marked a turning point in North Carolina's political history. After 1900, Republicans were relegated to a semipermanent minority status. Without their African American constituency, the party could no longer effectively run statewide campaigns, and the Democratic Party became the only avenue for political success from 1900 until the 1970s. At the same time, in the white primary, Democrats excluded blacks from party nominations. The solidification of one-party rule paved the way for another dimension of white supremacy, the institution of racial segregation in public spaces, accommodations, and institutions. In 1899, the legislature enacted its first so-called "Jim Crow" law, requiring segregation on the railcars and steamboats traversing the state. Although the law included a few exceptions—black servants, for one—it required "separate but equal" facilities for white and black passengers. Meanwhile, the legislature considered but ultimately refused to approve legislation that would have criminalized cohabitation by male and female members of different races.

* * *

In January 1901, after North Carolina's suffrage restriction had been passed, George H. White, an African American congressman from the Second Congressional District, rose to speak. Realizing that his term of office would soon expire, White offered a final plea for justice for black people. White North Carolinians, he said, should "measure the standard of the race by its best material, cease to mold prejudicial and unjust public sentiment" against them. He hoped for a future of racial harmony which would "obliterate race hatred, party prejudice, and help us to achieve nobler ends, greater results, and become more satisfactory citizens to our brother in white." Although this was "perhaps the negroes' temporary farewell to the American Congress," White predicted that "Phoenix-like he will rise up some day and come again." These were "parting words" on "behalf of an outraged, heart-broken, bruised, and bleeding, but God-fearing people, faithful, industrious, loyal people—rising people, full of potential force."[14]

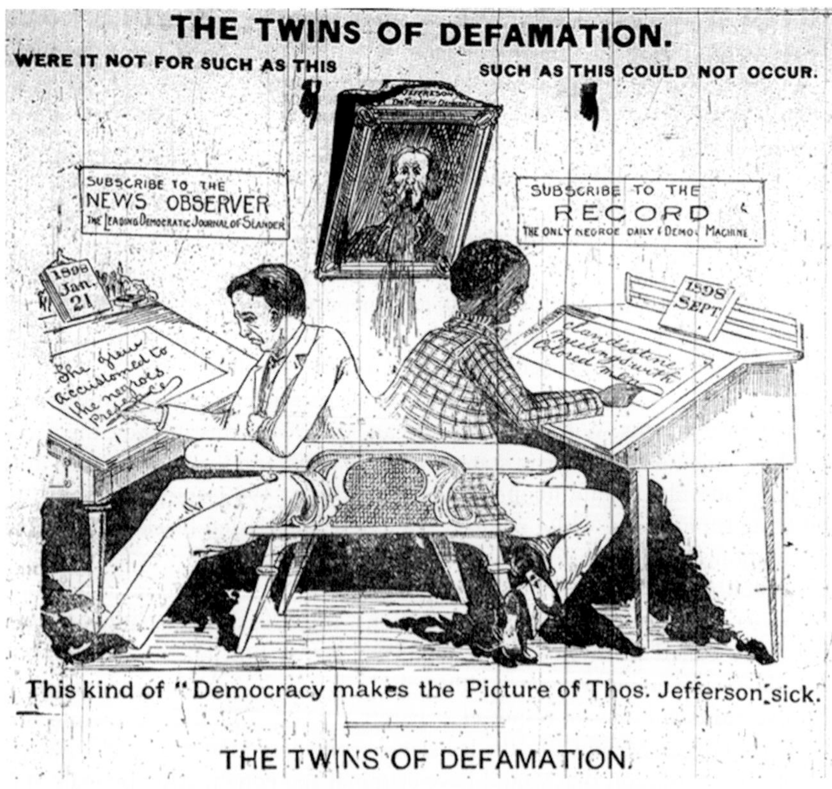

Figure 12.7 Cartoon appearing in the *Progressive Farmer*, October 25, 1898. *Source: North Carolina Collection, University of North Carolina Library at Chapel Hill.*

Disfranchisement and the advent of Jim Crow were landmark occurrences in North Carolina history. Black males were now effectively excluded from voting—and political power—and their political rights would not be fully restored until the civil-rights revolution of the 1950s and 1960s. Because the majority of Republicans were black, that party was rendered noncompetitive in statewide elections. Although pockets of white Republicanism persisted in North Carolina, between 1900 and 1972, no Republican would win a statewide election. Like most of the rest of the South, North Carolina became a one-party political state.

Notes

1 Quoted in Paul D. Escott, *Many Excellent People: Power and Privilege in North Carolina, 1850–1900* (Chapel Hill: University of North Carolina Press, 1985), p. 242.
2 Kent Redding, *Making Race, Making Power: North Carolina's Road to Disfranchisement* (Urbana: University of Illinois Press, 2003), p. 61.
3 Stuart Noblin, *Leonidas LaFayette Polk: Agrarian Crusader* (Chapel Hill: University of North Carolina Press, 1949), p. 99.
4 Escott, *Many Excellent People*, p. 244.
5 Quoted in Helen G. Edmonds, *The Negro and Fusion Politics in North Carolina, 1894–1901* (Chapel Hill: University of North Carolina Press, 1951), p. 61.
6 Quoted in Dwight B. Billings, Jr., *Planters and the Making of a "New South": Class, Politics, and Development in North Carolina, 1865–1900* (Chapel Hill: University of North Carolina Press, 1979), p. 177.
7 Quoted in Edmonds, *The Negro and Fusion Politics*, p. 138.
8 Quoted in Redding, *Making Race, Making Power*, p. 128.
9 Quoted in Glenda Elizabeth Gilmore, *Gender and Jim Crow: Women and the Politics of White Supremacy in North Carolina, 1896–1920* (Chapel Hill: University of North Carolina Press, 1996), p. 106.
10 Quoted in ibid., p. 107.
11 Quoted in Edmonds, *The Negro and Fusion Politics*, p. 165.
12 J. Allen Kirk, *A Statement of Facts Concerning the Bloody Riot in Wilmington, N.C. of Interest to Every Citizen of the United States* (Wilmington: n.p., 1898), p. 16. For a full account of the events at Wilmington, see the report of the 1898 Wilmington Race Riot Commission, which the North Carolina legislature established in 2000, at http://www.ah.dcr.state.nc.us/1898-wrrc/.
13 Quoted in Edmonds, *The Negro and Fusion Politics*, p. 183.
14 George H. White, *Defense of the Negro Race—Charges Answered. Speech of Hon. George H. White, of North Carolina, in the House of Representatives, January 29, 1901* (Washington, DC: Government Printing Office, 1901).

Suggested Readings, Part 4

Chapter 10

Roberta Sue Alexander, *North Carolina Faces the Freedmen: Race Relations during Presidential Reconstruction, 1865–67* (Durham, NC: Duke University Press, 1985).
Eric Anderson, *Race and Politics in North Carolina, 1872–1901: The Black Second* (Baton Rouge: Louisiana State University Press, 1981).
David Cecelski, *The Fire of Freedom: Abraham Galloway and the Slaves' Civil War* (Chapel Hill: University of North Carolina Press, 2015).
Gregory Downs, *Declarations of Dependence: The Long Reconstruction of Popular Politics in the South, 1861–1908* (Chapel Hill: University of North Carolina Press, 2011).
Laura F. Edwards, *Gendered Strife & Confusion: The Political Culture of Reconstruction* (Urbana: University of Illinois Press, 1997).
W. McKee Evans, *Ballots and Fence Rails: Reconstruction on the Lower Cape Fear* (New York: Norton, 1967).
J. G. de Roulhac Hamilton, *Reconstruction in North Carolina* (New York: Columbia University Press, 1914).
William C. Harris, *William Woods Holden: Firebrand of North Carolina Politics* (Baton Rouge: Louisiana State University Press, 1987).
Joe A. Mobley, *James City: A Black Community in North Carolina, 1863–1900* (Raleigh, NC: Division of Archives and History, 1981).
Steven E. Nash, *Reconstruction's Ragged Edge: The Politics of Postwar Life in the Southern Mountains* (Chapel Hill: University of North Carolina Press, 2016).
Scott Reynolds Nelson, *Iron Confederacies: Southern Railways, Klan Violence, and Reconstruction* (Chapel Hill: University of North Carolina Press, 1999).
Otto H. Olsen, *Carpetbagger's Crusade: The Life of Albion Winegar Tourgée* (Baltimore, MD: Johns Hopkins Press, 1965).
Horace W. Raper, *William W. Holden, North Carolina's Political Enigma* (Chapel Hill: University of North Carolina Press, 1985).

Allen W. Trelease, *White Terror: The Ku Klux Klan Conspiracy and Southern Reconstruction* (Baton Rouge: Louisiana State University Press, 1971).
Richard L. Zuber, *Jonathan Worth: A Biography of a Southern Unionist* (Chapel Hill: University of North Carolina Press, 1965).
Richard L. Zuber, *North Carolina during Reconstruction* (Raleigh, NC: Division of Archives and History, 1969).

Chapter 11

Dwight B. Billings, Jr., *Planters and the Making of a "New South": Class, Politics, and Development in North Carolina, 1865–1900* (Chapel Hill: University of North Carolina Press, 1979).
William K. Boyd, *The Story of Durham: City of the New South* (Durham, NC: Duke University Press, 1927).
Ron D. Eller, *Miners, Millhands, and Mountaineers: Industrialization of the Appalachian South, 1880–1930* (Knoxville: University of Tennessee Press, 1982).
Jacquelyn Dowd Hall et al., *Like a Family: The Making of a Southern Cotton Mill World* (New York: W. W. Norton & Co., 1987).
Dolores E. Janiewski, *Sisterhood Denied: Race, Gender, and Class in a New South Community* (Philadelphia, PA: Temple University Press, 1985).
Kent Redding, *Making Race, Making Power: North Carolina's Road to Disfranchisement* (Urbana: University of Illinois Press, 2003).
John F. Stover, *Railroads of the South, 1865–1900* (Chapel Hill: University of North Carolina Press, 1955).
Anthony Tang, *Economic Developments in the Southern Piedmont, 1860–1950* (Chapel Hill: University of North Carolina Press, 1958).
Phillip J. Wood, *Southern Capitalism: The Political Economy of North Carolina, 1880– 1980* (Durham, NC: Duke University Press, 1986).

Chapter 12

Deborah Beckel, *Radical Reform: Interracial Politics in Post-Emancipation North Carolina* (Charlottesville: University Press of Virginia, 2011).
Frederick A. Bode, *Protestantism and the New South: North Carolina Baptists and Methodists in Political Crisis, 1894–1903* (Charlottesville: University Press of Virginia, 1975).
David S. Cecelski and Timothy B. Tyson, eds., *Democracy Betrayed: The Wilmington Race Riot of 1898 and Its Legacy* (Chapel Hill: University of North Carolina Press, 1998).

Jeffrey J. Crow and Robert F. Durden, *Maverick Republican in the Old North State: A Political Biography of Daniel L. Russell* (Baton Rouge: Louisiana State University Press, 1977).

Helen G. Edmonds, *The Negro and Fusion Politics in North Carolina, 1894–1901* (New York: Russell & Russell, 1951).

Glenda Elizabeth Gilmore, *Gender and Jim Crow: Women and the Politics of White Supremacy in North Carolina, 1896–1920* (Chapel Hill: University of North Carolina Press, 1996).

James L. Hunt, *Marion Butler and American Populism* (Chapel Hill: University of North Carolina Press, 2003).

Robert C. McMath, Jr., *Populist Vanguard: A History of the Southern Farmers' Alliance* (Chapel Hill: University of North Carolina Press, 1975).

Stuart Noblin, *Leonidas LaFayette Polk: Agrarian Crusader* (Chapel Hill: University of North Carolina Press, 1949).

Adrienne Petty, *Standing Their Ground: Small Farmers in North Carolina since the Civil War* (New York: Oxford University Press, 2012).

H. Leon Prather, *We Have Taken a City: Wilmington Racial Massacre and Coup of 1898* (Wilmington, NC: NU World Enterprises, 1984).

Document Section, Part 4
The Klan

During the late 1860s and early 1870s, vigilante violence became epidemic in Piedmont North Carolina. The appearance of the Ku Klux Klan in North Carolina after about 1869 had a decisive political impact. Working closely with anti-Reconstruction political leadership, the Klan was dedicated to restoring a racial regime based on white supremacy. Existing on the scene until about 1872, when determined federal intervention prosecuted scores of perpetrators, the Klan could boast of major accomplishments—instigating violent reprisals against African Americans and their white Republican allies that provoked a clumsy attempt by Republican governor William W. Holden—known as the Kirk-Holden War—to reestablish order in Orange, Alamance, and Caswell Counties in central North Carolina during the summer of 1870.

The Klan's effort to reestablish white supremacy went far beyond purely political intentions, as the following documents illustrate. White fears about emancipation were linked to fears about the position of black men and women. How much power would freed black people possess? To what extent did freedom have sexual implications? White men possessed free sexual access to black women under slavery. What, white men wondered, would the freedom of black men mean? Many of the tensions after slavery connected to fears of black manhood—and their exaggerated sexual prowess—and feared threats to white womanhood. It was also connected to black womanhood and attempts to reestablish white control.

The documents in this section can be found in the volumes of testimony given to the Joint Committee of Congress investigating Klan violence in 1871–72, which was part of a general crackdown on the Klan. The testimony fills seventeen volumes, with the entire volume dedicated to North Carolina.

A Defense of the KKK's Motives, June 5, 1871[1]

Much of the Klan's strength rested on prevalent fears among whites about what emancipation really meant. In the years after the Civil War, uncertainty and anxiety prevailed about a new assertiveness among black people.

CHAIRMAN: What avowal of purpose was made to you by any one connected with the organization [the Klan]?

DR. PRIDE JONES: The purport of it was this: That barns were being burned, women were afraid to go about the country for fear of being ravished by negroes, and the law would not punish them; there was inefficiency somewhere; they could not get protection, and they got up this organization to protect themselves by punishing a few who were obviously guilty, and thereby preventing others from committing that sort of offenses. ...

CHAIRMAN: In judging whether it was a political organization or not, were you governed by the fact that most of the persons who were victims of these wrongs were of one political party; or how did you account for that?

DR. PRIDE JONES: I judged in this way; there were papers generally attached to the persons of those who were hung. In one case it would be, "You are hung for barn-burning;" in another case it would be, "You are hung for threatening to ravish" some one; or something to that effect. Those cards were attached to the bodies of the persons who were executed – or rather hung, not executed ....

MR. BLAIR: What did the threat of ravishment consist in; did he attempt to ravish her?

DR. PRIDE JONES: He met a girl in the road; she was living with her mother, a widow woman; they were the only persons in the family. This negro met the girl in the road and made propositions to her to have intercourse with her. She promptly declined, and tried to get rid of him as soon as possible. Finally he said, "I intend to have it, if not by fair means by foul. I expect to leave here" – at such a time – "and before that time I intend to have this thing."

CHAIRMAN: Was the rape committed?

---

1 From *The Condition of Affairs in the Late Insurrectionary States. North Carolina* (Washington, DC: Government Printing Office, 1872), pp. 3–11, http://books.google.com/books?id=PnEUAAAAYAAJ&printsec=frontcover&dq=Joint+Select+Committee+to+Inquire+into+the+Condition+of+Affairs+in+the+Late+Insurrectionary+States,+volume+2&hl=en&sa=X&ei=CIGQU4L1Co7msATqnIDADA&ved=0CCcQ6AEwAA#v=onepage&q&f=false

DR. PRIDE JONES: The rape was not committed.
MR. BLAIR: And the girl gave information of this?
DR. PRIDE JONES: Yes, sir.
MR. BLAIR: And the man was hung?
DR. PRIDE JONES: Yes, sir; and I presume hung by the Ku-Klux. I do not know whether they hung him, or some of her friends hung him.
MR. BLAIR: Was there great apprehension felt throughout that section of the State by the white women of the country?
DR. PRIDE JONES: There was.
MR. BLAIR: Apprehension of the commission of this crime?
DR. PRIDE JONES: Yes, sir . . . .
MR. BLAIR: There was very general apprehension felt?
DR. PRIDE JONES: Yes, sir; the poorer classes in the community, women who carry blackberries, cherries, eggs, butter, and things of that sort to town to sell, were afraid to go to town by themselves; they would only go when they could form large companies for mutual protection. Formerly, and even now, they could go singly just when they were ready. But just about that time they were afraid to go to town alone for fear of being insulted or ravished by negroes.
MR. VAN TRUMP: Was the conduct of the negroes of your county bold and aggressive in manner?
DR. PRIDE JONES: Yes, sir; it was.
MR. BLAIR: This very general apprehension irritated the people of the country, did it not?
DR. PRIDE JONES: Yes, sir, it had that effect . . . .
MR. BLAIR: Was the existence of this apprehension and of these crimes the cause, in your opinion, of the origin of those Ku-Klux societies, for the purpose of suppressing that kind of crime?
DR. PRIDE JONES: That is my opinion.

A White Republican Official's Perspective on the KKK, June 15, 1871[2]

Klan violence spread to much of central North Carolina, as this document indicates. The testimony here, of a white local official, Republican Webster Shaffer, indicates the extent of violence.

---

2 *Condition of Affairs in the Late Insurrectionary States. North Carolina*, pp. 31-49, http://books.google.com/books?id=PnEUAAAAYAAJ&printsec=frontcover&dq=Joint+Select+Committee+to+Inquire+into+the+Condition+of+Affairs+in+the+Late+Insurrectionary+States,+volume+2&hl=en&sa=X&ei=CIGQU4L1Co7msATqnIDADA&ved=0CCcQ6AEwAA#v=onepage&q&f=false.

CHAIRMAN: State, as briefly as you can, the facts that have come under your observation, and the condition of things as affected by those acts of violence, down to the present time.

A. WEBSTER SHAFFER: The warrants issued from my office have run into Johnson, Chatham, Harnett, and Moore Counties, chiefly against persons who had, during the night-time, disguised, assaulted the persons and houses of chiefly colored people, whipping, shooting, and otherwise mutilating them, in crowds from eight to twenty and twenty-five – sometimes thirty. I should think the number of cases was about twenty-five ....

CHAIRMAN: So far as you recollect individual cases that have been before you, proceed in order and give them.

A. WEBSTER SHAFFER: .... One is the case of Frances Gillmore, a colored woman from Chatham, in the vicinity of Locksville.

CHAIRMAN: When?

A. WEBSTER SHAFFER: About two months ago.

CHAIRMAN: What was her statement?

A. WEBSTER SHAFFER: She came to my office and complained that she had been whipped; that disguised persons had visited her house in the night-time, taken her out, and whipped her; laid her on the floor, taken her clothes off, and whipped her with a board; turned her over and whipped her again; then with matches burned the hair from her private parts, and cut her with a knife; and that she had been lying there about three weeks, unable to get to me before. I asked if she could identify any of the parties. She said she could not. I asked if there was anybody there who could do so. She said nobody was there who knew any of them except by suspicion. It is so very difficult to prove anything where they do identify them, that it is very discouraging to undertake to arrest persons purely on suspicion for such an offense as that. I desire to say that she was a colored woman, because I wish to make this case distinct; there were two cases very similar. Right after that there was another case in which another Frances Gillmore was interested.

MR. POOL: Was she a white woman?

A. WEBSTER SHAFFER: Yes, sir.

MR. POOL: From what county?

A. WEBSTER SHAFFER: Chatham County. In this last case the white woman belonged to a party of contractors on the Chatham Railroad. The principal contractor with the road was a man named Howle, from Richmond. These women were about the road; I do not know what they were doing. The Ku-Klux came there in the night-time – some forty or fifty of them, as the testimony showed – and entered the camp of these persons, firing right and left, and hooting and hallooing. The contractors, I think, got away. They did not catch them. ... They went to the house of this Mrs. Frances Gillmore and found two negroes there sleeping on a pallet.

Mr. Van Trump: Men or women?

A. Webster Shaffer: Men. They found one white man, named Gilmore, and four women.

Chairman: Did the testimony develop whether these were women of good or bad character?

A. Webster Shaffer: They were of rather bad character – rather worse than the generality of the country people, whose character is not always very good. They entered the house and took one negro out and whipped him. They shot him. That man was not able to travel when the parties were arrested and brought before me. He is still there, but recovering, I think. The testimony showed that one colored man was very severely whipped, and the women were whipped; also a girl, the only girl there was in the whole crowd; I should judge she was about sixteen to eighteen years of age; they took her clothes off, whipped her very severely, and then lit a match and burned her hair off, and made her cut off herself the part that they did not burn off with a match.

Mr. Pool: Was she a white girl?

A. Webster Shaffer: Yes, sir, a white girl . . . .

Mr. Pool: State how the victims of these outrages who were brought before you were injured.

A. Webster Shaffer: Those whom I personally examined were injured generally by whipping, as though they had been struck either with heavy knots, or ropes with knots in them, or with clubs with knots in them. They were mutilated in the back and arms. One or two had an arm broken, and one a finger broken, and they were otherwise cut.: . . . . The most outrageous cutting that I saw was the cutting of a woman, who was cut in her private parts. I did not see the marks, but, according to her statement and the statement of other witnesses, they first cut the hair off her head; then, when she would not furnish a pair of scissors for the purpose, they made her take a pocket-knife and mangle the hair off her private parts, and then they cut her with a knife.

A Northern White, June 26, 1871[3]

Northern whites sometimes became targets of Klan violence, especially if they employed blacks or if they were involved in the Republican Party. The

3 *Condition of Affairs in the Late Insurrectionary States. North Carolina*, pp. 51–55, http://books.google.com/books?id=PnEUAAAAYAAJ&printsec=frontcover&dq=Joint+Select+Committee+to+Inquire+into+the+Condition+of+Affairs+in+the+Late+Insurrectionary+States,+volume+2&hl=en&sa=X&ei=CIGQU4L1Co7msATqnIDADA&ved=0CCcQ6AEwAA#v=onepage&q&f=false

much-despised "carpetbaggers" symbolized northern insistence on freedpeople's rights; very often, as well, northern whites were involved in Republican politics and organizing. Not surprisingly, the Klan attempted to intimidate them into submission. In this case, a northern white railroad contractor, who employed black workers, became suspicious in the Klan's eyes because of a close congressional election.

CHAIRMAN: Have you lived in the State of North Carolina within the last year?
WILLIAM R. HOWLE: Yes, sir.
CHAIRMAN: In what business were you engaged?
WILLIAM R. HOWLE: In railroad contracting.
CHAIRMAN: In what part?
WILLIAM R. HOWLE: In Chatham County.
CHAIRMAN: How long were you occupied there?
WILLIAM R. HOWLE: About nine months; I arrived there the 22d of last September.
CHAIRMAN: State whether, during that time, you were visited by armed men in disguise; and if so, what they did and said.
WILLIAM R. HOWLE: In November, just after the election for member of Congress between Manning and young Holden, I was threatened by the Ku-Klux organization several times; told that I had better leave the State and not interfere with North Carolina politics. I paid no attention to it; thought it was only gotten up for show or brag. In fact I had a good force of hands there, and was not afraid of molestation, knowing that I was in the right.
CHAIRMAN: In what manner were the threats made?
WILLIAM R. HOWLE: To my men, not to me; they told them that if I interfered with North Carolina politics they would Ku-Klux me.
CHAIRMAN: To whom did they tell this?
WILLIAM R. HOWLE: I do not know, but principally negroes notified me that I would be Ku-Kluxed .... They said they would not be surprised if I was driven off the work for being suspected in my political principles .... When I got back I found my hands very much disturbed and alarmed; I could not get them to work. I had had twenty-five or thirty at work, but the number was reduced at last to six or seven. I told them not to be alarmed, that I was back with them. I supposed it was mere fright. On the night of the 29th of April, about 3 o'clock in the morning, I was aroused by heavy firing about a quarter or half a mile from the shanty where I was sleeping. I had been sleeping in the woods previously, in consequence of these apprehensions. Mr. Kelley had been sent for by my foreman to assist him in keeping off the Ku-Klux. He told me it would be unsafe for me to sleep in the house. So from that time till the 29th I slept out; but on the 29th

I ventured to sleep in the shanty. When I heard the firing I remarked to my foreman, who slept with me, that the Ku-Klux must have come. We got up, went across the railroad, and found our hands scattered about in the woods, lying in the underbrush that had been cleared from the track. There was a deep cut just there, and we got around on the side nearest to where the firing was. We heard the tramping of horses, and went off among the bushes and lay down, not wishing to be seen by the Ku-Klux. They came on hurrahing and yelling, forty or fifty of them, in disguise. They said they had just cleaned out one house; that this was a Ku-Klux country, and they would be damned if the Ku-Klux would not control it; all they wanted now was to drive the damned Yankee contractors off their work, and then they would have possession; that if they caught them they would hang them to the nearest tree they could find; and their stock should be killed. From their yelling and carrying on in that way I thought they must have been intoxicated .... After they struck the railroad cut they turned down the track and took a road that ran off into the woods. I saw no more of them that night. The next morning I went over to where the firing was heard. There I found that two negroes had been whipped, one white man, and three women, and that a negro had been shot. They told me it was done by this party of Ku-Klux that I saw coming away. There seemed to be three divisions of them; one party went toward Jonesboro, one toward Egypt, and the other toward my shanties, in the direction of Harnett County ....

CHAIRMAN: Did you know any of the persons that were there that night?

WILLIAM R. HOWLE: Yes, sir; we arrested some of them. After I returned on Sunday I sent my mules off in the country to a neighbor's to keep them from being shot. I also sent my child, fearing that they would burn my shanty during my absence during the night. I then proceeded to Raleigh with one of the party that was whipped, and carried him before United States Commissioner Shafer, when he swore out a warrant against some ten or fifteen of the party. I was appointed special deputy marshal by Shafer, went back to Chatham County, and arrested three of the men; the others ran and got into the woods, and I could not catch them. I caught two of the three men in the woods – Caberniss and Clark. I found that I could not complete my railroad contract, so I went to the company and asked them to settle with me, holding back 20 per cent. This they refused to do, and my contract remains unfinished ....

CHAIRMAN: What is the effect produced in that neighborhood, so far as you have observed, by the fact of these men riding armed and in disguise at night?

WILLIAM R. HOWLE: I think the whole of it is done for the purpose of keeping the negroes and white republicans from voting ....

CHAIRMAN: What is the effect of these outrages upon the sense of security enjoyed by the people?

WILLIAM R. HOWLE: The republicans feel particularly unsafe; they are afraid to talk politics at all; you can seldom get a white republican to express his opinions. I only know two in the whole neighborhood I was in, in parts of the two or three counties; they said they were republicans, but were afraid to have it known . . . .

MR. COBURN: Will you state what was the beginning of your trouble, what was the cause of it?

WILLIAM R. HOWLE: In the first place, there was a gentleman from Richmond got ahead of me a week or two at work on his contract on the road, and he reported all through the country that I was an irresponsible party and that I had been forced to leave Richmond on account of my political principles. He poisoned the minds of his men against me, and I found when I got there that my contract had been let to another party, I having been detained about ten days.

MR. COBURN: Had you made any political speeches then?

WILLIAM R. HOWLE: I did do so.

MR. COBURN: State about that.

WILLIAM R. HOWLE: To do so I must state that the negroes found out that I was a Republican from this man's reporting it; so, some ten days before the election in November, they came out and serenaded me, and I made a speech. I advised them on the day of the election to go to the polls and support the Republican nominee, and if they had any sick or disabled men I would send my carts and haul them to the polls to vote. After that I was threatened by the Ku-Klux.

Two Accounts of the Assault on Essie Harris, January 1871[4]

The Klan's assault on Essie Harris in January 1871 was typical of vigilante violence. Harris, a black tenant in Chatham County, was a Republican voter though not, by his account, an activist. More than likely his main offense was what whites often called "uppityness"—the tendency to aspire too much. Most likely the Klan wanted to teach him a lesson, and, failing that, to send a message to the black community about assertive black people. The accounts below come from

4 *Condition of Affairs in the Late Insurrectionary States. North Carolina*, pp. 31–49, 86–95; http://books.google.com/books?id=PnEUAAAAYAAJ&printsec=frontcover&dq=Joint+Select+Committee+to+Inquire+into+the+Condition+of+Affairs+in+the+Late+Insurrectionary+States,+volume+2&hl=en&sa=X&ei=CIGQU4L1Co7msATqnIDADA&ved=0CCcQ6AEwAA#v=onepage&q&f=false

testimony from white Republican Webster Shaffer, delivered on June 15, 1871, and by Harris himself, delivered about two weeks later.

Webster Shaffer, June 15, 1871

CHAIRMAN: Give us the general aspect of the cases, and then, if you can, the names of the parties.

SHAFFER: The case of Essie Harris, a colored man of Chatham County, is a peculiar one. The affair occurred some time in January last. A crowd from twelve to twenty approached the house and undertook to beat down the door. Harris had some corn in the house that he had put against the door. After one man had beaten the door, and broken in down, it went against the corn, and did not fall. Harris had a gun with him, and he shot the man through the door. The man fell. Some of the party gave the alarm that one of them was shot. They picked him up, put him on a horse, and rode away with him. When that case was brought before me, there were about eight or ten parties arrested. They all proved an *alibi*, as usual; and among them was this man Clark, who was shot .... This Clark was found; and from the fact of his being wounded, and the knowledge that Harris had shot some one, I thought it sufficient to arrest him. Harris did not know him .... He could not identity him. He saw some of them through a window whom he did identify, but he did not identify the man at the door, because he was disguised. He wore a false-face with horns on it, as Harris described it, so that he could not see his face.

Essie Harris, July 1, 1871

CHAIRMAN: Where do you live?

HARRIS: In Chatham County, North Carolina.

CHAIRMAN: Do you live in a town or out of town?

HARRIS: Out of town, about seven miles.

CHAIRMAN: What is your business when at home?

HARRIS: Farming ....

CHAIRMAN: State to the committee whether some men called upon you in disguise; tell the whole story about that.

HARRIS: Well, sir, they came the first time about last Christmas – the Wednesday night before Christmas—to take my gun .... They came to the door and knocked. I was asleep when they came .... Some said they reckoned there were about fifteen of them. They sort of scared me at first. Some of them had on some women's clothes. I was just awake, and they came right in and went right out.

CHAIRMAN: Did they wear disguises; had they something over their faces? ....

HARRIS: It looked like a sort of paper or sheep-skin; it was a sort of black thing; some had one thing and some another; it was not all of one sort .... They came back again. My wife said that they were going to fetch the gun back; but I did not understand them to say that. They went to another place about a quarter of a mile off, and took another fellow's gun; he lived on the same land; and this was on that same night .... They took his gun and ate something there. Some of them played a fiddle and danced awhile. They took another man's gun after that. They took about four guns from that settlement that night .... They went over to another hill. Some of the girls said they ravished them ....

CHAIRMAN: Did these men come to see you again? ....

HARRIS: They came after Christmas..... My wife woke me, and said, "Essic, you had better go to bed instead of sitting here by the fire in the way." .... She said, "Essic, the Ku-Klux is coming." I never said anything, but bounced out of my bed, and went to the door. I took my bar down and looked to see what was the matter. They cried, "Hello!" I peeped out and saw that my yard was full of men. I jumped against my door and fastened it .... My gun was at the head of my bed. As soon as I put my fire out I went back to the head of the bed and got my gun. By the time I had got my gun, they had knocked my window open .... I was then shot almost to pieces. My wife has got six children. Two of them were gone to school. I only had four children in there of my own; two of them were away at school. I had there with me a little boy, twelve or thirteen years old, my sister's son. I had him there to help me work. There were five children in the house. I never had time to see what they were all doing; but they all got out of the way. I thought they were all dead. My wife had got between the bed-ticking and the mat; my little children were in another bed; they had got in a pile, right on top of one another, like a parcel of pigs. ... The shots were flying all over where they were. The men poked their guns so as to make the range of the balls as nigh all over the house as they could. One thing that prevented them from killing my wife and children was, I reckon, this: I had four bushels of corn in my house, and I put them against the door, and also a little meal in a bag. When the door fell, it did not fall down. ... They shot the top of the door all to pieces. There are holes in my door that you can poke your finger in. ... They kept shooting and saying, "We have killed the old man, boys; let us go in and fetch them out." One would say to another, "Well, you go in." One would come around and say, "Yonder he is; I see him;" and then he would shoot. Another would say, "Boys, let us go in; I have killed him; I saw him fall; he is dead." But they didn't any of them come into my house. ... They said they had killed me. I felt it to be life and death anyhow. I thought my wife and children were all dead; I did not expect anything else. The shot just rained like rain. I raised my gun once to shoot; when I raised it I saw Miss Sally, Mr. Finch's sister, come along; and I laid my gun right down. I had my ax; it was lying on my right hand; my arm was shot so I could hardly use it; I drew it to me; and when Miss Sally passed I got my ax to me after a while. It was mighty heavy and my arm was sore so that I could hardly use it. I took aim at Clark's head.... Clark was cutting at the door, and I raised my gun to shoot his head. They always say in my country that a man could not kill a Ku-Klux; they said that they could not be hit; they if they were, the ball would bounce back and kill you. I thought though that I would try it, and see if my gun would hit one. It had no load in it to kill a man. I never loaded it to kill anything except squirrels, &c.... If I had put in a load to kill a man I could have killed him because I was very close to him. I shot this man, Joe Clark, and Mr. Burgess.... They said they were going to set my house on fire; that they did not intend to leave there till they had done it. I thought they were going to do it.... I had some shot. I have often heard people talk about a man being so scared that he could not shoot people; but they had been there so long my fear was over; I had no fear at all by that time – not a bit.... While I was loading they could hear me cramming the wadding down. After I had got it almost loaded I said, "Give me hold of my five-shooter." They said, "Boys, the old man is calling for his five-shooter, and loading his gun; let us leave." Upon that they went off....

CHAIRMAN: Have you had much to do with politics?

HARRIS: No, sir; I am no man for politics.

CHAIRMAN: You vote?

HARRIS: O, yes, sir; I always try to vote.

CHAIRMAN: Which party do you vote with?

HARRIS: The republican. That is the way I have always been voting....

CHAIRMAN: Have you anything to do with politics except going to vote?

HARRIS: No, sir; I never did. I have said to a good many people since that affair that I do not expect to vote any more.... The way things are we cannot vote. That is just the way it is. It is not worth while for a man to vote and run the risk of his life.

when going along, and [illegible] came right down. I had my axe; it was lying [illegible] hand, my arm was [illegible] I could hardly use it. I threw it [illegible] and when Miss Sally passed [illegible] my arm after a while. It was mighty heavy and my arm was so swelled that I could hardly use it. I took [illegible] Clarke's [illegible] Mr. Clarke [illegible] about my head. I had always [illegible] heard that [illegible] could not kill a [illegible]; they said that they could not be hit; they [illegible] would bounce back and kill you. [illegible] in the night [illegible] to try it, and see if my gun would hit them. When I find [illegible] to kill a man I never [illegible] [illegible] anything except squirrels, etc. [illegible] that gun and loaded it to kill a man I would have loaded him, because I was very close to him. I shot that man, Mr. Clarke, and Mr. Babcock. [illegible] They said they were going to set my house [illegible] but they did not [illegible] to leave there till they had gone [illegible] they were going to [illegible] at the same [illegible] I have often heard people talk about [illegible] being [illegible] that he would [illegible] of people; but they had [illegible] [illegible] and I had no fear of it. [illegible] While I was loading, they could hear me cramming the wadding down. After I had got it almost loaded I said, "Give me half of my five-shooter." They said, "Boys, the old man is calling for his five-shooter, and loading his gun; let us leave." Then that they went off.

CHAIRMAN: Have you had much to do with politics?

HARRIS: No, sir; I am not much for politics.

CHAIRMAN: You vote?

HARRIS: Yes, sir; I always vote.

CHAIRMAN: Which party do you vote with?

HARRIS: The republican. That is the way I have always been voting.

CHAIRMAN: Have you any thing to do with politics except going to vote?

[illegible]

that after that I do not expect to vote any more. The way things are we cannot vote; that is just the way it is. It is not worth while for a man to vote and run the risk of his life.

Part 5

Modernizing North Carolina

13

Progressive North Carolina

On December 17, 1903, Orville and Wilbur Wright made history in North Carolina. The Wright brothers were Dayton, Ohio, bicycle manufacturers and inventors who had come to Kitty Hawk, in the Outer Banks, to test new flying machines of their design. Beginning in 1900, they set up a tent colony on the North Carolina coast, hoping that the flat beach and consistently strong winds might help them get one of their airplanes aloft. After some success with gliders, the Wrights experimented with a new, machine-powered airplane, which they called the *Flyer*. At 10:00 a.m. on December 17, Orville Wright succeeded in sustaining flight for 12 seconds, in which time he traveled 100 feet. Three other flights followed, the last one by Wilbur Wright in which he covered 852 feet. The Wrights' successful experience in flying was a pivotal achievement, and it marked the arrival of the twentieth century—a new period of change and uncertainty.

The turbulent 1890s, with Fusionism, the White Supremacy campaign, and the overthrow of a legally constituted government in Wilmington in 1898, ended with the decisive victory of the Democrats and the institutionalization of their control after 1900. The advent of disfranchisement altered the political system: a large portion of the electorate, as much as half, was eliminated; a vibrant political party, the Republicans, was decimated; and racism triumphed in politics. In similarly radical fashion, the nature of government in North Carolina also changed after 1900. The triumph of white supremacy made government, both at the state and local levels, an active partner in the institutionalization of racism: government now *required* the segregation of public spaces, accommodations, and facilities across the state. This *de jure* (by law) segregation became a lasting legacy of North Carolina's turn-of-the-century social and political crisis.

Paradoxically, North Carolina's political leadership began during the next generation to embrace a model of change and progress. Its leaders, though white supremacists dedicated to the permanence of segregation, also became fervent advocates of modernization. Progressive-Era leaders realized that

North Carolina: Change and Tradition in a Southern State, Second Edition. William A. Link.

Figure 13.1 First flight, 120 feet in 12 seconds, 10:35 a.m., Kitty Hawk, North Carolina. This photograph shows Orville Wright at the controls of the machine, lying prone on the lower wing. Wilbur Wright, running along the machine to balance it, has just released his hold on the right wing. *Source: Library of Congress, LC-DIG-ppprs-00626.*

North Carolina, like the rest of the South, had fallen far behind the rest of the nation, and they promoted social, economic, and political modernization as their mantra of change. This generation, by the onset of World War I, successfully created a reputation—even a mythic status—that North Carolina sustained for many years afterward: that the state was more progressive, forward-looking, and open to change than anywhere else in the South.

The Advent of Progressivism

When Charles Brantley Aycock was inaugurated as North Carolina's first governor of the twentieth century, residents of the state generally felt that one era had passed and another had arrived. His inaugural speech, directed primarily to his white supporters, offered little hope of progress for black North Carolinians. In fact, Aycock blamed the social and political turmoil of the previous thirty years on the emancipation of thousands of blacks and their blind allegiance to the Republican Party. Like many of his contemporaries, Aycock was a white supremacist. During the 1890s, he claimed, the Fusionist alliance between

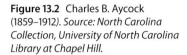

Figure 13.2 Charles B. Aycock (1859–1912). *Source: North Carolina Collection, University of North Carolina Library at Chapel Hill.*

Republicans and Populists had led to "lawlessness" that "stalked the State like a pestilence." The core of the problem, Aycock asserted, had been the political participation of blacks. "Death stalked abroad at noonday," he maintained, and the "sound of the pistol was more frequent than the song of the mocking-bird," the "screams of women fleeing from pursuing brutes closed the gates of our hearts with a shock."[1] Aycock nonetheless predicted a more hopeful future. The new governor advocated revitalized democracy through an expanded public-education system, but this reformed political system depended on the continued political disempowerment of black people. To Aycock, and many others who would call themselves "progressives," there was no inconsistency between the goals of voter restriction and greater progress for North Carolina.

Aycock's inauguration suggested a different style among the state's white leadership. In a period known nationally as the Progressive Era, that leadership now emphasized growth, development, and purposeful change. Starting during the 1890s and ending sometime before the Great Depression, the Progressive Era—and a phenomenon known as Progressivism—saw sweeping changes. As a movement, Progressivism was incredibly diverse, a diversity that confounds an adequate definition. The early twentieth century cannot be properly understood without comprehending that a new *Zeitgeist* (new spirit of the age) had swept through the United States. That *Zeitgeist* was optimistic, forward-looking, consciously modern, Protestant, and imbued with a certainty of the ability of the American people to shape their own destiny. This progressive spirit manifested itself in many ways, but it arose from the distinctive social and cultural environment created by the revolutions of the last half of the 1800s—the market revolution, the communications revolution, the transportation revolution, and the industrial revolution. Today, living through an information revolution, we should remember that late-nineteenth-century Americans lived through a period of even greater change. Those who lived in the years between the Civil War and World War I witnessed phenomenal changes: the completion of a national transportation and communication network; the extension of a new, integrated market for goods and services; the triumph of commercial agriculture; and the emergence of towns and cities as dominant centers of society. How, many asked, could the American republic function in this new environment? How would the new industrial society maintain the old bonds of community? What were the obligations of citizenship in this new society? And how active a role should government—at the state as well as the federal level—take?

Progressivism came to life in North Carolina as a series of local movements of national proportions. Reformers appeared almost everywhere in the United States at roughly the same time, and they resembled each other in their backgrounds and objectives. Progressivism first emerged as a movement seeking social and political reforms in American cities during the 1890s, as the country experienced a sharp economic depression (the Panic of 1893), widespread unrest, and social turmoil. Although it sounds contradictory, Progressivism was a movement that enjoyed considerable national coordination but whose energy lay at the local and state level. Progressives were aware of what was taking place across the country, to be sure. They were cosmopolitan in their habits: most reformers came from urban areas, were products of the new industrial age, thought and acted globally, and were generally educated and middle class in their orientation. This was not, on the whole, a protest group, but a group seeking to rebuild institutions from within.

The Progressive Era had as important an effect in North Carolina as anywhere in the United States. Known for its poverty, illiteracy, and underdevelopment, North Carolina had long suffered from its adverse geography, its inability to produce wealth, and its rigid political leadership. What makes North Carolina's modern history particularly remarkable is how the state acquired a reputation as the most progressive-leaning state in the South, with a political leadership committed to an agenda of improved education, better public health, and the development of a knowledge base resting on a superior public university system. The legacies of the Progressive Era are profound for North Carolinians.[2] As in the rest of the United States, reformers in North Carolina sought to revamp social and political institutions in response to the new world created by the Industrial Revolution. But while North Carolina reformers may have offered a mirror image of progressives elsewhere, there were distinctive qualities to the Progressive Era in North Carolina and the American South.

Aycock's inauguration marked the ascension of a generation of North Carolinians who were simultaneously white supremacists and reformers. They focused on a host of social problems spawned by the prevalence of rural poverty and its endemic social problems that, to Progressive-Era reformers, had too long dominated North Carolina life. Rural poverty was synonymous with ignorance, poor health, and intolerance—characteristics all incompatible with a "modern" frame of mind. The fact that North Carolina possessed a weak public education system only exaggerated its backwardness, and the high rate of illiteracy in the state was only one such example. Finally, rural poverty and the social and health problems it bred seeped into the new urban areas as poor people left the farm to find work in or near towns. Prior to the Civil War, North Carolina was overwhelmingly rural; unlike even some other southern states, it did not have a single community worthy of the term "city."

The Industrial Revolution saw hundreds of cotton mills spring up across the North Carolina Piedmont, and during the post-Civil War generation the new mills transformed life in the region, bringing new social structures to mill villages along with a highly stratified class system. As mentioned in Chapter 11, the cotton mills hired newly arrived workers as family units, and these people reconstructed their rural culture in the mill villages. But with long hours, unsafe working conditions, and a high incidence of child labor, the existence of mill villages presented Progressive-Era reformers with a list of social ills in need of remedying.

Race and poverty gave particular focus and emphasis to the way in which southern progressives approached reform. There was a strong consensus that, while the rest of the United States raced ahead toward wealth and modernity, citizens of North Carolina and the rest of the South would be content to be left behind to become a sort of third-world nation within a nation. More than any other region of the nation, southerners in general and North Carolinians in particular realized a need to reconstruct their society in order to liberate it from the oppression of the past. In North Carolina, reformers were of at least two generations. First-generation reformers were state patriots, doggedly attached to uplifting North Carolina out of poverty. In contrast, second-generation reformers were implementers—those charged with working through newly invigorated state bureaucracies to effect change at the local level.

Women and Reform

Between the Civil War and the Great Depression, North Carolina women greatly increased their roles in public life. Like their counterparts in the rest of the United States, North Carolina women became increasingly involved in voluntary organizations. Working within accepted Victorian gender roles, they focused many of their activities on matters related to the home and domesticity: education, temperance, and child welfare. The great majority of these women were middle class, and most of them were inhabitants of the growing urban areas associated with the post-Reconstruction economic transformation. But the new roles women assumed were by no means confined to middle-class whites. Working-class women, many of whom were employed in the textile and tobacco factories of the industrializing Carolinas, also redefined their roles, as did African American women, working- and middle-class alike. The changing role of North Carolina women was closely connected to a wider transformation occurring during the Progressive Era.

After the Civil War, women's activism grew noticeably. Many white women became involved as early as the 1860s in Ladies Memorial Associations dedicated to memorializing the Confederate dead and establishing Confederate Memorial Day as a holiday. Subsequently, during the 1880s and 1890s, white women participated in a statewide Lost Cause movement—a widespread cultural phenomenon exalting the Confederacy—and patriotic organizations such as the United Daughters of the Confederacy (UDC), Daughters of the American Revolution (DAR), and the Colonial Dames. The Lost Cause sought to bolster a demoralized southern (white) manhood by memorializing Confederate sacrifices and celebrating the bravery of white soldiers through commemorations, monuments, and other events in honor of military heroes and battles. Many of the people involved in the Lost Cause were women, many of whom were already involved in the women's club movement. In the late nineteenth century, women's clubs spread to North Carolina, and in May 1902 the leaders of seven white women's clubs organized the North Carolina Federation of Women's Clubs at a meeting held at Salem College, in Winston-Salem. The organization counted 50,000 members statewide by 1924.

African American women also enthusiastically joined in the club movement. In 1896, North Carolina women participated in the organization of the National Federation of Afro-American Women (later the National Association of Colored Women). In 1909, black women such as Charlotte Hawkins Brown, Minnie Pearson, and Julia McCauley Warren organized the North Carolina Federation of Colored Women's Clubs. Black clubwomen typically came from the upper tiers of African American society. Among the most important African American clubwomen in North Carolina was Charlotte Hawkins Brown, who founded the Palmer Memorial Institute (PMI), a private secondary school for male and female African Americans near Greensboro. Emphasizing their moral leadership, black clubwomen portrayed themselves as "earnest, intelligent, progressive colored women"—an attempt to distinguish themselves from white stereotypes about black women. They expressed a language of virtue, morality, and racial progress by middle-class black women. "Among colored women, the club effort," said one clubwoman, was "the effort of the few competent

Figure 13.3 North Carolina Federation of Women's Clubs, on the steps of the Capitol, Raleigh, 1909. *Source: North Carolina Collection, University of North Carolina Library at Chapel Hill.*

on behalf of the many incompetent." Although most were suffragists, black clubwomen advocated that they should serve as examples for racial uplift.[3]

The church became a forum for progressive reform, as well, for both white and black women. Some churchwomen helped to organize foreign mission work: the Methodists created the Women's Foreign Missionary Society in 1878 and the Women's Home Missionary Society in 1886. White Baptists and Episcopalians created similar organizations, as did Presbyterians, and all these groups sponsored the involvement of women as Christian missionaries at home and abroad. African American women also created missionary societies through their churches. The General Conference of the African Methodist Episcopal (AME) church created a Ladies' Home and Foreign Mission Society in 1880, while the state's black Baptists organized a Home Mission Convention four years later. African-American women were exclusively involved in domestic missionary activities, in contrast to their white counterparts. North Carolina white women went to Latin America and Asia, while other women became involved in home mission efforts focusing on education, moral uplift, and social uplift.

Another important arena for female activism during the 1880s and 1890s was temperance. The Women's Christian Temperance Union (WCTU), organized in Ohio in 1873, established itself in North Carolina in 1881 and by 1887 claimed 600 members, mostly in the Piedmont. The WCTU was part of a larger temperance movement that sought to encourage individual abstinence in the use of alcohol, and, by the late nineteenth century, it endorsed the growing movement of the prohibition of saloons. The WCTU was segregated, though African American women organized separate WCTU branches. In 1886, black women from Charlotte and Greensboro attended a statewide WCTU meeting at which Greensboro WCTU leader Florence A. Garrett spoke—the first time in North Carolina history that a black woman had addressed a white audience. By 1888, there were fourteen African American WCTU branches in the state, and in 1890—in large part because they believed that the white women's organization was not according them proper respect—black women organized a separate statewide organization known as "W.C.T.U. Number 2."

The North Carolina chapters of the WCTU were committed to the cause of temperance and, later, of prohibition, but their agenda expanded beyond this to include a range of moral reforms. WCTU leaders pressed for the application of a single standard of sexuality—that is, the belief that men should practice the same standard of morality that they expected from women. African American women called for the same standard, especially in denouncing white males' sexual exploitation of black women and in exploding myths and stereotypes about black sexual promiscuity. Black women actively challenged white supremacy's notions that black males were sexual predators and that black women practiced different standards of sexual morality. Black women should "rise in the pride of their womanhood and vindicate themselves," said black educator Nannie Helen Burroughs in 1904, and they should teach "all men that black womanhood is as sacred as white womanhood."[4]

For the most part, African Americans' efforts to dramatize these contradictions, even to white women, fell on deaf ears: there was little sense of sisterhood, as the color line prevailed over any common sense of gender. White women focused their social purity efforts on reforming the status of prostitutes, on raising the age of consent (the minimum age for girls to have sexual relations), criminalizing statutory rape, and on improving the status of "fallen" women. White women in the WCTU participated in various efforts to create houses for former prostitutes and to expose the problem to the public. The WCTU led the way in legislative campaigns, beginning in the 1890s, to raise the age of consent, which was set at age 10. In 1895, the legislature amended the law and raised the legal age to 14. A subsequent women's crusade brought legislation in 1913 that would raise this to 16, but this was defeated in the legislature. Not until 1923 did the General Assembly modify the law and raise the age of consent to 16.

These various experiences pushed women to the forefront of progressive reform. Involved in the most important reform crusades of this era in education, child welfare, public health, and prohibition, women were in the thick of leadership as well as grass-roots organizing. Many of these reforming women took the logical next step: to start a campaign to seek the vote for women. The suffrage movement exemplified a new sense of empowerment that women in North Carolina and elsewhere sought. Women reformers' efforts led naturally to an attempt to gain political power through the suffrage, as the rich experiences in social-reform crusades exposed mostly middle-class white women to political combat. An organized woman-suffrage movement had been in existence since the 1870s, but suffragists made their first attempt at converting the South after about 1910. They faced stiff resistance there, however, as white southerners feared a host of social changes that might accompany enfranchising women. In 1912, state senator Victor S. Bryant of Durham introduced a bill, which had the enthusiastic support of North Carolina white clubwomen, that would permit women to serve as members of school boards; after a two-month debate, despite determined opposition, in March 1913 the legislature enacted this measure into law.

In the wake of the new School Board Act, an organized suffrage movement emerged in North Carolina. One of its most important male supporters was Walter Clark, chief justice of the state supreme court, who had campaigned unsuccessfully for the Democratic nomination for US senator in 1912. During that campaign, Clark announced his support for woman suffrage. In 1913, a coalition of suffragists, including Clark, organized the Equal Suffrage Association (ESA) of North Carolina, which was associated with the mainstream National American Woman Suffrage Association (NAWSA). By 1914, seventeen chapters of the ESA existed in the state. Rejecting the more confrontational methods of Alice Paul, who split with the NAWSA in 1916 and formed the National Woman's Party—which gained national attention for its picketing, parades, and even hunger strikes, the Congressional Union, the ESA, and NAWSA sought to work through the mainstream political process, at first at the state level by enacting an amendment to the state constitution. In January 1915, supporters introduced the amendment to the legislature with great fanfare and extensive lobbying by suffragists. The legislature should provide political power for the "woman whose man does not protect her," said ESA president Barbara Bynum Henderson of Chapel Hill, and "who had been deprived of the power to protect herself."[5] But the woman suffrage campaign of that year failed, and two years later, in 1917, the legislature rejected a measure that would have permitted voting by women in the state's towns.

Woman suffrage continued to encounter significant opposition in North Carolina and other southern states. Most of the state's male leadership opposed it, but the movement also failed to attract a great many women activists. Many of the "antis"—those opposed to woman suffrage, who emerged as a powerful group in their own right after 1912—came from the same ranks of clubwomen, WCTU organizers, and other reformers. The most influential and largest white women's group, the North Carolina Federation of Women's Clubs, maintained its neutrality on woman suffrage. During World War I, the issue became a national one, as suffragists sought the passage of the Nineteenth Amendment, which would require woman suffrage on the national level. The United States Congress approved the amendment on June 4, 1919, and submitted it to the states; by August 1920, only one additional, thirty-sixth, state was needed for

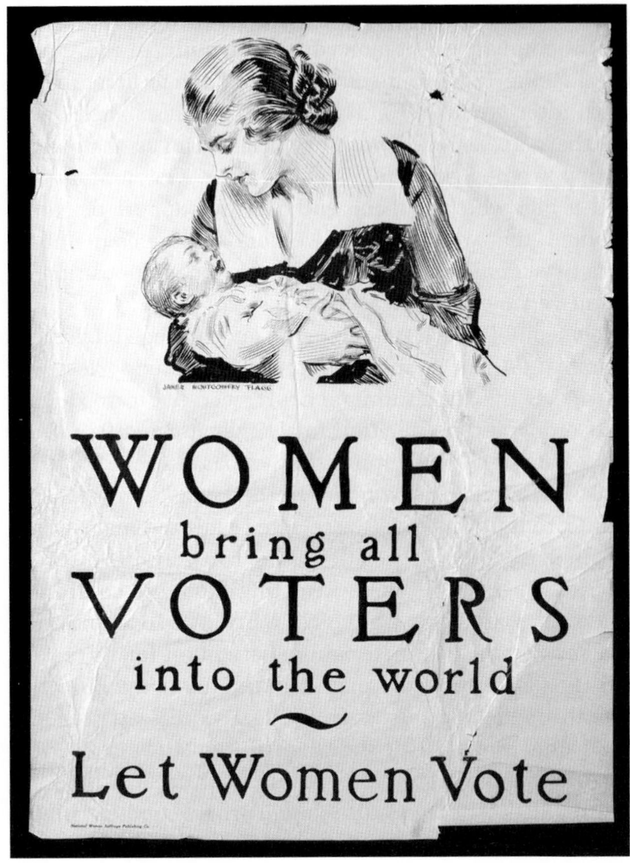

Figure 13.4 Woman suffrage poster. *Source: North Carolina Museum of History.*

ratification. Although North Carolina Democrats adopted a suffrage plank in their party platform in 1920, most of the leadership remained opposed: gubernatorial candidate Cameron Morrison, for example, was a firm "anti."

Throughout the spring and summer of 1920, the suffragists and the antis fought it out. The antis, having organized a state chapter of the Southern Women's Rejection League, contended that suffrage, by possibly enfranchising black women, would undermine women's place in the home and threaten the stability of white supremacy. Suffragists, in contrast, saw the vote as the logical fulfillment of women's widening influence in public life, arguing that the vote would protect, not threaten, white supremacy. There were notable African American women supporters—and a few opponents—of the Nineteenth Amendment. Charlotte Hawkins Brown became a prominent black suffragist, and she campaigned throughout the state. When the General Assembly convened in August 1920, however, it became apparent that the necessary votes for ratification did not exist. On August 11, a majority of the members of the lower house signed a "round robin" letter indicating their opposition, and six days later the state senate defeated ratification. North Carolina's action was, however, meaningless, for on August 18, 1920, Tennessee became the thirty-sixth state to ratify.

Charlotte Hawkins Brown and Black Women Reformers

Reform also opened up possibilities for African American women, and no individual better represents this than Charlotte Hawkins Brown. Born in Vance County, near Henderson, as a child, Charlotte moved to Cambridge, Massachusetts, where she graduated from Cambridge English High School in 1900. Under the sponsorship of the first woman president of Wellesley College, Alice Freeman Palmer, Brown attended the state normal college in Salem, Massachusetts, and then began work for the American Missionary Association in North Carolina. Moving to McLeansville in 1901, a year later she established her own school and named it the Alice Freeman Palmer Memorial Institute in Sedalia, North Carolina. The Palmer Memorial Institute (PMI) was originally established, adopting Booker T. Washington's educational philosophy, which emphasized vocational training in industrial arts and agriculture. Although the school always retained an emphasis on the good character and personal habits of its students—all of whom were required to work an hour a day for the school—over time the school began to put academics first. PMI filled an obvious need in North Carolina, where most African Americans had no access at all to a high school education, and eventually the school emphasized rigorous academic education and the training of black leaders. By 1915, PMI had graduated more than two hundred students, and it offered African American male and female students a high school education. Eventually, the curriculum at PMI expanded to include drama, literature, mathematics, and foreign languages.

With the support of Booker T. Washington, Brown successfully made Palmer Memorial Institute into an attractive beneficiary of northern philanthropy, and she was especially adept at presenting her case to northern white audiences. Her list of northern sponsors included influential people such as Harvard University president Charles William Eliot, who led a fundraising campaign, and Boston philanthropists Carrie and Galen Stone (who eventually gave the school $500,000). PMI also received funds from the leading northern philanthropies supporting black education, including the Jeanes Fund and the Julius Rosenwald Fund. Brown also cultivated white supporters from North Carolina, including Lula Martin McIver, a Greensboro reformer, and Frank Porter Graham, who served as president of UNC after 1931. A fire that destroyed two of the school's six buildings in 1917 proved to be only a

Figure 13.5 Charlotte Hawkins Brown, center (1883–1961) and the faculty of the Palmer Memorial Institute, c. 1907. *Source: Courtesy of the State Archives of North Carolina.*

temporary setback, for Brown remained successful at raising money, $300,000 in 1925 alone. By the 1930s, PMI consisted of a campus located on 350 acres of land that boasted more than a dozen buildings.

Brown was, by the 1930s, one of the leading African American women educators in the South. The Palmer Institute, though it struggled with financial instability for much of its existence, gained a reputation for producing several generations of black leaders, and after the 1940s it became an elite private school for African Americans, attracting students from around the nation. Brown was also a major figure in the black women's club movement. In 1909, she participated in the founding of the North Carolina Association of Colored Women's Clubs, serving for more than twenty years as the president of this organization. She was active in the formation of the National Association of Colored Women's Clubs, and worked closely with Mary McLeod Bethune in founding that organization. With her many white contacts and admirers, Brown was instrumental in the postwar interracial movement that sought to build bridges of respect and cooperation between reform-minded whites and blacks.

Brown was forthright about segregation, often more so than her African American contemporaries. In October 1920, while en route by train to the White Women's Missionary Convention in Memphis, Tennessee, Brown was evicted, against her will, from her sleeping-car berth and forced to go to the all-black Jim Crow car. At the meeting, she told an astonished audience of how she had been harassed on the train by a group of irate whites. "Put yourself in my place," she said, and "just be colored for a few moments." When the white people forced her to leave the sleeping car for the Jim Crow coach, she had felt "crushed and humiliated." Brown's Memphis speech had a huge impact, and many white women began to see, perhaps for the first time, what one of them recalled as the "gulf of distance, of mistrust and suspicion" that divided the races. When she heard the black women speak of their "aching hearts and unspeakable fear" at Memphis, said one white woman, "my heart broke, and I have been trying to pass the story on to the women of my race."[6]

Brown remained a strong opponent of segregation, even while she cultivated ties with many whites who supported the Jim Crow system. When women obtained the suffrage in 1920, Brown favored campaigns to register African American women to vote. She cooperated with the NAACP and other organizations in these efforts, and despite disfranchisement, she was at least partially successful. In addition, during World War II, she was one of the leaders that assembled a meeting that issued the Durham Manifesto, which declared that the time had come to end Jim Crow segregation. Brown suggested during the war that African Americans should serve their country but that their country, in return, begin to treat them as full—not second-class—citizens.

The Educational Crusade

Progressive governor Charles B. Aycock and his successors focused much of their reform effort on education, which they saw as a key to North Carolina's economic development and modernization. In 1897, North Carolina educational leader Charles Duncan McIver invited an old friend, Wake County's Walter Hines Page, to Greensboro to address the student body of the State Normal and Industrial College (of which McIver was president), then experiencing its fifth commencement exercises. Page had already lived an interesting life. A native North Carolinian, he attended Trinity College (now Duke University) and then Randolph-Macon College in Virginia. After some graduate work at the Johns Hopkins University, Page returned to North Carolina and became editor of the Raleigh *State Chronicle,* where he associated with other reform-minded North Carolinians. In 1885, he left the state in disgust, convinced—as he declared in a biting editorial—that the state was dominated by "mummies" who lived in and were bound by the dead traditions of the past. Page headed north, toward the publishing world of Boston and New York, where he became prominent in the Northeast's literary world. Later, during the presidency of Woodrow Wilson—Page's friend since his Johns Hopkins days—Page would serve with distinction as US ambassador to Great Britain before and during World War I. But intellectually and emotionally, Page never left his native South, and during the 1890s he became what his biographer deemed a sort of "intersectional ambassador" who explained the South to the North and the North to the South.[7]

Composed of young women from across the state, the State Normal graduates listening to Page represented Charles D. McIver's vision of the future, in which a new generation of white women mobilized into an army of reformers. McIver believed in what we would today call "empowerment." He was convinced that women's education fostered leadership and public activism. Not only could the State Normal educate women who would go on to be teachers, but it could also train a generation of women who might work toward changing and modernizing North Carolina. McIver's famous motto exemplified an overall strategy that lay at the heart of Progressive-Era reform: "Educate a man and you educate an individual," but "educate a woman and you educate a family."

Walter Page became intent on extending McIver's message of change for the entire state. Page believed that North Carolina should embrace the future rather than the past. In his address, he argued that a throwback to slavery and the mindset of the old South restricted the state's potential by perpetuating a rigid social structure, backward political leadership, and a stultifying economic system. North Carolina's main resource—its people—was wasted, its human capital neglected. He declared that the state's "forgotten" people were victims, and ordinary folk living in poverty and underdevelopment were locked into ignorance and hopelessness. Page's famous "Forgotten Man" address before the State Normal graduates became a clarion call for change, and during the next two decades reformers in North Carolina explored various dimensions of what it meant.

Even as Page spoke, the political reformers had begun to change the political landscape. What Page was suggesting really went far beyond a purification of the political system, and his vision extended beyond a single generation. It involved attempting to remake North Carolina's future by focusing on attitudinal changes at a basic level, remaking North Carolinians into a modernizing people, altering longstanding folk practices in a rural state.

Progressive-Era reformers' strategy, to an extraordinary extent, focused on children. During this time, Americans became fascinated with children and childhood, and one of the hallmarks of the era was a newfound appreciation of the importance of childhood. Simply put, social reformers agreed that investment in what Page called "human capital" meant improving education and health care for children. Backed by the new academic study of social psychology, reformers rallied to child-saving as a cause, one that meant protecting and fostering childhood and adolescence as a special, crucial period in human development. This sensibility is familiar to us in the twenty-first century but was largely alien to people of the early twentieth century, when it was still common practice for children to help their families by working at a young age—whether in the fields or the factories. Reformers believed that children, rather than entering the workforce at an early age, should be nurtured, first taught in kindergartens and then sent to structured elementary and secondary schools, where they could be educated in basic literacy and civic values and socialized

Figure 13.6 Frontispiece, 1909, *Yearbook for North Carolina State Normal and Industrial College. Source: North Carolina Collection, University of North Carolina Library at Chapel Hill.*

to appropriate behavior in an industrial society. Obviously, this approach made public education crucially important, but it also required restrictions on children working as part of the industrial labor force.

In fact, public education quickly emerged as a pivotal consideration of the Progressive Era. The lack of a system of public schools provided a telling example of the challenges of underdevelopment—but it also represented one of the opportunities for meaningful change, at least as reformers saw it. These first-generation reformers—men such as Charles D. McIver, Edwin A. Alderman, and James Y. Joyner—therefore attached great importance to public education, seeing it as North Carolina's gateway from chronic poverty to economic development. Their faith in schooling was nearly unlimited, and it came with a particular evangelical fervor. Reformers remained convinced that if North Carolinians could undergo a kind of conversion experience, that a social regeneration—a sort of social salvation—would occur. And they openly embraced evangelical methods of the revival: the careful organization and preparation of public opinion, the use of out-of-doors meetings (many of which resembled old-fashioned camp meetings), and the expectation of sudden, sweeping attitudinal changes. Key to this grand evangelical-style crusade were regional associations such as the Southern Education Board, which received significant backing from northern philanthropists but which also included crucial participation by North Carolinians. The result was the expansion of support for white schools.

Public Health and Child Saving

Relying on a combination of persuasion and coercion, North Carolina social reformers wanted to transform the folkways of ordinary people, not only those who lived in rural areas but also the rural migrants who inhabited the state's industrialized mill villages. Not always successful in their efforts, they often encountered indifference and sometimes opposition from people who resented the interference of outsiders. Two examples of the progressives' campaign were their attempts to regulate the use of child labor in textile mills and a campaign to transform public-health practices in the state. Both efforts confronted reformers with what they saw as the primary challenges in modernizing a population that often had little intention of being modernized.

Believing that "saving" children through education and social welfare would help to improve social conditions, reformers focused on the industrialized southern Piedmont, where the cotton-textile industry still relied on a family system of labor that employed large numbers of children. Male and female reformers alike were appalled at their discovery of working conditions for children. Young people formed the basis of society, wrote one reformer, upon whose shoulders rested the future; the "boy of today" would become "the man of tomorrow." Solving the problems that plagued children could mean having "solved all social problems."[8] The most important organization seeking to regulate child labor was the National Child Labor Committee (NCLC), a pressure group formed in 1904 with offices in New York City but which sought to organize a regional campaign in the South. Like other single-issue pressure groups, the NCLC turned out literature, dispatched field agents, and sponsored state committees. North Carolinians were especially active in their branch

Figure 13.7 November 1908, Lewis W. Hine photo of girls running warping machines in Loray Mill, Gastonia, NC. *Source: Library of Congress, LC-DIG-nclc-01342.*

of the NCLC, under the directorship of Alexander J. McKelway. Originally a Presbyterian minister, McKelway first came to reform as a prohibitionist. In 1898, he began work as editor of the *North Carolina Presbyterian,* based in Charlotte, during which time he took an interest in the child-labor issue. Like other reformers, McKelway exalted the status of children, and he embraced an evangelical zeal to change social conditions. The child, McKelway declared, was a "central figure" in the world's coming Golden Age. In contrast to this, he argued, was the emerging mill-village system, which had recreated a new "feudal" system of control that oppressed children. The cotton-mill people, warned McKelway, had become a "class apart," the mill villages pockets of "feudalism, sometimes benevolent, sometimes otherwise." In this system children occupied the bottom rung of society.[9]

The NCLC became especially active in North Carolina between 1909 and 1914. After 1910, moreover, the group hired a state agent, W. H. Swift, to work full-time on an anti-child-labor campaign. It focused its efforts on educating the public on the issue of lobbying for legislation that would limit the use of children in textile mills. NCLC-sponsored legislation sought to impose a higher age limit for child workers (from 12 to 14), a reduction in the maximum number of hours a child could work (from 66 down to 60 hours), the end to night work by children, and a system of factory inspection to enforce the law. Despite their best efforts, for the most part, the NCLC campaign in North Carolina failed. The North Carolina legislature had banned children working under the age of 12 and then raised that to age 14 in 1907, but the law provided for numerous exceptions. And while the legislation did reduce the maximum hours permitted to 60, the absence of any provision in North Carolina for factory inspection meant that the law remained largely unenforced. The practical result was that no effective system of regulating child labor in the state was created during the Progressive Era.

North Carolina reformers also focused on other outcroppings of rural poverty and underdevelopment: widespread ill health, malnutrition, and unsanitary practices. Of particular importance was the famous hookworm campaign, conducted in North Carolina between 1909 and 1914 and orchestrated by oil magnate John D. Rockefeller—the Rockefeller Sanitary Commission (RSC). The RSC received a $1 million grant in 1909 from Rockefeller, with which it set out to expose, organize, and propose remedies for hookworm infections across the South.

Hookworm infection had attracted considerable attention because of the work of medical zoologist Charles W. Stiles, well known as the "discoverer" of hookworms, who publicized the dangers and prevalence of hookworms, especially in the American South. Hookworms are parasites that live in human intestines and typically enter the body through bare feet in contact with fecal-contaminated soil. Although hookworms rarely kill their infected hosts, the latter do suffer anemia and debilitation. Stiles could thus describe hookworms as a "germ of laziness"—an expression he used to explain southern backwardness and underdevelopment—and hookworms became a focal point of public health reformers' efforts to transform folkways by altering the environment. The hosting of hookworms, after all, could be prevented by wearing shoes and, more important, by the sanitary disposal of human waste.

The hookworm campaign in North Carolina soon became one of the most successful in the South. North Carolinians such as Walter Hines Page and state school superintendent and school reformer James Y. Joyner—both members of the Southern Education Board—were also members of the RSC. It created field operations in each of the southern states to gather information about the extent of parasitic infection and make proposals for programs to eradicate hookworms. The RSC established strict requirements. The state programs were run under the oversight of state health officials and would be part of the state health system, though still subject to the influence of Rockefeller philanthropy. Each of the state campaigns had a semi-independent state director responsible for coordinating the campaigns. The state director in North Carolina was John A. Ferrell, who had been trained at UNC and at the Johns Hopkins Medical School and who had served as county public-health director in eastern North Carolina's Sampson County. Ferrell soon established a reputation as the most effective hookworm campaigner in the South. Indeed, North Carolina's hookworm campaign worked so well that it became a model for the rest of the South.

Ferrell appointed five field directors, who were generally young, enthusiastic, hard-working, and recently graduated physicians. Covering the entire state, the field directors investigated the extent of infection and, if possible, documented

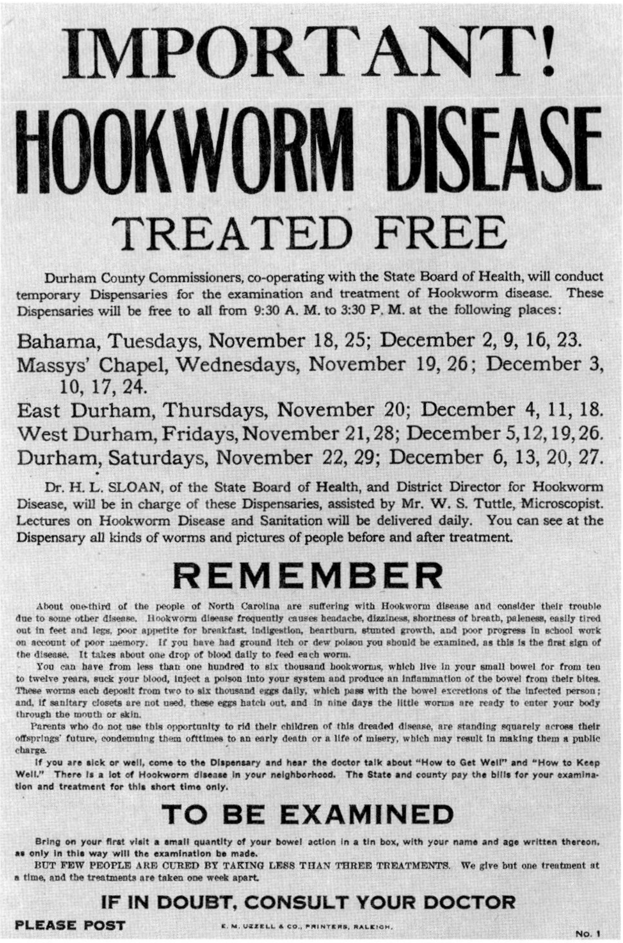

IMPORTANT!

HOOKWORM DISEASE

TREATED FREE

Durham County Commissioners, co-operating with the State Board of Health, will conduct temporary Dispensaries for the examination and treatment of Hookworm disease. These Dispensaries will be free to all from 9:30 A. M. to 3:30 P. M. at the following places:

Bahama, Tuesdays, November 18, 25; December 2, 9, 16, 23.
Massys' Chapel, Wednesdays, November 19, 26; December 3, 10, 17, 24.
East Durham, Thursdays, November 20; December 4, 11, 18.
West Durham, Fridays, November 21, 28; December 5, 12, 19, 26.
Durham, Saturdays, November 22, 29; December 6, 13, 20, 27.

Dr. H. L. SLOAN, of the State Board of Health, and District Director for Hookworm Disease, will be in charge of these Dispensaries, assisted by Mr. W. S. Tuttle, Microscopist. Lectures on Hookworm Disease and Sanitation will be delivered daily. You can see at the Dispensary all kinds of worms and pictures of people before and after treatment.

REMEMBER

About one-third of the people of North Carolina are suffering with Hookworm disease and consider their trouble due to some other disease. Hookworm disease frequently causes headache, dizziness, shortness of breath, paleness, easily tired out in feet and legs, poor appetite for breakfast, indigestion, heartburn, stunted growth, and poor progress in school work on account of poor memory. If you have had ground itch or dew poison you should be examined, as this is the first sign of the disease. It takes about one drop of blood daily to feed each worm.

You can have from less than one hundred to six thousand hookworms, which live in your small bowel for from ten to twelve years, suck your blood, inject a poison into your system and produce an inflammation of the bowel from their bites. These worms each deposit from two to six thousand eggs daily, which pass with the bowel excretions of the infected person; and, if sanitary closets are not used, these eggs hatch out, and in nine days the little worms are ready to enter your body through the mouth or skin.

Parents who do not use this opportunity to rid their children of this dreaded disease, are standing squarely across their offsprings' future, condemning them ofttimes to an early death or a life of misery, which may result in making them a public charge.

If you are sick or well, come to the Dispensary and hear the doctor talk about "How to Get Well" and "How to Keep Well." There is a lot of Hookworm disease in your neighborhood. The State and county pay the bills for your examination and treatment for this short time only.

TO BE EXAMINED

Bring on your first visit a small quantity of your bowel action in a tin box, with your name and age written thereon, as only in this way will the examination be made.

BUT FEW PEOPLE ARE CURED BY TAKING LESS THAN THREE TREATMENTS. We give but one treatment at a time, and the treatments are taken one week apart.

IF IN DOUBT, CONSULT YOUR DOCTOR

PLEASE POST   E. M. UZZELL & CO., PRINTERS, RALEIGH.   No. 1

Figure 13.8 Poster for hookworm campaign. *Source: North Carolina Collection, University of North Carolina Library at Chapel Hill.*

its existence. They found—and were able to publicize successfully—unsanitary conditions that prevailed generally across the state. Outhouses were still common, and typically these structures did not provide for sanitary disposal of human waste. Piedmont mill villages, for example, were found to have generally unhealthy conditions. Field director Benjamin Earle Washburn found, in a study of the textile-producing Alamance County, that nine-tenths of the homes in the county had unsanitary privies. Nor was this condition confined to the Piedmont: by the fall of 1910, the field reporters had found evidence of hookworm infection in all but two of North Carolina's counties.

Much of the hookworm campaign was directed toward exposure of the high rate of infection and publicizing effective methods of prevention. The North Carolina directors spread the word in various ways. Some of them used the public schools to promote their cause and to disseminate information, with the directors often appearing at teachers' meetings in attempts to enlist them in the cause. After 1910, the field directors conducted extensive surveys in most of the state. They discovered that hookworm infection afflicted nearly two-fifths of North Carolina's children. An important result of the hookworm campaign, then, was the use of schools as centers for the promotion of public health, as medical inspection of schoolchildren—some of whom had no other access to health care—became a routine part of public education.

A more spectacular method was the use of the county dispensary, which became the most successful and popular part of the Rockefeller hookworm campaign in North Carolina. Beginning in 1911, the dispensaries combined new medical science with an old-fashioned evangelical crusade. Early on, state director Ferrell realized that the greatest potential gains lay in public relations, in promoting the benefits of rural sanitation and of public health generally. The dispensaries became traveling road shows that provided speeches, exhibits, and demonstrations on public-health issues. The dispensaries also marked an experiment in free public health care, where thousands of North Carolinians could be examined and treated for hookworm infection. In August 1911, RSC officials ran dispensary campaigns in Robeson, Sampson, and Halifax Counties, in eastern North Carolina, and they succeeded in attracting large and enthusiastic crowds. By the end of August 1911, the hookworm campaigners had tested or treated some 12,500 people.

North Carolina's dispensary campaign became the most successful model for public health reform in the regionwide hookworm campaign. Subsequent dispensaries worked closely with fledgling local health officials, and the campaigners used intensive media and publicity to try to drum up a crowd. "See the Hookworms and the various intestinal parasites that man is heir to," read one handbill, while another warned that parents who avoided treating their children stood "squarely across their offspring's future, condemning them ofttimes to an early death or a life of misery, which may result in making them a public charge."[10] The dispensaries contained materials informing the public about the sources of hookworms and recommending solutions through better public health and sanitation. Most dispensaries included exhibits containing pictures of worms and describing how infection occurred. Lecturers provided further details, relying on visual aids such as charts and pictures and even preserved specimens of adult worms, and at many dispensaries speeches were followed by the singing of hymns. Participants even had the chance to view developing hookworm eggs through a microscope.

By 1915, when the Rockefeller Sanitary Commission had concluded its work, North Carolina's anti-hookworm campaign had become one of its leading success stories. By then, the commission had reached every county in the state, and the problem of hookworms had been fully exposed to the public. In the wake of the campaign, Rockefeller philanthropy had a decided effect on the structure of public health in the state. Although the RSC went out of existence, Rockefeller philanthropists remained involved in North Carolina public health through the International Health Commission (later the International Health Board). It focused much of its efforts on sponsoring the expansion of public health in sanitation, nutrition, and communicable diseases by building up the power of county health officials, and during the next fifty years state intervention in rural public health became common in North Carolina.

The Triumph of Prohibition

Writing in 1910, the North Carolina social reformer Alexander J. McKelway predicted that a time would come when a crow could fly across the South—from Cape Hatteras, west through Virginia, Kentucky, Tennessee, Arkansas, and Oklahoma, returning through Texas, Mississippi, Alabama, Georgia, Florida, and South Carolina, to the Atlantic Ocean—without seeing any saloons or flying over a wet country. By far, the most popular social reform of the Progressive Era was the crusade to institute the prohibition of the sale and manufacture of alcoholic beverages.

The prohibition movement ran against a strong tradition of alcohol consumption among many North Carolinians dating back to the colonial era. The production of spirits, ales, brandies, and wines had long had a place in rural parts of the state, and as towns expanded in the post-Reconstruction era, taverns and saloons became gathering places for workers in an industrializing North Carolina. There was also a class dynamic to prohibition: most of the reformers were middle class, most of the people who were their targets were working class. There was also a racial dynamic to North Carolina prohibition, as fears about a restive African American population fed the desire to establish a more stable basis of social order.

Prohibition drew on a rich tradition in the temperance movement, which had involved North Carolinians as early as the antebellum era and continued thereafter. After the Civil War, temperance reformers, emphasizing individual abstinence and restraint, focused primarily on efforts related to individuals. But by the 1880s, the temperance movement underwent a major transformation, as reformers came to favor government intervention that would ban saloons as well as the production and distribution of drink. In 1881, temperance advocates, with North Carolina Baptists and Methodists leading the way, proposed a statewide referendum that would prohibit the manufacture of liquors, wines, and ciders, except for medicinal purposes. The proposed laws met strong opposition from producers—many of whom had long produced spirits, ciders, and

Figure 13.9 Celebrating statewide prohibition, May 1908. *Source: North Carolina Collection, University of North Carolina Library at Chapel Hill.*

wines as a way to preserve their crops against spoilage—and in August 1881 the measure was defeated by a margin of more than three to one.

Prohibitionists would continue to favor legislation that would strike directly at the system of alcohol that they believed was corrupting social habits and impairing social progress. Reformers sought to destroy saloons because alcohol abuse had become the most important social problem of their time. For nineteenth-century Americans, alcohol use and alcoholism had become almost epidemic; prohibitionists were responding to a real social problem. The key to state prohibition, maintained Alexander J. McKelway in 1907, was changing a "total abstinence party" into a movement that attracted the support of ordinary people who believed that not all drinking was sinful but were, nonetheless, united in their opposition to saloons. Here, said McKelway, the "economic argument"—the notion that saloons bred disorder, crime, and inefficient labor—was paramount. This broad prohibitionist coalition had become convinced that saloons represented "everything that was abhorrent in politics and government."[11]

The prohibition crusade was spearheaded by the Anti-Saloon League (ASL), first organized in Ohio in 1895, becoming a national organization in the early

1900s. The ASL pioneered the mobilization of public opinion and established a model for Progressive-Era reform campaigns that relied on staged manipulation through intensive publicity, communication of a message through pamphlet literature and public meetings, and nearly constant pressure on legislators. Although a national organization, the ASL decentralized authority and gave state chapters wide latitude in executing their strategies. In general, these state-level campaigns, which began in the South after 1900 and continued until about 1910, focused first on expanding local-option prohibition and then on a statewide prohibition.

In North Carolina as elsewhere, church leaders took the initiative to organize the state chapter of the ASL. North Carolina Baptists were strong supporters of temperance and, by the 1890s, had become avid enthusiasts for prohibition. At their North Carolina state convention of 1901, Baptist leaders created a standing committee to consider organizing a state ASL chapter. Baptist prohibitionists then recruited other Protestant denominations, including the Methodists, Presbyterians, and Quakers, all of whom met in Raleigh on February 6, 1902, to establish the North Carolina Anti-Saloon League. The constitution creating the state chapter pledged to mobilize public opinion against saloons and the drink and to seek effective legislation. Pledging to act as a nonpartisan lobbying group, the ASL constitution also created an organizational structure designed to influence the political structure toward prohibition.

Operating between 1902 and 1910, the North Carolina ASL pursued a highly effective strategy. Years of experience in temperance agitation had convinced most of the membership of the complexity of enacting prohibition: they realized that public opinion could only be moved toward change incrementally. The ASL thus sought first to effect rural prohibition, then to abolish saloons, and finally to bring about statewide prohibition. Exercising influence in the legislative elections of 1902, ASL prohibitionists descended on the North Carolina legislature in the spring of 1903. They enjoyed the full support of US senator Furnifold M. Simmons, who had established himself as the most powerful political leader in the one-party system. In late 1902, Simmons announced his support for rural prohibition, and he favored legislation that would eradicate distilleries that existed in the remote countryside. Gov. Charles B. Aycock, in his annual message to the legislature in early 1903, also endorsed rural prohibition. When A. D. Watts introduced legislation early in the new legislative session of 1903, it carried the support of the Democratic leadership. ASL forces, however, countered with their own legislation that sought to eradicate liquor distilling and wine production; the ASL bill would also apply prohibition to towns of less than 1,000 inhabitants. The ASL forces, led by corresponding secretary and future US senator Josiah William Bailey, mobilized a massive petition campaign that enjoyed the strong and enthusiastic support of WCTU members across the state. The legislature was in this way inundated with the signatures of more than 100,000 voters. In the first two years of its existence, the ASL distributed more than 600,000 pieces of literature, 60,000 abstinence pledges, and 100,000 circular letters. More than 1,300 local leagues were organized.

The Watts bill eventually prevailed, and, though less than what the ASL favored, it brought rural prohibition to North Carolina. The new law banned the sale and production of alcoholic beverages outside of incorporated towns. Although the law excluded wines and ciders, along with fruit and grape brandies if sold in quantities larger than 5 gallons, it provided for wide discretion at the local level. The Watts law permitted towns to call special local-option elections that would permit urban communities to institute prohibition in their communities. In the aftermath of the law's passage, several urban communities instituted local-option prohibition, and prohibitionists prevailed in twenty out of twenty-eight local-option elections held in the summer and fall of 1903. In these campaigns, the ASL proved formidable in organizing and mobilizing voters, and they relied on a network of women's church groups and local denominational leadership. In July 1904, prohibitionists took their campaigns to leading urban Piedmont communities of Charlotte and Greensboro. In Charlotte, the ASL, headed by leading prohibitionist Heriot Clarkson, led a successful effort to vote for prohibition, which carried by a vote of 1,027 to 546. Similarly, in Greensboro, the drys carried the day by a vote of 741 to 315.

The Anti-Saloon League's campaign subsequently tightened the vise. In 1905, the legislature enacted the Ward law, which prohibited liquor manufacturing in towns of less than 1,000 people. The Watts and Ward laws helped to drive small distilleries out of business and to reduce the number of liquor dealers. Although there was some division among prohibitionists about the most effective strategy—ASL leader Josiah W. Bailey, for example, favored a slower, incremental approach, while prohibitionist John A. Oates, Jr., favored immediate prohibition—the successes of rural prohibition and local option emboldened reformers to press for statewide legislation. Public opinion, in the meantime, moved toward prohibition, as the ASL's grassroots campaign bore fruit. By 1908, only 26 of the state's 100 counties and 46 of the state's 328 incorporated towns still permitted saloons.

Reformers believed that these holdout "wet" areas were undermining effective prohibition, as "dry" areas were invaded with drink from nearby wet towns. "The saloon counties," wrote the *Raleigh News and Observer,* "do not confine the evils of the sale of liquors in their own communities, but they make it all the more difficult for the temperance counties to enforce their laws."[12] In 1908, a widespread movement for statewide prohibition emerged, with ASL leadership but also enjoying support from industrial leaders, who believed that prohibition would improve the efficiency of their workforce. In January 1908, the General Assembly enacted statewide prohibition in which the sale and manufacture of spirits, wine, and beers was made illegal, though the law provided exceptions in which wine and cider could be produced locally and in small quantities. Druggists were also permitted to sell alcohol with a doctor's prescription. The law went before the voters in a statewide referendum on May 26, 1908, and a vigorous campaign followed. Democratic governor Robert Glenn was an enthusiastic dry, traveling 4,000 miles and delivering more than fifty prohibitionist speeches, while women's groups and church organizations from around the state organized an effective public-relations campaign. In the end, the prohibitionists swept the state, carrying all but twenty-one of North Carolina's counties.

Looking back on prohibition, ASL president Heriot Clarkson declared that the prosperity of Charlotte, his hometown, had "never been greater." Local merchants received money that would have gone to the saloon, while workers were investing their savings in banks and building-and-loan associations. Charlotte's cotton-textile industry had profited by the good labor-management relations that prevailed because of a sober population. Prohibition was responsible for "wonders and untold benefit to the mill owner and the operatives, and all sorts and conditions of men." "I hope to live to see the day," Clarkson concluded, "when the saloon, 'the blot on the garment of our Country,' will be wiped away."[13]

* * *

After the Progressive Era, a good portion of North Carolina's leadership endorsed change and modernization through public education, public health, moral reform, and economic development. The state possessed an especially active group of reformers on many different fronts, and during the early twentieth century it acquired a reputation as the "Wisconsin of the South." Like Wisconsin, North Carolina boasted a public university in Chapel Hill which, after World War I, had become fully engaged in a mission of public service. Like Wisconsin, North Carolina also possessed leaders who wanted to accommodate their rural and small-town folk to the realities of an industrial society. But existing side-by-side with this new modernizing ethos were powerful forces that would seek to reassert the state's traditions.

Notes

1 Charles Brantley Aycock, inaugural address, January 15, 1901, in R.D.W. Connor, *The Life and Speeches of Charles Brantley Aycock* (New York: Doubleday, Page, and Company, 1912), pp. 229–30.

2 On reform and southern universities, see Michael Dennis, *Lessons in Progress: State Universities and Progressivism in the New South, 1880–1920* (Urbana: University of Illinois Press, 2001); Randal Hall, *William L. Poteat: A Leader of the Progressive Era South* (Lexington: University Press of Kentucky, 2000).

3 Leslie Brown, *Upbuilding Black Durham: Gender, Class, and Black Community Development in the Jim Crow South* (Chapel Hill: University of North Carolina Press, 2008), pp. 98–99.
4 Quoted in Anastatia Sims, *The Power of Femininity in the New South: Women's Organizations and Politics in North Carolina, 1880–1930* (Columbia: University of South Carolina Press, 1997), p. 67.
5 Donald G. Mathews and Jane Sherron DeHart, *Sex, Gender, and the Politics of ERA: A State and the Nation* (New York: Oxford University Press, 1990), p. 9.
6 William A. Link, *Paradox of Southern Progressivism, 1880–1930* (Chapel Hill: University of North Carolina Press, 1992), p. 263.
7 John Milton Cooper, Jr., *Walter Hines Page: The Southerner as American, 1855–1918* (Chapel Hill: University of North Carolina Press, 1977).
8 Quoted in Link, *Paradox,* p. 162.
9 Ibid., pp. 162, 169.
10 Quoted in William A. Link, "'The Harvest Is Ripe, but the Laborers Are Few': The Hookworm Crusade in North Carolina, 1909–1915," *North Carolina Historical Review* LXVII (January 1990): 14.
11 Quoted in Link, *Paradox,* p. 100.
12 Quoted in Daniel Jay Whitener, *Prohibition in North Carolina, 1715–1945* (Chapel Hill: University of North Carolina Press, 1946), p. 154.
13 *Prohibition in Charlotte* (Executive Committee of Anti-Saloon League, 1908), pp. 4–5.

14

World War I and the 1920s

Although American participation in World War I was brief, it had a pronounced effect on social, economic, and cultural life at home. The war unleashed forces that spurred far-reaching changes in the economy, cultural life, and politics. The changes that North Carolina witnessed during the 1920s evoked different reactions, as traditional ways of life underwent major changes and old assumptions appeared undermined. More than ever before, Tar Heels began to confront a cultural divide between what scholar Paul Luebke has called modernizing and traditionalist worlds, between largely external forces of change and a powerful internal will to maintain cultural conservatism. This cultural divide, first emerging in the decade after World War I, would remain a dominant theme in the history of the state for the remainder of the twentieth century.[1]

World War I and North Carolina

Nearly three years after the outbreak of general war in Europe, the United States declared war on Germany on April 4, 1917. The decision to enter the conflict followed a long period of neutrality, during which President Woodrow Wilson tried unsuccessfully to avert military intervention in the slaughter occurring across the Atlantic. There was strong sentiment favoring neutrality in North Carolina, and when Wilson delivered his war message before Congress on April 2, 1917, some North Carolina congressmen opposed US intervention. Claude Kitchin, a Democrat from Scotland Neck, North Carolina, had served in Congress since 1901 and held powerful positions of leadership; in 1917, he held a position as majority leader of the House of Representatives. Kitchin was one of several antiwar southern congressmen opposing Wilson's military buildup in his "preparedness program" of 1915. Kitchin described the war in Europe as a "slaughter-house for human beings" and urged that the United States remain out of the fight that it might serve as the "last hope of peace

North Carolina: Change and Tradition in a Southern State, Second Edition. William A. Link.

on earth" and the "only remaining compass to which the world can look for guidance in the paths of right and truth, of justice and humanity."[2]

Despite Kitchin's opposition—and the opposition of only a few others in Congress—the war resolution passed Congress by the overwhelming vote of 373–50. In North Carolina, public opinion rallied around the flag. Most North Carolinians supported intervention and the mobilization of manpower and economic resources taking place during 1917–18. On national Selective Service registration day, June 5, 1917—the beginning of a new national wartime draft—some 480,491 people in North Carolina, 337,986 white and 142,505 African American, registered for military service. Overall, 86,000 North Carolinians served in the military during World War I, with the largest numbers serving in the army's 30th Division, known as the "Old Hickory" Division, and the 81st Division, known as the "Wildcat" Division. Most Tar Heel soldiers were mobilized out of National Guard units or were draftees; many soldiers were housed at Camp Greene, outside Charlotte, which at its peak contained 65,000 men. Another greatly enlarged US Army camp was established for artillery forces at a 118,000-acre tract outside of Fayetteville; named for Confederate general Braxton Bragg, it became known as Fort Bragg. Gov. Thomas Bickett urged state residents to the war effort: he instructed communities to ring their church bells for two minutes every evening at 7:00 p.m. North Carolina's State Council of Defense worked, as did its counterparts in other states, toward mobilizing resources in support of the war effort. Patriotic fervor gripped the state: war officials even appointed a state music director responsible for encouraging communities to organize, among other things, a "Liberty Chorus" in each town.

More practically, the war provided new opportunities for activism and leadership by women, especially middle-class white women. In 1917, North Carolina women participated in war mobilization through involvement in the Woman's Committee, Council of National Defense, a national organization that served as a clearinghouse for women's organizations in support of the war effort. Laura Holmes Reilley, a Charlotte women's club leader, became state chair of the Woman's Committee, which oversaw organizing women's organizations, with 11,358 North Carolina women becoming involved during the first year of the war. With a slogan proclaiming the need for "A Garden for Every Home the Year Around," women urged local food production, while in other areas they extolled the need for sacrifice and patriotic activities. Women leaders also helped drive Liberty-Loan campaigns that sought to stimulate public support for war financing through bond sales.

The Woman's Committee, however, focused much of its efforts on the well-being and morale of the soldiers training in North Carolina. Many individual women participated through the Red Cross and Home Service Sections, helping to care for the wounded and disabled, while others worked in a canteen service that provided food and drink to wounded troops. Working with federal officials, women helped to organize a War Camp Community Service that

Figure 14.1 Salisbury Canteen, Christmas, 1917. This canteen gave a turkey dinner to every soldier passing through Salisbury on Christmas Day. *Source: North Carolina Collection, University of North Carolina Library at Chapel Hill.*

sought to improve the living conditions and moral environment surrounding the training camps. Community service workers attempted to shut down illegal drinking sites, as well as to uproot prostitution and vice near the camps. In general, relying on Progressive-Era standards of organized recreation, community-service women become social workers, of sorts, attempting to regulate the social environment for thousands of American soldiers. "The devoted work of these women—in snow and ice, heat and cold, at noon and at midnight," was remarkable, according to one observer. "Thousands of soldiers will never forget the cheer, the comfort and the sympathy which they dispensed."[3]

The strong feelings of nationalism and wartime patriotism emerging in North Carolina helped to spur along Progressive-Era reforms. Prohibitionists made the argument that national prohibition would assist the war effort. Earlier, in 1913, North Carolina congressman Edwin Y. Webb of Shelby co-sponsored the Webb-Kenyon Act, which prohibited shipments of drink from wet (nonprohibitionist) to dry (prohibitionist) states. Josephus Daniels, who owned the *Raleigh News and Observer*, in 1913 became Woodrow Wilson's Secretary of the Navy. In 1914, Daniels banned all drinking on navy vessels. Daniels's prohibitionism led to the derisive name for coffee, "Cup of Joe." The Eighteenth Amendment called for a national prohibition, and after its submission to the states in 1917, North Carolina quickly ratified it. The war stimulated a greater willingness to use governmental intervention and coercion. Public health, already high on the reform agenda, became a priority of the wartime governmental expansion, as county health officials, allied with a new state health bureaucracy, initiated programs of inoculation against a variety of communicable and often lethal diseases such as typhoid fever.

North Carolina agriculture and industry also benefited from the national war mobilization. The Wilson administration created the Food Administration, which controlled food resources to further the war effort, and the ensuing demand for food that the conflict created boosted farm prices. North Carolina possessed a small shipbuilding industry, with shipyards in Elizabeth City, Wilmington, and Morehead City, all of which experienced growth. An increase in cigarette smoking among soldiers and civilians alike benefited tobacco manufacturers and bright-leaf tobacco farmers. The textile industry also profited from the war-heated economy, as North Carolina mills operated around the clock to satisfy demand for cloth. The military mobilization resulted in an acute labor shortage, rising wages, and the migration of workers into the state. Mobilization also stimulated migration out of North Carolina, as thousands of North Carolinians—African Americans and whites alike—moved in search of work. What would become known as the Great Migration from the South had begun, initiated by the wartime boom.

With the armistice of November 1918, the 18-month American involvement in World War I came to an end, with North Carolinians having seen action in France for a few intense months in the summer and fall of 1918. Though brief, the war brought important changes. The military mobilization—the nationwide draft and the wholesale mobilization of economic resources—was unprecedented in its scope and impact. The war aroused intense nationalism that found expression not only in visible patriotism but also in a popular hostility toward religious, ethnic, and racial minorities. The Ku Klux Klan was reborn during the war years into a modern version at Stone Mountain, outside of Atlanta, Georgia, on Thanksgiving Eve 1915. Klan organizers found receptive audiences, and the organization attracted many members. A new cultural nationalism emerged during the war with the rise of Protestant fundamentalism. Rejecting modernism in theology and the secularization of American life, fundamentalists organized themselves after 1918 in the World Christian Fundamentals Organization, which assembled in Philadelphia.

World War I sped the onslaught of the modern world into the state, forcing North Carolinians to reconsider the role of the state. North Carolina became a sort of Progressive showpiece: in no other southern state was the impact of the social reforms in education, public health, and child welfare more significant, and North Carolina's state government possessed a reputation for efficient management. It became common for the state's economic and

Figure 14.2 World War I Homefront: Conserving cabbage in North Carolina. More than 1,000 pounds of cabbage were put up by these women in three ways—kraut in light salt; kraut in heavy salt, and cabbage in brine, or pickled cabbage. *Source: North Carolina Collection, University of North Carolina Library at Chapel Hill.*

political leadership to advertise North Carolina as the most progressive and forward-looking of any southern state. But North Carolinians retained a powerful traditionalism in society, culture, and politics. The resulting dialogue between modernizers and traditionalists would emerge prominently during the decade of the 1920s and remain a dominant tension.

Social Change in the 1920s

During the generation after World War I, North Carolina underwent significant social, economic, and cultural changes. Expanding industry and agriculture during the 1920s reflected much improved transportation, especially roads. North Carolina's roads remained little changed from the colonial and nineteenth-century system of haphazard, locally controlled, and erratically maintained dirt roads. The Transportation Revolution had been confined, for the most part, to the construction and expansion of a railroad network, and poor roads continued to characterize North Carolina. In 1928, an observer for the *Greensboro Daily News* described the "heart-cracking struggle, desolation, utter weariness of man and beast ... personified in the narrow sea of tortured red mud stretching from one impossible summit to another."[4] Modernizing reformers recognized that improving the road system was a prerequisite to economic development. In 1901–02, a "Good Roads Train," jointly sponsored by the Southern Railway and the US Department of Agriculture, toured the state, extolling the virtues of better, hard-surfaced roads. In February 1902, what became known as the Good Roads movement brought together supporters of expanded public financing for road construction. Joseph Hyde Pratt, a Connecticut native and professor of geology at UNC, was a key figure. Along with State Geological Survey director Joseph A. Holmes, Pratt favored expanding the use of convict labor as a low-cost instrument of road modernization, even going as far as to suggest that using convict labor, either directly or by leasing to private contractors, to build and maintain roads would also benefit the prisoners. There was a "considerable amount of evidence," Holmes wrote in 1901, suggesting that "this out-of-door work not only improves the physical health of the convicts but that their experiences as road builders have actually improved their general character and prepared them for better citizenship."[5] Holmes's views obscured the reality of the state prison system: in truth, it was a system that often brutalized prisoners and exploited them as a source of cheap labor. Since convicts were overwhelmingly African American, chain gangs became yet another component of the larger system of white supremacy.

While still supporting the continued use of chain gangs to build roads, Pratt called for a centralized and coordinated state highway system that would link the state together, improve communications, and attract a burgeoning tourist industry. Beginning in 1908, Pratt tirelessly campaigned on behalf of improved roads and for state control over road expansion. In October 1909, Pratt helped to organize a Southern Appalachian Good Roads Association in Asheville; the convention's invitation announced that without good roads the mountain region was "practically inaccessible to the tourist and pleasure seeker, and during certain months of the year is inaccessible to the people living in the mountains."[6] Pratt recommended building a scenic highway in western North Carolina, one that would attract tourists, along with a new, east-west highway linking Wilmington with the Tennessee border. In 1909, Pratt and the Good Roads Association endorsed a Good Roads platform. It recommended the creation of a centralized State Highway Commission controlling public funding and the use of convict labor. The election of Locke Craig as governor in 1912 marked the first time that a proponent of the Good Roads movement had occupied the governor's mansion.

Figure 14.3 Local roads, Mecklenburg County, 1912. *Source: North Carolina Collection, University of North Carolina Library at Chapel Hill.*

With the development and popularization of the gasoline-powered automobile during the 1920s, the ownership of cars and small trucks skyrocketed. At the beginning of the decade, automobile use had increased significantly, with more than 109,000 cars registered and 530 automobile dealers operating in North Carolina. By 1927, the number of registered vehicles had reached 430,000. The further spread of the automobile culture in the 1920s brought other changes, as North Carolinians, like all Americans, gained greater mobility. The spread of the personal automobile depended on the transformation of

North Carolina's roads, a process that began during the 1920s. Promoters of the state, seeking to attract new residents and businesses, advertised communities with good roads: thus, in 1910, Guilford County won a competition and a $1,000 prize, sponsored by the *New York Herald* and the *Atlanta Journal*, for the best stretch of road between Roanoke and Atlanta. The contest enthusiasm evidently stimulated competition among urban boosters, who, before and after, spent collectively about $500,000 in road improvements.

Much of the early impetus for road building originated from local governments. Urban counties led the way. In 1920, both Mecklenburg County (Charlotte) and New Hanover County (Wilmington) raised money for roads by floating public bond issues, and by 1920 some eighty counties in North Carolina had borrowed a total of $84.5 million to build and improve roads. These early efforts at highway financing were, however, irregular, scattered unevenly across the state. By the 1920s, road promoters favored a centralization of the system by the state government. Transforming the roads became a kind of mantra for North Carolina governors, and the state experienced a building boom and a burst of state expenditures. During the administration of Gov. Cameron Morrison, elected in 1920, the legislature appropriated money to construct 5,500 miles of roads across the state. Overall, between 1915 and 1925, government spending on roads grew at three times the national average, while the state's debt increased from $13 million in 1920 to $178 million by the end of the 1920s. In 1921, the General Assembly created a unified state system and ended what had been county autonomy in road construction and maintenance. The act provided for a 1-cent-per-gallon gasoline tax to finance roads, while it issued $50 million in bonds for new roads. The most important force stimulating the highway revolution, however, came through federal involvement. In the summer of 1916, Congress enacted its first Highway Act. It appropriated matching funds for the creation of a national highway system and required supervision by state highway officials. Federal funds created a sort of snowball effect, as state construction of highways accelerated during the 1920s and 1930s.

In a second Transportation Revolution, road building profoundly reshaped farming. Commercial agriculture suddenly became even more viable and profitable, and there was an expanded demand for service sectors in farming, especially in "truck" farming in vegetables grown for urban consumption. But even more important than truck farming was tobacco's heightened significance. During the 1920s and 1930s, flue-cured, bright-leaf tobacco grown to make cigarettes dominated the state's tobacco culture. Although cultivated in Piedmont North Carolina in the antebellum era, bright-leaf tobacco expanded rapidly after about 1910, especially in eastern North Carolina, where cotton culture had long dominated. A "New Belt" of tobacco markets arose in eastern towns of Wilson, Kinston, and Greenville, and, by the 1930s, North Carolina had grown into the single most important grower of bright-leaf tobacco, producing about 70 percent of the nation's total crop. The Big Four—American

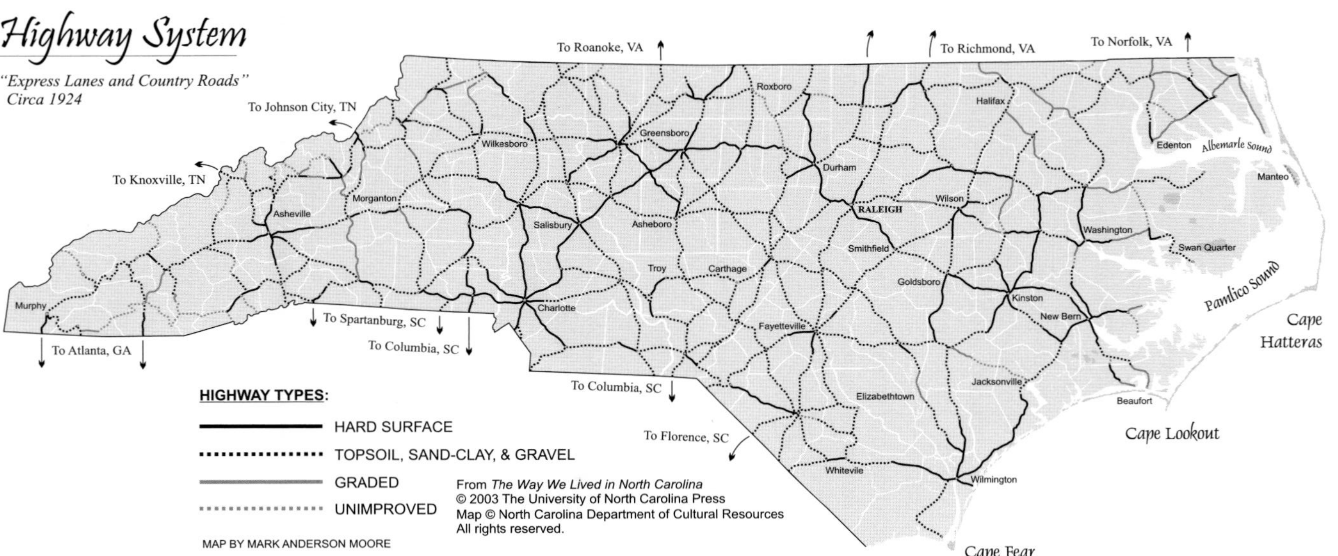

Figure 14.4 Map, highway system. *Source:* The Way We Lived in North Carolina *© 2003 The University of North Carolina Press Map © North Carolina Department of Cultural Resources.*

Tobacco (Reidsville), Lorillard (Greensboro), Liggett & Myers (Durham), and R. J. Reynolds (Winston-Salem), all located in North Carolina—accounted for a large portion of manufacturing wealth in the state. Although employing only one-tenth of North Carolina's workforce by the 1930s, tobacco manufacturing produced more than a third of the entire value of the state's manufacturing.

The boom in tobacco manufacturing made Winston-Salem and Durham nationally important. In addition, the presence of a large black labor force in tobacco factories sustained growing African American communities in both cities. In 1925, sociologist E. Franklin Frazier described Durham as the "capital of the black middle class." Frazier noted the existence of an "outstanding group of colored capitalists who have entered the second generation of business enterprise." Especially important was that Durham became a center of a black-run insurance industry. John Merrick, born a slave in Sampson County, worked as a brick mason and barber and succeeded in accumulating capital, which he used to start an insurance business, in partnership with Durham's first black physician, Aaron M. Moore, and Charles C. Spaulding. Eventually the company became, beginning in 1898, the North Carolina Mutual Life Insurance Company, what Frazier called the "greatest monument to Negroes' business enterprise in America."[7]

Other manufacturing enterprises also expanded after World War I. Furniture making and finishing matured into a major industry, with North Carolina becoming a national leader in furniture manufacturing during the 1920s. In 1921, High Point opened the Southern Furniture Exposition Building, and, with display space of 440,000 square feet, it soon became the third largest furniture mart in the nation. By 1923, High Point, with thirty-four furniture factories, had grown into a major center of manufacturing; the population of the city grew to about 37,000 people during the 1920s, a growth rate of 156 percent. The better-established textile industry also underwent drastic changes in the 1920s. During the depression of the 1890s, North Carolina cotton textiles had not only survived but had grown into a position of dominance, and the shift of textile manufacturing from New England to the South accelerated. The large Cone Mills operations, for example, had been founded in Greensboro during the depths of hard times in the mid-1890s. During the World War I boom, the production of unfinished cotton textiles continued to shift south, with the heart of the industry in the Carolinas. In the 1920s, the cotton textile industry experienced its most significant decade of reorganization, as producers integrated and amalgamated into larger operations. The most successful textile manufacturer that expanded through amalgamation was Burlington Mills, which textile magnate J. Spencer Love founded in 1924. Acquiring smaller mills, Burlington eventually became the largest textile manufacturer in the world. Cannon Mills, organized in Kannapolis in Cabarrus County, became a major manufacturer of sheets and towels. Consolidation in the industry continued throughout the 1920s and 1930s.

The Southern Renaissance and the University of North Carolina

After World War I, North Carolina developed into one of the South's leading centers of intellectual and cultural life, participating in what contemporaries and historians have since called a "Southern Renaissance." In a torrent of letters, southern novelists, poets, journalists, and public commentators began a flood of writing unprecedented in southern history. Appearing in state newspapers such as the *Greensboro Daily News*, the *Elizabeth City Independent*, and the *Raleigh News and Observer*, the work of editorialists such as Gerald W. Johnson, William O. Saunders, and Nell Battle Lewis exposed North Carolina's parochialism. Lewis regularly wrote columns in the *News and Observer* about women, agricultural conditions, and educational backwardness.

What united this diverse phenomenon was an embrace of modernism in literature, arts, journalism, and history. Modernists believed in the application of scientific, verifiable, and systematic methods as a tool in comprehending the behavior of humans and their society. The "moderns" possessed a faith in the ability of secular methods and science to determine the source of social problems. Modernism arose partly out of the revolution in higher education in Europe and the United States, and, not surprisingly, was closely associated with the rise of the University of North Carolina (UNC) as the leading public university in the South. The first public university to open its doors in the United States, UNC had long languished in a parochial and money-starved status. That changed when energetic UNC presidents, beginning with Edward Kidder Graham, who took the position in 1913, transformed the campus into an engine of modernization and revitalization.

After Graham's death during the influenza epidemic of 1918, Harry Woodburn Chase, a northern-born psychologist, was inaugurated president in 1920, determined to remake UNC into a modern university. He recruited leading scholars to help accomplish the task. Rural sociologist Eugene Cunningham Branson arrived in 1912 and founded a new department of rural social economics, which provided a platform for a program of education extension and rural improvement. Edgar Wallace Knight joined the UNC faculty in 1919 and helped to make UNC's School of Education a leading center. But the single most important figure was Georgia-born sociologist Howard Washington Odum, who came to Chapel Hill in early 1920, recruited to the university by Chase. Odum's arrival turned UNC into a social-scientific center of efforts to study social problems in the South. Head of UNC's Sociology Department, Odum also led UNC's newly established School of Public Welfare. Odum moved during the 1920s to apply modern social science to the study of longstanding problems, and he and his students discussed agriculture, labor, and race relations with remarkable candor. In 1924, Odum further expanded his reach by establishing the Institute for Research in the

Social Sciences, which, funded by the Laura Spelman Rockefeller Memorial (which was part of the Rockefeller philanthropic empire), supported the work of Odum's graduate students and faculty disciples.

Odum and his followers scrutinized various aspects of North Carolina life during the 1920s and 1930s. From the Institute came reports from Arthur Raper about lynching, Harriet L. Herring about mill life, and Thomas J. Woofter, Jr., about African-American folk life. Odum also shaped the study of southern history, and UNC historians—graduate students and faculty alike—began a detailed and candid examination of the South's distinctive past. In the 1930s, Odum's approach to studying social problems—one that urged students of the South to produce detailed, frank, and community-based studies of social structures and political economy—fell into what became known as the "Southern Regionalist" school of sociology.

In 1922, Odum extended his reach by establishing *Social Forces*, a journal intended to communicate, to a general audience, this new view of southern society. The purpose of *Social Forces*, wrote Odum, was to enable democracy to become more effective in "unequal places"—the many places in the South where poverty was overcoming everything else. Odum emphasized social scientific data collection and empiricism, "essential facts and broad bases upon which objective programs may be based." The purpose of *Social Forces* was to provide a "clear-thinking" guide to purposeful action by supplying a social-scientific basis for southern social policy.[8] Odum favored what he called a "frank, honest, scientific, stock-taking of ourselves, giving full recognition to strong points but also to weak points and deficiencies." He opposed the anti-intellectualism that gripped North Carolinians and southerners; this intellectual intolerance, he said, represented a "coercive, intolerant, reactionary religious and intellectual tyranny."[9] *Social Forces* attracted a wide readership: within two years of its founding, it boasted 1,700 subscribers, and it offered a combination of academic pieces and Odum's editorializing to this wide audience.

There were limits, however, to Odum's Southern Regionalism. His approach to race, though advanced for its day, did not seriously question white supremacy, locally or regionally. Odum's 1910 doctoral dissertation, "Social and Mental Traits of the Negro," was overtly racist in its assumptions, and one of his major conclusions was that whites and blacks had "different abilities and potentialities." Odum's views on race changed after World War I, and during the 1920s he sponsored folklore and anthropological studies of black communities across the South. Moreover, he participated in the activities of the Commission on Interracial Cooperation, founded in 1919 with a mission to improve race relations through increased contacts and cooperation across the color line. Yet Odum rarely questioned the premises of segregation, and he doubted the wisdom of efforts by civil-rights activists to change the system. Even as late as the 1950s, Odum continued to wonder about the effectiveness of openly challenging Jim Crow. He retained a faith in southern whites' ability to change the system from within, though events driven by those outside the old power base would soon challenge that faith.[10]

Eugenics and New Racial Policies

In 1922, the commissioner of the state board of charities and public welfare, Kate Burr Johnson, reported to the legislature about the social welfare system in North Carolina. Of prime importance to Johnson was a new effort to identify "weak" and "mentally unfit" members of society whom she claimed were genetically predisposed to poverty, crime, and immorality. The "undesirable elements of society, the delinquent, the defective and dependent," Johnson said, were "parasites—voluntary or involuntary—on the body social and politic."[11]

This statement reflects a dark side in Progressive-Era social reform, the emergence and widespread interest in eugenics, a pseudoscience of genetic management. Eugenics encouraged efforts to separate supposedly genetically "defective" people such as the poor and mentally ill, often to institutionalize them, and even to sterilize them by force. In 1924, the Virginia legislature enacted a sterilization statute that permitted the forced sterilization of persons deemed to be "feebleminded," including the "insane, idiotic, imbecilic, or epileptic." In 1927, the Supreme Court, in *Buck v. Bell*, upheld Virginia's law. "Three generations of imbeciles," wrote Justice Oliver Wendell Holmes, Jr., "are enough." Nationally, nearly 60,000 sterilizations had occurred by the 1970s.[12] Thirty states eventually created laws providing for involuntary sterilization on their books. By 1957, the most aggressive of these programs was that of Virginia, with 6,683 sterilizations, followed by North Carolina, with 4,472, and Georgia, with 2,490.

In February 1929, on the heels of the *Buck v. Bell* case, the North Carolina General Assembly enacted legislation authorizing state institutions, either charitable or penal, to require the "asexualization or sterilization" of "mentally defective or feeble-minded inmates" if such was deemed to be in the public interest.[13] But the 1929 law provided for no clear process for appeal, and on this basis the state supreme court declared it unconstitutional in February 1933. Within months, the General Assembly enacted new, much more specific legislation establishing an appeals process in a five-person Eugenics Board that approved and oversaw sterilizations. Significantly, the new law did not require that the persons declared as deficient be patients at state penal and charitable institutions. North Carolina had already created a system of public welfare that included county departments of public welfare; these could petition for sterilizations of non-institutionalized clients. With the Eugenics Board rarely denying requests, even in cases calling for forced sterilization, the 1933 law greatly accelerated the activities of the state's eugenics program.

Not all of the sterilizations conducted under this program were, however, involuntary; some women and a few men sought sterilization as a means of birth control. In an era in which methods of controlling pregnancy were limited, some poor North Carolinians took advantage of the program for their own reasons. According to a recent study, of the approximately 8,000 petitions for sterilization between 1937 and 1966, 468 of them were instances of voluntary sterilization—that is, either endorsed by patients, or sought out by them. The large majority of those opting for voluntary sterilization, about 70 percent of the total, were black women, suggesting that their options for birth control were even more limited than those for white women. In most instances, those who requested sterilization had already borne children but sought to limit family size.[14]

Especially prominent as the most aggressive advocates of the eugenics programs were women, many of them social workers or their supporters among women's clubs. A network of social reforming women—almost entirely white middle class—pushed this program as a leading feature of their efforts to improve society. North Carolina was among the first in the South to develop a state-supported social welfare through the North Carolina Board of Charities and Public Welfare, which was established in 1869 but altered to include "public welfare" in 1917. Kate Burr Johnson served as commissioner of public welfare beginning in 1921, becoming the first female state welfare commissioner in the nation.

Johnson, who was born in Morganton, became involved in welfare activities through participation in women's clubs. Serving as president of the Raleigh Woman's Club, Johnson became president of the North Carolina Federation of Women's Clubs between 1917 and 1919. Between 1919 and 1921, she directed child welfare for the state and was appointed commissioner of the Board of Charities and Public Welfare, serving in that post between 1921 and 1930. Over the course of her career, Johnson became an insistent advocate for the professionalization of social work, and she helped to reorganize state activities. Among her most important efforts included those associated with eugenics.

Under Johnson and after her, North Carolina's sterilization program became among the most ambitious in the nation. Continuing until 1975, it resulted in the sterilization of more than 7,000 people, a large portion of whom were women. Most were adults, though some were children who were sterilized despite parents' opposition. Both whites and blacks were sterilized, though over time the racial proportions of the program changed. Before the 1950s, the sterilization program targeted working-class white women; between 1929 and 1936, for example, only 17 percent of those treated were black. This was so because sterilization focused especially on genetically "inadequate" whites who threatened the purity of the race; sterilization was seen as a benefit, and black patients received less attention. But during the 1960s, the program sterilized more African American women. Disproportionately so, by this time most of those sterilized were poor women without legal protection or advice. The reasons for sterilizations conducted during the entire period 1929–68 included feeble-mindedness (71 percent), mental disease (24 percent), and epilepsy (5 percent).

Radio, Music, and Cultural Change

In the 1920s and 1930s, North Carolinians began to experience far-reaching cultural changes that continued full force into the remainder of the twentieth century. These changes were most apparent in the spread of radically new forms of media and musical entertainment. In each of these areas, new secular cultural forces reached into the lives of Tar Heels.

Radio began in North Carolina in 1920 when three men, Fred W. Laxton of General Electric, Frank L. Butler of Westinghouse Electric, and Earle J. Gluck of Southern Bell, formed a partnership and started broadcasting from Laxton's house in Charlotte. In 1921, they obtained an experimental radio broadcast licensing from the U.S. Department of Commerce. The next year the trio organized WBT radio, which began broadcasting with 100 watts from the eighth floor of the Independence Building in downtown Charlotte. In 1929, WBT became part of the CBS national radio network; by 1933, WBT was broadcasting with 50,000 watts. In Raleigh, WFBQ (later renamed WRCO) went on the air in 1924. In 1927, the Durham Life Insurance Company bought the station and changed its call letters to WPTF (for "We Protect the Family"). Broadcasting from Cary, by the 1940s, WPTF, like WBT, had a 50,000-watt transmitter and was affiliated with a national network, in WPTF's case, NBC.

Increasingly, radio came under corporate business control. In Greensboro, the Jefferson Standard Life Insurance Company, first organized in 1907, expanded into broadcasting when it purchased WBIG. In 1934, Joseph Bryan, the son-in-law of Jefferson Standard president Julian Price, convinced Price to move into broadcasting by organizing the Jefferson Standard Broadcasting Company, which expanded programming in sports, news, and entertainment.

The spread of radio offered an entirely new form of entertainment to people across the state, and by the 1930s one could find radio sets in the homes of most North Carolinians. The broadcasting of sporting events, such as college football, baseball, and boxing, became common. Radio shows featuring live music were especially well liked. Radio made Rocky Mount native James King Kern "Kay" Kyser a popular big-band leader, and in 1938 an estimated 20 million listeners tuned in to hear his nationally syndicated show, the "Kollege of Musical Knowledge." Kyser, the "Ol' Professor," appeared on the set wearing a mortar board and gown to introduce numerous musical acts. Other radio programming provided a new cultural market for North Carolina music that was

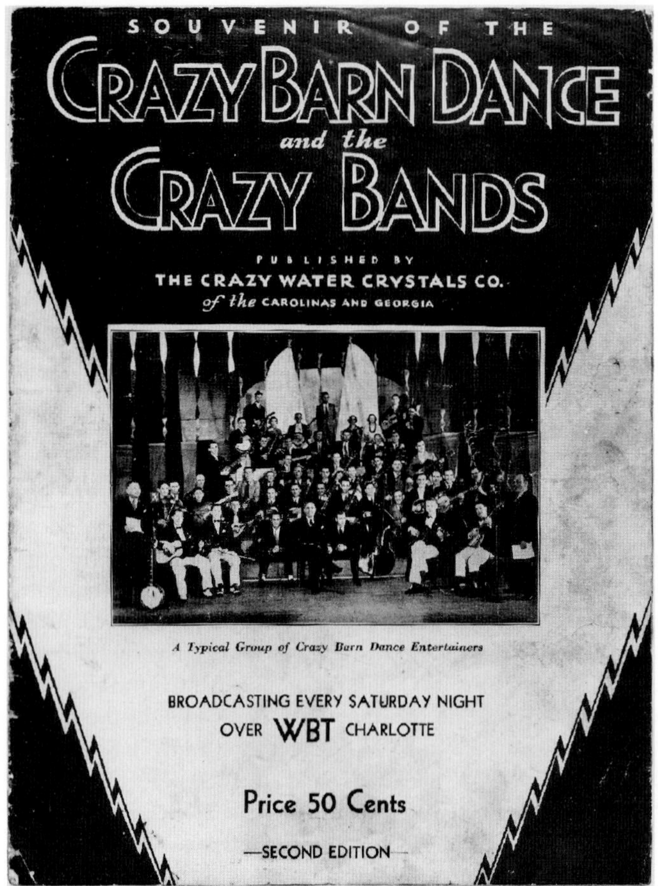

Figure 14.5 WBT radio, Charlotte. *Source: btmememories.com, courtesy of Jim Scancarelli.*

emerging in the twentieth century. White and black gospel music, the popularity of which had spread with the sharp growth in the number of evangelical and Pentecostal churches, was routinely aired on the radio. So, too, was bluegrass, a new musical genre that combined folk traditions with heavy banjo playing, first made popular in the 1940s by performers such as Bill Monroe and Earl Scruggs.

A distinctive form of African American music that emerged in the first half of the twentieth century was the blues, specifically what came to be known as the Piedmont Blues. In contrast to the blues of the Mississippi Delta, the Piedmont Blues possesses a style of guitar playing that relies on a steady, driving bass line (from the lower strings) played simultaneously with the melody (relegated to the higher strings). The songs of the Piedmont Blues tend to have a quicker,

Figure 14.6 Sonny Terry (1911–86) and Brownie McGhee (1915–96). Lincoln Folk Festival, July 24, 1971. *Source: Estate of Keith Morris/Redferns/Getty Images.*

more upbeat tempo than their Mississippi counterpart, but both forms of the blues express in ways that words alone cannot the African American experience, often one of dispossession, loneliness, and heartbreak. Although it had rural roots, the blues soon spread to urban markets, where it was played to enthusiastic city audiences in clubs along Durham's Pettigrew Street as well as in private clubs and at parties. Durham, with its tobacco factories and a large black working class, became a major blues center in the 1930s and 1940s. Among the most important blues artists playing in Durham in this era include Floyd Council, Richard and William Trice, and Alden "Tarheel Slim" Bunn. Others include Blind Gary Davis and Blind Boy Fuller, both of whom became well known in the state and nationally. The legendary blues duo of Sonny Terry and Brownie McGhee also got their start in the blues scene of urban North Carolina.

The Anti-Evolution Controversy

For much of the twentieth century, a tension existed between two North Carolinas: one, urban and cosmopolitan, oriented toward the social science of Howard Odum and UNC and connected to modernizing tendencies around the country; the other, inward-looking, traditional in its values, and clinging doggedly to longstanding rural and small-town values. After World War I, these two worlds, modernist and traditionalist, clashed repeatedly in North Carolina, and a struggle for the hearts and minds of the people of the state ensued. During the 1920s, Chapel Hill's intellectual renaissance contrasted with the strong reassertion of traditionalism in much of the rest of the state with the emergence of a powerful anti-evolution movement that drew on the strong support of many North Carolinians.

During World War I, a fundamentalist movement emerged on the national level composed of conservative evangelicals aroused by the spirit of nationalism that the war evoked. These conservative evangelicals reasserted the traditional authority of Protestantism on two fronts: they wanted to prohibit the teaching of the Darwinian theory of human evolution in public schools, and they sought to purge modernist interpretation and theology from their denominations. In 1920, the Mississippi evangelist and fundamentalist Thomas Theodore Martin attacked William L. Poteat in a series of articles that appeared in the *Western Recorder*, a Baptist publication appearing in Mississippi. Poteat, president of the Southern Baptist Wake Forest College, was a zoologist with a Ph.D. from the University of Berlin who had popularized the notion that it was possible to reconcile modern science and traditional Protestantism. Poteat taught evolution in his biology courses at Wake, and he became a nationally known supporter of reconciling religious faith and modern science. Claiming that Poteat belonged to a "fatal, Bible-warping, soul-destroying" conspiracy against traditional faith,[15] Martin objected to Poteat's theology, which was sympathetic to modernists and their conception of God and humankind. Martin especially objected to Poteat's views on human evolution. Although Poteat maintained sufficient prestige among North Carolina Baptists to withstand Martin's onslaught, fundamentalists mobilized across the state during the 1920s—this at a time when revivalism swept through small towns and rural communities and conservative evangelicals demanded the restoration of traditional cultural values.

The clash between modernism and traditionalism burst out into the open in January 1925, when two articles appeared in *Social Forces* that roused fundamentalists to action. The first was a piece by book-review editor Harry Barnes, which satirized Christianity and Victorianism; the second was a longer article by sociologist Luther L. Bernard, which examined the beginnings of religious faith. The publication of the *Social Forces* articles, which conservative evangelicals took as arrogant and offensive, coincided with the culmination of the anti-evolutionists' campaign in North Carolina. Elsewhere in the United States, anti-evolutionists tried to uproot the teaching of Darwinian biology from public schools. Charles Darwin's theory of the evolution of species, including all plants and animals, maintained that random processes in the chaotic, indeterminist world of nature—genetic mutation and the ability of species to adapt to their environment—explained the development of plant and animal life. The Darwinian worldview appeared to leave little room for divine creation or control of the universe, and anti-evolutionists focused on the teaching of evolution as a symbol of their overall objections to secularism. As public schools grew in size and importance in the socialization of American youth, moreover, anti-evolutionists saw their battleground. Across the nation, but especially in the South, Protestant fundamentalists in the mid-1920s launched efforts to ban, by law, the teaching of evolutionary theory and Darwinian biology in public schools and universities. In Tennessee, the legislature thus enacted a law in March 1925 forbidding the teaching of any theory that denied the biblical story of Genesis. Similarly, in North Carolina anti-evolutionists enjoyed considerable support. In January 1924, Gov. Cameron Morrison declared that he opposed the use of any textbook that printed a "picture of a monkey and a man on the same page," and, at his urging, the state textbook commission rejected two textbooks because they included discussions of evolution.[16]

Anti-evolutionists expanded their campaign in January 1925, when Hoke County's David Scott Poole introduced a bill opposing the teaching of Darwin by "any official or teacher in the State, paid wholly or in part by taxation, to teach or permit to be taught, as a fact, either Darwinism or any other evolutionary hypothesis that links man in blood relationship with any lower form or life."[17]

In the Poole bill, anti-evolutionists had focused their attention on uprooting secularism at UNC, the state's leading public university. Poole's resolution became deadlocked in the House Committee on Education, which in February 1925 reported unfavorably but nonetheless sent the bill to the house floor for a general vote. On February 19, 1925, after lengthy debate, the house defeated the bill by a vote of 67 to 46. One of the more vocal supporters of UNC in the house was Sam Ervin, later elected to the US Senate. Anti-evolutionists did not give up so easily, however, and during the mid-1920s organizations such as the Anti-Evolution League of North Carolina and the North Carolina Bible League were emboldened by the successes of opponents of modern science elsewhere in the South. In January 1927, the North Carolina Bible League came to Raleigh to deliver a petition with 10,000 signatures demanding the enactment of legislation banning the teaching of evolution. After fierce conflict in the 1927 legislative session, another anti-evolution bill sponsored by Poole failed in committee, and efforts by fundamentalists died thereafter.

From Gastonia to General Strike

By the close of World War I, North Carolina textile manufacturers had triumphed in a competitive struggle with New England producers, but now they confronted new challenges. With growth came new consumer preferences; Americans generally wore less clothing and lighter-weight apparel. Women opted for shorter hemlines and largely abandoned cotton stockings in favor of stockings made of synthetic rayon. All this meant a decrease in demand for cotton products. The rise of synthetics reflected a changed market for textile products, while significant competition from overseas cotton producers in Asia created pressures on prices and profitability. Therefore, on the heels of a boom during the war, the textile industry in North Carolina suffered a severe postwar recession followed by a decade of cutbacks seeking to reduce costs. Now managers of textile mills adopted newly minted corporate tactics that involved the reduction of the labor force combined with devising ways to raise worker productivity. Owners and management at textile mills employed new methods of welfare capitalism in the mill villages: under a cloak of sociological expertise, managers tried to supervise the private lives of workers. But mill managers' main objective remained their desire to reduce costs and remain competitive.

In an industry-wide shakeout, smaller operations did not survive, and the textile companies that came to dominate the sector were larger operations, such as Burlington Industries, which J. Spencer Love had transformed into the largest textile company in the world. Large textile operations were even more cost conscious, a mindset that led to the implementation of the hated "stretch out," in which workers were required to tend more machines for the same pay. The stretch out was the worst of several measures managers imposed on textile workers, who grew markedly disgruntled during the late 1920s and 1930s, among the most confrontational years in labor/management history. The tense equilibrium that had come to characterize the mill villages of North Carolina was broken wide open by a period of unprecedented labor violence. In June 1929, textile workers openly revolted with strikes at Marion, in the western North Carolina foothills, and at Gastonia, in the heart of the textile belt, just north of the South Carolina border.

In Gastonia, cotton mills had sprung up during the post-Civil War period because of the town's proximity to power provided by the Catawba and South Fork Rivers and, after the 1870s, easy access to railroad transportation. Gastonia attracted workers to the mills from farms of the Piedmont and Carolina hill country, and after the Civil War a profusion of small mills dotted the Gaston County landscape. By World War I, these smaller mills had given way to larger, consolidated enterprises in which workers were strictly segregated into mill villages that ringed the town's outside perimeter, with housing, stores, churches, and schools provided by mill management.

In the 1920s, Gastonia's mill-village paternalism turned sour, as management made concerted attempts to cut costs and workers objected to the introduction of the stretch out and the added pressure on workers that came with it. Gaston County, North Carolina, which by the end of the decade comprised more than 100 mills and 25,000 workers, lay at the center of the state's textile industry. Beginning in 1919, the county's largest textile plant, the Loray Mill, was taken over by a northern company, the Jenckes Spinning Company of Rhode Island, which in 1923 merged with the Manville Company. The Loray Mill employed workers who had recently immigrated from farms and villages; in its large operations, few shreds remained of traditional paternalism. Beginning in 1927, the Loray Mill cut its workforce from 3,500 to 2,200 and slashed

Figure 14.7 Exterior view of Cannon Mills, 1920s. *Source: North Carolina Collection, University of North Carolina Library at Chapel Hill.*

wages by 25–50 percent. The situation at Loray became desperate from the point of view of workers, who were primed for radical protest. In a spontaneous protest on March 5, 1928, fifty weavers walked off the job, and later that year workers marched through downtown Gastonia to protest the practices of mill management. Neither protest had much impact. Aggrieved workers discovered an effective vehicle for their protest with the arrival of union organizer Fred Beal and the National Textile Workers Union (NTWU) in early 1929. Even though the NTWU was affiliated with the Communist Party of America, industrial workers found its rejection of the system of industrial capitalism appealing.

In April 1929, the Loray workers went on strike, and management responded, with the cooperation of local authorities, by summoning the state militia to protect the use of replacement workers (derided by strikers as "scabs") and to suppress the strike. With a strike led by a Communist union, class tensions in Gastonia worsened. "This strike is a first shot in a battle which will be heard around the world," said a Communist publication, much to the horror of most of Gastonia's and the state's political leaders. "It will prove as important in transforming the social and political life of this country as the Civil War itself." Strongly militant against any form of Communism, local authorities banned parades, and when workers attempted to march in late April they were met by a brutal police response. Soon managers began to fire striking workers and evict them and their families from mill-owned housing.

Especially prominent among the strikers were young female workers. "If Gastonia has never realized that militant women were within its bounds," wrote a *Charlotte Observer* reporter, "it certainly knows it now." The reporter noted that the strike rallies had attracted numerous women in their "gay Easter frocks and a few with spring coats."[18] Ella May Wiggins, a legendary strike leader and balladeer, was originally from eastern Tennessee but moved to work in Piedmont textile mills, where she became a single mother of nine children. In 1929, Wiggins, a maverick who was already known as fiercely independent, became one of the union leaders. Wiggins sang about working conditions, and the strike became legendary. "We leave our homes in the morning/We kiss our children goodbye," went the lyrics to her "Mill Mother's Lament," "While we slave for the bosses/Our children scream and cry."[19]

As the strikers evicted from mill housing established a tent colony and local authorities allied themselves with the mill's management, tensions heightened. Intent on crushing the strike, the Gastonia police force invaded the strikers' tent colony on June 7, 1929, but the workers resisted the onslaught. In the ensuing melee, shots were fired from both sides: Gastonia police chief Orville F. Aderholt was fatally wounded and four police officers were injured. The response of Gastonia townsfolk was swift. Some seventy strikers were rounded up by vigilante mobs; the strikers' tent colony was destroyed. Days later, 5,000 townspeople attended Chief Aderholt's funeral. Fred Beal fled the scene and was arrested in Spartanburg, South Carolina; meanwhile calls went up for the trial and execution of him and other strike leaders. Between June and September 1929, a reign of terror prevailed in Gastonia as freedom of assembly was suspended, union organizers were jailed or expelled, and union property was dynamited.

The Gastonia strikers became internationally known, as the Communist Party represented the strike and its suppression as a class struggle against capitalist tyranny. In August 1929, Beal and other strike leaders were tried for murder, and, after a trial in Charlotte, a mistrial resulted. In the retrial, Beal and three other defendants were convicted and received long prison sentences. The violence in Gastonia continued, and in September 1929 Ella May Wiggins was shot and murdered by an angry mob while on her way to a union rally. No one was ever tried for her killing. While on appeal, Beal and his codefendants fled to the Soviet Union. Subsequently disaffected with what he found in the Soviet system, Beal returned to the United States in 1942 and served his term in prison.

But the labor troubles of the Carolina Piedmont did not disappear with Beal's departure. As workers grew more aggrieved with the onset of the Great Depression—and the disappointing results of the New Deal—they again turned to strikes. In 1934, the National Textile Workers Union (NTWU) organized a general strike affecting the entire textile industry from Maine to Alabama, with the epicenter in the Carolina Piedmont. In September 1934, "flying squadrons" of union workers traveled, caravan style, in cars and trucks, sweeping through North Carolina to urge fellow workers to join the strikers. According to some estimates, as many as 85,000 of the state's 110,000 textile workers participated, and in some areas, such as Gaston County, about 90 percent of workers struck. But the union failed to shut down the mills completely. On September 5, 1934, Gov. J. C. B. Ehringhaus called out the National Guard, and the troops, along with private detectives hired by the mills, protected strikebreakers as they entered and worked in the mills. There were instances of violence, including a bombing, supposedly the work of strikers, in Burlington on September 14 that resulted in arrests of the local union leadership. By the end of September the strike had collapsed, and employers succeeded in laying off union leaders and preventing any further inroads by labor organizers.

World War I and the 1920s ushered in many changes for North Carolinians, but the eruption of bitter conflict between the industrial working class and management in the state's textile industry clouded the future. Meanwhile, the rise of Protestant fundamentalism suggested a widespread, popular resentment of modernization, especially the dominance of secularism over religious authority. The clash between modernizers and traditionalists became fully pronounced in North Carolina during the 1920s, and during the end of the decade it coincided with a larger economic collapse that came with the Great Depression. During the 1930s and 1940s, the state faced more changes that would come with the New Deal and World War II.

Notes

1 Paul Luebke, *Tar Heel Politics 2000* (Chapel Hill: University of North Carolina Press, 1998).

2 Quoted in Alex Mathews Arnett, *Claude Kitchin and the Wilson War Policies* (Boston: Little, Brown, and Company, 1937), p. 229.

3 Archibald Henderson, *North Carolina Women in the World War* (Raleigh, NC: North Carolina Literary and Historical Association, 1920), p. 4.

4 Quoted in Harry Wilson McKown, Jr., "Roads and Reform: The Good Roads Movement in North Carolina, 1885–1921," M.A. thesis, University of North Carolina at Chapel Hill, 1972, p. 1.

5 Robert E. Ireland, "Prison Reform, Road Building, and Southern Progressivism: Joseph Hyde Pratt and the Campaign for 'Good Roads and Good Men,'" *North Carolina Historical Review*, LXVIII (April 1991): 131.

6 McKown, "Roads and Reform," p. 32.

7 E. Franklin Frazier, "Durham: Capital of the Black Middle Class," in Alain Locke, ed., *The New Negro: An Interpretation* (New York: Albert and Charles Boni, 1925), pp. 333–35.

8 Morton Sosna, *In Search of the Silent South: Southern Liberals and the Race Issue* (New York: Columbia University Press, 1977), pp. 45–46.

9 Daniel Joseph Singal, *The War Within: From Victorian to Modernist Thought in the South, 1919–1945* (Chapel Hill: University of North Carolina Press, 1983), p. 123.

10 Sosna, *Silent South,* p. 45.

11 Quoted in Anna L. Krome-Lukens, "A Great Blessing to Defective Humanity: Women and the Eugenics Movement in North Carolina, 1910–1940," M.A. thesis, University of North Carolina at Chapel Hill, 2009, p. 2.

12 *Buck v. Bell* 274 U.S. 200.

13 *North Carolina General Assembly Session Laws of 1929,* Section 1, Chapter 34, pp. 28–29.

14 Johanna Schoen, "Between Choice and Sterilization: Women and Sterilization in North Carolina, 1929–1975," *Journal of Women's History* 13 (Spring 2001): 132–56; Johanna Schoen, *Choice and Coercion: Birth Control, Sterilization, and Abortion in Public Health and Welfare* (Chapel Hill: University of North Carolina Press, 2005).

15 Willard B. Gatewood, Jr., *Preachers, Pedagogues, and Politicians: The Evolution Controversy in North Carolina, 1920–1927* (Chapel Hill: University of North Carolina Press, 1966), p. 32.

16 "Governor Vetoes Evolution and Board Cuts Out Books," *Raleigh News and Observer,* January 24, 1924.

17 North Carolina General Assembly, "Joint Resolution Restricting the Teaching of Darwinism in the Public Schools of North Carolina," 1925.

18 John A. Salmond, *Gastonia, 1929: The Story of the Loray Mill Strike* (Chapel Hill: University of North Carolina Press, 1995), p. 31.

19 Ibid., p. 62.

15

Depression, New Deal, and World War II

With the onset of the Great Depression, North Carolinians confronted the most serious economic crisis in their history. During the 1930s, the collapse of banking, industry, and agriculture affected virtually every aspect of life. Like other Americans, Tar Heels confronted an epidemic of bank failures, farm and home foreclosures, high unemployment, and thousands of people in desperate straits. The election of Franklin Delano Roosevelt as president—the first Democratic president since Woodrow Wilson—brought an attempt to confront the economic collapse, and the advent of the New Deal shook the political system, creating tensions and reconfiguring political alliances. Nonetheless, the New Deal helped to set in motion a series of forces that would transform North Carolina and the rest of the South. So did the advent of World War II, the occasion of the most extensive civilian mobilization in United States history.

The Great Depression

Following the Great Stock Market Crash of October 1929, the American economy went into a tailspin, with collapsing farm income, high employment, and, ultimately, a general financial collapse and a banking crisis. Between 1929 and 1933, some 215 North Carolina banks failed, and so severe was the financial crisis that the legislature empowered the state banking commissioner, Gurney P. Hood, to slow withdrawals. Elsewhere in the nation, governors were declaring bank holidays, suspending the operations of banks in order to slow the crisis by precluding "runs" on banks. On March 6–8, Gov. J. C. B. Ehringhaus declared a bank holiday in North Carolina, the last governor in the nation to do so. This coincided with President Roosevelt's declaration of a national bank holiday after his inauguration on March 4, 1933.

The financial crisis tore into the agricultural economy, as farmers found it all but impossible to meet the heavy debt obligations that they had incurred during the previous decade of expansion. Many of them fell victim to mortgage

North Carolina: Change and Tradition in a Southern State, Second Edition. William A. Link.

foreclosures—losing their homes, farms, or both—and their inability to pay their debts reflected a collapse of crop prices, which declined by about a third between 1930 and 1933. For example, the price of cotton was 20.2 cents per pound in 1927; in 1931, it was a mere 5.97 cents. Total income for North Carolina cotton farmers declined from $62.4 million in 1929 to $19.5 million in 1932. Income for tobacco farmers similarly collapsed, mostly because overseas demand for American leaf—two-thirds of which was grown in North Carolina—slipped sharply, as exports dropped by about 40 percent between 1930 and 1932. Prices dropped from around 20 cents per pound in 1927 to a low of a little more than 8 cents per pound in 1931. The value of the tobacco crop, because of low prices, declined from $88.6 million in 1929 to $34.8 million three years later. Especially hard hit were tobacco farmers of eastern North Carolina. In Nash County, the heart of the tobacco country, some 3,500 of the county's 5,280 tobacco farmers suffered foreclosures in 1930. A wave of bank and building-and-loan association closings gripped the state in the early 1930s. Between 1930 and 1933, some 194 banks failed, most of which had been closely associated with the farm economy, and depositors lost a total of $103 million in hard-earned savings.

Because of the popularity of smoking, tobacco manufacturing remained "depression proof," and most of the 150,000 tobacco-factory workers in the state kept their jobs. Amazingly, the Big Four tobacco manufacturers reported record profits during the 1930s, and in January 1933 the chairman of R. J. Reynolds, S. Clay Williams, crowed that the company was in the "strongest financial condition in its history."[1] Utilities such as electric power and telephone service reported continued strong profits and employment, as did the Vick Chemical Company of Greensboro. Vick introduced two new products, Vicks Nose-drops and Vicks Medicated Cough Drops, in the early 1930s, and the strong sales of these new products sustained the company's profitability throughout the Depression.

Other industries were not so fortunate. Furniture manufacturing in the state declined in value from $53.6 million in 1929 to $26.6 million three years later. The Great Depression also ravaged North Carolina's textiles. The value of cotton textiles dropped from $317 million in 1929 to $190 million in 1933, and three-quarters of the textile firms in North Carolina were losing money in 1932. Especially in furniture and textiles, factory closings and layoffs became common, with most factories on a reduced workweek. During 1930, industrial unemployment tripled, with an estimated 100,000 out of work by the following year. By 1932, more than 144,000 heads of family were on relief in North Carolina, about 25 percent of the population. By the early 1930s, the Depression had brought a terrible crisis to North Carolina. A newspaper editor visiting the state in January 1930 described a "trail of poverty" he had witnessed in the northeastern part of the state. There was "little money passing, taxes are not being paid to any great extent, mortgages and property liens are being foreclosed in greater volume than in many a year, ... pauper lists are swelled, and local charity organizations are doing a record business." These observations were not an overstatement, as virtually every dimension of economic activity suffered.

The ability of the North Carolina state government to respond to the economic crisis was limited. In 1929, Gov. O. Max Gardner announced a "live at home" program that urged farmers to reduce the production of cotton and tobacco crops, thus reducing supply and raising prices. As part of this program, Gardner envisioned that North Carolina farmers could become more self-sufficient in producing food and raising livestock—and thus produce less of the overabundant cash crops of cotton and tobacco. But the "live at home" plan remained voluntary, and while it may have resulted in higher food production, it did little to raise the rock-bottom farm prices. Gardner opposed mandatory production controls over agriculture, despite rising demands among desperate farmers. Similarly, cotton-textile manufacturing had campaigned in the 1920s for more industry cooperation in setting production quotas and limiting the amount of product on the market. Textile manufacturers organized the Cotton Textile Institute (CTI) in 1926 to encourage limited production and discourage ruinous competition. But the CTI had little effect in checking declining prices, and the drive for industrial stabilization looked in other directions by 1932.

Origins of the New Deal

In response to the Great Depression, Franklin D. Roosevelt, who had been elected president in 1932, advanced sweeping legislation and policy that he announced to the American people as a "New Deal." The first Democrat elected to the White House since Woodrow Wilson, Roosevelt won four terms as president. His New Deal sought to generate recovery in manufacturing, agriculture, banking, and other sectors of the economy. Although the New Deal was diverse and experimental in its approach and proposed remedies, the common theme accompanying all the measures it comprised was the massive intervention of the federal government in areas that previously had been the exclusive preserve of state and local authorities.

During the course of the Depression, the implications of these changes in Washington eventually became apparent in North Carolina. O. Max Gardner, a textile executive from the southwestern Piedmont town of Shelby, had been elected governor in 1928. Gardner succeeded Sen. Furnifold M. Simmons as the kingmaker of North Carolina politics; Simmons lost reelection in the Democratic primary of 1930 after he opposed Democratic presidential nominee Al Smith of New York—and broke party ranks to vote for Republican Herbert Hoover—because Smith was a Roman Catholic. Gardner's political organization—what became known as the "Shelby Dynasty"—relied on appointments to newly centralized state agencies. Gardner's organization dominated Democratic Party politics in North Carolina from the late 1920s to the late 1940s. The Shelby Dynasty elected a succession of governors that included Gardner, J. C. B. Ehringhaus, and Clyde Hoey (who was Gardner's brother-in-law). All from Shelby with the exception of Ehringhaus (who was from Elizabeth City), these men served as governors of North Carolina consecutively from 1929 to 1941. Gardner constructed a powerful political machine, with a strong, county-based organization, that emphasized businesslike efficiency with support for modernization in education and road building. The Shelby Dynasty represented the political power of the industrialized Piedmont, and it defended the business interests of textile and tobacco manufacturers and banks, as well as strongly opposing labor unions.

As governor, Gardner favored measures to reorganize state government and obtain corporate-style efficiency in organization, management, and budgeting. But the governor was soon forced to confront the economic crisis. The Stock Market Crash of October 1929 made measures more urgent, and, in addition to cutting the state's budget, during the budget crisis Gardner favored the cause of governmental reform combined with efforts to reduce expenditures. In 1929, the Brookings Institution of Washington conducted a comprehensive study of North Carolina government. Its report, issued in 1929, recommended a program of the reorganization of state government and cost cutting, achieved through centralization. In 1931, the General Assembly acted on these recommendations by restructuring the most important agencies of state government, including health, agriculture, and highways. In addition, in a major change, the legislature reorganized the state university system by creating a consolidated University of North Carolina system composed of three campuses: Chapel Hill, Raleigh (North Carolina State), and Greensboro (the women's college and formerly the State Normal and Industrial College, and, after 1919, the North Carolina College for Women).

Its efforts at reorganization notwithstanding, the Depression had a devastating impact on the ability of the North Carolina state government to function. With declining tax revenues, the state had no choice but to respond with a massive cutback in services. By 1932, state employees experienced a 10 percent pay cut. Although Gardner maintained state support for education, public schools and universities suffered. The expansion of road building, in which North Carolina recently had poured millions into the construction of a system of hard-surfaced roads, came to a halt. By 1933, the state, in many respects, was experiencing the worst crisis in its history.

The crisis also affected local government in North Carolina. The growth of governmental expenditures during the 1920s had expanded the state's debt, which rose from $13 million in 1920 to $178 million in 1929. State and local taxes rose nearly 200 percent during the decade, although property taxes as a percentage of all taxes plummeted from 85 percent in 1920 to 60 percent in

1929. As at the state level, the economic crisis placed severe pressure on county governments' ability to pay off their heavy debt burden. As a result of the fiscal crisis, seventy-seven towns and thirty-four of the state's one hundred counties had defaulted by 1932, even as hard-pressed North Carolinians demanded greater relief from property taxes. In 1931, in reorganizing state government, the legislature assumed control of all state roads and guaranteed funding in public schools for a six-month term. Meanwhile, the legislature also reduced property taxes by $12 million, the biggest tax cut in the history of the state, making up for the loss in revenue by increasing levies on corporate income, gasoline, and franchises. In addition, the legislature also enacted a 15 percent ad valorem tax on property. Although, at Gardner's insistence, the legislature refrained from enacting a state sales tax, additional fiscal pressures prompted the passage (after Gardner left office) of a 3 percent sales tax in 1933, the highest such tax in the nation.

These measures reassured lenders who were holding North Carolina's public debt, and unlike many other states in the early years of the Depression, North Carolina kept its state government solvent. But Gardner's fiscal conservatism limited the state's ability to respond to the Depression, and the measures that his administration took involved budget cutting and more regressive taxation. Balancing the budget meant slashing state expenditures, which were reduced by 30 percent between 1930 and 1932. Despite the presence of 100,000 unemployed North Carolinians, along with 20,000 displaced tenants and sharecroppers, the state government did nothing to abate the deprivation of the Depression. Gardner's "live at home" program had little impact on the hardship experienced by the rural masses. Ideologically opposed to a welfare role for state government, Gardner and other North Carolina leaders made little provision for unemployment relief. Late in the Gardner administration, a relief program came instead through federal intervention. Congress enacted the Reconstruction Finance Corporation (RFC) Act in July 1932, which supplied funds for work relief, and in 1932–33 North Carolina received roughly $6 million in RFC funds. Gardner created the Governor's Office of Relief (GOR) to process these appropriations, and by the fall of 1932 nearly 57,000 workers were either employed or received relief, while another 40,000 benefited from RFC farm loans.

The economic crisis had political consequences. For the first time in a generation, the dominant faction of the Democratic Party—by the early 1930s, this was O. Max Gardner and the Shelby Dynasty—experienced voter restiveness. Encouraged by Josephus Daniels's anti-Gardner message in the *Raleigh News and Observer*, in the Democratic primary of 1932 an insurgent candidate for governor, Lt. Gov. Richard T. Fountain, challenged Gardner's handpicked successor, J. C. B. Ehringhaus. Unable to obtain a majority of Democratic votes in the first primary against Fountain, Ehringhaus narrowly won a second primary. In the primary for US senator, former governor Cameron Morrison had been appointed to office after the death of longtime senator Lee Overman in December 1930. Morrison faced Robert "Our Bob" Reynolds, who had no political program except to repeal prohibition. Nonetheless, Reynolds criticized Morrison for having lost touch with ordinary North Carolinians, and, during hard times, for his wealth and elitism. In a standard stump speech, Reynolds described how Morrison rode in a limousine to a Washington, DC, hotel, where he went to eat a caviar breakfast. Reynolds reminded voters that caviar were "fish eggs from Red Russia."[2] Reynolds gained a landslide victory to the US Senate with a 108,000 vote margin.

The New Deal and North Carolina Agriculture and Industry

The New Deal brought an unprecedented expansion of the power of the federal government. The balance of power between individual states and the government became tilted in favor of federal control, and after the 1930s, in most areas of policy, the national government reigned supreme. New Deal officials exerted unprecedented controls and attempted new ones over the economy. To help farmers, the New Deal put governmental controls on the production of crops in an attempt to buoy prices. To help industrial workers, federal policy sponsored cooperation among manufacturers and unionization among workers. For the destitute, the New Deal offered a massive program of relief that employed thousands of North Carolinians and kept the wolf from the door. The restructuring of federal-state relations was especially important in the South, America's poorest region and the scene of pronounced efforts to address basic problems in industry, agriculture, and social welfare.

Congress's adoption of the Agricultural Adjustment Act in May 1933 (cosponsored by Rep. John H. Kerr of North Carolina) marked a historic change in federal agricultural policy. The federal government became committed to increasing farm income, the newly created Agricultural Adjustment Administration (AAA) oversaw voluntary and mandatory controls over crop production that aimed to raise prices and farm income. The AAA cajoled and persuaded farmers to sign contracts in which they agreed to future participation in a program of production quotas; as participants, they paid a processing tax that financed benefit payments, or subsidies, which went to farmers who agreed to reduce their acreage in production. With millions of farmers participating, the AAA promised a radical new experiment in managing agriculture.

In the spring of 1933, AAA officials moved to restrict production by cotton farmers. Looking at bumper crops and large surpluses during the early 1930s and an expected large crop in 1933, the AAA initiated a crash program to persuade a million cotton farmers nationwide to plow under 10 million acres of cotton already under cultivation. In North Carolina, the federal agricultural extension service campaigned to convince the state's 150,000 cotton farmers to destroy much of their crop and join the AAA program with signed contracts. The sign-up campaign represented a huge public-relations effort, which by and large succeeded. Cotton prices rose to nearly 11 cents a pound in 1933, from just over 7 cents a pound a year earlier. In 1934, the program of crop controls in cotton became compulsory with the enactment by Congress of the Bankhead Act; henceforth, farmers who refused to sign up in the AAA program would pay a new tax. In the long term, the AAA's cotton program yielded less successful results, as throughout the 1930s supply continued to exceed demand. Moreover, cotton production in North Carolina and the South had entered a period of permanent decline. In the 1930s, 1940s, and 1950s, the traditional cotton-plantation system, which depended on the crop-lien system, sharecropping, and tenancy, and the impoverishment of the rural masses, was eroding. Thousands of North Carolina cotton farmers moved to towns and cities, joining a general exodus from the cotton South. By encouraging landowners to modernize and reduce cultivation, the AAA did little to arrest this decline and much to encourage it.

The effect of the New Deal on tobacco farming in North Carolina told a different story. Many tobacco growers eagerly signed up for the AAA program; by September 1933, some 95 percent of them had agreed to participate. Negotiating with cigarette manufacturers, the new tobacco growers' association succeeded in raising tobacco prices from 11.6 cents per pound in 1932 to 15.3 cents per pound a year later. The system became compulsory in 1934, when Congress enacted the Kerr-Smith Tobacco Control Act, which imposed taxes as high as 33 percent on growers who had not signed on with the AAA. By the mid-1930s, the basic components of what became known as the "tobacco program" were in place: tobacco growers who had signed up acquired allotments, which enabled them to grow tobacco under a regime that planned production to maximize growers' income. The tobacco program was a success—the most successful of any New Deal agricultural program—and, for the next sixty years, it grew into a political article of faith in North Carolina. Despite the US Supreme Court's ruling in 1935 that the AAA was unconstitutional, the tobacco program survived, with the strong support of growers. After World War II, the system became institutionalized with the establishment of the Flue-Cured Tobacco Cooperative Stabilization Corporation, a federal agency that bought and resold tobacco that failed to reach a designated support price.

Defenders of the New Deal's tobacco program often pointed out that this was a self-administered and self-financed system: growers voted on crop controls, and their fees financed the buying and selling of surpluses. For the next generation, the tobacco program provided for prosperity in the tobacco regions of eastern North Carolina. But the system also had adverse long-term consequences. Under federal protection, the tobacco program sponsored monopoly control in tobacco farming. Those growers who had signed on with the original AAA program acquired a kind of license that permitted them, rather than their competitors, the right to grow tobacco, and their allotments became frozen in time. Holders of allotments could permanently maintain their holdings, sell them, or even bequeath them to their children. The tobacco program heavily privileged landowners; no provision was made for tenants and sharecroppers, and crop reductions were accompanied by evictions of landless farmers, with owners pocketing the cash payments. For the most part, the system of agricultural extension—county agents, the extension service, and the local committees of tobacco growers—remained unconcerned about the needs of the rural poor. Over time, the tobacco farmers of North Carolina became noncompetitive with growers in South America and Africa; many years later, in the 1980s, the difference between the support price and the market price grew to the point that the self-financed subsidies became increasingly difficult to sustain.

The New Deal also brought massive intervention in North Carolina industry. The National Industrial Recovery Act, which Congress enacted in June 1933, created a National Recovery Administration (NRA), whose main purpose was to foster economic recovery by manufacturers. Like the AAA, the NRA assumed that self-regulation provided a path to prosperity, and the federal agency tried to promote labor-management cooperation. In the textile and tobacco industry, codes were written creating production goals, at the same time establishing minimum wages and maximum hours for industrial workers. Yet the NRA program in North Carolina nearly collapsed because of clashing expectations among manufacturers and workers. Cotton textile manufacturers, for example, were initially enthusiastic about the NRA because they saw it as a way to reduce overproduction and bolster chronically low profit margins. Labor unions saw the NRA as a first step toward federal protection, and organized labor moved aggressively. These clashing expectations partly contributed to the bitter General Strike of 1934, which manufacturers crushed but which left a residue of bad feelings among workers. The General Strike also coincided with a loss of confidence in the NRA by manufacturers, who came to resent the federal intervention that the agency represented. When the Supreme Court struck down the NRA as unconstitutional in 1935, the program had already become unworkable and untenable.

Despite the end of the NRA, federal intervention in industry expanded in other ways. The Wagner Act of 1935 established a National Labor Relations Board (NLRB) that recognized the right of unions to exist and offered federal protection to them. Three years later, the Fair Labor Standards Act created national standards for maximum hours, established a minimum wage, and created a system of federal enforcement for labor policy. Although the New Deal had brought North Carolina manufacturers and businessmen significant benefits by stabilizing the financial system, averting more drastic political responses, and fostering public confidence in capitalism, the New Deal polarized the political spectrum. Textile manufacturers opposed federal intervention in labor relations, and they fought unionization. In 1937, an ambitious organizing drive by the Congress of Industrial Organizations (CIO) made little headway after it was met by unified opposition by textile managers. In 1939, only 4.2 percent of North Carolina's nonagricultural work force belonged to unions, and the state ranked forty-seventh out of forty-eight states in union membership. Many of North Carolina's financial and industrial leaders believed that FDR's programs constituted a first step toward socialism. The stage had been set for a backlash, the rise of a new, antigovernment conservatism.

The New Deal and the Welfare State

In response to the massive unemployment of the Great Depression, the New Deal provided unprecedented amounts of federal expenditures: between 1933 and 1938, some $440 million was spent in North Carolina, a huge amount for that era. The New Deal also created a new structure of public welfare and relief. Prior to the 1930s, problems of poverty were considered outside of the role of government at any level. The Depression changed this, and government began to provide a "safety net" for the unemployed through relief, public works, and, eventually, a social security system. Early in FDR's administration, the president established the Federal Emergency Relief Administration (FERA) to coordinate relief efforts, and it distributed its largesse through state governments, according to new federal standards. Governor Ehringhaus created the North Carolina Emergency Relief Administration (NCERA), which spent nearly $41 million in relief that sustained 300,000 people a month over the next two years. The Civil Works Administration, the most important New Deal public-works agency before 1935, was also active in North Carolina, and NCERA distributed more than $800,000 of its funds and hired 70,000 people to build schools, hospitals, airports, sewers, parks, and schools across the state. NCERA also ran camps that housed 120,000 transients in North Carolina and provided rehabilitation loans for poor farmers.

Perhaps the most successful public-works project in North Carolina was the Blue Ridge Parkway. Good Roads reformers such as Joseph Hyde Pratt had advocated a Crest of the Blue Ridge highway as a way to stimulate economic development and tourism in western North Carolina, but it was not until the economic crisis of the Depression that the project was undertaken. In 1933, with the support of the North Carolina and Virginia congressional delegations, the New Deal's Public Works Administration (PWA) provided funding to begin a parkway. But wrangling ensued in Congress over the details of the new highway, in particular its route and the extent of federal control. By 1935, there was agreement that the newly named Blue Ridge Parkway would connect the Shenandoah National Park in Virginia to the Great Smokies National Park in North Carolina (significantly North Carolina's congressional delegation won a major political victory by routing the parkway through North Carolina). In addition, and unusual for American highways, the Blue Ridge Parkway was to be constructed with "scenic easements" that would prevent commercial development along the road, which was preserved as a park.

Hiring through FERA and public-works projects, parkway construction provided work for thousands of young men throughout the 1930s. The absence of modern highways in the mountains made the engineering challenges daunting, and the process of buying and obtaining easements was time-consuming, with work slowing during World War II but continuing through the 1960s. By 1968, the parkway was complete except for a 7-mile stretch near Grandfather Mountain in North Carolina, and it included 26 tunnels, 200 scenic overlooks, and a total of 469 miles of highway. The completion of the Linn Cove Viaduct, finished in 1987, provided a 1,200-ft portion of the highway that crosses Grandfather Mountain without inflicting serious environmental damage in the process. The completion of the Blue Ridge Parkway marks the creation of one of the most successful highways in American history.

Government-funded relief and public works expanded even further with Congress's establishment of the Works Progress Administration (WPA) in 1935. The WPA represented the largest and most ambitious attempt in American history to deal with poverty. Between 1935 and 1939, the WPA employed 40,000 unemployed North Carolinians in public-works projects in roads, bridges, schools, armories, stadiums, swimming pools, gymnasiums, airports, hospitals, and rural sanitary privies. The WPA also supported less conventional public-works projects. The Federal Theater Project (FTP), headed by state director John A. Walker, hired unemployed playwrights and actors to stage productions in Raleigh, Greensboro, Charlotte, Wilmington, Wilson, and Kinston. The FTP supported the production of *The Lost Colony*, an outdoor drama written by UNC playwright Paul Green and staged at Manteo. Another WPA agency, the Federal Arts Project (FAP), hired artists to paint murals in schools, post offices, and other public buildings. From 1935 to 1937, it was estimated that 353,000 people took part in four FAP projects in North Carolina by attending galleries, enrolling in courses, and hearing lectures. The WPA's Federal Writers Project (FWP) employed writers; in its Historical Records Survey, 110 historians and archivists were hired to catalogue archival collections in North Carolina under the direction of historian Christopher Crittenden in Raleigh. The FWP also conducted an extensive oral history project to collect the memories of ex-slaves, interviewing hundreds of ordinary North Carolinians. Between 1935 and 1942, the WPA spent more than $175 million in the state.

The New Deal also created a permanent system of social welfare. Although the state's political leadership had long resisted establishing a state system of welfare, the Social Security Act of 1935 created a system of pensions for the elderly, unemployment insurance, and welfare for children and the infirm. The Act required that states contribute matching funds to the Social Security system, which was implemented in North Carolina in 1936–37. The New Deal,

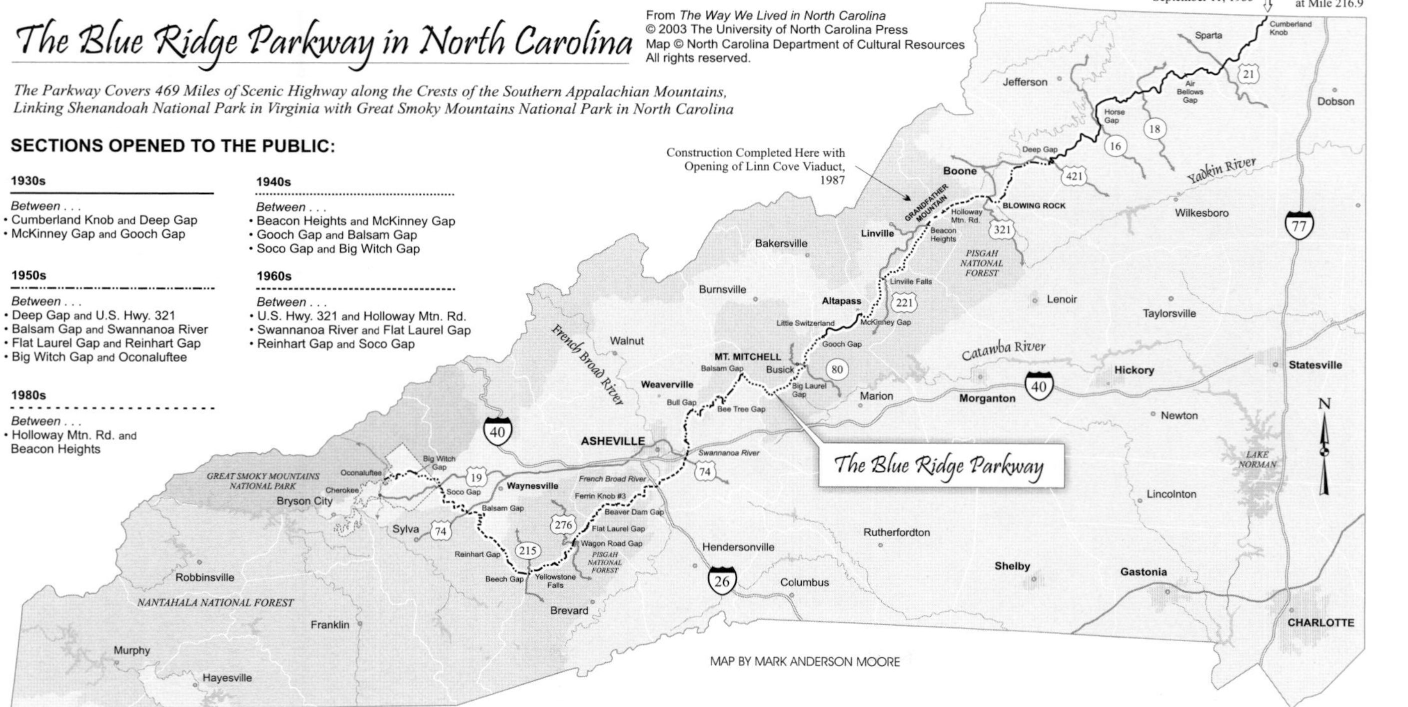

Figure 15.1 Map, Blue Ridge Parkway. *Source:* The Way We Lived in North Carolina *© 2003 The University of North Carolina Press Map © North Carolina Department of Cultural Resources.*

Figure 15.2 *The Lost Colony* souvenir program, 1937. *Source: North Carolina Collection, University of North Carolina Library at Chapel Hill.*

in addition, initiated programs for young people. The Civilian Conservation Corps, created in 1933, hired unemployed young men in work camps that sought to maintain and improve national and state forests, and they built trails, constructed fire towers, and planted trees. By September 1935, the CCC operated eighty-one camps and employed 16,200 workers in North Carolina. The National Youth Administration (NYA) came into existence in 1935 under the rubric of the WPA, and it employed young North Carolinians and provided a substantial program of aid to students through scholarships, jobs, and loans. By June 1940, nearly 12,000 students in North Carolina were enrolled in the NYA's student aid program.

Neither the NRA nor the AAA made much effort to challenge the state's ingrained white supremacy. The NRA codemakers generally ignored black workers in the tobacco industry, while the AAA did little to help displaced black farmers, and its committees typically did not include black representatives. The CCC also hired few African Americans, and those blacks who did participate were housed in segregated facilities. In addition, even the black CCC camps were led by white officials and administrators. Even so, North Carolina whites frequently complained about the presence of black CCC camps—and the supposedly threatening presence there of a large number of young black males. By the late 1930s, the New Deal increasingly confronted the problem of southern rural poverty and of race. The WPA, in contrast to other New Deal agencies, was notable for its efforts to include African Americans, and in 1938 a quarter of its employees were black. The NYA, a part of the WPA's operations, had the best record of any New Deal agency in hiring African Americans, and the agency paid whites and blacks equal wages. In North Carolina, the NYA employed nine African Americans in administrative posts.

It was partially the New Deal's turn to the left that alienated much of the political leadership in North Carolina, and a conservative backlash against the New Deal was in full swing by the late 1930s. The state's business elites in manufacturing, banking, and electrical utilities were thoroughly alarmed by what they regarded as "creeping socialism" with the intrusion of federal authorities—and especially the New Deal's insistence on new policies by the state government. This leadership remained opposed to labor policies that encouraged unionization, to efforts to assist marginal farmers and sharecroppers and tenants, and by what they perceived as efforts to encourage challenges to white supremacy.

Both of North Carolina's senators, Josiah W. Bailey and Robert Reynolds, became outspoken critics of the New Deal by 1937. In December of that year, Bailey, along with other conservative Democrats and Republicans in Congress, issued a Conservative Manifesto that asserted the property rights of business and denounced the New Deal. Instead of governmental intervention, the Manifesto called for reliance on "the American system of private enterprise and initiative, and our American form of government." Rather than public spending, the Manifesto urged fiscal and tax policies that encouraged private investment and free-market capitalism. Finally, the Manifesto demanded that taxes on capital gains and undistributed profits be lowered, that federal expenditures be slashed, that "unnecessary" competition between business and government be eliminated, and that states' rights and local control be restored.[3]

Women and Political Power

A key figure in the transition from the suffrage movement to postsuffrage activism was Gertrude Weil. Born in Goldsboro, Weil grew up in a wealthy Jewish family who operated a popular general merchandise store. Attending high school in New York City, Weil graduated from Smith College in 1901—the first

Figure 15.3 Josiah W. Bailey. *Source: Courtesy of the State Archives of North Carolina.*

North Carolina graduate from that institution. Returning to Goldsboro, Weil recalled, she wondered why women did not possess the right to vote. "Women breathed the same air, got the same education; it was ridiculous, spending so much energy and elocution on something rightfully theirs."[4] Weil became an activist in North Carolina, endorsing welfare and labor reforms. She founded and served two terms as the president of the North Carolina Equal Suffrage League, and she led the unsuccessful fight to ratify the Nineteenth Amendment. In the 1920s, Weil helped to found the North Carolina Federation of Women's Clubs and the Legislative Council of North Carolina Women.

Other white women in North Carolina became activists by participating in public service and the expanding state government. Born in Raleigh in 1867, Jane S. McKimmon graduated from the Peace Institute at the age of 16, and she married two years later. Serving as the director of the women's division of the state Farmers' Institutes between 1908 and 1911, she became in the latter year North Carolina's first home demonstration agent. In this capacity, McKimmon oversaw the expansion of home demonstration, which NC State College, state agricultural officials, and the US Department of Agriculture provided for in fourteen counties in the state. The extension service included efforts to encourage farm women to participate in commercial agriculture by growing and canning their own vegetables. McKimmon ran home demonstration

Figure 15.4 Equal Suffrage League of North Carolina, 1920. Gertrude Weil is on the far left.
Source: Courtesy of the State Archives of North Carolina.

in North Carolina between 1911 and 1937, and she also served as assistant director of the North Carolina extension service from 1924 to 1946.

Kate Burr Johnson represented a new, postsuffrage woman active in public affairs and power, as part of the new social welfare bureaucracy. Born in Morganton, Johnson graduated from Queens College in Charlotte, and, after marrying and raising children, became involved in the cause of social welfare and women's club activities. In 1915, she was elected vice-president of the North Carolina Conference for Social Service. Four years later, Johnson began work for the newly reorganized Board of Charities and Public Welfare, where she served as director of child welfare. In 1921, Johnson became the agency's first female commissioner, the first woman state welfare commissioner in the United States, and the first woman to be in charge of any state agency in North Carolina. Under Johnson's leadership, North Carolina expanded its system of public welfare, and she helped to begin the first stages of the professionalization of social work in the state. Johnson enjoyed the support of groups such as the Legislative Council of North Carolina Women, which rallied women's organizations and lobbied for improved state programs of social welfare. Johnson served as state commissioner of public welfare until 1930, when she left the state to work as superintendent of the New Jersey Home for Girls.

The New Deal offered new avenues for white women in public activism. Annie Land O'Berry offers one such example. Originally from Goldsboro,

O'Berry had a background as an activist in women's clubs and supporter of state welfare activities. She also worked in Democratic Party activities, and she helped to organize women in political activities. Along with her mentor, former suffragist and political activist Cornelia Jerman, O'Berry supported the insurgent candidacy of Josiah W. Bailey, who successfully defeated incumbent US senator Furnifold M. Simmons in the state's Democratic primary in May 1930. In 1933, O'Berry was appointed head of the North Carolina FERA, and a year later she worked for the CWA. O'Berry exerted considerable power, dispensing nearly $40 million in federal relief funds. O'Berry engaged in political combat over the distribution of these funds, as Democratic Party leaders wanted to use the money for patronage purposes, while she insisted on providing relief on a nonpolitical basis.

Harriet W. Elliott, a political scientist serving on the faculty of the Woman's College of the University of North Carolina, became an important force in the Democratic Party and the New Deal. Originally from Illinois, Elliott came to Greensboro in 1913 and joined what was then the State Normal and Industrial College (later the North Carolina College for Women and the Woman's College of the University of North Carolina). Elliott was a suffragist, and in the 1920s became part of a network of women political activists. At Woman's College, she mentored a generation of activist women involved in North Carolina public life. For example, Gladys Avery Tillett, a 1915 graduate of the State Normal College, was an Elliott protégée, later serving as vice-chair of the North Carolina Democratic Committee and as director of the Speaker's Bureau of the Democratic National Committee. In 1934, Elliott organized the Institute for Democratic Women, a New Deal organization that mobilized women nationwide. Elliott's contacts with the FDR administration were extensive, and she was closely involved with First Lady Eleanor Roosevelt's most important political adviser, Molly Dewson. Elliott served as delegate-at-large to the 1932 and 1936 meetings of the Democratic National Convention, and in 1935 she was appointed director of study groups for the women's division of the Democratic National Committee. At the 1936 Democratic National Convention, Elliott and Tillett promoted an agenda seeking greater economic power for women and measures against gender discrimination.

World War II and North Carolina

Only a few weeks after the Japanese attack on Pearl Harbor, on December 7, 1941,the Rose Bowl game, usually played in Pasadena, California, was held instead at Duke Stadium because of fears of a Japanese attack on the West Coast. The game attracted 56,000 fans who, in a cold and steady drizzle, watched Duke lose to Oregon State by a score of 20 to 16. The only Rose Bowl ever played outside of California suggested the depth of the wartime emergency. In World War II, hundreds of thousands of North Carolina men and women enlisted in the largest military mobilization in US history, dwarfing that of World War I and creating new military training camps in the state, converting industry to a wartime footing, providing for full employment, and spurring on migration from the countryside to cities. The war, in short, ushered in significant changes that would have lasting effects on the state.

In 1939, with the eruption of general war in Europe, the United States inaugurated a large-scale mobilization of human and economic resources. The Selective Service Act of September 1940 required all males between the ages of 21 and 36 to register for the draft, and in October 1940 more than 450,000 North Carolina men had done so. By war's end, more than 650,000 had registered, while 370,000 men and women served. About one-third of all employed workers in North Carolina served in the military during the war. The draft was segregated: whites and blacks registered separately and underwent separate physical examinations. About 43 percent of the registrants in North Carolina were disqualified—a rate exceeded only by South Carolina—and the high rejection rate indicated a lingering prevalence of health problems among inductees.

As part of the military mobilization, the US government established new training facilities throughout North Carolina. Indeed, by the end of the war, more military personnel were trained there than any other state in the Union. College campuses were transformed into training centers. At UNC-Chapel Hill, the Navy established a pre-flight training center, and nearly 19,000 had completed the program there. A building boom, employing tens of thousands, ensued in the state. The army base at Fort Bragg, originally established in 1918, was expanded, becoming the largest artillery base in the world, with 122,000 acres, 3,135 buildings, and housing for 100,000 soldiers. The army also established a new base roughly 30 miles northeast of Wilmington in December 1940, and it eventually housed more than 20,000 men, with 3,000 buildings, 30 miles of paved roads, a hospital, four movie theaters, and two 5,000-ft runways. Known as Camp Davis, it served as one of the army's most important anti-aircraft artillery training centers. Meanwhile, the army established facilities at Camp Sutton in Monroe and Camp Mackall near Hoffman. At Cherry Point and Camp Lejeune, military authorities created two major US Marine facilities. In March 1943, the Army Air Force established a base at Greensboro with 650 acres leased from Cone Mills. Beginning as a basic-training base, some 90,000 recruits passed through before it became an overseas replacement depot (ORD). By the end of the war, 330,000 soldiers had spent time at Greensboro's ORD. The Army Air Force also established and maintained major bases at Goldsboro (Seymour Johnson Field) and at Fayetteville (Pope Field). A total of fourteen new bases were constructed across the state during the war.

The enormous military mobilization created new opportunities for women, many of whom took jobs outside the home for the first time in their lives, filling jobs left behind by men in military service, endorsing the wartime slogan

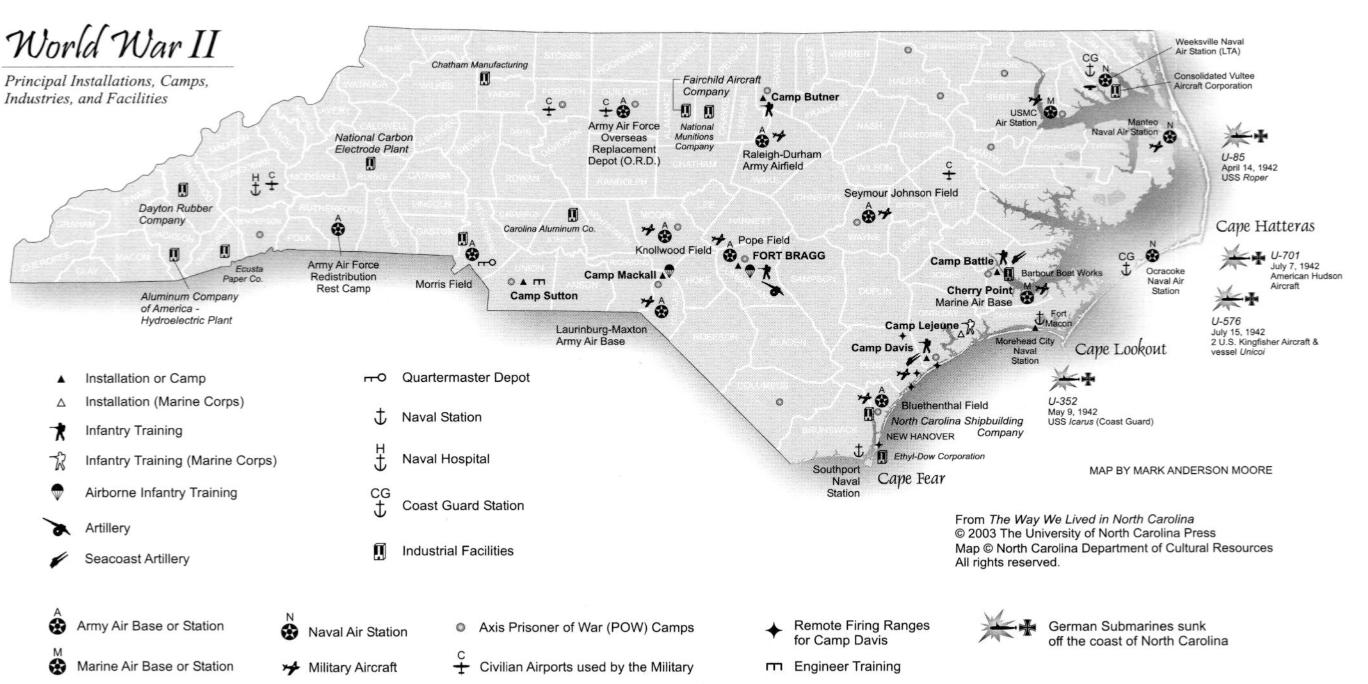

Figure 15.5 Map, World War II. *Source:* The Way We Lived in North Carolina *© 2003 The University of North Carolina Press Map © North Carolina Department of Cultural Resources.*

that a woman working would "free a man to fight." Many women worked in agriculture, with the percentage of women in farming increasing during wartime from 8 percent to 22.4 percent. Even more women worked in North Carolina's tobacco factories, and when workers struck at the R. J. Reynolds plant in Winston-Salem in 1943, it was a black woman, Theodosia Simpson, who led the workforce—four-fifths of which was female—off the job. Many North Carolina women volunteered for military service, first, as nurses in the army. The army's 38th Evacuation Hospital, composed of nurses recruited from the Charlotte area, served behind the front lines of North Africa and Italy, while the 65th Evacuation Hospital, with nurses from Duke University, served as an air evacuation unit during D-Day. Beginning in the spring of 1942, women could serve in the newly minted Women's Army Auxiliary Corps (WACs); Women Air Force Service Pilots (WASPs); the navy's Women Accepted for Voluntary Emergency Service (WAVES); the marines' Women Marines; and the Coast Guard's SPARS.[5] In North Carolina, women drawn by patriotic fervor and a desire to join an exciting adventure, rushed to volunteer for these units, overwhelming recruiting stations. Dorothy Hoover, who grew up in Asheville, had always dreamed of being a pilot. WASPs gave her the chance, and, with her husband in the Pacific theater and with 200 hours of flying experience, she joined up. Like other female pilots in North Carolina, she towed gliders that were used in the D-Day invasion, and she also pulled targets for anti-aircraft practice. Although she knew that some men resented her, Hoover said she did not care, "as long as they let me fly." A total of 7,000 North Carolina women joined the military, the largest portion, some 4,000 women, serving in WAACs. The volunteers included women from all walks of life, including African American women who joined up in segregated units, though they were barred from serving in the Women Marines or the WASPs.

Scores of other women also accompanied their husbands, sometimes with their families, to the bases. As servicemen's families filled up available housing, they competed with thousands of new migrants employed in war industries. Soon there was a housing shortage in most of the cities of the state, and the federal Office of Price Administration (OPA) in 1942 froze rent increases. The military mobilization also brought thousands of young men into North Carolina, and the soldiers filled movie theaters, hotels, grocery stores, transportation facilities, and department stores. Colleges and universities, whose enrollments declined because of the absence of college-age males, also participated in military training programs. While Duke University ran a naval ROTC program and an army finance school, UNC operated training for navy preflight and navy V-12s. Other campuses became involved in training military personnel.

The war also created cracks in the system of white supremacy. Camp Butner, an entirely new base constructed during the war to house 40,000 trainees, also contained 7,500 African American soldiers. The black soldiers filled the streets of Hayti, the African American business and residential district of

Figure 15.6 Rachel Leuella Summers McGee, of Greensboro, in WACS uniform. *Source: Martha Blakeney Hodges Special Collections and University Archives, the University of North Carolina at Greensboro.*

nearby Durham, and they found housing and entertainment at black-owned hotels and restaurants. Black women organized themselves in the local Harriet Tubman YWCA (the local African American "Y" in town) and formed USO units that attended to the black soldiers, while a local Colored Travelers Aid Society assisted the thousands of African Americans arriving at the base. Local black women's clubs engaged in other activities in support of the black troops. Like their white counterparts, black women participated in the patriotic fervor that prevailed during World War II by supporting Victory Gardens, rationing, and civic defense—all in support of the war effort.

Black women also participated in a meeting at the North Carolina College for Negroes in Durham in October 1942, in which fifty-nine southern blacks examined the problem of race during wartime. The meeting issued a call for action, the Durham Manifesto, which declared that the war had accelerated tensions between whites and blacks and urged the reestablishment of political enfranchisement for African Americans, equal access to economic resources, an end to white primaries, and the destruction of white supremacy. The Durham Manifesto suggested the existence of larger tensions and a wider erosion of segregation and Jim Crow.

Fighting World War II required a total mobilization of economic resources, with federal expenditures in the state totaling $2 billion for goods and services during the war years. For its part, North Carolina produced military items such as bombs, radar and aircraft parts, and ships, along with textiles used to make tents, uniforms, towels, and blankets. Cannon Mills in Kannapolis provided yarn for 15 million machine-gun belts, while it also produced cloth for camouflage, bandages, and towels. The P. H. Hanes Knitting Company, a hosiery mill in Winston-Salem, employed 3,300 workers in the manufacture of underwear for soldiers. With demand soaring, the cotton-textile industry underwent a boom, and mills operated on three shifts and doubled their payrolls. Some seven-tenths of the textile industry's production went toward the war effort. Another critical war material was mica, a mineral used in the manufacture of insulators for radio tubes. As early as the 1890s, Spruce Pine had become the leading national center of mica mining, and during World War II a boom occurred in the mining of mica in western North Carolina. By the end of the war, the state was producing half of all the mica mined in the United States. North Carolina farmers also found a market for their products, and, despite a general shortage of labor, the state's farmers produced a greatly expanded crop during the war years. In Burlington, the Fairchild Aircraft Plant helped to assemble war planes. The coastal ports of North Carolina served as centers for shipbuilding. While Morehead City and Southport ran naval repair stations, Wilmington was home to the North Carolina Shipbuilding Company, and Elizabeth City manufactured small, wooden-hulled submarine chasers. The Wilmington shipyard, which produced cargo ships, the Liberty Ships, was operating at peak efficiency and, by the end of the war, was producing a ship a month. Like other Americans, North Carolinians during World War II lived under a strict regime that limited their access to consumer goods and even basic commodities. Essentially, no appliances or automobiles were manufactured domestically during the war, as the nation's entire productive capacity had been turned to the production of all things war-related. The federal government managed a program of rationing in which North Carolinians (like their counterparts in other states) used books of ration stamps to buy fuel, butter, meat, sugar, coffee, and canned goods, among other items. Drivers were limited to three gallons of gasoline a week; many people left their cars at home and rode buses instead. People on the home front, after 1943, were even rationed shoes—no more than three pairs per person annually. Meanwhile, urged by war mobilization authorities, North Carolinians enthusiastically participated in the Victory Garden program, designed to increase food production at home and, this way, free up more food resources for the troops abroad. In 1944, Tar Heels canned 28 million quarts of food, dried 8 million pounds of fruits and vegetables, and cured 30 million pounds of meat. The city of Raleigh boasted 4,000 Victory Gardens by 1945.

During the war's early years, the Germans conducted an all-out submarine assault on American shipping, and many of these attacks occurred off the

North Carolina coast. Favorite targets were oil tankers traveling from Texas to East Coast ports north of the Carolina coast. In the early months of the war, coastal residents frequently saw evidence of the sea war in the oil and debris that washed up on beaches. Much of the US sea battle against submarines occurred without public knowledge, in order to forestall public panic. Before the German submarine war ended, in August 1942, the US military imposed a blackout on all residents within 20 miles of the coast; all outside lights were turned off, and locals were ordered to run automobiles on reduced lighting. Driving on the beaches was prohibited. In early 1942, the submarine war off the North Carolina coast reached a peak, with American military forces attempting to root out prowling German subs, and the Germans ferociously assaulting American ships. Some 287 people died off of Cape Hatteras during these attacks that sank eight ships off the coast, an area known to sailors as "Torpedo Junction." The submarine war resulted in the sinking of four U-boats off the North Carolina coast, the most of any state in the Union.

North Carolinians also housed a significant number of foreign prisoners of war (POWs). Nationally, by late 1943 about 50,000 Italian POWs were in camps in twenty-three states, with North Carolina housing 3,000 Italians at a prison facility at Camp Butner. Later, once the Italian fascist regime of Benito Mussolini collapsed, the American military formed Italian Services Units (ISUs) composed of Italian POWs willing to swear loyalty to the Allied cause, and Camp Sutton (no longer in existence) served as a training facility for about 3,500 of them. By the end of the conflict, camps across the nation housed 378,000 German POWs, and by 1945, North Carolina held some 10,000 Germans, along with Czechs, Poles, Dutch, French, Austrians, Lithuanians, and Luxembourgers who had served in the armies of the Third Reich. Twenty-nine POWs in North Carolina attempted to escape, but only one of them, Kurt Rossmeisl, succeeded; he eventually turned himself in to the FBI (in 1953). These prisoners worked on farms and in agricultural processing on a contract basis, and, though their presence went largely unnoticed and unreported in the press, they provided about 2 million man-days of work in the state.

Like other Americans, North Carolinians lived under a strict system of wartime rationing of crucial foodstuffs and materials. Residents of the state were given ration stamps, with which they bought limited amounts of coffee, sugar, gasoline, groceries, and tires. Because of gas restrictions, North Carolinians were encouraged to carpool and to ride buses and trains. As ridership on buses increased, the segregated public transportation system experienced increased tensions: black riders were forced to move to the back of the bus, and frequently confrontations occurred because black and white passengers were not permitted to sit next to each other. Recycling became a patriotic activity: in Charlotte, the Salvage for Victory Committee encouraged residents to recycle aluminum, rubber, iron, steel, tin, newspapers, and cloth rags. As a byproduct of wartime rationing, a system of auctioning of produce arose during the war,

Figure 15.7 New African American recruits at Camp Lejeune, New River, North Carolina, 1943. *Source: Library of Congress Prints and Photographs Division.*

with farmers' markets emerging—along with a burgeoning market for truck farming across the state that survived during the postwar era.

North Carolina made a major contribution to the nation's military effort in World War II in both the European and Pacific theaters. Marines trained at the base in Camp Lejeune, North Carolina, participated in the Allied invasion of Japanese-controlled islands. In Normandy, France, Elmo Jones, a US Army sergeant, took part in a crucial reconnaissance mission prior to the D-Day invasion on June 6, 1944. The Thirteenth Infantry, which had been a National Guard unit in North Carolina, became known as the "Workhorse of the Western Front" because of its heavy involvement in European fighting. Eight North Carolinians won the Congressional Medal of Honor, awarded for battlefield valor, for their service. The western North Carolina town of Canton was home to two of these Medal of Honor recipients, Max Thompson and William David Halyburton, Jr. A native of Greensboro, Maj. George Earl Preddy, Jr., flew a P-51 Mustang for the Eighth Air Force in Europe. Preddy became one of the Army Air Force's most accomplished fighter pilots—he recorded more air victories than did any other American P-51 ace of World War II—but he was accidentally shot down by US anti-aircraft artillery on Christmas Day 1944. All told, nearly 370,000 North Carolina men and women served their nation in World

Figure 15.8 50-cal. anti-aircraft gun guarding Beach Head, Camp Lejeune, NC. *Source: North Carolina Collection, University of North Carolina Library at Chapel Hill.*

War II, a number that includes about 75,000 African Americans. Of the North Carolinians who served, roughly 7,100 of them lost their lives in the conflict.

The end of war with Germany and Japan in 1945 ushered in a new period in the history of North Carolina and the nation. The war had effectively ended the Great Depression, and prosperity returned to farms and factories across the state. But World War II also brought far-reaching changes in many aspects of life in North Carolina. Wartime mobilization resulted in jobs, but it also drove large numbers of people in search of work to migrate from the countryside to cities, and from one state to another, and the intense wartime population mobility tested the social fabric. The military buildup stoked the economy, but it strained resources and aggravated racial tensions. The war also raised expectations among the state's African Americans, who saw a fight against fascism and Nazism as part of a larger global struggle against racism that had obvious implications at home for white supremacy and, in their eyes, Jim Crow.

Notes

1 Anthony J. Badger, *North Carolina and the New Deal* (Raleigh, NC: Division of Archives and History, 1981), p. 6.

2 Quoted in Joseph L. Morrison, *Governor O. Max Gardner: A Power in North Carolina and New Deal Washington* (Chapel Hill: University of North Carolina Press, 1971), p. 107.

3 Carl Abrams, *Conservative Constraints: North Carolina and the New Deal* (Jackson: University Press of Mississippi, 1992), p. 247.

4 Margaret Supplee Smith and Emily Herring Wilson, *North Carolina Women: Making History* (Chapel Hill: University of North Carolina Press, 1999), p. 260.

5 The acronym came from the Coast Guard's motto "Semper Paratus, Always Ready."

Suggested Readings, Part 5

Chapter 13

John Milton Cooper, Jr., *Walter Hines Page: The Southerner as American, 1855–1918* (Chapel Hill: University of North Carolina Press, 1977).
Lee A. Craig, *Josephus Daniels: His Life and Times* (Chapel Hill: University of North Carolina Press, 2013).
Robert F. Durden, *Reconstruction Bonds and Twentieth-Century Politics: South Dakota v. North Carolina, 1904* (Durham NC: Duke University Press, 1962).
Michele Gillespie, *Katharine and R. J. Reynolds: Partners of Fortune in the Making of the New South* (Athens: University of Georgia Press, 2012).
Rose H. Holder, *McIver of North Carolina* (Chapel Hill: University of North Carolina Press, 1957).
Angela Hornsby-Gutting, *Black Manhood and Community Building in North Carolina, 1900–1930* (Gainesville: University Press of Florida, 2011).
Spencer Bidwell King, Jr., *Selective Service in North Carolina in World War II* (Chapel Hill: University of North Carolina Press, 1949).
William A. Link, *Paradox of Southern Progressivism, 1880–1930* (Chapel Hill: University of North Carolina Press, 1992).
William Mabry, *The Negro in North Carolina since Reconstruction,* Trinity College Historical Papers, vol. 23 (Durham, NC: Duke University Press, 1940).
John R. Moore, *Josiah William Bailey: A Political Biography* (Durham, NC: Duke University Press, 1962).
Oliver H. Orr, Jr., *Charles Brantley Aycock* (Chapel Hill: University of North Carolina Press, 1961).
Thomas C. Parramore, *First to Fly: North Carolina and the Beginnings of Aviation* (Chapel Hill: University of North Carolina Press, 2002).
Leonard Rogoff, *Gertrude Weil: Jewish Progressive in the New South* (Chapel Hill: University of North Carolina Press, 2017).

North Carolina: Change and Tradition in a Southern State, Second Edition. William A. Link.

Anastatia Sims, *The Power of Femininity in the New South: Women's Organizations and Politics in North Carolina, 1880–1930* (Columbia: University of South Carolina Press, 1997).

Marjorie Julian Spruill, *New Women of the New South: The Leaders of the Woman Suffrage Movement in the Southern States* (New York : Oxford University Press, 1993).

Walter B. Weare, *Black Business in the New South: A Social History of the North Carolina Mutual Life Insurance Company* (Urbana: University of Illinois Press, 1973).

Chapter 14

Alex Mathews Arnett, *Claude Kitchin and the Wilson War Policies* (Boston: Little, Brown, and Company, 1937).

Jessica A. Bandel, *North Carolina and the Great War, 1914–1918* (Raleigh: North Carolina Office of Archives and History, 2017).

William J. Breen, "The North Carolina Council of Defense during World War I, 1917–1918," *North Carolina Historical Review* 50 (January 1973).

Robert L. Dorman, *Revolt of the Provinces: The Regionalist Movement in America, 1920–1945* (Chapel Hill: University of North Carolina Press, 1993).

John R. Finger, "'Conscription, Citizenship, and 'Civilization': World War I and the Eastern Band of Cherokee," *North Carolina Historical Review* 63 (July 1986).

Willard B. Gatewood, Jr., *Preachers, Pedagogues & Politicians: The Evolution Controversy in North Carolina, 1920–1927* (Chapel Hill: University of North Carolina Press, 1966).

Randal L. Hall, *William Louis Poteat: A Leader of the Progressive-Era South* (Lexington: University Press of Kentucky, 2000).

Archibald Henderson, *North Carolina Women in the World War* (Raleigh, NC: North Carolina Literary and Historical Association, 1920).

Charles J. Holden, *The New Southern University: Academic Freedom and Liberalism at UNC* (Lexington: University Press of Kentucky, 2011).

Robert E. Ireland, "Prison Reform, Road Building, and Southern Progressivism: Joseph Hyde Pratt and the Campaign for 'Good Roads and Good Men,'" *North Carolina Historical Review*, LXVIII (April 1991).

Sarah McCulloh Lemmon, *North Carolina's Role in the First World War* (Raleigh, NC: Division of Archives and History, 1966).

Harry Wilson McKown, Jr., *"Roads and Reform: The Good Roads Movement in North Carolina, 1885–1921,"* M.A. thesis, University of North Carolina at Chapel Hill, 1972.

John A. Salmond, *Gastonia, 1929: The Story of the Loray Mill Strike* (Chapel Hill: University of North Carolina Press, 1995).

Joanna Schoen, *Choice and Coercion: Birth Control, Sterilization, and Abortion in Public Health and Welfare* (Chapel Hill: University of North Carolina Press, 2005).

Daniel Joseph Singal, *The War Within: From Victorian to Modernist Thought in the South, 1919–1945* (Chapel Hill: University of North Carolina Press, 1983).

Chapter 15

Douglas Carl Abrams, *Conservative Constraints: North Carolina and the New Deal* (Jackson: University Press of Mississippi, 1992).

Anthony J. Badger, *Prosperity Road: The New Deal, Tobacco, and North Carolina* (Chapel Hill: University of North Carolina Press, 1980).

Anthony J. Badger, *North Carolina and the New Deal* (Raleigh, NC: Division of Archives and History, 1981).

John L. Bell, *Hard Times: Beginnings of the Great Depression in North Carolina, 1929–1933* (Raleigh, NC: Division of Archives and History, 1982).

Janet Irons, *Testing the New Deal: The General Textile Strike of 1934 in the American South* (Urbana: University of Illinois Press, 2000).

Harley E. Jolley, *The Blue Ridge Parkway* (Knoxville: University of Tennessee Press, 1969).

Sarah McCulloh Lemmon, *North Carolina's Role in World War II* (Raleigh, NC: Division of Archives and History, 1985).

Julian M. Pleasants, *Buncombe Bob: The Life and Times of Robert Rice Reynolds* (Chapel Hill: University of North Carolina Press, 2000).

Julian M. Pleasants, *Home Front: North Carolina during World War II* (Gainesville: University Press of Florida, 2017).

Liston Pope, *Millhands and Preachers: A Study of Gastonia* (New Haven, CT: Yale University Press, 1942).

Elmer L. Puryear, *Democratic Party Dissension in North Carolina, 1928–1936* (Chapel Hill: University of North Carolina Press, 1962).

John A. Salmond, *The General Textile Strike of 1934: From Maine to Alabama* (Columbia: University of Missouri Press, 2002).

Richard D. Starnes, *Creating the Land of the Sky: Tourism and Society in Western North Carolina* (Tuscaloosa: University of Alabama Press, 2005).

Patricia Sullivan, *Days of Hope: Race and Democracy in the New Deal Era* (Chapel Hill: University of North Carolina Press, 1996).

Gregory S. Taylor, *The History of the North Carolina Communist Party* (Columbia: University of South Carolina Press, 2009).

Clifford Tyndall, *Greetings from Camp Davis: The History of a WWII Army Base* (Chapel Hill, NC: Chapel Hill Press, 2006).

Document Section, Part 5
The Debate about Darwin

During the 1920s, a fierce conflict emerged across the country over the teaching of the ideas about human evolution. A powerful movement, led by conservative evangelicals who rejected the growing secularization of American life, sought to ban the teaching of Charles Darwin's theory of evolution by legislative enactment. The debate about evolution revealed a sharp cultural divide in North Carolina: a gulf between those advocating the use of science to understand their surroundings and those who insisted on the traditional cultural authority of biblical inerrancy. In North Carolina, the controversy engulfed public-supported colleges and universities. In the state's higher education system, the University at Chapel Hill had been remade into what soon became the South's leading university. UNC presidents Edward Kidder Graham, Harry Woodburn Chase, and Frank Porter Graham remade UNC into a vehicle for modernization. While anti-evolutionists were able to limit the teaching of Darwinian biology in public schools, they encountered fierce resistance among UNC supporters when they turned their attention to the university. The attempt to enact legislation that would prohibit the teaching of Darwinian biology on college campuses, embodied in the Poole bills of 1925–27, involved a larger debate about the future of the state.

The following documents explore the debate about Darwin.

A Biology Textbook (1919)[1]

The following selection comes from a textbook, Elementary Biology, *approved by the North Carolina textbook commission in 1919, but then rejected, because*

1 Benjamin Charles Gruenberg, *Elementary Biology: An Introduction to the Science of Life* (Boston: Ginn and Co., 1919), pp. 494–96, http://www2.lib.unc.edu/ncc/evolution/elementarybiology.html

of its depiction of evolution, by Governor Cameron Morrison and the State Board of Education. Morrison, elected as an advocate of modernization through improved roads and education, was a stout anti-evolutionist. He declared that he would not want his "daughter or anybody's daughter to have to study a book that prints pictures of a monkey and a man on the same page."

Fifty years ago much of the discussion among thinking people centered around the question of the validity of the evolution theory as applied to man. There were many who were prepared to believe that evolution has taken place among plants and lower animals, but who hesitated to accept the same explanation for the appearance of man upon earth. One of the strongest objections urged against the theory was the fact that it had been impossible to produce a complete record of a graded series connecting man of to-day with his supposed non-human or prehuman ancestors. This argument of the "missing link" carried a great deal of weight with people who did not appreciate how unlikely it would be for complete series of specimens to be preserved through geologic times. Of the millions of human beings and other vertebrates that die in a given region during a century, how many skeletons are likely to remain sufficiently intact to be recognized from ten thousand to fifty thousand years later? From a scientific point of view it would be sufficient if the scattered pieces found at widely different levels (geologic ages) do actually fit in with a supposed species.

T. T. Martin, *Hell and the High Schools*[2]

The growth of high schools raised the ante for people uncomfortable with the idea of evolution, and during the 1920s anti-evolutionists began to campaign to suppress its teaching in public-supported schools. Born in Mississippi in 1862, Thomas Theodore Martin was a leading conservative evangelical. In the 1920s, he led a national anti-evolution campaign. In 1922, he attacked Wake Forest College president William L. Poteat for his attempts to reconcile science and religion. Although moderates defeated attempts to condemn evolution and Poteat at the state convention, anti-evolutionists articulated a critique of evolution linking it to social disintegration and moral decline. In his widely read book, Hell and the High Schools, *Martin laid out his case.*

WHAT can be done? Where is our hope? The pussyfooting apologies for the Evolutionists will say "Don't do anything drastic. Educate the people, and the

2 T. T. Martin, *Hell and the High Schools: Christ or Evolution, Which?* (Kansas City: The Western Baptist Publishing Co., 1923), pp. 156–65.

thing will right itself." Educate the people? How can we, when Evolutionists have us by the throat? When they have, while we were asleep, captured our tax-supported schools from primary to University, and many of our denominational colleges?. . . .

What is a war, what is an epidemic that sweeps people away by the hundred thousand, compared to this scourge that under the guise of "science," when it is not science, at all, is sweeping our sons and daughters away from God, away from God's word, taking from them their Redeemer and Saviour, to spend eternity in hell?

The two pillars are:

First, the local Board of Trustees of every public school. They are absolutely sovereign. Even the Governor of the State, even the President of the United States, cannot force any teacher upon any public school. It is in the hands of the local Board of Trustees. Let the fathers and mothers see that only men and women shall be put on Boards of Trustees who will protect our children from this scourge, this "scholastic paganism." It can be done in two ways: first, employ no teacher who believes in Evolution; second, obligate every teacher to post himself and expose the claims of Evolution every time it comes up in the text books that are being used, for many of them are poisoned with it. This can be easily done. At the close of this book a list of books will be given that will enable the teachers to combat this deadly-damning curse.

Second, elect to the legislatures men who will cut off all support from all tax-supported schools where Evolution is taught, and require that in all tax-supported schools only teachers shall be employed who will post themselves and combat this terrible curse every time it comes up in the text books being used. Too drastic? Do you fight a scourge of small-pox with halfway measures. A scourge of small pox and yellow fever combined would be slight, as a. curse, compared to this scourge that is sweeping our young men and women, boys and girls, away from God. . . .

Fathers and Mothers!

DO YOU remember the first faint cry from a tiny little life, when the doctor told you that you were a parent? Can you ever forget the thrill, the inexpressible joy? No language can ever describe it. Did you realize then that there was a being whom you had brought into existence who would spend eternity in Heaven or in hell? Do you realize it now? Do you realize your responsibility for the eternal destiny of that child? Do not hide behind excuses; do not try to shirk responsibility; do not, as the ostrich, when about to be captured, who sticks his head in the sand, to avoid capture, try to escape by sticking your head in the sands of infidelity and saying you do not believe there is any hell. There is as much evidence for believing there is a hell as for believing there is a heaven. Many books will convince you that there is a heaven and a hell. If you will get and read honestly John Urquhart's "Wonders of Prophecy," or Walker's "Philosophy of the Plan of Salvation," you will realize that there is a heaven and a hell, and that your child will spend eternity in one or the other.

Do you realize not only the duty but the privilege of keeping out of your child's life every influence that could possibly lead to its spending eternity in hell, and of putting into its life every possible influence that would lead to its spending eternity in heaven?. . . .

But what have the High Schools of the land to do with the child spending eternity in hell? Many books being taught in the High Schools teach Evolution that all species or kinds of beings, from the smallest insects up to man, have developed, evolved, from the lower species up to the higher; that the first living thing, not as large as the point of the finest needle, only one one-hundred-and-twentieth part of an inch in diameter, multiplied for ages, each generation differing very slightly, until a new species or kind was evolved, developed; and that this process continued till at last man was evolved; that the first man was "midway between the anthropoid ape and modern man;" that the first man did not speak a plain language, but chattered as animals in trees, having only exclamation of pain or pleasure. If this is true, then Jesus Christ was the bastard, illegitimate son of a fallen woman, not Deity, not really God's son, not really our Redeemer and Saviour at all; for three reasons: ten times in the first chapter of Genesis there is the positive statement that everything brought forth "AFTER HIS KIND." If Evolution is true, that each brought forth, not "after his kind," but differing slightly till there was evolved a new kind, a new species; then there are ten lies in the first chapter of Genesis. Then the first chapter of Genesis says that God made the first man in His own image; but Evolution says that that is another lie, that the first man was "midway between the anthropoid ape and modern man." Then, Genesis states positively that the first man spoke in a plain language, but Evolution states that that is another lie in Genesis, that the first man did not have a plain language but only chattered as animals, having only exclamations of pain or pleasure. Now the Saviour endorsed Genesis as the word of God. These twelve lies COULD NOT BE THE WORD OF GOD. If, when the Saviour endorsed Genesis as the word of God, He knew there were twelve lies in it, then He was not Deity, not really God's Son, but a vile liar and deceiver, and only the illegitimate, bastard son of a fallen woman; and not our Redeemer and Saviour. If these twelve statements are lies (and they are, if Evolution is true) and the Saviour did not know it when He endorsed Genesis as the word of God, then He was a goody-goody ignoramus and fool, who honestly thought that He was God's Son, when He was only the bastard, illegitimate son of a fallen woman, and not Deity, not God's Son, not our real Redeemer and Saviour at all-and we are left in our sins. There is no escaping these conclusions by any honest man or woman, boy or girl who accepts Evolution as the truth. Some boys and girls who are taught Evolution in the High Schools, and believe its teachings to be true, may not think clearly, and may continue to believe in the Bible and in the Saviour; but those who are taught it and believe it, and who think clearly, will be forced to give up the Bible and the Saviour as real Redeemer. From respect for the feelings of their Christian fathers and mothers, of their pastors, and of Christians generally, they may not come out frankly and declare their convictions; but they cannot accept as Deity a being who would endorse twelve lies as the word of God; then, if He was not Deity, He was no real Redeemer at all, and we have no Saviour and are left in our sins. . . .

The boasted builders of the *Titanic* boasted that it could not sink, and great throngs crowded on it and defied God that Sunday night with their revelry and sin; but the horrible death struggles in those icy waters bore tragic testimony to their fearful deception. The boasted builders of your *Titanic*, Evolution, are causing thousands to crowd on board, but as certain as God is God the fearful iceberg is ahead, and many will sink beneath the gloomy waves of hell, and you fathers and mothers are to blame.

It is in your power to save your children from this deadly, soul-destroying teaching. The Baptist, Catholic, Congregational, Disciple, Episcopalian, Lutheran, Methodist, Presbyterian and other fathers and mothers can, in twelve months, drive Evolution out of every tax-supported school in America and out of every denominational school. Will they do it?. . . .

The fathers and mothers of America, some to appear "broad and liberal," some to appear "up-to-date," some, because brow-beaten by these Evolutionist high-brows and their pussy-footing apologists and defenders, are standing silently by while our children are being eternally damned. As I said in the beginning of this book, the Germans who poisoned the wells and springs of northern France and Belgium that the little children might drink and die, were angels compared to the text-book writers and publishers who are poisoning the books used in our schools that our children who go there to drink in a little learning, may have their souls poisoned and sent down to eternal death; that the Germans who poisoned candy and poured it out from aeroplanes that the starving Belgian and French children might eat it and die, were angels compared to the teachers, paid by our taxes, who feed our children's minds with the deadly, soul-destroying poison of Evolution. But the Belgian and French mothers and fathers who could have prevented the wells and springs being poisoned and the poisoned candy from being scattered, who could have prevented their children from drinking and eating and dying, and would not have done it, would have been equally guilty with the Germans. And the father and mother, who will stand by, and not go to the limit to protect their children from the soul-destroying poison of Evolution, are equally guilty with the text-book writers and publishers and the Evolution professors in our schools.

Governor Cameron Morrison and Evolution, January 24, 1924[3]

This newspaper account, appearing in the Raleigh News and Observer, *describes the State Board of Education's decision to ban Darwinian biology in textbooks. Morrison played a central role in the decision, which had the effect of strictly limiting what could be taught in North Carolina high schools.*

With Governor Morrison standing flatly against any book that "prints a picture of a monkey and a man on the same page" illustrating a line of descent, the State Board of Education yesterday rejected from the report of the sub-committee of the Text Book Commission two works on biology. As adopted the list of 700 odd books from which the counties may select for State high school purposes, contains four biologies. While Governor Morrison indicated little favor for any of the books containing evolution theories, his first choice was the first choice also of the Text Book Commission.

"One of those books," said Governor Morrison, speaking of the rejected text, "teaches that man is descended from a monkey and the other that he is a cousin to the monkey. I don't believe either one of them.

"You don't think much of evolution?" the Governor was asked.

"I believe in evolution if you will let me define evolution," he continued. "Evolution is progress, and I believe in the development of man from a lower form of human life to a higher. I don't believe in any missing links.

"If there were any such thing as a missing link, why don't they keep making them?" the Governor asked.

It was the Governor's feeling on the subject of evolution and the text book teachings that moved him Tuesday night to carry all six of the proposed volumes to the mansion for some intensive study. The results of his study he gave to the board of education yesterday afternoon.

The Poole Bill, 1925[4]

D. Scott Poole, legislator from Hoke County, first proposed legislation restricting the teaching of Darwin in 1925. Poole was an active Presbyterian churchman,

---

3 "Governor Vetoes Evolution and Board Cuts Out Books." *Raleigh News and Observer*, January 24, 1924, pp. 1, 2, http://www2.lib.unc.edu/ncc/evolution/textbooks1-24-24.html.

4 North Carolina General Assembly, "Joint Resolution Restricting the Teaching of Darwinism in the Public Schools of North Carolina," 1925. Courtesy of the North Carolina State Archives, http://www2.lib.unc.edu/ncc/evolution/poolebill.html.

and North Carolina Presbyterians became the most vociferous advocates of suppressing the teaching of Darwinian biology. The proposed resolution included all state-supported institutions, including public schools, as well as state-supported colleges and universities. Yet the resolution contained no specifics—and no sanctions if the law were violated.

JOINT RESOLUTION RESTRICTING THE TEACHING OF DARWINISM IN THE PUBLIC SCHOOLS OF NORTH CAROLINA.

Resolved by the House of Representatives, the Senate concurring:

1. That it is the sense of the General Assembly of North Carolina that it is injurious to the welfare of the people of the State of North Carolina for any official or teacher in the State, paid wholly or in part by taxation, to teach or permit to be taught, as a fact, either Darwinism or any other evolutionary hypotheses that links man in blood relationship with any lower form or life.
2. That this resolution be in effect from and after its ratification.

Legislative discussion, February 11, 1925[5]

The introduction of the Poole bill rallied UNC supporters in the legislature. Led by UNC alumni and by legislators such as Sam Ervin of Morganton—later a US senator—the UNC forces were able to beat back the anti-evolutionists. The UNC president, Harry Woodburn Chase, led a coordinated lobbying effort. Below, in this newspaper account, Chase argued for free speech on the university campus.

Representative Poole, patron of the bill, declared that he could produce affidavits supporting the statement of a young man who entered the North Carolina A. & E. college last year and did not return because "a professor told the young men that the Bible was a myth and the Christian religion a superstition." The representative stated that the young man informed him that this professor said that the Christian religion was accepted "just like Santa Claus."

Representative Madison declared that evolution is being taught in some of the public schools of the state and that he was prepared to prove it.

Dr. Chase began by stating that he was not a student of biology, but that he did think something ought to be said on "the other side." He asked: "Why should it be unlawful to teach in the week what is not unlawful to preach from the pulpits

5 "Anti-Evolution Bill Fails of Committee O.K.," *Charlotte Observer*, February 11, 1925 pp. 1, 13, http://www2.lib.unc.edu/ncc/evolution/charlotteobserver2-11-25.html.

on the Sabbath day?" He declared that even Christianity has suffered because of some of its over zealous advocates; that all great causes have so suffered. Men like Gallileo were persecuted, he said, and declared that the Catholic church in Gallileo's time thought his doctrine to be worse than a denial of the incarnation of doubting the Holy Trinity.

He declared that under the constitution men and women are guaranteed the right of free speech; that the freedom of the press should remain unabridged, and asked if the constitution meant to say that everybody should have the right of free speech except school teachers.

Dr. Chase was asked if he thought teachers had the right to teach atheism and to this he replied that this was a matter of conscience....

Scott Poole Defends the Poole Bill, October 1926[6]

In this document, Poole offers a spirited defense of his bill, articulating the vital importance anti-evolutionists attached to public schools, youth, moral decline, and fears of secularization.

Prevented by illness from making a scheduled address before the student body of the University, Mr. D. Scott Poole, originator of the famous "Poole Bill," replied to a request for the manuscript of his address with the brief presented on this page.

In printing this article, which should represent the candid opinions of the fundamentalists of this state as held by their acknowledged leader, there has been no attempt at editing. The brief was printed as it came to the office.

I object to a mode of creation being taught in the public schools of this state for the following reasons:

1. Because parents, not the state, have the right to teach their children religion. Parents are responsible for the religious training of their children.
2. Because Evolution as taught in the schools, teaches a mode of creation, of the Creator, the Bible, and the philosophy of life, may be classed as religion.
3. Because state schools have no right to teach religion.
4. Neither the Evolutionist, nor the Christian Fundamentalist has a right to teach his peculiar views at public expense.
5. Because debarring Evolution from the public schools will not infringe upon the right of any Evolutionist from teaching or writing at his own expense.

---

6 D. Scott Poole, "Why the Opposition," *Carolina Magazine* 57 (October 1926): 19–20, http://www2.lib.unc.edu/ncc/evolution/poole.html.

This is the reasons for debarring evolution, legally, and now as further reasons, it is not fair to taxpayers to defray the expense of teaching their own peculiar doctrine, and then by a state supported educational system have all their work undone, and that also at their expense.

It is plain to be seen, that this conflict of view will amount to a menace of the welfare of the Commonwealth if allowed to go on.

From the writings of evolutionists we make the following deductions:

1. All gods and devils are the creations of human imaginations.
2. There never has been a divine relation of God's will to man.
3. No extant moral code possesses Divine authority.
4. The Christian's hope of heaven is based on myth.
5. The fall of man is mythical.
6. Conscience is the product of group opinion.
7. Christianity is wrong in its basic purpose of moral conduct.
8. Christian teaching as to purity and modesty is wrong, based on mysticism and superstition.
9. Christianity has degraded woman, and retarded progress.
10. The world has no true code of morals.

In reviewing these extreme views, you may call them, is it any wonder that Church has arisen to oppose such teaching? Scientists say the Bible was not given to teach science. I grant this. Neither should scientists undertake to teach the Bible. The Bible is supernatural. It must be what it is believed to be, the revelation of God's will to man. The Scriptures teach what a man is to believe concerning God, and what duties God requires of man.

By following the teaching of the Bible a man does not become a worse citizen; but rather, he who follows more closely the teaching of this wonderful Book is the highest specimen of the race. The Bible is the only source of light that shines across the cold, dark silence and shadow of the death. Surely none would extinguish this.

J. R. Pentuff Defends the Poole Bill, March 4, 1925[7]

A Concord Baptist minister, Pentuff was born in 1864 and attended Furman College and later did graduate work at Southern Baptist Theological Seminary, Shurtleff College, and the University of Chicago. A professor of history and Greek at Burlington Institute and later president of Stephens College, Pentuff was a distinguished evangelical. He took a major part in supporting the Poole bill. In this

---

7 J. R. Pentuff, "Dr. Pentuff on Poole Bill," *Biblical Recorder*, 4 March 1925, p. 10, http://www2.lib.unc.edu/ncc/evolution/biblicalrecorder3-4-25.html.

letter to the Biblical Recorder, *the North Carolina Baptist newspaper, Pentuff outlined his ideas*

Dear Dr. [Livingston] Johnson:–In the main I agree with you in what you say about the Poole Bill in your historical sketch. But there are two points on which I do not agree. To my mind the Poole Bill was not and is not in any sense a religious Bill and that is the main reason I spoke in favor of the Bill. The Bill, so far as I observed, made no reference to religion, no reference to the Bible, no word about any body's faith. To claim "blood kin" to the lower animals places the one who claims it out side the Bible, for it makes no such claims. It is begging the whole question to say that the Legislature cannot bar the teaching of such "blood kin" without infringing on somebody's religion, on the Bible, or on Christianity.

The Darwinian Theory of Organic Evolution and Descent of Man from the animals is Scientific, or it is pseudo-scientific and has no connection with the Bible, except that it was invented as a weapon with which to fight the Bible … Mr. [D. Scott] Poole's aim was to try to stop the State from teaching things that are against the Bible, and irreligious propaganda… .

Dr. [Harry W.] Chase endeavored to twist the whole discussion over to his fallacious interpretation of the freedom of speech and over on religious grounds… That is a favorite dodge of Evolutionists when asked to give a sensible argument for their theory. They at once pose as martyrs to the cause of science. And they begin to call us "pious hoodlums," "religious bigots," "suspicious," "prejudiced," and "uninformed," while they are the wise, good, and the persecuted…

In the second place, the legislators were made to believe that the passage of such as Bill would violate the freedom of speech measure in the Federal Constitution. The good men of those days when the Constitution was made, probably did not dream that the time would ever come in our country when Agnostics, Atheists, or traitors, or others who would destroy our homes, subvert our government, destroy peoples' faith in the Bible, would invoke the protection of the Constitution and Stars and Stripes while doing such work. …

J. R. Pentuff
Concord, N. C.

Frank Porter Graham Opposes the Poole Bill[8]

Ultimately, however, the Poole bill was narrowly defeated in the house by a vote of 67-46, with most of the opponents graduates of UNC and Wake Forest. In this

8 Frank Porter Graham, "Evolution, The University and the People," *Alumni Review* 13 (1924–1925): 205–207, http://www2.lib.unc.edu/ncc/evolution/fpg.html

document, Frank Porter Graham, then a member of UNC's history department, argued for defeat of the bill.

Evolution was taught at the University by North Carolinians before President Chase was born. Though modified from time to time with the increase of knowledge, the theory of evolution has moved from conquest to conquest and is now an important part of the teaching of geology, physics, chemistry, biology, psychology, and sociology. It is taught in most of the colleges in every civilized nation in the world. It is taught by Christian missionaries in the colleges of Asia and Africa. Today students in many of the high schools in both hemispheres accept the theory as freely as they do the Copernican system and the circulation of the blood. By papal edict it was handed down that the earth did not move around the sun and by solemn law it was enacted that the blood did not circulate from the heart through the body. But fortunately for the human race the earth continued on its celestial course and the blood went on its arterial way. Despite reports to the contrary, ex cathedra in medieval times and ex lege in modern times, the earth revolves, the blood circulates, and life evolves not only biologically, from simpler to more complex organisms, but also socially, with restless searchings of men for the kingdom of God. The great evolutionary process wins its way to acceptance around the world in accordance with laws higher than the constitution, whether joined or opposed by the misconceptions of men and the laws of states.

The Poole Bill raises issues older than the State of North Carolina. The inquisition, the index, and the stake are the unclaimed ancestors of the Poole Bill. Bruno chose to be burned to death rather than be saved on ecclesiastical terms. The teachers and the youth of North Carolina today would revolt against this ancient tyranny in its latest form. A tyranny that commanded them to be dishonest with themselves is not their idea of the way of salvation. All honor to President Chase for speaking clearly and standing squarely to the issues raised. May we also salute with equal respect President William Louis Poteat, who, by his stand at Wake Forest, as been, for all our colleges, the buffer state against unreason, the shock absorber of intolerance, and the first line trench against bigotry lo! these many years. President Chase, confronted with the issue, went out to meet it - 'God helping him, he could do no other.' Then and there he revindicated his leadership and holds more tightly to his side the fighting loyalty of university men. Let us all close ranks solidly about him. He has raised the University standard to be seen of all our people. Freedom to think, freedom to speak, and freedom to print are the texture of that standard. That freedom the great Virginians led the way in writing into the first amendment to the constitutions of the United States. It was one of the conditions of North Carolina's ratification of the federal instrument. Upon this three-fold freedom Thomas Jefferson founded our oldest national political party. It is the cornerstone of the motto of the first American university to open its doors in the name of the people - in a little North Carolina village one hundred and thirty years ago.

Anti-Evolution Broadside[9]

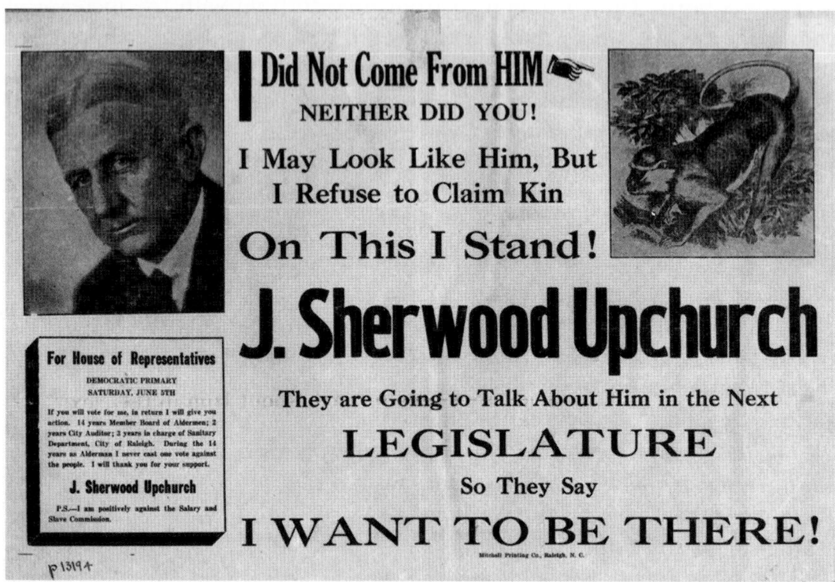

The Poole Bill, 1927[10]

The Poole bill of 1925 was defeated in the legislature, mostly because of opposition by UNC's legislative supporters. However, the anti-evolutionists were not yet finished. A second Poole bill of 1927 provided even stronger language, specifically banning the teaching of Darwin in schools and universities. In the end, however, the same political pattern prevailed, and the bill went down to defeat in the state house.

A BILL TO BE ENTITLED AN ACT TO PROHIBIT THE TEACHING OF EVOLUTION IN CERTAIN SCHOOLS AND COLLEGES IN THE STATE OF NORTH CAROLINA

---

9 http://docsouth.unc.edu/nc/upchurch/upchurch.html.

10 North Carolina General Assembly, "A Bill to be Entitled an Act to Prohibit the Teaching of Evolution in Certain Schools and Colleges in the State of North Carolina," 1927. Courtesy of the North Carolina State Archives, http://www2.lib.unc.edu/ncc/evolution/poolebill1927.html.

The General Assembly of North Carolina do enact:

Section 1. That it shall be unlawful for any professor, teacher or instructor, to teach in any school, college or educational institution within the State of North Carolina, receiving aid from the State, any doctrine or theory of evolution, which contradicts or denies the divine origin of man or of the universe, as taught in the Holy Bible: PROVIDED, however, that nothing in this act shall be construed to prohibit the teaching in said schools, colleges or educational institutions of all useful arts and sciences, unless the same are taught in such a manner as to contradict the fundamental truths of the Holy Bible.

Sec. 2. That any professor, teacher or instructor violating the provisions of Section One, of this Act shall be guilty of a misdemeanor and upon conviction shall be fined or imprisoned in the discretion of the Court, and in the discretion of the court may be disqualified from teaching in such schools, colleges or educational institutions upon such terms and conditions, and for such a time as the court in its discretion may order.

Sec. 3. That this act shall be in force from and after its ratification.

Part 6

Toward the Twenty-First Century

16

Postwar North Carolina

In the half century after the end of World War II, North Carolina underwent a social, economic, and political transformation. Continuing a trend that had begun during World War I, many rural black North Carolinians left their homes for the city, either in North Carolina or in the North. Peaking during the period between World War II and the 1970s, the exodus of African Americans became one of the most significant social trends of modern North Carolina. But the state's population expanded, in large part because of an unprecedented spate of in-migration to the state of non-native southerners, a trend that continued into the early years of the twenty-first century with the arrival of thousands of Latinos. The North Carolina economy also experienced dramatic changes during the era. The demise of the plantation economy meant that traditional cotton culture entered irreversible decline, while new, highly capitalized forms of agriculture became more prevalent. Industrialization continued in North Carolina with the spread of manufacturing. In politics, serious cracks emerged in the political consensus of white supremacy, and by the 1960s North Carolina was becoming a more competitive political environment with the reemergence of the Republican Party.

Growth and Change in Postwar North Carolina

North Carolina's economy combined industrial manufacturing—by World War II, the state was the most industrialized of any state in the South—and labor-intensive agriculture. In 1947, some 42 percent of the workforce was employed in agriculture and 28 percent in manufacturing. By the 1970s, the agricultural sector was much smaller, and only 8 percent of North Carolinians worked in farming, as opposed to "agribusiness." Industrial manufacturing, in contrast, continued to expand into the 1970s, and North Carolina remained one of the most industrialized states in the United States. By 1970, the portion of North Carolinians working in manufacturing had increased to 40 percent. Between

North Carolina: Change and Tradition in a Southern State, Second Edition. William A. Link.

Table 16.1 The North Carolina Population, 1940–2005

Year	Population
1940	3,571,623
1950	4,061,929
1960	4,556,155
1970	5,032,059
1980	5,881,776
1990	6,628,637
2000	8,049,313
2005 (July)	8,683,242

1940 and 2008, the state's population more than doubled, from about 3.5 million to more than 8 million people (see Table 16.1). The growth in population was significant, indicating North Carolina's emergence as the nation's tenth largest state. These demographic changes were accompanied by significant differences in the characteristics of the population. Reflecting a trend that began after the Civil War, towns and cities attracted rural migrants, and North Carolina became decidedly more urbanized.

Indeed, by 1960, nearly 40 percent of North Carolinians lived in urban areas as compared with about 26 percent in 1930. Correspondingly, there was a steady decline of traditional rural living. The farm population declined from 59 percent of all North Carolinians in 1920 to 18 percent in 1960. The concentration of urban population across the state yielded a steady growth in the size of major cities, especially along an urban corridor stretching along Interstate 85, between Raleigh and Charlotte, and including Greensboro and Winston-Salem (see Table 16.2). The urban corridor—what became a sort of metro Carolina—included six counties along I-85: Wake, Durham, Orange, Guilford, Forsyth, and Mecklenburg. Comprising the center of industrialized North Carolina, these counties accounted for about 30 percent of the state's population. The largest city in North Carolina, Charlotte, became a magnet for population. In addition, after the 1980s, Raleigh and the surrounding counties, driven by the expansion of service, technology, and information industries, became major centers of growth.

Table 16.2 Standard Metropolitan Statistical Areas (SMSAs), 1960–1980

SMSA	1960	1970	1980
Charlotte	443,855	557,785	637,218
Greensboro/Winston-Salem/High Point	622,086	724,129	827,252
Raleigh/Durham/Chapel Hill	324,047	419,254	531,167

North Carolina, especially in the latter of the half of the twentieth century, essentially became two states—one, poor and underdeveloped, the other, dynamic and booming. Especially between the 1940s and the 1970s, large numbers of residents left North Carolina for northern cities. The migrants were white and black, though about twice as many African Americans left North Carolina as did whites. Between 1940 and 1970, the state experienced a net outmigration of approximately 440,000 nonwhites, part of the so-called Great Migration of African Americans from the South that began around the time of World War I and ended in the early 1970s. Most of these migrants were men and women in their twenties and thirties. Disproportionately, the migrants left the poorest parts of North Carolina: the eastern part of the state, where rural African Americans were eager to escape from the collapsing plantation system and the poverty that had historically characterized their lives. Although some of the rural migrants of the 1950s and 1960s moved to North Carolina cities, the majority of them moved north to the cities of the Eastern Seaboard.

Along with the exodus out of rural North Carolina, there was also a significant migration into the state. Since the late eighteenth century, North Carolina had seen few newcomers arrive from the North or from outside the country. After 1945, that changed substantially. Some post-1945 migrants came to serve in and then remained in the state's military bases. Also attractive were counties with a mixture of new industries, retirement communities, and resort and tourist developments in the mountains and on the coast. Migrants moved in significant numbers to mountain communities near Asheville, Hendersonville, and Boone, as well as to eastern coastal communities near Wilmington and New Bern, helping in each community to create a different population mix and economy. Manufacturing and extractive industries continued to dominate the North Carolina economy between 1940 and 1980, but during the last two decades of the twentieth century service, finance, retiree, tourist, and high-tech industries spurred economic development. Charlotte became a national banking center with a series of mergers that created a new Bank of America in 1998. In addition, a merger brought Wachovia Corporation (which originally was in Winston-Salem) to Charlotte in 2001. Economic change attracted the greatest numbers of migrants into the state. Between 1990 and 2005, some 1.4 million people migrated to North Carolina. Migrants increasingly came to North Carolina's population centers. Between 1980 and 1987, Raleigh and Charlotte attracted a third of all new residents. Between 1990 and 2004, the population of both Wake and Mecklenburg Counties (home to Raleigh and Charlotte) grew by nearly 60 percent, more than double the state's growth rate of 25 percent. By 2004, Charlotte had almost 600,000 residents, while Raleigh claimed 326,000—making them the largest metropolitan centers of the state.

The emergence of finance, service, and tourism as dominant industries in North Carolina coincided with the decline of traditional manufacturing and agriculture during the 1980s and 1990s. While manufacturing provided more

Figure 16.1 Charlotte skyline, 2006.

than 36 percent of all nonfarm jobs in 1975, that figure had declined to 15.4 percent in 2004. This economic transition was especially acute in the textile, apparel, and furniture industries, all of which began to experience devastating foreign competition in the 1980s. Between 2000 and 2004, these industries lost a combined total of more than 214,000 jobs. The number of North Carolinians employed in agriculture continued to decline during the 1970s and 1980s; by 1987, only 3 percent of the state's workforce was employed in farming. At the same time, the proportion of employees working in manufacturing decreased from 40 percent in 1970 to 30 percent in 1987. Meanwhile, new jobs were created in North Carolina completely outside of agriculture and industry; four-fifths of new jobs created between 1970 and 1987 came from the so-called service sector. Although North Carolina led the nation by the 1990s in industrial employment, by the dawn of the twenty-first century, foreign competition led to a shrunken employment base in textiles, apparel, furniture, and tobacco manufacturing.

The Expanding University System

One of the most important and powerful engines of social change after World War II was the growth of the University of North Carolina. For much of the nineteenth century, the University at Chapel Hill had been a sleepy, remote backwater; in 1900, the institution had only 512 students enrolled and a thirty-five-member faculty. By the time of World War I, however, the Chapel Hill campus changed radically. In the 1920s, Chapel Hill became renowned regionally and even nationally, and in the 1930s its enrollment grew to 2,600 students, with more than 300 full-time and part-time faculty members. Intellectual centers such as the Institute for Research in Social Science (founded in 1924), the Institute of Government (founded in 1932), and the School of Public Health (founded in 1936), helped to involve the university directly in the public affairs of the state.

Table 16.3 Enrollment at North Carolina Colleges and Universities, 1960–2006

Year	Public Institutions	Private Institutions
1960	35,894	31,679
1970	92,597	47,888
1980	132,381	55,133
1990	170,422	63,881
2000	201,130	70,507
2006	247,309	83,304

In 1931, university consolidation established a multicampus system with branches at Chapel Hill, Raleigh, and Greensboro. The returning World War II veterans after 1945, followed by the burgeoning numbers of Baby Boomer students in the 1960s and 1970s, accounted for the surges in student enrollments (see Table 16.3). Even as existing public colleges grew, more were founded to meet the needs of the state. By the 1950s, North Carolina had nine more public colleges. In 1961, Gov. Terry Sanford appointed a Governor's Commission on Education Beyond the High School. Headed by Winston-Salem attorney Irving E. Carlyle, the commission delivered its report to Sanford in August 1962. The report urged that North Carolina make higher education available to a greater share of its population; only a tenth of the state's young people in the early 1960s had earned a college or university degree. Acknowledging the "sudden and substantial rise" of Baby Boomer-era students, the Carlyle Commission wanted to see university enrollment double. Specifically, it called for the establishment of a new community college system that could supply technical education beyond

Figure 16.2 Terry Sanford. *Source: Bettmann/Getty Images.*

high school. In addition, the commission recommended that UNC expand its campuses to other locations in the state.

The General Assembly had established the first community colleges in 1957 with the Community College Act. At the same time, the legislature created a system of Industrial Education Centers (IECs) designed to provide technical training and vocational education. In 1961, when the Carlyle Commission was created, there were seven IECs and five public junior colleges in the state. The public junior colleges at Charlotte, Asheville, and Wilmington all had ambitions to become full-fledged public colleges. While the commission acknowledged those goals, it recommended merging the public junior colleges and the IECs under one system of community colleges. In May 1963, the General Assembly acted on those recommendations by creating a Department of Community Colleges that functioned under the State Board of Education. The community college system grew rapidly over the next twenty years, and by 1978 there were fifty-eight campuses across the state. In 1981, the community colleges came under the control of a new state Board of Community Colleges.

Acting on the Carlyle Commission report, the multicampus UNC system in 1965 expanded with the creation of a new campus at Charlotte; in 1969, the system incorporated senior public colleges at Asheville and Wilmington (which became UNC–Asheville and UNC–Wilmington). The expansion of public colleges and universities continued outside of the University, and in the 1960s East Carolina College, which had been founded as a teacher's college in 1907, tripled in size during the presidency of Leo M. Jenkins, from 1960 to 1978. Jenkins successfully made East Carolina into an independent university by legislative enactment in 1967. After a long campaign in the legislature, Jenkins succeeded in establishing a medical school at East Carolina, despite a turf fight and intense opposition from UNC supporters.

The rivalry between East Carolina and UNC culminated in the General Assembly's session of 1972, in which it completely restructured higher education in the state. Under the new legislation, all senior public colleges and universities came under the control of a new entity—the Board of Governors—known as the University of North Carolina. Containing sixteen institutions, it included the six UNC campuses at Chapel Hill, Raleigh, Greensboro, Charlotte, Asheville, and Wilmington; five historically black colleges at Durham, Greensboro, Winston-Salem, Elizabeth City, and Fayetteville; East Carolina and former teachers' colleges at Boone (Appalachian State), Cullowhee (Western Carolina); and historically Indian Pembroke College. The new UNC system also included the North Carolina School of the Arts in Winston-Salem, which opened in 1965.

Private colleges and universities have always been important in North Carolina. Many of these institutions were denominationally affiliated schools founded in the 1800s. By 1945, denominational schools educated nearly as many students as did public institutions. Private colleges and universities remained important in the post-1945 era. Davidson College (Presbyterian),

Duke University (Methodist), Wake Forest University (Baptist), Elon University (Church of Christ), Lenoir-Rhyne College (Lutheran), and Guilford College (Quakers) all represented the denominational heritage. Other private institutions, such as Bennett College in Greensboro, St. Augustine in Raleigh, and Johnson C. Smith in Charlotte, are historically African American. In total, some thirty-six colleges and universities belong to the North Carolina Association of Independent Colleges and Universities.

Research Triangle Park and the New Economy

In the post-1945 era, it became increasingly clear that the traditional occupations prevailing in North Carolina were low-income ones, and by the 1950s the state ranked among the lowest in the nation in per capita income. Traditional livelihoods for North Carolinians—work on small farms and in mills and factories—had locked many people into a low-wage cycle. In 1952, only two states, Arkansas and Mississippi, had lower levels of income than North Carolina. In the post-Reconstruction era, the Industrial Revolution had brought manufacturing to the state, which became a national center for cotton textiles, tobacco, and furniture. Yet these industries, even as early as the 1940s, faced an uncertain future, and although employment continued to grow in these industries between the 1940s and 1970s, international competition and the general decline of manufacturing in the United States would eventually undermine their existence. The creation of Research Triangle Park (RTP) in the 1950s thus takes on great importance in North Carolina's history, for RTP eventually became a force for growth and development and set the pattern for future economic development.

Research Triangle Park was a creation of the three universities in the Raleigh–Chapel Hill–Durham area—NC State, UNC, and Duke. In 1952, Howard Odum, the distinguished UNC sociologist, proposed research cooperation between UNC and State. The real impetus for the creation of RTP came from North Carolina's political leadership, especially Gov. Luther Hodges. Elected as lieutenant governor in 1952, Hodges became governor on the death of William B. Umstead in November 1954. Subsequently, in 1956, Hodges was elected to a second term as governor, and President John F. Kennedy would in 1961 appoint him as secretary of commerce. A former executive with Fieldcrest Mills, in Eden, North Carolina, Hodges was a businessman's governor, and one his primary objectives was economic development; he worked tirelessly to promote North Carolina trade, both domestic and international. The crown jewel of Hodges's program, and his most lasting legacy, would be RTP, what he called the "heart and the hope of North Carolina's industrial future."

Hodges endorsed the concept of the RTP only after energetic efforts by Romeo Guest, a Greensboro contractor who had worked as an industrial

Figure 16.3 Luther H. Hodges. *Source: Courtesy of the State Archives of North Carolina.*

recruiter for the state's Commerce and Industry Division during the 1940s and early 1950s. Guest wanted to convert the undeveloped pinelands between Chapel Hill, Durham, and Raleigh into an area that would attract high-tech industry. Working with another industrial recruiter, Brandon Hodges (no relation to Luther), Guest tirelessly worked to persuade state leaders to endorse the concept of a "Carolina Triangle," which, by 1953, Guest was calling a "Research Triangle." In the case of Harvard and MIT, he pointed out, the technological and research facilities of major universities had brought tangible economic benefits to their home state of Massachusetts. Furthermore, the most successful partnership between university expertise and the private sector was already up and running in the Stanford Research Institute, which later figured prominently in the development of the Silicon Valley as a center of the computer hardware and software industries. In 1953, according to another recruiter, Walter Harper, Guest and his supporters "more or less stumbled on" a 1,000-acre tract of land in Durham County. This was, according to Harper, "pure luck," a matter of the existence of an available tract of land. "We were off to a running start," recalled Harper.[1]

With Guest promoting the idea, a delegation visited Hodges in late 1954 to push the Research Triangle. Although initially unenthusiastic, the governor had endorsed the idea by February 1955. That spring, a Research Triangle Council (which about a year later became the Research Triangle Committee) was created, with UNC sociology professor George Simpson taking leave to serve as its first director. In 1959, the Research Triangle Institute, which pooled research resources from the three campuses, was established. In the late 1950s, a private company, the Pinelands Company, began assembling tracts of land for a Research Triangle Park; its stock would be controlled by the committee, which in 1958 became the Research Triangle Foundation. Winston-Salem banker Archie Davis led the effort to raise more than $1.4 million to break ground on the park and the Research Triangle Institute, which subsisted through research contract work with industry and government.

Research Triangle offered a new approach to economic recruitment, as the Park would house new companies interested in relocating to an area with extensive support for research. In 1959, Chemstrand Corporation, a manufacturer of chemical fibers, became the first occupant of the park when it purchased a 100-acre site. Thereafter, new arrivals came slowly. In 1965, the National Institute of Environmental Health Sciences created a $70 million research center. In April 1965, IBM announced that it would locate a 600,000-sq ft facility there. Other facilities relocated at a faster pace during the next decades, and the RTP effectively transformed the economy of the Raleigh-Durham-Chapel Hill area and made it a population magnet. In 1978, in a major development, the American Academy of Arts and Sciences located the National Humanities Center at RTP. By 2000, tenants in the nearly 7,000-acre RTP occupied more than 18 million square feet of space—a dramatic increase from just over 2 million in 1970. In 2000, more than 44,000 people worked in RTP.

Sports in Postwar North Carolina

In one of the most important social changes during the fifty years after 1945, the sports and entertainment industry emerged prominently in North Carolina's social, cultural, and economic life. The Wilmington-born Charles Kuralt, who went on to have a long career as a CBS news reporter and commentator, remembered: "Wherever you lived, no matter what school you went to or what you did for a living, there was a baseball team playing nearby." Baseball teams before 1945 existed at the neighborhood, high school, collegiate, and minor-league level, and the game held the attention of athletes and spectators alike.[2] The Piedmont League, which came into existence in 1920, had franchises in Durham, High Point, Winston-Salem, Greensboro, Charlotte, and Asheville, while other "minors" such as the South Atlantic and Eastern Carolina leagues, thrived in North Carolina towns and cities. By 1949, at the peak of baseball's popularity, there were forty-nine minor league teams in the state. Today, the (AAA) Durham Bulls, an affiliate of the Tampa Bay Rays, are one of the most popular minor league clubs in the nation. In 1995, to the delight of their steady fans and visitors to Durham alike, the Bulls moved into a $16 million brick ballpark, the Durham Bulls Athletic Park—in the heart of the city's

Figure 16.4 James King Kern "Kay" Kyser and cheerleader cheering for UNC team at a Duke University–North Carolina football game, Durham, 1939. *Source: Library of Congress, LC-USF33-030683-M3.*

downtown. North Carolina also produced successful major leaguers, including Greensboro's Rick Ferrell, High Point's Luke Appling, Roxboro's Enos Slaughter, and Tarboro's Burgess Whitehead. Later, in the 1960s and 1970s, North Carolina natives—and Hall of Famers—included Hertford's Jim "Catfish" Hunter, Huntersville's Hoyt Wilhem, and Williamston's Gaylord Perry.

Beginning in the 1960s, North Carolina hosted other professional sports teams. In 1969, the American Basketball Association's Carolina Cougars became North Carolina's first major sports franchise. Formerly the Houston Mavericks, the Cougars alternated home-court play in Charlotte, Greensboro, and Raleigh during the five years of their fledgling existence. In the 1973–74 season, the Cougars attracted 340,000 fans, though the owners moved the franchise in the 1975 season. Thirteen years later, professional basketball returned with the arrival of a National Basketball Association team, the Charlotte Hornets. After the Hornets moved to New Orleans in 2002, another NBA expansion team, the Charlotte Bobcats, began in North Carolina. In professional football, the Carolina Panthers, arriving in Charlotte as an expansion team during the 1995 season, became the first NFL team in the Carolinas. The next year the Panthers moved into the 73,504-seat Carolina Stadium, now the Bank of America Stadium, and saw postseason play that year, making it to the NFC Championship game. In 2004, the young franchise made it all the way to the

Super Bowl, which they lost only narrowly to the New England Patriots. In 1997, the National Hockey League's Hartford Whalers moved to North Carolina. Renamed the Carolina Hurricanes, they played one season in Greensboro and thereafter at the new Entertainment and Sports Arena in Raleigh.

Competing with professional sports for the time and interest of Tar Heels was a long and storied tradition of sports at the intercollegiate level. Throughout the 1920s and 1930s, the "Big Five" in North Carolina—which included UNC, Duke, Wake Forest, NC State, and Davidson—maintained intrastate sports rivalries. The beginning of the Southern Conference in 1921 extended competition across state lines with campuses across the South. College football surged in popularity after World War I, and at UNC in 1925 the team went 7-1 and attracted 16,000 fans in its final game against the University of Virginia. In 1927, football had become so popular at UNC that the university constructed Kenan Stadium, which held crowds as large as 28,000. At Duke, Coach Wallace Wade helped to build a nationally competitive football program after he was hired in 1931. By the 1950s, college football was beginning to overshadow baseball. From 1946 to 1949, UNC's football team was led by All-American running back Charlie "Choo-Choo" Justice of Asheville, one of North Carolina's greatest athletes ever.

Intercollegiate athletics in North Carolina gained fan support thanks to two key developments after World War II. First, in December 1953, North Carolina's Big Four—UNC, Wake, Duke, and NC State—joined Maryland, Clemson, South Carolina, and Virginia to form the Atlantic Coast Conference (ACC). Then, in 1971, South Carolina left the ACC, but the conference subsequently expanded with the addition of Georgia Tech in 1978, Florida State in 1991, Miami and Virginia Tech in 2004, and Boston College in 2005. The ACC's success provided a wider market and regular regional competition for all intercollegiate sports, but especially for the high-interest, high-revenue sports of football and basketball. Finally, the dramatic increase in the marketing of college sports broadcasting, especially on television, injected huge amounts of money into North Carolina's college football and basketball programs.

In the post-World War II era, college basketball grew wildly popular in North Carolina. The most successful programs were those at the Big Four schools. In the late 1940s and 1950s, Everett Case, originally a high school coach in Indiana, built a highly successful basketball program at NC State. Case managed to recruit players from all over the country, and his teams dominated both conference play and contests with in-state rivals (he defeated UNC, for example, fifteen consecutive times). In 1949, the opening of the William Neal Reynolds Coliseum, with 12,400 seats, made it the largest basketball arena in the Southeast, and Case's teams included All-Americans such as Dick Dickey, Ronnie Shavlik, and Bobby Speight. In 1953, UNC responded to NC State's triumphs by hiring Frank McGuire of St. John's University in New York, and, by recruiting almost entirely from the New York City area, he built powerful teams. UNC's legendary

1957 national championship team, with New Yorkers Lennie Rosenbluth, Tommie Kearns, Joe Quigg, Pete Brennan, and Bob Cunningham, bested Kansas and its superstar, Wilt Chamberlain, in a dramatic triple-overtime victory, ending the season with a stunning 32–0 record. In the late 1950s, meanwhile, Duke, coached by former Case assistant Vic Bubas, began to build a highly competitive basketball program.

But as college basketball emerged as the leading sport in North Carolina, it also became entangled with problems related to money and fan hysteria. Intense competition for recruits led to irregularities. Case's program at NC State was clouded by sanctions placed on it after the National Collegiate Athletic Association (NCAA) imposed a four-year ban on postseason play after charging that Case offered gifts and cash to Louisiana basketball sensation Jackie Moreland in 1956. At UNC, McGuire also came under sanction (in 1961) for recruiting violations. Even more serious were the point-shaving scandals of the early 1960s, in which players at both UNC and NC State were bribed to manipulate the margin of victories so that gamblers could beat the point spread. In 1961, a point-shaving scandal forced McGuire out, but his replacement, assistant coach Dean Smith, went on to build a basketball dynasty at UNC. Perhaps the worst display of point shaving involved the Dixie Classic, a holiday basketball tournament run by NC State at Reynolds Coliseum. The Dixie, which first ran in 1949, attracted the best teams in the nation, was the subject of fanatical fan interest, and generated some $31,000 in annual profits for the State's basketball program. Between 1949 and 1961, the Dixie Classic drew 713,800 spectators. In May 1961, after it was disclosed that gamblers had infiltrated the tournament, UNC system president William Friday cancelled the Dixie Classic and sharply reduced the playing schedules of both UNC and NC State.

In the face of the controversies, however, college basketball fever continued to grip North Carolina. In his thirty-six-year tenure, from 1961 until his retirement in 1997, Dean Smith's teams met with spectacular success, with 879 victories, twenty-three consecutive NCAA tournament appearances, eleven Final Four appearances, and national championships in 1982 and 1993. Smith coached a series of All-Americans and NBA players, including Billy Cunningham, Larry Brown, James Worthy, Sam Perkins, Phil Ford, Bob McAdoo, Kenny Smith, Walter Davis, Jerry Stackhouse, Antawn Jamison, Rick Fox, Vince Carter, and Rasheed Wallace. Perhaps the greatest basketball player of all time, Wilmington's Michael Jordan, played under Smith at UNC from 1981 to 1984. Rivaling Smith's success and dominance at UNC was Mike Krzyzewski, who has coached Duke since 1980. By 2008, he had become the most successful active coach in college basketball, with more than 800 wins, ten Final Four appearances, ten ACC championships, and national championships in 1991, 1992, and 2001. His Duke players have included such NBA standouts as Danny Ferry, Christian Laettner, Carlos Boozer, Grant Hill, Luol Deng, Shane Battier, and Elton Brand.

Figure 16.5 Left to right: Michael Jordan, Matt Doherty, and Sam Perkins, with Coach Dean Smith, October 14, 1992. *Source*: Raleigh News and Observer.

College football and basketball were not the only sports attracting attention in North Carolina—and college sports was not an exclusively male domain. In 1972, Congress enacted the Education Amendments Act, Title IX of which required colleges and universities that accepted federal funding to grant more equal support and access to women's sports programs. In the wake of the "Title IX" legislation, women's athletics grew at the high school and college level throughout the 1970s, 1980s, and 1990s. Especially noteworthy has been the success of women's soccer, which became a major high school sport. At UNC, women's soccer, which began at that campus in 1979, stepped on the path to a long era of dominance. After having won the national championship in 1982, between 1983 and 2003 UNC's women's soccer team went on to claim seventeen out of twenty-two national championships. The longtime UNC coach, Anson Dorrance, helped his teams achieve their remarkable level of success. Perhaps his best-known player, Mia Hamm, played soccer at UNC between 1989 and 1993.

In the late twentieth century, one of the most popular and most successful sports in North Carolina has been stock car racing, especially what became the National Association for Stock Car Auto Racing (NASCAR), which by 2008 had become the second most-watched sport on television, second only to professional football. With 75 million fans worldwide in 150 countries, NASCAR is a billion-dollar industry that has its roots in North Carolina.

According to lore, stock car racing began during the Prohibition era, when moonshiners tried to outrace their police pursuers. By the 1930s, scores of local tracks began appearing in North Carolina to host races, and with the end of Prohibition ex-moonshiners moved into professional racing. Thus, Robert Glen "Junior" Johnson, of Wilkes County, worked for his father as a moonshiner and began racing as a teenager. Johnson became one of the early heroes of the emerging stock car industry. Racing took off in the late 1940s, after William France and Ed Otto organized NASCAR and began sponsoring large-scale race events in North Carolina and across the rest of the South. NASCAR's first-ever sponsored event was held at the dirt Charlotte Speedway on June 19, 1949. Ten years later, the Charlotte partners Curtis Turner and O. Bruton Smith constructed the new Charlotte Motor Speedway (in Concord), a 1.5-mile-long racetrack that hosted a 600-mile race, the longest of any NASCAR event. The Charlotte Motor Speedway became an important venue for NASCAR and helped to center much of the sport's activity in North Carolina. Other tracks subsequently opened in the state, including the North Wilkesboro Speedway and the North Carolina Speedway in Rockingham.

The most important North Carolinian in stock car racing was Richard Petty. A member of a NASCAR family dynasty, Petty hailed from Level Cross, in Randolph County. His father, Lee Petty, won the first Daytona 500 in 1959 and earned NASCAR championships three times, in 1954, 1958, and 1959. During a career that spanned several decades after the 1950s, Richard Petty won 200 races, taking both the Winston Cup championships and the Daytona 500 seven times, the latter a record number. Known as "the King," Richard Petty is considered by most racing fans the greatest stock car driver of all time. Retiring in 1992, Petty remained a major presence in NASCAR. A number of other NASCAR drivers were native North Carolinians; among them was Dale Earnhardt, born in Kannapolis, who went on to become a highly successful and popular driver after the 1970s. His tragic death (at the age of 49) in Turn 4 of the final lap of the Daytona 500 still haunts his many fans, but his legacy lives on in his son, Dale Earnhardt, Jr., another native-born North Carolinian. "Junior," as he is known to those who follow racing, won his first Daytona 500 in 2004.

Labor in the Postwar Era

In the 1920s and 1930s there were various attempts by unions to organize the cotton textile industry, efforts that had culminated in the General Strike of 1934. After its failure, unions were able to make few inroads during the 1930s. In the last years of the decade, the Congress of Industrial Organizations (CIO) initiated an aggressive effort to organize tobacco workers in North Carolina, and during World War II African American and white workers in Winston-Salem responded by embracing the union and organizing the R. J. Reynolds tobacco factories. The victory of the CIO in part reflected favorable conditions during World War II, when federal authorities protected labor unions in order to maximize production. The CIO's progress in North Carolina tobacco factories was matched by gains by union organizers in textile mills. Beginning in 1937, the Textile Workers Organizing Committee (TWOC) initiated an ambitious effort to organize southern mills, but they had little success. By 1941, the newly organized Textile Workers Union of America (TWUA) enjoyed some success. In that year, only 500 of North Carolina's textile workers were employed in mills that had collective bargaining agreements, and the National Labor Relations Board could do little in the face of determined anti-union sentiment among mill owners and managers.

As a result of a labor shortage combined with intense demand for textiles from war orders, the balance of power tipped during World War II. The National War Labor Board (NWLB) was energetic and efficient in supervising fair union elections and protecting collective bargaining. In the interests of preserving war production, NWLB brought unprecedented opportunities for organized labor in North Carolina. Nonetheless, there was a price paid for federal protection. Unions were required to sign no-strike pledges, which restricted their leverage with employers. In addition, the TWUA made its most strenuous efforts outside of the South, and, even with federal protection, by 1945 only 10 percent of North Carolina's 200,000 mill workers belonged to the union. Despite federal mandate, North Carolina mills continued to resist vigorous labor inroads by forcing extended union elections, rejecting election results, and delaying contract talks. In 1943, Burlington Mills even shut down two plants to avoid complying with an NWLB order to recognize the union with a new contract.

Set against a context of continuing tensions between workers and managers and substantial gains by unions, the post-World War II era brought renewed conflict. The CIO's ambitious plans to expand union power in the unorganized South foundered, as anti-union forces emphasized that these unions were left-wing and favored racial integration. The tobacco-factory union in Winston-Salem encountered a concerted campaign by factory owners in the immediate postwar years to uproot the CIO union by associating it with Communism; opponents also fanned racial tensions, both in the Winston-Salem community toward the union and between white and black workers.

Following a wartime and postwar boom, the textile industry in North Carolina underwent slow but steady change. In 1948 and 1949, cotton textiles were hit hard by a recession in which employment in mills declined from 230,000 to 200,000 between May 1948 and August 1949. Some manufacturers eliminated the third shift as a way to reduce employment. Although the recession ended by 1950, structural problems in the industry remained. In part because of declining demand for American textiles abroad, increased international competition, and a continuing shift to synthetics, consumption of cotton textiles declined. A number of textile manufacturers raised productivity

Figure 16.6 Workers in Winston-Salem during the 1947 strike. *Source: Courtesy of Forsyth County Public Library Photograph Collection.*

by modernizing equipment and by increasing workloads. The stage was thus set for even further conflict between management and labor. Unions were only weakly established; in the mid-1950s, about 13,000 of the 220,000 textile workers were organized, and the numbers dwindled during the postwar years.

Race and Anticommunism in Postwar North Carolina

In the aftermath of World War II, North Carolina experienced significant turmoil. During the war, the traditional social structure had come under duress. Workers were challenging managers for control on the shop floor, and under the protective umbrella of the federal government, union membership in North Carolina expanded. Some unions were associated with the CIO, which succeeded in organizing a biracial union at R. J. Reynolds tobacco factory in Winston-Salem. After World War II, the CIO continued its efforts with Operation Dixie. Operating in twelve southern states between 1946 and 1953, Operation Dixie sought to extend the wartime gains and solidify organized labor's position in the anti-union South.

Operation Dixie ran squarely into some important post-World War II trends. In the late 1940s, much of white opinion solidified against desegregation and rallied around white supremacy. President Harry S. Truman's desegregation of the American military and the Democratic National Convention's adoption of a pro-civil rights plank in July 1948 led to a walkout by the entire Alabama and Mississippi delegations, along with other delegates. The breakaway group formed a separate convention, created the States' Rights Democratic Party, or "Dixiecrat" Party, and nominated Gov. Strom Thurmond of South Carolina to run as its presidential candidate. In 1948, former vice-president Henry A. Wallace ran on a left-wing Progressive Party ticket which was organized in December 1946. The Progressives favored accommodation with the Soviet Union, economic justice, protection for labor unions, and an end to segregation. Attracting African Americans, union organizers, and women, the Progressive Party in North Carolina adopted the slogan "Jim Crow Must Go!," and it nominated Mary Price as the party's gubernatorial candidate in 1948, the first time that a woman had run for this office in the history of the state. In 1947, opponents of the Progressive Party claimed that the Southern Conference for Human Welfare (SCHW)—an organization founded in 1938 to liberalize the system of segregation, many supporters of which were Progressives—had been dominated by Communists, and in June 1947 the US House Committee on Un-American Activities described the organization as a "red front." Elizabeth Bently, a former Soviet agent turned informer, charged in 1948 that Price had worked as a spy since 1941. Although Price described Bentley's charges as "fantastic," the declassification of Soviet espionage records in 1995, after the end of the Cold War, strongly indicated Price's involvement in Soviet spying. While working as an assistant to journalist Walter Lippmann in New York City, Price had passed information to the Russians. In addition, she worked as a Soviet courier, according to these records. Although some Communists participated in the SCHW, these charges were a gross exaggeration, but the damage had already been done. When Henry Wallace visited North Carolina in August 1948, he was greeted by menacing crowds of whites, and in every city that he visited hecklers disrupted his speeches and threw eggs and tomatoes. In addition, with the onset of the Cold War, anticommunism and fears of subversion merged with fears of racial change, and labor organizers—who endorsed integration—faced the strong opposition of southern whites.[3] The reaction to Wallace's visit, wrote an African American, demonstrated that whites despised "anyone, white or black," who favored "better conditions for brown Americans." Black North Carolinians could not rely on the good intentions of whites: "If we have to pull ourselves up by our bootstraps, WE WILL DO IT."[4]

The convergence of opposition to desegregation and a wave of anticommunism in North Carolina played out in the Senate race of May 1950. Two years earlier, in 1948, W. Kerr Scott had been swept into office as an insurgent in the Democratic gubernatorial primary, and his campaign left the political system

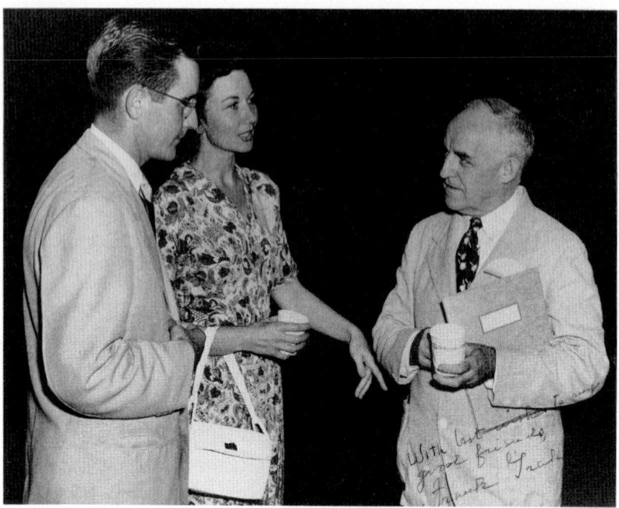

Figure 16.7 William Friday, Ida Friday, and Frank Porter Graham, at Graham's swearing-in as a US Senator, 1949. *Source: North Carolina Collection, University of North Carolina Library at Chapel Hill.*

badly shaken. Organization Democrats, generally conservative in their stance on white supremacy and anti-union issues and unsympathetic to urban and industrial interests, dominated politics until the ascendancy of Scott, who ran in the Democratic gubernatorial primary as a left-leaning populist, a political outsider promising true reform. An Alamance County dairy farmer and commissioner of agriculture, Scott challenged the political establishment—the famous "Shelby Dynasty" that had run the state since the 1930s—and he appealed to a broad coalition of farmers, organized labor, and urban African Americans. As governor, Scott initiated a "Go Forward" program that provided for 15,000 miles of farm-to-market roads. At the time, while Scott was governor, 31,000 rural telephone lines were added, along with 150,000 rural power connections.

On March 22, 1949, only a few months into his governorship, Scott appointed UNC president Frank Porter Graham to the US Senate seat to replace J. Melville Broughton, who had died suddenly on March 6, 1949. Much admired by many North Carolinians, "Dr. Frank" was also widely disliked by conservatives for his support of controversial causes in labor and race relations. Although Graham did not favor integration—he preferred a more cautious, gradualist approach—many North Carolinians branded him a turncoat on white supremacy, and he remained vulnerable politically. His appointment to the Senate galvanized the anticommunist and staunchly segregationist wing of the Democratic Party, which rose up in revolt against him. In Frank Graham, the opponents of New

Deal liberalism had found a target that embodied their fears about labor relations and race; these joined with rumors about communist subversion in the Truman administration.

Appointed to office in 1949, Graham faced a special election to retain the Senate seat in the Democratic primary of May 1950; the election would divide the state along modernizer/traditionalist lines. Raleigh attorney Willis Smith, a World War I veteran, respected attorney, and former legislator, rallied conservatives and decided, on February 24, 1950, to challenge Graham. Representing many of the state's largest business interests, Smith held views typical of the conservative wing of the Democratic Party. One of the bitterest elections in modern North Carolina history, the 1950 contest defined ideological differences. Early on, Smith ran an aggressive campaign that accused Graham of subversion for his connections with liberal/left organizations and Communists. Smith further suggested that Graham favored federal intervention through a revived Fair Employment Practices Committee (FEPC) and questioned his devotion to white supremacy. Graham responded defensively—and, in general, ineffectively—to Smith's attacks, though he carefully documented his denunciations of Communists and his support for gradual and voluntary, not compulsory, desegregation. Smith linked Graham with the left-wing tendencies of the unpopular Truman administration on issues of race, labor, and taxes, and the campaign for the primary election turned decidedly nasty. Smith supporters ran ads and circulated handbills that emphasized the race issue and Graham's weakness on segregation. In one of the most notorious incidents, rural white North Carolinians received a handbill with pictures of black soldiers dancing with white women in England during the war, with the suggestion that Graham approved of such interracial contact. In another such example, Smith's operatives sent out postcards from New York City, supposedly from the NAACP, to heavily white areas urging voters to support Graham because he had "done much to advance the place of the Negro in North Carolina." Meanwhile, rumors were circulated that Graham had appointed an African American to West Point. (In fact, Graham had turned such appointments over to a selection commission, and it had named the black student, Leroy Jones, as a second alternative, though he never received the appointment.) On May 27, Graham earned a decisive plurality of 53,000 votes (nearly 49 percent to Smith's 40.5 percent), but since Graham had not received a majority, under North Carolina's election laws Smith was entitled to call for a second, runoff primary.[5]

After nine days of indecision, on June 7, Smith—having been urged on by campaign workers, especially his young supporter Jesse Helms—called for a runoff. At this point, a seventeen-day campaign led up to the second primary. In this campaign, as in the first, Smith went on the attack, suggesting that Graham was soft on Communism, sympathetic to the relentless expansion of federal control under Presidents Roosevelt and Truman, and only a weak defender of segregation. As was true in the first primary, local Smith campaign committees emphasized the race issue. A fictitious "Colored Committee for Dr. Frank Graham" placed an ad announcing their support. Handbills and circulars reproduced photographs of the black-majority South Carolina legislature of 1868. In the most outrageous of these circulars—no copy of which has survived—a photograph of Graham's wife, Marian, was superimposed on the picture of a white woman dancing with a black soldier during World War II. Only verbal reports remained about many of these race-based materials, which were flashed from wallets and pockets, representing what the historians of the 1950 election have called "political pornography." The pace of the second primary led to an even more frenzied use of the explosive issue of interracial sex designed to fan white fears. "WHITE PEOPLE WAKE UP," read one broadside.

> DO YOU WANT Negroes working beside you, your wife and daughters in your mills and factories? Negroes eating beside you in all public eating places? Negroes riding beside you, your wife and your daughters in buses, cabs and trains? Negroes sleeping in the same hotels and rooming houses? Negroes teaching and disciplining your children in school?

Radio ads reinforced the message: voting for Graham meant a vote to end segregation. Despite efforts by Graham supporters to counterattack, the Smith campaign relentlessly pursued the race issue. Since the end of disfranchisement, black voters had made increasing inroads in registration, especially in urban areas, and there was a significant (though still, in many parts of the state, restricted) African American voting force by the middle of the twentieth century. Smith supporters frequently reminded white voters that a "bloc vote" of African Americans composed an important part of Graham's coalition.

And, as before, the Smith campaign successfully fused the race issue with anticommunism. In a final campaign rally on June 23, 1950, Smith supporters reminded voters that big government—and federal intervention in matters of race—had become the campaign's central issue. Smith, the voters were assured, opposed "all unnecessary encroachments of big government upon the lives of all the people." Nell Battle Lewis, speaking at the rally, also framed the issues in terms of unnecessarily expanding government. Lewis, a crusading liberal journalist for the *Raleigh News and Observer* during the 1920s, had now become a strong anticommunist. Did voters want to follow a trend to the left, she asked, "Or do you want to preserve that way of life which despite its many obvious imperfections gives to both individualized nations and states the maximum of freedom and initiative consistent with stability and order?" In the end, voters agreed with Lewis, and, in a large turnout in the second primary, Smith carried the state by nearly 20,000 votes.[6]

This victory of the conservatives—who had ruthlessly exploited racial issues to win, even linking federal control to Communism—presaged a larger, and continuing, struggle in North Carolina; throughout the remainder of the 1950s

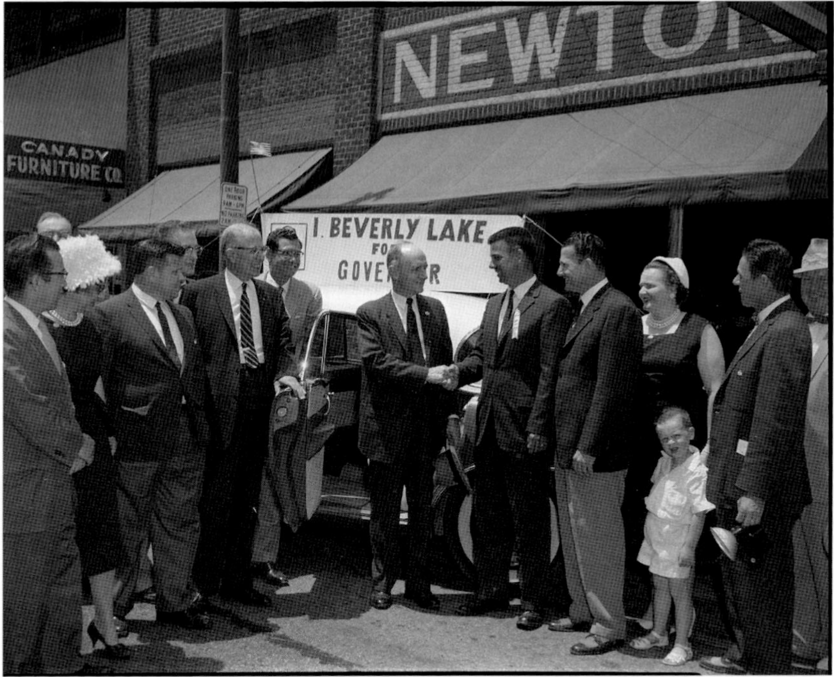

Figure 16.8 I. Beverly Lake, Sr. *Source: Photo Edward J. McCauley/*Daily Times-News *(Burlington NC)/Wilson Library, University of North Carolina at Chapel Hill.*

and 1960s the divisions aggravated by the senatorial election of 1950 persisted. After two and a half years in the Senate, Smith died in July 1953. His seat was then won by Kerr Scott in the Democratic primary of May 1954 and general election of November. In 1960, Terry Sanford, promising a "new day" for North Carolinians, was elected governor over conservative I. Beverly Lake. The Sanford-Lake contest was a bitter one, however, and with the advent of the civil rights revolution, the political tensions in North Carolina persisted.

The Harriet-Henderson Strike

The most significant labor conflict since the Gastonia strike of 1929 occurred in Henderson, North Carolina, in 1958. There, workers had taken advantage of the World War II growth in unions by organizing a chapter of the TWUA in 1943, and it continued to represent them during the 1940s and 1950s. The managers of the Harriet-Henderson mills, owned by the powerful Cooper family, grew unhappy with the union's presence. The mill was under terrific pressure by the

1950s; some seventy-four mills in the state had gone under between 1952 and 1956. Competition had narrowed profit margins, and mills competed with each other by producing increasing quantities of cotton yarn and cloth. Managers attempted to reduce costs by raising workloads, but the union filed numerous grievances in order to slow down management's changes. The Harriet-Henderson mills stood out among its competitors because so many of its workers were unionized; indeed, union members in these mills accounted for about one-seventh of all union membership in North Carolina. Now the managers of the Harriet-Henderson mills concluded that their very survival depended on reducing labor costs by uprooting the presence of the TWUA.

Conflict over workload issues and the management's reluctance to let union officials participate in decision-making led workers at Harriet-Henderson to a strike that began on November 16, 1958. For the rest of the year and into early 1959, no negotiations occurred, and the company shut down operations at the mill. Then, on February 9, 1959, when a truck attempted to cross picket lines to deliver a load of cotton, the driver was surrounded by pickets and pulled from the truck. Mill managers then secured an injunction from a local judge prohibiting the union from barring entrance to the mill grounds and limiting the number of pickets on the scene at any given time. With the injunction in hand, the mills announced on February 12 that they would reopen, and they invited strikers to return to work. The mill imported strikebreakers, or nonunion workers, to break the strike, and the scabs enjoyed the protection of the state police, who had been sent in by Gov. Luther Hodges.

The situation in Henderson grew tenser over time. On February 26, windows at the Henderson mill were destroyed by gunfire, while a few days later someone threw dynamite at a strikebreaker's residence. Other bombings occurred during the spring of 1959, including one that destroyed a Harriet mill boiler room. Governor Hodges dispatched additional state police: by March 1959, the town brimmed with 150 patrolmen, one-quarter of the state's force. While Hodges privately urged the Cooper family to negotiate with and to make concessions to the strikers, he ordered the State Bureau of Investigation (SBI) to conduct surveillance of TWUA strike leader Boyd Payton. The local community was alarmed by the outbreak of violence, and public opinion, in general, turned against the strikers. Meanwhile, the deadlock continued.

The strike took a new turn in June 1959, when state officials indicted Payton and seven others—including the most prominent strike leaders—on charges that they conspired to conduct a bombing campaign of another boiler room and an electrical substation. The state made its case based on the testimony of Harold Aaron, a union member who worked as an undercover agent for the SBI. Aaron had a dubious arrest record. As was often the case with informants, he had an active hand in planning the bombing. Aaron identified Payton as the head of the conspiracy based on a phone call that defense attorneys were able to show never occurred. At the trial, the defense contended that Aaron was the primary perpetrator of the conspiracy and that there would have been no criminal activity without his leadership. The *Raleigh News and Observer* claimed that the trial had "put a stain on the reputation of the State Bureau of Investigation" and that its role was to "obtain evidence not to manufacture evidence."[7] Following a three-day trial, the jury convicted Payton and his co-defendants, and Payton was immediately given a stiff sentence of six to ten years. "Fear has run rampant in Henderson and Vance County," said the judge. "It must end right here."[8] After exhausting appeals, Payton served nine months in Raleigh's Central Prison, before Gov. Terry Sanford paroled him in 1961. In 1964, during his last day in office, Sanford granted Payton a full pardon. But the result of his conviction had been that the strike collapsed and union power in Henderson, North Carolina, came to an end.

* * *

The postwar generation witnessed a social, cultural, and economic remaking in the way that Tar Heels lived, and few things escaped the transformative impact of change. But the social transformation of the mid-twentieth century also brought new tensions, as North Carolinians continued to disagree about the state's future. While unprecedented wealth came to the state, poverty persisted. In no area was the disparity between heady change and a gritty reality more apparent than in matters of race. The uprising of African Americans against white supremacy in the 1950s and 1960s in fact constitutes a major part of the post-World War II social transformation. That uprising, and the civil rights movement, would have profound consequences for the next generation.

Notes

1. Sabine Vollmer, "Early Developers 'Stumbled Upon the Land' for RTP," *Raleigh News and Observer*, March 18, 2007.
2. Jim L. Sumner, *A History of Sports in North Carolina* (Raleigh, NC: Division of Archives and History, 1990), p. 45.
3. Sayoko Uesugi, "Gender, Race, and the Cold War: Mary Price and the Progressive Party in North Carolina, 1945–1948," *North Carolina Historical Review* LXXVII, no. 3 (July 2000): 269–311.
4. Patricia Sullivan, *Days of Hope: Race and Democracy in the New Deal Era* (Chapel Hill: University of North Carolina Press, 1996), p. 264.
5. Julian M. Pleasants and Augustus M. Burns, *Frank Porter Graham and the 1950 Senate Race in North Carolina* (Chapel Hill: University of North Carolina Press, 1990), pp. 174–87.
6. Simmons Fentress, "Smith Ends Campaign with Rally," *Raleigh News and Observer*, June 24, 1950; Herbert O'Keef, "Smith Wins Senatorial Nomination,"

Raleigh News and Observer, June 25, 1950; Pleasants and Burns, *Graham*, pp. 221–22.

7 *Raleigh News and Observer*, July 25, 1959, quoted in Daniel J. Clark, *Like Night & Day: Unionization in a Southern Mill Town* (Chapel Hill: University of North Carolina Press, 1997), p. 198.

8 Boyd E. Payton, *Scapegoat: Prejudice/Politics/Prison* (Philadelphia, PA: Whitmore Publishing Co., 1970), p. 83.

17

The Civil Rights Revolution

During the generation after World War II, a revolution occurred in relations between white and black people. Beginning with the Supreme Court's *Brown* v. *Board of Education* decision in 1954, the federal government intervened, eventually, in the adoption of the Civil Rights Act of 1964 and the Voting Rights Act of 1965. Federal intervention forced the end of legally enforced segregation, but the civil-rights revolution had originated at the local level—in a community-based uprising across North Carolina. Across the state, black people rose up against white supremacy, and it was their bravery and defiance that proved decisive in finally upending Jim Crow.

Origins

On May 17, 1954, the US Supreme Court unanimously ruled that the segregated public schools of the South were "inherently unequal." In a follow-up to this decision a year later, the court ordered that desegregation of public schools should take place "with all deliberate speed." Although the *Brown* decision, perhaps the most important that the Supreme Court ever reached, had major repercussions, change had been a long time in coming. For decades, black activists had fought white supremacy, using whatever tools existed at hand. Starting in the 1920s, the Legal Defense Fund, Inc., the NAACP's group in charge of civil-rights litigation, mounted court challenges that eroded the legal basis for segregation.

Even under the oppressive system of segregation, black leadership matured and developed—and by the 1930s was organizing itself against Jim Crow. Pauli Murray, who was born in Baltimore but grew up in Durham, was at the head of her class at the all-black Hillside High School, and then graduated from Hunter College in New York City. Murray then took the bold step of applying for admission to the University of North Carolina in 1938. Murray's application dramatized the inherent conflict between white liberals' support for racial progress

North Carolina: Change and Tradition in a Southern State, Second Edition. William A. Link.

Figure 17.1 Pauli Murray, civil rights activist, feminist, and Episcopal priest. *Source: North Carolina Collection, University of North Carolina Library at Chapel Hill.*

and their adherence to white supremacy. A case in point was UNC president Frank Porter Graham, one of the South's best-known southern liberals. In the face of an official university policy that refused admission to African Americans, he refused Murray's application. Her unsuccessful campaign to obtain admission to UNC, bold and brave, was not part of any organized effort. Murray would subsequently go on to a career as an activist, lawyer, and writer. In 1977, she became the first black woman to become an ordained Episcopal priest.

Other activists spearheaded the campaign against segregated education. In 1933, the NAACP sponsored an attempt by a graduate of the North Carolina College of Negroes (NCC), Thomas R. Hocutt, to study at UNC's pharmacy school. Although no pharmacy school in the state admitted African Americans, Hocutt filed a lawsuit—the first litigation challenging segregated higher education in the South. The lawsuit was supported by NAACP lawyers based in Durham, Conrad Pearson and Cecil A. McCoy, but Hocutt's application was dismissed in North Carolina Superior Court after the NCC president, James Shepard, refused to send UNC his transcript. But this rebuff was only the beginning of the NAACP's campaign. By the late 1940s, the NAACP was sponsoring applications by groups of students to UNC graduate programs as well as its law school. These cases were not resolved until the Supreme Court, in *Sweatt* v. *Painter* of June 1950, ruled against segregated-but-equal graduate education in a case involving an applicant to the University of Texas's law school. The *Sweatt* case meant that UNC and other all-white public universities would immediately have to desegregate. In 1951, following a lawsuit by Harold Epps and Floyd McKissick, the first African Americans were

Figure 17.2 Left to right: Leroy Frasier, John Lewis Brandon, and Ralph Frasier, following their enrollment at UNC, September 1955. *Source: North Carolina Collection, University of North Carolina Library at Chapel Hill.*

admitted to UNC graduate programs and the law school. In the *Frasier* case, decided in 1955, three black students, brothers LeRoy Benjamin Frasier, Jr., and Ralph Frasier, along with John Lewis Brandon, became the first African Americans admitted to Chapel Hill as undergraduates.

The *Brown* decision of 1954 might have completed a process that was already well underway, but the reaction of North Carolina whites was mixed. Gov. William Umstead announced he was "terribly disappointed" by the Supreme Court's ruling, but he did not recommend defiance, saying this was "no time for rash statements or the proposal of impossible schemes." In Greensboro, the school board declared its intention to abide by the court's decision. It was "unthinkable," said the city's school superintendent, that "we will try to abrogate the laws of the United States of America." "We must not fight or attempt to circumvent this decision," the chairman of the Greensboro school board added.[1] Most of the white leadership was proud of the state's moderate tradition. Although much of the reputation for racial moderation reflected a self-created mythology and congratulatory image-making, whites had constructed a system of segregation that provided ample room for black leadership. The state also had supplied some funding for segregated facilities; though in no way equal to white higher education, five historically black campuses, more than any other southern state, operated in North Carolina by the 1950s. Gov. Luther Hodges, who took office on the death of William Umstead in late 1954 and served another term thereafter, saw his state as forward-looking and progressive, yet he and other leaders saw no contradiction in the values of moderation and white supremacy. There was further evidence that North Carolina would diverge from the rest of the South in response to the court's mandate to desegregate. Four days after the *Brown* decision, for example, Irving Carlyle, a Winston-Salem lawyer and Democratic leader, declared that North Carolinians had "no other course except to obey the law laid down by the United States Supreme Court."[2]

Once the news of the *Brown* decision had sunk in, however, the end of segregation seemed profoundly alarming to many whites. In August 1954, Governor Umstead appointed a nineteen-member Governor's Advisory Committee on Education, chaired by state senator Thomas Pearsall, to recommend legislation in response to *Brown*. It issued a report in December 1954. In 1955, after Governor Umstead's death, the legislature authorized a new, six-member committee, also chaired by Pearsall. Known as the North Carolina Advisory Committee on Education, a year later it produced the Pearsall Plan.[3] It supplemented the Pupil Assignment Act of 1955, which assigned all authority over public schools to local school boards, and which made school desegregation suits more difficult by providing criteria that could be used to deny black students access to white schools. Adopted by the legislature during a special session in July 1956 and then enacted into law by popular referendum in September as a series of state constitutional amendments, the Pearsall Plan complied only nominally with the *Brown* decision. It permitted voluntary desegregation in those few, mostly urban communities willing to tolerate it. The Pearsall Plan also gave ammunition to segregationists by extending public funding for private schools to those communities which, by popular referendum, chose to close their public schools rather than desegregate them. Although these segregationist measures were less extreme than those in other southern states, in the mid- and late-1950s the state's white leadership worked hard to evade the high court's mandate.

North Carolina's Pearsall Plan reflected a hardening of attitudes among whites about desegregation. In a speech in Asheville in 1955, Wake Forest College law professor and segregationist I. Beverly Lake urged the decentralization of public education through state subsidies for private schools. Lake described his proposals as a sort of "GI Bill" designed to protect segregated schools. Jesse Helms, then executive director of the state banking association and later a five-term US senator, enthusiastically embraced Lake's ideas. While the Pearsall Committee deliberated, Helms wrote a controversial editorial in the banking association periodical, the *Tarheel Banker*, suggesting alternatives to desegregation. Helms anticipated the Pearsall Committee's eventual remedy—and the "massive resistance" approach of segregationists. Rather than destroying the school system, Helms suggested, there existed "another way": privatizing the public schools by providing state support for all-white schools.[4] The Pearsall Plan provided for extreme measures that white school boards could use as a last resort against integration. Control of the public schools was devolved into the hands of local school boards, which now possessed the power to close schools. In place of public schools, moreover, local school boards were authorized to provide state tax funds to operate segregated private schools.

By the late 1950s, the white leadership remained committed to white supremacy. The Pearsall Plan's provisions authorizing school closings and publicly supported private schools were never invoked, but the message was clear: North Carolina would block integration. Little change thus came in the immediate aftermath of *Brown*. The Pearsall Plan may have provided a means for local communities to avoid integrating schools, but it also opened the door for the few communities willing to make changes. The first schools to integrate were in urban communities—the three cities of Greensboro, Winston-Salem, and Charlotte, which, in July 1957, announced simultaneously that they would permit black students to transfer to all-white schools. The school boards in these communities worked in concert. The desegregation of these schools—some of the first in the entire South—involved a limited number of students; in the fall of 1957, Greensboro's school board permitted five black pupils to enroll at an elementary school and one other black student at Greensboro Senior High School. This desegregation effort was a "token"—that is, it involved few black students and did not represent an effort to integrate in any significant way. Indeed, token integration reinforced the segregated system rather than changed it. The Charlotte school board explained that desegregation sought to "preserve the public schools," while a Raleigh newspaper declared that the urban schools' decision would "make it possible for schools in areas where integration is surely not possible ... to continue completely separate schools."[5] There was little more integration beyond this, which involved only a handful of students in urban North Carolina. And there was no trend toward greater desegregation: fewer blacks were enrolled in white schools in 1959 than had been two years earlier. Nonetheless, even integration was met with strong resistance by local whites with threats of violence and abuse. In 1959–60, four additional school systems admitted black students to white schools, but of these, two of them, Wayne and Craven Counties, possessed large military installations that were relatively easy to desegregate. In hundreds of other cases, requests for transfers into white schools by African American students were denied, and the state courts showed little inclination to intervene. In 1960, only 1 percent of the black school population in North Carolina attended integrated schools, and the state ranked twelfth out of sixteen southern and border states with historically segregated public schools.

Black Student Activists and the Movement

While obstructionism and tokenism characterized the response of North Carolina's white leadership in the wake of *Brown*, African American leaders heard

Brown as a clarion call for change. The NAACP doggedly pursued its case in the courtroom, though its efforts languished during the late 1950s. Increasingly, the legal and political approach of the NAACP seemed less relevant, and many black activists looked for different, more direct approaches to challenge white supremacy. In Monroe, North Carolina, a town near the South Carolina border 25 miles east of Charlotte, NAACP leader Robert F. Williams contested Jim Crow militantly. When threatened by the local Ku Klux Klan, Williams helped to organize and arm local African Americans, and the real threat of an armed resistance seemed to stall the Klan's activities. Williams, a veteran of World War II and the grandson of a black Republican leader, was, like many black veterans, impatient with the pace of change. Williams became an NAACP organizer in Monroe, but his tactics clashed with the organization's national leadership. In 1958, two young African Americans were accused of assault after kissing a white girl, and Williams conducted a national campaign in their defense. In 1959, Williams debated Martin Luther King, Jr., who had become a national celebrity because of his advocacy of nonviolence. Williams argued for the value and effectiveness of militancy—what he called "armed self-reliance"—and his views were subsequently published in his book, *Negroes with Guns* (1962). It had long been an "accepted right" of Americans to take up arms "where the law is unable, or unwilling, to enforce order." Black people, he wrote, could "act in self-defense against lawless violence" by the Klan. Williams had not abandoned nonviolence, but he asserted that

> a man cannot have human dignity if he allows himself to be abused, to be kicked and beaten to the ground, to allow his wife and children to be attacked, refusing to defend them and himself on the basis that he's so pious, so self-righteous, that it would demean his personality if he fought back.[6]

Williams hosted activists in the Freedom Rides movement—an effort by white and black activists to ride buses across the South and integrate in bus station restaurants and restrooms—when they traveled through Monroe. In August 1961, during a tense confrontation, he helped a white couple to escape after they had been encircled by an angry group of black people. Local authorities charged Williams with kidnapping, and he fled the country for Cuba, where he ran a radio show, "Radio Free Dixie." Four years later, he moved to exile in China.

At historically black campuses in North Carolina, young blacks, restive about the slow pace of change, demanded an immediate end to segregation. The NAACP's Ella Baker, native of Littleton and a Shaw University graduate, played a major role in organizing the Student Nonviolent Coordinating Committee (SNCC), and she mentored student leaders to mount extralegal challenges around the state between 1960 and 1965. The black students experienced rising

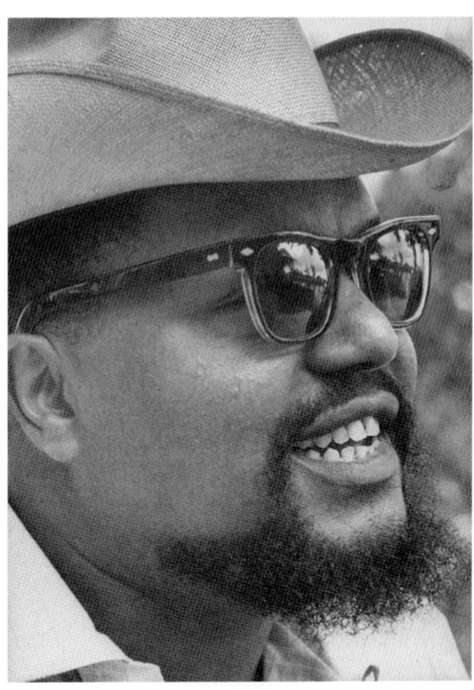

Figure 17.3 Robert F. Williams.

expectations that flowed from the new post-1945 world of greater prosperity, transportation, and new media. On February 1, 1960, four students at North Carolina A&T State College in Greensboro walked into the downtown F. W. Woolworth's five-and-dime store, sat down at its lunch counter, and asked to be served. When they were asked to leave, the black students refused to do so, and a standoff ensued. Word spread quickly among other black students in Greensboro, and during the next weeks hundreds of activists joined the "sit-in," while student demonstrations spread across the state. In Winston-Salem, a group of about twenty-five black students from Winston-Salem State sat-in at downtown lunch counters; demonstrations continued during the next month, and on February 23 twenty-two protesters were arrested for trespassing. Supported by mass meetings of as many as five hundred students, the Winston-Salem African American community also endorsed a boycott of segregated downtown businesses. On the same day that sit-ins began in Winston-Salem, they also erupted in Durham, in a movement led by North Carolina College students. On February 9, students from the all-black Fayetteville Teachers College sat-in at Fayetteville's downtown businesses; on the same day in Charlotte, students from the all-black Johnson C. Smith University initiated sit-ins. The Charlotte students' pressure eventually led to desegregated lunch counters in July 1960. Other sit-ins occurred in High Point, Shelby, Salisbury, and Henderson.

Figure 17.4 Left to right: the Greensboro Four (David Richmond, Franklin McCain, Ezell Blair, and Joseph McNeil) at the Greensboro sit-in, February 1, 1960. *Source: Jack Moebes/©* Greensboro News and Record.

The student-led movement continued during subsequent years. In Greensboro, student activists from North Carolina A&T, including the football star and future black presidential candidate Jesse Jackson, organized a movement in the spring of 1963 seeking to mobilize the entire African American community. The movement succeeded beyond their wildest imaginations. Between May 11 and June 7, 1963, scores of demonstrators paralyzed Greensboro's downtown, provoking arrests and demanding the desegregation of businesses. The demonstrations began with the picketing of a local McDonald's, but they eventually expanded to downtown chain stores and cafeterias. Scores of demonstrators eventually participated, almost all of them black and including ordinary people, professional and working class. The movement's strategy was to clog the jails by provoking arrest of large numbers of demonstrators, and on May 17, 1963, demonstrators conducted sit-ins in all-white movie theaters and cafeterias. Mass arrests soon led to a crisis. At one time, Greensboro's jails were holding some 1,400 black demonstrators, and local authorities were forced to open temporary facilities to house the protesters. In a huge "silent march" taking place on May 22, 2,000 demonstrators lined up, two by two, stretching over eight city blocks. The crisis ended only on June 13, when Greensboro mayor David Schenck formally endorsed desegregation of downtown businesses.

The African American uprising of the spring and summer of 1963 spread across the state, with major demonstrations occurring in Fayetteville, Greenville, High Point, and Kinston. In many of North Carolina's towns,

African Americans engaged in impromptu and smaller-scale challenges to white supremacy. Black demonstrators often faced violent opposition. When civil rights activists marched in Lexington to protest downtown segregation, they were met by a crowd of some 2,000 angry whites who assaulted them with bottles, rocks, and sticks. In May 1963, black students from the North Carolina College in Durham spearheaded a citywide movement to desegregate that city's downtown. On May 18, 425 activists staged sit-ins at six downtown Durham restaurants, with protesters conducting thirty consecutive days of demonstrations. City leaders and civil-rights activists remained deadlocked into 1964. In Raleigh, African American students from Shaw and St. Augustine colleges led street demonstrations in parts of downtown. Demonstrators in Raleigh made a particular point, in the spring of 1963, of protesting near the Sir Walter Hotel, where most of the North Carolina legislators took up residence during the General Assembly that was then in session.

In Chapel Hill, beginning in April 1963, activists formed the Committee for Open Business and boycotted thirteen segregated businesses. Street demonstrations subsequently accompanied the boycott. White UNC students such as John Dunne, a Morehead Scholar, and Pat Cusick, head of the campus Student Peace Union, rallied UNC students. Dunne and Cusick combined forces with Quinton Baker, a black student leader at NCC in Durham. Both of these white UNC students had visited Birmingham, Alabama, and witnessed the citywide movement, led by Birmingham African Americans and Martin Luther King, Jr., challenging white supremacy. That same month, in April 1963, demonstrators protested the segregation of UNC's Memorial Hospital. During the following summer, thirteen weeks of demonstrations occurred; in December 1963, the Congress of Racial Equality (CORE) and NAACP organizers launched more sit-ins. Between December 19 and January 7, 1964, 133 people were arrested in Chapel Hill. With local authorities arresting demonstrators, in early 1964, the marches were renewed, and protesters demanded a local ordinance banning segregated businesses. The Chapel Hill movement culminated in February 1964 with a street blockade that disrupted the arrival of fans to a Wake Forest-UNC basketball game.

The Freedom Struggle uprising of 1963–64 experienced its greatest successes in urban areas, where business leaders feared the disruptive impact of demonstrations and worried about their image. In North Carolina's largest city, Charlotte, the business leadership quietly desegregated public accommodations in 1962; they did so not out of a sense of justice and fair play, but because of their desire to avoid unfavorable publicity. This was not the case in eastern North Carolina, where most whites, even in towns, opposed change. Located on the southern bank of the Roanoke River, in northeastern North Carolina's Martin County, Williamston was a small town holding tightly to a rigid system of segregation. In July 1963, African Americans, led by Southern Christian Leadership Conference (SCLC) organizer Golden Frinks, mobilized for twenty-nine consecutive nights of street demonstrations against segregated public accommodations in restaurants, theaters, and retail businesses. Although the Williamston demonstrations paused on July 30, they resumed on August 9, and the police continued to arrest demonstrators. The conflict culminated on August 30, 1963, when three hundred children marched in a protest that was greeted by violence and mass arrests.

In contrast to urban North Carolina, demonstrators encountered frustration in Williamston. Blacks and whites there remained highly segregated, with blacks in menial occupations, whites in positions of power. The Williamston Freedom Struggle had ambitious goals that encompassed ending employment discrimination and school segregation, and during the next year and a half the movement conducted boycotts of schools and businesses. The social, cultural, and political environment of Martin County was unlike that of the towns and cities of Piedmont North Carolina. Few Williamston blacks could vote, segregation was more rigid, and the advocates of white supremacy were more determined to maintain the Jim Crow system. During the movement, one of the targets of Williamston activists had been the town's public library. Although the local government was willing to desegregate the library, it caused an uproar among local whites. The town council responded by cutting off public funding to the library and operating it under private support.

The Williamston experience thus illustrated how the Freedom Struggle, aside from the well-publicized successes in the state's largest cities, encountered frustrations. Public school desegregation, which seemed so promising with the *Brown* decision, had stalled, and even in communities where whites showed tolerance, it had not progressed much beyond the token level. Significant change came only after federal intervention in the administration of Lyndon B. Johnson in the Civil Rights Act of 1964 and the Voting Rights Act of 1965. Enacted in July 1964, the Civil Rights Act ended segregated public accommodations, banned discrimination in employment, required the integration of public schools, and empowered the federal government to oversee desegregation. This legislation represented one of the most sweeping federal interventions in state and local affairs in American history. The Voting Rights Act, enacted in August 1965, required federal supervision of voting in the South and ended disfranchisement. Federal intervention ended the outward manifestations of white supremacy, though the struggle against its legacy would continue for many decades.

White Responses: The North Carolina Speaker Ban

In the wake of changes coming during the Civil Rights Era, there were new configurations, new political alignments, and new ways of thinking in North Carolina. Among whites, the changes brought by federal intervention eventually ushered in major changes in daily life: by the late 1960s, the "white-only" and "black-only" Jim Crow signs that once hung over water fountains, public parks and swimming pools, and in the windows of restaurants, theaters, and public transportation had disappeared. In the generation after the Civil Rights Act, however, North Carolinians struggled to come to grips with the meaning of the new, desegregated world. For many whites, the disruptions of daily life caused by the African American uprising of 1960–65 and federal intervention seemed profoundly troubling. Their world, it seemed, had turned upside down.

Civil rights protest and white reactions emerged in the North Carolina Speaker Ban law and the controversy that followed it. On a sultry summer day near the end of an acrimonious legislative session, on June 25, 1963, the North Carolina General Assembly enacted legislation barring any "known Communist" or person who had taken the Fifth Amendment from speaking at any public college or university. The Speaker Ban law, as it soon came to be known, targeted the University of North Carolina, widely perceived as a center of white liberalism that sponsored the black rebellion. White fears focused on Communism: there had been some Communists at UNC in the 1930s and 1940s, and during the early 1960s it housed a few left-wing student organizations. But the real fears behind the passage of the Speaker Ban sprang from white anxieties about the African American rebellion, and they were woven into fears about the implications of racial change. To many whites, UNC had become a symbol of how white liberalism, a "Trojan horse" in which subversion—a metaphor for racial change—could enter society. Fears of Communism came to embrace fears of social change and the eroding system of white supremacy.

In June 1963, when the Speaker Ban was enacted, Raleigh experienced street demonstrations in the downtown district surrounding the capitol and the legislative session. Marches regularly moved past the Sir Walter Hotel, where most legislators lived in temporary quarters during the session. North Carolina's white political leadership became outraged as African Americans conducted sit-ins in the lobby of the Sir Walter. Many of them blamed UNC, and they grew determined to put the university in its place. Leaders of the state senate, such as Clarence Stone, along with state house leaders, such as Clifton Blue, sought to replace a 1941 law outlawing anything in speech or print advocating the violent overthrow of government. Also playing a key role was Jesse Helms, who by that time had become a vice president at WRAL, a Raleigh television station that was aggressive in expressing a conservative, anti-civil rights point of view. Beginning in November 1960, Helms broadcast nightly five-minute editorials opposing civil rights, federal intervention, and UNC liberalism. The North Carolina General Assembly enacted the Speaker Ban as a result of what amounted to a sort of conspiracy. On June 25, as legislators were preparing to adjourn, Rep. Phil Godwin introduced the Speaker Ban bill; the house passed it four minutes later. Barely an hour after its introduction in the house, the law moved through the senate, as Stone gaveled down protests among some senators. Despite last-minute attempts by UNC president Bill Friday to undo the legislation, the Speaker Ban became law, exposing major tensions in post-1960 North Carolina.

The election of Terry Sanford as governor in 1960 aroused fears about the possibilities of integration. Sanford, a Fayetteville attorney and former FBI agent, had been closely associated with Kerr Scott and the liberal wing of the North Carolina Democratic Party. Promising a "New Day" for the state, Sanford had embraced the cause of education. Promoting an increased sales tax, he boosted funding for elementary and secondary education, while also initiating efforts to reorganize higher education. While Sanford was governor, he was able to keep a lid on the ensuing white backlash. The Speaker Ban represented the will of the countermovement, which encompassed frustration over the civil rights movement and a strong opposition to liberalism, as embodied by UNC. Despite opposition by UNC and the daily newspapers of Raleigh, Charlotte, and Greensboro, the Speaker Ban stuck. Sanford and his allies found the law difficult to undo; white opinion sympathized with this blow against Chapel Hill liberalism. The Democratic gubernatorial primary of 1964 involved a contest between conservative Dan Moore and moderate Richardson Preyer, a Sanford supporter and federal judge from Greensboro. Moore won decisively, with the election becoming a symbolic referendum on the Sanford administration, and especially its racial policies.

After Moore's election, the Speaker Ban continued to polarize public opinion. As a law, it was, however, nearly impossible to enforce. Who was a "known Communist"? Did the ban include visiting artists from Russia and eastern Europe? Who would enforce the ban, and how would it be enforced? And, most important, how could the Speaker Ban be squared with UNC's academic traditions and its protection of free speech? Although most of the political leadership of the state saw nothing wrong with the law—and feared political repercussions if they attempted to change it—most UNC supporters saw the Speaker Ban as an outrageous interference in university affairs. After the regional accrediting agency, the Southern Association of Colleges and Schools (SACS) threatened to revoke UNC accreditation unless the law was revised, Governor Moore convened a legislative commission chaired by Rep. David Britt. In August 1965, the Britt Commission recommended amending the law to award more control to UNC administrators. A special session, convened in November, enacted these changes, yet UNC students refused to accept the Britt compromise. In early 1966, student activists provoked a conflict by inviting as speakers Herbert Aptheker, a historian and member of the Communist Party, and Frank Wilkinson, who had taken the Fifth Amendment and refused to testify before Congress. When UNC trustees voted to ban Aptheker and Wilkinson from speaking, students launched a campuswide protest movement. As well, they initiated a lawsuit against the Speaker Ban, and two years later a federal court struck down the law.

That the only way out of the Speaker Ban conflict had been a lawsuit and a court decision indicated how polarized North Carolina had become by the mid-1960s. The university became a kind of lightning rod for white frustrations, and the struggle over the law revealed larger tensions about not only higher education but also liberalism.

School Desegregation and Busing

The enactment of the Civil Rights Act of 1964 altered the discussion about school desegregation. After the *Brown* decision, little was done affirmatively to end school segregation. The Pearsall Plan provided for the token integration of a handful of black students into white schools, but this happened only in a few selected white communities in urban areas. For the rest of North Carolina, the Pearsall Plan signaled that the state leadership would resist desegregation. But the Civil Rights Act required much more extensive desegregation and, under Title VII of the law, committed the resources of federal authorities to enforcement. Beginning in 1964, all federal agencies were required to ensure that their funds were spent without discrimination, and in 1965 the United States Department of Health, Education, and Welfare (HEW) issued new guidelines requiring school boards to write plans stating how they intended to integrate their school systems.

Federal intervention enhanced the leverage of NAACP attorneys pushing for school desegregation. Leading the NAACP's efforts in North Carolina was attorney Julius Chambers, who eventually became one of the most successful civil-rights lawyers in the South. Chambers grew up in a small town northeast of Charlotte, Mount Gilead, and he attended the North Carolina College for Negroes in Durham. He then was among the first African Americans admitted to the UNC Law School. First in his law school class and editor of the *North Carolina Law Review*, Chambers graduated in 1962 and became part of the Legal Defense Fund (LDF) offices in New York City. In 1963, he returned to Charlotte, where, joined by white lawyer Adam Stein, he began a new civil-rights law firm, Chambers and Stein. Chambers soon became involved in scores of lawsuits seeking to desegregate North Carolina's public schools.

School boards tried to satisfy federal pressure by writing "freedom-of-choice" plans, under which black students could cross attendance lines in order to increase the integration of schools. The school boards' plans represented a significant departure from token integration, and white anger at "mixing" the schools soon surfaced. On November 22, 1965, in Charlotte, unknown perpetrators bombed the houses of state NAACP president Kelly Alexander, his brother Fred Alexander, Julius Chambers, and local civil-rights leader Reginald Hawkins. But Chambers and the LDF continued to challenge the freedom-of-choice plans, claiming that they were intended to perpetuate the segregated system. The HEW ratcheted up the standards of what constituted an acceptably

Figure 17.5 Julius L. Chambers at the University of North Carolina at Chapel Hill, Feb. 13, 2007. *Source: Wikipedia/Public Domain.*

desegregated school system, and the federal courts backed up this view. The Supreme Court's decision in *Green* v. *New Kent County* (1968) required school boards to seek to integrate schools, rather than adopt a race-neutral posture. The case ended the freedom-of-choice plans and required that federal officials would require new, "unitary" school systems in which the racial composition of the school population would roughly equal that of the general population.

The *Green* case altered the balance of power substantially. Now the NAACP pressed lawsuits against school segregation across the South, but their key case would be in Charlotte, North Carolina's largest city. Appointed federal judge in Charlotte in 1968 by President Lyndon Johnson, federal district court judge James McMillan operated under a new Supreme Court directive: in *Alexander* v. *Holmes County* (1969), the court ruled that there should be no further delays, fifteen years after the *Brown* decision, in desegregating public schools. Rejecting a series of school board plans, Judge McMillan in February 1970 imposed his own plan on the city. He believed that direct judicial intervention was necessary, and the plan that he approved was the most complete desegregation effort ever attempted in the United States. The plan was written by John A. Finger, a consultant from Providence, Rhode Island.

The Charlotte-Mecklenburg school board then appealed the case. Taking it up in October 1970, the Supreme Court listened to Chambers present the NAACP's case on behalf of 6-year-old James Swann and nine other African American families in Charlotte, while President Richard Nixon's solicitor-general, Erwin Griswold, made contrary arguments. In April 1971, in a 9–0 decision, the Supreme Court upheld McMillan's intervention, ruling that the use of massive, cross-town school busing was a legitimate tool of integrating the dual public-school system. The *Swann* decision empowered district court judges to oversee the implementation of new integration plans that relied on radically reconfigured attendance zones and pupil assignment plans. It also legitimized the use of busing on an unprecedented scale. McMillan's plan for Charlotte provided a model for other school systems around the South; more than forty judges issued desegregation orders shortly after the *Swann* decision, while, within four months of the decision, HEW negotiated some thirty-seven plans to desegregate schools in other communities. All of this occurred with remarkable speed: when schools opened in the fall of 1971, many of them were now fully integrated.

The use of school busing reshaped public education in the South, but many parents were deeply troubled by the consequences of such radical change. Not all black parents were happy with school desegregation, as the burden of integrating schools fell disproportionately on black schools, many of which—often because these facilities were very inferior—were closed as a result of integration. Many whites were alarmed by the end of all-white neighborhood schools and the prospect of their children attending school across town with black children. Busing was very unpopular among voters, and most of North Carolina's political leaders opposed it. North Carolina senator Sam Ervin denounced court-ordered busing as an instance of "the old issue of governmental tyranny versus liberty."[7]

Black Power and the Wilmington Ten

Although the civil-rights crusades of 1960–65 had overthrown many of the outward symbols of white supremacy, vestiges of the old social order nonetheless remained. Public schools remained segregated, black people still lived in the poor neighborhoods of North Carolina cities that were largely walled off from expanding white suburbs, to which whites largely fled, leaving inner urban cores with large minority populations. Programs labeled as urban renewal, adopted in North Carolina in the late 1950s and 1960s, brought the destruction of historic black neighborhoods and the African American business districts that once served them. Replacing these neighborhoods were expressways and vacant lots. The criminal-justice system became increasingly racialized, as white fears about black crime fueled anxieties—real and imagined—about the post-Jim Crow South. Even the results of the spectacular Freedom Struggle now seemed ambiguous. Sit-ins and street demonstrations might have opened lunch counters, restaurants, and movie theaters to African Americans, but many whites simply responded by fleeing the downtown districts where protests had taken place. School desegregation came in the late 1960s, but it, too, seemingly had occurred at the expense of black-community schools, many of which were closed when black students were transferred to white schools.

Seen from this perspective, it should not be surprising that North Carolina blacks were generally frustrated over the failure of significant change. After the apparent victory of the movement in 1964–65, much of the focus of black activism remained political. In the Democratic gubernatorial primary of May 1968, Charlotte dentist and black activist Reginald Hawkins conducted a grass-roots campaign, as the first black candidate for governor in the history of the state, and attracted 130,000 votes. In Chapel Hill, Howard Lee won election as mayor in May 1969—the first African American elected to head a predominantly white town. Originally from Georgia, he moved to Chapel Hill in 1964 when he enrolled in UNC's graduate program in social work. Lee, who was harassed and had a cross burned on his lawn when he tried to buy a home in a predominantly white neighborhood, decided to enter politics. Although African Americans composed only one-tenth of Chapel Hill's population, a mobilization of black voters, in combination with sympathetic whites, led to a narrow victory for Lee, who gained election by about 400 votes.

More militant black leaders such as Golden Frinks of the Southern Christian Leadership Conference (SCLC) and Ben Chavis of the United Church of Christ were key figures in post-1965 protests. Frinks was an unstoppable fighter for change in eastern North Carolina; in the course of various marches and protests, he was reportedly jailed eighty-seven times. One historian has called him "the most important civil rights organizer in eastern North Carolina in the 1960s."[8] Originally from Horry County, South Carolina, Frinks served in the US Army during World War II, after which he moved to Edenton. Working as a truck driver and a night club manager, in 1956 he became chairman of the Chowan County NAACP. Adopting the nonviolent tactics of Martin Luther King, Jr., Frinks helped to organize protests in Edenton against the segregation of public accommodations, and he continued to press the issue in 1961–62 in what became known as the "Edenton Movement," a full-scale assault on white supremacy in the small southern town. Frinks then became North Carolina field secretary of the SCLC in 1963, in which capacity he worked throughout the state, but especially in eastern North Carolina. He played a major role in the Williamston movement, and participated in efforts in Plymouth and Greenville to desegregate public facilities and public schools.

Frinks and Chavis were schooled in the language and style of "Black Power"—a term coined by SNCC leader H. Rap Brown that came to embody African American impatience with the slow pace of change. Frinks, in his fifties by the early 1970s, was of a different generation, and Chavis articulated a rhetoric that called for armed resistance, if necessary, to white supremacy. Black Power threatened many whites, who saw it as a menacing symbol of black criminality and violence. Black Power, African American frustration with continued white supremacy, and a new phase of the civil-rights movement—one that grew deeply fractured and often violent—led to a tense period of race relations during the late 1960s and 1970s. During these years, the clash between North

Carolina's image of moderation and a reality of racial conflict—and between modernizers and traditionalists—stood in stark contrast to one another.

During the late 1960s, African American activism focused on the impact of school desegregation. As white officials closed black schools in the name of integration, school boycotts erupted across eastern North Carolina, many of them organized by Golden Frinks. In Hyde County, in 1968, African Americans protested by marching and conducting a highly successful school boycott after white school officials attempted to respond to mandates for school desegregation by closing the Davis School in Engelhard and O. A. Peay High School in Swan Quarter. The Hyde County protests expanded into demonstrations that resulted in mass jailings. In February 1969, 600 protesters marched to Raleigh, objecting to the school closings. By the fall of 1969, the protests had succeeded in keeping schools in the black community open.

In Oxford, North Carolina, violence broke out in 1970 when a returning black Vietnam veteran, 23-year-old Henry Marrow, was murdered with a shotgun blast; locals suspected two whites, local merchant Robert Gerald Teel and his son, Robert Larry Teel. Obtaining justice for Marrow became the objective of a young 21-year-old African American leader, Ben Chavis. An Oxford native, Chavis was the great-great-grandson of the fabled John Chavis, who had attended Princeton and run a school in Wake County for white and black students in the early 1800s (he taught whites by day and blacks by night). Ben Chavis, who was substitute teacher at the all-black Mary Potter High School in Oxford, had become impatient, like many other younger black activists, with the slow pace of meaningful change. In 1961, Chavis took part in an unsuccessful effort to integrate Oxford's all-white public library. Attending the historically African American St. Augustine College in Raleigh for a year, where he worked for the Southern Christian Leadership Conference, he became one of the first black students to attend UNC-Charlotte, where he was graduated with a degree in chemistry in 1969.

Chavis was soon spearheading civil-rights activism. In Charlotte, he helped to organize local blacks into the Black Panther Party (BPP). Founded in Oakland, California, in 1966, the Black Panthers called for black nationalism, armed resistance, and militant opposition to white oppression; they appealed to African American militants of the late 1960s who had lost patience with incremental change. The Panthers were originally formed as a self-defense group against white police, but their agenda extended further. The BPP established nationally recognized affiliates (which required a lengthy certification process by the Oakland headquarters) in Winston-Salem and High Point, along with other groups in Greensboro, Charlotte, and Lumberton. They soon came to embody the rising militancy of younger African Americans.

Although the Charlotte Panthers dissolved in 1969, Chavis returned to Oxford in 1970, when the murder of Marrow threw the town into a period of violent conflicts that involved school boycotts, arson, and a violent uprising of

Figure 17.6 Benjamin Chavis, part of the campaign to free the Wilmington Ten. *Source: North Carolina Collection, University of North Carolina Library at Chapel Hill.*

African Americans that resulted in bottle-throwing, fist fights between whites and blacks, and the burning of downtown white businesses. Propelled to fame, Chavis became the Southern Regional Program Director of the United Church of Christ Commission for Racial Justice (UCC-CRJ) after the fall of 1970, and he led protests and school boycotts in the eastern North Carolina towns of Henderson, Warrenton, and Elizabethtown. In late 1970, Chavis moved to Wilmington, where he organized black resistance to school closings.

Spectacular violence occurred in Wilmington in February 1971. Wilmington, which had been the scene of a racial massacre and *coup d'état* in 1898, erupted into conflict after local school authorities closed the popular, historically black Williston High School. Black students, working with Frinks, organized a school boycott in January 1971 that heightened tensions between whites and blacks. Chavis had come to Wilmington as a UCC-CRJ field organizer and helped to organize the boycott. By February 1971, the Wilmington school boycott had escalated into community-wide violence, including shootings, looting, bottle-throwing, and bombings. Two white businesses were burned soon after Chavis's arrival; he and fellow black militants were immediately blamed. A white backlash resulted. Along with the Ku Klux Klan a group calling itself the Rights of

Figure 17.7 The Wilmington Ten. *Source:* Raleigh News and Observer.

White People (ROWP) opposed school integration, and armed white groups patrolled the downtown district of the city and fired shots at blacks. Armed groups of whites and blacks threatened to plunge the city into further conflict, and violence prevailed between February 2 and 12. On the evening of February 6, the white-owned Mike's Grocery—which was operated by a Greek American, Mike Poulos, in a historically black neighborhood—was firebombed. Snipers on the roof of Chavis's headquarters at the Gregory Congregational Church shot at firefighters on the scene, the gunfire preventing them from extinguishing the fire. In the ensuing melee, a policeman was wounded in the leg, while a black teenager was killed by police fire. Now Chavis and his supporters barricaded themselves in the church, after having rolled concrete pipe into the street to block access. When police and National Guardsmen stormed the church, they found its defenders had fled but left behind ammunition, blasting caps, and dynamite. Having suffered the destruction of more than $500,000 of property, Wilmington remained occupied by the state police and National Guard for five days. Prosecutions of white and black rioters proceeded. The leaders of ROWP were tried and subsequently convicted of bombing white-owned businesses. About a year later, in the spring of 1972, Chavis and fourteen others were charged with conspiracy and arson. Tried about 35 miles north of Wilmington, in Burgaw, the case against Chavis, who was now an ordained minister, rested on the testimony of an informant, a 17-year-old high school dropout named Allen Hall, and two other witnesses.

Chavis and nine others, the so-called Wilmington Ten, were tried for arson and conspiracy, convicted, and in 1972 given prison sentences that totaled 282 years; Chavis's sentence was twenty-nine years. While in prison between 1976 and 1980, Chavis became a folk hero, and a national campaign to free the Wilmington Ten became a *cause célèbre.* In April 1977, Amnesty International adopted the case as an instance of "prisoners of conscience," and this appeared as an example of how the United States was holding political prisoners—at a time when President Jimmy Carter was making human rights a centerpiece of his foreign policy. After a 1977 investigation by the CBS news television program *60 Minutes,* there were suggestions that the case had been based on fabricated evidence. In the same year, Hall and the other two recanted their testimony against the Wilmington Ten. Gov. Jim Hunt ordered the State Bureau of Investigation to conduct an inquiry, and it concluded that the defendants were indeed guilty. Nonetheless, Hunt reduced their sentences enough to parole all of the defendants except Chavis. Finally, in 1980, a federal appeals court voided the Wilmington Ten's convictions and freed them.

The upsurge of conflict and racial violence in North Carolina in the late 1960s and throughout the 1970s suggested the collapse of the modernizers' model for racial harmony. Until that time, the state's leadership had nurtured an image of racial harmony, and they had insisted that the "North Carolina way" of moderation and compromise had made their state one of the most tranquil in the South. But the uprising of African Americans against Jim Crow had exposed the "North Carolina way" as nothing more than paternalistic smokescreen, and the convulsive changes that accompanied the end of de jure segregation brought a period of raised expectations, pronounced disappointment, and unremitting tension in the state. And the modernizers' formula for racial harmony rang even more hollow in the troubling period after the mid-1960s federal intervention.

The Greensboro Massacre, November 1979

The struggle between moderate and traditionalist North Carolina also played out in the eruption of violence in Greensboro on November 3, 1979, when five members of the Communist Workers Party (CWP) were killed and another ten wounded by members of the KKK and the American Nazi Party at the Morningside Homes public housing project. The CWP was composed of white activists, many of them graduates of Duke Medical School, such as Paul Bermanzohn, Jim Waller, and Mike Nathan, who had been radicalized by the late 1960s movements against the Vietnam War, economic injustice, and racism. Joining them were other activists such as Bill Sampson, who had been involved in community organizing and labor activism in Greensboro textile mills. In 1974, Durham black activist Howard Fuller moved Malcolm X University, a black liberationist institution based in Durham, to Greensboro, where it became a center of black radicalism. Originally from Milwaukee, Fuller moved in 1968 to Durham, where he worked as a labor organizer and civil rights activist. Another African American activist in Greensboro, Nelson Johnson, was a former North Carolina A&T State University activist who founded the Greensboro Association of Poor People (GAPP) in the early 1970s. Other Greensboro African Americans involved in the CWP were Willena Cannon, a former A&T student who had participated in the 1960 sit-ins, and Sandi Smith, a former Bennett College student. Joyce Johnson, Nelson's wife, was a Duke graduate and, through GAPP, established an alliance with the Duke white radicals. The CWP became a biracial organization that sought to fight for labor unions and civil rights in Greensboro, but did so while espousing a Marxist-Leninist revolutionary ideology.

Some months earlier, the Workers Viewpoint Organization—which in October 1979 became the CWP—had disrupted a Klan meeting in China Grove, a small town northeast of Charlotte, and the activists conducted an anti-Klan demonstration. After one of the demonstrators grabbed a Confederate flag and burned it, tensions escalated, and a number of Klansmen appeared armed with rifles and shotguns. Ultimately, the KKK backed down at the China Grove confrontation, with Paul Lucky, one of the CWP members, exclaiming, "Death to the Klan!" This soon became the slogan of the CWP's wider anti-Klan campaign. A few months later, in October 1979, the CWP arranged a "Death to the Klan" rally in Greensboro, having obtained a parade permit from city officials. At 11:20 in the morning, soon after all the police officers assigned to the parade had mysteriously been pulled away, about fifty demonstrators conducted a protest in which they denounced the KKK with chants such as: "People, people have you heard? Black and white is the word!" At this point, a caravan of cars filled with Klansmen and members of the American Nazi Party pulled up to the scene. One of the Klansmen, Eddie Dawson—who had worked as an FBI informant—yelled to Bermanzohn: "You wanted the Klan, you Communist son-of-a-bitch, well you got the Klan!"

With the Greensboro police inexplicably absent, violence followed, as demonstrators rushed the caravan, attacking with sticks, and the Klansmen and Nazis poured out of the vehicles to engage the CWP. A Klansman fired a shot into the air, then shots rang out from both sides. The Klansmen had come prepared for violence, with numerous pistols, shotguns, pick handles, chains, and brass knuckles in their car trunks. After 88 seconds of gunfire, CWP members Waller, Sampson, Smith, Cesar Cauce, and Nathan lay dead, with Johnson and others wounded, and the police arrived on the scene to arrest twelve people in the Klan/Nazi band. Meanwhile, Nelson Johnson, though wounded, was arrested for having incited the crowd to riot.

The massacre immediately became front-page national headlines, with Greensboro mayor Jim Melvin trying to downplay the murders as "an isolated, senseless, barbaric act of violence." In the days after the shootings, the city entered into a state of emergency. The CWP, in response, described the attack as a "premeditated political assassination by the capitalist state" of its leadership, and it organized a funeral march through the city on November 11.[9] As the murder trials of the Klan/Nazi members proceeded, the local press uncovered reports that the racist organizations had been infiltrated by FBI and police informers. The CWP, refusing to cooperate with prosecutors, would not testify, insisting that the murders had occurred with the cooperation of local and federal officials. Defense attorneys, meanwhile, claimed that CWP demonstrators had fired shots and the KKK/Nazi group had responded in self-defense. On November 27, 1980, a trial in North Carolina Superior Court resulted in acquittal on all counts of murder charges for all eleven defendants. The defendants were tried again in early 1984 on federal civil-rights charges, but again were acquitted on April 15, 1984. A year later, however, the CWP survivors won a civil case in which, for the first time, they testified against the city of Greensboro. The city eventually settled by paying a judgment of $351,500 in November 1985. The case revealed no evidence of deliberate conspiracy, but it did suggest a lack of coordination among federal, state, and local law-enforcement agencies, as well as a general indifference to protecting the left-wing protesters from violence.

The civil rights movement challenged, among other things, the obvious, outward displays of white supremacy that characterized early- and mid-twentieth-century North Carolina. By the mid-1960s, the racial segregation in public transportation, schools, and accommodations had disappeared as a result of unprecedented intervention by federal authorities through the Civil Rights Act of 1964. Yet the problems of racial oppression did not disappear, and as North Carolina entered the last third of the twentieth century, the state continued to struggle with problems of race. The state would face new challenges about its future on other fronts as well. It would experience a greater degree of racial and ethnic diversity than had ever existed in its history, and, like other parts of the world, would struggle with how to respond to climate change and a debased environment.

Notes

1 William Chafe, *Civilities and Civil Rights: Greensboro, North Carolina, and the Black Struggle for Freedom* (New York: Oxford University Press, 1980), p. 16; Davison M. Douglas, *Reading, Writing, & Race: The Desegregation of the Charlotte Schools* (Chapel Hill: University of North Carolina Press, 1995), p. 27.
2 Chafe, *Civilities and Civil Rights*, p. 66.
3 Ibid., p. 67.
4 "There Is Another Way," *Tarheel Banker*, XXXIV, no. 3 (September 1955): 24.
5 Douglas, *Reading, Writing, & Race*, p. 45.

6 Robert F. Williams, *Negroes with Guns* (originally published 1962; Detroit: Wayne State University Press, 1998), pp. 3, 83.

7 Douglas, *Reading, Writing, & Race*, p. 179.

8 David Cecelski, *Along Freedom Road: Hyde County, North Carolina, and the Fate of Black Schools in the South* (Chapel Hill: University of North Carolina Press, 1994), p. 83.

9 Elizabeth Wheaton, *Code Name Greenkill: The 1979 Greensboro Killings* (Athens: University of Georgia Press, 1987) pp. 165, 169.

18

Modernizers and Traditionalists

During the second decade of the twenty-first century, North Carolina was a study in contrasts. The state contained nearly 10 million residents in 2015, rising from less than 6 million in 1980, with the population increasing especially in the urban belt that follows the Interstate 85 corridor. Between 1970 and 2000, the state's urban population grew from 45.4 percent to 60.2 percent. Much of the population increase, especially in the twenty-first century, resulted from out-of-state migrants moving to the state's cities. Between 2000 and 2008, 65 percent of population growth came from immigration. The character of the state's population was growing more diverse, as well. Whites constituted 76 percent of the population in 1980; that percentage had declined to 67 percent in 2008. Urban North Carolina became a magnet for new immigrants from around the nation and, by the 1990s, a home for a large and growing number of Latin Americans.

A longtime bastion of rural prosperity in North Carolina, the tobacco program, came to an end. Since the New Deal, federal largesse had subsidized tobacco farmers, supporting higher prices and farm incomes through subsidies paid directly to farmers and incentives to limit production. The Fair and Equitable Tobacco Reform Act of 2004 replaced the New Deal system with the Tobacco Transition Payment Program (TTPP). In money provided through a settlement with tobacco manufacturers, farmers were awarded $9.6 billion over ten years to ease the transition to different forms of agriculture. TTPP payments came to an end in 2014, however, and North Carolinians looked forward to a different model of farming, one based completely on the free market and less dependent on tobacco.

Despite these changes, many North Carolinians expressed an intense loyalty to past traditions, with the conflict between modernizers and traditionalists remaining a central theme. As it long had, this dichotomy manifested itself politically, focusing on a cluster of issues. The civil-rights revolution exposed major divisions: traditionalists opposed changes in segregation and, even after federal intervention in the mid-1960s, remained opposed to the

North Carolina: Change and Tradition in a Southern State, Second Edition. William A. Link.

legacy of the civil-rights movement. Modernizers favored a moderate degree of state intervention in the economy; traditionalists were libertarian and favored low taxes and as little governmental interference as possible. Traditionalists also promoted a cultural agenda that appealed to more conservative traditions of local control, the authority of Protestant Christianity, and opposition to feminism and gay rights. Until the 1970s, the modernizer-traditionalist conflict was played out inside the Democratic Party, which retained a monopoly on power. Thereafter, during the 1970s and 1980s, this same conflict emerged in a revitalized Republican Party, which, in its new, conservative form, became strong enough to mount competitive and increasingly successful statewide political campaigns, making North Carolina—after nearly 100 years—once again a two-party state.

The New Immigration

Major demographic changes have reshaped North Carolina in the past three decades. At the turn of the twentieth century, more than nine out of every ten people living in the state were born in the South. By 2010, that proportion had declined, as 70 percent of North Carolinians were southern-born. In addition, a majority of American-born immigrants into North Carolina arrived from the Northeast and West Coast, outnumbering those from elsewhere in the South.

North Carolina, despite the outmigration of thousands of African Americans, remained a state of racial diversity. In 2000, blacks comprised nearly 30 percent of the state's population, a proportion that placed North Carolina among the states with the largest African American population in the nation. The state also had retained a large population of American Indians, especially of Cherokees and Lumbees, ranking North Carolina first among the Eastern Seaboard states. And in the last two decades of the twentieth century, North Carolina diversified further with the arrival of new racial and ethnic groups. Combined with a steady infusion of immigrants generally from outside the state, the arrival of a great many nonwhite newcomers constituted perhaps the most significant social change of the twentieth century. Among the most important groups immigrating to North Carolina were Asians, who arrived in significantly greater numbers after 1980. During the 1990s, the number of people of Asian descent more than doubled.

A steady stream of Hispanic immigration also signified major demographic changes in recent North Carolina history. After the 1990s, North Carolina possessed the fastest-growing Latino population of any state in the nation. Between 1980 and 2008, this group grew from 57,000 persons to nearly 700,000 in 2008. Most of the new arrivals came from Mexico: in 2000, 65 percent of all Latinos in North Carolina were of Mexican descent. Of these Latino migrants, about 64 percent were foreign-born, and 58 percent noncitizens. In 2000, about one-third of Latinos living in the Tar Heel State spoke little or no English, with about half of them telling surveyors that they did not speak the language well.

Immigrants from Central America to the United States tended to concentrate in particular counties and cities of the South. In Mecklenburg County, North Carolina, which includes the city of Charlotte, the Latino population grew from 7,000 in 1990 to about 45,000 in 2000, an increase of 570 percent. In the Raleigh-Durham area, Latinos increased by 1,180 percent between 1980 and 2000, while in Atlanta during the same years the growth rate was 995 percent. These same trends also occurred outside large cities. The late 1990s brought an economic boom, with low unemployment, which made the South—expanding even more rapidly than other parts of the country—an attractive location for immigrants. The population of Latinos in the state grew from about 77,000 to nearly 638,000 between 1990 and 2007—an increase of 732 percent. Rural areas and small towns saw the sudden appearance of Spanish-language stores, churches, and community groups. By 2004, in some parts of eastern North Carolina, one-fifth of the population was Latino, while in other communities, such as Siler City, the Latino population was close to two-fifths of the total. In Alamance County, the number of Latinos increased from 736 in 1990 to 14,000 (close to one-tenth of the county's total population) in 2005, with most of them living in Burlington or Graham.

Latinos filled the demand for labor in a variety of occupations, including textiles, manufacturing, construction, and farm work. "If it weren't for immigrants, there wouldn't be an agriculture industry in North Carolina," said a North Carolina Farm Bureau official, "because picking tobacco is hot and hard, and harvesting Christmas trees is cold and hard. Farmers can't hire enough local people to do the work anymore."[1] Beginning in the early 1980s, Mexican immigrants appeared in significant numbers in North Carolina fruit, vegetable, and Christmas tree farms, and by the late 1980s Mexican were displacing African American workers in these employment sectors. North Carolina employers recruited Mexican workers under the guest-worker provisions of the Immigration Reform and Control Act (IRCA) of 1986, as way to supply cheap labor in agriculture and industry.

During the 1980s, Mexican immigrants to North Carolina worked in rural poultry processing plants, pork meatpacking, and blue crab processing. By the 1990s, they found employment in urban and industrial enterprises such as construction, furniture manufacturing, landscaping, and restaurants. After 1986, when Congress enacted the IRCA, which provided for amnesty for illegal immigrants, the flow of Mexicans into North Carolina—and to the Southeast generally—accelerated, reaching a peak after 1990. The numbers of Mexicans in North Carolina grew from 76,726 in 1990 to 328,963 a decade later. Across the state, the Mexican population was significant, as their immigration constituted about one-fifth of the population increase in the state during the 1990s.

In that same decade, the expansion of the Latino population reflected an extended migrant network that provided transportation and support for migrants once they moved to North Carolina. Spread across the state, the highest concentrations of immigrants were located in the central Coastal Plain and the Piedmont. In 2000, there were five counties in the state whose population was more than 9 percent Latino, while another fourteen counties possessed a Latino population greater than 6 percent. Although early migrants tended to be male, over time Mexicans immigrated as families. Nonetheless, by 2000, three-fifths of North Carolina's Latinos were male (whereas 49 percent of the North Carolina population as a whole was male). With the expansion of Mexican communities around the state, a network of services oriented toward Mexicans came into existence, including communication and financial services, grocery stores, Spanish-language media, churches, restaurants, and entertainment. According to one estimate, in 2006 Latinos purchased a total of $5 billion in goods and services in North Carolina.

The immigration of large numbers of Latinos into North Carolina was not a smooth process. Compared with other groups in the state, Latinos were disproportionately poorer and, though more fully employed than any other ethnic group, concentrated in low-wage jobs. In 2002, although Latinos composed about 5 percent of the total population of North Carolina, they constituted over a tenth of the state's poor people. According to the 2000 census, 27.4 percent of all Latinos lived below federal poverty guidelines, a rate higher than any other ethnic group. By comparison, 25 percent of African Americans and 8.5 percent of whites lived in poverty.

The large number of Mexican immigrants placed severe strain on public schools, which were ill-equipped to educate non-English-speaking children. Between 2000 and 2005, Latinos accounted for 57 percent of the growth in public school enrollment in North Carolina; in the period 1990–2000, they accounted for 15 percent of enrollment growth. Whereas public schools spent about $10 million a year in 1999–2000 to educate illegal immigrants—most of them Spanish speakers—by 2006, the annual cost of educating them had reached $210 million.

Most of the post-1990 Latino immigrants, nearly two-thirds of them, were undocumented. North Carolina alone had 300,000 undocumented immigrants in 2000, only a minority of which arrived in the state speaking English. Generally poor, many Latino immigrants were also undocumented and worked illegally in the country, often with the encouragement of employers, and living on the margins of society. The precise number of illegal immigrants is difficult to estimate, but one source asserts that, as of 2007, there were as many undocumented as documented Latinos in North Carolina. An indicator of the large number of undocumented immigrants was that the Mexican consulate in Raleigh annually issues more than 20,000 *matricula consulars*, or identification cards, that illegal immigrants use in order to obtain bank accounts.

Across the state, law-enforcement officials stepped up efforts to apprehend undocumented workers in order to deport them. Under Section 287 (g) of the 1996 Immigration and Nationality Act, local law enforcement was authorized to arrest undocumented aliens, and some localities began aggressive anti-immigrant campaigns. In North Carolina, in addition, the legislature in 2006 prohibited illegal immigrants from obtaining driver's licenses. The law of 2013 loosened these restrictions somewhat. Under this new law, the 325,000 undocumented immigrants in North Carolina would be able to obtain a driver's license if they had lived in the country for a year, but the law added a host of new restrictions. Modeled on a tough Arizona law upheld by the Supreme Court in a 2013 decision, the new law authorized police officers in North Carolina to detain persons on "reasonable suspicion" that they were undocumented. The law also made possessing a false driver's license a felony, while it tightened requirements for employers to confirm workers' identity status. The law was passed in July 2013, but vetoed by Gov. Pat McCrory. The legislature then overrode the veto in September 2013.

Mexican immigration has caused a backlash in North Carolina, as anti-immigration positions became polarizing political issues. In 2004, the state government initiated a crackdown on undocumented aliens obtaining driver's licenses by requiring that all applicants produce a valid Social Security card or official visa. Some of the state's counties with the largest Mexican populations began deportation programs designed to identify illegal immigrants. Beginning in 2006, twelve local law enforcement agencies in the United States participated in a program with the federal Immigration and Naturalization Service (INS) that gave local authorities the power to enforce federal immigration laws. Three of these twelve law enforcement agencies were in North Carolina, in Mecklenburg, Gaston, and Alamance Counties, whose officers proceeded to verify the immigration status of persons they arrested for other crimes. By early 2007, Mecklenburg's program alone had resulted in the deportation of 1,000 illegal immigrants.[2]

Environmental Challenges

The modernizer-traditionalist dialogue ignored, for the most part, the most important challenge facing North Carolinians as they entered the twenty-first century: the environment. Natural population growth combined with the high rates of migration into the state resulted in overdevelopment. As early as the 1980s air pollution started to become a significant problem in North Carolina, especially during the May–September summer season. In 1998, a study by the US Public Interest Research Group reported that North Carolina had the second-worst ozone levels in the nation, second only to California! In the summer of 1999, North Carolina ranked fifth among states in the Union for the number of days during which ozone levels exceeded federal standards. In 2000, a study by the American Lung Association rated Charlotte as the eighth worst and Raleigh the seventeenth worst in air quality in the nation's urban areas. State environmental authorities regularly issued air-quality alerts in Charlotte, Greensboro, and Raleigh, and during the heat of the summer they repeatedly urged children, the elderly, and those with respiratory problems to remain indoors. The main source of increased ozone levels was nitrogen oxides (NO_2), half of which were emitted into the air from automobiles, the other half from coal-fired power plants. Lacking an effective public transit or intercity rail system, North Carolinians overwhelmingly relied on automobiles. The state was also home to prominent polluting coal utility plants: Duke Power's Belews Creek steam station was the nation's third largest producer of nitrogen oxide emissions, Carolina Power & Light's plant at Roxboro ranked tenth.

These air-quality issues forced the state's political leadership to reconsider the traditional lack of regulation that it had exerted over the utilities. Along with popular outcry and grassroots mobilization in favor of vigorous state action to improve air quality, pollution threatened to undermine tourism—a leading North Carolina industry. The Southern Appalachian Mountains Initiative (SAMI) was a multistate effort that encouraged stiffer air-quality requirements. The North Carolina state senate enacted a version of a Clean Smokestacks bill in 2001, but it failed in the state house. Only after Gov. Mike Easley met with the CEOs of utilities and agreed to permit their companies to write off costs for new pollution controls—calculated at $2.3 billion—did a compromise emerge that made the passage of the bill possible. In June 2002, the General Assembly enacted the Clean Smokestacks Act, which required that the worst-polluting coal plants reduce their nitrogen oxide emissions by 77 percent by 2009 and sulfur dioxide (SO_2) emissions by 73 percent by 2013. The Act also empowered the state attorney general to pressure neighboring states to reduce air pollution moving across borders into North Carolina. Coal-fired power plants in the Midwest were one source of air pollution in North Carolina, especially in the state's western half. Federal regulators required the two largest utilities in North Carolina, Duke Power and Progress Energy (formerly Carolina Power & Light), to reduce emissions at the fourteen power plants that they operated in the state.

The growth of the state's economy, as well as its modernization of the agricultural sector, were achieved at a great cost to the environment. Throughout the state, questions of air and water quality came to dominate public dialogue, and the state's leadership faced the challenge of how to sustain the modernizers' commitment to development and economic growth while maintaining North Carolinians' environmental quality of life. Particularly exposed to urban, industrial, and agricultural pollutants was the Neuse River basin, which runs through the highly urbanized counties surrounding the Raleigh-Durham-Chapel Hill area and then flows through 4 million acres of eastern

North Carolina farmland. The Neuse, as early as the 1970s, experienced high levels of nitrogen as a result of animal waste and fertilizer runoff. Despite a statewide ban on the use of phosphate-based detergents in 1988, high levels of nitrogen in the river water spawned toxic algae blooms, a sprawling scum; during the summer of 1995, large fish kills occurred on the lower Neuse where the river empties into Pamlico Sound. The dinoflagellate algae, or *Pfiesteria piscicida*, poisoned the fish and then ate their flesh. Other species of algae also multiplied rapidly, including one prevalent in the river between Vanceboro and New Bern that was found to cause rashes in humans and made the water smell like rotten eggs. Other algae blooms produce "red tides," which began to afflict the North Carolina coast as early as 1987, forcing the closure of beaches and driving off tourists. Striped bass, a popular game and food fish once abundant in the Neuse River, disappeared, while another, sea trout, became rare. Massive pollution from agricultural runoff in the Neuse River basin was supplemented by contaminated runoff from homes, roads, and automobiles, along with the discharge into the river of contaminated wastewater. The explosive growth of the Raleigh-Durham-Chapel Hill area figured importantly, and by the 1990s it was estimated that businesses and residences in the Triangle produced one-third of the harmful runoff into the Neuse.

Along with real estate development, pollution caused by agribusiness in eastern North Carolina also affected water quality. A significant contributor to the problem was the hog industry, as eastern North Carolina by the 1980s and 1990s became a center for the massive, industrial production of pork, as many farmers shifted to hog farming from growing tobacco, a livelihood beset by antismoking efforts and foreign competition. By 1995, North Carolina had become the second leading hog-producing state in the nation, with annual revenues in excess of $1 billion, in a broad region extending between the Triangle and the coastal counties. The triumph of "Boss Hog" brought prosperity to eastern North Carolina with rising land prices, incomes, and tax revenues. By the mid-1990s, some 25,000 North Carolinians worked directly or indirectly in the hog industry. The growth of hog production came with the spread of highly capitalized, large operations, many of them owned by out-of-state companies. By 1994, some 12 million hogs were slaughtered annually in North Carolina.

In some cases, hog farms indiscriminately disposed of animal waste; as a standard practice, millions of gallons—perhaps as many as 22 million gallons a week—were sprayed as fertilizer onto fields. The overspraying contaminated groundwater and caused algae blooms in waterways, while fecal matter turned up in high doses in the state's rivers. In 1995, an NC State study concluded that 21 of 100 counties were spraying fields with more nitrogen or phosphorus than crops could absorb. Other hog farmers collected excrement in the more than 2,400 waste lagoons that existed in North Carolina. Many, perhaps most, of these lagoons lacked synthetic or clay liners, so the waste ended up contaminating water supplies. On some occasions during wet periods the dams holding the hog ponds threatened to burst, with the possibility of massive amounts of waste spilling into local waterways. Only after a series of such spills of animal waste resulting in environmental catastrophes in the 1990s did the state try to intervene in the practices of the industrial-scale producers of hogs, dairy, and poultry. On June 21, 1995, a 10,000-head hog farm near Richlands owned by Oceanview Farms, Ltd., saw a dike holding back a waste lagoon burst after heavy rains. Thirty million gallons of hog waste spilled into the New River, and the state suddenly became aware of the devastating environmental implications of the modern pork industry. Four other major spills occurred during that same summer.

Although some called for the greater regulation of the hog industry, modernizers certainly favored agricultural expansion, seeing it as vital for rural North Carolinians in the eastern part of the state. After an explosion of publicity about hog pollution, algae blooms, and fish kills in 1995, the General Assembly considered new legislation expanding controls over the hog industry. Pork producers responded with a campaign that brought 2,000 hog farmers to Raleigh for "Pork Appreciation Day" and intensive lobbying efforts. Ultimately, the efforts to regulate the industry were defeated in the legislature. Heavy political contributions by agricultural interests had an effect, too, as legislators were reluctant to take on the state's huge farmer bloc. Apparently, the modernizers' rhetoric of progress did not include state protections for the environment. In 1996, one study found that when it came to protecting the environment, the North Carolina state government spent less than all thirteen southern states save Alabama and Georgia.

After the mid-1990s, the extent of river pollution in North Carolina decreased, though fish kills continued. In 2003, some 3.2 million fish died in the Neuse near New Bern. Clearly something had to be done. In 1997 the state-run North Carolina Environment Management Commission initiated a Neuse River cleanup plan, the first mandatory state water-pollution controls ever put in place. The plan required a 30 percent reduction in nitrogen levels in the river by 2003, by which year roughly half of the croplands were enrolled in nitrogen-reduction conservation programs. The program's goals were basically met: according to an NC State study, nitrogen levels in the river declined by 27 percent between 1995 and 2003. Nonetheless, some experts claimed the decline in nitrogen had less to do with governmental regulation than with the effects of the particularly intense Hurricane Fran—which, in September 1996, became the strongest hurricane to hit North Carolina since Hurricane Hazel in 1954—and Hurricane Floyd, which in September 1999 caused massive flooding in eastern North Carolina. It may have been that these violent torrential storms and the large amount of water that they spawned had the effect, at least in the short term, of purging the river systems of nitrogen pollutants.

The unknown implications of climate change have raised the increased possibility of damage to North Carolina's coastline through beach erosion and

Figure 18.1 Satellite image of coastal NC, September 23, 1999. Hurricane Floyd caused massive sediment and pollutant runoff. *Source: NASA/Goddard Space Flight Center Scientific Visualisation Studio/Public Domain.*

submersion and the threat of more frequent—and more powerful—hurricanes. The impact of humans on the North Carolina environment has been pronounced. On the coast, climate change, according to many scientists, has resulted in rising sea levels. Worldwide, oceans rose by 6–8 inches during the twentieth century, while in North Carolina they rose by 8 inches. In 2007, scientists predicted that the oceans would rise further—perhaps as much as 30 inches—because of climate change. Increasing sea levels of this scale, according to one estimate, would submerge as much as 770 square miles of eastern North Carolina—an area about the size of Great Smoky Mountains National Park.

Climate change might also affect interior North Carolina, as periods of intense drought and high rainfall seem to have become more common. In general, summers have become drier and hotter, with intense downpours but less water available. In eastern North Carolina, heavy water demands from wells led to a new state mandate, in effect after August 2002, requiring that well users reduce their demands on aquifers by 25 percent over the next six years. As North Carolina grows in population, its urban residents in the Piedmont will likely find water supplies harder pressed, especially during periods of drought. Both Greensboro and Raleigh suffered from water supplies that could no longer keep up with their populations, and both sought to alleviate their

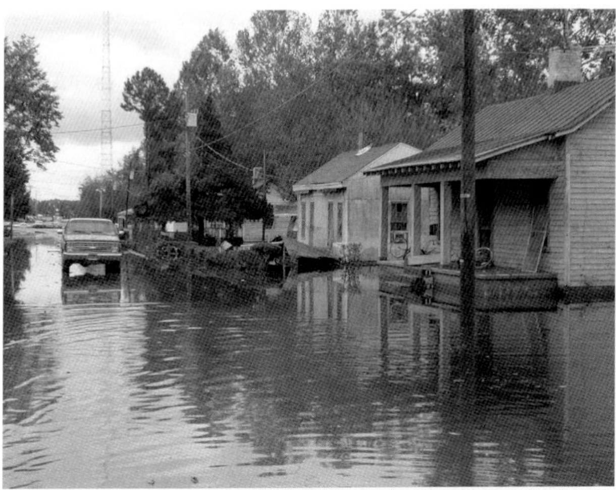

Figure 18.2 Flooded Tar River at Princeville, NC, in the aftermath of Hurricane Floyd, September 1999. *Source: Dave Saville/FEMA News Photo.*

problems through inter-basin transfers. In 2005, for example, Raleigh requested an inter-basin transfer from Kerr Lake on the Roanoke River to help satisfy rising water demands, while Greensboro constructed water pipelines to Reidsville and Burlington, as well as a new reservoir on the Deep River, the Randleman Dam. North of Charlotte, in Cabarrus County, the towns of Concord and Kannapolis, in another inter-basin transfer, wanted to drain some 38 million gallons of water a day from the Catawba River.

On the fragile Outer Banks, rising sea levels with sinking land and beach erosion threatened much of the beach housing, as it is especially susceptible to storm-related flooding. By 2007, according to one account, some 22 miles of beach were collapsing on Hatteras Island, Ocracoke, Pea Island, and Rodanthe, and the beaches were sustained only through massive bulldozing of sand. Rising sea levels have brought other adverse consequences. The influx of salt water into estuaries and rivers has spelled the doom of many freshwater swamps and cypress groves. In 2001, during a drought, saltwater was detected as far as 16 miles up the Cape Fear River, nearly 50 miles from the ocean.

Like the rest of the globe, North Carolina will continue to face environmental cataclysm, and preserving its environmental quality remains a challenge for the state's leadership. The traditional dichotomy between modernizers intent on economic growth and relatively open to new ideas, and traditionalists opposed to changes that undermined the state's social and cultural structure seemed increasingly untenable. North Carolinians will need, as they progress through the twenty-first century, new approaches, ideas, and models for leadership.

Figure 18.3 In 1870, the Cape Hatteras Lighthouse was built 1500 feet from the sea, but by the 1990s erosion had brought the coast within 100 feet of the structure. In the summer of 1999, the National Park Service, at the cost of nearly $10 million, moved the lighthouse 2,900 feet inland. Cape Hatteras Lighthouse, October 22, 1999. *Source: Courtesy of Jones Airfoils.*

Political Patterns in the Twenty-First Century

Patterns of change and tradition dominated North Carolina's politics during the late-twentieth and early-twenty-first centuries. As in many other areas of life in modern North Carolina, there were sharp contrasts and an increasing degree of polarization. Like much of the rest of the South, North Carolina tended to vote Republican in national elections after 1970. Between 1972 and 2004, North Carolina voted for only one Democratic presidential candidate, Jimmy Carter of Georgia, in 1976, and in presidential contests no Democrat mustered more than 42 percent of the vote. Jesse Helms, a Republican, was elected to five terms as a US senator, beginning in 1972, while none of the three Democrats elected to the Senate during this period—Robert Morgan (elected in 1974), Terry Sanford (elected in 1986), and John Edwards (elected in 1998)—served more than one term. Republicans won nine of twelve Senate races between 1972 and 2004. At the same time, however, Helms was the only senator of either party who achieved reelection: Republican John East committed suicide on June 29, 1986,

Figure 18.4 President Ronald Reagan and North Carolina Governor Jim Martin.

and was succeeded by Rep. James T. Broyhill, who lost in November 1986 to Sanford. After Lauch Faircloth defeated Sanford in 1992, six years later he lost to John Edwards.

Still, in contrast to other southern states, North Carolina maintained strong two-party competition. In gubernatorial and legislative elections, the Democrats tended to prevail. Between 1972 and 2008, only two Republicans, Jim Holshouser in 1972 and Jim Martin in 1984 and 1988, won the North Carolina governorship. Sixteen years of the Democratic governorships of Jim Hunt (1992–2000) and Mike Easley (2000–08) then followed. After the elections of 1994, when Republicans became dominant across the South, North Carolina Republicans controlled the lower house of the legislature for the first time in a century, a majority they maintained until 1996. Although Republicans narrowly recaptured the house in 2002, they lost control after a Republican member, Michael Decker, switched sides. (Decker was later convicted of having accepted more than $63,000 in cash and campaign checks from Democratic leader Jim Black to switch parties.) Throughout the 1990s and 2000s, Democrats hung onto control of the state senate and the governorship. By the twenty-first century, with Democrats constructing a coalition of African Americans, rural whites, and suburbanites, North Carolina remained the most politically competitive state in the South. During the 2004 elections, exit polls revealed just how competitive the state remained: 39 percent of voters identified themselves as Democrats, 21 percent as independents, and 40 percent as Republicans.

Figure 18.5 Jim Hunt in campaign for Lieutenant Governor in 1972, Greenville, NC. *Source: Joyner Library, East Carolina University.*

Much of this political competitiveness expressed North Carolina's demographic diversity. After the adoption of the Voting Rights Act of 1965, the percentage of black voters—who voted Democratic by large majorities—in the North Carolina electorate steadily increased from 14.5 in 1966, to 19.1 percent in 2000, to more than 21 percent in 2008. While rural counties and small towns trended Republican, the urban Piedmont, over time, trended Democratic. The state's rapid population growth was matched by an expanded electorate, which grew from 3.3 million registered voters in 1990 to 6.2 million in 2008. These Democratic tendencies were accentuated by the arrival of new suburban white immigrants, swing voters who were leaning Democratic. Latino immigrants, a majority of whom voted Democratic, also figured significantly in North Carolina elections.

In the changing politics of twenty-first-century North Carolina, women played a central role. Because women composed a large proportion of swing voters, their political preferences could—and did—decide elections. In addition, the numbers of women candidates sharply increased. In the 2008 elections, for example, four out of five candidates for county commissioner in the Research Triangle were women, while in Wake County five women ran for the legislature. By 2008, North Carolina ranked first among southeastern states in the number of female legislators. In 2000, Bev Perdue of New Bern became North Carolina's first female lieutenant governor. Reelected to that post in 2004,

Figure 18.6 Kay Hagan, official campaign photo. *Source: Wikipedia/Public Domain.*

Figure 18.7 Beverly Perdue, official photo. *Source: Wikipedia/Public Domain.*

she became the first female governor in 2008, when she won election as a Democrat over Republican opponent Pat McCrory.

The election for the US Senate in 2008 pitted two women candidates against each other, Republican incumbent Elizabeth Dole and Democratic challenger Kay Hagan. Dole was elected in 2002 as the first female US senator from North Carolina, occupying Jesse Helms's seat. At the start of the campaign Dole was considered as a lock to win reelection. In 2007 and early 2008, the conventional wisdom said that Dole was unbeatable, and prominent Democrats refused to run against her. As late as September 2008, Dole maintained a double-digit lead over her Democratic challenger, state senator Kay Hagan of Greensboro. Below the surface, Dole had political problems. While her predecessor Jesse Helms had maintained one of the best constituent services operations in the Senate, Dole seemed unresponsive and preoccupied with events outside North Carolina.

Elected to the state senate in 1998 in a close contest against an incumbent Republican, Hagan rose to become chair of the state senate's powerful appropriations committee. Like most successful North Carolina Democrats, she ran a moderate-conservative campaign, stressing education, economic development, and environmental issues. Buoyed by $6.6 million from the national Democratic Senatorial Campaign Committee, Hagan pulled ahead in the polls in October. Dole reacted with sharply negative television ads, one of which claimed that Hagan had accepted "godless money" from atheist supporters; the ad connected her with an organization called Godless Americans. "Godless Americans and Kay Hagan," declared the ad. "She hid from cameras. Took godless money. What did Hagan promise in return?" The ad concluded with a woman in the background saying "There is no God." Dole's ad backfired. Hagan asserted that Dole was "attacking my strong Christian faith" and should be "ashamed" of herself. Filing a defamation suit, Hagan also assured voters that she, a Presbyterian elder and Sunday school teacher in Greensboro, was by all means a church-going Christian. The backlash from the "Godless" ad helped to push along a decisive Hagan victory, and in the end she won by a 362,000 vote margin, or by 53 to 44 percent.

For most of 2007 and 2008, Barack Obama and Hillary Clinton had battled it out in a campaign for the Democratic Party's presidential nomination. In March and April 2008, Clinton had scored big victories in Texas, Ohio, and then Pennsylvania, threatening to overcome Obama's lead in delegates. But primary election day in North Carolina, on May 6, 2008, brought a decisive victory for Obama, who, fueled by the state's sizable African American vote—about 21 percent of the electorate—carried the state by more than 14 percentage points (56 to 42 percent). Obama's victory in North Carolina, which gained him a larger share of the state's 115 convention delegates, combined with a narrow loss in Indiana, seemed to assure his control over the nominating process.

In the general election, Obama faced an uphill struggle for North Carolina's fifteen electoral votes: in 2004, incumbent Republican George W. Bush had carried the state by twelve percentage points. During the primary campaign, Obama's supporters successfully registered new voters, energizing African Americans and young North Carolinians. In the general election, moreover, Obama attracted 17,000 volunteers and four hundred paid staff that spurred voter registration efforts and an ambitious get-out-the-vote campaign. His opponent, John McCain, had, in contrast, only thirty-five staff members. The national Obama campaign poured resources into the state, staffing sixty field offices in North Carolina, as compared to forty offices for Republican presidential candidate McCain.

Prior to the May 2008 Democratic primary, Obama organizers registered 120,000 new voters. Thereafter, the Obama camp accelerated its efforts. By November, 970,000 people had filed new or updated registrations, the overwhelming proportion of them (by a more than two-to-one margin) Democratic. While Obama aired a steady stream of television ads, McCain visited infrequently during the summer and fall months of the campaign, assuming that North Carolina was solidly Republican. Toward the end of the campaign, Obama drew very large crowds as he visited the state frequently: attracting 20,000 at a rally in Charlotte on September 21 and 28,000 in Asheville on October 5. All told, by early October more than 128,000 people had attended Obama's rallies in North Carolina.

As was true in other states, in North Carolina, the Obama campaign urged its supporters to participate in early voting. These efforts folded nicely into intense voter registration efforts; about two-thirds of new registrants in 2008 were new voters or people who had moved to North Carolina. In a new law that came into effect in 2008, North Carolina became one of seven states that permitted same-day registration during the early voting period (creating an early voting period of seventeen days)—discarding the previous provision that required registration twenty-five days prior to elections. During the early voting period, about 92,000 voters registered. About a third of these new registrants were black, and about 93 percent of these voters cast ballots for Obama. In the two weeks of early voting before November 5, more than 2.4 million voters voted early—more than did so on Election Day. All told, 4.4 million ballots were cast, a turnout of better than 70 percent and a 21 percent increase in the vote over 2004. This was by far the largest number of North Carolinians ever voting in an election, and early voting—a large proportion of which went to Obama—proved decisive. Obama polled well among African American voters, receiving more than 90 percent of their vote. Nearly three-quarters of black voters turned out, while about 42 percent of Obama's voters came from African Americans. Obama also attracted about 35 percent of the white vote, succeeding in attracting the suburban white vote in the Triangle, Triad, and Charlotte. Obama carried North Carolina by the narrow margin of 14,177 votes, or by 49.7 to 49.38

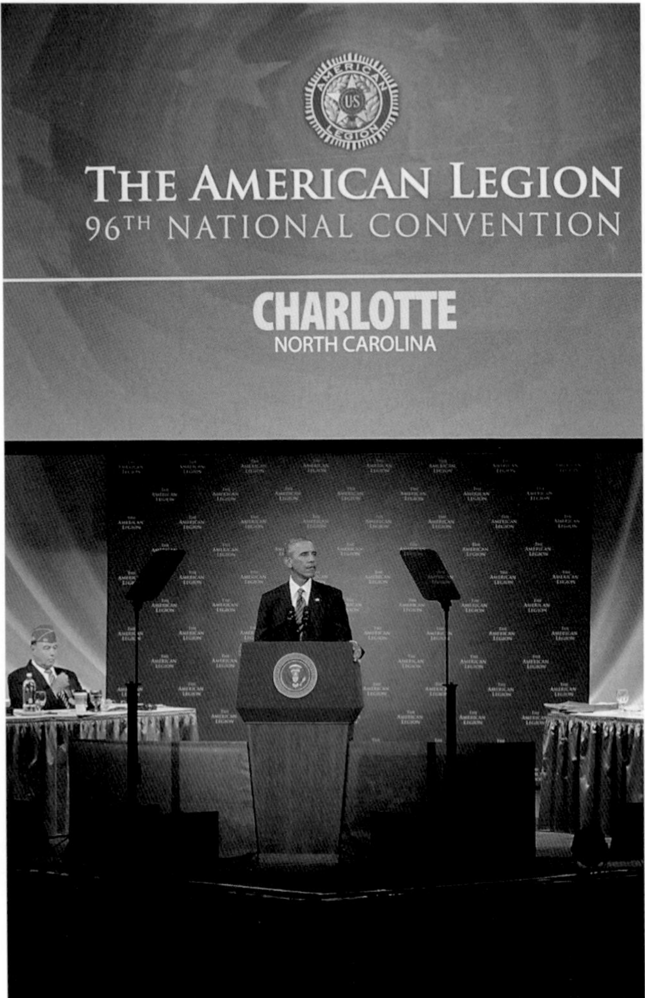

Figure 18.8 Barack Obama at the American Legion in Charlotte.

percent of the vote, to become the first Democrat the state helped send to the White House since 1976. Once again, North Carolina had surprised people.

Republican Resurgence

The Democratic victories in 2008 were short-lived, and North Carolina Republicans quickly rebounded. President Obama was suffering from contentious battles with Congress, an economy in deep recession. Throughout the early 2000s, North Carolina lost manufacturing jobs. The outlook for workers got only worse after the Great Recession that began in 2007 and lingered for the next couple of years. In 2010, although technically the economy had moved out of recession, North Carolina still reported an unemployment rate of 10.5 percent.

As a result of relentless Republican attacks, Obama saw his approval rating sink in North Carolina within eighteen months of his inauguration. In particular, the Affordable Care Act, passed over strenuous Republican opposition and signed by Obama in March 2010, suffered from widespread disquiet. By November 2010, with mid-term elections approaching, nearly the majority of North Carolina voters disapproved of his performance in office.

Perhaps of greater consequence was the implosion of the North Carolina Democratic Party. John Edwards, elected senator in 1998 and Democratic vice-presidential candidate in 2004, admitted to having had an extramarital affair which resulted in an out-of-wedlock child. Indicted for using campaign contributions to hide the affair in June 2011, his trial a year later resulted in an acquittal. Several state leaders experienced corruption charges, including Mike Easley, who was Democratic governor from 2001 to 2009. Accused of failing to report contributions and the use of aircraft, Easley settled the charges by paying a $1,000 fine. In 2006, the Democratic speaker of the house, Jim Black, who served four terms in office, pled guilty to federal charges of public corruption, including bribery, and was sentenced to five years in prison. In March 2004, State Agriculture Commissioner Meg Scott Phipps, the daughter of former governor Bob Scott and granddaughter of Kerr Scott, was sentenced to four years in prison after admitting that she had received bribes from carnival operators at the North Carolina State Fair.

As governor, Bev Perdue suffered plummeting approval ratings because of the economy and charges of campaign irregularities. In 2009, Perdue also proposed, and the legislature enacted, an increase of a penny in the state sales tax, along with severe cuts in health care and education. In February 2010, after just one year in office for Perdue, only 30 percent of North Carolina voters approved of her performance in office. The governor also suffered from accusations of financial irregularities including charges that she took more than three dozen flights that she failed to report to campaign authorities. As a result of a criminal investigation, four of her aides were indicted, including her 2008 campaign finance director. Perdue was in constant combat with the legislature, especially after the Republicans were swept to power in November 2010. Riding a tide of popular discontent, the Republicans captured both houses of the legislature—their last majority in the state senate was in 1898—and they had decisive majorities of 31–19 in the senate and 67–52 in the house. Perdue stymied this legislature with sixteen vetoes in 2011, but in February 2012 she announced that she would not seek reelection—the first time a sitting governor had declined to do so since a constitutional amendment in 1977 permitted governors to serve more than one term.

The Republicans pressed forward with their agenda, despite Perdue's opposition. The legislature permitted the 2009 sales tax increase to expire, resulting in large cuts to public schools, state agencies, universities, and community colleges. These amounted to 15 percent, the largest budget cuts since the Great Depression. The legislature also reapportioned districts in the state house and in Congress in 2010. Under Democratic control, the legislature had always been apportioned to provide the party an electoral advantage. In 1990, the General Assembly, under pressure from the Justice Department, drew the black majority 12th Congressional District in such way that it snaked along Interstate 85 Durham to Charlotte, including portions of Greensboro, High Point, and Winston-Salem.[3] Now, with the Republicans in control, the impact of reapportionment was substantial, as in 2012, despite a popular vote of 51–49 percent Democratic to Republican, the congressional delegation was controlled by Republicans 9–4.

The Republican General Assembly also moved forcefully into the politics of sexuality. In September 2011, the legislature approved a constitutional amendment to be submitted to voters—known as Amendment One—that stated that "marriage between one man and one woman is the only domestic legal union that shall be valid or recognized in this State." The vote on the amendment during the May 2012 primary reflected a sharp cultural polarization in North Carolina. Only eight of the state's one hundred counties—all of them urban counties—voted against the amendment, while in the rest of the state the amendment rolled up large majorities, with 61 percent of state voters approving the measure. Amendment One, which also invalidated domestic unions among heterosexual couples, was declared unconstitutional in October 2014 after the 4th Circuit Court of Appeals in Richmond invalidated a similar ban in Virginia in July 2014.

North Carolina approached the elections in 2012 deeply divided. Facing Republican challenger Mitt Romney, the Obama campaign devoted substantial resources to repeating the 2008 formula for victory, which included a large field force of staff and volunteers, along with the heavy use of social media. In the end, though, Romney narrowly carried the state, with 50.6 percent of the vote compared to Obama's 48.4 percent. The number of people voting increased to 4.5 million, but Republican turnout exceeded that of the Democrats. Obama attracted a large African American vote, but he also attracted white votes in urban and suburban areas, carrying Charlotte, Greensboro, Durham, Asheville, Fayetteville, Raleigh, and Winston-Salem by substantial majorities. In Durham County, Obama won 76 percent of the vote. In centers of modernizing North Carolina, Obama attracted a coalition of young, African American, urban, and tech-savvy voters. Outside of modernizing North Carolina, Romney was favored, often by large majorities that reflected the persisting traditionalist small town and rural presence. After winning 35 percent of the state's white vote in 2008, four years later Obama received only 30 percent.

In the gubernatorial election in 2012, Republican candidate Pat McCrory defeated lieutenant governor Walter Dalton by 54.7 percent to 43.2 percent. In control of the legislature and governorship, the General Assembly consolidated its control. On July 25, 2013, the legislature enacted sweeping changes in the state law regarding voting. Perdue had vetoed a measure adopted in June 2011 requiring all those wishing to vote to present a valid photo identification at the polls; requiring a photo ID for voting demonstrably affected minorities (who voted Democratic), who were less likely to own cars. Another Republican measure reduced the number of early voting days passed the house, but the law failed in the senate. Proponents of these new measures claimed that they would limit voter fraud. Rep. Ric Killian of Charlotte, a co-sponsor of a voter ID law, maintained that making sure that "a person is who they say they are" was "a crucial first step toward validating elections."[4] Others argued that eliminating same-day registration and limiting early voting would enable election officials to prevent fraud. Yet little evidence of voter fraud in recent elections existed. Between 2000 and 2012, according to a study by the North Carolina Board of Elections, there were only 629 examples of improper voting and only two instances of voter impersonation out of millions of votes cast. The Democratic legislature's liberalization of the franchise between 1997 and 2007 had had a significant effect in increasing turnout. Before the 2000s, North Carolina was in the bottom third of voter turnout among the fifty states; by 2010, it ranked in the top third.

After the legislature convened in early 2013, the house enacted a voting law that focused mainly on requiring photo identification for voting beginning in 2016. On June 25, 2013, in *Shelby County v. Holder*, after the US Supreme Court struck down the "preclearance" provisions of the Voting Rights Act—which empowered the Justice Department to review changes in voting procedures in forty counties in any state with a history of disfranchisement—the state senate rushed to enact the bill. Emboldened by Shelby's elimination of federal preclearance, the senate transformed the house bill. The senate version required the use only of driver's licenses (the house version permitted other identification), limited early voting, and eliminated same-day registration. The measure was enacted in the senate three days after it left committee, and the house concurred with little discussion.

Nearly two years later, on March 23, 2016, the North Carolina legislature attracted national attention when, in a rushed vote taken during a special session, it enacted House Bill 2 (HB2). A day later, McCrory signed the bill into law. It repealed Ordinance 7056, which the Charlotte City Council adopted on February 22, 2016, and which banned discrimination on the basis of sexual orientation and gender identity in public accommodations and city transportation, or by city contractors. Charlotte was following a national trend of localities instituting protections for LGBTQ people; seventeen of the nation's biggest cities had already enacted similar legislation. One of the law's features was that it theoretically permitted transgender people to use the bathroom of their choice—though this was not an explicit part of the bill. HB2 voided the Charlotte ordinance, mandating that all people must use a public bathroom that corresponded to their gender, according to their birth certificate. But HB2 went further by prohibiting local governments in North Carolina from increasing the minimum wage or limiting child labor above the state level, instituting workplace protections for municipal employees, and providing for paid family leave. The law also banned any lawsuits in state courts that charged discrimination.

Republican legislators lined up behind HB2, claiming that it protected against the threat of sexual predators in public bathrooms—a claim that possessed no basis in fact. Contending that the law violated municipal autonomy, Democrats protested by walking out on the day of the vote on HB2. Dan Blue, Senate Democratic leader, described the law as an "affront to equality, civil rights, and local autonomy." On March 28, the American Civil Liberties Union filed a suit against the law. Meanwhile, state attorney general Roy Cooper, a Democrat, refused to defend the law because, he claimed, of its unconstitutionality.

HB2 caused a national furor. Entertainers and sports organization objected. Filmmakers and television producers cancelled work in the state. The popular circus Cirque du Soleil cancelled their shows in Greensboro and Charlotte. Musical performers such as Bruce Springsteen cancelled a Greensboro concert scheduled for April 10. Other acts such as Pearl Jam, Ringo Starr, and Ani DiFranco followed suit. "Some things are more important than a rock show," Springsteen announced on his website, describing his cancellation as part of a "fight against prejudice and bigotry." Other performers did not cancel their acts but donated part or all of the proceeds to LGBTQ organizations. Meanwhile, the National Basketball Association threatened to cancel the All-Star Game, which was scheduled to be played in Charlotte in 2017.

The backlash to HB2 also extended to business leaders. More than a hundred corporate leaders signed a manifesto denouncing the bill. Deutsche Bank cancelled the construction of a planned facility in Cary, resulting in the loss of 250 jobs. The tech giant PayPal cancelled its plans to establish a $36 million operations center in Charlotte with 400 employees. "The new law perpetuates discrimination," PayPal CEO Dan Schulman declared, "and it violates the values and principles that are at the core of PayPal's mission and culture. As a result, PayPal will not move forward with our planned expansion into Charlotte." Meanwhile, federal officials intervened in early May, bringing suit against North Carolina for violating Title VII of the Civil Rights Act, Title IX of the Education Amendments Act of 1972, and the Violence Against Women Act.

Government officials also objected to the law. Five states and the District of Columbia, along with numerous municipalities, prohibited non-essential state travel to North Carolina. More serious was the prospect of federal intervention. For a few years, officials in various federal bureaucracies had moved to extend civil rights protections to LGBTQ people. Responding to HB2, federal officials threatened proceedings to cut off billions of dollars of federal funds, including $1.5 billion for UNC. Despite this pressure and a mounting national boycott of the state, legislators refused to change or repeal the law through the spring and summer of 2016. In addition, they contested federal intervention with a vigorous legal defense.

The controversy over HB2 spilled over into the gubernatorial and presidential elections of 2016. North Carolina became a key battleground state, with Democratic presidential candidate Hillary Clinton and insurgent Republican candidate Donald Trump visiting the state twenty-nine times during the campaign. Despite Clinton's appeal in urban and suburban counties, Trump enjoyed powerful support outside the state's urban areas. In the elections of November 8, Trump won the state and its fifteen electoral votes by more than 177,000 votes, or by 50.5 percent to Clinton's 46.7 percent. While Clinton carried Charlotte, Raleigh-Durham-Chapel Hill, Greensboro, Winston-Salem, Asheville, and Boone by significant majorities, she lost most of rural and small-town North Carolina by large majorities, with the exception of counties containing a large African American population.

Nonetheless, the 2016 elections also showed that North Carolina was becoming a more politically competitive "purple" state. The controversy surrounding HB2 had an effect on state elections—as public opinion polls showed that 66 percent of voters disapproved of the law—and a significant number of Trump voters cast ballots for Democratic gubernatorial candidate Roy Cooper against Republican incumbent Pat McCrory. In a razor-close election, Cooper won the state by about 10,000 votes out of 4.6 million votes, while McCrory lost by bigger margins than did Trump in urban counties. In Mecklenburg County, for example, Cooper won fifty precincts that McCrory—who calls Charlotte home—had carried in 2012. McCrory challenged the results of the election, claiming voter fraud. Yet no evidence of fraud surfaced despite numerous challenges by the McCrory campaign, and the contested precincts that canvassed or recounted their votes brought a slightly larger margin for Cooper.

On December 7, 2016, McCrory finally conceded the election, and Cooper was declared the victor. Almost immediately the Republican legislature moved to strip Cooper of some of his powers, including the power to appoint local boards of elections and judges. Cooper and the legislature wrangled for two months about the fate of HB2, and the prospects of further boycotts by the NCAA loomed large. On March 30, 2017, the General Assembly repealed HB2, but in new legislation that outraged LGBTQ leaders in the state, also prohibited cities from enacting ordinances regulating discrimination in employment or public accommodations until 2020. This partial repeal was enough to result, within weeks, in the lifting of the NCAA's and the ACC's ban on postseason tournaments in the state.

* * *

North Carolinians can look back on nearly four centuries of change and tradition. A thoroughly southern state, its history parallels that of the American South, with a common heritage of agriculture, slavery, Civil War, and Jim Crow. But North Carolina, especially in the past century and into the twenty-first century, has led change in the region, becoming a center of the industrial revolution, especially in the cotton textile industry, the spread of railroad and highway transportation, and the expansion of the service and the high-tech sectors. North Carolina's increased presence on the national stage throughout 2008 was no accident. A far cry from its days as a regional "backwater," the state in recent decades has become one of the most vibrant in the Union, with a dynamic and resilient economy, a leading system of public and private universities, and natural beauty that attracts thousands of tourists (who annually contribute more than $1 billion to the state's economy). Many of the migrants were younger, with 557,000 eligible voters moving to North Carolina between 2000 and 2015; two-thirds of these were aged between 18 and 44. With a rapidly increasingly population, by 2015, the state had become the tenth largest in the nation. Possessing excellent higher education, research institutes, and the presence of high-tech firms, the state continues to be a mecca for new ideas and the information revolution. North Carolinians, like other southerners, have become a much more diverse population that includes immigrants from the rest of the United States, Latin America, and Asia. Even as it maintains powerful traditions, North Carolina remains an engine of change.

Notes

1 Rick Martinez, "Immigration Hits 'Critical Mass' in NC," *Carolina Journal Online*, December 12, 2005, www.carolinajournal.com/exclusives/display_exclusive.html?id=2983.

2 Karin Rives, "Businesses Meet Immigrants' Needs," *Raleigh News and Observer*, March 5, 2006; Marti Maguire, "Schools Bear Burden of Immigration," *Raleigh News and Observer*, February 27, 2006.

3 In *Shaw v. Reno* (1992) and *Shaw v. Hunt* (1996), plaintiffs claimed that the district was a racial gerrymander. After the Supreme Court ruled in favor of the plaintiffs, the district was altered.

4 Rob Christensen, "Legislators to Take up Voter ID—Republicans and Democrats Debate the Extent of Voter Fraud in the State," *Raleigh News and Observer*, March 13, 2011.

Suggested Readings, Part 6

Chapter 16

Daniel J. Clark, *Like Night & Day: Unionization in a Southern Mill Town* (Chapel Hill: University of North Carolina Press, 1997).
John Ehle, *Dr. Frank: Life with Frank Porter Graham* (Chapel Hill: Franklin Street Books, 1993).
Robert Rodgers Korstad, *Civil Rights Unionism: Tobacco Workers and the Struggle for Democracy in the Mid-Twentieth-Century South* (Chapel Hill: University of North Carolina Press, 2003).
Albert N. Link, *A Generosity of Spirit: The Early History of the Research Triangle Park* (Research Triangle Park, NC: Research Triangle Foundation of North Carolina, 1995).
———, *From Seed to Harvest: The Growth of the Research Triangle Park* (Research Triangle Park, NC: Research Triangle Foundation of North Carolina, 2002).
William A. Link, *William Friday: Power, Purpose, and American Higher Education*, 2nd ed. (Chapel Hill: University of North Carolina Press, 2013).
Malinda Maynor Lowery, *Lumbee Indians in the Jim Crow South: Race, Identity, and the Making of a Nation* (Chapel Hill: University of North Carolina Press, 2010).
Paul Luebke, *Tar Heel Politics 2000* (Chapel Hill: University of North Carolina Press, 1998).
Boyd E. Payton, *Scapegoat: Prejudice/Politics/Prison* (Philadelphia, PA: Whitmore Publishing Co., 1970).
Julian M. Pleasants, *The Political Career of W. Kerr Scott: The Squire from Haw River* (Lexington: University Press of Kentucky, 2014).
Julian M. Pleasants and Augustus M. Burns III, *Frank Porter Graham and the 1950 Senate Race in North Carolina* (Chapel Hill: University of North Carolina Press, 1990).

Sayoko Uesugi, "Gender, Race, and the Cold War: Mary Price and the Progressive Party in North Carolina, 1945–1948," *North Carolina Historical Review* LXXVII no. 3 (July 2000).

Chapter 17

William J. Billingsley, *Communists on Campus: Race, Politics, and the Public University in Sixties North Carolina* (Athens: University of Georgia Press, 1999).

Leslie Brown, *Upbuilding Black Durham: Gender, Class, and Black Community Development in the Jim Crow South* (Chapel Hill: *University of North Carolina Press*, 2008).

David C. Carter, "The Williamston Freedom Movement: Civil Rights at the Grass Roots in Eastern North Carolina, 1957–1964," *North Carolina Historical Review* 76 (Jan. 1999), 1–42.

David S. Cecelski, *Along Freedom Road: Hyde County, North Carolina, and the Fate of Black Schools in the South* (Chapel Hill: University of North Carolina Press, 1994).

William Chafe, *Civilities and Civil Rights: Greensboro, North Carolina, and the Black Struggle for Freedom* (New York: Oxford University Press, 1981).

Davison M. Douglas, *Reading, Writing, & Race: The Desegregation of the Charlotte Schools* (Chapel Hill: University of North Carolina Press, 1995).

John Ehle, *The Free Men* (New York: Harper & Row, 1965).

Frye Gaillard, *The Dream Long Deferred* (Chapel Hill: University of North Carolina Press, 1988).

Christina Greene, *Our Separate Ways: Women and the Black Freedom Movement in Durham, North Carolina* (Chapel Hill: University of North Carolina Press, 2005).

Kenneth Robert Janken, *The Wilmington Ten: Violence, Injustice, and the Rise of Black Politics in the 1970s* (Chapel Hill: University of North Carolina Press, 2016).

Robert Korstad and James Leloudis, *To Right These Wrongs: The North Carolina Fund and the Battle to End Poverty and Inequality in 1960s America* (Chapel Hill: University of North Carolina Press, 2010).

William A. Link, *Righteous Warrior: Jesse Helms and the Rise of Modern Conservatism* (New York: St. Martin's Press, 2008).

Richard Rosen and Joseph Mosnier, *Julius Chambers: A Life in the Struggle for Civil Rights* (Chapel Hill: University of North Carolina Press, 2016).

Sarah Caroline Thuesen, *Greater than Equal: African American Struggles for Schools and Citizenship in North Carolina, 1919–1965* (Chapel Hill: University of North Carolina Press, 2013).

Timothy B. Tyson, *Radio Free Dixie: Robert F. Williams and the Roots of Black Power* (Chapel Hill: University of North Carolina Press, 1999).

Elizabeth Wheaton, *Codename GREENKIL: The 1979 Greensboro Killings* (Athens: University of Georgia Press, 1987).
Miles Wolff, *Lunch at the Five and Ten: The Greensboro Sit-Ins, a Contemporary History* (New York: Stein and Day, 1970).

Chapter 18

Rob Christensen, *The Paradox of Tarheel Politics: The Personalities, Elections, and Events that Shaped Modern North Carolina* (Chapel Hill: University of North Carolina Press, 2008).
Tom Eamon, *The Making of a Southern Democracy: From Kerr Scott to Pat McCrory* (Chapel Hill: University of North Carolina Press, 2014).
Leon Fink, *The Maya of Morganton: Work and Community in the Nuevo New South* (Chapel Hill: University of North Carolina Press, 2003).
John L. Godwin, *Black Wilmington and the North Carolina Way: Portrait of a Community in the Era of Civil Rights Protest* (Lanham, MD: University Press of America, 2000).
Wayne Grimsley, *James B. Hunt: A North Carolina Progressive* (Jefferson, NC: McFarland & Co., 2003).
Jack Temple Kirby, *Mockingbird Song: Ecological Landscapes of the South* (Chapel Hill: University of North Carolina Press, 2006).
Rick Martinez, "Immigration Hits 'Critical Mass' in NC," *Carolina Journal Online*, December 12, 2005, www.carolinajournal.com/exclusives/display_exclusive.html?id=2983.
Donald G. Mathews and Jane Sherron DeHart, *Sex, Gender, and the Politics of ERA: A State and a Nation* (New York: Oxford University Press, 1990).
Timothy B. Tyson, *Blood Done Sign My Name: A True Story* (New York: Three Rivers Press, 2004).

Document Section, Part 6
School Desegregation and Its Legacy

In the aftermath of the Brown *decision of May 1954, the Supreme Court mandated school desegregation. Yet little progress occurred for the next seventeen years until 1971, when the Supreme Court's landmark* Swann v. Charlotte-Mecklenburg *required drastic solutions involving the use of school busing. Thousands of students in North Carolina were bused away from segregated high schools in order to achieve racial balance. The* Swann *formula—court-required plans which measured desegregation against existing racial demographics and which employed busing as the most important tools—became prevalent across the South. Busing evoked white backlash across the country, as parents objected to these drastic changes, sometimes because of racial fears, sometimes because they feared any disruptions in their children's education.*

Immediately following the Swann *decision, the Charlotte-Mecklenburg school board implemented plans affecting school children beginning in the fall of 1971. Among the schools most affected were traditionally African American schools, such as West Charlotte High School. Established during the Jim Crow era, West Charlotte served as a bastion of the black community, and many of its graduates became high achievers. Excerpts of the following documents come from a series of oral-history interviews conducted by the Southern Oral History Program's Pamela Grundy at the University of North Carolina at Chapel Hill in 1999. As these interviews suggested, desegregation occurred with mixed consequences.*

Charlotte African Americans Remember Desegregation

Interview with Saundra Davis, May 12, 1998[1]

PAMELA GRUNDY: So you were mentioning, when you were talking about the two sides of the road, the beginnings of school integration, and I guess in the earlier years of it when the first white kids started to come to West Charlotte, that was a pretty turbulent time. A lot of things went on.

SD: Yes. A lot of things went on, but normally West Charlotte was really quiet. I think West Charlotte was more like a model school for everybody else. Any time something would happen that they needed to try something out, they would try it at West Charlotte. West Charlotte is number one. We always make things go smooth. It seems like we had the personnel to do it. I wasn't there when the integration started, but my children came into it when they were in elementary school. My baby girl, Angela, had to go to Rama Road, and that's way, way on the other side of town. She was bussed all the way over there. We've just been fortunate, blessed, lucky because in the end they got to go to school right across the street. They came right back home. They had to be bussed a few years, but you put up with that.

PG: What did you think about that when it first began to start and when you were faced with having to send your children away? What was your feeling about that?

SD: I'm going to tell you right now. I'm frank. I'm honest. I'm blunt. I'm going to tell you what's on my mind. I didn't want my children to have to be bussed out of the neighborhood. I really didn't. But if that meant my children getting a better education, yes. Let them be bussed. Somebody had to do it. The ice had to be broken somewhere. For the simple reason the white schools have had the better things. When they finished with them they passed them to our kids. I know my children are just as good as anybody's children. Not only my children, every child in the world should be treated equal, because they're taking our tax money just like they're taking everybody else's tax money to do these things with, so why make our children suffer? They've suffered enough all the years of their life. No, I didn't want my children to be bussed, but I didn't let them know that that

1 Interview with Saundra Davis, May 12, 1998 (Interview K-0278), Southern Oral History Program Collection, Southern Historical Collection, Wilson Library, University of North Carolina at Chapel Hill, http://docsouth.unc.edu/sohp/K-0278/excerpts/excerpt_709.html.

was the way I felt because if I had let them know what I felt they wouldn't have learned as much as they could have. I always instilled in them, go to school, learn everything you can, and do the best you can. I felt good about them going, the computers and everything. They enjoyed it, too. It wasn't the hand-me-downs. They got it first hand.

PG: Do you think that made a big difference?

SD: I think so. But the only thing that bothered me, and still bothers me, our children, the black children as a whole, they are bussed, and bussed, and bussed. But in the white neighborhoods they do all they can to keep their children there. I don't care how they try to break it down or what they do. I can see it. Nobody is crazy. But if it's taking the bussing to get our kids where they should be, fine. But you have to think about it, too. How can a child get up at five o'clock in the morning, catch the bus, got to be at school at seven or seven-thirty, how in the world can they learn what they should be learning because they're are not getting enough rest? They are not. And that's sad. And everybody's saying they want to go back to the neighborhood school. I know they do. It would please me nothing more in the world than for our kids to go back to the neighborhood school, but by God, make sure that everything that is in one school is in all schools. Even if you go back to the neighborhood schools, it's still going to be integrated some. It may not be at a seventy/thirty basis, it's going to be integrated some because people are moving everywhere all around now. But, I don't trust the people. I don't.

Interview with Arthur Griffin, May 7, 1999[2]

PG: All right. I guess just start, before you get to Second Ward, with where you grew up.

AG: I was born in Good Samaritan Hospital, which was located on the site where Ericcson Stadium is currently located. It was located on Mint Street. I grew up on 6th Street, which is in First Ward. I entered public schools in 1954. That was called Alexander Street Elementary School. That was, I guess, the colored elementary school at that time for folk that lived on that part of the city, which was the eastern part of the city?–I'm not real sure about the directions right now. I went to Alexander Street, and black people that lived on the other side, in Brooklyn, went to what's

2 Interview with Arthur Griffin, May 7, 1999 (Interview K-0168), Southern Oral History Program Collection, Southern Historical Collection, Wilson Library, University of North Carolina at Chapel Hill, http://docsouth.unc.edu/sohp/K-0168/menu.html.

called Myers Street. So I did know a little about that. And I went to Alexander Street up until about the 4th grade. At that time, the upper end of First Ward, Ninth Street, Tenth Street, Brevard Street, that was white. The southern part of First Ward was black. Davidson Street, Alexander Street, the McDowell Street was black. So as whites sort of migrated or left the area, they left what's now the First Ward Elementary School. It was an older school, but when we moved to Alexander Street to First Ward, we thought it was a brand new school because conditions are so much different with regard to quality of facility. That's why this whole desegregation thing was really unique. Simply because First Ward Elementary was an older school, but their facilities, their books and everything were a hell of a lot better than the facilities at Alexander Street. As a matter of fact, going to Alexander Street, since all of the black kids had to go to one school, we had a double shift, and you would go to school from 8 to 12, and another shift would come in at 12 o'clock and would go from 12 to 4. And that went on until the guys who went to First Ward–it was like being delivered and going to Heaven. Going to First Ward, and living in First Ward, you'd be blind, deaf, dumb, not to know about Second Ward, because there was an event called the Queen City Classic, and that was like a huge homecoming. And living in First Ward, walking to what was called the Park Center–now it's called Grady Cole Center–it was the Charlotte Armory, at one point while I was growing up, then they changed it to Park Center. But you could just walk up Seventh Street, [ ] Sixth Street, and walk all the way up to the Park Center. And right behind Park Center was Memorial Stadium, which was this huge event for little kids–to even think about looking at something as great as the Queen City Classic, which was your two black high schools, West Charlotte versus Second Ward. And it would fill up Memorial Stadium. So for us growing up, I mean, that was the event. All these black people just filling up a big huge arena, it was just unheard of. So every year you'd just wait till the Queen City Classic. Growing up, Second Ward was the school closest to my home, although it was a couple of miles to get there, a mile and a half, two miles to get to Second Ward. You just grew up knowing you were going to go to Second Ward High School. As I said, I entered school in '54, so I graduated from elementary school in 1960 and went to Second Ward. Second Ward was 7th grade to 12th grade when I was there. And urban renewal came about in Charlotte in the middle and late '50s. So we knew some things were going on because you could read in the paper where some places, people were telling, "You got to tear these houses down, they're not safe, decent and sanitary by the government's standards." . . . .

PG: Do you remember when you first heard that Second Ward had been closed?

AG: I remember. We thought that it was the utmost in betrayal, because no one had indicated at any time that the school was going to be closed. The best news we had received was that the students were having contests, trying to decide what's the name of the school. What was the new name going to be? And I've even looked through school board minutes, back in the late '60s, where students came before the board of education and suggested that the school be called Metropolitan High School. So even up to the very last moment, students, families in the community felt, and were promised, that the school would continue. And not until many many years later, and even now, going back, reading the case, the Swann desegregation lawsuit, it became a casualty of the lawsuit. And this is an opinion, although it's not written anywhere, but certainly a lot of older people who were around at the time have shared the same opinion, when we were talking about school desegregation, which were the closest schools to desegregate with Second Ward? I don't know if you–are you familiar with Charlotte at all?

PG: I wouldn't be familiar enough to know which would be the closest.

AG: The closest school is Myers Park. Myers Park would have been desegregated, so you'd have white students from Myers Park coming to Second Ward, and students from Second Ward going to Myers Park. And I think, like in many other decisions back then, folks just said, "No, we're not going to a school that looks like this." Because a school was not in great repair, didn't have nearly the things that Myers Park High School had. And I just believe that economics decided that, no, this one's going to close, our kids, if they go anywhere, might go to West Charlotte. And that's what happened, ultimately. The kids around the east, over in the Myers Park area, were assigned to West Charlotte High School as opposed to Second Ward. Whereas it would have been a shorter trip and a whole lot of other things had they been paired with Second Ward. But the politics just didn't make it. I think we just were on a losing end. As I said to you earlier, Second Ward didn't have all the affluent African Americans, and a lot of the African Americans that were somewhat affluent were being urban removed to the west side. And it left, generally, the lower-income African Americans around Second Ward, around First Ward, and around Brooklyn, to the very, very end. Because ultimately they started to urban renew First Ward, and they moved my family from First Ward to Fairview Homes, so that tells you about the economic level of Arthur Griffin's family as opposed to moving into a new home somewhere on the west side. So it was a sense of betrayal. We had–Dr. Grigsby was the principal for a very long time, then Dr. Spencer Durant was the principal for a long time. When I started in 7th grade, Dr. Durant was the principal. And up until about the 10th grade, I believe, 10th or 11th grade, he left, and Dr. E. E. Waddell became the principal. So there's always been a sense that something must have been said, because Dr. E. E. Waddell's brother–he has a twin brother–was Vernon Sawyer's deputy director, or deputy whatever it is, of the whole urban renewal program. So it's always in the back of my head that perhaps he knew something about what was going to occur to that area of the city. But I'm not real sure if he knew. But it's just in the back of my head: this guy's twin brother's working for the city's arms that's going for the entire black community, wiping it out, then maybe they could have talked. But I don't really know if that occurred. Just a sense of betrayal and loss, because that's all I've ever thought about. When we were urban removed, for example, over to Fairview Homes, the public housing community, off of Oaklawn Avenue, that was West Charlotte's attendance area. But I continued to want to go to Second Ward, despite being in West Charlotte's attendance area, and I paid my ten cents every morning to ride the [ ] buses back across town and go to Second Ward. . . .

PG: Well, integration came. What did you think at the time? I guess you weren't really here.

AG: I wasn't here. As I said to you, I came back in '71 from Vietnam, and started going to school out in UNC-C, when I got back, on the GI bill. And it was here. I mean, it was here. Politically, I didn't pay any attention, other than the fact that schools were desegregated, black kids were going to formerly all-white schools, and white kids were going to formerly all-black schools. The only thing I noticed was that progress caused all of the black schools to close. I mean, you just–Second Ward was gone, a number of elementary schools were closed, they were black elementary schools. And I didn't pay a whole lot of attention to that. . . . I started going to school board meetings, trying to find out what's happening. Jim Hunt introduced public kindergartens in about '77 or '78. He had the competency test, the California achievement test was introduced. And the first administration of the California achievement test, the gap between blacks and whites was about 60 points. And I said, "This is crazy. What's going on? We're being desegregated, but what's going on?" I was saying, "This is wrong." I was hot-headed, young, I even used a word that politicians don't use these days: I was calling people racist, and this is racism, and–I didn't know back then that you don't say that publicly in North Carolina, and particularly in Charlotte. . . .

The white community really supported magnet schools. The suburban community, they loved it. The business community, loved magnet schools. The black community was so afraid of that. They just packed the school board meetings saying, "Don't have magnet schools. This is just a way to go back to segregated schools."

PG: Why did they see that as a way to go back to segregated schools?

AG: Because it created magnet schools in the black community. And it forced black kids out, for the most part. It was a change from mandatory. They felt that if whites were given a chance to voluntarily select schools, that they wouldn't do it. That was the sense in the black community. And as the program grew, with a lot of restrictions, their realization became true. Because as you built a brand new school in the suburbs–if you had a math-science theme for a magnet school, you have good math-science teachers at a new elementary school in the suburbs, why would you go to a math-science school? The curriculum's the same, basically. The communications magnet school we have now. If you have good language arts, good English teachers, at your neighborhood school, why would you go to a Communications–? Over time, that's true. You could see, if you put a quality, brand-new, bells and whistles schools out in the suburbs, those folk will stay. They won't come in. Where you have people coming in right now are in unique curriculums: your performing arts, where you can dance, where you can do plays of one denomination or another. And that's unique. The academically gifted magnet school is a unique school. But your other schools are not as unique. And that's why you have your ratios changing the way they are, over time. I even wrote an article in Community Pride, in late '92, saying that this is not the way to go, with magnet schools. Because we opened a magnet school, and I think it was Ashley Park or Oaklawn, where the ratio was like 44 percent African American. And I said, this is Day One. It's supposed to be 40 percent. This is not a good sign. So. They just didn't have the restraints and the control necessary to maintain diversity on a long-term basis. . . .

PG: As someone who went to Second Ward, what does West Charlotte mean to you now?

AG: It's a school that, on the school board or not on the school board, I would fight to save it. They will never close West Charlotte. Because schools mean so much to communities, and in particular high schools. This is the place you graduated from. Elementary schools, not as much. And it means a lot to Charlotte. It means a tremendous–it's our last historically black high school. So I think you'd get every African American, at least who grew up in Charlotte, to walk up and down Trade Street if that school was threatened in any way, because it's like family. It's like your distant cousin. You still love your distant cousin, you know your cousin's over there, you haven't seen her in ten years, but you still love your cousin. West Charlotte is like a distant cousin. Maybe a first cousin that's across town. But it's a school that I have very fond memories of, and would want to make sure that those fond memories remain, as an operating, regular, comprehensive high school. Not a warehouse, not a special program, but an operating comprehensive high school here in Charlotte, North Carolina.

Interview with Latrelle McAllister, June 25, 1998[3]

PG: And where did you go to school as you [microphone obstructed]. Where did you go to school before West Charlotte?

LM: Okay, well, because my mother was a teacher I didn't have the benefit of going to the neighborhood elementary school. I went to school with her. I went to Druid Hills elementary school. University Park was right behind our house, really, but–. I could jump the fence, cross the fence and just go, maybe, three or four blocks. But, I went across town with my mother who taught. I spent one year at J. T. Williams Junior High School and two years—I was bussed to Wilson, which is now Wilson Middle School. But, it was Wilson Junior High at that time.

PG: What was that experience like?

LM: Oh, it was great. I enjoyed it. It was, as I remember, a fairly long bus ride, but it gave us an opportunity to socialize. And, for me, it was important because I got the opportunity to establish relationships with young people in my neighborhood. I hadn't had that experience in elementary school. I really enjoyed it. It was fun. We were pretty wild. We probably would have been most bus drivers' worst nightmare. But, it was fun. We walked to the bus stop together, came home together. So, it was interesting. And, it gave me a different–. A chance to talk with folks with different orientations. Not just of different races, but different economic classes, but really different orientations. So, I enjoyed that experience, as well. . . .

PG: But you look forward to returning to West Charlotte, obviously?

LM: Oh, yes. Oh, yes. My husband and I were talking about an article that appeared in the paper, I guess about three weeks ago, about the

3 Interview with Latrelle McAllister, June 25, 1998 (Interview K-0173), Southern Oral History Program Collection, Southern Historical Collection, Wilson Library, University of North Carolina at Chapel Hill, http://docsouth.unc.edu/sohp/K-0173/menu.html.

coaches at West Charlotte recruiting students. There was an issue as to whether or not the coaches were recruiting students for their athletic ability or if students really, naturally, wanted to go there. For me, it was a desire. It was part of a rich heritage in the Charlotte community. There is an extensive alumni association. People who were my father's contemporaries were members of it and it's a very active group. So, people who graduated from West Charlotte thirty years, forty years before I did, still get together and socialize and do fund raising. When I was in junior high school I participated in a march. It was my first civil rights protest. They were considering closing West Charlotte due to integration. We have pictures of us marching up Beatties Ford Road to–. And, it was the whole community that gathered around and the House of Prayer's church band came, as I believe it. We all gathered around to rally around our neighborhood school. That was very important. It was a very important part of it. And so, that was important. I think that had I not been assigned there I would have sought to go to school there. . . .

PG: Did you have a sense that people in the white community really didn't understand how important a place like West Charlotte was?

LM: I'm not sure about the white community, but I think, certainly our sense was that the school board, the administrators, didn't understand the value that the school had. I mean, I grew up being able to hear the band practice. I grew up watching the band go away. I grew up seeing the football team come back to the games after the victories. I grew up with people whose parents had been athletes, whose parents had been scholars there. Because my mother was an educator I knew people who taught there. And so, it was just such an integral part of my life that I'm not sure that the administration thought that there was that much attachment to the building. And, perhaps, there wasn't that much attachment to the building. You remember, West Charlotte—. When my father attended West Charlotte it was where Northwest Middle School is now. So, it probably-. Had they offered to build a brand new school and campus somewhere in that proximity people would have gone with that. But the idea of closing the school down all together certainly wouldn't be accepted.

PG: No. When you were growing up did your parents and the other graduates of West Charlotte, was that something that was always important in their lives, that they talked about or–?

LM: Well, they did. I think part of what happens anyway in the black community is there is a strong oral history. So, I did get a lot of what happened, their antics, their experiences from my parents and my friends' parents. Actually from my father. My mother's not a native Charlottean. But, from my father and his brothers and sisters who attended West Charlotte. So, I did get a strong sense of what when on there, the quality of the education, the quality of care from people. In fact, I'll tell you an interesting story. One of the people who had been one of my father's teachers, Miss Marjorie Belton, was my guidance counselor. It was, I guess, to me a very memorable moment, because as outgoing as I am now, I was a very shy teenager. I had my father walk me to school the first day. He took my hand and placed it in Miss Belton's hand. That was a very historic moment, but it also–. The symbolism went further than that. She took his gesture of his entrusting me to her very seriously. In fact, helped to mold my academic career there at West Charlotte. That was very important to me, too. . . .

LM: Well, you know, part of–. From an adult's perspective, from a person who grew up in a predominantly black elementary school where the teachers that I still see and interact with still come up to me and hug me and call me "Precious" and tell me I'm beautiful. Even thirty-five years later they still see their role as affirming me and nurturing me. They still have that role. I don't know that my son will have that at school. There is probably in the black community, and certainly in our household, an ongoing debate about the degree to which integration helps our children or hurts our children. We don't know. I think that as long as there's some mechanism for keeping the resources, the resources equitable, then the make-up, the racial make-up of the school really isn't as important. However, one of the things that I think is important, though, is that students do have the opportunity to exposure to cultures outside their own. That's–. I work in human resources and a lot of the issues that I see in my job come from cultural clashes. Not necessarily racial clashes, but cultural clashes. I was brought up differently from you and so I see things differently than you. I approach problems differently. I communicate differently. I think that integrated situations are beneficial to African-American children because it gives them the opportunity to develop those skills that they need as they work and live in the society at large. So, I think there's some benefits to integration, although, I'm not sure–. My husband and I have chosen not to put our child on the bus. We take him to school. But there are children who have to get up as early as 5:15 to do that. And for those parents who aren't able to get their children to school in any other way, I imagine that is a concern for them. So, from a humanistic standpoint I really don't advocate children having to get up that early and have maybe three, four hours of their day spent on a bus. I think that there are a lot of bright minds in the education community and I think there are some ways to come together and partner to solve those problems. I think those problems are those that are easily attacked. But, like I said, I just don't know. There's still some debate about the benefits of it. For instance, if in school, especially elementary school, if I got in trouble–. If I got in trouble on the way home, or if I got in trouble in the community at large, I could be sure that my mother would know about it or my father would know about it and that something would be done about it. There's not that type of support. There's not that village that we talk about that's important in raising and nurturing and shaping young minds. Perhaps a part of the movement away from bussing is the movement toward establishing those villages where we can nurture our children. That's probably not a bad approach. But, I do think that there's value in exposure to other cultures.

Appendix

State Symbols

State capital:	Raleigh
Origin of name:	North Carolina is named for King Charles I of England, from the Latin "Carolus"
State nickname:	The "Tar Heel State"
Song:	"The Old North State" by Judge William Gatson
Motto:	*Esse Quam Videri* ("To Be Rather Than To Seem"). The North Carolina General Assembly adopted the motto in 1893
State bird:	Cardinal
State flower:	Dogwood

Governors

Roanoke Island Colony
Ralph Lane, 1585–1586
John White, 1587

Commander of the Southern Plantation
Samuel Stephens, 1662–1664 (later governor under Lords Proprietors)

Lords Proprietors
William Drummond, 1664–1667
Samuel Stephens, 1667–1669 (previously Commander of the Southern Plantation)
Peter Carteret, 1670–1672
John Jenkins, 1672–1675
Thomas Eastchurch, 1675–1676

John Jenkins, 1676–1677
Thomas Miller, 1677
John Harvey, 1679
Henry Wilkinson, 1680
John Jenkins, 1680–1681
Seth Sothel, 1682–1689
John Archdale, 1683–1686
John Gibbs, 1689–1690
Thomas Jarvis, 1690–1694
Philip Ludwell, 1690–1691, 1692–1693, 1693–1695
Thomas Harvey, 1694–1699
John Archdale, 1695–1696
Henderson Walker, 1699–1703
Robert Daniel, 1703–1705
Thomas Cary, 1705–1711
William Glover, 1706–1710
Edward Hyde, 1711–1712
Thomas Pollock, 1712–1714
Charles Eden, 1714–1722
Thomas Pollock, 1722
William Reed, 1722–1724
George Burrington, 1724–1725 (later royal governor)
Richard Everard, 1725–1731

Royal Governors

George Burrington, 1731–1734 (previously governor under the Lords Proprietors)
Nathaniel Rice, 1734
Gabriel Johnston, 1734–1752
Nathaniel Rice, 1752–1753
Matthew Rowan, 1753–1754
Arthur Dobbs, 1753–1763
William Tryon, 1765–1771
James Hasell, 1771
Josiah Martin, 1771–1775

Governors of the State of North Carolina

Richard Caswell, 1776–1780 (first of two terms)
Abner Nash, 1780–1781
Thomas Burke, 1781–1782
Alexander Martin, 1782–1785 (first of two terms)
Richard Caswell, 1784–1787 (second of two terms)
Samuel Johnston, 1787–1789

Alexander Martin, 1789–1792 (second of two terms)
Richard Dobbs Spaight, Sr., 1792–1795
Samuel Ashe, 1795–1798
William Richardson Davie, 1798–1799
Benjamin Williams, 1799–1802 (first of two terms)
James Turner, 1802–1805
Nathaniel Alexander, 1805–1807
Benjamin Williams, 1807–1808 (second of two terms)
David Stone, 1808–1810
Benjamin Smith, 1810–1811
William Hawkins, 1811–1814
William Miller, 1814–1817
John Branch, 1817–1820
Jesse Franklin, 1820–1821
Gabriel Holmes, 1821–1824
Hutchins Gordon Burton, 1824–1827
James Iredell, Jr., 1827–1828
John Owen, 1828–1830
Montfort Stokes, 1830–1832
David Lowry Swain, 1832–1835
Richard Dobbs Spaight, Jr., 1835–1836
Edward Bishop Dudley, 1836–1841
John Motley Morehead, 1841–1845
William Alexander Graham, 1845–1849
Charles Manly, 1849–1850
David Settle Reid, 1851–1854
Warren Winslow, 1854–1855
Thomas Bragg, 1855–1859
John Willis Ellis, 1859–1861
Henry Toole Clark, 1861–1862
Zebulon Baird Vance, 1862–1865 (first of two terms)
William Woods Holden, 1865 (first of two terms)
Jonathan Worth, 1865–1868
William Woods Holden, 1868–1870 (second of two terms)
Tod Robinson Caldwell, 1870–1874
Curtis Hooks Brogden, 1874–1877
Zebulon Baird Vance, 1877–1879 (second of two terms)
Thomas Jordan Jarvis, 1879–1885
Alfred Moore Scales, 1885–1889
Daniel Gould Fowle, 1889–1891
Thomas Michael Holt, 1891–1893
Elias Carr, 1893–1897
Daniel Lindsay Russell, 1897–1901

Charles Brantley Aycock, 1901–1905
Robert Broadnax Glenn, 1905–1909
William Walton Kitchin, 1909–1913
Locke Craig, 1913–1917
Thomas Walter Bickett, 1917–1921
Cameron Morrison, 1921–1925
Angus Wilton McLean, 1925–1929
Oliver Max Gardner, 1929–1933
John Christoph Blucher Ehringhaus, 1933–1937
Clyde Roark Hoey, 1937–1941
Joseph Melville Broughton, 1941–1945
Robert Gregg Cherry, 1945–1949
William Kerr Scott, 1949–1953
William Bradley Umstead, 1953–1954
Luther Hartwell Hodges, 1954–1961
Terry Sanford, 1961–1965
Dan Killian Moore, 1965–1969
Robert Walter Scott, 1969–1973
James Eubert Holshouser, Jr., 1973–1977
James Baxter Hunt, Jr., 1977–1985 (first of two terms)
James Grubbs Martin, 1985–1993
James Baxter Hunt, Jr., 1993–2001 (second of two terms)
Michael F. Easley, 2001–2009
Beverly Perdue, 2009–2013
Patrick Lloyd McCrory, 2013–2017
Roy Cooper, 2017–present

United States Senators

Samuel Johnson (Federalist), November 27, 1789–March 3, 1793
Alexander Martin (Democratic-Republican), March 4, 1793–March 3, 1799
Timothy Bloodworth (Democratic-Republican), 1795–1801
Jesse Franklin (Democratic-Republican), 1799–1805
James Turner (Democratic-Republican), 1805–1816
Montfort Stokes (Democratic), 1816–1823
John Branch (Democratic), 1823–1829
Bedford Brown (Democratic), 1829–1840
Willie P. Mangum (Whig), 1840–1853
David S. Reid (Democratic), 1854–1859
Thomas Bragg (Democratic), 1859–1861
Vacant, 1861–1868 Civil War/Reconstruction
Joseph C. Abbott (Republican), July 14, 1868–March 3, 1871

Matt W. Ransom (Democratic), 1872–1895
Marion Butler (Populist), 1895–1901
Furnifold M. Simmons (Democratic), 1901–1931
Josiah W. Bailey (Democratic), March 4, 1931–December 15, 1946
William B. Umstead (Democratic), 1946–1948
Joseph M. Broughton (Democratic), 1948–1949
Frank P. Graham (Democratic), 1949–1950
Willis Smith (Democratic), 1950–1953
Alton A. Lennon (Democratic), 1953–1954
William Kerr Scott (Democratic), 1954–1958
B. Everett Jordan (Democratic), 1958–1973
Jesse Helms (Republican), 1973–2003
Elizabeth Dole (Republican), 2003–2009
Kay Hagan (Democratic), 2009–present

Benjamin Hawkins (Federalist, later Democratic-Republican), 1789–1795
Timothy Bloodworth (Democratic-Republican), 1795–1801
David Stone (Democratic-Republican), 1801–1807
Jesse Franklin (Democratic-Republican), 1807–1813
David Stone (Democratic-Republican), 1813–1814
Francis Locke (Democratic-Republican), 1814–1815
Nathaniel Macon (Democratic), 1815–1828
James Iredell, Jr. (Democratic), 1828–1831
Willie P. Mangum (Democratic, later National Republican), 1831–1836
Robert Strange (Democratic), 1836–1840
William Alexander Graham (Whig) 1840–1846
William H. Haywood, Jr. (Democratic), 1843–1846
George E. Badger (Whig), November 25, 1846–March 3, 1855
Asa Biggs (Democratic), 1855–1858
Thomas L. Clingman (Democratic), 1858–1861
Vacant, 1861–1868
John Pool (Republican), 1868–1873
Augustus S. Merrimon (Conservative Democrat), 1873–1879
Zebulon B. Vance (Democratic), 1879–1894
Thomas J. Jarvis (Democratic), 1894–1895
Jeter C. Pritchard (Republican), 1895–1903
Lee S. Overman (Democratic), 1903–1930
Cameron A. Morrison (Democratic), 1930–1932
Robert R. Reynolds (Democratic), 1932–1945
Clyde R. Hoey (Democratic), 1945–1954
Sam J. Ervin (Democratic), 1954–1974
Robert B. Morgan (Democratic), 1975–1981
John P. East (Republican), 1981–1986

James T. Broyhill (Republican), 1986–1986
Terry Sanford (Democratic), 1986–1993
Lauch Faircloth (Republican), 1993–1999
John Edwards (Democratic), 1999–2005
Richard Burr (Republican), 2005–2009
Kay Hagan (Republican), 2009–2015
Thom Tillis (Republican), 2015–present

North Carolina Population, 1790–2010

	Black	White	Latinos	Asian	Total
1790	105,547	288,204			393,751
1800	140,339	337,764			478,103
1810	179,152	377,374			556,529
1820	219,629	419,200			638,829
1830	265,144	472,834			737,987
1840	268,549	484,870			753,419
1850	316,011	553,028			869,039
1860	361,522	629,942			992,622
1870	391,650	678,470			1,071,361
1880	531,277	867,242			1,399,750
1890	561,018	1,055,382			1,617,949
1900	624,469	1,263,603			1,893,810
1910	697,843	1,500,511			2,206,280
1920	763,407	1,783,779			2,559,123
1930	918,647	2,234,958			3,170,276
1940	981,295	2,567,635			3,571,623
1950	1,047,353	2,983,121			4,061,929
1960	1,116,021	3,399,285			4,556,155
1970	1,126,478	3,901,767			5,089,059
1980	1,318,857	4,457,507	56,667	21,153	5,881,766
1990	1,456,323	5,008,491	76,726	50,593	6,628,637
2000	1,737,545	5,804,656	378,963	113,689	8,049,313
2010	2,048,628	6,528,950	800,120	208,962	9,535,691

Index

North Carolina: Change and Tradition in a Southern State, Second Edition. William A. Link.